Management for Professionals

More information about this series at http://www.springer.com/series/10101

Kai Jacob • Dierk Schindler •
Roger Strathausen

Editors

Liquid Legal

Transforming Legal into a Business
Savvy, Information Enabled and
Performance Driven Industry

 Springer

Editors
Kai Jacob
SAP SE
Walldorf, Germany

Dierk Schindler
NetApp B.V.
Schiphol-Rijk, The Netherlands

Roger Strathausen
Dr. Strathausen Consultancy
Berlin, Germany

ISSN 2192-8096   ISSN 2192-810X   (electronic)
Management for Professionals
ISBN 978-3-319-45867-0   ISBN 978-3-319-45868-7   (eBook)
DOI 10.1007/978-3-319-45868-7

Library of Congress Control Number: 2016956208

Printed on acid-free paper

This Springer imprint is published by Springer Nature
The registered company is Springer International Publishing AG
The registered company address is: Gewerbestrasse 11, 6330 Cham, Switzerland

At the beginning of my career, I became a lawyer. A key reason for taking that direction was that I have always believed that this profession along with the other functions in legal systems plays a key role in the cohesion, balancing, and evolution of societies. Even though I am today a CFO by heart, due to both my past and present occupations, the nature of the legal function within corporations and beyond is of high interest to me, especially because I see them changing. That is why I count myself as part of the legal community as I share my thoughts here.

Yes, lawyers pursue the particular objectives of their clients, and yes, there are many legal and professional boundary conditions—both for good reasons—but I still believe there is quite some room for lawyers to actively shape how we serve our clients and society at large. Much of that potential is still to be realized in particular when it comes to the legal function in enterprises and organizations.

I therefore applaud how this book purports to lure legal professionals out of their comfort zone. For me, the concept of liquid legal means dissolving the rigid demarcation lines of what legal is and does. It is about bridging the gap between on the one hand the legal, compliance, and risk management departments[1] and on the other hand all the adjacent functions in corporations, especially the customer-facing ones.

Compliance and protecting our organizations against risk, as true stewards do, have always been and will remain the core tasks of legal, and we have to keep delivering these services against the regulatory backdrop, in the most effective and efficient way possible. The law is the law, and we have to observe it. Period. That core remains stable.

But there are ways to better bridge what legal is doing and the efforts of the rest of the enterprise, without compromising the steward role. For many this may sound like a vision far away from today's corporate reality, but the shift of mind-set has started, one reason being that there is pressure on us to increase our relevance, or else we risk being viewed as cost factors.

We are able to and are increasingly called upon to enlarge our contributions to the organization we work in and for. We must go the extra mile, cross the bridge,

---

[1] I will refer to these functions collectively as legal for simplicity's sake.

and fully understand both the business and the culture we serve in. If we manage to do that, the traditional corporate lines of defense can turn into enablers that add more value than ever before and even become sources of competitive edge. And we are not the only so-called enabling function that is hearing that call.

If we look at corporate culture as an expression of who we are and what we believe—often codified in purposes, values, missions—then it becomes clear that legal does not have to remain a reactive defender of the law, but can turn into a proactive leader that drives not only financial performance but corporate reputation as well, simply by "enacting" corporate culture.

I believe there is an inherent potential in the role of the legal function, of general counsels and lawyers in a company, as well as of the legal firms working for them: Every move we make in these functions has both a business side (which easily translates into money to be earned or saved) and a reputational side. That latter aspect deserves much more attention than it is currently receiving.

For too long we have neglected the influence of legal on how the companies they serve are perceived. The way a company deals with legal issues, the language it uses in legal contexts, in contracts and clauses tells a story that we are often not aware of. So do our legal decisions: when and how we negotiate, litigate, settle, and appeal and when we "interpret" the rules—all of that constantly produces context that employees and the outside world read as indicators of our corporate culture. Legal decisions and discourse clearly have strong ramifications in what the external codified law requires and what financial gains or losses may come with them for our companies, but they also have a lot to do with what a company stands for or rather would like to stand for, that is, with its purpose and its values.

Hence, legal is an *actor* not just in court rooms, but on the stage of corporate culture and reputation. Culture is about what people think and do, and so is legal. The link is evident. When we see large corporations in legal trouble today, often enough their corporate culture is pulled into the limelight, and their reputations incur severe damages. Corporate culture can easily become the accused these days, especially when a single human culprit cannot be identified. Especially in such highly public scenarios, the question is not just whether a company will be *sentenced* or *acquitted* in court but also what will either do to its reputation. And to make things worse, the correlation is not clear-cut—on the contrary: It is highly ambiguous.

Looking at legal in seemingly nonfinancial terms as I am suggesting here is in line with a fast-spreading trend to look at business holistically. Many companies today have started to do that. They report not just on financial KPIs, but also look at factors relating to people and corporate culture and reputation. The financial communities have an increasing interest in this full story. Investing in such KPIs is a win-win proposition. Metrics such as employee retention and employee engagement come into the focus, all of them very much related to corporate values and culture. How legal speaks, acts, and decides can be viewed as contributing to these. Hence efforts to *simplify* and *humanize* legal can be expected to make a real difference, particularly when it comes to integrity, trust, fairness, equality, and sustainability as core values. Living up to them takes more than abiding by the rules.

Again, when I say legal I of course mean any function that is somehow part of a company's set of lines of defense, including compliance offices and stewards of integrity of any ilk. My call is for these functions to pass two tests whenever they act or speak: the legal boundary conditions, of course, but also the cultural boundary conditions within a company.

In the end—you probably guessed it—we can safely close the loop, because culture, corporate values, and employee engagement are linked to business performance.

What in the beginning looked like a dichotomy or conflict really is not. Business is culture and culture is business. And legal is both. We need to run legal as a business, founded in a distinct corporate culture and purpose.

We have an incredible opportunity in front of us to open up and reach the next level of our profession and of the value we deliver by breaking down the walls around that very profession. I am convinced we will win that case. It is our own.

Chief Financial Officer, SAP SE   Luka Mucic
Walldorf, Germany

Luka Mucic is a member of the Executive Board and chief financial officer of SAP SE and has served in this function since July 2014. He is responsible for finance and administration as well as for IT and processes of the company. He began his career at SAP in 1996 as a member of SAP's Corporate Legal department, where he focused on corporate and commercial law. Mucic holds a joint executive MBA from ESSEC, France, and Mannheim Business School, Germany, and a master's degree in law from the University of Heidelberg, Germany. He has completed the second legal state examination in Germany.

Foreword: Creating Your Path—Building Towards Liquid Legal

Finally—a book not only telling us that legal teams must change to be relevant in a data-driven digital world, but also offering us a blueprint on how to do it. The authors of *Liquid Legal* are all accomplished and innovative leaders who are making their clients more efficient, agile, and competitive. This book challenges traditional views of the role and purpose of lawyers. It promises new levels of innovation, service, and efficiency to businesses willing to ignore historical biases and demand that their law departments stretch and grow.

I believe deeply in this vision and have dedicated years to realizing it. Proving this simple but powerful concept—that "legal" can be just as effective and innovative as any other part of the company—has been a huge element of my life and career. I have taken on sacred cows and deeply held biases about lawyers and "legal" and seen our team go from barely tolerated to openly valued. This is not a quixotic journey; it is a chance to make a real contribution to the success of the enterprise.

I had a special opportunity to put my ideas into practice in 2010 and try them "at scale," when I left my position of General Counsel at JDS Uniphase to take the same role at NetApp. I had many reasons for leaving after 11 years at JDSU, but a big motivation was the opportunity to take on the challenge of delivering a world-class organization to a company that already had a strong corporate culture and, as such, was a hard place for outside executives to come and flourish.

I learned two key things in my first stint as a general counsel. First, I learned how important company culture was to me. As I looked for my next professional opportunity, I realized that would be an absolutely critical factor. I hoped to find a company where culture was viewed as fundamental to the company's success, not something that lazy people griped about because they wanted excuses for poor performance. As the chief lawyer—and chief compliance officer—I also knew that companies with great cultures also tended to have fewer episodes of misconduct and violations, and I wanted to be part of one of those companies.

Second, I discovered that I was no longer satisfied with the traditional limits and role of corporate legal teams. There was a certain way that legal teams were "supposed" to run, and that way seemed to be defined more by tradition than reason, by conservatism than creativity, and by the biases of others than the ambition and potential of the team itself. I wanted to break the traditional game plan and try to remake corporate legal in a fundamental new way.

When I joined NetApp, I became part of a company deeply focused on its people and values. I felt the difference in the conversations I had with the executive team during the interview process. Culture really seemed to matter; they talked about it, tracked it, guarded it, and considered it essential to the future of the company. It was fresh and exciting, and I heard "the click."

Another thing I heard early on during my very first conversations with NetApp was that the legal team had lost its way. NetApp had grown from a Silicon Valley startup to a global enterprise quickly, powered by the two drive trains of sales and engineering, knitted together by an empowering culture. The company's legal function, however, had failed to keep up. Service had dropped off and the group had become internally dysfunctional and disconnected from the enterprise, which viewed it as an obstacle to doing business. I will never forget my last interview at NetApp. Taking a chance, I told my future boss, "NetApp deserves a world-class legal team. I do not think you have one today, but I think I could help create one."

Once I joined the company, the work began in earnest. I inherited a large global team. Most of the organization was cynical and untrusting after years of working in a dysfunctional environment. The team was generally skeptical, and some people were openly hostile to my leadership and direction.

The first step was to move the legal department, which had reported into the CFO, to report directly to the CEO. I saw this as a critical change that would help ensure visibility and drive accountability. No more hiding behind a strong and highly respected CFO.

My next move was to get a clear picture of our effectiveness and impact. This involved "100 interviews in 100 days," with clients in every geography of our business, designed to give us a real sense of how the team was performing. I flew around the world twice in the first few months, meeting with key customers. I asked simple questions. What are your expectations from this team? Your experiences? How big is the gap between those? And finally: are you willing to give us another chance?

This discovery period also included a survey of a broader client group as well as the legal team itself. Our clients rated us low across a few dozen metrics. I heard feedback like "you act like the 'department of no,'" "you tell me what I can't do but never tell me what I can do," and so on. Revealingly, the legal team also scored its own effectiveness and impact very low. There was virtually no spirit of partnership or service towards other groups, just a sense of "that's not my job." The attitude of the team—in sharp contrast to the engaging, collaborative culture of NetApp overall—was to take the most limited interpretation of their role.

So everyone knew there was a problem but no one was taking ownership over it. How will we turn it around?

I have never worked as hard as my first 12 months at NetApp. Our change began in late 2010, and it started with a new mindset. "We will be lawyers who do windows," I first told my team at one of those early all-hands meetings and then declared to all 13,000 employees at the corporate all-hands that introduced me to the company. What I meant was that we would do the hard, thankless work that needed to be done. We would change our mentality from that of experts in ivory towers to that of partners willing to do anything to support our business stakeholders in their success, just like the rest of the company.

Over the next several years, we restructured the global team, hired or promoted new leaders to my leadership team, and introduced technologies that automated manual processes and sped up the velocity of the business. It was not easy and it did not happen overnight. Institutional resistance remained strong in pockets of the department. By the end of the first year, a quarter of the team—including all of the 13 direct reports that I inherited—either left or were asked to leave.

As a renewed leadership team, we changed the culture of the group from what it had been—a loosely organized collection of lawyers—to a true team of business partners and counselors. We found new ways to work with outside counsel, getting better returns and accountability by using data in powerful new ways. We implemented a new "legal ecosystem" that integrated legal operations professionals alongside traditional legal experts into a single, coherent global team.

And the results came. Our restructured team quickly gained traction internally. People were bringing us to the table. We were actually being invited to strategic meetings and into key projects that we had to watch from the sidelines in the past. We improved our relationships, built trust, and scored some major wins leveraging new technology and processes.

I knew we were making progress when Tom Mendoza, a longtime leader and executive at NetApp, acknowledged our team onstage during a company all-hands. "Something good is happening over there," he said. "In 20 years of being here, not once did I ever give a shout out to anyone in the legal department. And now I've done it for four quarters in a row." That comment was pure gold.

When I look back nearly 6 years at all the hard work, I am so grateful to the NetApp legal senior team: Connie Brenton (Operations), Tim O'Leary (Field), Beth OCallahan (Corporate), Valerie Velasco (APAC), and Dr. Dierk Schindler (EMEA). They each brought intense personal commitment with the trust and vision that our team can achieve so much together. Thank you!

I also extend a big "thank you and congratulations" to Dierk, Kai Jacob, and Roger Strathausen, the driving forces behind this book and the inspiration for much of the content. Dierk challenges all of us to strive to be our best and has built a loyal team and grateful clients who value his energy, vision, and leadership.

I am grateful to the entire NetApp legal team for giving so much of themselves every day for the company and our clients. Even today, our journey continues. At NetApp, we like everything we have achieved, but still see plenty of areas to develop and improve. We are still in the beginning stages of defining what we can become as a legal team.

   This book is about your journey and finding your path. It is about understanding and embracing the challenge of remaking our industry in a substantial way. I hope you embrace the journey, and I hope you will let me know how it goes.
   Matt. Matthew.fawcett@netapp.com

General Counsel, Chief Compliance Officer,   Matthew Fawcett
and Secretary for NetApp Sunnyvale, CA, USA

Matthew Fawcett is responsible for all legal affairs worldwide, including corporate governance and securities law compliance, intellectual property matters, contracts, and mergers and acquisitions. He has overseen the development of NetApp Legal into a global high-performance organization with a unique commitment to innovation and transformation.

One of the leading voices on the intersection of law, technology, and business, he was named "One of America's Top 50 General Counsels" by the *National Law Journal* and is widely recognized for redefining the role of legal counsel in the modern corporation. He speaks at international and national legal and technology trade conferences and writes regularly on innovation in the legal industry, managing data governance in the cloud era, and defending against patent trolls.

Before joining NetApp, Matthew was the senior vice president and general counsel of JDS Uniphase Corporation, where he built a worldwide legal organization, managed dozens of acquisitions and strategic transactions, and oversaw a patent program with thousands of issued and pending patents.

Foreword: Need a Lawyer? Use a Robot Instead!

The rule of law is fundamental to human society. Today, we see apparently endless growth in law and regulation. Surely this must mean the role of the lawyer is safe.

The answer to that is yes, but only if lawyers adjust and adapt. Legal and regulatory complexity is challenging the ability of business and society to function. Traditional court systems, forms of contract, and methods of risk evaluation and dispute resolution are too slow and too expensive. A global economy demands new approaches.

There will be many changes in the near future. Examples may include online courts, industry standard agreements, and digital contracts. But fundamental to social progress is the readiness and ability of the legal profession itself to lead the change agenda. Ultimately, human and social progress will not be held back by the reluctance of lawyers to adapt.

A Revolution in the Making

At a conference last year, someone posed the question "Should the general counsel of the future be a lawyer?" A lively debate followed, with about 50 % concluding that they should not. This might not be surprising—except that the audience consisted of general counsel and their immediate deputies.

So what is going on? Why would senior in-house lawyers suggest that the current top job should go to the non-lawyer?

The answer, in part, may rest in the term "non-lawyer." As one speaker observed, "We are the only profession to see the world in such simple terms— you are either a lawyer or a non-lawyer." And in this simple depiction, he perhaps highlighted the big challenge that the legal profession faces today and which threatens its future. Lawyers have a tendency to see themselves as "special," as an elite with unique and valuable knowledge on which business and society depends.

Even if this belief could ever be justified (and I believe it could), technology is transforming the situation. Knowledge is rapidly becoming an easily accessed commodity. It is the application of knowledge that increasingly has value, which differentiates the "trusted counselor" from the "mere specialist." Here we have the explanation for that question about the general counsel; should he or she be the most senior specialist, or perhaps the intermediary who links legal opinion with business context?

Responding to the Needs of Our Clients

A fundamental principle in the digital age is that society increasingly expects "ease of use." The technology in our hands is simplifying so much that used to be complex, including instant access to advice or information. It is fundamentally different from the formality and discipline associated with the typical "legal consultation."

Several years ago, I was preparing a conference presentation and wanted to offer the audience a sense of the changes that technology introduces. I focused on a previous age, the shift from medieval to early modern, when the world was being stirred by the printing press and the earliest automation. While undertaking research, I came across the origins of the word "mystery." It was apparently used in the Middle Ages in its plural form, to describe the craft unions. "The mysteries" were the ways that they retained their stranglehold on the craft professions—jobs that had survived for centuries, yet rapidly disappeared as new technologies changed what was needed and how work was performed.

For the majority of the world's population (those vast numbers of "non-lawyers"), the legal profession remains a mystery, shrouded in complexity of tradition, wording, and procedure. This may make us necessary, but do we really believe it makes us popular? Instead, the common view is that we slow things down and we are expensive. Too often, we thrive on fear—the fear of an expensive mistake.

The clients for our services want to avoid problems, but legal work is typically more about containing or controlling them. In other words, we fight to limit the consequences if things go wrong. As one business executive recently observed: "My legal team is very good at explaining and managing consequences, but if I ask them to assess the probabilities (of something going wrong), they are reluctant to comment."

And in this digital age, that comment summarizes the problem. Business and society is focused on how we achieve favorable results or outcomes, not just about protecting against events that may never occur. Technology is changing the environment due to its increasing ability to capture and analyze data, to provide predictions.

The Challenge for Lawyers

The legal profession is perhaps more challenged than many because of its past reluctance to adopt and use technology to streamline operations and to increase the value of its contribution. To illustrate this point, I was speaking recently with the general counsel of a major corporation who observed that top management today has limited respect for opinions—they want facts. And in many cases, lawyers lack facts, which explains their reluctance to offer clear advice. In the world of contracts, a lawyer will be confident when talking about potential consequences of a particular action or inaction. They are knowledgeable about precedent and the precise wording that should be used in a contract or a letter. But when it comes to probabilities, they are reluctant to be drawn. And as for the impact that their contracts (and wordings) may have on behavior or acceptability, that is often outside their realm of expertise or training.

Yet these are the functions that are increasingly demanded in a world where success is judged on outcomes. Business—and society at large—is wanting more than simply to be protected if things go wrong. As the many contributors to this book explain, today's technologies are enabling new capabilities, such as predictive analytics and wide-ranging portfolio review that transcend the experience of any one individual, legal department, or law firm.

Lawyers have been trained in a way that makes them risk averse, because their trade is essentially to protect their client's interests and assets. As one law school dean observed: "We don't teach win-win." They have flourished because they protect their clients from the uncertainty, unpredictability, and ambiguity of our world. But as with medicine, artificial intelligence will increasingly offer far more insight than any lawyer. Indeed, law firms are already starting to employ artificial intelligence to undertake document analysis and review on an unprecedented scale, offering transformations in speed and affordability.

So what remains? Can lawyers still be "special"? Interpreting data, formulating new approaches, and creating alignment between the law and other disciplines or perspectives—these will remain as fundamental issues. For those who embrace technology, high-value service offerings are emerging. In many cases these are simply providing traditional services far more cheaply through combining technology with low-cost labor resources. Yet as this book describes, others are working on issues such as contract standards and automated data extraction—the sort of initiatives that make contracts and legal advice faster, more affordable, and of direct relevance to today's business challenges.

Case Study: Reduced Cycle Times and Increased Compliance

Some lawyers and legal teams are focused on the real business risks and are transforming their approach. Contract design is a good example. The in-house legal group at one global corporation was challenged to reduce the cycle time for on-boarding new suppliers. They discovered that it was taking on average more than 3 months to sign agreements—even after a traditional "simplification" exercise (e.g., shorter agreement and simpler language). In addition, the growth of regulation in their industry was resulting in increased business risk—and suppliers were showing poor compliance levels.

Hiring more staff to deal with these problems was not an acceptable option. The general counsel realized that the issue was one of understanding. The suppliers were mostly medium-sized companies, with staff who spoke limited English and where there was no in-house lawyer. The main reason they did not sign or comply with the contract terms was because they could not understand them. She therefore commissioned a contract redesign project, including restructuring of the agreement (it actually became longer) and use of supporting guidance documents and videos. Time to signature reduced from 3 months to 3 weeks; compliance rates have risen by over 60 %.

Case Study: Designing for Users in a Global Economy

In today's global economy, economic prosperity depends on the ability to offer reliable and high-quality services. For companies in Africa, new technologies have enabled them to compete internationally, especially in areas such as food supply. But it is challenging to find workers who meet the standards required and meet the demands of growing international regulation.

In southern Africa, farmers were struggling to manage the performance of their labor force. Punctuality, hygiene standards, and safety procedures—these were among the problems they needed to fix. Workers were asked to sign comprehensive employment agreements with all the rules and procedures spelt out, as well as the consequences of failure to perform. This made no difference.

A local lawyer decided to investigate. He quickly realized that many of the workers were semiliterate—it didn't matter how many words went into the contract; they could not read them. He drafted the employment terms as a comic strip. His colleagues were worried—what will the courts say? So he consulted leading barristers and asked for their review. The result? A comic-strip contract, gauged to be far more enforceable than the previous traditional contract. And of course, a much more productive workforce.

Conclusion

The digital age requires a readiness to adjust, to embrace the potential that technology offers, rather than to resist it. Of course there are risks—but not as great as the risks of failing to think and act differently. Lawyers survived the elimination of the craft guilds; now they must adapt again and embrace the concepts of "liquid legal."

Technology is transforming what lawyers do, how and where they do it, and how much they are paid. In many cases, it is challenging whether a physical lawyer is needed at all or whether Robert the lawyer becomes Robot the lawyer.

And that is why, for those who love their profession, fundamental change is not an option; it is a necessity.

President and CEO of IACCM   Tim Cummins
(International Association for Contract
and Commercial Management)
Ridgefield, CT
USA

As CEO of IACCM, Tim Cummins leads global research on the future of contracts and trading relationships. He works with major corporations and advises the government on commercial trends and policies. His prior career included management and executive positions in technology, aerospace, automotive, and banking sectors. A native of the UK, Tim has worked in more than 60 countries and lived in France and the USA.

Preface

Much has been said about the digital transformation, disruption, machine learning, and artificial intelligence, about the flat world. But what does that mean to us, the **legal professionals**—working in an in-house legal department (LD), for an international or small law firm (LF) or for a legal process outsourcer (LPO) in 2016? Will we still have job in 2020? Likely. But what will this job look like? Will we be surrounded by the same people, doing the same work the same old way, or will we perform tasks like legal research, legal drafting, collaboration, etc., significantly differently from today? If so, in what way? Is this something we can influence or will we be "moved" into this future without much influence? And will we have the right skills to do the "new job"? And beyond, what is the role of the legal ecosystem surrounding those legal professionals? Will law schools of the future adjust their legal education? Will there be the war for talents and, if so, how is legal recruitment changing? What is the state of the legal associations and what is going on the world of legal academia?

When the three coeditors of this volume met in Walldorf in February 2015 for a conference, we started to exchange on the questions above and observed: The picture portrayed on stage, supported by fancy power points, and shared eloquently in panel discussions looked innovative, attractive, and almost too perfect. The arguments made sense, everything flowed nicely, and in the end, even though the presentations or speeches were criticizing one or the other aspect, or argued for innovation or change, the audience was left with the overall feeling: "We are doing ok. Legal is fine, everything is under control, and we know what to do."

But when one starts asking the same questions to colleagues around the world in direct and personal conversations, the picture suddenly looks very different: At least the lawyers we talked to are actually very concerned about the state of the industry, and not few of them wonder if they will still have a job in a couple of years, and if so, what this job will look like.

One friend working for an international law firm stated: "We hear all these bold statements about the disruption and the necessity to change, followed by very little tangible actions. It seems everyone is carefully watching his peers—and as long as they don't change, why should we?"

An in-house lawyer claimed: "Getting things done in the most efficient and effective way is the aim—but the reality looks quite different! We have all this simplification programs and initiatives, which seem to result only in greater complexity. Projects claim 'massive savings' and 'huge efficiency gains' and they may do so on paper—but then they too often result in insular simplification here, while adding complexity there—while the calculated head-count cuts still happen. I'm open to new technology, as long as it truly positively impacts my work!"

A colleague working for a world leading LPO, however, has a very different perspective: "We wouldn't exist without the change you described: The flattened world, the rise of the Internet, the new technology are the foundation on which LPOs are built, today. Data extraction, data analytics, machine learning, and even AI are not only buzzwords—I'm dealing with new technology every day! We always adopt, learn, take on new services, and constantly challenge ourselves and the status quo. So instead of hunting for the best law graduates in terms of high marks, we are looking for a specific mindset: 'some problem-solving-techies' with legal background."

When sharing all of our findings, conversations, and observations, the three of us concluded that legal reality is quite different from the way it is being portrayed officially and that we should take the initiative to create a platform for these strong voices to be heard and to create an initial holistic picture of the change that is coming towards the legal industry.

So we sent out a call for paper, presenting our view of the status quo of the legal profession, and invited friends and colleagues from our legal network to share with us an abstract with their ideas for book articles. The "by invite" approach and the assessment of the received abstracts allowed us to carefully steer and maneuver in the direction which we considered as most beneficial for the book intent: provide a platform for strong and future oriented leaders and their views concerning our legal profession.

Based on all abstracts we received, we carefully developed the book outline, and upon passing the critical mass in terms on consents to publish, we gave it a go! A publisher was soon found and all formalities with Springer cleared.

Right from the beginning we considered law firms, in-house legal, and LPOs as the basis—with academia, legal HR, and the associations being added to ensure a holistic representation of the legal ecosystem. A few months into our journey, we noticed that we had forgotten to include voices from the legal tech scene—a huge omission, as Legal Tech is far more than solution providers; they are rather change agents of their own kind! So we did a second round of call for papers to fill the gaps.

With that addition, we also reconsidered the title of our book: *Run Legal as a Business* was a catchy header, but did not quite cover our intent, because it seemed to focus exclusively on in-house-legal departments. We explained to our authors the new book title: "Liquid Legal—Transforming legal into a business-savvy, information-enabled and performance-driven industry," and we got the feedback that it resonates. We intend to establish the term "liquid legal" as a brand for our joint idea—a kind of *meme* that evokes open and dynamic interfaces, holistic resource views, and a nonhierarchical and process-oriented culture of collaboration across departmental and organizational borders.

Although supported by our senior management, such a private engagement comes on top of an already busy workday—so smooth collaboration was key: We three co-editors conducted weekly update calls to monitor the progress of article submissions, and we held in person editorial board meetings in different venues to set the golden thread, go through all articles over and over again, discuss timing and marketing options, and make adjustments in the book structure and positioning, where required.

What started as a formal commitment to jointly go the extra mile for the better of our profession turned into a remarkable experience. First of all, the editor onsite meetings were an intense, creative, and joyful exercise; we often forgot the hour, skipped lunch, and spent even the whole dinner to discuss our authors' thoughts and ideas and the bigger picture that this could create.

For each author, one editor was appointed the main point of contact, and the work started: 30+ authors (some single writers, some teams) had to be managed. We edited the articles and provided detailed comments to the authors, making sure the article included a new message or line of thought that propels the development of our legal profession and that it was also easy, ideally even fun, and entertaining to read . . . And the authors followed us: With fantastic drive and commitment, they thought through our comments and provided new drafts. We developed an *esprit de corps* that motivated them as much as they motivated us!

True to the motto *divide et impera*, we also shared responsibilities on the constitutive elements of the book, but selected one main author: The preface was written by Kai, Roger contributed the Call for Papers,[2] and finally Dierk created the bridges between the articles.[3]

Although all three of us invested private time and money to realize this book, Dierk and I want to thank our NetApp and SAP chain of commands for their support of the book, especially Luka Mucic, Matthew Fawcett, and of course also Tim Cummins from IACCM who open the book with their forewords. This executive support provides proof to our initial agenda: Our collective strong voices have been heard!

We thank all authors for their hard work and dedication and would like to end with the words of a student that supports us in driving the messaging in social media on this book. After spending only an hour in a restaurant in Rome with her, explaining to her the vision that we want to spread with this book and the great panel of authors, this is what we got back:

> . . . I assume we all agree, that liquid legal is not just supposed to be a book title. [. . .].
> Liquid legal will become the common noun for 'future legal', encompassing its digitaliza-
> tion, transformation, and more. It will be known as the one source of accumulated
> knowledge and information people worldwide will think of and reach out to. Liquid legal
> will indicate trends and thus give guidance regarding future legal for companies, industries,

---

[2]The original Call for Papers is included in this volume as *Introduction: "Run Legal as a Business!"*.

[3]These bridges between articles are referred to in the book as "Liquid Legal Context."

for millions of people. [...] Establishing the brand LL is the first step to create value and more value around it. [...] Liquid legal will be a leader of change.

She reflected back what we did not dare to state. Well, if this is what a young talent in our industry has taken from Liquid Legal, we are eager to hear what you will take from this book. We hope that we encourage the readers to be leaders of change towards "liquid legal."

It's time to lead!

Walldorf, Germany	Kai Jacob
Munich, Germany	Dierk Schindler
Berlin, Germany	Roger Strathausen
July 2016	

Liquid Legal Acknowledgments

First and foremost I would like to thank you, my teammates at SAP. Fighting the "urgent" distracts many people from the "important"—that's why I shared my "Q2 goals," the top 5 personal priorities with you. I wrote: "transformation cannot be imposed from the outside, it has to come from us: we have to find new ways to operate, to engage with people, to organize ourselves, to get the work done...." And you delivered! You have pushed forward the transformation; we will come out stronger. Your dedication, creativity, and endurance really make the difference. I'm honored to lead such an amazing team!

Many thanks as well to my wife Eva for having my back and to my kids Elli and Justus for giving me the extra space for finishing this book project!

Kai

Moving into the unknown requires creativity, trust, and a lot of work. I am humbled and grateful to my team members—in Europe and the USA—for giving me plenty of all three. Without them, I would have had no story to tell.

My team knows how much inspiration I take from my "coach"—I quote her very often. I believe that kids can see through things, and that is what my 12-year-old *Emily Joy* does for me, often triggering new thoughts and always a smile!

Last but not least I want to thank my wife *Christina*, my soul mate, in daring to question anything in order to see, if it can be made a little bit better for the benefit of all.

Dierk

I want to thank my lawyer friends Thorsten, Thomas, and Stefan who, from different angles, introduced me to the world of legal. Also, many thanks to my coeditors Kai and Dierk who turned this book project into a fascinating collaboration which was as educational as it was fun!

Roger

Contents

Kai Jacob, a lawyer by education, joined SAP in 2008 and heads the Global Contract Management Services team since 2011. In 2015, he assumed additional responsibility for Legal Information Management, aiming to support the digital transformation of the legal function. Kai joined IACCM (International Association for Contract and Commercial Management) in 2004, became a member of its Board of Directors in 2012, and since January 2014 has been serving as Officer and Vice Chair EMEA. Kai is a regular speaker at conferences and engaged in various round tables, boards, and initiatives in support of his vision of liquid legal.

Dr. Dierk Schindler is the head of Legal and Deal Management for Europe, Middle East & Africa and the head of Worldwide Contract Management and Services at NetApp, a leading data management company. He has transformed the legal department by combining legal and deal management including the development of a deal and case management application that supports the working processes and provides legal analytics. His teams have been awarded the "IACCM Global Innovation Award" in 2014 and 2015. Between 2009 and 2016, Dr. Schindler also served as a member of the Board of NetApp Deutschland GmbH, an organization that has acquired top ranks in the Great Place to Work-ranking in 2014 and 2015. Dr. Schindler regularly presents both at business and peer group meetings and at various universities throughout Europe on the innovation of legal and the vision of liquid legal.

Dr. Roger Strathausen is a business consultant with expertise in leadership and legal strategy whose clients are multinational companies. He was previously a senior manager at Accenture and an employee at SAP. Dr. Strathausen lectured at the Technical University of Berlin, the Universities of Heidelberg and Kaiserslautern, and the Berlin School of Economics and Law (HWR) where he promotes his vision of liquid legal. He took his PhD from Stanford University while on Fulbright and Stanford Fellowships and his MA from the University of Tübingen. His website is www.strathausen.com.

List of Contributors

Sven von Alemann rfrnz, Munich, Germany

Stephen Allen LexFuturus, London, UK

Thomas D. Barton California Western School of Law, San Diego, CA, USA

Lucy Endel Bassli Microsoft Corporation, Redmond, WA, USA

Connie Brenton Corporate Legal Operations Consortium, Las Vegas, NV, USA

Liam Brown Elevate Services, Inc., Los Angeles, CA, USA

Micha-Manuel Bues LEVERTON GmbH, Berlin, Germany

Arne Byberg EVRY, Oslo, Norway

Barbara Chomicka Arcadis LLP, London, UK

Kunoor Chopra Elevate Services, Inc., Los Angeles, CA, USA

Christophe Collard EDHEC Business School, Roubaix Cedex, France

Ron Dappen Elevate Services, Inc., Los Angeles, CA, USA

Jack Diggle Elevate Services, Inc., Los Angeles, CA, USA

Peter Eilhauer Elevate Services, Inc., Los Angeles, CA, USA

W. Jon Escher Solutus Legal Search, Redwood City, CA, USA

Arne Gärtner Linklaters LLP, Frankfurt, Germany

Suzanne Ganier Elevate Services, Inc., Los Angeles, CA, USA

Helena Haapio Department of Economics and Business Law, University of Vaasa, Vaasa, Finland
Lexpert Ltd, Helsinki, Finland

Ulrich Hagel KonsensKanzlei Berlin, Berlin, Germany

Markus Hartung Bucerius Center on the Legal Profession, Hamburg, Germany

Kai Jacob SAP SE, Walldorf, Germany

Rainer Markfort Dentons Europe LLP, Berlin, Germany

Bruno Mascello Executive School of the University of St. Gallen, St. Gallen, Switzerland

Emilio Matthaei LEVERTON GmbH, Berlin, Germany

Gerrit Mauch RETENCON AG, München, Germany

Jan Geert Meents DLA Piper UK LLP, Munich, Germany

Pratik Patel Elevate Services, Inc., Los Angeles, CA, USA

Christine Pauleau Radio Frequency Systems (RFS), Nokia, Nozay, France

Elisa de Rocca-Serra Capgemini, Paris, France

Christophe Roquilly EDHEC Business School, Roubaix Cedex, France

Mark Ross Integreon, Woodland Hills, CA, USA

Isabelle Roux-Chenu Capgemini, Paris, France

Mari Sako Saïd Business School, University of Oxford, Oxford, UK

Dierk Schindler NetApp B.V., Schiphol-Rijk, The Netherlands

Roger Strathausen Dr. Strathausen Consultancy, Berlin, Germany

Ivar Timmer Amsterdam University of Applied Sciences, Amsterdam, Netherlands

Andranik Tumasjan Technische Universität München, Lehrstuhl für Strategie und Organisation, Munich, Germany

Isabell M. Welpe Technische Universität München, Lehrstuhl für Strategie und Organisation, Munich, Germany

Christina Wojcik Seal Software, San Francisco, CA, USA

Ulf Zetterberg Seal Software, San Francisco, CA, USA

Introduction: *"Run Legal as a Business!"*

Roger Strathausen, Kai Jacob, and Dierk Schindler

Abstract

The authors argue that the new legal function will shift from a paradigm of security to one of opportunity; that future corporate lawyers will no longer be primarily negotiators, litigators and administrators, but that instead they will be coaches, arbiters and intrapreneurs; that legal knowledge and data-based services will become a commodity, and that analytics and measurement will be key drivers of the future of the profession.

In Franz Kafka's short story *"Before the Law"*, a country man requests entry into the law. A doorkeeper responds that he cannot allow the man to enter the law at that time. So the man waits his whole life to gain entry, and when he is finally near death, he asks why all these years no one else ever requested entry into the law. Only then the doorkeeper tells him that this gate had been intended specifically for him, and that after the man's death, the gate will be closed.

Kafka's story expresses a general feeling of alienation typical for the *Zeitgeist* at the beginning of the twentieth century. It also conveys an image of the law as opaque, mysterious, and inaccessible. People want to understand and access *the law*, but *the law* is guarded, and the doorkeepers decide if and when people can enter.

R. Strathausen
Dr. Strathausen Consultancy, Berlin, Germany
e-mail: dr.strathausen@gmail.com

K. Jacob (✉)
SAP SE, Walldorf, Germany
e-mail: kai.jacob@sap.com

D. Schindler
NetApp B.V., Schiphol-Rijk, The Netherlands
e-mail: dierk.schindler@netapp.com

© Springer International Publishing AG 2017
K. Jacob et al. (eds.), *Liquid Legal*, Management for Professionals,
DOI 10.1007/978-3-319-45868-7_1

Lawyers in the past have very much acted like the doorkeeper in Kafka's story. Emphasizing their institutional role and their certified qualification, they have guarded the law and minimized risks and costs of non-compliance. The law, in turn, has provided lawyers with *"Herrschaftswissen"* (literally "domination knowledge")—a special knowledge that gives them power. This domination knowledge has allowed lawyers to define their own work environment as subject matter experts who value professional freedom and often work without much managerial supervision.

It is normal for people to put themselves at the center of things. And in enterprises, it is the task of leadership, and the purpose of organizational design and process engineering to use this natural pre-disposition of individuals to create the largest value for the organization as a whole. Bundling legal competencies in one department creates economies of scale, and one might say that Legal contributes to the overall efficiency of the organization simply by being a centrally funded function. After all, it would be much more costly to allow each line of business to have its own fully staffed legal department.

Also, many lawyers choose to work in large organizations precisely because these organizations allow them to focus on internal client relationships and on legal subject-matters instead of on revenue and costs. We have heard corporate colleagues say that, if they had wanted to become business men and think about numbers more than paragraphs, they would have opened their own law firm.

And while it is true that lawyers need freedom to work holistically and satisfy clients' needs, it is not the whole truth. It is perfectly legitimate for executives and senior partners to demand, in the name of company owners and shareholders, that legal be run as a business. Increasing both efficiency and effectiveness is expected of Human Resources, Finance, IT departments and other central functions—why should Legal be different?

The traditional self-understanding of lawyers as *doorkeepers* and isolated case workers has created not only legal silos in many companies, but also redundancy of back-office work within these silos. As doorkeepers, lawyers often exhibit a mentality averse to innovation and resistant to change. Statements like *"Better safe than sorry"* and *"The law is the law"* are legitimate—but when overused, they lead to a perception of Legal as inefficient, bureaucratic and, in fact, a business constraint rather than a business enabler. And instead of leveraging the opportunities provided by technology, project management and leadership theories to improve the efficiency and effectiveness of their own work, lawyers appear to rather stick "to whet they know"—the law.

Today, Corporate Legal is changing. Legal departments are downsized, manual tasks are automated with intelligent software and workflows, and new business models appear around outsourcing and shared services, causing thought leaders like Richard Susskind to reflect on *the end of lawyers and the future of the profession.* Underlying this change are business trends and the usual ups and downs of markets. Certainly, in the aftermath of the 2008 financial crisis, this continuous volatility of global markets forces legal departments to be agile and innovative in their operations. And increasing internal cost pressure, in turn, requires continued sim- plification and automation of legal processes and efficient service delivery.

It is important to realize, however, that the ongoing change in macro-economics and its impact on the business models in the legal industry is of a more fundamental and long-lasting nature than normal economic cycles, and it affects the very essence of the legal profession. Globalization and the internet have created a dynamic that exponentially increases complexity and demands fast reactions to change. In a highly complex and constantly changing business environment, Legal can no longer remain simply a doorkeeper of the law; *instead, Legal needs* to *lead and pro-actively further the business!*

The fast development of information technology is both a driver and an enabler for the changing role of Legal. IT systems not only automate and streamline work processes; they also provide the basis for measuring all aspects of the business and balancing the conflicting goals of agility and control. Leveraging information technology creates transparency for governance, improves decision-making, and provides the basis for scaling operations.

To get a seat at the executive table, Legal must change its *mindset*, its *roles*, its *services* and its *mode of operation*. Further down, we present four theses on the *Future of Legal.*

Often when we talk to corporate lawyers about the future of legal and the role of IT, we encounter a mixture of disinterest and fear. In working on the concept for this book, we discussed the possibilities of increased efficiency through legal software with a colleague working as a corporate lawyer for a German DAX company. As he listened to our ideas, his face became more and more skeptical. In the end, he frowned and said that he was not sure if he should endorse our initiative—he felt that the focus on efficiency could endanger his own job.

This reaction seems quite common for many corporate lawyers. The profession does have a tendency to ignore the change, hoping it will go away by itself, like so many corporate initiatives in the past, from LEAN to Knowledge Management, have appeared in Legal—and then disappeared again without leaving much of a trace.

By ignoring the benefits of IT, lawyers actually hurt themselves. Increasing workloads and lack of resources are already the biggest challenges in corporate legal departments. Lawyers are flooded not only with service requests from internal clients, but also with more and more administrative tasks consuming a large amount of time and effort. The complexity of legal work requires concentration, and the interruptions caused by the continuous influx of e-mails and phone calls pertaining to other matters make it difficult to deliver high quality documents on short notice.

One way to address the issue of increasing workload is to define clear client engagement rules and intake criteria. Another way is to increase lawyers' compe- tency in time and project management through training and professional develop- ment. Improved time and project management can free up capacity by streamlining work towards time, money and value delivered, improving collaboration among lawyers and allocation of limited resources, and by optimizing the engagement of external counsel.

The most effective and sustainable way for lawyers to free up time and get back in the driver seat is the use of software. *Legal Case Management (LCM)* and *Contract Management Solution (CMS)*, for example, are only two examples of software solutions that enable the scaling of legal operations by creating an information-base for the preparation, execution, and follow-up of legal case work (LCM), and for the handling of written contracts for all lines of business and across the whole contract lifecycle (CMS). The possibilities of IT-support for Legal are virtually limitless—but instead of using workflows, apps and platforms, still lawyers prefer to collaborate via phone and the exchange of emails.

When Legal is run as *a* business, we believe it will be a huge step towards Legal becoming a strategic partner of corporate executives, and for the whole legal profession to regain economic momentum. In order to spark the interest to contribute, to foster a discussion and to provide some initial structure for the book, we put the following four theses in front of our potential authors, when we sent out our call-for-papers:

1   Thesis 1: The Legal Function Will Shift from a Paradigm of *Security* to One of *Opportunity*

For decades, lawyers have been educated and trained to be *reactive*. Legal is triggered from outside and usually becomes active *after* something has happened, when there is a *legal need*—when clients ask questions, when contracts must be closed, when claims are made. No plaintiff, no judge. Lawyers then analyze the situation and provide advice on compliance and the mitigation of risk. This reactive attitude grew out of management theories and the managed organization of the twentieth century. In a fixed structure of hierarchical positions, everybody knows his and her exact role, and future tasks are expected to be very similar, if not identical, to present tasks.

Yet the managed organization is a relic of the past. The agile organization of the future will be much less hierarchical and much more tolerant of complexity. It will consist of self-organized teams defining their tasks according to abstract company goals. These autonomous teams will establish networks and fast feedback-loops along the value chain and constantly re-align in response to changing environments.

In such an agile organization, Legal can no longer remain passive and wait for issues to be brought before it, like a court waits until there is a case to be decided. Instead, Legal will have to become pro-active, combining legal expertise with business acumen to seek out new playing fields and provide value to external and internal clients. Complexity and ambiguity will be the natural state of business, and Legal will help master uncertainty by providing options and suggesting alternative paths of action.

Under the current *security* paradigm, however, legal work often is a zero-sum game. The goal of negotiations and litigations is to "win"—more security for one side means less security for the other side. Under the *opportunity* paradigm, lawyers will cooperate to create win-win results. Documents will be produced online and collaboratively across departmental and organizational borders. Lawyers will educate clients and enable them to think *legal* at the outset of business endeavors. Lawyers will help avoid the emergence of conflicts by setting proper expectations and moderating diverging interests, and they try to resolve conflicts *before* they turn into litigation cases and go to court.

2 Thesis 2: Future Corporate Lawyers Will No Longer Be Primarily Negotiators, Litigators and Administrators— They Will Be Coaches, Arbiters and Intrapreneurs

A Legal departments operating under the paradigm of opportunity instead of security will change the role and the tasks of lawyers. A good example for an area in which lawyers are increasingly acting as pro-active coaches and arbiters is *Contracting*.

Contracts and contracting are becoming more performance and outcome-based, shifting away from *risk allocation* and *price* towards *risk sharing* and *value*. *Contract management* is booming—as a software product, as a corporate service, and as topic of academic research. Business professors analyze similarities and differences of organizational contract management practices. Non-profit think-tanks like the *International Association for Contract & Commercial Management* (IACCM, representing over 40,000 members and more than 8000 international companies) calculate the business impact of inferior contract management, estimating an overall revenue loss of 9.5 %. And contract management professionals start communities of practice, exchanging ideas and learning from each other on how to create value through contract management. There is truth in the words of an Fortunate 500 CEO who claims: "If you are not in control of your contracts, you are not in control of your business."

As part of the agile organization, *dynamic contracting* describes a new contracting mindset with wide-reaching effects for contract management. Instead of competing for maximum protection against all possible risks, legal parties engaging in dynamic contracting put business cooperation and common goals and outcomes in the center of contracting. The whole of the contract becomes more important than its individual clauses which may be adjusted and augmented as needed at a later point in time. Values, guidelines and principles replace endless fine print and imaginary bones of contention.

Dynamic contracting enables parties to adjust contract contents to changing situations. Reality is always more complex than any argument, and actual events often differ from what even experts predicted. No disclaimer, no single clause, or single contract can 100 % ensure the achievement of unilateral goals. It is the totality of an organization's contracting landscape and its underlying contract management structure, processes and tools that will ensure mutual benefits of contacting parties within and between organizations.

Besides being coaches and arbiters, future lawyers will also be *intrapreneurs*. The term *intrapreneur* is derived from *entrepreneur*, an innovative person pursuing new opportunities and leading others to realize a vision. The Austrian economist Joseph Schumpeter defined entrepreneurship as creative destruction. Such creative destruction also happens within organizations—like entrepreneurs, intrapreneurs must sometimes tear down what exists in order to create something new.

Lawyers become intrapreneurs when they seize business opportunities and influence the perspective of executives and other stakeholders. For example, working with external law firms and managing them for value might be seen as an intrapreneurial task. The financial crisis has heightened corporate sensitivity towards third party costs and the actual value delivered from external counsel. Lawyers engaging with external counsel need to define clear criteria for what, when and how to outsource; they should follow a Request for Proposal (RFP) process, build a RFP database, compare prices of outside counsel, and negotiating success-based fee arrangements.

3 Thesis 3: Legal Knowledge and Data-Based Services Will Become a Commodity

Like other disruptive innovations, the information-enablement of legal departments will make some legal jobs disappear. Most administrative back office functions around managing and processing data, for example, can be done more efficiently by machines than humans. And separating routine and high volume activities from high value legal activities improves the allocation of limited legal resources and increases service transparency.

Shared Service Centers (SSC) are a proven way to scale operations and reduce the workload of senior personnel and expensive experts. At the same time, SSC establish a clear career path for junior staff. Shared services rest on a unified service delivery platform. For each service in the portfolio, a process model must define which activities are strategic and should be kept in the (global or regional-local) legal line function, and which activities are executed by the SSC; client engagement, service level agreements (SLA) and escalation paths between experts in Legal and the SSC must be defined with clear KPIs; the SSC funding model (e.g. central budget, co-funding above a base load, pay-per-service) need to be decided; roles, responsibilities and interactions between the SSC front-office (client engagement) and back office (service delivery) must be clarified, and SSC hubs in low-cost countries must be identified. Legal Process Outsourcing (LPO) companies have been entering this market niche quite successfully in the recent decades.

Bringing about such change and actually information-enabling legal departments and creating shared services is by no means trivial. Making Legal *lean* by standardizing and automating recurring activities requires a thorough understanding of subject matter, work processes and IT capabilities. To encourage knowledge sharing and usage of best practices beyond teams and departments, Legal must also actively communicate and market its services and provide easy access to collaboration sites.

Underlying shared service centers is software which often must be customized to fit specific needs. Yet when it comes to legal software development, many organizations today suffer from a knowing-doing gap. On one side are legal experts, considering their work too complex to be executed by a machine, and on the other side are IT teams, unable to gather the required information to build programs that could ease the lawyers' work. Even if IT and the legal department do jointly define functional blueprints, technical specifications and programming work, the end result often is not as expected. Traditional software development usually lacks clarity or business formalization, takes too long and consists of too many isolated phases to create value for the clients.

For example, a specialized legal team at SAP, a global software company, ran their "business" on MS Excel for more than 5 years because their efforts to develop a simple case management solution together with internal IT failed. Using a rapid prototyping approach with frequent feedback loops between legal experts and developers allowed a specialized team to build such a solution in only 12 man days—from start to finish!

When software is used intelligently, it bridges the gap between those who *know* and those who *do*. Software opens up time for lawyers to think, and thinking creates opportunities for new legal services and jobs. While legal knowledge is ready-at-hand and can be searched in databases and shared in communities, lawyers will still be needed to apply this knowledge in varying business contexts and to communicate emphatically with people. Gathering facts to get a holistic understanding of the situation, weighing interests and claims, seeing the general in the specific, and the specific in the general—these legal skills will be more valuable than ever in the agile organization.

Basically, lawyers of the future must be able to translate legal into business, and business into legal.

4   Thesis 4: The Legal of the Future Will Measure Everything It Does

The Legal of the future will deploy strategic tools such as the *Balanced Scorecard* approach to design service portfolios and measure service impact in terms of *clients*, *costs*, *processes*, and *learning*. The legal department of another large software company uses, for example, a 3-year strategy and a scorecard with 30 indicators spread across seven headings (Economic, IQ and IP, Software and Additional Services, Citizenship, Inter-Operability and Anti-Trust, Operational Excellence and People and Culture) to tie its activities to business goals.

In partnering with the business, Legal will deploy the client engagement model that works best in any given situation. In some cases, it will make sense to define practice areas, and let the lawyers engage directly with the clients; in other cases, it will be smarter to assign Legal business partners to division or line of business and let these business partners orchestrate the access of clients to legal services. Partnering with the business generally means to integrate lawyers and legal procedures as much as possible into corporate or local governance, product and infrastructure activities. For example, significant business unit teams should include a lawyer as a participating member; lawyers should have a formal role in the development of new products or services and contribute to annual business unit plans; and the law department should review major policy decisions before they are announced.

In all these activities, Legal can improve its performance and its organizational standing by developing metrics and actively communicating and marketing its achievements. Possible key performance indicators (KPI) include the revenue generated through legal deal support, vendor expenses reduced, operational costs saved (e.g. through process automation), compliance fines avoided, risks mitigated, litigation cases won, and many others.

People will continue to be Legal's most important assets. It is time to acknowledge, though, that traditional performance management has failed. It makes little sense to define individual and team objectives once a year and then never revisit them again until the next annual performance review. Since the business environment constantly changes, the once-a-year performance management approach forces employees to either turn off their brain and simply ignore changing conditions, or to adjust to new situations, thus deviating from defined goals at the risk of upsetting their bosses and losing their bonuses.

Gallup reports that 51 % of corporate employees are not engaged at work, and 58 % believe that their current performance management approach drives neither employee engagement nor high performance. Employees need feedback on their work all year around, and not only, or even primarily, from their managers, but from the people they work with, most importantly from their internal and external clients. And the metrics used to assess performance must themselves be based on relevant and current data, and they must be adjusted to changed circumstances.

In agile organizations, many people management positions will become obsolete. The online retailer *zappos* with 1500 employees, for example, in 2015 abolished all people management positions in the company, arguing they are no longer needed in an organization driven by talented employees and self-aligning work processes. IT systems manage data and processes, people engage in their jobs, and teams perform.

Legal departments can optimize the return on their human capital by promoting leadership and improving overall engagement across the whole talent management process, from recruitment to learning, performance, compensation and succession. Measures may include conducting employee engagement surveys; establishing clear job profiles and career paths; regularly assessing individual skills and competencies (e.g. negotiation, communication, time and project management, etc.); measuring output and client satisfaction; ensuring healthy work-life balances, and others.

The lawyers of the future are business-minded and well aware of the challenges in their profession. They are leaders, not doorkeepers, they lead by example, and they are eager to learn from each other!

Masters of Ambiguity: How Legal Can Lead the Business

Roger Strathausen

Abstract

This chapter of *"Liquid Legal: Transforming legal into a business-savvy, information-enabled and performance driven industry"* takes a systemic approach to the legal function in business enterprises. Defining *law* as a set of rules to govern human behavior, *legal* as the social system with the ideal of *justice* as normative reference, and *laws* as the medium through which this norm is operationalized, the article proposes to view both *the dissolution and creation of ambiguity as legal modus operandi*.

Ambiguity is simultaneously dissolved and created in legal contexts which frame the interactions of agents such as governments, courts, law firms, business enterprises, and private citizens. A legal context centers on a case or matter. Cases emerge when the law (the abstract set of rules) is applied to events (concrete facts in time and space). Cases are thus instances of the law, and they are always situated in a specific context that is defined through interest-driven relations of law and event, of the general and the particular. Like all self-referential systems which take their own output as new input, legal, through ambiguity as its modus operandi, primarily produces *more legal*.

I interpret the current pressure on in-house legal departments to *"do more with less"* as a symptom for the dis-functionality of the self-referential legal function within a business enterprise.

For legal to overcome this dis-functionality and to take a leadership role in business, I propose to shift the legal mind set from *adversarial* to *collaborative*. Looking at the constructive side of ambiguity, corporate lawyers can learn from each other and develop standards for simpler legal transactions. By focusing on "win-win" rather than "win-lose" relations, legal will create new business value instead of self-referential output.

R. Strathausen (✉)
Dr. Strathausen Consultancy, Berlin, Germany
e-mail: dr.strathausen@gmail.com

© Springer International Publishing AG 2017
K. Jacob et al. (eds.), *Liquid Legal*, Management for Professionals,
DOI 10.1007/978-3-319-45868-7_2

Technology and the ability to streamline and automate workflows, leverage the scalability of digitalized legal assets, and create transparency across the whole enterprise will enable such an increase of legal value contribution. Transparency can help establish a corporate culture built on trust, fairness and equality of opportunity—a culture which I believe is conducive to doing business in a globalized, complex and polycentric world.

1   "What?" "Who?" "Why?": An Introduction to *Legal*

Webster online dictionary defines the meaning of the term *legal* as *"established by or founded upon law or official or accepted rules."*[1] The adjective can be used in a predicative way, as in: *"Her action was legal,"* or in an attributive way: *"She took legal action."* When used in an attributive way, *legal* no longer expresses the legality of a thing or action, but, together with the noun, creates a new specific meaning. We talk about "the legal system" and "the legal industry," about "legal disciplines," "legal practices," and "legal institutions," and it appears we are all fine with this usage and understand each other rather well.

However, latest when, as in *Liquid Legal*, a genuine noun is missing, the meaning of *legal* becomes ambiguous. As a nominalized term, *legal* may refer to jurisprudence or the profession of law in general; it may also refer to in-house legal departments, to law firms and legal process outsourcers (LPO), to law-making bodies or agencies, to courts, or to any other organization or activity somehow related to *the law*. The title of this book further enhances this linguistic ambiguity by qualifying *legal* as *liquid*—as something fluid, amorphous, and without shape.

Such ambiguity appears to be fundamentally opposed to the concept of law and the goal of the legal profession. The purpose of law is to govern behavior, and this purpose only seems achievable if the meaning of laws is clear and can be univocally understood. Using terms with unclear meaning, let alone intentionally creating ambiguity, appears counterproductive to that goal, and one of the deadly sins of lawyering. The below statement from Escher[2] expresses the negative connotation which the term *ambiguity* carries for most legal professionals[3]:

> Lawyers must be capable of advanced legal reasoning, they must know the law, and, because so many in-house positions are transactional in nature, clients look to lawyers to effectively memorialize business agreements. By "effectively" the clients mean that the

---

[1] Webster WordNet Dictionary. http://www.webster-dictionary.org/definition/legal. Accessed Oct. 15, 2016.

[2] Jon Escher, "Building a Legal Department in a Metrics-Driven World," in LL, p. 363–364.

[3] Throughout my article, I will quote other articles of "Liquid Legal" to connect the individual texts and help create a network of ideas. However, the selected quotes and references are primarily intended to support my own theses; it is not my intention to summarize or even capture the main theses of these other articles. To understand the authors' intentions and to do justice to their ideas, readers are advised to read the original articles themselves.

lawyers will draft agreements that accurately reflect the business understanding while at the same time shielding the company from undue risk, ambiguity, and misunderstanding.

While it is true that, in each single case, ambiguity is problematic for achieving agreements and thus should be reduced to the minimum, I want to make a structural argument for why ambiguity also, in principle, is unavoidable and a necessary constituent of all legal activity. The simultaneous dissolution and creation of *ambiguity*, that is the central thesis of this article, *is the basic legal modus operandi*, an operation without which legal could not even exist.

Part one of this article, entitled *"Justice, Law, and the Legal System,"* compares the functioning of legal to the functioning of language. Just like speech acts are situational linguistic instances which presuppose a whole system of language in the background, cases are situational legal instances which presuppose a whole system of law in the background. And just like the meaning of a particular speech act depends on the situational context, the meaning of single rules and the assessment of individual cases (who and what is "right or wrong," "legal or illegal") also depends on the context which the agents create. Legal cases and contexts are in a state of flux, constantly dissolving and, at the same time, producing ambiguity.

In the second part of this article, entitled *"'Win-win' versus 'win-lose': The Systemic Predicament of In-house Legal Departments,"* I explain the difference between a business and a legal frame of reference. I structure legal services in a 2×2 matrix and review two areas in which legal can take a proactive role in serving clients and delivering more value to the business: *Risk management*, i.e. switching between legal and business frames of reference and turning legal issues into quantifiable business issues, and *project management*, i.e. improving individual and group performance in legal service delivery, especially when working with external counsel.

The third and final part of the article *"Corporate Culture and The Business of Legal"* calls for a mind shift of legal professionals, a shift which I deem necessary to *run legal as a business*. I am sharing thoughts on what *Liquid Legal* could look like in corporate practice, showing what legal practitioners can do to advance the role, its relevance and the leadership potential of in-house legal departments. In essence, I argue that legal should make corporate culture its business and help create what, in another publication, I have called a *Culture of Lines*,[4] characterized by abundant information, pervasive communication, and transparent rules.

2   Justice, Law, and the Legal System

Law[5] is one of mankind's greatest inventions. Regardless of the structural and material differences between common law, civil law, and religious law, and independent of the specific procedures of how, when, and by whom national and

---

[4]Strathausen (2015).

[5]There are numerous definitions of *law*, none of which can claim to represent the last word on the subject. In our context here, whenever I talk about *law* or *the law* (singular), I mean an institutionally sanctioned set of rules to govern human behavior.

international laws[6] are being created, implemented, and sanctioned—the fact that human communities and cultures of all times have given themselves rules to govern their behavior separates us from all other species on earth.

Of course, people do not always accept or adhere to the law; if they did, police, courts and prisons would be superfluous. Criminals intentionally break the law to gain a personal advantage, and even among law-abiding citizens, conflicting opinions exist within one and the same jurisdiction as to what exactly *is* or *should be* the law, and whether or not particular forms of behavior do or should constitute a legal offense.

Such conflicts are an integral part of the legal system. Laws not only refine and complement but also oppose and contradict each other. The meaning of a particular law may appear abundantly clear when looked at in isolation; but when a given law is applied to a particular case, several other laws may apply as well, and legal meanings start to shift. The individual right to freedom of speech must be balanced with personality rights and ends where other individuals are being insulted.[7] The right of an organization to enter into contracts with employees, suppliers and clients is limited by national labor laws and civil laws. If and how particular laws matter, and what exactly they mean, depends on the particular circumstances of the case, and on the relations between one law and other laws. Legal ambiguity leads to dissolution attempts via new laws, and new laws lead to ambiguity because they change the overall system of law on which the meaning of individual laws depends.[8]

Conceptually, one opposite of ambiguity is *clarity*; the other conceptual opposite of ambiguity is *obscurity*. The ambiguity created through contexts stands between clarity and obscurity. Multiple legal meanings of a matter are only possible because contexts first of all create *the possibility of legal meaning per se*. Legal contexts dissolve and, at the same time, create ambiguity because they constantly shift and are ultimately contingent. Even if one assumes that the facts of a matter can be objectively established, and that laws are fairly applied, the interests of the parties will always remain unforeseeable and idiosyncratic. Law itself, as a set of rules, is dead. Law comes to live only when parties express their interests, when event and

---

[6]By *laws* (plural) I mean all kinds of institutionally sanctioned national and international social rules, including constitutions, statutes, decrees and regulations, etc.

[7]The defamation law suit launched by the Turkish president Erdogan against the German satirist Jan Böhmermann (see Böhmermann affair), a law suit which was explicitly sanctioned by the German government, provides proof that even in art, not everything is allowed, at least in the eyes of the state.

[8]For example, the September 2015 ruling of the EU Advocate General dissolved the ambiguity around the question whether or not the previously existing Safe Harbor agreement between the United States and the European Union (EU) provided adequate protections for data privacy. The court ruled that it did not—and in doing so, it created ambiguity in other legal contexts, as attested by an Accenture study: "Now, however, US companies may be at risk if their technology suppliers are not compliant with the tougher standards." (https://www.accenture.com/us-en/insight-spend-trends-privacy-protection-compliance.aspx).

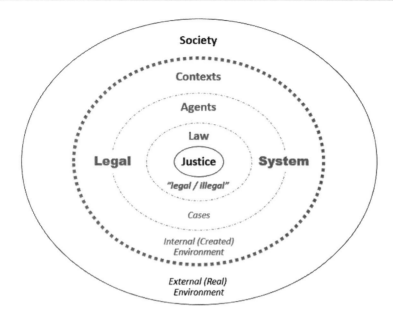

Fig. 1 The Legal System (own material)

rules, the particular and the general, are connected in a particular context and create legal meaning—*when the case emerges.*

Following the German sociologist Nilkas Luhmann[9] who has transferred the biological concepts of autopoiesis and self-referentiality to social systems, I regard the legal system as operationally closed and structurally open (or coupled). Like all systems, legal is "blind" towards its real environment because the distinction between itself and the environment is internally produced, "a re-entry of the form into the form," as the English mathematician George Spencer Brown famously formulated. The environment (politics, the economy, science, etc.) stimulates the legal system and causes changes (structural openness), but such changes themselves are always the result of legal's own internal operations (operational closure), i.e. of dissolving and creating ambiguity through the continuous application of the binary code "legal or illegal" (Fig. 1).

At any given moment, law embodies different perspectives and conflicting interests which must be balanced for "the greater good." As one of the three independent forces in modern democratic states, the *judicative* includes court trials and other mechanisms to resolve legal disputes and achieve justice. Every case contains pros and cons for each position. In Western art, *Justitia* is represented as a goddess with three attributes: a blindfold, symbolizing the irrelevance of the wealth and status of the parties involved, a scale indicating the weighing of competing

---

[9]Luhmann (1992), pp. 1419–1441.

positions, and a sword showing the power of the courts. When judges deliver a verdict, not everyone, least of all those convicted, will necessarily *agree* that justice has, indeed, been served. Justice is an idea, a cognitive construct; yet exactly as an unattainable ideal, justice remains indispensable for the legal system to operate and to ultimately decide what should be *legal* or *illegal*. Elusive and contested, justice represents the ultimate norm which is operationalized as law and which legitimizes individual rules. Justice is a never-ending process and no fixed state. Subjectively, as individuals, each one of us may believe to be just, but collectively, as a society, we can only agree on operational procedures which we think will increase the likelihood that legal outcomes may be just. Timmer[10] remarks on the relation between law and justice:

> Throughout the ages, the law and legal culture have hugely benefited the development of individuals, organizations and democratic societies. Although one can, even in the most advanced legal cultures, be critical of many aspects of the law, an advanced and balanced legal system raises the overall standards of justice and fairness in society. Studies also show that the efficacy and independence of a country's legal system contribute significantly to a country's economic prosperity (cf. Veld & Voigt 2003).

Laws are complex and difficult to understand for laymen. As a group of experts with special education and knowledge, and with the state-certified ability to practice law, lawyers help apply laws to social reality. Paradoxically, the self-understanding of lawyers as being "special" is one of the reasons why the legal profession has come under scrutiny in business environments, as Cummins[11] remarks:

> Why would senior in-house lawyers suggest that the current top job should go to the non-lawyer? The answer, in part, may rest in the term 'non-lawyer'. As one speaker observed: 'We are the only profession to see the world in such simple terms – you are either a lawyer or a non-lawyer'. And in this simple depiction, he perhaps highlighted what is wrong with the legal profession today and what is threatening its future. Lawyers have a tendency to see themselves as 'special', as an elite with unique and valuable knowledge on which business and society depends.

In my view, the current crisis of in-house lawyers is primarily an identity crisis, created by uncertainty about w*ho or what is a lawyer?*[12] While having passed the bar distinguishes lawyers socially, such distinction is mostly irrelevant and, in fact, often counter-productive in a business environment. Corporate lawyers rarely represent their companies in court, and often work with external counsel instead.

---

[10]Ivar Timmer, "Look to the moon. Managing and Monitoring the Legal Function," in LL, p. 344.

[11]Tim Cummins, "Need a lawyer? – Use a robot instead!", in LL, p. xiii.

[12]The debate in Germany about whether or not corporate counsels are allowed to remain exempt from public old age insurance can be seen as an expression of this identity crisis. In 2012, the German Federal Social Court (BSG) had ruled that corporate counsels do *not* practice law, thus could not become members of insurances for lawyers and, consequently, could not be exempt from public insurance. This BSG ruling was adjusted in 2015 by parliament which strengthened the legal status of corporate counsel as lawyers. See www.syndikusanwaelte.de (only in German).

Later in this article I will argue that the special skills of lawyers, the ability to see different sides of a matter and to think through ambiguity, still possesses huge value for companies—provided that it becomes increasingly embedded in a business frame of reference.

To fulfill their social function, laws, which serve as the social medium through which the ideal of justice is implemented, must themselves be coded into a communicable medium. Social rules can also be tacit and implicit, as is the case in cultural habits and norms which will play a crucial role for the arguments advanced later in this article. But only when rules are explicitly expressed some-where, for all to see and comprehend, a society can reasonably demand of its members to follow them, and only when non-compliance of these rules is sanc-tioned through official social institutions such as police and courts do we commonly speak of *laws*.

Stating that laws must be *coded* does not mean that all law is *codified*. The codification of rules into a complete body or *code of law* which can only be changed through legislators is the defining characteristic of civil law jurisdictions like Germany. In common law jurisdictions such as the UK and the US, not only legislators, but also courts can *make law* by setting precedents which must then be observed in later court rulings.

The difference between codified civil law and non-codified common law pints to the basic operation of any legal system: *the reconciliation of the particular with the general*.[13] For law to govern all possible human behavior, it must consolidate similar forms of behavior into abstract categories (e.g. fraud) and define general rules of legal assessment (e.g. intent and financial gain). Social reality, on the other hand, is concrete, not abstract. The real life situations out of which legal disputes arise are always local, specific, and bound to a certain time and place. Any legal case represents a unique set of related facts, and each case demands to be looked upon as a whole, as something which is more than the sum of its part and which may ultimately differ from seemingly identical cases. Killing a person for money constitutes a very different legal case than killing a person out of self-defense.

Through their ability to adjust to the social environment and through the hierar-chical structure of laws, legal systems allow for flexibility and change. The less fundamental a law, the easier it can be adjusted if public opinion shifts or political

---

[13]Common law, by allowing judges to set precedents and create law, emphasizes the particular case, while civil law, restricting judges to the mere application of existing laws, emphasizes the general rule. Yet even civil law jurisdictions develop mechanisms to use court decisions for legislative purposes. In Germany, the "Bundesverfassungsgericht" (Federal Constitutional Court) over the past 60 years has become the de facto last instance to resolve political conflicts, reaching from military draft and freedom of speech to abortion and issues of social equality. While political scientists lament the seeming dissolution of the division of powers, the political parties themselves consciously use the path to the *Bundesverfassungsgericht* to avoid making unpopular decisions, e.g. regarding European integration. It appears that in common law jurisdictions, perceived inadequacies of existing laws to do justice to single cases is dealt with immediately by lower courts, while in civil law jurisdictions, such perceived inadequacies are escalated upwards and dealt with only on the highest court level.

processes require it. In federal countries, state and communal laws may differ in certain practice areas, reflecting the values and beliefs of the respective constituencies, and such state and communal laws can also be changed more easily than the national constitution embodying the values and beliefs of the whole population.[14]

Of course, even constitutions do evolve over time, along with the human experience upon which they are built. The US constitution was put in effect in 1789 and has been amended 27 times, last in 1992. Throughout human history, technological advancement, most of all in the areas of transportation and telecommunication, enabled and also forced states, companies and individuals to collaborate across different jurisdictions. The twentieth century has seen alignment of national criminal, tax and finance laws to common standards established and upheld by the United Nations, the European Union and other inter- and supranational organizations. International private law becomes increasingly important since, for example, more and more people with different nationalities get married and divorced. Technological innovation like the internet have enabled new social practices and created new legal subject areas. The high volume electronic trading of ill-rated derivatives which caused the Great Recession in 2007/08 has led to the Dodd-Frank Act and other legislation that imposes stronger regulations on financial markets.

On the other hand, globalization also caused, and continues to cause, ideological counter movements insisting on regional, local and religious identities. The vote of the British people to leave the European Union (EU) is the latest example of this widespread desire to maintain a sense of national self in the face of increasing globalization and integration. In the Middle East, revolutions and warfare have led to radical changes of legal systems, a recent example being the establishment of the Sharia, the Islam religious law, by the terror organization "Islamic State" in large parts of Syria, Iraq and Libya.

But such abrupt and fundamental changes of legal systems are few and far between, and they remain restricted to times of social crisis and war. Law can *claim* to govern everyday life precisely because the majority of people experience the law as relatively stable during their lifetime. By providing security, fostering trust and enabling people to work together, law is both, an expression and a fundamental driver of human civilization.

---

[14]Linguistic vagueness and ambiguity in fundamental laws and frame contracts is often intentional to leave space for refinement in subordinate laws and contracts. Through such ambiguity, the frequent and rather insignificant changes on the lower level do not require changes on the higher level—which could create severe uncertainty and instability. The wording in constitutions will be rather abstract, vague and ambiguous (for example, §1 of the German constitution states: *"The dignity of man is untouchable"*), and the wording in traffic decrees will be rather concrete, clear and unambiguous (*"Parking cars outside of designated parking areas will result in a fine of 5 Euros"*).

Because laws must be explicit and communicable, they are usually coded in written language.[15] Philosophical attempts to define laws more abstractly, e.g. as "a particular kind of assemblage of signs" or as "signification of volition" appear to be problematic and have met widespread criticism.[16] The coding of laws in language does not mean that language is the only medium relevant to the legal professional. When lawyers practice law, for example by drafting contracts or advancing arguments in court, they do so primarily in language and with words, but not exclusively.

We all know from personal experience that it matters in which medium a "message" appears. Reading a Harry Potter book, and watching a Harry Potter movie, are two very different experiences, although both media carry the same content in terms of characters and plot. Language conveys information sequentially and creates a relative clear cognitive understanding while images convey a totality of information instantaneously through an aesthetic impression, but are also more open to interpretation and different meanings. As the Canadian media theorist Marshall McLuhan famously stated: *"The medium is the message."*

A specific medium of communication can thus further or hamper legal intentions. Haapio and Barton[17] convincingly argue that the use of images can make the meaning of written contracts more intuitively understandable for laymen. However, images may also blur cognitive nuances which can matter in contracts, and Haapio and Barton thus also point out that images should only support and not replace language as the primary form of contracting. In court, the showing of video footage depicting, for example, a physical assault certainly conveys a more objective account of what happened than a verbal description by a witness (provided, of course, that the video has not been tampered with). On the other hand, the strong emotional impact of such images may cause jurors and judges to deemphasize, or even overlook, other facts of the case, perhaps making it more likely that the defendant is being convicted.

Thus in legal, there always exist uncertainties, trade-offs, and pros and cons for each position. As the seemingly least ambiguous medium, language is privileged over images and other forms of legal signification. Linguistic proficiency and good communication skills are central to the work of lawyers, and they represent important hiring criteria which companies use to assess the quality of job applicants. Also, the semantics (meaning) and pragmatics (usage) of legal language differ from everyday language. Sheila Hyatt from the University of Denver points out that the legal system creates new words like "judicata" and "mens rea," and also gives a specific meaning to ordinary words. Legal language demands a high degree

---

[15]Oral laws only exist in primitive cultures. The unwritten rules of illegal or otherwise secret organizations like the Mafia are not sanctioned through official social institutions and thus cannot be called *laws*.

[16]Stanford Encyclopedia of Philosophy: Law and Language. http://plato.stanford.edu/entries/law-language (2016). Accessed Oct. 15, 2016.

[17]Helena Haapio, Prof. Thomas D. Barton, "Business-Friendly Contracting," in LL, p. 389.

of precision, down to the use of commas, to ensure that intentions are expressed correctly.

> (A) person who leaves $50,000 'to each of my children who took care of me,' has a different intention than a person who leaves $50,000 'to each of my children, who took care of me.'[18]

Finally, the meaning of many legal terms such as "resident" depends on the particular practice area (e.g. getting a driver's license, or getting a divorce) and on the nation or state in which it occurs. The German political theorist Carl Schmitt has used the Greek concept of *Nomos* to express this *unity of location and law* (in the German original: *"die Einheit von Ortung und Ordnung"*).[19]

To clarify the importance of context, I want to compare the functioning of legal to the functioning of language. My thesis is that both function as a systemic structure in which the context ultimately determines the meaning of single elements. Like all languages, English consists of different kinds of words (nouns, adjectives, verbs, conjunctions, prepositions, etc.) and a set of rules (grammar) prescribing how these words can be combined to sentences. In order to speak and write, and for participating in the social practice of communication, the speaker or author must know the whole system of language even though he or she only uses a very small subset of the linguistic possibilities. The reason is that words (in linguistic terms: the signifiers) have no intrinsic reference (in linguistic terms: the signified), and that linguistic meaning is an effect of formal differences. A single word alone does not mean anything. There is nothing intrinsic to the signifier "house" that signifies a house, the real object with walls and a roof that people live in. Rather, the signifier "house" can only signify a real object *because* it differs from other signifiers, e.g. from "louse," "mouse" and all other words in the English language. *Linguistic meaning rests on a system of difference between signifiers, and meaning, therefore, is always dependent on context.*

In the following part, I will take a closer look at *legal in business*. If the meaning of single laws depends on the whole system of law—what happens when this whole system of law is framed by economic and financial interests?

3   "Win-Win" Versus "Win-Lose": The Systemic Predicament of In-House Legal Departments

One of my friends is a corporate lawyer in a logistics enterprise. Occasionally, we have lunch together, and one time he told me about his work.

---

[18]Sheila Hyatt: Legal Language. https://www.law.du.edu/index.php/law-school-learningaids/legal-language. Accessed Oct. 15, 2016.

[19]See: Schmitt (2003).

"I love my job," he said, *"but it also stresses me. The stakes are high. One mistake in my contracting and litigation cases could have devastating effects for the whole company – we are talking millions, and in some cases hundreds of millions of Euro! But that's not the problem. I actually like big cases because all parties send their best lawyers, and together, we usually settle things in a good way. And the few times we don't settle, I take my case to court, and I enjoy that as well. No, my problem is not the work as such – it is the quantity of work! I do not just have three or four cases in parallel, I have a dozen of them, and they keep getting more. It's simply too much, I drown in cases!"*

I tried helping my friend by telling him the story of *The Busy Woodchoppers*, a story my first manager told me when I started out in the software industry about 20 years ago.

The Busy Woodchoppers *A man encounters a group of feverishly working woodchoppers in the forest. "Why are you working so hard?" he asks one of them. "Well," the woodchopper answers, "we have to cut down all these trees, and we are behind schedule."—"Why are you behind schedule?" the man asks. "It always happens," the woodchopper sighs, "when we work hard, our axes become blunt, and then we must work even harder to make up for the lost time."—"So why don't you take a break and sharpen your axes?"—"Oh no," the woodchopper exclaims, "that would take far too much time – I told you, we are already behind schedule!"*

As investors, we know it takes money to make money. As project managers, we ought to know that *it takes time to make time*. My friend's situation reminded me of the woodchopper story because, like these hard working men, he seemed to focus too much on the execution of single cases, and too little on creating the tools that would enable him to scale case execution.

Why have legal in-house departments come under such extreme pressure to increase their performance?

On the surface, the demand to "do more with less" was the result of the Great Recession in 2007/08 and the increased financial strains on business enterprises. But underlying this effect of the financial crisis is what I would like to call the *systemic predicament of in-house legal departments*, a conflict of two frames of references: business and legal. To illustrate the systemic difference between business and legal, recall the definition of legal as a self-referential and operationally closed system that maintains its own identity against the environment by relying on the binary code "legal or illegal." I use the example of *contracts* to first of all illustrate the systemic interdependence of dissolving and creating legal ambiguity in a business enterprise.[20]

---

[20]A plethora of literature exists on the topic of ambiguity in contracts which I will not deal with here. In general, the discussions center around the questions how ambiguity can be avoided in the first place and how it is best dealt with once it is perceived (see, for example, Contra Proferentem). This article, however, is primarily concerned with the *systemic function of ambiguity* and seeks to show that ambiguity is constitutive for legal operations per se.

While contracts are intended to express a joint desire of the contracting parties and to create a clear understanding of mutual rights and obligations, such unambiguity is, in principle, unattainable. During all phases of the contract cycle, the legal meaning of the contract and its clauses depends on contexts: on the explicit context documented in the contract itself, and on implicit contexts assumed by the parties. The diversity of such implicit contexts become apparent when claims are made, e.g. when real events reveal opposing interests of the contracting parties and create legal conflicts.

Personally, I like the old-fashioned way of contracting: You look each other in the eyes and shake hands on a joint goal—and if there's a problem down the road, you take care of it then. Of course, that is the business person speaking. For lawyers, such an attitude is reckless at best and clearly contradicts the mandate to reduce the legal risks of clients. In a contractual situation, the desire to prevent such risks and to ensure maximum legal protection for each party motivates lawyers to turn implicit contexts ("What if...?") into explicit contexts, for example by adding new clauses to the contract. Over time, contracts thus become larger, more complex—and again more ambiguous.

The increase in government regulations and compliance laws can itself be seen as a consequence of the self-referentiality of the legal system. For *public institutions* like parliaments and courts, self-referentiality presents no problem because legal is their sole purpose. Financial and other restrictions may indirectly affect their activities, but they are merely means to an end. The law remains the only normative frame of reference.

Law firms are in a different situation. They are commercial entities that sell legal services to external clients. As businesses, their ultimate frame of reference is financial, and legal services are only the means by which law firms achieve this financial end. But since legal is their core service, the business of law firms largely coincides with legal competence. Legal and business performance are strictly proportional in law firms and can be measured in billable hours and revenue.

Such a direct connection between legal and business does not exist *for in-house legal departments* in complex enterprises. Legal departments are cost-centers providing an internal support function for selling non-legal products and services, and in doing so, they must observe corporate requirements and economies of scope and scale. By having to reconcile two often conflicting normative frames of reference, legal in-house departments find themselves in a predicament which can best be expressed as the conflict between two relational paradigms: *win-win* versus *win-lose*.

In a market economy, business rests on the idea that all parties, e.g. seller and buyer, benefit from a transaction—otherwise the transaction would not occur. Money, the medium through which the economic system functions, is expandable[21]

---

[21] Similar to the hierarchical structure of laws (from constitutions down to decrees), the concept of *money* includes different levels of supply: M0 is the name for the money base, the sum of cash and central bank reserves; on this level, money is closest to its function as concrete payment method.

and allows for win-win relations, i.e. both parties can "make money" through one and the same transaction. Public corporations, for example, can simultaneously increase both their respective stock value through a merger or acquisition. From an economic perspective, rational agents will only spend money if they believe the transaction possesses value that equates or exceeds the costs of consumption (e.g. buying a private car) or investment (e.g. buying a company car). Just like the ideal of "justice" serves as norm in the legal system, with laws (and the binary code of "legal or illegal") as medium of social implementation, the ideal of "value"[22] serves as norm in the economic system, with money (and the binary code of "gain or loss") as medium of social implementation. In the economic system, "win-win" relations, expressed as monetary gains through business transactions, are possible and, in fact, the norm.

The legal system, on the other hand, is characterized by adversarial relations and the binary code of "right or wrong" (legal or illegal). If one party *wins* a case in court, it normally means that the other party has *lost*. Laws, the medium through which the legal system functions, are fixed, and opposing claims cannot both be right—otherwise laws would lose their ability to govern human behavior.[23]

Because the outcome of legal cases is hard to predict, rational agents such as business enterprises think twice before going to court and risking losing a case. Instead, they will try to quantify their legal risks and consider alternative means of dispute resolution. Hagel[24] provides detailed examples for how legal disputes can be translated into a business case of monetary gains and losses, and he also emphasizes the importance of communication for avoiding costly court cases.

> The goal in dispute management is to minimize the risks while maximizing the profit. (...) Except for rare cases, avoiding conflicts and disputes makes commercial sense. In order to effectively avoid conflicts, the main causes of disputes need to be known. Disputes are often caused by miscommunication. Parties communicate (1) on the wrong subjects, (2) in the wrong way and (3) at the wrong time.

Yet even though conflicting parties seek to avoid miscommunication by collaborating and settling legal conflicts outside of court, they only do so because they *fear losing the case in court*. "Win-lose" is the relational paradigm in the legal

---

The higher levels of money supply, from M1 to M3, are increasingly more removed from everyday life and include abstract forms of money such as credits and stocks. See Wikipedia on Money Supply.

[22]The understanding of economic terms depends on the theoretical framework applied, and thus there are numerous definitions of "value." Mark Skousen in "The Making of Modern Economics," New York 2009, presents a good overview of economic theories and their terminology.

[23]In some cases, courts may rule that both parties are partly "right" and partly "wrong," and occasionally, both parties may feel, or at least say, they "won" the case. But such psychological "win-win" outcomes are not the norm and simply illustrate that parties can only do one of three things in reaction to a court ruling: they can either accept the ruling (and maybe declare victory to feel better), file an appeal (if legally possible, thus producing more costs and more uncertainty), or disobey the court ruling—and risk social sanctions like fines and imprisonment.

[24]Dr. Ulrich Hagel, "The Dispute as a Business Case," in LL, p. 242.

system, and it contrasts sharply with the "win-win" relational paradigm of the economic system. In this systemic perspective, the increase of alternative dispute resolutions suggests that businesses prefer to remain within their own economic system of "making or losing money" and seek to avoid entering the legal system of "being right or wrong" in the first place. Lawyers are not only averse to risk but to change in general. Byberg[25] remarks:

> Lawyers are notoriously skeptical about change, and while there are honorable exceptions, my experience is that the general public is more right than wrong when thinking of the legal community as change-resistant. My favorite quote to this point is a Danish Supreme Court Judge allegedly having stated that he was resisting all change—including change for the better!

Going forward, I structure the activities of in-house legal departments in a 2×2 matrix. On one axis, I distinguish two frames of reference: law (being right or wrong), and business (making or losing money). The business frame of reference includes internal rules which a company gives itself in order to advance its goals and produce positive outcomes. Such internal business rules are often expressed in corporate value and mission statements as well as internal policies and guidelines which are considered "good" for business, or else the organization would not impose these rules on itself. How a company understands and practices social responsibility, the ways it deals with diversity and other ethical norms may have no immediate connection to revenue and profit. But by investors and employees alike, these activities are increasingly seen as crucial for branding and competitive advantage, as Mucic[26] argues:

> For too long we have neglected the influence of Legal on how the companies they serve are perceived. The way a company deals with legal issues, the language it uses in legal contexts, in contracts and clauses tells a story that we are often not aware of. So do our legal decisions: when and how we negotiate, litigate, settle, appeal, and when we "interpret" the rules—all of that constantly produces context that employees and the outside world read as indicators of our corporate culture. Legal decisions and discourse clearly have strong ramifications in what the external codified law requires and what financial gains or losses may come with them for our companies, but they also have a lot to do with what a company stands for or rather would like to stand for, that is with its purpose and its values.

On the other axis of our 2×2 matrix, I distinguish two kinds of client engagement in rendering legal services: By "downstream engagement" I mean that lawyers react to a request *coming down from the clients*, and by "upstream engagement" I mean that lawyers work pro-actively *towards the clients*, trying to promote "right" behavior and seeking to avoid the emergence of legal issues in the first place (Fig. 2).

---

[25] Arne Byberg, "Change Management for Lawyers," in LL, p. 175.
[26] Luka Mucic, "Bridging the Gap – The New Legal," in LL, p. xi.

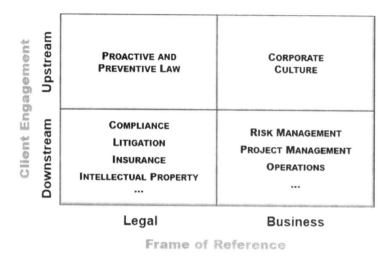

Fig. 2 In-house Legal Service Portfolio (own material)

When we look at legal services in this 2 × 2 matrix, it becomes clear that most activities fall in the lower left quadrant: In litigation, insurance, compliance and intellectual property issues as well as in all other traditional practice areas, legal departments' frame of reference is the law, and its normal mode of engagement is to react to ad hoc service requests (downstream). Lawyers seek to achieve their internal clients' explicit goal by reconciling the facts of the case at hand with the law.

It is less common that legal departments refer to external law in a proactive mode and deliver upstream services with the goal to prevent the emergence of legal issues or cases in the first place (upper left quadrant). Nonetheless, *Proactive and Preventive Law* is a growing discipline, as Haapio and Barton[27] remark:

> Preventive Law focuses on dysfunctional cycles that generate recurring losses. It seeks to identify and understand the conflicting elements of a system, as we have done above, that unless somehow resolved will continue to generate problems. Proactive Law adds a focus to achieving positive goals and value. Together, PPL can alter mentalities and harness tools toward smoother operations and successful outcomes.

In the lower right quadrant, the frame of reference is business, so self-imposed rules supporting monetary gains, and the mode of client engagement is reactive (downstream). I have put risk management and project management here as two examples for such legal services. By assessing the likelihood and financial impact of legal risks, risk management helps convert legal issues into business issues. Meents and Allen[28] differentiates pre-engagement legal risks, referring to a

---

[27]Helena Haapio, Prof. Thomas D. Barton, "Business-Friendly Contracting," in LL, p. 376.

[28]Jan Geert Meents and Stephen Allen, "The Value of Everything," in LL, p. 232.

company's breach of regulatory obligations, and post-engagement legal risks, referring to situations in which a company fails to carry out contractual obligations. Mascello[29] remarks on the changed role of general counsels:

> (T)he general counsel is now perceived as a risk manager. He is also expected to provide general problem-solving beyond legal subject-matter tasks and to act as a co-designer of the company's strategic development. Consequently, legal strategies are being integrated into corporate strategies.

Besides risk management, project management is becoming increasingly important to legal departments. As a reaction to the financial crisis, many companies have reduced internal legal staff and outsourced work to law firms. While externalizing service delivery reduces the need for subject matter expertise, it also requires corporate counsels to use proven methodology and IT tools to manage a high number of parallel projects and to deliver results on time and budget. In-house lawyers must have a good market overview and select the right law firm, get contracts in place and check invoices, set up the case strategy together with external counsel, keep deadlines in mind, validate work results, and solve all kinds of problems and operational hick-ups along the way.

The upper right quadrant of the in-house legal service portfolio matrix shows *corporate culture* as a practice area. I use corporate culture as an umbrella term for proactive (upstream) legal activities in a business frame of reference—activities enabling and promoting internal and sometimes even tacit rules for collaboration and win-win relationships. For many enterprises, culture holds high and unrealized value potentials, and we will explore these value potentials in the last part of this article.

4 Collaboration, Corporate Culture, and the Business of Legal

In Berlin, I often walk by a second-hand store called "Goods without Fault" *("Waren ohne Mängel")*. The naiveté of this marketing approach has always baffled me. *Why should a fundamental requirement of any product ever be worth mentioning, let alone entice customers to buy?* Basically all goods, second hand or not, must function and be without fault—or else one could only use them for spare parts. It seems to me that the owner of this store has little understanding of fundamental marketing principles.

It's similar with legal departments: To present the legal department's achievements to executives, as many general counsels do, by saying "We do legal well," or "We protect our clients from legal risk," etc. actually offers little marketing value—*because protection from legal risk is why legal departments*

---

[29]Dr. Bruno Mascello, "Procurement of legal services – How customers professionally procure legal services today," in LL, p. 292.

exist. Companies hire and pay lawyers because they are expected to do legal well—
it's a fundamental requirement of the job!

Of course, legal departments possess a certain degree of freedom in how exactly
they organize the work. Lawyers may specialize in certain practice areas, or
become generalists with a broad knowledge over many practice areas. And general
counsels may choose to insource or outsource case work. Sako[30] has investigated
the conditions under which general counsels tend to internalize or externalize legal
work:

> Evidence from Fortune 500 companies reveal that internalizing corporations have more
> intangible assets (such as brands and intellectual property) to defend, and are more
> international in their presence. Moreover, companies that externalize legal resources have
> developed more stable relationships with fewer law firms, each providing legal services in a
> broader range of practice areas.

Yet regardless of how and by whom the work is done: If legal departments want
to lead the business, they must deliver value above and beyond what is expected of
them, and they have to start promoting their achievements. My impression is that in
order to repair their damaged image, legal departments should make a stronger
effort to market themselves—even though, or rather *because* most lawyers seem to
frown upon such activities. Endowed with a special education prescribed and
sanctioned by society, lawyers used to offer what Timmer calls *credence services*:
services whose quality clients cannot assess because they lack the knowledge to do
so. Now however, legal departments stand next to Legal Process Outsourcers (LPO)
and other alternative legal service providers, and therefore, in the eyes of many
executives, in-house departments *"need to earn the right to exist."* This right should
be earned not by competing but by collaborating with LPOs. Ross'[31] argument for
strategic collaboration between law firms and LPOs applies equally to in-house
legal departments because like law firms, legal departments will use LPOs only for
the effective delivery of internal services and not for representing their companies
in court:

> The theory behind strategic collaboration is not rocket science, just the premise that the
> whole is greater than the sum of the parts. Contrary to early concerns that LPO providers
> would compete directly with law firms, it has become abundantly clear to those firms
> embracing strategic collaboration that the most effective legal services delivery model is a
> symbiotic ecosystem in which law firms and LPO providers both play crucial roles. LPO
> providers do not practice law and so are not true alternatives to law firms. (Ross, p. 6)

For in-house legal departments, there is absolutely nothing dubious or shameful
about doing good things for the company—*and talking about them*. Legal
departments must promote themselves to their clients, to corporate executive and

---

[30]Mari Sako, "Globalization and the Changing Role of General Counsel," in LL, p. 33.
[31]Mark Ross, "Legal Process Outsourcing," in LL, p. 83.

to their own team members just like all other lines of business do. Brown[32] points out that legal can benefit hugely simply by learning from others:

> Successful legal departments address the growing "more for less" challenge by adopting proven, relevant practices from other business functions. The most effective General Counsel and senior legal department leaders have stepped into their 'C-suite of Legal' shoes, running the legal department with business discipline.

I want to pick up Brown's idea of a "C-suite of Legal" and illustrate what and how legal can learn from three other established business functions: management, operations, and human resources.

4.1   The Management of Legal

Many general counsels have reacted to executive pressure by measuring and managing legal performance and by trying to involve legal in strategic business decisions. Pauleau, Collard and Roquilly[33] write:

> The legal performance of a company can be understood in two different ways. In a narrow sense, it refers to the performance of its LD, in other words the capacity of that department to achieve its own missions and objectives. (...) A broader – and perhaps more appropriate – understanding is to see legal performance as the company's ability to deploy legal resources (especially intangible resources such as a specific legal capability) and combine them with the other types of resources at its disposal in order to achieve its objectives, in particular its strategic objectives. In this sense, legal performance can be considered as an important factor in the overall performance of the company. And the performance achieved by the legal team significantly contributes to the legal performance of the company as a whole.

Bassli[34] emphasizes that general counsels must pay more attention to financial metrics and business planning, for example by questioning traditional models of engaging and paying for law firms, and by considering managed services as an alternative:

> Switching from a traditional hourly based billing model to a managed legal services model yields business benefits for both sides of the engagement. One benefit that immediately comes to mind is the predictability of a recurring monthly billing. A flat fee for services eliminates the peaks and troughs of normal hourly billing, making forecasting easier and more reliable for both parties.

---

[32]Liam Brown, "Running the Legal Department with Business Discipline," in LL, p. 397.
[33]Pauleau, Collard, Roquilly, "KPIs: Run Legal with Business Metrics," *in LL*, p. 119.
[34]Lucy Endel Bassli, "Shifting Client Expectations of Law Firms," in LL, p. 66.

Meents[35] cautions against a purely cost focused approach in managing legal and emphasizes the importance of delivering effective services that secure value realization and prevent value leakage:

> Measuring cost is important. Legal functions need to be more efficient, and their failure to do so has only increased the level of scrutiny they face. Almost all commentary on legal departments, to date, has focused on the cost of legal and its failure to leverage technology and alternative ways of working. However, if everything is viewed only through the 'cost lens' then effectiveness is often overlooked - and 'value' not understood.

The orientation towards finances and performance also brings up the question if future general counsels must be lawyers at all, as asked by Hartung and Gärtner[36]:

> Nowadays, most GCs are lawyers. Is this a necessary prerequisite for a GC? Rather not. The GC has to advise the board on the best, or most appropriate, way forward with regard to risk and compliance management. Many legal and/or regulatory questions have to be taken into account. However, a GC who only focuses on legal issues would miss the point. Hence, being a lawyer can be one of the preconditions of being a good GC but it is not a conditio sine qua non.

Finally, Chomicka[37] points out that the separation of tasks from education not only allows non-lawyers to work in legal, but also enables lawyers to work in other lines of business, thus creating new job opportunities:

> What if a contract administrator, contract manager or even a project manager, rather than a construction professional with an appreciation of legal issues, happens to be a law practitioner trained in basic construction 'stuff'?

4.2 The Operations of Legal

Since its inception some years ago, the Corporate Legal Operations Consortium (CLOC), a non-profit community of legal professionals, has looked at legal departments as true business units whose internal operations must be optimized for efficiency and strategic relevance. Brenton,[38] two of the founders of CLOC, describe leading legal departments as being proactive and business minded:

> These teams don't simply solve the problems that their internal clients bring them – they anticipate and plan. They don't just try to run more efficiently – they innovate and experiment. They listen to their "customers" – the internal client teams – but don't limit their contributions simply to addressing their issues. Their numbers are few, but growing.

---

[35] Jan Geert Meents and Stephen Allen, "The Value of Everything," p. 227.

[36] Hartung, Gärtner, "The Future of In-house Legal Departments and their Impact on the Legal Market," in LL, p. 283.

[37] Barbara Chomicka, "A rose under any other name," in LL, p. 142.

[38] Connie Brenton, "Sharing Best Practices and Setting Standards," in LL, p. 304.

Roux-Chenu and de Rocca-Serra[39] argue along the same lines and call for legal departments to become business creators:

> Every Legal Department should be looking to not only be a business enabler but it should be a business creator in order to make a real difference. This is possible because very often the Legal Department is involved in contract negotiations with the whole ecosystem, in the case of Capgemini this would mean clients, procurement and alliances contracts. This unique central position allows Legal to have a 360° view, to foresee the needs of the market, and to develop solutions for its internal and external clients.

von Alemann[40] stresses that both, the challenge and the opportunity to improve operations through communication with other business functions applies equally to legal departments in large corporations and in small and midsize enterprises (SME):

> The need to constantly communicate with other departments of the company may be even more important for members of small legal departments than for members of bigger legal departments. That is because small legal departments – as opposed to large legal departments – usually do not have a formalized process for alignment with other departments. Through communication, members of small legal departments can therefore detect legal issues early and prevent non-compliance instead of only reacting to legal problems after they are discovered. By communicating with other corporate functions as business partners, legal departments of all sizes can actively shape the direction of the business, for example by providing options, by communicating legal problems early and by making sure all stakeholders are involved.

Such constant communication of legal with other departments is facilitated by information technology (IT) and the increasing digitalization of legal service delivery. Although technology is only part of a systemic solution mix which must also include governance, process and people aspects, it is in this area that legal departments can have the greatest impact and fastest success for satisfying business expectations. The English anthropologist Gregory Bateson defined information as "a difference that makes a difference," i.e. a change that matters to an observer. IT improves legal operations not only by providing the tools for scaling communication, i.e. the exchange of information, but also by creating new insights and shifting basic forms of legal reasoning from humans to machines, as Zetterberg and Wojcik[41] remark:

> There is an entirely new type of software, very different than office automation or efficiency tools, and it changes the way lawyers work. It leverages a new set of technologies referred to as Artificial Intelligence (AI), and combines Machine Learning (ML) and Natural

---

[39]Isabelle Roux-Chenu, Elisa de Rocca-Serra, "How the Legal Department Can Be a Business Enabler," in LL, p. 203.

[40]Dr. Sven von Alemann, "LegalTech Will Radically Change the Way SMEs Handle Legal," in LL, p. 215.

[41]Ulf Zetterberg, Christina Wojcik, "How Emerging Technology is bringing In-House Legal Counsel into Modern Legal and Business Practices," in LL, p. 326.

Language Processing (NLP) in a way to help lawyers change what they do in their engagement with clients, not just make what they do more efficient.

However, Matthaei and Bues[42] point out that for the foreseeable future, lawyers will not be replaced by robots since the definition of a problem domain, i.e. the setting of a context within which legal meaning arises, requires a form of strong AI which currently is still beyond reach:

AI currently used in LegalTech tools is far away from strong AI. [Therefore, when we speak of AI in the context of LegalTech, we mean technologies which seem intelligent but have defined functions, i.e. weak AI.] It uses models of its problem domain given to it by programmers. Weak AI cannot perform autonomous reduction, whereas strong AI has a real understanding of a problem domain. Therefore, weak AI requires an expert who performs all required reduction in advance and implements it into a system. As a result, weak AI will only have a specific set of tasks it can solve.

4.3   The Human Resources of Legal

As important as technology and efficient operations are for legal departments, Hartung and Gärtner are absolutely right in stating that "*processes and structure won't save the company's life in a crisis. It is instead the human workforce that makes the difference.*" Telling his own career story, Fawcett[43] provides a real life example of how leadership and team work can transform a legal department:

As a renewed leadership team, we changed the culture of the group from what it had been – a loosely organized collection of lawyers – to a true team of business partners and counselors. We found new ways to work with outside counsel, getting better returns and accountability by using data in powerful new ways. We implemented a new "Legal Ecosystem" that integrated legal operations professionals alongside traditional legal experts into a single, coherent global team.

Tumasjan and Welpe[44] maintain that, in order to lead and act entrepreneurially, lawyers must shift from a predominantly preventive to a predominantly promotional mindset:

Regulatory focus theory posits that individuals use two different mindsets to guide their behavior: promotion vs. prevention focus (Higgins, 1998). In a promotion focus, individuals concentrate on gains, advancement, growth, and positive outcomes. They act with an open mindset toward novel opportunities, consider many different alternatives, and "think big". In contrast, in a prevention focus, individuals concentrate on losses, security, safety, and negative outcomes. They exhibit high vigilance, are prone to behave and think conservatively, and focus on details and accurateness (Halvorson & Higgins, 2013).

---

[42]Dr. Emilio Matthaei, Dr. Micha-Manuel Bues, "The Bright Future of LegalTech," in LL, p. 93.

[43]Matthew Fawcett, "Creating Your Path: Building Towards Liquid Legal," in LL, p. xi.

[44]Dr. Andranik Tumasjan, Prof. Dr. Isabell M. Welpe, "The Legal Entrepreneur," in LL, p. 130.

Individuals act in both mindsets – depending on the task and situation – but usually, one of the mindsets is dominant.

While entrepreneurial spirit transcends race and gender, Markfort[45] points out that in most legal departments, promoting diversity and gender equality is still in its infancy:

Lawyering, for a long time, has been a masculine domain. We are just starting to take stock of the real negative impact inflicted on our global society by gender inequality. Whether viewed from an ethical, economic or managerial perspective, statistics demonstrate the benefits we are collectively and individually missing if we don't give this matter the consideration it truly deserves.

The below diamond-shaped model of Liquid Legal summarizes what legal departments can learn from established business functions like management, operations and human resources. It combines the four dimensions of principles, people, portfolio and processes into a holistic approach for transforming traditionally reactive and law-focused silos into agile networks that not only satisfy increasing demands for service efficiency and effectiveness, but also, as announced in the title of this paper, reverse the situation and actually start leading the business (Fig. 3).

Fig. 3 Liquid Legal Model (own material)

---

[45]Dr. Rainer Markfort, "Shifting the Mind Set of Lawyers," in LL, p. 52.

Liquid legal is not defined by departmental borders, hierarchical reporting and an "us versus them" mentality, but by dispersed communities in all lines of business which share the same norms and values. From proactive and preventive law, liquid legal takes over *"(t)he goal (...) to promote 'legal well-being': embedding legal knowledge and skills in corporate culture, strategy and everyday actions to actively promote success, ensure desired outcomes, balance risk with reward, and prevent problems."* (Haapio and Barton, p. 17)

I want to use the term *corporate culture* to denote implicit and often tacit behavioral norms that promote creativity, collaboration and self-organized teams, a culture in which processes and the interaction of people are more important than fixed structures and managerial ranks.

Seen from a business perspective, law is at least as much collaborative as it is adversarial. One does not have to be an expert in idealism to understand one of the German philosopher Hegel's basic ideas, namely that *giving ourselves a rule is the highest form of human freedom*. Law not only means freedom *from op*pression, but also freedom *for ex*pression. It is because of the trust in law that foreigners interact and do business with each other although they are not personally acquainted. In cultural artefacts throughout human history, from religious texts thousands of years old to contemporary Hollywood movies, *good* wins over *evil* because the villains, by abusing their fellow men and only seeking their own advantage, fail to create lasting communities and ultimately always turn on themselves. Trust is the ultimate legal currency, and the greatest value delivered by law!

Let lawyers be the ones to prove to employees, executives and the whole organization that pursuing business opportunities does not have to be at the expense of legal security. Legal departments of the future can start improving their internal standing by promoting a culture of trust. Just like the heart pumps blood through physical organisms, legal, by establishing fair and transparent rules among people, departments, lines of businesses, divisions and subsidiaries, *can carry trust through business organisms. Liquid legal* is the belief that trust is the essence of business—and that together, we are better off than alone.

Legal can lead the business because lawyers are masters of ambiguity—trained to see different sides of a matter, to understand varying interests of different parties, and to lay the foundation for win-win situations. When it comes to mergers and acquisitions, to corporate strategy, to product lines and service portfolios, in fact: with regard to all business decisions that require assessing scenarios and weighing alternatives, lawyers should stop limiting themselves to legal aspects only. Instead, they need to go above and beyond what is expected of them and simply start applying their key skill in a business frame of reference: the ability to reason and to think through ambiguity.

5   No Conclusion

In this article, I have tried to outline basic ideas for a theory of Liquid Legal: systemic reflections on why and how corporate legal departments should transcend the confinement of traditional practice areas and apply their ability to think through ambiguity in a business frame of reference. Legal can lead the business if it stays conscious of its role to *serve*. The new theory of *servant leadership*[46] stresses the importance for any leader to selflessly serve an ideal. Lawyers, by definition, serve the law and the ideal of *"doing the right thing."* And in an increasingly complex world, lawyers, as *servants*, might be just the kind of leaders that today's businesses need: smart, committed, and prepared for the unexpected.

References

Luhmann, N. (1992). Operational closure and structural coupling: The differentiation of the legal system. *Cardoso Law Review, 13*, 1419–1441.
Schmitt, C. (2003). *The Nomos of the Earth.* Telos Press (original publication: 1950).
Strathausen, R. (2015). *Leading when you're not the boss – How to get things done in complex corporate cultures.* New York: Apress.

Dr. Roger Strathausen is a business consultant with expertise in Leadership and Legal Strategy whose clients are multinational companies. He was previously a senior manager at Accenture and an employee at SAP. Dr. Strathausen lectured at the Technical University of Berlin, the Universities of Heidelberg and Kaiserslautern, and the Berlin School of Economics and Law (HWR) where he promotes his vision of LIQUID LEGAL. He took his PhD from Stanford University while on Fulbright and Stanford Fellowships and his MA from the University of Tuebingen. His website is: www.strathausen.com

---

[46]See "Servant Leadership" in Wikipedia.

Globalization and the Changing Role of General Counsel: Current Trends and Future Scenarios

Mari Sako

Abstract

Globalization and digital technology have transformed the role of general counsel in the past few decades. This chapter presents a series of studies to explain in what ways the general counsel has transformed the in-house legal function and its relationships with law firms. In response to demands to deliver more legal work for less cost, corporate legal departments have either internalized or externalized legal work. Evidence from *Fortune 500* companies reveal that internalizing corporations have more intangible assets (such as brands and intellectual property) to defend, and are more international in their presence. Moreover, companies that externalize legal resources have developed more stable relationships with fewer law firms, each providing legal services in a broader range of practice areas. As corporate clients enhance their international presence, particularly in newer emerging markets, some of them are finding the global mandate of large law firms, which are far less international than other professional service firms in accounting and consulting, less than satisfactory. The chapter concludes by briefly laying out four possible future scenarios in global legal services markets. We identify under what circumstances the corporate legal department is likely to grow and remain powerful in relation to external providers of legal services.

1   Introduction

Globalization and digital technology are pervasive forces that present challenges and opportunities for lawyers in the twenty-first century. Digital technology has transformed professional work in ways unimaginable several decades earlier. It is

M. Sako (✉)
Saïd Business School, University of Oxford, Park End Street, Oxford OX1 1HP, UK
e-mail: Mari.sako@sbs.ox.ac.uk

© Springer International Publishing AG 2017
K. Jacob et al. (eds.), *Liquid Legal*, Management for Professionals,
DOI 10.1007/978-3-319-45868-7_3

also a key enabler of the globalization of law firms as they strive to offer legal services to business corporations operating internationally. Relatively new in this scene are the so-called legal process outsourcing (LPO) providers who combine digital technology and global presence to deliver legal support services from low cost locations, onshore and offshore.

In this context of an increasingly internationalizing legal services market, what role has the general counsel, or the chief legal officer, played to transform the in-house legal function and its relationships with law firms? This chapter uses management theories to interpret a series of studies I conducted on this question. We begin with findings from *General Counsel with Power?*, a study of general counsel at major corporations and financial institutions in Britain and the United States. Next, we present evidence from *Fortune 500* companies, to glean the reasons behind different sourcing strategies. Focusing on satisfying the legal needs of corporate clients with international presence, we note a tension between large law firms with a global mandate and law firms that are largely nationally based. Last but not least, I draw implications for the future, by highlighting different roles that company lawyers might play in different future scenarios. As I argue below, company lawyers can be a key agent of change in transforming legal practice if they respond proactively to the global wind of creative destruction. In doing so, however, company lawyers remain beholden to a world that is far from being flat.

2   General Counsel with Power? A Study of Internalizers and Externalizers

When I first began researching about legal services, the corporate pressure to do "more for less", a secular trend accelerated by the 2008 financial crisis, was the talk of town at legal industry conferences and workshops. How are in-house lawyers reacting to these pressures to deliver more effective legal services at less cost? Industry analysts' consensus at the time was that corporate legal departments were bringing more work back in-house to avoid soring billable hours charged by global law firms.[1] I set out to find out for myself in 2010 and 2011 by conducting 52 interviews with in-house lawyers at major global corporations and financial institutions headquartered in Britain and the United States.[2] I discovered that the central trend identified in the industry disguised important variations.

Over the decade up to 2007, the majority of organizations I interviewed increased the number of in-house company lawyers, reflecting general business

---

[1] Association of Corporate Counsel (ACC) and Serengeti found greater reliance on insourcing in the United States, from 33 % of total corporate legal spending in 2004 to 38 % in 2008. *Legal Week* also found similar insourcing trends, with corporate respondents shifting from 49 % of total legal spending on average in 2004 to 58 % in 2008 in Britain.

[2] The full study is reported in Sako (2011).

Table 1 Size and shape of in-house legal departments in 2010

Sector	Number in sample	Number of in-house lawyers (range)	External to total legal spending (range)
Construction	4	25–61	20–83 %
Manufacturing	2	150–314	30 %
Energy	7	10–650	12–57 %
Financial services	11	80–1068	50–77 %
ICT	9	2–400	27–93 %
Professional services	2	11–12	60 %
Public sector	3	n.a.	n.a.
Retailing and wholesale distribution	5	8–35	60–90 %
Utilities	2	n.a.	20 %
Other sectors	7	7–72	40–60 %
Total	52	2–1068	12–93 %

Source: M. Sako (2011) *General Counsel with Power?* Available from: (http://eureka.sbs.ox.ac.uk/4560/1/General_Counsel_with_Power.pdf) Author's interviews; *n.a.* not available

growth. In financial services in particular, corporate legal departments grew enormously, reaching a peak in 2007 before the financial crisis led to a contraction in lawyer headcount. Despite a common aim to cut costs, my study revealed a wide-ranging variation in how the general counsel were responding to the "more for less" challenge (see Table 1), reflecting different logics of action co-existing in parallel. The study captured these different logics by classifying general counsel into three types.

First, *"Internalizers" brought legal work back in-house, with at most 20 % reliance on external legal resources.* They developed a strong in-house legal function that conducted most of the legal work for the corporation. The key advantage of this approach lies in in-house lawyers' intimate knowledge of the business. Transacting with many outside counsel, constantly keeping them up to speed on what the business was doing, was considered very expensive. Internalizers advocated fit-for-purpose lawyering, which involved staying very close to internal clients in business operations, and keeping tight control over external legal resources. Some corporations reduced reliance on external lawyers by increasing the size of the internal legal department, but others did so whilst cutting back also on the size of the internal legal department. On first reading, this appeared counter-intuitive. However rather than merely shifting legal work from external to internal lawyers, the general counsel in a small number of cases achieved heavier reliance on in-house legal resources at the same time as reducing in-house lawyer headcount. These Internalizers therefore took seriously the following dictum by the management guru Peter Drucker: "there is nothing more wasteful than doing more efficiently that which need not be done".

Second, *"Mid-Rangers" are more even-handed in their reliance on internal and external lawyers.* They typically work for financial services firms, including investment banks and commercial banks, which are the biggest spenders on big law firms in absolute terms. Their even-handed reliance on internal and external lawyers might conflate clear patterns in different lines of work, for example, heavier reliance on external lawyers in corporate finance than in sales and trading due to large amounts of complex documentation and the use of syndicates in the former. Nevertheless, apart from "big ticket" items such as major litigation cases, internal and external legal work was considered fungible. As a general counsel at an investment bank asked rhetorically:

> What has to be done in-house? Nothing! A few years ago, I said to my bosses when we were having a debate about the structure of the legal department. I said we can hire another 200 lawyers and bring more of the work in-house, or we can fire all in-house lawyers and you two can manage all the outside counsel. Those are the two ends of the spectrum. The question to me is where do you want to be in the middle.

However, apart from consideration for managing the existing capacity and internal lawyers' careers, the general counsel admitted to not being able to "articulate where on the spectrum we should be".

Third, *"Externalizers" depend on external lawyers for 90 % or more of their legal resource needs*. These externalizers fall into two types with different logics. Type 1 externalizers do not have an active legal department of their own and use external lawyers in place of in-house general counsel. For example, a US retailer did not have an in-house lawyer at all until recently. Another retailer in the UK had a small in-house legal department that was often bypassed by the CEO and business managers who went direct to external lawyers for advice. According to the general counsel:

> Our legal function was a little bit like an outside law firm dropped in here, and we sort of sat and waited for people round the business to come and talk to us, and then we'd give them some advice and then they'd go away. That was one part of the model. The other part was, we had outside lawyers that were more like in-house counsel.

Type 2 externalizers rely heavily on external legal resources but take a proactive stance to managing them. Typically, the general counsel hosts an annual conference of major law firms, and encourages lateral communication amongst the law firms in what they call a "legal community", a "legal network", or a virtual law firm. These general counsel are adept at balancing collaboration and competition, in order to induce law firms to work effectively and efficiently for the corporate client.

Besides classifying general counsel into these types, I was curious what power they were exerting in order to bring about sustainable change, hence the study title *General Counsel with Power?*. One measure of GC power is with respect to external law firms, which we might call *external GC power*. Another is GC power inside the corporation; let us call this *internal GC power*. The most temporary of external GC power lies in being in the buyer's market during an economic downturn. Much of the bargaining power resulting from an adverse economic climate is likely to erode when the economy picks up. This implies that to exert sustained external GC power, making law firms compete with each other in a buyer's market may be necessary but not sufficient. External GC power for the long term is based on proactively managing a network of law firms, so that they are made to collaborate as much as compete. This is consistent with the way Type II Externalizers think.

GC power inside the corporation depends on the capabilities of the GC and his or her staff in the legal department. More specifically, the general counsel may enhance his internal power to become a sustainable force for change by proactively investing in capabilities such as project management and risk management. In relation to top management, the test of internal GC power lies in the general counsel's ability to influence CEO's strategic decisions. This requires offering advice based on deep legal knowledge in the business context of the corporation. It is also predicated on the legal department holding legal information, in the form of meta-data, metrics, and analytics, that enables the general council to provide evidence-based strategic advice. The managerial theory of the firm states that managers have a propensity to grow their firm for reasons of prestige and status. We might apply this theory to company lawyers, with the general counsel wishing to grow their legal department to signal their power. Indeed, some corporate legal departments have increased their headcount to take on more legal work, which in turn multiplied the work put out to law firms, in part as company lawyers seek a second opinion from external lawyers. For sustainable internal GC power, however, we would expect the large size of the legal department to be underpinned by broad capabilities of company lawyers to execute legal work effectively for internal clients.

3 Why General Counsel Vary in Sourcing Strategies: *Fortune 500* Evidence

The discussion above still leaves us with an unanswered question: why do company lawyers react differently using different logics of action to the same pressure to do "more for less"? A casual inquiry with industry analysts and other insiders tended to yield stories that were unique to a particular corporation or a particular lawyer. Typically, the story might go as follows: a charismatic in-house counsel was responsible for growing the legal department at Corporation X, and was able to continue to do so even after a new CEO took office. As a social scientist, I was looking beyond the personal idiosyncratic stories, to seek patterns in my data so that I could explain why some general counsel were internalizers and others were externalizers. I began this enquiry by analyzing the survey data from ALM (the media company that publishes *The American Lawyer*) on legal departments at *Fortune 500* companies.[3]

The study provides explanations based on theories of the firm, in particular those that address the make-or-buy decisions. Here, we glean these explanations without

---

[3]The full study is reported in Sako et al. (2016, forthcoming).

presenting the full study involving econometric analysis. Put simply, multiple regression analyses enable us to examine the impact of multiple factors on a specific variable, here the size of in-house corporate legal department as indicated by the number of lawyers employed. We can see if the impact of each factor is significant or not, whilst taking account of the impact of all other factors, including many control variables such as the size of the company and the sector in which the company is in. I report on four significant results that have a bearing on where we are likely to find general counsel who are internalizers or externalizers.

First, we examined Research and Development (R&D) expenditure as a proportion of corporate sales (i.e. R&D intensity) and advertising expenditure as a proportion of corporate sales (i.e. advertising intensity). Amongst the *Fortune 500* companies, those with high R&D intensity and high advertising intensity were found to employ more in-house company lawyers, controlling for size and other things. This makes intuitive sense: as compared to external attorneys, in-house lawyers have better knowledge of the business of the company they work for, enabling them to use their legal knowledge to advise on what to patent and how to defend patents and copyrights, and how best to advertise within legal constraints and to defend brands. According to one interviewee:

> [W]e have a large research center on this site, where we do R&D and test tubes and all that kind of stuff, and we have patent attorneys sit here, supporting them. . . . We have a process by which all the guys on the test tubes over in the lab, when they invent something, will write up their lab notebooks. . . .We have a patent attorney, an inventor and a business manager all sitting in the same room, because then the strategic relevance of the patent is tested rather than just that it is chemically a great idea.

Thus, internalizing general counsel tend to work for companies that have intangible assets to defend, typically in the form of intellectual property and brands.

Second, this study looked at sourcing strategies as characterized by three things: (1) whether external legal work was concentrated in a small number of law firms or dispersed across a large number of law firms, (2) how stable relationships with law firms were over time, and (3) how broad or narrow the capabilities of law firms were, as measured by the number of practice areas. We found that at *Fortune 500* companies, externalizers were adept at developing more stable relations with a smaller number of law firms than internalizers. These chosen law firms also provide legal advice across a broader range of practice areas. By contrast, internalizers tended to retain a larger number of law firms, each providing a narrower range of legal advice, with no guarantee of stable flow of work. This result has implications for "panel reviews" which often lead to "convergence", i.e. a reduction in the number of law firms retained. In particular, our study suggests that a reduction in the number of law firms is perfectly consistent with relying more on external legal resources, as Type 2 Externalizers do, as long as they can design multi-year transactions in multiple practice areas by surviving law firms in the panel. This requires building relationships of trust and commitment.

Third, general counsel who also carried a senior management job title (Executive Vice President or Senior Vice President) tended to be Internalizers, heading a relatively large legal department, controlling for other things. This could be a reflection of GC's internal power, set in a corporate setting with "legal astuteness", referring to corporate top management's proactive stance to use internal legal resources to make strategic decisions.[4] Although the proportion of general counsel who sit on the board of directors or executive committee of large global corporations is very small,[5] that is too strict a test of how chief legal officers are exerting influence in corporate top management teams. Using a weaker test in our sample, the proportion of general counsel who also carried a senior management job title is widespread, covering just under 80 % of our *Fortune 500* sample companies.

With a backdrop of a vigorous debate on the role of general counsel,[6] we hear about powerful GCs such as Ben Heineman at the US giant General Electric and David Drummond at Google. Corporate executives turn to the GC to pre-empt going to jail and to fend against endless threats of lawsuits, including from patent trolls. More generally, in-house lawyers are expected to increasingly play a dual role of being a lawyer and a business partner, as legal work in compliance and risk management increases.[7] Our study of *Fortune 500* companies indicate that these expectations by corporate executives have created GCs who are Internalizers, finding it easier to use internal rather than external legal resources to deliver what is expected of them.

Last but not least, the *Fortune 500* companies study examined the link between international presence and the size of the legal department. The degree of internationalization, measured by the number of countries in which the corporation has a subsidiary, was found to be positively correlated with a larger legal department, controlling for other things. Thus, on the whole, as companies become more global, they employ more company lawyers, over and above the size one would expect with general business growth. The reason lies in advantages of dealing with complex managerial tasks inside the global corporation. As multinationals enter more foreign markets, complexity multiplies with the number of jurisdictions in which they operate, each with a different set of regulations. At the same time, through interjurisdictional coordination, international presence creates opportunities for generating value through regulatory arbitrage, when firms exploit locational differences to reduce or avoid regulatory costs, for example in corporate taxation. A strong legal expertise within the corporation helps to identify and exploit such opportunities in the process of company lawyers interacting frequently with the corporate accounting department (for international tax planning) or the strategic planning department (for foreign direct investment or M&A). Arguably, external counsel would be just as knowledgeable about such regulatory issues in general. However, managers can be better assisted in exploiting market opportunities by the

---

[4]Bagley (2008).
[5]Litov et al. (2014).
[6]See Veasey and Guglielmo (2012).
[7]Kurer (2015).

in-house counsel who has an intimate knowledge of the business. Hence, the potential to exploit opportunities from the co-specialization of legal and other firm resources favors the insourcing of legal services. This advantage of internal coordination within the corporation increases with greater multi-jurisdictional international presence.

4   Law Firm Perspective: The Global Mandate

Large law firms, so-called global law firms, are relatively recent globalizers and remain less global than their major client corporations. For example, Unilever opened its international operations over a century ago, and sells its products in 190 countries. Its arch US rival, Procter & Gamble, began to internationalize after the Second World War, and is less international with operations in 80 countries, touching the lives of people in 180 countries. Compared to this, the most global of law firms, Baker & MacKenzie, had 77 offices in 47 countries in 2015.[8] The English "magic circle" law firms, Allen & Overy and Freshfields, have 32 and 28 international offices respectively. These figures indicate that law firms are not as global in their physical presence, even compared to other professional service firms. For instance, in audit and accounting, PwC employed 208,000 people in 157 countries, whilst EY similarly had 211,450 employees at 700 offices in 150 countries in 2015.

Law firms at the top of the ranking aspire to become more global, and consider such "global mandate" as a no brainer for continued success and survival. A word of caution against this mindset comes from a principle in Strategy, which states that firms should enter new national markets only if such entry enhances the overall profit of the firm. Evidence from the Global 100 law firms indicate that this management principle is not taken seriously amongst top law firms. As Fig. 1 shows, greater international presence does not lead to higher profits. In fact, an overwhelming majority of Global 100 law firms have less than 15 % of their lawyers outside the home country. The most international, as measured by the percentage of lawyers working outside the firm's home country, is Baker & MacKenzie which employs just over 80 % of its lawyers outside the United States. By contrast, the least international, is Wachtell, Lipton, Rosen & Katz, with one office in New York City, making profit per equity partner of $4.5 million, which is three times that of Baker & MacKenzie. (Note that Wachtell's corporate clients are global themselves.) Whilst this is an extreme comparison, it helps to make the point that operating internationally is highly challenging for law firms.

Major law firms think that they have to increase their global presence in order to serve their global corporate clients. This might seem to make a lot of sense, but only if law firms themselves develop their capacity to manage their strategy and operations at a global level, rather than have a federation of national offices that do not create synergy for the overall enterprise. From the perspective of corporate

---

[8]The American Lawyer, "Special Report: The 2015 Global 100", 28 September 2015.

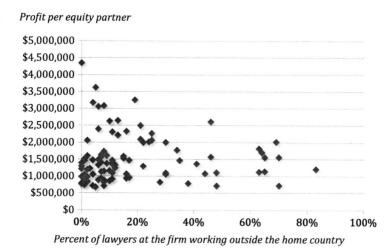

Profit per equity partner

Fig. 1 Internationalization and profit per partner at large (*Global 100*) law firms in 2011. Source: *Global 100* in 2011, www.law.com

clients that have implemented "convergence" (i.e. a reduction in the number of law firms retained) during panel reviews, some general counsel note the problem of false aggregation. According to one general counsel interviewed for the *General Counsel with Power?* study:

> When we focus on a very small number of (law) firms, those firms in turn go out and hire local counsel anyway. So it looks like it is aggregated, but it truly always is not.

More traditional forms of managing law firms internationally, including a Swiss verein form or an international network (such as Lex Mundi (http://www.lexmundi. com/) and Multilaw (https://www.multilaw.com/)) and "best friends" arrangements, continue to exist for a good reason. The jury is still out on whether a global law firm or a federation of law firms would better serve globalizing corporate clients, especially as those clients look increasingly to new high-risk emerging markets in Africa, Asia, and Latin America.

5 The World Is Not Flat

A global corporation with a panel of global law firms might be the way to go for dealing with an increasingly globalizing legal services market. However, although 45 % of the $600 billion turnover global legal services market in 2014 is in the Americas and a further 30 % in Europe, growth markets are in emerging economies in the Asia-Pacific and Middle Eastern regions, according to MarketLine.[9] This trend creates new demand for corporate legal services, for example to facilitate South-South trade and investment (e.g. Chinese companies investing in Africa). Even before the current phase of globalization, the world has been far from flat, due to the persistence of nationally based jurisdictions with the license to practice law given at the national (or subnational state) level. Added to this is national difference in the way lawyers are treated when they go in-house to work for business corporations. A brief account of Japan, a major industrial nation, illustrates this point.[10]

Japanese corporations, many with global presence, of course have in-house legal departments, but they are not staffed by qualified lawyers. The in-house legal department staff may have studied law at top universities, but they have never practiced law, not passed a bar exam, nor admitted to the bar. Just a handful of corporations have a qualified lawyer heading the legal department. A career in a corporate legal department is considered a life-long job, on a par with any other white-collar lifetime employment jobs in large corporations. Legal training necessary to be able to draft contract documents and to comply with government regulation, has been provided largely on-the-job in-house. One consequence of this system is that legal department staff have a deep understanding of the business of their employer.

There is, however, wind of change in Japanese legal departments, due to both demand-side and supply-side reasons. On the demand side, Japanese corporations have realized that they need to better manage their risk and reputation, and some major corporations have increased the size of their legal departments significantly to enforce compliance, in some cases following a corporate scandal or mismanagement. From the supply side, there have been pressures to make the legal system serve societal needs better, for example by reducing the time to get a case heard. This led to reforms in legal education, creating law schools and increasing the number of those who pass the bar exam, with a recent figure of just over 36,000 admitted to the bar. This is still a relatively low number in a country with a population of 120 million. Nevertheless, an increase in the flow of qualified lawyers has led to an addition to the core career aspiration of freshly minted lawyers, to become a judge or a partner in a law firm, in the form of becoming a company lawyer.

The legal education reform therefore began to impact corporate legal departments gradually. First, a trickle of qualified attorneys went in-house, mostly for the Tokyo offices of foreign banks and subsidiaries of foreign multinationals such as IBM and GE. More recently, an accelerating flow of qualified lawyers choosing to join business corporations meant a thirteen-fold increase in in-house

---

[9]MarketLine (2015) *Global Legal Services*, MarketLine Industry Profile, Reference Code 0199-0423.

[10]This ongoing study is based on a few dozen interviews conducted by the author in Tokyo with Japanese lawyers and legal department heads in 2014 and 2015.

lawyers during 2005 and 2016. But the total number of lawyers who work in-house remains low, at just over 1000 in 2014, according to the Japanese Bar Association. Lawyers used to have to seek permission to go in-house from its professional association until 2004, but this permission system was changed to a notification and registration system more recently.

Today, major Japanese corporations and trading companies thus have a legal department whose head came through the old system of internal training and promotion, with a small number of younger qualified lawyers. The jury is still out on how the balance between non-lawyers and lawyers will pan out in the future. There appears to be no consensus yet among Japanese legal department heads on how best to use the newly available legal knowledge and expertise of qualified lawyers in-house. But in a work environment in which legal department work is carried out by both lawyers and non-lawyers, it surely concentrates our mind on what it is that only qualified lawyers can do, or permitted to do, in corporate legal services.

6   Implications for Structuring the Legal Function in Global Corporations

Given that the world is not flat, what are the choices available to the general counsel in charge of delivering legal services for global corporations? One way of answering this question is to attempt to be a futurologist with a foresight of a single most likely future. Another approach, which I take here, is to adopt a scenarios planning thinking, imaging more than one plausible futures, say in 2030. There are two critical uncertainties for global legal services, one of which is the extent to which legal services markets become deregulated, for example with other countries adopting something akin to the UK Legal Services Act which permits non-lawyers to own and manage law firms in the form of Alternative Business Structures. Another critical uncertainty is the extent to which the delivery of legal services becomes truly global in part with the use of digital technology. See Fig. 2 for the four possible scenarios given these two dimensions.

The two scenarios to the left present a world with limited deregulation. Starting with the top left quadrant, the Saville Row I scenario is with little deregulation and local delivery, indicating little change in the current state of play with an emphasis on bespoke advice provided by eminent lawyers supported by traditionally trained lawyers. Going to the lower quadrant, the Saville Row II scenario is similar to Saville Row I but with a difference that bespoke legal advice is supported by "legal process factories" to conduct legal research and document review, located in different parts of the world to take advantage of low-cost non-lawyer talent and digital technology.

To the right are two scenarios in a world of extensive deregulation in legal markets. In the top right quadrant scenario of Lawyers as Consultants, legal service delivery remains local, but deregulation means that lawyers compete with other professionals, such as accountants, to provide integrated advice to corporate clients.

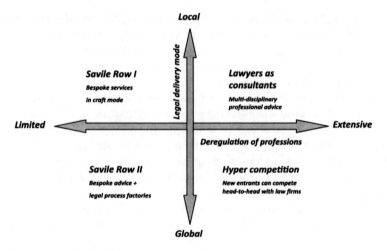

Fig. 2 Future scenarios for global legal services in 2030

The distinction between legal advice and non-legal advice becomes blurred. The lower right quadrant scenario of Hyper Competition is perhaps the most challenging, with the pressure from new entrants in global delivery of legal services adding to inter-professional rivalry due to deregulation.

From the perspective of the general counsel working for global corporations headquartered in the United States or Europe, these four scenarios present different challenges and opportunities. There are at least two implications for the legal function in global corporations which are worth noting. First, in the two scenarios Saville Row II and Hyper Competition, the general counsel might do well to exploit the availability of global legal service delivery. However, this global delivery might be carried out inside the global corporation, rather than by law firms or LPO providers, especially if the corporation exploits advantages that come from the co-specialization of legal and other expertise inside the corporation. This implies a significant growth in the size of corporate legal departments in the future. Internalizers among general counsel have a head start in preparing for this future.

Second, in the two scenarios Lawyers as Consultants and Hyper Competition, the general counsel might welcome extensive deregulation if it implies receiving legal, tax, audit, and compliance advice in an integrated manner. The key unknown in these scenarios is the extent to which the corporate legal department internalizes or externalizes compliance officers, risk managers, and other semi-professionals who come to work with, but independently of, in-house lawyers. Moreover, the world of law is likely to continue to be divided into national jurisdictions, unlike the world of other professionals such as accountants with their international standards. Therefore, company lawyers are likely to remain beholden to a world that is far from being flat.

Liquid Legal Context
by Dr. Dierk Schindler, Dr. Roger Strathausen, Kai Jacob

Sako provides an interesting perspective on what makes GC's gravitate towards keeping work in-house (internalize) or towards finding resources outside of the company (externalize). She also reveals a correlation between the degree of embracing legal technology and the need—or tendency—to localize the delivery of services. How does the change of services in the (external) legal environment influence the decision to externalize?

This question connects to Bassli's clear and convincing call to action to law firms: *Provide managed legal services to retain your relevance for us!* If we accept that, we find ourselves in a legal ecosystem that undergoes fundamental transformation and brings about new types of service providers, e.g. Legal Tech or LPO's. Are changing service offerings and billing practices the key to a prosperous future also for law firms?

As we all wait for final answers, another very practical question for any leader in legal arises: How do we deal with uncertainty, while simultaneously being asked to run a successful business in today's legal industry, be it as a leader in legal in-house, in legal tech or in a law firm? Mari Sako concludes by introducing a model for scenario planning which rests on two of the most impactful variables in the transformation: (1) the degree of deregulation and (2) the degree of true globalization in delivery of legal services.

How does a partner in a global law firm address these issues? In the upcoming article, Rainer Markfort opens up a fundamental dimension for the future success of "big-law": *Polycentrism*, an emerging business practice that consists of networking international talent, capital, and ideas to meet global and local demands for new products and services. Networking connects well to the challenges we know from global corporate organizations as they battle for the necessary talent and competencies to remain future-ready. Is shifting the mindset of lawyers also the approach that global law-firms and in-house teams must take to succeed in transforming the industry?

References

Bagley, C. E. (2008). Winning legally: The value of legal astuteness. *Academy of Management Review, 33*(2), 378–390.

Kurer, P. (2015). *Legal and compliance risk*. Oxford: Oxford University Press.

Litov, L. P., Sepe, S. M., & Whitehead, C. K. (2014). Lawyers and fools: Lawyer-directors in public corporations. *Georgetown Law Journal, 102*, 413–480.

Sako, M. (2011). *General Counsel with Power?*, Said Business School, University of Oxford, http://eureka.sbs.ox.ac.uk/4560/1/General_Counsel_with_Power.pdf

Sako, M., Chondrakis, G., & Vaaler, P. (2016, forthcoming). How do plural-sourcing firms make
    and buy? The impact of supplier portfolio design. *Organization Science*. http://pubsonline.
    informs.org/doi/full/10.1287/orsc.2016.1079
Veasey, E. N., & Guglielmo, C. T. D. (2012). *Indispensable counsel: The chief legal officer in the
    new reality*. New York: Oxford University Press.

Mari Sako is Professor of Management Studies, and member of the Professional Service Firm Hub at Saïd Business School, University of Oxford. Previously, she taught at LSE, and held visiting positions in Japan and at MIT Sloan School of Management. She holds a BA in Philosophy, Politics, and Economics (Oxford), MSc in Economics (LSE), and a PhD in Economics (London). Her research on global strategy, comparative business systems, and labour markets are published in five books and journal articles. Her most recent work is on the outsourcing and offshoring of professional services and their impact on the professions.

Legal Advisor–Service Provider–Business Partner: Shifting the Mindset of Corporate Lawyers

Rainer Markfort

Abstract

Clients' expectations towards their lawyers have changed, and they will keep on changing. Clients want solutions, not opinions, so lawyers have had to shift from legal advisors to service providers. As the needs of clients are continually evolving, they now want legal solutions to fit into their company's processes and procedures. So today's legal service provider needs to transform into the client's real business partner, to support management in reaching their goals and moving the business forward.

External advice is becoming more and more internal, as lawyers become part of the client's project team. While qualifications, expertise and availability are a necessary basis for cooperation, adapted team structures and good team management are also required to make that cooperation work.

To become part of the client's projects, lawyers and law firms need to prepare well. This involves strategic thinking on how to serve clients in their global activities, how to use technology effectively, and how to integrate other service providers and manage projects efficiently. They also need to build trust and credibility through thought leadership and transparency around legal spending.

This will not take place without shifting the mindset of corporate lawyers towards a forward-looking and client-oriented attitude. Developing this attitude, however, requires an optimistic approach in a disruptive environment, mindful thinking about the ethical and economical challenges and a strong belief in the fundamentals of our profession.

R. Markfort (✉)
Dentons Europe LLP, Markgrafenstraße 33, 10117 Berlin, Germany
e-mail: rainer.markfort@dentons.com

© Springer International Publishing AG 2017
K. Jacob et al. (eds.), *Liquid Legal*, Management for Professionals,
DOI 10.1007/978-3-319-45868-7_4

47

1   Introduction

Expectations of lawyers and legal services have changed and will continue to do so. When I started in private practice some 25 years ago, a lawyer's role was one of a legal advisor in the narrow sense of the term. He/she provided the legal answer to a question of law and the client just had to cope with it. The standard work product was a memorandum outlining the legal situation under a given set of facts or assumptions, reflecting the jurisdiction and authorities, formulating concerns, and showing the most likely position a court would take if it would come to litigation.

Within one generation, this attitude was no longer appreciated by clients. Instead of opinions, clients asked for solutions, and instead of legal advisors they looked for service providers. The service rendered became advice on how to solve a given problem. A memo could still summarize facts and reasoning, but the work product was now in the form of a presentation to the board, a step plan, or another text for immediate use by the client.

Clients today ask for even more, as providing a solution to a problem is no longer enough. Clients desire the next step where such a solution fits within and can be implemented into the company's processes and procedures. Lawyers need to be business oriented, understanding not only the goal but also the means available—such as people and resources—and how they can be utilized. The legal service provider needs to transform into a real partner within the client's business.

In past years, we have observed the transformation of in-house legal departments. Today's in-house lawyers are closer to business; they are involved in the project team at an early stage, and are consulted on business decisions. At the same time, the relationship to external lawyers has changed correspondingly. External advice is becoming more and more "internal", as lawyers are becoming part of the client's team, and part of the project. Qualifications, expertise and availability are a necessary basis for successful cooperation. Team structures at the law firm must be adapted to the client's teams, and good team management is required. Responsiveness, transparency and effectiveness are the crucial factors in integrating.

The challenge for a company when choosing a law firm is to examine which lawyers would fit best into an integrated team and will cooperate in a transparent and effective way, as this will ensure a successful transaction. Lawyers should make this task as easy as possible, through thoughtful preparation in order to increase their chances of being retained. This requires, most of all, a shift in mindset. Many lawyers still think that a presentation means talking about oneself ("We are global, we are qualified and experienced. Look at all our famous clients and big transactions.") Instead, reflecting a change in attitude, they should talk about the client and the project to come, and present their thoughts and approach. Smart law firm managers are offering sales training to their partners and smart lawyers benefit from soft skill seminars. Some, like Dentons, even have a Director of Talent and a Director of Innovation who are constantly working on the shift in mindset.

Lawyering has become a business and therefore has to follow the rules of business. Pitching for work has become part of life for today's lawyers. Whereas in the past, an individual lawyer was retained due to his good personal relationship with the general counsel or management (and certainly because of his good reputation), there is rarely an interesting mandate today that will be assigned without a procurement process. To get invited to such a process more frequently requires having qualified to be on the law firm panel. The panel process reveals qualifications, expertise and competitive conditions. It is the battle for "better, faster, and cheaper".

To win this battle, lawyers need to engage in strategic thinking on how to serve global clients in their global activities, how to use technology to be cost efficient and effective, and how to manage projects and integrate other service providers. At the same time, thought leadership, predictability on legal spending, and trust are the pillars of a successful client relationship.

2 Polycentric: The Contemporary Approach for a Global Strategy

The legal services business is inevitably entwined with and closely correlated to our clients' evolution. Multinational corporations are competing globally and are being pressured to leverage economies of scale to maximize profits, but at the same time, they still have to adapt to local customer needs and regulations which cannot be disregarded. This is precisely what a global law firm should do: adapt and swiftly respond to the requirements of mid-sized enterprises and big, multinational corporations, accurately understand their business models and mirror their modes of functioning by being both responsive locally and present worldwide.

Business management strategies have been evolving significantly over the last two decades. Globalization has made the frontier between domestic and international markets extremely diffuse. We cannot talk about a single way of doing things when everything is interconnected and integrated. A lawyer's primary goal is to understand and respond to clients' needs. If a law firm wants to serve globally active, multinational corporations, it also needs a global presence. On the other hand, just being global and having a geocentric philosophy with a "one size fits all" approach also does not work. If a law firm wants to serve modern global corporations, the process of how to render legal advice cannot be defined solely out of a London or New York headquarters.

Back when corporations from western countries made their first steps into foreign markets, they appreciated a lawyer from their home jurisdiction at their side who served as a legal interpreter, arranged for local legal advice, and made great efforts to structure a transaction in the same way the client was used to at home. Over the years, many of these corporations have evolved into decentralized business organizations. Legal departments have built sophisticated teams with specialist in-house lawyers for different regions, and both business and in-house lawyers have become more confident in looking for legal advice from local lawyers—and at local rates. They have also become more open to business standards and transaction structures customary in other parts of the world. Law firms today must take into account their clients' regional constraints and opportunities, thus also adopting a multi-domestic view. In short, global law firms must develop strategies that reflect their complex environment.

Polycentrism is an emerging business practice that consists of networking international talent, capital, and ideas to meet global and local demands for new products and services. It may sound obvious for our modern way of doing business, but the implications are far reaching. Indeed, being in and of the community implies openness and understanding of intercultural differences, opinions and ways of life from a multi-dimensional perspective as well as accepting differences in values, customs, languages and currencies. Essentially this relates to seeing the whole picture from different perspectives without losing track of a common global strategy. A polycentric law firm is able to pay close attention to regional drivers of differentiation, and give prime importance to local approaches. Polycentrism unlocks regional opportunities and integrates them into an innovative network to drive successful synergies on a worldwide scale.

3   Technology: A Laptop and a Smartphone Are Not Enough

Shifting our mindset will require new systems to support and enhance our thinking towards increased capability and efficiency. Unless we embrace new, powerful and fit-for-purpose information systems, we will not achieve this aim. The global demand for complex and cross-border legal advice seems healthier than ever, but while the market may be growing, the allocation of market share is very much up for grabs. Indeed, the corporate legal advice landscape is being reshaped and is entering a new era, where client pressure for constant price reduction and digitization of legal data is the new norm. Multinational corporations will expect more and better services for less money as they see new opportunities emerging. Legal process outsourcing providers and legal-tech vendors will only add to the pressure. Investing in legal technology solutions and redefining our business models, are therefore fundamental if we want to sustain success and respond to clients' expectations.

Servicing clients more cheaply ultimately means fewer billable hours and thus a need to work more efficiently. The Boston Consulting Group and the Bucerius Law School[1] report that 30–50 % of the tasks currently performed by junior associates, even on bespoke cases, could be automated through tech-based tools. Furthermore, the volume of data used in legal advice has increased exponentially. This offers us a unique opportunity to leverage our talent and capabilities by adopting new technologies to automate standard legal tasks, such as discoveries, contract and legal reviews. Legal technologies are now advancing towards providing

---

[1]Veith et al. (2016).

sophisticated and integrated features, which support the more specialized tasks to be conducted by a lawyer while saving time and money on the standard legal tasks.

Mobile- and web-based legal technology solutions, such as e-discovery, legal review tools, practice management apps and big data analytics, along with clouds and databases, support and promote the digitization of legal data. Moreover, progress in cybersecurity will certainly strengthen this trend. Collaboration platforms have also been created to respond to specific needs of the legal profession. Support-process solutions optimize case-management and back-office work, and substantive law solutions can support or even replace lawyers in executing core legal tasks in transactions and litigation cases. Big data analytics unlock great new opportunities by supporting legal professionals in capturing valuable insights from large data sets and ultimately enable them to make more accurate, better and faster decisions. For example, business partner compliance checks today can be run automatically by integrating structured and unstructured data from internal and external sources, analyzing them with sentiment algorithms and evaluating the results according to KPIs like identity, quality, solvency and integrity.[2] This and other examples show that big data analytics might reveal correlations we would never have thought of. Eventually, the future of legal technology will likely see the emergence of supportive applications powered by artificial intelligence.

Therefore, in addition to offering on-site training to help lawyers leverage legal technology and executive education programs focused on technology literacy, a change in the business model is needed. This is exactly what Dentons decided to do with NextLaw Labs—a global innovation platform focused on developing, deploying, and investing in new technologies to transform the practice of law—in which Dentons is the lead investor and supporter. Providing financing to ground breaking legal technology projects is one objective, providing user input in the development and product design phase the other. NextLaw Labs also works with IBM to provide access to IBM Cloud and the IBM Global Entrepreneur Program for Cloud Startups. One of NextLaw Labs' portfolio companies[3] is developing ROSS, an IBM Watson-powered legal advisor app that will streamline legal research. Watson's cognitive computing and natural language processing capabilities will enable ROSS to listen to lawyers' research questions in natural language, read through the law, gather evidence, draw inferences and return evidence-based answers. NextLaw Labs also works together with Apperio,[4] which is a powerful, smart-analytics dashboard to provide clients with real-time transparency on legal fees that is accurate and meaningful. Thereby Apperio provides support to all project partners, lawyers and clients' teams, in their project management with real-time and consistent data. This solution will remove information asymmetry from legal services.

---

[2]Solution based on DEUS© and provided by HP enterprises and Dentons.

[3]www.nextlawlabs.com/portfolio/rossintelligence/,ROSS Intelligence Inc.

[4]www.nextlawlabs.com/portfolio/13104/, Apperio Ltd.

NextLaw Labs serves as the global testing ground for new products, services and other ideas to be vetted, piloted and scaled. This is an innovative platform where technology providers, venture capitalists and other stakeholders come together to work on changing the legal market for the benefit of clients. The example of NextLaw Labs demonstrates how we can develop an effective and powerful toolkit for the sake of our clients and the future of our profession. Developing and adopting these tools also requires a shift in mindset from a traditional lawyer towards a partner in business.

4 Integration: External Services for High Quality Solutions

Clients no longer accept skyrocketing bills as the hours of legal work mount, so if a law firm wants to compete, it must demonstrate cost-efficiency. This may imply using contract attorneys or outsourcing research and less-specialized tasks to third-party providers.

Law remains our core business and the underlying connection of our services and deliverables. But as we start to integrate and coordinate external legal service providers, we create an opportunity to streamline our legal processes. This effort of integration requires once more a shift in mindset and a greater emphasis on business project management capabilities—improving communication, prioritizing efficiency, and engineering our external provider networks to support the meaningful integration of our legal services to meet client needs.

Outsourcing relevant legal services will enable law firms to tighten cost control, and in doing so, will strengthen competitiveness and ultimately help mitigate risks. Using specialized service providers for specific tasks will enable us to deliver higher quality at reduced cost. The lawyer will concentrate on quality control and managing interfaces, just as our clients do when managing their supply chain. Indeed lawyers will have more time and space to design sound action plans, and to work on implementing them in collaboration with the client. Thus, integrating external providers into our systems will give our service offering a greater chance of success and allow us to focus on delivering quality. It's a win-win.

In the area of science, the times of polymaths like Leonardo da Vinci are long behind us. In industry, no manufacturer produces all elements of a product independently, and in the digital world, new software solutions are the result of many people working together. In the legal profession, the time of integrated work products is still to come.

5 Diversity: Many Good Reasons, Profit Is One

For a long time, lawyering was a masculine domain, but today we are fortunate to have many talented women in the legal profession. However, women lawyers still experience salary inequality and are under-represented in management. Whether viewed from an ethical, economic or managerial perspective, it is clear that we are collectively and individually missing out on numerous benefits if we do not empower women to achieve their full potential.

According to the Department of Economics and Social Affairs,[5] women work longer hours than men, if we take into consideration unpaid work. Women work roughly twice as much or more on domestic chores alone, including meal preparation, cleaning and childcare. These figures are also relevant in developed countries. In Europe, for example, women employed full-time work an extra hour on average per day compared to men. This point clearly shows that women are hard-working, committed, and responsible. In short, women are potential leaders, and yet the gender pay gap is still significant worldwide. Figures vary considerably between industries and geographic regions, but if we focus solely on the legal services sector in Europe, women earn on average 15 % less than men.[6]

Besides being ethically and objectively unfair, we are missing out not only on women's tenacity and courage but also on their tremendous experience in supporting and sustaining growth if we do not bring them into more executive positions and involve them in key strategic decisions. In a survey of 800 business leaders worldwide, McKinsey & Co, in its *Women Matter* series,[7] confirmed that leadership styles and behaviors typically adopted by women are critical for companies to make a difference and perform well in our post-crisis world. According to the American Psychological Association,[8] women's leadership style tends to be akin to mentoring and coaching, while men's style revolves around command and control. Progressive, diverse, reactive, flexible, smart and therefore sustainable company boards of directors have lively debates and challenge each other, without breaking the harmony of the group. From a corporate governance perspective, prioritizing diversity on company boards will enable us to harness these opportunities from angles that were potentially inaccessible before.

Making sure that women's voices are heard in the boardroom is a strategic issue. While in many European law firms there is almost a 50:50 split of women and men at the fee earner level,[9] women are dramatically underrepresented in management and partner level positions. Simply put, quite often there are just no women on the board. Besides appearing obviously unfair to women, this status quo poses a risk to the organization. A study[10] published in 2012 revealed that those firms with at least one woman on their board outperformed those with no women by an average of 5 %. Another study[11] on Fortune 500 companies found that companies with the highest percentage of women board directors outperformed by 53 % on return on

---

[5]Department of Economic and Social Affairs (2010).

[6]Foubert et al. (2010).

[7]Desvaux et al. (2010).

[8]The American Psychological Association. (2006). Introduction to Mentoring, A Guide for Mentors and Mentees.

[9]Legal Profession (2013).

[10]Curtis et al. (2012).

[11]Joy (2007).

equity, 42 % return on sales and 66 % return on invested capital. This is in addition to the positive corporate image and message sent to the stakeholders, and the benefit (however difficult to quantify) of having a diverse range of thinkers.

Why should this priority for diversity be any different in the legal profession? These facts call for a mind shift, because gender equality is simply good business. Furthermore, matching diverse client teams is difficult when the law firm has only male partners. Increasingly, large corporates ask for gender equality and diversity and make it a prerequisite to qualify for the panel. Law firms should take this seriously, being aware that it will take some time to change the structure of a firm and prepare for the future—a future that has already started.

6   Project Management: A Lawyer's Second Hat

Clients expect lawyers and legal advisors to provide more than legal solutions. They want this paired with a concrete and sound business plan, and a clear-cut position where lawyers share the risks. This represents a dramatic shift away from the old paradigm.

To simply offer legal advice, propose a solution and then leave clients alone to face the consequences is no longer relevant. We are definitely witnessing the dawn of a new era in our profession. Clients are asking their lawyers to behave as real partners in business—to not only share the risks, but to help design and implement effective processes and programs that solve the issue or prevent it from occurring. Corporate clients expect quality law firms to provide high quality legal advice, and also to deliver quality service. This entails lawyers taking on a role as a member of the client's team and not remaining aloof from it. It also means sharing knowledge and expertise to achieve a common goal: the successful execution of the business plan—from its development to implementation. And it means wearing two hats— that of the lawyer, and that of the project manager.

Many factors are disrupting our old paradigm: cost-reduction pressures, work internalization, unbundling of services and the increasing and diverse number of market players are but a few. If we want to remain ahead of the field, and to provide clients with direction, continuity and coordination, we must make legal project management part of our expertise. This means adopting more effective planning, budgeting, cost control, communication, and appropriate staff and risk management throughout the case or project. Lawyers need to reframe their thinking—away from exhaustively scoping the project towards improving awareness of timing, budgeting and staffing aspects.

This new focus represents a major strategy shift, away from a preoccupation with chargeable time towards the value to be delivered to the client. This value-orientation is the core principle of project management.

7 Legal Spending: The Desire for Predictability

Clients are looking for better, faster and cheaper services, but what they expect first and foremost is better predictability in their legal expenditure. The shifting realities of the corporate environment are forcing law firms to revise their internal operations in much the same way as their clients have to. Over time, lawyers have had to develop their business acumen and provide legal advice aligned with their clients' strategic goals. At the same time, clients have been consistently demanding greater efficiency, consistency and predictability.

Predictability obviously implies that lawyers can no longer just give clients various options; external counsel needs to look ahead to the outcome of implementing a strategy and go for it. So far business people have been left alone with the execution, but today we talk about risk-sharing. In our clients' eyes, this goes hand in hand with predictability. When these two ingredients—risk-sharing and predictability—are part of the agreement between legal advisors and their executive counterparts, then—and only then—can their relationships be built on trust.

8 Trust: The Art of Delivering Legal Advice Will Persist

Trust has always been a synonym for a client-lawyer relationship, at least in western communities. And trust will remain the primary KPI. You cannot "deliver" trust, you can only build it, but the ways to gain, build and maintain trust have changed.

Trust is the backbone of sustained relationships, which can only be built over time if we adhere to strong core principles such as cooperation, transparency, and efficiency. Trustworthiness, a fundamental value of our daily business, can be improved with techniques and constant learning. Genuine exchanges will happen if our clients sense our authentic care for their concerns, and if they feel our true commitment to satisfy both their business, and their personal needs.

Reliability is also central. If we meet our clients' expectations, deliver on time, and respect what we agreed on—we will build a reputation for consistent efficiency and reliability, which can become one of our best assets. There can't be trust without intimacy. Confidentiality and transparency are absolute musts for building a safe and secure environment and capitalizing on our relationships with clients.

If our ability to screen, analyze and interpret unprecedented volumes of data in order to serve our clients faster, better, and more cheaply is becoming crucial to our success, so is the "art of delivering" legal advice. This cannot be done by machines or software; human relationships will remain a cornerstone of our client interactions. How can lawyers achieve this if they are not perceived as credible? Professionalism is obviously reflected in the words we speak. They have to be accurate, respectful and meaningful. Weighing and practicing our speech and vocabulary will strengthen our credibility, which in turn will enable the cooperation process between the two parties.

Ultimately, lawyers' self-orientation should be minimal. Truly caring about clients is about responding to their needs and not about putting our personal agendas in the foreground. Trust can be sown and benefits reaped if we care about these clients in the first place. Mindfulness and trustworthiness go hand in hand and are sine qua non if we want to successfully and wisely shift our mindset towards meaningful and solid collaborative achievement.

9   Thought Leadership: Thinking Ahead to Show the Way

All in all, we are witnessing the need for lawyers to broaden their skill set. Not only must they maintain their legal expertise, they also have to sharpen their strategic and business thinking as well as understand and integrate the valuable lessons from their emotional and social intelligence. In one word, they have to become great leaders!

It will not suffice to help clients implement solutions and take on the role of project manager. We must think ahead, engage with the client's team, share knowledge and support the client's growth, because their success is ours too. Leaders mentor—they instill values and develop strategic thinking in the people they work with. Lawyers must become part of a trusted think-tank to which clients can turn for reliable and valuable insight. Achieving this is no small feat.

In order to build a solid reputation, lawyers must consistently meet their targets and long term goals. Becoming a leader is also about knowing your collaborators' strengths and weaknesses, not being blindsided, being consistent and even-tempered in every decision and interaction, and being trustworthy and likable. On top of this, lawyers should never avoid speaking the hard truths or listening to them; candid and frank conversations are part of the process. Listening to clients' needs and aspirations is fundamental—and such listening, in turn, will require an individualized and appropriate answer. This will help develop a better leader within the lawyer.

A good leader will always think ahead. What will come next? What will be my clients' needs in the future? What will be the appropriate legal service to address those future needs? Lawyers need to be creative and innovative, and to be a thought leader they need vision. Clients will not be successful without envisaging future market trends and planning accordingly, nor will their lawyers. This two-step process requires, firstly, careful observation and strategic thinking, and secondly, diligent planning and realization. Food for thought will emerge out of a trustful client-lawyer relationship.

Above all, we must give a strong and positive impression, nourished by a thoughtful attitude and strategic thinking, always aiming to stay at the top of the game. It may not be easy, but it is what it takes to be seen as a trusted, respected and valuable resource for our clients and to secure the top position lawyers held in the past as trusted advisors.

10   Conclusion

In just one generation, the work of a lawyer has evolved beyond measure. Looking back 20 years ago, lawyers were sole practitioners and individual centers; they managed everything on their own, from administrative tasks to pitching to clients, and were willing to take on a wide variety of cases.

Globalization and trade liberalization have prompted a revolution in the business practices of our clients. Law firms have had to adapt accordingly in order to keep up with the needs and expectations of global corporations. These multinationals, dealing with ever more complex and sector-specific matters, need specific legal expertise—which the traditional legal services model is not able to deliver. Lawyers have responded by specializing and reorganizing, and big law firms have pooled talent and built sector and practice groups through well-connected international networks. Today, lawyers are supported by business people, who assist them in pitching to clients, attracting and growing talent, hitting targets and designing sound business strategies.

While those changes have taken place incrementally over two decades, this evolution is accelerating. Law firms are adopting even more specialized, strategic, integrated and efficient business models. And some, like Dentons, have opened up to the world as a whole, and to the communities, becoming polycentric. The mindset of corporate lawyers has begun to shift. But to make this change sustainable requires constant self-reevaluation, clarity of mind and an eagerness to adopt new tools. Developing this attitude, however, requires an optimistic approach in a disruptive environment, mindful thinking about the ethical and economical challenges and a strong belief in the fundamentals of our profession.

Liquid Legal Context
by Dr. Dierk Schindler, Dr. Roger Strathausen, Kai Jacob

There is pressure on the traditional model of how law firms serve corporate clients. However, the debate about this very often gets reduced to the cost-element, i.e. how the budget pressure on in-house leaders translates into a rapidly decreasing willingness to accept the high rates and traditional ways of billing by law firms. This exclusive focus on cost is trying to cure the symptom while remaining ignorant about the root cause.

Markfort overcomes the traditional way of thinking and offers a range of aspects on how the DNA of legal service providers has to change in order to succeed in a changing market. His point of departure is the fact that clients want solutions, not opinions—so lawyers have had to shift from legal advisors to service providers. Markfort concludes that the main traits of a legal service provider to manoeuvre in a globalized industry are: polycentrism, project management skills and savviness in technology, as much as diversity and trust.

How does Markfort's thoughtful and innovative approach from a big law-perspective resonate with an in-house leader? Is the service provider

(continued)

approach a match to the expectation that Lucy Bassli voices when she expects law firms to become managed services providers?

It is also interesting to add the perspective of Jan Meents and Stephen Allen into the picture, who—in defining new types of services from providers in the legal industry—make a strong case for not falling into the trap of only focusing on cost and to measure value creation instead.

References

Curtis, M., Schmid, C., & Struber, M. (2012, August). *Gender diversity and corporate performance*. Zurich: Credit Suisse AG.

Department of Economic and Social Affairs. (2010). *The World's Women 2010, trends and statistics*. New York: United Nations.

Desvaux, G., Devillard, S., & Sancier-Suttan, S. (2010). *Women leaders, a competitive edge in and after the crisis*. McKinsey & Company 2009, Women Matter 3, April 2010.

Foubert, P., Burri, S., & Numhauser-Henning, A. (2010, October). The Gender Pay Gap in Europe from a Legal Perspective, European Network of Legal Experts in the Field of Gender Equality commissioned by the European Commission.

Joy, L., Carter, N. M., Wagner, H. M., & Narayanan, S. (2007). *The bottom line: Corporate performance and women's representation on boards*. Catalyst Inc. http://www.catalyst.org/system/files/why_diversity_matters_catalyst.pdf. Accessed 3 Oct 2016, http://www.bcg.de/documents/file204646.pdf. Accessed 3 Oct 2016.

Legal Profession. (2013, March). Key Figures of Six Countries of the European Union, Avocats. BE, Conseil national des barreaux, Bundesrechtsanwaltskammer (BRAK), Deutscher Anwaltverein (DAV) e.V., Soldan Institut, Consiglio Nazionale Forense, Ordre des Avocats du Barreau de Luxembourg, Abogacia Espanola.

The American Psychological Association. (2006). Introduction to Mentoring, A Guide for Mentors and Mentees.

Veith, C., Bandlow, M., Harnisch, M., Wenzler, H., Hartung, M., & Hartung, D. (2016). *How legal technology will change the business of law*. Munich: Boston Consulting Group.

Dr. Rainer Markfort is a corporate partner in the Berlin office of Dentons. He focuses on advising corporations in critical situations. He supports companies' management in internal investigations and in setting up compliance management systems. Rainer has years of experience in advising on the restructuring and refinancing of companies. His practice covers providing insolvency advice to creditors, shareholders and management as well as developing and implementing insolvency plans, and advising on MBO and M&A transactions. Rainer studied law at the University of Münster (Germany) and Université Paris II (Maitrise en droit) and received his PhD in law from the University of Münster in 1993.

Shifting Client Expectations of Law Firms: Morphing Law Firms into Managed Services Providers

Lucy Endel Bassli

Abstract

It's good to be the client. We dictate what we want from the law firms and when we want it delivered. That may have been true for decades, if not centuries, but now it is becoming more complicated. As pressure continues to mount on internal legal departments to do more with less, and as legal professionals are functioning more and more like business professionals, we have to think differently. Legal departments need to ask for different outputs from their outside counsel firms, and the law firms need to deliver legal services in a different way.

It is no secret that in-house lawyers love their jobs because we get to be close to the business and contribute to how the company works. We have first-hand sight of how businesses operate and how businesses outsource their non-critical work. So why are we not learning from our business partners about how to operate the legal practice? It is a business, after all. Well, we are learning, and that is forcing a change in how legal services are delivered in-house and in the expectations we have of our law firms. We are learning that we can expect operational excellence from law firms, just like we expect it from our professional service providers in other parts of the companies we work in.

It is time for a radical shift... It is time for law firms to deliver services with the quality of a law firm but with the operational excellence of an outsourcing company. Besides doing away with the billable hour, in-house teams need to get more back than we have gotten before from the law firms for the same amount of money. In addition to high quality legal services and advice, we need to get insight into the work of the law firms in a way we have never had before. The law firms are full of valuable information and data about the legal services that we procure from them, which could inform in-house teams about the business of the company they work for more broadly. Yet, that information is not being

L.E. Bassli (✉)
Microsoft Corporation, One Microsoft Way, Redmond, WA 98057, USA
e-mail: lucyB@microsoft.com

© Springer International Publishing AG 2017   59
K. Jacob et al. (eds.), *Liquid Legal*, Management for Professionals,
DOI 10.1007/978-3-319-45868-7_5

harvested and business is continuing as usual: deal by deal, legal memo by legal memo.

Slowly, change is happening. At Microsoft, we have stratified our legal services for procurement contract review in a way that allows us to optimize our external and internal resources and learn about our legal transactional practices in a way we have not done previously. The most radical change we made is moving our law firm support for contract review and negotiation into a managed service engagement. Like the IT managed services that have been around for decades, we are now beginning to engage law firms to deliver to our department as a managed service, the contract review service they had been doing for us for years, but in a very different way. Let's dive in deeper.

1   Stratifying the Work

Before contemplating which work to outsource and to whom, legal departments need to regularly assess if any legal involvement is necessary, at all. We all want to help internal business clients with their contracts, but sometimes legal becomes a sort of a crutch for the business and finds itself completely overloaded. The triangle in Fig. 1 is a view on how work can be allocated and resourced based on the complexity of the transaction.

At the very base of the triangle is the large volume of work that is not complex and frankly requires no involvement from the legal department. This sort of contracting work can be handled by the business owners by following some simple guides and pre-populated templates. The next level up is the work that the in-house legal professionals, either junior attorneys or paralegals, should stop handling because the work becomes quite predictable and stops being challenging. That work is conducive to documenting in a playbook and can rather easily be

Fig. 1 Stratification of work

outsourced to a legal process outsourcing company, which utilizes low-cost experienced legal professionals across a variety of skill levels.

The next level up is the premise of this whole article. It is the combination of high-level law firm legal services with the operational efficiencies of an LPO. This work should be the type that is commonly handled by law firms, but could benefit from the recurring themes and learnings' making the delivery of the legal services more predictable and efficient. While playbooks are very helpful, the law firms are in a position to make judgment calls and legal advisory assessments, such that playbooks are not the only basis for the work delivery.

Finally, there are those transactions that require the subject-matter expertise of legal experts and the unique business insight that only the in-house legal team can bring. Regardless of the changes in the legal services delivery models, there will always be the need for these most complex transactions to be handled by certain experts at law firms or by those legal advisors closest to the business.

2   Myth Buster: Managed Services Can't Work for Legal

It is common to hear about outsourcing to India. That is old news. But outsourcing has a unique concept buried within it: managed services. A managed service is a type of delivery model for outsourced services. Outsourcing should be thought of very broadly. Companies pay for service providers to deliver services across a variety of areas. Everyone pays external service providers to do certain things for them. It is *the way* in which the services are delivered that defines if it is just regular outsourcing or if it is a managed service provided by that third party.

Most companies outsource janitorial services, real estate maintenance, catering and other non-core work that is needed to run the business. Typically, those are outsourced as a managed service. What does that mean? The customer relies on the supplier to deliver the service end-to-end without getting involved in *how* they perform their duties. The customer has no say into which workers are deployed, how much those workers are paid or how those workers perform their tasks. The customer looks to the supplier to handle all of the "how" details, and in return expects outcomes. The outcomes have to be agreed upon and documented, but really it is all about answering the following question as a customer: "Are my objectives being met?"

In the past decade it has become more common to see companies disaggregating some of their core work and outsourcing even certain segments of core work. Manufacturing companies are hiring manufacturers overseas and are shifting entire operations to those companies. Tech companies are hiring software development service providers across the globe and trust them with delivering core testing functions. Like those companies, legal departments have historically been outsourcing to law firms forever in time, but we have not really taken that outsourcing practice along the continuum to a managed service, like the other industries have.

The one area where we have seen some examples of managed legal services is in the models delivered by Legal Process Outsourcing ("LPO") companies. LPO's have been providing "back-office" services for law firms for well over a decade now. Back-office can be anything from pure word processing up to some services related to data management of the financial processes for the law firm (i.e. overseeing e-billing, or managing procurement). Slowly, LPO's moved up the value chain to do work that is closer to the "core" of legal services, like document review and discovery. LPO's were stepping in to provide lower cost resources for high-volume tedious work. Most of that work was being handled offshore, in India, and proved to be quite successful. Still, there was a reluctance to outsource any work that was considered core to the law firms.

As the recession approached and pressure increased to do more with less, there was some expansion in the use of LPOs. At Microsoft, we were early adopters in a way and pushed the envelope of what could be outsourced to an LPO. When other legal departments and law firms were outsourcing only document review or contract extraction, we chose to outsource the legal analysis and written negotiations of contracts. This was *"real"* legal work, that is core to in-house practitioners. It was work that was handled by our internal paralegals and lawyers, and some of this work was being done by our outside counsel. We made significant changes to how this contract review work is handled and redesigned the internal legal support model within our department.

Outsourcing is not something to be jumped into. It cannot be a bunch of work that is tossed over the fence to an LPO, with the hopes of a neat and tidy outcome. In fact, it takes a lot of work on behalf of the client to prepare for outsourcing, and then a significant amount of work to manage the relationship. That work, however, is very different from the work of actually doing the legal substantive analysis. The work to be done by the client after outsourcing is all about managing expectations and reviewing the results together with the service provider. It requires project management skills and business operations experience. Later in the article, we review the best practices for outsourcing.

3   What's in It for the Client?

For decades, legal departments have bought services in the way that they were sold by the law firms. There is nothing to say that the client shouldn't or can't dictate what services it needs and how to receive those services, within the limits of the current legal market of course. In fact, now is precisely the time for clients to redirect the law firms and ask for more, and different services. It is time we get more for our money. Note that moving to a managed service is not necessarily done to save money. In fact, cost reduction should be secondary so that law firms don't get scared away by the thought of lost revenues. The goal is to get more from the law firms for the same amounts spent. For example, there is arguably a body of work done today by junior associates that can be done at lower costs, and the savings can then be applied to delivering different skill-based professional services.

Legal departments that have enough volume going to law firms can require that law firms provide additional services traditionally not thought to be within the expertise of legal professionals. For example, data analytics, associated with spreadsheets and "people good at math" is becoming a common request from clients. In-house teams are hungry to know more about their own companies' business, and much of that knowledge sits with the law firms. The in-house lawyers know what legal work is being handled outside, but they lose sight of some of the business problems and issues that are associated with that legal work because the outside lawyers are working directly with the business owners. Over time, law firms who provide a significant amount of recurring work for companies begin to learn valuable insights about that company's (aka, their client's) business and legal needs. In fact, it is that unique insight that makes those law firms so valuable to the companies and why in-house legal departments become dependent on their outside counsel. Truth is that there are many scenarios where the law firms know more about their clients' business than the client's in-house legal team.

So, why not demand that knowledge to be shared back with the client? It is not enough to hope that the best partners will see the benefit in educating the client about the law firm's learnings, it must be a requirement of the engagement. In-house legal teams can request that the law firms provide back some basic information about the work handled outside. For example, in a transactional practice, the law firms should, as standard practice, provide the following basic data points on a regular basis: how many transactions were handled, some break-down on the types of transactions, feedback about the documents/templates used, common negotiation topics, etc.

This sort of information is already at the hands of the law firms, and it just needs to be gathered and collated in a consumable format. That is where the function of data analytics comes in. Once foreign to law firms, it is now being developed across the industry and nurtured, as more clients begin to request this insight. The client benefits immediately from such information because adjustments can be made to templates, and trainings can be delivered to internal business clients who are misusing/abusing the outside legal services.

A perhaps easily overlooked benefit in receiving this sort of data is that the in-house team discovers the gaps in knowledge within their own company. Often it is the outside legal team that becomes familiar with the business contacts within the client company and can relay back to the in-house legal team where there are gaps in experience where training or further education would help. Senior business leaders will be better informed by their legal counterparts about trends in the industry. In-house legal teams would no longer be paying law firms to spend their time educating the business clients on matters that they can be trained on by the in-house team. This presumes that the in-house attorneys can consume such data, and act on it effectively.

Training opportunities are just some of the many benefits of receiving data analytics information back from the law firm. A more tangible benefit is the learnings from repetitive work handled by law firms. In a transactional practice, law firms are often doing similar types of deals over and over again. Sure, each one is somehow unique, but all deals start from some sort of template, or sample used before. As law firms try to accommodate and please their corporate clients, they often fall into the trap of using the client's preferred forms and may shy away from telling the painful truth that the templates are outdated or they waste negotiation cycle time on the same issues regularly. Experienced and confident partners may raise these concerns, but it is not systematic in how law firms deliver services. So, corporate clients pay for the repeated use of basically "bad" templates. Once law firms get into the practice of proving this sort of feedback, as would be required in newly documented engagement letters and statements of work, in-house teams can update their documents more regularly, reducing cycle time of negotiations significantly, which results in savings.

If these benefits are not enough, then the one that is sure to convince even the biggest skeptic is the benefit of predictable fees. Later in the article, we examine the financial benefits of this managed service arrangement.

4 What's in It for the Law Firm?

For this section, two law firms[1] who have partnered to deliver a managed service together to a global client have provided their perspective on why they have invested in this new model.

4.1 Sustainability (Chosen over Short Term Profitability)

The challenges facing law firms since the 2008 banking crisis are widely reported. In the most part, there are simply too many corporate law firms whose business models have been overly reliant on customer loyalty and unchallenged hourly rates. As in-house legal departments face ever-increasing pressures of tighter budgets and greater workloads, coveted work is being secured through points-based procurement assessments which place sometimes disproportionate emphasis on price. It is a race to the bottom that law firms cannot afford to win (or lose). It is also of no benefit to clients who want to secure long-term supply partners. A market survey carried out by Legal Week Intelligence,[2] recently revealed that, despite budget pressure, clients still identify "quality of service delivery" and "commercial approach and understanding my business" ahead of "value for money".

In short, the lawyer/client model has to change, and it will. It needs to move from one of simply winning on price to a sustainable, mutually beneficial outcome. In the

---

[1]Davis Wright Tremaine LLP (Seattle, Washington) and Addleshaw Goddard LLP (London, UK) contributed their perspective.

[2]http://www.legalweek.com/legal-week/analysis/2439097/legal-week-best-legal-advisers-2015-law-firm-rankings, December 2015.

This report is based on a survey of the 13/15 of the UK's largest companies and 8/10 of the world's largest investment banks.

new world, the winners will be those law firms who can offer real value and quality service to legal departments by reducing workloads while containing the risks and costs. The managed services model offers just that. Those law firms who can offer managed services alongside a sustainable pricing model (for both the law firm and the client), and who do it well, will have a clear and compelling point of differentiation.

The lessons learned by the law firm from one particular engagement translates into other work for the same client by showing that law firms take seriously the charge to do more for less. These lessons can also turn into new work for other clients as the constant iteration of this new delivery model yields more learnings. Further, if the client is willing to speak publicly about the successes of the managed-service delivery model (or allow the law firms to do so), there is a great advantage when competing with other law firms for new work. There is a big competitive difference between saying "we know how to improve processes and provide greater value, and we hope to do this one day soon for a client" and saying "we have a record of success improving processes for clients, and here is what client X says about the additional value we have provided."

4.2   Relationship Building

Law firms providing managed services are given a unique opportunity to be part of a client's "business as usual" in addition to their big-ticket deals. This day-to-day contact (otherwise achieved only through often costly and precious secondments) leads to much tighter, more focused client relationships (and with it, to a competitive advantage of winning big-ticket deals). Such relationships are also formed through multiple touchpoints between a law firm and its client (at all levels: senior and junior, business and legal) which affords much more stability than the traditional over-reliance on a single point of contact. Clients also appear to welcome a team-based offering. The Legal Week Intelligence survey (above) also revealed that partner-level contact is a decreasing priority for many clients, with only 63 % of survey respondents selecting it as important.

Law firms learn a great deal from these sorts of managed services arrangements. That learning might concern the client's policies and positions, or something more specific about how individual in-house attorneys like to work, and their views on particular issues. As an added benefit, the law firms also learn something about their own processes and how to cut waste and increase value as perceived by the client. Developing greater skill in listening to the voice of the client and designing solutions in close collaboration with clients to deliver greater value helps law firm lawyers become better lawyers. Naturally, there is a presumption that the client in-house teams are interested in these new arrangements.

4.3   Opportunities for a Broader Service Offering

Law firms delivering managed services usually sit in the "engine room" of the legal function, dealing with the volume of day-to-day contracts that drive the productivity of the business. With this position comes a unique insight with which law firms can identify opportunities to add further value and win further work. Many in-house counsel underestimate the value outside counsel place on becoming more of an integral part of the in-house team. Law firm lawyers like to solve real problems for their clients; and they like helping in-house counsel succeed. This includes helping in-house lawyers move up the value chain within their own organizations. Managed legal service lawyers find this in itself to be enormously satisfying and believe it will help their relationship with these clients and in-house lawyers for years to come.

Any successful managed service offering should set continuous improvement (both legal and non-legal) as one of its goals. In this regard, law firms are given a platform not only to suggest improvements but also to deliver them. Law firms can and should use this opportunity to widen their service offering to new categories of work (and revenue) beyond traditionally "legal" work. Examples of such new categories of work are: process mapping; legal project management; risk management; horizon scanning; document automation and artificial intelligence. All of these services are complementary to the core managed service and can drive further growth for both the law firm and the client.

5   Financial Benefits of the Managed Services Model

Switching from a traditional hourly based billing model to a managed legal services model yields business benefits for both sides of the engagement. One benefit that immediately comes to mind is the predictability of a recurring monthly billing. A flat fee for services eliminates the peaks and troughs of normal hourly billing, making forecasting easier and more reliable for both parties. In Fig. 2, we examined our monthly invoices for legal services over the course of 2014.

One can see that there is no discernable pattern to the hourly billing, in stark contrast to the flat rate scenario. To be sure, the nature of flat fee pricing means that at times one party will see financial favorability, since fee setting is not always an exact science. For instance, in the example above, a managed services provider would have come out of the year more favorably than we would have, as the total flat fee for the year would have exceeded the total we paid under traditional billing. However, our full year variance would have been within 15 % of the flat fee, and we would have had the benefit of being able to forecast accurately if we had a flat fee model, so it still would have been a win-win for both sides of the engagement.

Law firms moving to a managed services model can also see a windfall resulting from the base fee calculations. If the fees are based on total hours of anticipated work, typically a blended rate will be used to calculate the annual fee. Blended rates are often calculated as the average rate of all legal staff who are expected to provide

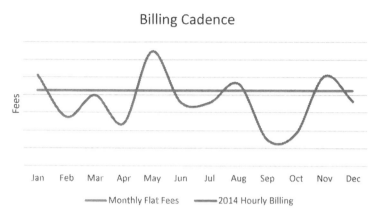

Fig. 2 Billing Cadence

Sample Blended Rate Scenario				
Legal/Non-Legal	Position	Hourly Rate	Number of Resources	Total Cost
Legal	Partner	$ 550	2	$ 1,100
Legal	Associate	$ 350	5	$ 1,750
Legal	Paralegal	$ 200	3	$ 600
Legal	Contractor	$ 150	5	$ 750
Non-Legal	Project Management	$ 85	1	$ 85
Non-Legal	Administrative	$ 50	1	$ 50
Non-Legal	Technical	$ 75	1	$ 75
Legal	Total	$ 280 Blended Rate	15	$ 4,200
Non-Legal	Total	$ 70 Blended Rate	3	$ 210
Combined	Total	$ 245 Blended Rate	18	$ 4,410
	Delta in Hourly Rate	$ 35		

Fig. 3 Blended rates

services. This can run the gamut from contractors and paralegals up to partner level attorneys. There are a couple of financial benefits that a managed services firm can realize from this. For one, this calculation sets aside non-legal personnel who are required for a managed services model to run smoothly. Project managers, administrative staff, and technical staff are all critical to start up, manage, and improve the outsourcing program. By excluding non-legal staff, blended rates end up higher than they would be otherwise. In the hypothetical scenario below, a $35 per hour windfall is built in to the blended rate. While it may seem small, a large scale arrangement will magnify that favorability over the course of the work (Fig. 3).

Another benefit of the blended rate is that it assumes that some number of senior level resources will be required. Early assumptions about the level of senior level involvement may shift, however, as the law firm gains familiarity with the client and the incoming matters. The initial start-up period may indeed require the expertise of senior level resources, but over time, the law firm should be able to assign the work to less costly resources, all while billing under the pre-set fees that

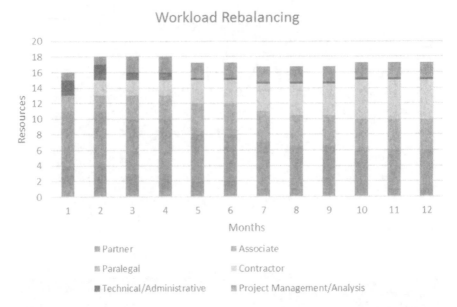

Fig. 4 Workload balancing

were based on the blended rate. Per the sample above, the client still has access to all levels of resources, but the balance of work should evolve so that the bulk of the work can be provided by lower cost resources (Fig. 4).

Since the commodity purchased by the client is the managed service, it does not matter what level of resource is providing the service, provided the quality meets the designated service levels. This allows the law firm to have scalability and be better able to handle a client's varying flow of work without overly relying on a handful of resources. For these reasons, it behooves the managed services firm to aim for a higher margin by quickly ramping up and distributing the work to less costly resources.

We should note here that an increase in a law firm's efficiency is made possible with data collection and analysis, two key components of a well-run managed services program. While business intelligence, or BI, may seem to be a buzzword more apt for other industries, it is a concept that is well suited for the legal services industry. Data can surface information such as how much time a transaction takes from start to close, what level of resources are used, what types of contracts are most common, which contractual provisions are consistently problematic, and so on. This type of data can inform the law firm and the client where there might be room for improvements, or even demonstrate the success of the program. BI has also quantitatively shown the benefits of our program. For example, in the chart below, we have data showing that our outsourcing partner was able to increase volumes per resource while decreasing escalations back to our in-house staff (Fig. 5).

The overall improved efficiencies shown above give us more confidence in the service and the value that the outsource partner provides. The more efficient the

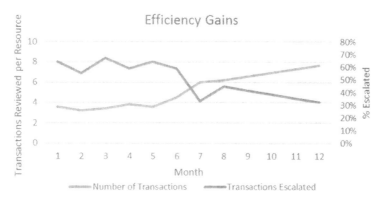

Fig. 5 Efficiency gains

program is, the more likely it is that we will send a larger quantity of matters into the program, even if the matter would not have previously risen to the level of sending it to outside counsel. Increases in volume can increase revenue for the law firm, so efficiency gains are a win for all.

Whether the fees are built on annual transactional volume or annual hours, the managed services model provides business advantages for both the client and the law firm. The new client-firm relationship is not just about the law firm providing more for less; it is the intersection where predictability, positive efficiency incentives, scalability, and smart use of the client's limited resources drives a mutually beneficial relationship.

6 The Basic Steps Every Successful Managed Service Engagement Needs to Take

Once convinced that outsourcing legal work to a managed service provider is right for your legal department, some very critical steps must be taken in order to achieve measurable success. Figure 6 is a rough timeline for outsourcing a sizeable operation. Granted, this was our first time outsourcing contract legal review, and subsequent processes were outsourced on a slightly compressed schedule, but the steps taken are all quite similar.

6.1 Understand What You Are Outsourcing

There is no faster way to fail in outsourcing than to expect the service provider to take on processes that internally the client team cannot understand or explain. It is critical for the client team to spend a significant amount of time learning their own process. This step is something that does not come naturally to attorneys because we are used to doing what lands on our plates. We receive a problem to solve or a

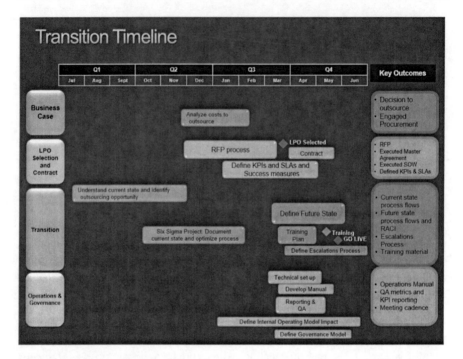

Fig. 6 Transition timeline

contract to review, and we jump in. There is no time taken to review how to get to the end results. In order to outsource effectively, the current process must be clearly documented in some details. Specifically, pay attention to the "special" cases that arise, and unique scenarios that are outliers, but should be noted for full transparency.

Once the current state is defined, that is the perfect time to identify inefficiencies and process gaps. There is no reason for the processes to stay the same in preparation for outsourcing. Make as many easy changes as possible at this point. Revise the process maps to reflect a better process than the one that you started with. There will be ample opportunities to refine it once the service provider is engaged, but for now it is important to have as clean of a process as possible in order to share it during the RFP engagement with potential suitors.

Uncommon to the practice of law are process maps. This exercise may require the help of a Six Sigma or other process expert. Many project managers have this skill-set, and there are automated tools that can help as well. Documenting a process in prose, using Word, would be very natural to an attorney because we live in Word documents and paragraphs, but real process efficiencies are best analyzed in a visual representation that depicts the various players involved and the key steps taken in each role.

Figure 7 depicts 7 stages on the NDA process touched by 6 different roles. It demonstrates the complexity that can become apparent when breaking down what

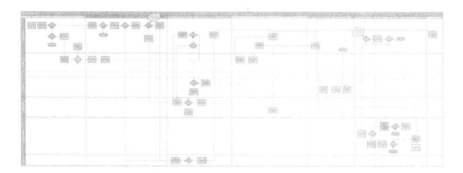

Fig. 7 Sample workflow

otherwise would appear to be a fairly simple process of creating and executing an NDA. Needless to say the process was simplified tremendously!

6.2   Decide What Outcomes You Seek

It is important to think through within the legal department exactly what is intended from the outsourcing process. These outcomes will be unique to the department depending on what the goals are for outsourcing. Consider whether this is just an alternative resourcing structure to free up the time of the internal employees or to save money on outside counsel, or whether there is a goal to gather deeper insights into the legal work currently handled in-house. Of course, it could be a combination of these and others. Regardless of the stated goals, the desired outcomes must be reasonable and within the scope of capabilities sought from the providers.

It is very easy to come up with a grandiose wish-list of goals, but care should be taken that the goals are actually achievable. Naturally, a good service-provider will advise on the goals and should honestly describe what is and isn't possible. An easy trap for clients to fall into is the "metrics buffet:" all the data you want for one set price. This is not as great as it sounds, and certainly not always very helpful. Often the client is overjoyed with the prospect of receiving data about the work that for years has been completely unmeasurable that they want everything tracked and measured. This is a cumbersome task for the service-provider and often yields data which the client does very little with. Consider requesting the data that will actually inform changes within the legal department or the outsourced process.

6.3   Select the Right Partner

While most attorneys are familiar with RFPs (Requests for Proposals), because our business clients do these, we still only rarely use them for legal services. Only recently have RFPs for legal services from law firms become more common. Law firms are getting better at responding to them, and legal departments are getting better at issuing them. Still, we have a long way to go. Legal departments should engage their company's procurement team to leverage those best practices for sourcing services. There is still the perception that legal services are so unique, but there is a lot that can be learned for the standard procurement process of running an RFP. The legal team should modify the RFP documents to make sense for the purchase of legal services, but certainly can benefit from the more generic process well-established by procurement professionals.

Spend time with the respondents and learn about their capabilities and innovative solutions to deliver legal services, but also spend time getting a sense of their culture. Will the law firm's culture match the culture of the legal department? Preferences for communication styles, drafting styles and risk tolerances are just a few of the attributes that can quickly signal whether or not there is a match. Also an important factor is the law firm's policy for conflict checks and seeking waivers. That will become critical, and is unique to law firms, since most LPO's can provide dedicated teams walled off from other clients, so that conflicts are not an issue. With law firms, it is critical to define the alternative solutions when the law firm will have a conflict, and to set timelines for the conflict checks to avoid delays in processing.

6.4 Plan the Transition

Once you see the light at the end of the tunnel (it is a bright future of the legal department handing off a bunch of work to a capable external service provider), you must be careful not to skip on the transition plan. Work backwards with the service-provider from an agreed-upon go-live date, and focus on the communication to the impacted business owners across the company and the hand-off between the client and the provider. There will be questions thrown back and forth, and both parties have to agree on timing of those exchanges and set SLA's, so that no one holds up the other, especially in the early days after transition.

Another critical ingredient for success is a clearly documented governance plan that will guide how the client and service provider will interact on a regular recurring basis. At a minimum the following must be agreed upon: (1) How will success be measured? (2) How will issues be resolved? (3) What is the escalation process back into the legal department to resolve inquiries from the service-provider? And (4) How will the process be reviewed for efficiencies and improved upon continuously? There are many more questions to consider, and the service provider will likely suggest some goals for the governance model as well. This is an opportunity to have the service provider share best practices from the industry and learnings from other engagements.

6.5 Stay Connected

Once the confetti is cleared off the floor and champagne flutes are discarded after the go-live party, be ready to stay closely connected with the service provider. The first "problem" is likely to arise within hours. Someone in the business will be confused about the new outsourced process, and complaints will begin. Understand that complaints about any change are natural and not a sign of failure. In fact, consider preparing a survey for key stakeholders within the business who will be using the newly outsourced service. Track those survey results and identify patterns.

Most importantly, do not blame the service provider for failures when there is a good likelihood that the client had something to do with the issues that arise. Do post mortem reviews and alter direction as needed. Be agile and open to critical feedback. Work through problems with the service provider as one unified team, and over time, the relationship will yield results beyond those anticipated.

The law firms also provide their perspective in the challenges that law firms face as they try to move in this direction.

While the rewards are great, the "change curve" will be steep. For those law firms looking to offer managed services, there are at least a few key challenges to overcome:

1. Mindset shift. Law firms (and their finance departments) need to reassess how they measure "profitability". For almost all firms, this means focusing less on hours-based realization and near-term profits and more on guaranteed revenue and long-term sustainable relationships. Still, successes with great clients (including projects generating substantial fees on a recurring basis) pave the way for additional innovation by and within our law firm. There is nothing like a client win to get the attention, interest and support of our partners.
2. Delivery. Implementing a managed service will require a significant investment in operational and technological efficiencies, which quickly distinguish between legal/non-legal work and "triaging" matters as (a) standardized; (b) specialist; (c) bespoke so assigned appropriately at the outset. This is particularly critical for recruitment/retention because good lawyers don't want repetitious low-level work.
3. Sourcing. To be agile to client's needs, law firms will need to establish a flexible approach to multi-sourcing through a combination of both legal and non-legal personnel such as project managers, paralegals, consultants (flexible resource) or external specialists (e.g. tech partners).
4. Measuring success. Finally, for any managed services project to be successful, both partners need clear objectives and incentives. At the outset, law firms and clients should not be afraid to discuss the metrics of success and what the rewards will be (for both parties).

7   In Conclusion

There is no template for delivering a managed legal service by law firms. This offering has to be crafted in partnership with a willing and invested client. It cannot be overstated how important it is for the consumer of an innovative service (aka, the in-house team) to be willing to invest the time and insights necessary for a law firm to be successful. In our case, my team had a very transparent conversation about the need to change and what that would be mean for the internal legal professionals that were doing the work prior to the transition. Everyone has to be committed to making such a transformation successful. Law firm and in-house legal team must align interests and goals to jointly develop a successful managed service delivery model. Law firms can't market this sort of delivery model in the abstract, without specific experience already in progress, and in-house teams can't demand this delivery model without being very clear on the desired outcomes and planning. What law firms can market is a willingness to try something new and curiosity for experimentation.

Liquid Legal Context
by Dr. Dierk Schindler, Dr. Roger Strathausen, Kai Jacob

Lucy Bassli has a clear vision when she talks about the changed expectations of corporate clients for law firms: It is time for a radical shift. *"It is time for law firms to deliver services with the quality of a law firm but with the operational excellence of an outsourcing company."* And with Markfort and Meents/Allen, two prominent voices of big law firms agree with her.

But what about the LPO's, specifically the new type of LPO's that mix up the legal industry and are often referred to as the change agents? To be provocative: May we interpret Bassli's statement as pointing out the limits of the future market for LPO's? Are LPOs lacking the depth and breadth of substantive legal advice—or simply the license to practice law—to become true contenders of law firms?

Well, this is where Mark Ross' provocative question comes in, when he asks "what is in a name?" Ross claims there is essentially no difference between LPOs and managed legal services. To be fair, Ross makes a strong and convincing case for how LPO's will become a strong and *complementary* player in the legal industry by constantly combining the cutting edge of legally trained resources and technology. But he also points us to a very valid question, especially considering developments like the UK Legal Services Act, which permits non-lawyers to own and manage law firms in the form of Alternative Business Structures: Could at some point a law firm become "just" one arm of the offering of an LPO?

Lucy Endel Bassli joined the legal department of Microsoft in 2004, providing legal support to the central procurement organization globally and across all lines of business at Microsoft. In recent years, she has focused extensively on complex and global outsourcing contracts and gained first-hand experience in outsourcing by engaging an outsourced legal services provider (LPO) to assist her with high-volume contract transactions. She recently launched a new "managed services" engagement with law firms. She oversees a centralized contracting office in the legal department of Microsoft, specializing in contracting tools, and process efficiencies and automation.

Legal Process Outsourcing: Redefining the Legal Services Delivery Model

Mark Ross

Abstract

In-house legal departments and their outside counsel are under pressure—and have been since before the global financial crisis in 2008—to do more with less. Much more. The great recession only exacerbated this pressure and led to a surge in the exploration of innovative legal services delivery models. As a result, two key questions came to the fore for in-house legal:

- Can we reduce or eliminate the requirement to undertake certain legal services; and
- For the services we must have, how can we perform them as efficiently and as cost-effectively as possible?

Subsequently, a new legal ecosystem has emerged in which, alongside outside counsel and corporate legal departments, legal process outsourcing (LPO) has arisen to play a crucial role in the transformation, re-engineering and cost-effective delivery of legal services.

This chapter will examine how advances in technology and the growth of LPO are closely aligned. It will hopefully put to rest any mistaken assertions that LPO providers are somehow threatened by technology's ability to automate processes and reduce the need for human labor. It will then go on to address the journey that the traditional bastion of legal services delivery, law firms, have undergone in exploring the LPO phenomenon and what the profession can expect over the next few years. It is clear that if law firms wish to remain the first port of call for corporate legal departments and the primary conduit for the delivery of legal services, this is predicated on their acceptance of the LPO operating model. In a profession that has historically embraced change at a

M. Ross (✉)
Integreon, Suite 1100, 1450 Broadway, New York, NY 10018, USA
e-mail: mark.ross@integreon.com

© Springer International Publishing AG 2017
K. Jacob et al. (eds.), *Liquid Legal*, Management for Professionals,
DOI 10.1007/978-3-319-45868-7_6

glacial pace, this acceptance can be characterized as a four-phased process, each of which is covered below.

Finally, this chapter will survey the latest practice frontier being explored by LPO providers—compliance. Much has been written and discussed over the years on the role of LPO in e-discovery, document review and contract lifecycle management. At each and every conference covering these topics, LPO provider sponsors and LPO panel sessions abound. However, given the perilous nature of burgeoning regulation and associated enforcement, it is not surprising at all that the LPO industry has been quick to step up to the compliance plate. However, before diving into these areas, it is important to try to define what the LPO industry actually represents within today's legal ecosystem.

1   What's in a Name?

While initially the focus of the LPO industry was on the labor arbitrage benefits available from outsourcing certain routine legal tasks to lower-cost locations, such as India and the Philippines, the industry has matured dramatically and transformed itself over the last few years. Today, LPO is best characterized as a global operating model, combining a best-practices framework with process efficiency, quality control, consultative expertise and enabling technology at its core. The leading LPO providers today support multiple practice areas from onshore, offshore and onsite delivery platforms and are no longer constrained by the shackles of a particular geography or restricted to e-discovery. There has even been discussion in the marketplace as to whether the acronym LPO is still appropriate, given the expanding array of services on offer. In an attempt to differentiate from LPO and, by association, from the world of e-discovery, some utilize terminology such as "managed legal services", or "alternative legal services provider". Well, if it looks like a duck, waddles like a duck, and quacks like a duck, then as the saying goes. ... it probably roasts up well with an orange glaze. In my opinion, LPO providers, managed legal services providers and alternative legal services providers are one and the same—essentially new legal market entrants providing innovative, efficient, technology-enabled legal services.

2   Technology vs. LPO: Compatible or Opposing Trends?

It is indisputable that developments in enabling technologies are reducing the need for manual labor in legal services and speeding up their delivery. These include: predictive coding, automated contract abstraction, deal rooms, e-billing software, data analytics, ever-more sophisticated search and knowledge management technology, and document assembly. While some might argue that technological advances represent a competitive challenge to LPO, nothing could be further from the truth.

Back in 2004–2006, it was technology that led to the advent of LPO by enabling offshore locations to interact with clients thousands of miles away. It is the LPO industry that has since continued to embrace and incorporate technology into virtually every element of its legal services delivery offerings, including assisting and advising corporations and law firms on the selection and implementation of labor-saving technologies. It is the LPO industry that now pushes the envelope to redefine the art of the possible, providing expert consultants who weave together advanced technologies as part of an overall legal process transformation. A few examples below aptly illustrate how LPO providers are achieving this.

Litigation The days are quickly fading in which, as part of the e-discovery and document review process, huge teams of attorney reviewers tackled hundreds of thousands—or millions—of seemingly unfiltered documents. Some industry commentators would have you believe that there is a battle for supremacy between advocates of inefficient, overly costly manual document review and the knight in shining armor that is technology assisted review (TAR), but this has little consideration for practical realities. The leading LPO providers have long been proselytizers of TAR workflows and have been constantly developing, testing and refining these very workflows to deliver smarter and less costly review processes.

The choice for corporate clients is no longer "should I employ a TAR workflow?" but rather "when should I employ it, and which combination of technology and workflow best suits my needs?" Utilizing these tools is not always about reducing the size of the overall document corpus or finding the proverbial smoking gun. In fact, LPO providers deploy these technologies in a variety of ways, such as to support a quality control process. The LPO industry, being both technically proficient and oftentimes technology agnostic, is well-placed to provide the insights their clients need to choose and deploy these technologies wisely.

Contract Lifecycle Management (CLM) For many corporations, the traditional model for contract lifecycle management is both labor-intensive and cost-prohibitive. Often, there are no formalized processes, standard templates, accepted language, back-up provisions or guidelines for turnaround times for CLM workflows. However, by using Lean and Six Sigma techniques to reengineer contract review processes, applying best practices and flexible resources, and optimizing the mix and utilization of technology, the LPO industry has led the way in CLM transformation.

The different CLM software platform providers offer varying degrees of functionality, including searchable repositories, clause libraries and workflow communication and obligations management, with dashboards that provide customizable views and reporting capabilities. These platforms can facilitate effective communication and collaboration between those involved in each step of the contract creation, review and negotiation process.

The degree of sophistication and functionality, and the associated cost of implementing the technology, varies dramatically across CLM platform providers. The role of LPO providers is to be the conduit to the efficient and appropriate utilization and implementation of these technologies. Whether through customizing their own proprietary CLM technology or by partnering with best-of-breed third-party providers, LPO providers work with corporate legal departments to help them understand which platform is the best fit for their environment, budget and tolerance for change. Enterprise-wide, multi-functional platforms may be just what the doctor ordered for some, whereas others may find such systems far too complex (and expensive) for their needs—especially if they only use a fraction of the tool's functionality.

Contract Review and Data Extraction The LPO industry is also at the forefront of technological innovation in contract data extraction and migration. Often triggered by the implementation of a CLM platform, or following an acquisition, or as a response to an audit, corporations can be faced with the need to locate, review and then extract information from thousands of contracts. LPO providers employ subject matter experts, who in addition to the requisite legal training, also possess a comprehensive understanding of the applicability of the range of technological tools available that can support such an engagement.

The first consideration for a contract review and data abstraction project should be to determine whether technology can assist in the process. While historically the process of extracting data from volumes of contractual documentation has been a manual one, this is no longer the case. There are tools that can be utilized to locate and collate contracts stored on hard drives, file shares, network drives and various software platforms. Once contract files are found, these tools can index them and render any text fully searchable using optical character recognition (OCR) technology. Then, the information important to the client needs to be extracted from each contract. Automated meta-data extraction and categorization technology can be used to speed up this process and reduce the costs associated with traditional manual contract review. This technology auto-triages contracts based on certain business rules (e.g., the exclusion of expired, duplicate, unsigned or immaterial contracts), groups like-contracts together and prioritizes the most critical contracts for review before automatically extracting the metadata. However, it is the LPO providers' combination of legally trained resources and leverage of technology that provides the most effective end-to-end solution. The software alone cannot extract every single piece of data that is important to the business. For the data the software does extract, a manual quality control process is essential to ensuring it is accurate and in the form that the business requires.

Legal Spend Analytics This is another example where LPO providers are leveraging technology to support a more cost-effective and re-engineered delivery of legal services. Data analytics technology, incorporating specialized visual techniques, can facilitate the analysis and presentation of historical and ongoing e-billing data to help a legal department achieve overall legal spend reduction. Although some software companies operating within the legal spend analytics space offer stand-alone analytics services, the more innovative LPO providers are offering consultants, expert in the delivery of cost-efficient legal services, who can organize and interpret this data in support of overall legal process transformation. By digesting, analyzing and then presenting (in a dashboard format) the intelligence gleaned from legal invoices, it is possible to benchmark outside counsel and vendor performance. With access to the right data, one can create business intelligence reporting and management information that provides in-house legal and finance teams with updates on outside counsel spend, breakdowns of matters by firm, practice area and timekeeper, as well as savings opportunities, performance against budgets, benchmarking and many other key metrics.

Knowledge, as they say, is power, and by utilizing software-enabled data analytics and dashboard reporting, corporate legal departments are empowered to revisit the entire gamut—the identification, selection, retention, management, cost and evaluation—of their relationship with outside counsel and other legal services providers. The end-game is one where resource allocation planning is optimized, ensuring that the right technologies and the right legal professionals, based on a combination of expertise, cost and availability, are assigned to the delivery of the requested legal services, given the type and complexity of the matters at hand.

3 Redefining the Law Firm Delivery Model: A Journey of LPO Acceptance

In order to survive in today's economy and thrive in the future, many law firms are actively re-thinking their business models. This frequently includes an embrace of LPO and a re-examination of the traditional law firm pyramid structure (partners at the top, junior associates and paralegals at the bottom) as the usual modus operandi for legal services delivery. Although some believe LPO providers will increasingly contract directly with corporate clients, it is important to consider that LPO providers do not practice law and therefore cannot replace law firms. A more natural fit for LPO is to supplant the lower tiers of the law firm pyramid. This is not to suggest the only benefit of LPO is labor arbitrage, in which expensive junior associates are simply supplanted, on a like-for-like basis, by less expensive offshore lawyers in India and the Philippines. As discussed above, LPO providers are leading the way in the incorporation of technology and process transformation into legal services delivery. And, likewise, law firms are evolving towards greater acceptance of LPO (Fig. 1).

Kicking or Screaming In or around 2006, it was not law firms but corporate legal departments that were the first proponents of LPO. Back in those early days, a cocktail of incredulity, mixed with a dash of disdain and served in a frosted glass of tradition, was the tipple of choice for many a law firm partner confronted with the

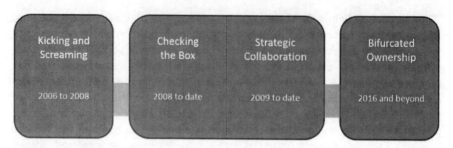

Fig. 1 Law firm adoption timeline for LPO

LPO elevator pitch. Senior executives at leading law firms would protest that LPO was win-win-lose. A win for the firm's clients, a win for the LPO provider, yet a "lose" for the law firm. This viewpoint presupposes the adequacy of two hypotheses that simply do not hold water any longer, namely the zero-sum game, where the more the client loses, the more the law firm wins, and that every penny of revenue generated by an LPO provider is a penny of revenue lost by a law firm.

In any event, these first few years can be characterized, perhaps somewhat harshly, as the phase where law firms were dragged kicking and screaming into the arms of LPO providers. On a case-by-case basis, in-house counsel started to advise their outside counsel that to retain their corporate client business they must begin to utilize LPO providers. In fairness to Big Law, this phase of forcible reluctance has largely passed and did so fairly quickly. Whether the great recession was the dominant catalyst or merely a sidebar to a change in partners' mind sets is a debate for another day.

Checking the Box Law firms have many constituencies but their clients always come first. Major firms' clients are, by and large, cost-sensitive in-house counsels. Firms can gain both a perceived and actual advantage with clients by making clear they understand and are responding to the cost pressures their clients face. In-house counsel muscle-flexing manifested itself not only in ad hoc requests that outside counsel use LPO providers but also in the increasing prevalence of requests for proposals (RFPs) asking outside counsel whether they had relationships in place with LPO providers. Law firms responded in turn by undertaking selection processes of their own to choose one or more preferred LPO providers so they could respond in the affirmative. This is the Checking-the-Box phase and for many firms, once a Master Services Agreement was put in place between the firm and the LPO provider, it was considered a job well done, with no further action required. Many firms today are still struggling with how to navigate the transition from this phase to the one that follows, Strategic Collaboration.

Strategic Collaboration In 2011, my employer, Integreon commissioned research through Legal Week (Legal Week, 5 May 2011), tracking the adoption of LPO among law firms and in-house counsel. While a small minority of firms seemed to worry that using an LPO might send clients the wrong signal, the results of the research showed such fear to be unfounded. A significant majority, about 75 %, of both in-house and law firm lawyers believed using an LPO did not "diminish the brand." Rather, those that embraced LPO were perceived as cognizant of the cost, efficiency and quality demands of their clients, and consequently appeared to gain a competitive advantage. A small yet growing number of innovative law firms have begun publicly to acknowledge their relationships with LPO providers. These firms are at various stages of the phase that can be termed as Strategic Collaboration.

Under the strategic collaboration phase, law firms can work with LPO providers to expand their offerings and deliver a complete, end-to-end approach, efficiently providing the appropriate level of legal services required for each type of work product. The end of this phase, one that arguably no firm has yet reached, is when LPO solutions are so closely integrated into the firm's overall value proposition that they are simply viewed as part of a suite of re-engineered solutions that the firm provides to its clients across all its practice groups. This requires a firm to embrace LPO at a strategic level, welcoming the LPO provider into the firm, lifting open the hood and working with the provider, as Richard Susskind, a preeminent commentator on the future of the legal profession, would say, to "decompose" legal functions. During this process, the provider and the firm map out "as is" workflows and then re-engineer the processes to incorporate LPO best practices, technology and, where appropriate, lower-cost labor.

The theory behind strategic collaboration is not rocket science, just the premise that the whole is greater than the sum of the parts. Contrary to early concerns that LPO providers would compete directly with law firms, it has become abundantly clear to those firms embracing strategic collaboration that the most effective legal services delivery model is a symbiotic ecosystem in which law firms and LPO providers both play crucial roles. LPO providers do not practice law and so are not true alternatives to law firms. They do not have the ability to provide advocacy or strategic, across-the-table, one-to-one legal advice. Law firms, on the other hand, do not generally bring a best practices approach to efficient, technology-enabled, legal services delivery with the same rigor as LPO providers. Neither side can individually deliver the holistic, end-to-end services corporate clients are now demanding. While one could argue that law firms with their own, fully integrated, "captive" LPO units can do so, there are limits to the capabilities of even the world's largest law firms and their captives.

A common misconception held by proponents of captives is that working with a third-party LPO provider means a loss of control. This is not the case. Control is more about governance than ownership. For example, some captives are out-of-control because they have not been properly set up with service level agreements (SLAs) and rigorous metrics. Conversely, a proper SLA and governance structure can give the law firm more control over a third-party LPO provider than they might typically have over their own staff. Running a captive center, especially offshore, requires a scale that only the largest law firms possess. LPO providers typically offer several other advantages over a captive as well. These include better capacity utilization by aggregating demand across many clients, converting fixed to variable costs, ongoing investments in technology and continuous improvement, and, of course, business continuity assurance through having multiple delivery locations.

Bifurcated Ownership Companies are increasingly finding that, as the saying goes, you can either shape the change or be shaped by it. Unrelenting cost pressure, deregulation, disaggregation, globalization and technological advances have been the genesis of LPO. Over the next 3 to 5 years, the challenge and opportunity for LPO providers and their law firm clients is to develop new service delivery models that will drive even greater innovation. It is thus incumbent upon all the key constituent stakeholders in the legal services industry to find better ways of working together.

In coming years, there is no doubt we will see even closer collaboration between law firms and LPO providers, with the lines of ownership in the legal services delivery model becoming increasingly blurred as stakeholders invest in and enter into joint ventures with one another. This I call the Bifurcated Ownership phase. How long will it be before an LPO provider acquires a major law firm in the UK now that external investment in law firms is permitted via the Legal Services Act? Hardly a week goes by without the rumor mill spinning a story about this or that law firm seeking to monetize either their captive LPO operation or their high-volume practice group. For many of the reasons cited above, it is likely that the majority of those law firms with captive LPO providers today will look to divest these operations in the coming years. The most logical acquirers of these entities may well be global LPO providers.

As time progresses, there is a growing optimism about, and enthusiasm for, reshaping the way legal services are delivered, making the rise of the new, bifurcated model inevitable. The end result of the journey to this fourth and final phase is a seamlessly integrated delivery model, with both corporate and lay clients benefiting from better, faster, more readily accessible and lower-cost legal services.

4   Corporate Compliance: The Latest Frontier for LPO

Agencies like the Department of Justice (DOJ) and Securities and Exchange Commission (SEC) in the US, and the Financial Conduct Authority (FCA) in the UK, along with a plethora of other regulators, are policing corporate conduct with ever-increasing voracity. The implications for the future are significant, including an expanding role for LPO. Compliance no longer simply requires instituting appropriate policies and procedures. In order to stay one step ahead of regulatory enforcers, it is essential to demonstrate these policies will be adhered to proactively. It also serves corporations well to try to anticipate the compliance programs they will need to meet changing regulatory obligations in the months and years ahead. With all of this to think about, efficient and cost-effective compliance processes that meet the regulatory requirements of today—and those of tomorrow—are a business essential.

The development of sophisticated LPO compliance offerings has occurred in tandem with the maturation of the LPO industry itself. LPO-based compliance solutions are often characterized as enterprise-wide endeavors rather than single-service transactional engagements. To achieve compliance, regulations increasingly demand both quantitative and qualitative reporting, as well as regular audits. This requires collaboration between the key constituent stakeholders, namely corporate legal, compliance and the internal audit, accounting and/or finance departments. Global LPO providers are stepping in and facilitating this collaboration by providing end-to-end managed services and support. The programs they provide offer much more than merely labor arbitrage and include process reengineering, multi-lingual support and enabling technologies. As corporations struggle to ensure their systems, processes and policies are compliant with the Foreign Corrupt Practices Act (FCPA), UK Bribery Act, Dodd Frank, anti-money laundering and data privacy legislation, LPO providers are leveraging their global delivery platforms and process transformation know-how to assist their clients in evaluating current compliance initiatives, implementing new ones and even consolidating jurisdiction-specific processes into global compliance programs.

Third-Party Due Diligence In the midst of ongoing legislative changes, third-party due diligence support for know your supplier (KYS) and know your customer (KYC) initiatives have emerged as perhaps the premier LPO compliance offerings. Outsourcing third-party due diligence tasks to LPO providers allows the business to understand and accurately budget, on a predictable basis, the full cost of ensuring third-party compliance.

The financial services industry for example, is increasingly looking to LPO providers to help meet their anti-money laundering requirements. This includes outsourcing elements of the customer onboarding process, with LPO providers undertaking research and analyzing data pertaining to politically exposed persons, negative news searches, source of wealth determination, high-risk jurisdictions or any other red-flag issues. The outputs from this process can range from basic red-flag indicator reports to much more detailed reports where high risks have been identified, including in-depth profiling of the corporation, directors, shareholders or other relevant entities. Once again, the value-add the LPO industry brings to the table is marshalling resources with the domain expertise needed to comprehend the forces driving the demand for compliance programs. The combined research, analytics, multi-lingual and general legal capabilities of top-tier LPO providers make them the logical port of call for this type of support.

Greater vigilance by anti-corruption regulators is also increasing the liability associated with third-party suppliers, which, in turn, is driving the outsourcing of compliance work. In connection with FCPA or other anti-corruption legislation, outsourced compliance support can include the design, distribution, assistance in completion, and collection of surveys of a company's global supply chain. This can be further supplemented by supplier response fact-checking and red-flag analysis. The skillset required by the LPO resources engaging with third-party suppliers calls for not only an understanding of the anti-corruption laws in play, but also the interpersonal skills necessary to facilitate successful interactions with third-parties who may be wondering why they're being asked to jump through hoops beyond the normal supplier selection process. With "global" being the operative word, those LPO providers that offer multi-lingual capabilities are even better placed to assist corporate clients with anti-corruption compliance certification of their global supply chain.

When all of this information is finally obtained, it needs to be organized, categorized, hosted and maintained in an easily accessible platform. This is where best practices, process improvement and fit-to-purpose technology, an integral element of the LPO offering, can also help.

Contractual Compliance New regulatory changes, mergers, acquisitions and divestitures frequently demand that corporations undertake a comprehensive review of high volumes of contracts to ensure compliance with both internal corporate policies and jurisdiction-specific requirements. These reviews can pertain to any number of issues but some of the most frequently encountered include:

- Ensuring a client's customer and supplier contracts include appropriate data privacy provisions
- Reviewing International Swaps and Derivatives Association (ISDA) agreements to ensure compliance with the European Market Infrastructure Regulation (EMIR)
- Ensuring compliance with contractual notice and consent obligations pertaining to change of control and assignment, in connection with an acquisition or divestiture.

LPO providers are able to provide teams of onshore and offshore lawyers and support staff to not only review these contracts and ascertain whether they are compliant, but also aid in remediation as needed to render them compliant. This remediation activity can include reaching out to third parties to obtain informed consent to a change in control of ownership, or negotiating an amendment to a contract to ensure compliance with a specific piece of legislation. As with other key areas of support in compliance LPO, having access to a global pool of multi-lingual, legally trained resources provides the corporation with a huge value-add in the arena of contractual compliance.

Regulatory Compliance Research and Gap Analysis Multi-national corporations are responsible for staying abreast of, and complying with, changes in the law in every jurisdiction in which they operate. It's a never-ending challenge for businesses in highly-regulated fields. Monitoring changes in regulatory requirements is another area of legal compliance that is now routinely outsourced to LPO providers.

Compliance professionals and in-house counsel know their business better than anyone and are keenly aware of both the issues that are most important to them and the kinds of legal changes they need to look out for. But tracking these legal issues in a systematic way can be a fairly rote, time-consuming process. By contrast, LPO providers can efficiently track, research and summarize current and pending statutes and regulations in multiple countries across the globe. In essence, the LPO provider is mapping a given organization's regulatory universe. In non-English speaking countries, this requires the ability to locate and understand legislation in the local language. Here again, global LPO providers with multi-lingual and dual-qualified legal resources are able to deliver a valuable service.

Once the regulatory universe has been charted, it can serve as a foundation for making informed corporate compliance decisions. LPO providers can then go a step further and perform a gap analysis wherein they analyze a corporation's existing compliance programs to determine their adequacy and alignment with the mapped-out regulatory universe. Any inadequacies or red flags pertaining to existing compliance programs can then be highlighted for remediation.

5   What's Next for LPO?

Five years ago, hardly a day passed without an article extolling the benefits of LPO and predicting this nascent industry's transformative impact on the legal profession. Perhaps the news mill is simply tiring of the story, but much of what has been written recently in the legal press has been prophesying the demise of LPO, referencing survey results that appear to show law firms now overwhelmingly engaging in captive operations or that advances in technology are obviating the need for LPO services. However, when those surveyed come from within private practice, asking them whether their clients prefer captive law firm operations or third-party LPO providers is a bit like asking the turkey where it prefers to spend Thanksgiving. And, as discussed above, given that LPO providers have so readily embraced technology over and above all other legal industry players, technology is unlikely to sound the death knell of the LPO industry any time soon.

Although LPO might not these days be the darling of the press, its prospects remain as bullish as ever, if not more so. The LPO industry has matured and transformed over the last ten years, but that journey has, in reality, only just begun. Out of all of the different stakeholders providing legal services within the new legal ecosystem, it is the LPO providers that have the deepest experience deconstructing and re-engineering legal processes using Lean and Six Sigma techniques, applying best practices and flexible resources, and optimizing the mix and utilization of technology. It is the LPO providers that have the demonstrated expertise to analyze which aspects of the work done by lawyers, paralegals and support staff add value and which should be eliminated, automated or delivered by alternative resources. As the rollercoaster of legal services innovation and techno-logical advances continues to pick up pace, not only will LPO providers be along for the ride, they'll have front-row seats.

Liquid Legal Context
by Dr. Dierk Schindler, Dr. Roger Strathausen, Kai Jacob

Ross takes the widely known sore spots of inhouse departments as his point of departure: (1) how can we get rid of some work (at least manually)? and (2) how can we increase efficiency and cost-effectiveness? Adding the rapidly increasing opportunities created by new legal technology, he describes the ecosystem in which the new type of LPO's can blossom.

Is this a threat to law firms, or is it rather an opportunity as a new player has emerged with which law firms can augment their services? My interpretation of Ross' article is that he thinks it is may be both: If law firms embrace the opportunities that a collaboration with LPO's brings to them, both parties will benefit. However, if law firms ignore the new expectations of clients for a much broader range of managed legal services and push their traditional business model, they might find themselves becoming just one arm of a multitude of services of an LPO, as LPO's benefit from a deregulated legal marketplace.

If Ross' is right, we are looking at a converging legal industry: LPO providers, managed legal services providers and alternative legal services providers are one and the same—essentially new legal market entrants providing innovative, efficient, technology-enabled legal services. This seems to resonate with what we have read from Bassli in terms of the changing inhouse expectations, and it also seems to link into the line of thought Markfort and Meents are pursuing.

It is now time for a "double click" on the aspect of (emerging) legal technology! Is it an enabler and a change agent—or the beginning of the end of lawyers who will be replaced by artificial intelligence? In the next article, Bues and Matthaei will kick off the discussion with an insightful definition of LegalTech.

Mark Ross is an authority on the future of the legal profession and the only person to have been invited to address the ABA, Law Societies of England & Wales and South Africa, the Solicitors Regulation Authority and the International Bar Association on the topic of LPO. He developed the first MCLE and CPD courses on the ethical implications of outsourcing legal work.

Mark is on the Advisory Boards of Suffolk Law School's Institute on Law Practice Technology and Innovation, and Northwestern University Law School's Center for Practice Engagement and Innovation. In 2016, Mark was elected as a Fellow in the College of Law Practice Management.

LegalTech on the Rise: Technology Changes Legal Work Behaviours, But Does Not Replace Its Profession

Micha-Manuel Bues and Emilio Matthaei

Abstract

For some time, the authors of this article discussed the understanding of LegalTech, its foundation and its impact on the legal profession. This paper aims to provide an overview of the global LegalTech development in an integrative manner. First, we elaborate on a definition of LegalTech and its history in recent centuries. Thereafter, the authors introduce the key technological foundations of LegalTech including artificial intelligence, machine learning and natural language processing. We also highlight the use of LegalTech in practice, ranging from e-discovery to automated legal reasoning. Our understanding from the technological foundation and practical applicability of LegalTech postulates that LegalTech changes, but does not replace, the way lawyers work, and leads to disruptive change of the profession.

1 Introduction

Undeniably, technology has revolutionized the business world, rapidly changing and expanding in every field imaginable. When it comes to the legal industry, technological innovation is no exception. However, much of the discussion around the use of technology in the legal industry focuses on the battle between humans (lawyers) and machines (robots). On January 20, 2016, The Telegraph titled: *"Doctors and Lawyers could be replaced by Robots"*. This article claims that lawyers and other white collar workers face being left on the scrapheap as advances in artificial intelligence (AI) trigger "terrifying changes" in the jobs market. According to this article, jobs commonly perceived as smart will be replaced by

M.-M. Bues (✉) • E. Matthaei
LEVERTON GmbH, Mauerstr. 79, 10117 Berlin, Germany
e-mail: micha.bues@lvn.com; emilio.matthaei@lvn.com

© Springer International Publishing AG 2017   89
K. Jacob et al. (eds.), *Liquid Legal*, Management for Professionals,
DOI 10.1007/978-3-319-45868-7_7

computers which will automate many tasks. Such claims have become increasingly popular in the last years. Richard and Daniel Susskind, for instance, argue that "*increasingly capable machines, autonomously or with non-specialist users, will take on many of the tasks that are currently the realm of the professions*" (Richard & Daniel Susskind, The Future of the Professions, 2015, 231). Other authors predict that "*once we have fully artificial intelligence enhanced programs [. . .], there will be no need for lawyers, aside from the highly specialized and expensive large-law-firm variety*" (Paul Lippe & Daniel Martin Katz, 10 Predictions about how IBM's Watson will impact the Legal Profession, 2014). A recent study by the Bucerius Law School and The Boston Consultiong Group titled "How LegalTech Will Change the Business of Law" suggests that LegalTech solutions could perform as much as 30–50 % of tasks carried out by junior lawyers today.

These developments challenge the common idea that lawyering is inherently a human activity and that lawyers are immune to the changes sparked off by the digital revolution. Today, it is almost common wisdom that computers will change the way law is practised and how lawyers work. The use of technology in the legal practice will have far-reaching effects. Hardly anybody will doubt that. However, it would be too easy—as many articles do—to just vaguely assume that lawyers will be somehow replaced by computers or robots using AI. Some commenters rightly demand to "*cut the hysteria surrounding AI in law*" (Ryan McClead). AI is not "magic" and it does not change by waving a magic wand.

Therefore, this article will try to give a nuanced and careful analysis as to how technology will change the way lawyers perform their work. In doing so, this article seeks to explain what LegalTech is, and it will engage, as far as possible here, with technical details. While these details may be difficult to understand or even uninteresting to lay readers, they are crucial to understand the kinds of lawyering tasks computers can and cannot perform (at the moment).

2   About LegalTech

2.1   Definition of LegalTech

There is no universally recognised definition for legal technology (short: LegalTech). In this article, we will define the term LegalTech broadly as technology and software used in the legal profession. LegalTech can be applied to almost all working steps that a necessary to render legal services. This definition of LegalTech encompasses the high end uses of technology, such as AI, for legal reasoning, as well as the apparently more mundane use of software for billing or case management. In practice, other terms like "law tech", "legalIT" or "legal informatics" might be used synonymously. The term LegalTech is not to be confused with information technology law or the substantive law relating to the use of information technology. As Wikipedia describes it: "*Legal technology, also known as Legal Tech, refers to the use of technology and software to provide legal services. Legal Tech companies are generally startups founded with the purpose of disrupting the traditionally conservative legal market."*

Broadly, three solution categories can be distinguished within LegalTech (cf. Bucerius/BCG Study): (a) technologies facilitating the access to and processing of legal data and lawyers (b) support solutions, and (c) substantive law solutions. The first category offers solutions which provide a better access to lawyers and legal data ranging from vertical legal marketplaces to legal research and information retrieval. The second category comprises supportive tools which enhance case management and back-office work, ranging from human resources management, accounting, billing, and financing to business development. The third category includes solutions which support or even replace lawyers in the execution of specific legal tasks. This category contains numerous subfields like, for example, automated contract drafting and analysis, e-discovery, online dispute resolution, legal analytics and blockchain-based solutions (smart contracts etc.). This article will primarily focus on the third category without implying that tools of the first and second category are of minor importance. However, we assume that the third category will have a more profound impact on the way lawyers will work in the future.

2.2   Brief History of LegalTech

Until the late 1950s, the use of information technology in law—especially regarding substantive law solutions—can be broadly described as an evolutionary process from deductive to data driven approaches. The deductive approach (also called rules-based logic) expresses information processing as a logical, step-by-step procedure. Example: If a certain condition X is fulfilled, Y needs to be verified. In the early days of LegalTech, it was assumed that most tasks could be described in deductive instructions by attempting to replicate computer-based versions of human cognitive processes (Stuart Russel/Peter Norvig, AI: A modern approach, 2010, 3–10). Behind this focus was a belief that computers have to "work" the same way as the human brain. The attempt was to create an artificial version of the human brain functionality. As the deductive approach did not show the envisaged outcome, the data driven approach became (until today) increasingly popular and more promising. The data driven approach is used to describe information processing that cannot be articulated as a mere series of logical steps. These inductive rules take the form of statistical equations that model the relationship between the information inputs and the processed output. The equations are estimated or trained with samples of historical cases. The estimated equations are then used to process new cases.

In the mid-1980s, legal expert systems—being a deductive approach—were *en vogue*. A legal expert system is a computer system that emulates the decision-making ability of a human expert in the field of law. Legal expert systems employ a rule/knowledge base and an inference engine to accumulate reference and produce expert knowledge. Expert system builders gather expertise and knowledge from (legal) experts. They then incorporate the knowledge and expertise into a software application in order to make the expertise and knowledge easily replicable. Some legal expert systems, like Susskind and Capper's, The Latent Damage System, became publicly accessible (cf. Philip Leith, The Rise and Fall of the Legal Expert System, EJLT 2010, 1 ff.). Many saw legal expert systems as an opportunity to provide inexpensive and easily accessible legal knowledge and advice. Expert systems are (early) forms of AI software.

In the 1980s and later, soft computing, a combination of technologies such as fuzzy logic, probabilistic reasoning and neural networks, became fashionable without sustained success. In the 1990s and beyond, expert systems were considered a failure because they only seem to work if (a) the legal rules are straightforward enough, (b) there is no ambiguity or vagueness regarding the inputs, and (c) there is clarity about which rule applies in each situation. Expert systems could not account for some of the most important performances of legal cognition: making analogies, applying vague and imprecise standards, using insufficient or contradictory data, learning through examples and experiences. What followed was the so-called AI winter of the late 1980s, a period of reduced funding and interest in legal AI research. The initial hype was followed by disappointment, criticism and funding cuts. Today, legal expert systems (sometimes also referred to as decision support systems) still play an important role by standardizing, formalizing and modelling expert knowledge. Nowadays, however, the aim is not to eliminate the human factor but to build expert systems that augment and facilitate the decision making process of lawyers.

Another trend in the 1990s was the development of formalisations of domain conceptualisations (so-called ontologies). A legal ontology tries to indicate concepts that exist within the legal domain and seek to explain how these concepts are related to one another. In other words, legal ontologies are used to express the common understanding of concepts and relations among them in a formal and structured manner. Ontologies can be used to, for example, create a common gateway facilitating exchange between domains such as taxes and property administering. Ontologies can be also very useful for information retrieval as it is possible to detect similar things that are named or called something else. Early examples include Valente's functional ontology and the frame based ontologies of Visser and van Kralingen (both 1995). There are many examples ranging from generic top-level and core ontologies to very specific models of particular pieces of legislation.

Even though not all early approaches to enhance legal work with technology were equally successful, they all contributed some important spadework for current LegalTech tools. They especially lead to the conclusion that it is not promising to only re-model an "intelligent" process that replicates the thinking of the human specialists to achieve "intelligent" outcomes. Today's LegalTech focuses on whether a computer system is able to produce accurate, appropriate, helpful and useful results which could be considered as "intelligent". In the following, we will explain which "modern" technologies are used nowadays to imitate intelligent processes.

3   Basics of Machine Intelligence

3.1   Definition of AI

As already pointed out, it is essential to understand a set of basic ideas in AI before we set out to explore the impact of those technologies in greater detail. Accordingly, we begin with a selected overview of AI capacities and limitations. We then review the current capacity of technology and/or software to automate various lawyering tasks.

AI was famously defined by John McCarthy as *"the science and engineering of making intelligent machines"* (John McCarthy, What is Artificial Intelligence?, 2007, 2). AI could also be defined as "cognitive technologies". However labelled, the field has many branches, with many significant connections and commonalities among them. The most important fields are currently machine learning, including deep learning and predictive analytics, natural language processing (NLP), comprising translation, classification & clustering and information extraction.

There is a lot of buzz around the term AI. It is an idea that has oscillated through many hype cycles over many years. AI seems almost magical and a bit scary. In 2015, a group of high-profile scientists and entrepreneurs warned that AI might be the last invention of the human race. In his bestseller *Superintelligence: Paths, Dangers, Strategies* (2014), Nick Bostrom warns about the potential threat of AI. He fears that an intelligence explosion through AI could lead to machines exceeding human intelligence. In Bostrom's view, superintelligent AI systems would quickly dominate the human species.

Even though the discussion of "superintelligence" is extremely interesting and sometimes mind-boggling, it has nothing to do with AI in law (at least at the moment). When the use of AI in law is discussed, it is important to bear the one distinction between "weak" and "strong" AI in mind. AI used in LegalTech is commonly referred to as "weak" (or "shallow") AI. It seems intelligent, but it still has defined functions. It has no self-awareness. Weak AI has to be distinguished from "strong" AI, also known as artificial general intelligence (AGI) or "deep" AI. Strong AI would match or exceed human intelligence which is often defined as the ability *"to reason, represent knowledge, plan, learn, communicate in natural language and integrate all these skills toward a common goal"*. In order to achieve strong AI status, a system has to be able to carry out these abilities. Whether or when strong AI will emerge is highly contested in the scientific community.

AI currently used in LegalTech tools is far away from strong AI. Therefore, when we speak of AI in the context of LegalTech, we mean technologies which seems intelligent but have defined functions, i.e. weak AI. It uses models of a problem domain given to it by programmers. Weak AI cannot perform autonomous reduction, whereas strong AI would have a real understanding of a problem domain. Therefore, weak AI requires an expert who performs all required reduction in advance and implements it into a system. As a result, weak AI will only have a specific set of tasks it can solve. A chess computer would, for instance, not be able to solve legal problems. The problem statement is outside of its capabilities. A

LegalTech tool using weak AI would only be able to "understand" the specific problem domain it was designed for. Therefore, modern AI algorithms are only able to replicate some of the human intellectual abilities. This is also true for IBM's cognitive computer Watson which famously won the quiz show "Jeopardy" against human competitors in 2011. IBM's Watson is a (very advanced) machine learning algorithm not a computer with human-level intelligence. Current AI tools are not able to mimic advanced cognitive processes, such as logical reasoning, comprehension, meta-cognition or contextual perception of abstract concepts that are essential to legal thinking. We should bear these limitations in mind when we proceed exploring which techniques are used to "produce" weak AI.

In addition, the work of lawyers is (sometimes) highly complex. Lawyers need to process convoluted sets of facts and circumstances, consider applicable legal rights and obligations and render reasoned opinions and guidance on the best course of action based on all of that information. A lawyer (ideally) has the ability to understand the background and context of events, general knowledge of how the world works, and knowledge of the law and its application. The work of lawyers involves a lot of automatic filtering out of irrelevant noise and focusing in on the signal. For computers it is generally highly challenging to perform these tasks. To completely replicate a (human) lawyer would mean to re-engineer a process that could produce creative, imaginative and innovative ideas and results, whilst drawing on a comprehensive set of legal information and an "experience database" comparable to an experienced lawyer. As lawyers know, it can be an extremely complex task to render legal advice. Thus, it will be an extremely difficult task to replicate this with computers using weak AI. Current LegalTech tools are far away from achieving this.

However, even though it is important to understand the current limitations of AI, it is equally important to understand the evolving technological progress which is unfolding at rapid speed. Computational power is growing exponentially. And, exponential growth is difficult to comprehend for humans as we generally think in linear terms. The most famous equation which stands for this exponential growth is Moore's law. Moore's Law states that CPU processing power will increase exponentially by a factor of 2 every 18–24 months. In other words, Moore's Law claims that CPU processing power will double approximately every 2 years. Assuming that computers continue to double in power, their hardware dimension alone will be over two hundred times more powerful in 2030. Differently put, the next decade will witness more than thirty times as much increase in power as the previous one.

Regardless of whether this growth will continue and whether the growth of computational power means that the abilities of AI systems will grow exponentially, as well, people have the tendency to underestimate the potential of tomorrow's applications by evaluating them in terms of today's enabling technologies. This tendency is sometimes referred to as "technological myopia" (Richard & Daniel Susskind, The Future of the Professions, 2015, 44). This should be born in mind, when we discuss the application of technology in the legal realm. Even though there are some substantial limitations today, this does not mean that these limitations will still exist in 5 or 10 years. The ability of technology might change more radically and sooner than we expect. Hence, although machines are just beginning to perform legal tasks, it is likely that we can expect substantial progress in the coming years. Until computers are able to mimic intelligent legal reasoning, the question is not whether they may or may not replace lawyers, but how they will impact how a lawyer will work.

The techniques used in LegalTech tools are called machine learning (including deep learning and predictive analysis) and NLP.

3.2 Machine Learning

Machine learning refers to a subfield of AI and involves *"computer algorithms that have the ability to "learn" or improve in performance over time on some task"* (Harry Surden, Machine Learning and Law, Washington Law Review 2014, 88). Machine learning algorithms predict outputs based on previous instances of relationships between input data and outputs. A machine learning algorithm will be gradually improved by testing and correcting its predictions.

Researchers have successfully used machine learning to automate a variety of sophisticated tasks that were previously presumed to require human cognition. These applications range from self-driving cars, facial recognition, fraud detection, speech recognition and spam filter to automated language translation. These algorithms cannot learn in the human sense. The algorithms are only able to "learn" in a functional sense as they can change their behaviour to enhance their performance on a specific task through experience (Stuart Russel/Peter Norvig, AI: A modern approach, 2010, 693). Machine learning algorithms cannot, however, replicate the human cognitive system. Machine learning techniques have been able to produce "intelligent" results in complex, abstract tasks, often not by engaging directly with the underlying conceptual substance of the information, but by engaging indirectly with this information, through detecting proxies and patterns in data that lead to useful results.

The rise of machine learning was enabled by advances in processing capacity and better availability of teaching data (Big Data). Big Data refers to *"a massive volume of both structured and unstructured data that is so large it is difficult to process using traditional database and software techniques"* (What is Big Data? A Webopedia Definition, www.webopedia.com). The advent of Big Data is a game-changer for many industries. Google, for instance, processes more than 100 petabytes (100 million gigabytes) of data every single day. In law, however, Big Data might be misnomer. The legal industry does not have enough data to label it as "big." The legal datasets are still mostly measured in gigabytes or maybe terabytes, nowhere near the petabytes and exabytes of Google. Some authors, therefore, suggest using the term Medium Data in a legal context to clarify that Big Data techniques in a narrower sense are not applicable. This Medium Data is equally valuable to streamline and automate legal work, and is hence also referred to as "Smart Data". That such Smart Data plays an increasingly important role in the legal industry can be seen when looking at companies like *Lex Machina*, *Juristat, eBrevia, Justly* and *LEVERTON*.

3.3   Natural Language Processing

Another technology used in LegalTech is natural language processing (NLP). It is the application of linguistics, statistics, and computer science to problems related to spoken or written language. NLP systems are able to convert samples of human language into machine readable format, and to convert information from computer databases into readable human language (cf. Ela Kumar, Natural Language Processing, 2011, 1). NLP is at work if someone asks Siri on his IPhone. NLP is challenging because computers traditionally require a programming language that is precise, unambiguous and highly structured. Human speech, however, is often ambiguous and the linguistic structure can depend on many complex variables, including slang, regional dialects and social context.

Many NLP applications today use "shallow NLP" or "statistical NLP" techniques. These applications do not "understand" the meaning of a word, phrase or sentence. They have just memorized certain words, patterns, or statistical associations between words. For a NLP tool to show "intelligent" behaviour (for example, interpreting a legal contract), the tool would need to understand legal concepts. In addition, it would need to be able to reason or combine information from different sources. NLP researchers are working in two areas—semantics and pragmatics—that may eventually enable computers to "understand" written text or spoken language. NLP may lead to applications that can acquire knowledge on their own, or are able to reason in an intelligent manner. If this occurs, lawyers could potentially use NLP to build applications that are capable of understanding contracts and cases, researching legal topics on their own and making predictions about potential outcomes.

To sum up, LegalTech applications might use AI techniques, such as machine learning or NLP, to replicate intelligent behaviours. However, other tools or "normal" software solutions might be deployed as well to improve the way legal work and supportive activities are carried out.

4   LegalTech in Practice

The technology described above can be used in two ways. In its more basic form, technology *automates* processes that once required significant human effort. Typewriters replaced handwriting, and later word processors replaced typewriters. This kind of technology has (only) incremental value to lawyers. The change to work brought about by this technology is not radical but will transform the work of lawyers in many different ways. But sometimes technology does more than (just) automate; sometimes it *innovates*. This occurs when technology creates a completely new way of handling the same task, even though the actual impact might be small in the beginning. In the words of Clayton Christensen, author of the book *Innovators Dilemma*, LegalTech might not be sustaining but disruptive. Most LegalTech tools used in practice fall into the improvement category. LegalTech tools help lawyers to render a certain task faster and more efficient, with higher quality and fewer costs, compared to performing the task manually.

There are, however, several LegalTech tools that will challenge and completely change the way in which certain legal services are delivered. Collectively, they will transform the entire legal landscape. In what follows, we will briefly describe a selection of these tools and their use cases. Other tools which will not be described in detail include knowledge management, e-learning, online legal guidance, legal open-sourcing, workflow, case and project management, and contract management.

4.1   E-Discovery/Forensic Investigations

Machine intelligence in a legal context is most advanced in electronic discovery (or e-Discovery). It can be used in a variety of ways, including streamlining aspects of document review, analysing a document production received from an opposing party, preparing for depositions and expert discovery. E-discovery was the first (big) data application for law, emerging in the early 2000s. Nowadays, it is a multi-billion-dollar industry in the U.S. alone with many companies and notable exits. The e-discovery industry also continuously attracts new funding rounds. E-discovery has already significantly changed and disrupted the document review process which consumed much time of associates years ago. Law firms set up e-discovery units or outsource this work to third-party providers.

E-discovery is, simply put, the application of general methods of machine search to the review of legal documents. In its simpler form, it uses keyword search terms employing Boolean logic to find relevant documents. Search terms are then electronically applied to a set of documents. Lawyers will—based on this preselection—review those documents manually to determine if they are relevant.

Predictive coding (or Technology-Assisted Review, TAR) has fundamentally transformed the prospects for e-discovery. Predictive coding has proven to be faster, better, cheaper and more consistent than Human Powered Review (HPR) by applying methodologies including contextual searching, concept searching and metadata searching to document review. Predictive coding matches the text of entire documents (rather than individual words) to other documents using statistical sampling and modelling. Predictive coding involves a machine learning and various algorithmic tools. In general, experienced lawyers "train" the software by identifying relevant documents (seed set) from a broader set of potentially relevant documents. Drawing on the seed set, the algorithm learns to identify relevant documents. Through an iterative process of several learning cycles, the software is "trained" with additional documents.

Predictive coding has its downsides and limitations. Currently, predictive coding cannot effectively evaluate spreadsheets or documents without searchable text or other file types, such as videos, graphics and audio files. Predictive coding has some well-known problems which apply to machine learning in general. It will only be useful if the class of future cases has pertinent features in common with the previously analysed cases in the training set. The kind of relationship between future and past cases within a data set is an important dimension for the success of predictive coding. In addition, predictive coding generally requires a relatively large sample of past examples before robust generalisations can be inferred. Another common problem is overgeneralization (overfitting) which might occur when a model is excessively complex, such as having too many parameters relative to the number of observations. Overfitting happens when a model begins to "memorize" training data rather than "learning" to generalize from trend. Similarly, problems occur when the machine learning algorithm is trained with a biased data set and is therefore unable to infer useful rules for predictive purposes.

The same techniques used in e-discovery can also be applied to forensic investigations. This kind of investigation focuses on internal investigations as well as compliance programs. Forensic investigations tend to be more specific, targeted, less voluminous and much more technical. They can require a deeper inspection of lower data into operating systems, applications and server activity. The tools can not only be used in reactive scenarios where noncompliant or fraudulent activity has already happened. Legal analytics tools can also be used to proactively detect and head off potentially improper transactions before employees, third parties, or even criminals engage in the activities.

4.2   Legal Search

Legal research is a key aspect of legal practice, particularly for litigators. The average associate may spend up to 35 % of her time conducting legal research (cf. American Bar Association's 2013 Legal Technology Survey Report). According to several discussions with leading law firms, clients are also increasingly unwilling to pay for legal research. This might explain why legal search tools is the "dinosaur" of LegalTech applications and are available in all (industrial) countries at least in some form. The purpose of legal search tools is to make different types of static legal content available for human consumption. Computerized legal research began in the mid-1960s. Through the years, computerized legal search has become more sophisticated, efficient and precise. Previously, legal search depended on determining the right keyword. The major step was the change from keywords to semantics. Semantic search is normally defined "*as a kind of data searching technique in which a search query aims to not only find keywords matches* [. . .] *to determine the contextual* [and intent] *meaning*" of words (Marios Polycarpou et al., Hybrid Artificial Intelligence Systems, 2014, 540). By understanding and connecting intention and context, semantic search engines are able to understand the different motivation and expectation behind queries. A lawyer may input a query in natural language, and the search engine is still able to make sense of it.

Legal search is challenging for many reasons. In order to work, legal search tools require a great deal of manual encoding of the legal knowledge. Ideally, the knowledge-encoding could be done automatically, using some kind of NLP system. In practice, automatization is not possible, yet. Additionally, and this is a fundamental problem, law and judicial decisions are not objective and unambiguous. There might be disagreement about the meaning or the implications of a certain case or word. In general, judicial decisions, for instance, do not contain a fixed set of facts and/or rules which can be enumerated a priori.

4.3 Automated Document Assembly and Analytics

Traditionally, document creation and assembly were the bread and butter business of associates in big law firms. It is time-consuming and error-prone, if done manually. Document automation is a design of systems and workflows that assist in the creation and assembly of (legal) electronic documents, contracts and letters. In short, document automation is targeted at replacing the manual creation of documents with template-based and highly standardized systems. Document automation might involve machine learning tools and NLP techniques. Also, logic-based systems use segments of pre-existing text and/or data to assemble a new document. Document automation will—like every application using machine learning—require very substantial additions and rewriting in the beginning. But the software will "learn" and improve over time, and will deliver better and better results. Advanced document automation systems allow users to create their own data and rules (logic).

4.4 Online Dispute Resolution/Mass Procedures

Online dispute resolution (ODR) is a branch of dispute resolution which uses technology to facilitate the resolution of disputes between parties outside the courtroom in an online fashion. In short, ODR refers "*to the use of IT and the internet to help resolve disputes.*" (U.K. Civil Justice Council, Online Dispute Resolution, 2015, 4). When disputes are resolved by using ODR, the settlement process is entirely, or largely, conducted through the internet. Human beings might be occasionally involved in the ODR process, but they are not essential to the process. ODR is suitable for relatively low value disputes which can be resolved more quickly and for less costs with ODR than with ordinary courts. Broadly, ODR methods could be grouped into two consensual and adjudicative methods. Consensual methods involve automated or assisted negotiation. Automated negotiation relates to those consensual methods in which technology "negotiates" cases in which parties do not dispute on liability but need to agree on the value of remedies. Automated ODR services offer so-called "blind-bidding" services, including double blind bidding and visual blind bidding through a sophisticated auction mechanism. Blind-bidding services match offers and demands. Disputants might have, for example, three opportunities or rounds to settle a claim. One demand or offer is entered for each round. The service provider compares the demands to the opposition's corresponding offer. When the offer is greater than or equal to the opposition's demand, the claim instantly settles.

Another form of consensual ODR methods is the so-called "expedient non-adjudicative online resolution" which prioritizes expedience and dispenses with adjudication altogether. The ODR method recognizes the litigants' desire to simply dispose of the matter as quickly as possible. An algorithm automatically determines a fair settlement to be accepted by each party. The concept of "crowdjustice" has also recently taken shape as a means to leverage social norms and the wisdom of crowds to determine the outcome of a dispute. The most prominent adjudicative method is online arbitration, i.e. a process where a neutral third party (arbitrator) delivers a decision online which is final, and binding on both parties.

4.5   Standardized Claim Management

Standardized claim management is an area which has attracted a lot of attention recently. The claim manager offer LegalTech enhanced online services for highly standardized legal cases, mainly in consumer law. These services are offered in areas where the eligibility for compensation can be easily determined, such as compensation claims due to delayed flights. The business model of these services normally implies that the claim manager bears all the financial risk and is only compensated with a contingent fee if the claim is successful. These services will use LegalTech and process management tools to ensure that the handling cost for every standard case is as low as possible.

4.6   Legal Predictive Analytics

After the use of data analytics has become usual in other industries, predictive analytics is now coming to law. "*Predictive analytics is the use of data, statistical algorithms and machine-learning techniques to identify the likelihood of future outcomes based on historical data. The goal is to go beyond descriptive statistics and reporting on what has happened to providing a best assessment on what will happen in the future.*" (Predictive Analytics: What it is and why it matters, retrieved from www.sas.com). Law contains huge amounts of data from judicial decisions, briefs, articles, commentaries, legislative texts and other documents. Legal data includes fact patterns, precedents and case outcomes. This data is the foundation of legal predictive analysis. One form of legal analytics could be, for example, the use of fact patterns and precedents to predict a case's outcome. This prediction could help lawyers to assess the likely results of a patent litigation.

4.7 Blockchain and Smart Contracts

Blockchain is the latest LegalTech trend. The Harvard Business Review recognizes the blockchain technology as one of the top technology trends to watch out for, concluding that they will disrupt entire industries (HBR, 8 Trends to Watch in 2016, December 2015). The term "blockchain" refers to a *"decentralized digital ledger that combines powerful cryptography algorithms with a system of decentralized computing power that redundantly verifies transactions, which are ultimately recorded on a public digital ledger available to the world."* (Joe Dewey/Shawn Amuial, Blockchain Technology Will Transform the Practice of Law, retrieved from bol.bna.com). In short, blockchains can be used to replace anything that needs authentication or a signature. The core innovations of blockchain technology lie in the principles of decentralisation and trust. A fundamental prerequisite of any transaction is trust. If a person enters into a transaction with a stranger, he needs some underlying trust-building mechanism. We trust transactions even with complete strangers, because we trust centralised intermediaries (such as banks) and the legal system. The blockchain technology makes centralised intermediaries redundant by providing a digital ledger which ultimately verifies every transaction.

The blockchain technology is a platform upon which many applications can be built. There are some use cases of the blockchain technology which are of special interest or relevance to lawyers. The most interesting use case for lawyers is probably smart contracts. Smart contract *"is a set of promises, specified in digital form, including protocols within which the parties perform on these promises."* (Nick Szabo, Smart Contracts: Building Blocks for Digital Markets, 1996, 1). In other words, a smart contract is a software application that replaces part of or all of the contract through sets of computer codes that, essentially, automate contractual functions among parties. Many smart contracts are self-executing and self-enforcing which means that they do not need inputs to be executed or enforced. This could mean, for example, to conclude a smart insurance contract when hiring a rental car. The smart contract would automatically adjust the premium upon predefined risk factors (average speed, driving style etc.) which are automatically gauged and processed without any human involvement.

The blockchain technology can also be used for notary and registry services. The blockchain, as a decentralised ledger which cannot be altered by third parties, may be used to give unique digital identifier to documents. That identifier verifies all subsequent versions of the document without the need to share the document.

4.8 Automated Legal Reasoning/Decisions Support

A legal automation process (an expert system as described above) formalizes and models expert knowledge, i.e., it automates the human legal decisions process. It consists of modelling legal decisions and transferring these into a formalized comprehendible structure. These tools can be used when dealing with highly frequent cases, complex assessment structures or huge amounts of data.

5   Overview of Current LegalTech Market

Developments in the LegalTech industry differ across countries. While the U.S. is very advanced with more than 1'000 LegalTech companies, Europe clearly lags behind. Germany has around 15 LegalTech providers currently. The LegalTech market sees rapid growth. In a recent study, *Mitratech* estimated that corporate law departments and law firms currently spend $ 3 billion on LegalTech solutions (excluding legal research) and that the addressable market in the U.S. is $ 16 billion. It would be impossible here to give a complete market overview. The companies represented in this market are a diverse group in terms of whom they serve, what technologies they apply and how innovative their products and services are. In the following, we grouped companies together in a few clusters which might have the greatest impact on the way legal services are rendered in the future.

5.1   E-Discovery/Forensic Investigations

There are well over 100 companies offering e-discovery and forensic investigation services around the globe. It would be impossible to name them all. The e-discovery industry is the most developed LegalTech niche in terms of the maturity of products and the revenue generated. In the U.S. alone, the e-discovery market is worth several billion dollars depending on the survey. E-discovery solutions are mostly used in litigation, and less often in due diligence procedures.

5.2   Legal Search

The legal research landscape is changing. Prominent providers like *Westlaw*, *LexisNexis* and *Thomson Reuters* are challenged by start-ups like *Casetext*, *Fastcase*, *Judicata* and *Ravel Law*. Since 2012, *Ravel Law*, for instance, uses data-driven, interactive visualization and analytics tools to help lawyers find, contextualize, and interpret legal information. These tools assist in analysing judges and cases, and in visualizing the search results. *Casetext* is a mix between a legal research platform and a publishing platform on which users, mostly lawyers, are able to publish commentaries and annotations within the text of cases. Other features include a crowd-sourced citation, automatically generated case summaries, and a heat map feature that highlights often-cited portions of texts.

ROSS Intelligence applies IBM Watson's Q&A technology to legal research on bankruptcy topics. After building and training the data set, *ROSS Intelligence* invites users to evaluate search results. It then feeds those evaluations back into the engine to pursue tuning in the manner of recommendation engines (known, for instance from *Netflix* or *Amazon*). With this process, *ROSS Intelligence* tries to build a "super intelligent lawyer" which is able to provide answers to legal questions in natural language—which would be a revolutionary step for LegalTech.

5.3 Legal Marketplaces

Like in other industries, vertical legal marketplaces are a crowded and diverse space. Some platforms focus on consumers, and others target lawyers. Some platforms offer low-cost and quick legal advice, and others provide more demanding legal representation. These legal marketplaces try to create transparency in the way clients select their lawyer. Their aim is to offer more affordable, accessible, fast, and transparent legal services. These new vertical marketplaces will serve what Richard Susskind has called the "latent market" for legal services. This unaddressed market remains significant. The prediction is that over time, legal services provided by legal marketplaces will move up the value curve, serving small business and eventually larger business entities and more affluent clients.

Popular platforms are, for example, *Avvo, Frag-einen-Anwalt, Hire an Esquire, Jurato, LawDingo, LawGives, Legalbase, LegalHero, LegalZoom, PrioriLaw, RocketLawyer, SmartupLegal* and *UpCounsel*. There are two basic business approaches. Some companies seek to link consumers with lawyers who charge their regular hourly rates. Other companies offer limited legal services for a fixed fee, powered by technology to keep legal fees low. The latter companies have the opportunity to scale their business. The impact of legal marketplaces, particularly on soloist and small law firm practitioners, will be huge. Fierce competition will force them to continually lower their fees. Lawyers will lose control of their client base, as clients are attracted and won over by the new legal marketplaces.

5.4 Automated Document Assembly and Contract Analytics

Companies like *Contract Express, Exari, HotDocs, KnowledgeTools, Neota Logic* and *SmartLaw* apply procedural rules and some inference engines to generate legal documents. *Contract Standards, eBrevia, Kira Systems, LegalSifter, Seal Software, LEVERTON* and others use statistical and machine learning techniques as well as NLP to analyse contracts automatically. The machine learning models used by these companies are trained by experts to recognize provisions with a high degree of accuracy. The products can be used in due diligence, contract management, lease abstraction, and document drafting.

Lex Machina, recently acquired by *LexisNexis*, creates structured data sets from public data to help its users predict the outcomes of different legal strategies and scenarios by categorizing, tagging, mining, and enhancing millions of federal court dockets and documents. The technology used by *Lex Machina* allows for data-driven decisions and derives, for example, litigation strategies from data on case law, parties, counsels, jurisdictions and presiding judges. *LexPredict* builds models to predict the outcome of Supreme Court cases, and it is doing so at accuracy levels challenging experienced Supreme Court practitioners. *Huron's Sky Analytics* and *Legal Operations Company* use their big databases of law firm cases and billing data to offer outcome predictions as well as cost and rate benchmarks. Other companies, like *LEVERTON*, specifically aim to streamline due diligence processes though machine learning (including deep learning) technology and to build smart data platforms.

5.5   Case and Practice Management

Several companies use technology to automate common routines in legal practice. *Clio* offers comprehensive practice management, including timekeeping and billing, calendars and deadlines, collaboration, workflow, task management and reporting. *LegalTrek* provides tools for timekeeping, expense tracking, billing, financial reporting, client management and communications, case management, document management, calendaring, contract management.

5.6   Standardized Claim Management

Companies like *Compensation2Go, EUclaim, Flight-Delayed, Flightright, Gopogo* and *Refund.me* help air plane passenger to easily claim compensation when a flight is delayed without any risk for the claimant. This concept has been transferred to other areas like loan agreements (*Bankright* and *Recht-ohne-Risiko*), parking tickets (*Fixed*) and car related fines (*Geblitzt*).

5.7   Online Dispute Resolution

A prominent provider of Online Dispute Resolution is *Modria*. It provides low-cost resolution processes to provide valuable outcomes to case stakeholders. It has processed hundreds of millions of disputes, 90 % through automation—without human intervention. Modria is a cloud-based platform on which businesses and public bodies can customize and build their own ODR services. It supports various ODR methods, including diagnosis, negotiation, mediation, and arbitration, and also offers a configurable case management and workflow system that handles case intake, document generation and management, scheduling, reporting, and status messaging. Other providers are *Cybersettle, Online Schlichter, Nominent* and *Resolver*.

5.8   Automated Legal Reasoning/Decisions support

Companies like *ComplianceHR, Neota Logic* and *Lexalgo* offer decision support systems. For example, *Neota Logic* offers a platform to build rule based functions and applications (expert systems) that can be used for various purposes. The law firm *Norton Rose Fulbright*, for example, built a ContractorCheck based on Neota Logic's platform. *Thomson Reuters* offers an expert system called Checkpoint Catalyst to research tax issues. There are many other examples of automated legal reasoning based on rule-based functions with a significant share in the LegalTech market.

6 LegalTech Changes How Lawyers Work

LegalTech will massively influence how lawyers work. Some even suggest that technology—especially the rise of AI—will render many lawyers obsolete. Richard Susskind predicts that traditional lawyers will in large part and in the long term be *"replaced by advanced systems, or by less costly workers supported by technology or standard processes, or by lay people armed with online self-help tool"* (Richard Susskind, The End of Lawyers, 2008, 2). There is no doubt that LegalTech will rapidly automate, computerize and streamline manual tasks and, thus, will reduce the work for (human) lawyers in various evolutionary steps. LegalTech effects on legal work flow will vary widely, according to the type of work that lawyers perform. The effects will be felt by big law firms to solo practitioners, from litigation to M&A, from associates to partners, from task to task.

Whether and to which degree a task could be automated by machine intelligence depends on how structured and repetitive it is, and whether contingencies are predictable and manageable. Tasks which require capabilities such as creativity and sensing emotions (emotional intelligence) are difficult to automate. It will, therefore, be hard to automate tasks like, for instance, investigation, legal writing, advising and communicating with clients, court preparation and appearances, interview claimants to get information related to legal proceedings and supervise activities of other legal personnel. When legal work cannot be automated, clients will still call upon a traditional lawyer. However, the speed with which advances in AI and machine learning develops will continue to challenge our assumptions about what is automatable.

In our view, low-level and repetitive tasks, such as document management and review, billing, filing, and accounting, for which genuine lawyering is hardly required, will be automated or outsourced, soon. It's likely that client-contactless, commoditized and process level work will be industrialized using LegalTech. Many other tasks will be partly automated, including document drafting, due diligence on deals, legal research and legal analysis. In advanced LegalTech, we will see that even areas of the legal industries which at first seem difficult to automate will be partly automated gradually.

Owing to the rise of machine intelligence, lawyers will have the opportunity to shift their focus from mundane and repetitive work to the more meaningful, creative and high-value tasks of legal practice. Some of these task may even be completely new. LegalTech offers the chance to move routine work to the machines. Lawyers will be increasingly able to engage in the analytical, creative, and strategic parts of legal practice, i.e. the work of the intellect. In other words, a successful lawyer of the twenty-first century will be a lawyer who knows how to harness LegalTech to do the mundane tasks of fact-gathering and filtering, and then apply his unique skills to frame issues and arguments, and represent a subtle point of view that

LegalTech, alone, cannot provide. It is time to re-elevate the legal profession, as the work behaviours and routines are required to change.

The impact of LegalTech on the legal profession should not be viewed as a battle between machines vs. lawyers. As already pointed out, LegalTech should be regarded (at least for the time being) as an enabler which helps lawyers, not as a replacement of real lawyers who advise people. There will be a new partnership between computers and people. This does not mean, however, that lawyers will continue to work as in previous years. LegalTech will transform the job description and behaviours of lawyers, amend routines and processes and will require new forms of organizational structure upon service delivery. In short, LegalTech (and other drivers of change) will alter the legal profession in its current foundation.

Lawyers will need to understand the technologies, methodologies and concepts behind LegalTech, as the ability to use LegalTech will be a rapidly increasing competitive advantage. They need to comprehend its benefits and risks and they also must understand how the different technologies and tools can be used to guarantee the best service results with a competitive price. It will not be enough for a lawyer to harness legal knowledge in the future. Lawyers need to develop a new mind- and skillset to ensure that they are able to render their services in an efficient way.

To develop this new mind- and skillset, lawyers need a basic understanding of coding and the underlying techniques and methods deployed in legal described as described above. They should be able to understand what code is and how it fits legal design. Lawyers should know which LegalTech tools exist and to which extent they might be deployed in their daily work. This primarily means to understand that legal work is not "monolithic". It is possible to decompose or disaggregate legal work into various tasks without undermining quality. LegalTech will require a new working attitude that fosters the decomposition of legal tasks. Lawyers have to discern whether and to what degree each task should be computerized, standardized or automated or really needs a handcrafted solution.

As legal task will be decomposed, there will be new ways to source legal work. Lawyers will be confronted with third party providers willing to offer their services in areas which are prone to standardization and automatization. They will put price pressure on the market. As the standardization and automatization of legal work continues, third legal parties will take on tasks which have been "lawyer-exclusive" in the past. The tightened competition and price pressure exerted by clients will lead to new pricing models which will hugely influence how lawyers work. In light of automatization, increased competition by third-party providers and price pressure, the market will most likely no longer tolerate the inefficiencies of the traditional law firm models and lawyering. The current prevailing pricing model (billable hour approach) is inherently in conflict with maximizing efficiency and fostering innovation in law firms. Under a billable hour approach, a law firm would lose revenue if certain services are rendered in less time. Clients will insist that the fees bear a more reasonable relationship to the value provided. As a result, law firms and lawyers will introduce new pricing models which will replace billable hours with fee arrangements based on the value delivered, i.e. the outcomes. Therefore, future pricing models will be based on outcomes, such as fixed fees for an entire engagement or specific tasks.

Pricing models which focus on outcomes will force lawyers to become more efficient. One means to become more efficient could be the use of LegalTech. However, there are more techniques and methodologies which could be borrowed from other industries. Project management will become important in law firms. A legal project manager would be responsible for leading, guiding and monitoring the business side of delivering legal service. It can be a separate role to the lawyer that actually does substantive work or a new skill set that most lawyers need to bring to the table in the future. Possible responsibilities and tasks include, among others, developing a project plan (including a work breakdown structure and budget), monitoring the matter against timelines, deadlines, and budget as well as ensuring sufficient communication with the client and matter team.

In addition, a range of new opportunities and new careers for people trained in law will emerge due to LegalTech (cf. Richard Susskind, Tomorrow's Lawyer, 2013, 109 ff.). Standardized and computerized legal services will require "legal knowledge engineers" to organize and model complex legal materials and processes. These lawyers will develop legal standards and procedures in organizing and representing legal knowledge in computer systems. Other individuals, labelled as "LegalTechnologist" by Richard Susskind, will bridge the gap between law and technology. The "LegalTechnologist" is trained and experienced both in the practice of law and in the profession of systems engineering and IT management.

In order to ensure that lawyers are well equipped for the challenges imposed by LegalTech, legal education needs to amend its curriculum. Many universities and law schools are ill-equipped to train their students on LegalTech and on the applications that are already available. Law schools have to revise their curriculums as part of a larger interdisciplinary approach. They should, for example, introduce LegalTech lectures, courses, clinics, internships, conferences and workshops which provide the theoretical and practical knowledge for the future jobs describe above. In particular, universities would need to train future lawyers on how to more be effectively and efficiently in delivering legal services.

As LegalTech will have a profound effect on the future of the legal profession, it seems wise to embrace it now, so that it can be a tool as opposed to an impediment. If LegalTech is understood as an enabler and as a "partner" for lawyers, it might be easier to embrace LegalTech tools and the changes that follow. Lawyers and law firms which become expert in combining human expertise with machine intelligence will lead the way to a more efficient and affordable future. The focus should not be on the question whether lawyers are replaced by robots but how lawyers may proactively use LegalTech and other innovative methodologies to automate mundane and repetitive legal work to be able to focus on the analytical, creative, and strategic parts of the legal practice. LegalTech will not only revolutionize the way lawyers work, but make their work more enjoyable.

Liquid Legal Context

By Dr. Dierk Schindler, Dr. Roger Strathausen, Kai Jacob

Bues and Matthaei make an important point right at the start: very easily, legal tech gets boxed into the corner of specific, maybe the most broadly known solutions, e.g. eBilling, contract management etc. This approach bears significant risk: first, it obscures the view to many other new solutions that emerge at ever faster pace in legal technology, and secondly—and even more importantly—it prevents us from looking at the bigger picture behind legal technology, i.e. its force to fundamentally change the industry.

Against that background, Bues and Matthaei point out a distinct effect of adopting legal tech: It might "just" improve the world for lawyers, meaning it might only automate certain tasks that lawyers had to spend (more) manual time on before. Alternatively, it might introduce true innovation, by challenging and completely changing how legal services are being delivered. The broad landscape in which legal tech is having an impact, already today, does inevitably lead back to the question: How does legal tech change the job of a lawyer in the industry?

Too often, this gets discussed from a defensive position: "machine intelligence is taking my job away". Bues and Matthaei create a broader and more balanced view, also describing the opportunities. Lawyers will have the opportunity to shift their focus from mundane and repetitive work to the more meaningful, creative and high-value tasks of legal practice, i.e. the work of the intellect.

With that view, the silver lining emerges of a lawyer serving as a strategic business advisor, as an orchestrator of the various aspects of delivering legal services provided by the different players in the legal industry. If legal tech is the enabler of running legal with a business mind, will legal tech also be the enabler to run legal with business metrics? Pauleau, Collard and Roquilly answer this question with a clear and convincing "yes" in their upcoming article.

Dr. Micha-Manuel Bues is Managing Director at Leverton, a LegalTech-company with offices in Berlin, London and New York which is specialised in data extraction from contracts. From 2013 to 2016 he worked as a lawyer at the international law firm Gleiss Lutz. He studied law at the universities of Passau, Bonn and Oxford and wrote his doctoral thesis at the University of Cologne. For many years he has been engaged in the theoretical and practical interfaces between law and technology and digitalisation trends in general. He runs a blog on the subjects of LegalTech, Legal Innovation and Legal Start-ups (www.legal-tech-blog.de).

Emilio Matthaei is CEO of LEVERTON. As a passionate data strategist, entrepreneur, ex-banker and researcher, Emilio revolutionizes how individuals work with data and documents. With LEVERTON, he brings innovative technology to various industries—LegalTech, PropTech, CRETech, FinTech.

LEVERTON develops and applies disruptive deep learning/machine learning technology to extract and manage data from corporate documents in more than 20 languages. Global clients from the legal, financial, and real estate sectors optimize their contract management significantly and process transactions faster. Asset documentation with an underlying face value of more than €40 billion is managed with LEVERTON's smart data technology.

Clients such as Bilfinger, Clifford Chance, Deutsche Bank, Freshfields, Goldman Sachs, JLL and Strabag trust LEVERTON's smart data solution.

Before LEVERTON, Emilio spent 6 years with Houlihan Lokey and Goldman Sachs in Investment Banking in London. He was involved in >20 financial transactions (incl IPOs, M&As, Capital Increases and Restructurings).

Emilio studied Economics and Management in Bonn and Leipzig and graduated with a PhD (summa cum laude) in the field Strategic Management. He wrote two books ("Strategies for Innovators" and "The Nature of Executive Work") and spent a year as Visiting Researcher at the University of Oxford.

Contact LEVERTON at www.LVN.com.

Key Performance Indicators (KPIs): Run Legal with Business Metrics: Will the Legal of the Future Measure Everything It Does?

Christine Pauleau, Christophe Collard, and Christophe Roquilly

Abstract

Gone are the days when company lawyers were isolated in their ivory tower. In our fast-paced competitive environment, the aspiration of in-house counsels is to go beyond their specialist role and become relevant business advisors aligned with the company strategy and committed in bringing value to the business. Today, the concept of "legal performance" has become part of both the vocabulary and the practice of many general counsels. But how many of them have engaged in legal performance measurement through figures and metrics?

In many corporate functions, performance is measured to ensure that teams contribute to the business objectives and strategy. Incidentally, one can question whether it is appropriate to measure intellectual outcomes such as the results of legal services. Yet, it certainly seems critical for legal departments to understand *why* they need to assess their performance, *what* should be measured, and *how*.

Legal KPIs are often defined without sufficient consideration of what they are supposed to demonstrate, and to whom. It is necessary to start from the vision statement of the legal department, thereby identifying the objectives that support this vision, before defining the relevant indicators, which help to monitor the achievement of these objectives. By doing this, the Legal of the future should not measure everything it does, but simply demonstrate to what extent it contributes to business and strategic objectives. The execution of a "program" will actually

C. Pauleau (✉)
Radio Frequency Systems (RFS), Nokia, Route de Villejust, Centre de Villarceaux, 91620 Nozay, France
e-mail: christine.pauleau@rfsworld.com

C. Collard • C. Roquilly
EDHEC Business School, 24 Avenue Gustave Delory, CS 50411, F-59057 Roubaix Cedex 1, France
e-mail: christophe.collard@edhec.edu; christophe.roquilly@edhec.edu

© Springer International Publishing AG 2017   111
K. Jacob et al. (eds.), *Liquid Legal*, Management for Professionals,
DOI 10.1007/978-3-319-45868-7_8

help the successful implementation of legal KPIs and ultimately facilitate the transition to running legal departments like real Business Units.

1   Introduction

Paris, January 2016, annual seminar of the Group Legal Department of company "X" (a listed company, operating in 28 countries, that we shall call in what follows "the Company", to protect its anonymity). In his opening speech initiating the seminar, which most of the Group Legal Counsels are attending, the general counsel presents the team with a detailed picture of the Group Legal Department as it stands: staff, average age, gender diversity, training, as well as the number of trademarks and patents managed, volume of questions addressed, amount of fees invoiced by law firms, litigations initiated and defended, amounts of fines and damages for which the Company was held liable, payments retrieved within litigations, etc. It is clear that only a very few number of attendees have such comprehensive visibility on *who they are* and *what they do*. Each of the points raised is clearly outlined and commented, often in a positive way, and potential areas of improvement are identified. All relevant key figures are reflected on the presentation flyer used to promote the operational activities of the Group Legal Department internally. The general counsel shares one specific reason for satisfaction with his team: an informal benchmark based on legal departments in other similar companies shows that the Company is achieving the same results with half of the internal legal staff and half of the budget for external counsels. In other words, *"you are achieving more with less (or at least less than the others)!"* Above all the general counsel highlights the fact that he has managed to secure a commitment from the Company's senior management that it will maintain the Group Legal Department's budget and headcounts at current levels. This is certainly excellent news in a climate of restructuring, budget cuts and staff reduction within the Company. This internal success was made possible by demonstrating the performance of the Group Legal Department and the value created by its team, which would have been impossible without the metrics at its disposal. In this respect, the general counsel reminds each team member about the importance of properly entering all necessary input into the database in order to be able to extract and calculate the Key Performance Indicators (KPIs). While this requires some effort, it is most definitely useful for the whole of the legal team!

Communicating, demonstrating the value generated by legal departments (LDs, or "legal"), and thereby reinforcing their role and influence... these are some of the possible uses and examples of potential usefulness of legal KPIs illustrated by the above short story (a true story, apart from a few details). Gone are the days when company lawyers were isolated in an ivory tower, disconnected from the reality of business and the way it works. In our fast-paced, changing and competitive environment, LDs are increasingly embracing the opportunity to effect a significant transformation. The aspiration of modern LDs is to go beyond their traditional role as specialists in legal disciplines, and to become relevant and trusted business advisors with a true "sense of purpose". As in the case of other corporate departments (such as finance, marketing, human resources, R&D, etc.), the modern in-house legal teams understand how critical it is to be business-oriented, aligned with company strategy and fully committed to bringing true value to the business.

Today, the concept of "legal performance" has become part of both the vocabulary and practice of many general counsels (GCs) and in-house counsels. But how many of them have engaged in legal performance measurement? When GCs want to be acknowledged for adding substantial value to the business, how many of them offer transparency regarding the performance of their legal teams through figures and metrics? At the end of the day, how does the LD, together with the entire organization, know if it really brings true value to the business and the company as a whole?

In many corporate units, performance measurements are used to ensure that teams contribute to the business objectives and strategic goals. From this perspective, key performance indicators (KPIs) are used to assess and demonstrate workload, required resources, results, productivity, client satisfaction, process efficiency, cost effectiveness, effective avoidance of value loss, long-term revenue generation/protection, etc. Incidentally, one can question whether it is relevant, or even appropriate, to measure the performance of intellectual outcomes such as the results of legal services: measuring the total amount of monetary penalties paid is one thing, judging the quality of the strategy adopted on legal matters quite another. Indeed, a widespread argument stresses that legal outcomes are of such a specialized nature that it makes it very difficult, if not impossible, to realistically assess them. But before trying to measure legal performance, it certainly seems critical for LDs to understand *why* they need to assess their performance. Section 2 of this chapter is dedicated to this simple but essential question.

Section 3 focuses on *what* should be measured. Far too often, legal KPIs are merely based on the data traditionally available within in-house legal teams, without giving adequate consideration to what such KPIs are supposed to demonstrate and to whom. We believe that it is necessary to adopt a "top-down" approach: starting from the vision statement of what the LD should do to be in line with the business strategy, thereby making it possible to identify the objectives to target in order to support this vision. Once the goals and missions of Legal have been properly defined, relevant indicators may be identified which will help to monitor the achievement of the objectives set out.

Finally, by sketching out the key factors for the successful implementation of legal KPIs Sect. 4 addresses the question of *how* LDs can measure their performance. It proposes solutions allowing for the execution of a transformation program that enables the transition to running LDs like real Business Units.

2   Why Should Legal Departments Assess Their Performance?

Although this might be considered as regretful, performance has become a kind of mantra in modern society, affecting all of us—whether individuals or organizations. Companies are mainly affected by the increasing demand for performance: they are probably even largely contributing to this demand. Whereby this trend seems to dangerously dominate our life in general, focusing on performance may be seen as legitimate in the area of business: in an unstable and globalized environment where future is uncertain, there is hardly room for rentier models. In today's corporations, all departments are mobilized to contribute as effectively as possible to the performance levels expected of them. LDs are not an exception to this underlying trend.

But what exactly does "performance" mean? Three different but complementary meanings are traditionally attributed to "performance": (1) the execution of an action, (2) the outcome achieved, and (3) the successful achievement of it. In the business field, "performance" often refers to the extent to which something is accomplished according to the targeted objectives (i.e. effectiveness) as well as to the ability to perform under optimized conditions in terms of quality and costs (i.e. efficiency). For the purpose of this chapter, the term "performance" will be used to refer to the achievement of company objectives (whether such objectives are strategic or operational) as well as to the processes that enable such achievement.

Within companies, performance has become a common criterion for assessing value creation, and there is no reason for legal teams to remain excluded from such a pervasive development. Here are some of the basic reasons that should motivate general counsels to use KPIs:

1. Performance measurement has become a standard business practice. It is probably the most basic consideration: *"everyone is doing it, so we will too"*. At least, it is about standardizing communication, which requires a certain level of normalization.
2. In-house legal counsels themselves increasingly tend to act, think and speak like their chief executives, chief financial officers, and any other company executives with responsibility for P&L. By sharing the same language and using the same tools, legal teams can properly reinforce their positioning as real business partners within the company.
3. There is ongoing pressure on LDs (like any other departments in business organizations) to reduce costs, improve efficiency and demonstrate value. It is also vital for LDs to cope with the need to be "smarter-better-faster": in our fast-paced, changing and competitive business environment, LDs have no other choice than to embrace this significant transformation. This need to be "smarter-better-faster", combined with the ongoing focus on reducing costs, has led to what Richard Susskind, in *Tomorrow's Lawyers* (Oxford, 2013), calls the "More-for-Less Challenge": deliver more and better legal services at

a lower cost. Responding to all these challenges (by demonstrating that the LD does more for less) requires the increasing use of relevant tools and metrics.

LDs have certainly neither the need nor the interest to measure everything they do, but they have much to gain from using robust analytics to demonstrate their working efficiency and the effectiveness of their results, i.e. to what extent they contribute to strategic, operational and financial corporate goals.

This being said, the implementation of KPIs within LDs may serve different purposes (all of which answer the question: why measure?). KPIs can help LDs to:

- develop a self-diagnosis of the legal function and therefore improve its management;
- demonstrate and communicate the value generated by the legal team;
- improve LDs' effectiveness and efficiency;
- align Legal & Strategic objectives;
- reinforce the role, positioning and influence of the internal legal function.

Each of the above aims underpinning legal KPIs (except the last point—reinforcing the role, positioning and influence of the LD—which is the natural outcome of all the previous achievements) can be analyzed in more detail as follows:

2.1 "Know Thyself": Self-Diagnosis, Monitoring and Management

The management guru, Peter Drucker, is often quoted for having said: "*If you can't measure it, you can't manage it.*" Whatever opinion we may have of this famous business maxim, we should recognize that GCs, as well as legal teams themselves, need to access data which provide an answer to the following basic questions: "*Who are we?*", "*How have we become who we are?*" and "*Where do we want to be in the future*"? Measured data offer an overview of the current state of play and a clear picture—through some sort of "mirror effect"—of the in-house legal function: staff, activity, productivity, budget, etc. Most importantly, the data collected in a reporting system allow for proper monitoring of changes, progress and improvements over time. Metrics also help to identify trends for the future and issues to be addressed by the LD. Finally, metrics should allow for benchmarking between LDs of comparable companies against a set of common references (as soon as implementing meaningful metrics within LDs will become a standard practice among the broadest number of companies).

Data collected through KPIs basically provide information about the effective contribution of each member of the legal team, including the GC. In that sense, legal KPIs should not be automatically seen as monitoring tools: it is not the tool itself that is relevant, but what the GC decides to do with it! Regarding management of the legal function and its workload, metrics make for better staffing and optimal legal coverage of the business over time by identifying the following:

- the right profiles, competences and skills at the right cost for each of the company's legal tasks (attorneys vs. paralegals, specialists vs. generalists);
- the right proportion of internal resources and the right allocation of work to external counsels (law firms) and other service providers (legal process outsourcing vs. insourcing) at the right cost to reflect the value ascribed to each task.

By using metrics, a language that top management understands, the general counsel may be able to more objectively support and justify the existence of the LD as an essential corporate function, as well as defend current headcounts, budget and structure, or change them as required. Last but not least, promoting the value they bring to the business is probably the most efficient way to motivate members of LDs and therefore increase their commitment to succeed.

2.2 Demonstrating and Communicating the Value Generated by the Legal Team

Legal KPIs bring transparency to an LD's performance and value. Such transparency does not only benefit the legal team, but also other corporate functions and business units, and obviously the company's top management and Board of Directors. Legal KPIs serve two different but closely linked purposes in this regard: *demonstrate* and *communicate* the added value provided by the LD.

2.2.1 Demonstrating the Value

"*In God we trust, all others must bring data*" is a famous quote attributed to a renowned American statistician, W. E. Deming. In-house counsels commonly believe that they play a key role in terms of value creation, but how many of them can really prove it? KPIs can help LDs to demonstrate the reality of this assertion, as well as how this happens: how in-house counsels—and their external advisors—create value, what kind of value they create and whether such value is created with efficiency/effectiveness.

It is obviously impossible to properly address the value that an LD can enable (or contribute to enable) without referring to a common standard of value at the company level. As a matter of fact, the nature of the value enabled by the LD cannot be "decoupled" from the overall value enabled and/or protected at the company level. It is thus necessary to determine which type of value the company prioritizes, and how the company assesses it.

At a principle level, two value categories can be identified: financial value and strategic value.

(a) Financial value can be expressed through a broad range of financial targets: e.g. economic value generated, return on investment, invested capital return rate, cash-flow generation, proportion of revenue generated by new products or services, etc. In this respect, the LD can seek to show how it contributes to financial value, either directly (e.g. cash retrieved through litigations or disputes resolutions, or by (re)negotiating or implementing penalty or delay clauses) or indirectly, for example by describing how it enables the launch and development of new products. It can also be relevant for an LD to show how it helps to avoid or mitigate the destruction of financial value (e.g. through the implementation and management of intellectual property rights, or the implementation of compliance and business ethics programs). This can become an integral part of KPIs.

(b) Strategic value refers to the acquisition, preservation or loss of a competitive advantage in the medium or long term. It can relate to the company's reputation (with respect to the different stakeholders, public authorities, NGOs, etc.), its leadership on the market, its international development, etc. In this regard also, the LD intends to show how it helps enable value creation (or how it avoids value destruction). As an illustration, the LD can assess the impact of training performed by legal staff to avoid non-compliant behaviors within the company. This training can result in a reduction of efforts in terms of investigations and external inspections and therefore mitigate negative press exposure. The LD can also use adjusted property rights and contractual mechanisms to promote innovation and market leadership. The LD can finally build the proper legal argumentation to open a new market or to promote deregulation, etc.

2.2.2 Communicating the Value

Metrics help executives and directors to understand why and how the role of the LD is key for the company. By increasing the visibility of the Legal function, metrics also help increase its influence within the company. It is up to the LD to identify the proper metrics—and they are not all of a financial nature—in order for its contribution to be easily understood both by the leadership team and the Board of Directors. Should LDs limit themselves to metrics that are exclusively their own, communication could become challenging. Legal KPIs have to be defined with this in mind: they need to be shared—and also consolidated into the global KPIs of the company—and must therefore be easy to share. It may happen that the LD's internal reporting presents certain shortcomings: whenever it provides the leadership team (or equivalent) with a report of more than 30 pages for example, highlighting ongoing/successful/unsuccessful litigations, the number of projects or contracts managed by members of the legal team, the list of law firms engaged and the amount of legal fees invoiced by such firms, the LD is simply revealing how high its current workload is and how it steers its activities. Yet, what does the LD actually want to demonstrate through such reporting? The significant amount of information and the fact that such information is not analyzed together with the strategic objectives of the company may significantly affect the capacity of others to properly understand the report produced by the LD. This is especially true whenever the addressees and stakeholders have little time to dedicate to such reports and therefore need reading material which is clear and easy to understand. Reporting by the LD on its own performance is an act of management—and therefore also an act of communication and even education. By demonstrating the value enabled by the Legal team based on "state-of-the-art" communication materials, KPIs ultimately allow it to achieve its aspiration to be a relevant and valuable business advisor within the company. In all cases, the value that LDs define and integrate as part of performance objectives and indicators needs to be properly aligned with the strategic goals of the company.

2.3 Improving the Efficiency and Effectiveness of the Legal Department

LDs cannot assess their performance without measuring their efficiency and effectiveness in respect of the objectives defined as part of the company strategy. Such efficiency and effectiveness cannot be "absolute": they depend on several factors, such as (1) the company missions, business(es) and strategy; (2) the company values, and (3) the LD's missions, as these are pre-defined.

Whatever the method used to define such missions, they all have the following elements in common: the LD processes incoming information flows (input) and proposes solutions (output). For example, the decision to operate in a new country is linked to an overall strategic objective, which is impacted by a whole set of input data: the business targets, the political, economic and legal environment, the resources available to implement the project etc. The related outputs may be the legal engineering scheme proposed by the LD (contracts, structures, legal entities), its proposals to avoid or mitigate potential legal/business risks, etc. In order to turn input into output, it is necessary to define the complete list of actions—and associated costs—required to implement the transformation process (this is outlined in Sect. 4 below). By analyzing all of their missions and by dividing them into as many processes and sub-processes as necessary, LDs can define their own value chain and provide answers to several questions:

- What objectives have been achieved based on the output delivered by the LD?
- To what extent do these objectives contribute to value creation (or help avoid value destruction) at the company level?

The answers to these first two questions will make it possible to assess the LD's effectiveness.

- What are the costs incurred to achieve such output?
- To what quality level do these costs correspond?

The answers to these two questions will make it possible to assess the LD's efficiency.

Whenever the LD has identified a clear chain of value showing which resources are used to achieve which results and to enable which value creation (or - non-destruction of value), it is able to identify both its performance (in terms of efficiency and effectiveness) and the legal mission(s) in relation to which it is capable of enabling the most value.

The LD cannot identify the complete value creation process in its own "chain" without including external service providers such as law firms. Consequently, the contribution made by external service providers to value creation has to be properly assessed. Such information is critical for the LD to deploy—or re-deploy—its resources in the most optimized way (staffing, internal and external expertise, budget, etc.).

2.4   Aligning Legal and Strategic Objectives

The role of the legal team is not only to provide legal services in the most efficient and effective manner, as it is monitored by specific operational KPIs. The LD also needs to demonstrate that its organization, as well as its overall operations (which are guided by the LD's missions and objectives), are entirely focused on achieving the top priorities of the company and driven by the achievement of its strategic goals. Metrics enable the LD to demonstrate to what extent it contributes to these strategic corporate objectives. This is a fundamental aspect of what may be called the legal performance of the company.

The legal performance of a company can be understood in two different ways. In a narrow sense, it refers to the performance of its LD, in other words the capacity of that department to achieve its own missions and objectives. This aspect is at the core of the present chapter. A broader—and perhaps more appropriate—understanding is to see legal performance as the company's ability to deploy legal resources (especially intangible resources such as a specific legal capability) and combine them with the other types of resources at its disposal in order to achieve its objectives, in particular its strategic objectives. In this sense, legal performance can be considered as an important factor in the overall performance of the company. And the performance achieved by the legal team significantly contributes to the legal performance of the company as a whole.

In view of the above, and as already highlighted in this Section, the correct use of metrics by Legal seems to trigger a common effect: it contributes to reinforcing the role, positioning and influence of the LD as a key player, influencer and business partner within the company.

This Section has helped us understand *Why* measuring is important, which in turn helps to identify *What* should be measured.

3   What Should Legal Departments Measure?

This is certainly the most important question from an operational perspective. It is twofold:

- What method should LDs adopt to identify critical performance indicators?
- What are relevant indicators for LDs to measure?

3.1   How to Identify Relevant Indicators

As already described in Sect. 2, relevant indicators can only be identified if and when the LD's missions and responsibilities are properly pre-defined. These can be defined in different ways, yet they must be linked to how the LD understands its fundamental purpose: *why does Legal exist* and *what is the scope of its responsibilities* in order to achieve this vision? To the question *"What is our mission statement?"*, Legal may answer, for example: *"We exist to turn our knowledge into value for the benefit of the company"*, or *"We partner with our internal clients to successfully navigate through important business challenges and to protect the company"*.

Based on this understanding of their fundamental purpose, LDs can better define the missions they need to fulfill. Regardless of the type of company or industry concerned, we believe that the different missions of an LD can be described in terms of two essential elements:

1. the avoidance of value destruction—and thus of reduced performance—by (legally) managing risks (whether such risks are legal or not);
2. the promotion of value creation—and thus of increased performance—by (legally) managing opportunities (whether such opportunities are legal or not).

Such missions will be executed through the responsibilities incumbent upon the LD. These responsibilities can roughly be summarized as follows:

1. draft legal assessments of the external framework and the company's internal matters;
2. identify, analyze and manage legal and business risks through the adjusted implementation of "legal tools";
3. create legal solutions best suited to the company's needs and targets;
4. influence the external legal framework;
5. and promote legal awareness within the company.

Based on the defined missions and responsibilities, it is possible to identify the individual objectives and targets to be achieved by the LD—in alignment with the strategic company objectives—and the extent to which such objectives and targets are being achieved, i.e. the performance of the department. The data collected

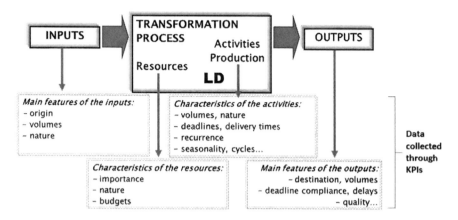

Fig. 1 LD's performance measurement: what kind of indicators?

through KPIs will actually provide transparency regarding the LD's performance (actions taken, outcomes achieved, extent of achievements), as described in Fig. 1 below.

For example, regarding one possible responsibility/mission defined for the LD—*"provide clear, constructive and reliable answers/solutions according to internal clients' expectations"*—the associated objectives can be defined as follows: (i) *"provide an answer within the agreed deadlines"*, (ii) *"improve information-sharing by using the Legal intranet"*, etc. Compliance with the agreed timeframe is obviously an indicator that makes it possible to monitor the achievement of objective (i). It can easily be calculated using the right metrics.

It is generally accepted (and certainly useful to keep in mind) that indicators can only be relevant if they are "defined, objective and measurable".

According to Andrew Likierman ("The Five Traps of Performance Measurement", Harvard Business Review, 2009, 10), best practices in terms of performance measurement are as follows:

- Measuring performance by comparing it with the past can be useful. Yet a performance measurement system above all should support the assessment of whether decisions made today can be useful for the future;
- It is not appropriate to use financial metrics to measure what belongs to non-financial activities. It is critical to identify the most relevant metrics and resist the temptation of reducing everything to a figure of Return on Investment;
- The unit which implements metrics needs (i) to use measures which are accurate regarding what is assessed, (ii) to be explicit on the metrics themselves, and (iii) to be certain that all concerned parties are perfectly aligned with the first two elements under (i) and (ii).
- Benchmarks are relevant when they are set against competitors or external stakeholders. Membership in professional associations can help LDs to define the benchmark criteria.

Following the method and practices described above, it is possible to properly identify relevant indicators to be measured by LDs.

3.2   Relevant Indicators for Legal Departments to Measure

The definition of relevant indicators to be measured by an LD will largely depend on the individual business context. Beyond this general observation, and in the interest of being a bit more specific, it is worth identifying different groups of possible relevant indicators.

As highlighted in Sect. 2 above, when assessing legal performance, indicators can be essentially divided into two main groups, whether they are used to measure (a) the working efficiency of LDs, or (b) the effectiveness of their contributions.

3.2.1   Indicators Measuring the Working Efficiency of Legal Departments

"Efficiency KPIs" will often assess and demonstrate the efficiency of LDs based on data traditionally available within them.

As an illustration, relevant "efficiency KPIs" can be of a financial/quantitative nature, measuring:

- the extent to which the LD has performed according to its budget: beyond the obvious usefulness of such an indicator, it is essential to stress that it may also be quite "unproductive", unless it is assessed in conjunction with other indicators which can be used to determine whether the possible costs overruns have helped create, or avoid the destruction of, greater value;
- cost savings achieved in relation to, for example, adjusted internal staff or the engagement of external counsels.

When focused on efficiency, relevant KPIs can also measure non-financial/ qualitative objectives such as:

- the legal workload, the necessary internal staff and external resources, and the optimized allocation of tasks among them for an efficient coverage of legal matters within the relevant business organization. Such KPIs can help to address some potentially critical questions: should internal clients involve the LD in all contractual activities? Do business stakeholders sometimes avoid involving the LD on the basis that it is understaffed and therefore a *bottleneck*? Does the LD currently have the staff capacity to be involved in all of the company's key projects?
- the legal team's productivity, and especially negotiation cycle times, reaction times in contracting processes, number/value of contracts signed and reviewed by the legal team. These "efficiency KPIs" can, for example, help to assess the relevance of the actual "legal tool box"—templates, models of clauses,

processes—and its adjustment to business realities, whether the LD uses state-of-the-art technology to manage its activities, etc.;

- internal client satisfaction when involving or interacting with legal team members. Beyond the most common limitations of this kind of survey, it is critical that the LD assesses how it complies with its mission statement: as a service provider and a (hopefully trusted) business partner, the LD needs to build the correct network among all internal business stakeholders (and not only within the professional community), and act in a way that is client-centric, collaborative and transparent when delivering legal advice. Developing qualitative "empathy" towards business stakeholders and asking lots of questions in order to help them reach the objectives is necessary to achieve relevance and value.

3.2.2 Indicators Measuring the Effectiveness of Legal Departments' Contributions

Modern LDs increasingly focus on aligning the way they apply their knowledge of the law with business objectives and strategic goals, whether it is to ensure growth or to enter into new markets for example. By focusing on purpose and context, LDs can make their contributions with relevance and value, based on the definition of creative plans and viable alternatives and the implementation of proper concepts and ideas. As a result, legal team members can expect to achieve their aspiration to be given much broader attention by business stakeholders.

Wherever legal teams intimately understand the business objectives and goals, and the missions of the LD are properly pre-defined, relevant indicators can be identified, using not only the data traditionally available within LDs but also the increasing volume and detail of information obtained from customers, partners, the global ecosystem, suppliers, etc. This makes it possible to measure the effectiveness of legal contributions towards the different objectives, and consequently the actions to be undertaken to improve legal performance towards their achievement.

From this perspective, modern legal departments should not measure every input/output they provide, but should simply demonstrate through robust analytics to what extent they contribute to key goals and protect the company. Obviously the associated Indicators will greatly depend on the nature of such business objectives and goals. It is yet possible to classify "effectiveness KPIs" into different sub-groups.

Some of such Indicators will measure whether by executing their missions and responsibilities LDs actually help avoid value destruction (negative risks), while others will measure whether they help create value (positive risks/opportunities).

In order to easily give several illustrations of relevant "effectiveness KPIs", we will start from the main matters that are typically under the LD's responsibility:

1. It is probably in relation to contractual matters that analytics appears most advanced at this stage. Modern contract analytics can include, among other things, the measurement of:

- the impact of contractual deviations from standard terms or preferred contractual positions;
- long-term revenue generation/protection and therefore long-term relationships with customers/partners/suppliers;
- working capital to be reduced;
- payment cycle times to be shortened;
- the effective avoidance of value loss and the control of revenue leakage by documented "add-on sales" and/or cost effectiveness;
- the mitigation of delays in delivery and the minimization of liquidated damages or exposure to delay penalties;
- the avoidance of uncovered contract non-compliance;
- hidden costs and unbilled spending;
- supplier performance.

2. Analytics can also be performed regarding litigation matters, measuring among other things:

- litigation avoidance rate through effective settlement agreements;
- settlement cycle times.

3. When applied to Intellectual Property (IP) management, analytics can for example track IP spending as well as the creation of IP value.
4. Compliance analytics can measure among other things:

- the impact of compliance programs on the prevention/occurrence of the related legal risks;
- the impact of business targets and employee reward schemes, which may tend to "promote" specific (i.e. ethical/unethical) conduct.

5. Finally, analytics can assess the transmission of key legal knowledge by LDs to the rest of their business organization by measuring, for example:

- legal awareness-raising throughout the organization via regular training of non-legal staff and communications which are clear and accessible;
- the impact of such legal awareness on, for example, the level of disputes and claims, the efficiency of business decision-making processes, or compliance costs.

4 How Can Legal Departments Measure Their Performance?

Implementing KPIs is not a one-off exercise. It requires the execution of a transformation program to make the successful transition to running LDs like real Business Units. In this respect, LDs need to follow the guidelines applicable to all business transformation programs. For example, KPI programs need to be constantly improved. Different implementation phases can be defined: starting with a "soft" initial phase and at the next stage undertaking a core transformation phase. They also need to be regularly adjusted to the evolving business objectives and strategic goals. All this does take time, but the transparency rewards are meant to far outweigh the investment, as highlighted in Sect. 2 above.

When narrowing down the possible indicators to be monitored, it is critical to determine whether the data needed to calculate them can be gathered easily and in a timely manner. Section 3.2 above explains how possible relevant KPIs can be based not only on working data traditionally available within in-house legal teams, but also on the increasing volume and detail of information obtained from customers, partners, the global ecosystem, suppliers, etc. Facing such a significant amount of data, it is critical to be able to access and gather it automatically where possible. For this purpose, the most efficient automation method will need to be carefully identified and implemented, whether it is an existing system or a new one to be introduced. KPIs can be implemented by means of multiple valuable tools. Some organizations use a multi-quadrant presentation method, which scores the different indicators. This can become a powerful tool when used alongside the implementation of a proper dashboard.

In terms of allocating responsibilities, LDs do not necessarily have to be responsible for the design and updating of all the relevant KPIs identified in Sect. 3.2 above. This is especially the case when indicators are aimed to demonstrate the full effectiveness of contractual activities in achieving business objectives and goals. Yet, a strong and active role played by LDs regarding all these matters is always recommended, not only to avoid building "legal silos" decoupled from the reality of the business context, but also to increase LDs' intimate knowledge of the business strategy and objectives and ultimately achieve their aspiration to be relevant and valuable business advisors who create value and address the most significant risks. The willingness to embrace such a strong and active role in assessing performance represents a real opportunity for company lawyers, as highlighted in Sect. 2 above.

Finally, it is impossible to drive a successful KPI program without properly addressing cultural aspects within the relevant business organization. From this perspective, it is critical to anticipate internal resistance to KPI monitoring and to ensure that, when calculated, proper actions will be consequently undertaken to improve the measured performance and to facilitate the achievement of business, strategic or financial goals. Some company lawyers may question the transparency sought by measuring KPIs: what if KPIs are wrongly understood or used by other departments or by top management? For example, in environments with a weak collaborative and team culture, KPIs could be feared as merely serving to point the finger at the potentially poor legal performance, and then to reduce legal resources while ignoring the optimized "legal coverage" needed by the business. KPIs could also be seen as allowing the simple negative observation that lawyers are not sufficiently equipped with critical skills (e.g. contract & commercial management, project management, cyber security) without undertaking any consistent action plans.

It is also essential that change management forms an integral part of KPI implementation programs. Experience shows that changes within legal teams require an assessment of their history, as well as their readiness and capacity to change. Changes will be mostly initiated from the top, enlisting executive advocates for support and direction (sponsorship) within and outside the legal team and different change agents within the legal team itself. It is also important to generate a data-driven business case for the implementation of KPIs to motivate the program and consult the LD's internal clients. Ultimately, the message needs to be clearly and regularly communicated to and received by all legal team members as well as the entire business organization.

Liquid Legal Context
by Dr. Dierk Schindler, Dr. Roger Strathausen, Kai Jacob

Take a moment and capture what came to your mind when reading Pauleau/Roquilly/Collard's introductory story about the GC's speech at the all hands: "Utopia!"? Or: "The scenarios described are possible, but not part of the vision."? "Talked about but not consistently pursued."? Or are you already there? I guess all of us who work in an inhouse environment and who look at the wind of change as an opportunity to accelerate and see GCs as an image of a true and modern leader, who can demonstrate by means of relevant KPI's not only the value that Legal has created for the company, but also that and why the function could be shielded from the cost reduction pressure to a certain extent.

A great strength of the article by Pauleau/Roquilly/Collard is that the three authors resist the temptation to take a shortcut to a glorified image of KPI's. They start with the hardest questions and thereby with the questions that every single team member will ask as a department embarks on the journey of performance management: Why should legal departments measure their performance? What does "performance" mean?

As they then emphasize the need to link performance back to the creation of value, there is an interesting connection to Bassli's article on what inhouse expects from lawfirms, and also to Markfort's and Meents'/Allen's article on how law firms focus much more around outcome-based services. As law firms reshape their offerings in light of that principle, should we think more aggressively about not only exchanging "question and answer", but also requesting data associated with it that will talk to the KPI's we have defined for ourselves inhouse?

Well, isn't data something that the new LPO's are actively using to demonstrate their added value, as much as to help their clients move towards a much more data-driven world? Both, Ross and Brown, representing two strong and innovative players in the LPO-industry, make a case for that. So,

(continued)

let's look at it from an inhouse perspective: If our law firm partners and our LPO partners enable or even pursue a KPI-based collaboration—why do we not take them up on the offer and use their data as the first step into a KPI-enabled management of our work?

However, taking a step back, we must realize that all tectonic plates in the industry are moving: cost-pressure, outsourcing, automation and artificial intelligence through legal tech, performance management based on KPI's enabled by data. Can our people deal with that? Is this an environment that is perceived as holding broad opportunity, or rather threat? We will need to make sure that we hire talent that embraces the opportunity in this—and such talent will likely be individuals that embrace a dynamic entrepreneurial element of constant evolution in their jobs. Tumasjan/Welpe inform us about when "corporate lawyers act entrepreneurially."

Christine Pauleau is the General Counsel of Radio Frequency Systems (RFS), a global Nokia affiliated group of companies.

Christine is a dual-qualified legal counsel with PhD (France and Spain) and education in German law. She has developed an extensive practice in commercial, contract and licensing law throughout Europe, Middle East, Africa, the USA and Asia.

After joining the law firm Cuatrecasas in Barcelona, Christine became in 2001 a legal professional of the technology industry: at Infineon Technologies in Munich, then at Ericsson in Middle East and Northern Africa.

Before RFS, Christine was the General Counsel of Ecomouv', a PPP project company for the eco-tax in France.

Christophe Collard is a Professor of Law at EDHEC Business School, and the director of the LL.M. "Law & Tax Management". He teaches Antitrust Law, Contract Law and Legal Management, delivering courses to a wide range of publics, with a genuine experience of teaching in foreign countries. A member of the LegalEdhec Research Centre, Professor Collard maintains an active research agenda in the areas of Legal Management and Strategies. He has presented numerous papers at French and international conferences and his research have appeared in a variety of academic and professional journals. He is the co-author of one of the best selling books in France dedicated to the concept of "legal performance".

Professor Roquilly is currently Dean for Faculty and Research at EDHEC Business School. He is also Director of LegalEdhec Research Centre and in charge of the Business Law & Management Program. He has performed different functions at EDHEC: creating, managing and developing the Legal Studies Department; acting as Dean for Graduate Programs; and managing major projects (e.g. EDHEC's first EQUIS accreditation). His research examines relationships between law and strategy, legal management, legal risks, compliance and ethics. He received the EDHEC Foundation Award for best research paper in 2001. Author of books and papers in academic and professional journals and the business press, Christophe serves on a number of boards (Scientific Committee of the Business and Legal Forum, Advisory Board of Arsened Taxand Law Firm, Advisory Board of the World Council for Law Firms and Justice, Advisory Council of the European Company Lawyers Association).

The Legal Entrepreneur: When Do Corporate Lawyers Act Entrepreneurially?

Andranik Tumasjan and Isabell M. Welpe

Abstract

Corporate lawyers are increasingly aiming at being involved in adding value to the business "bottom line". To be able to create or add business value, corporate lawyers have to identify, evaluate, and exploit opportunities for value creation— they have to act as internal entrepreneurs in their field. Using extant research findings and frameworks, this chapter will outline individual and organizational conditions which foster entrepreneurial behavior. Based on our analyses, we will derive concrete managerial implications for organizations that aim at stimulating corporate lawyers' involvement in value creation.

1 Introduction

In today's competitive and complex business environments, in-house legal departments are increasingly expected to create and demonstrate their value to business success. A recent UK-based study including more than 100 general counsels, heads of legal, and other senior in-house lawyers in different firms illustrates this trend (Nabarro 2011): whereas in 2010 only 3 % of the participants reported that they already perform tasks with high-level strategic value (e.g., strategic business planning, change and process management, introducing commercial opportunities), 29 % of them expected to perform such activities in 2015. In the same vein, 54 % of the participating CEOs deemed it "very important" that the legal function contributes economic value to the organization (Nabarro 2011).

A. Tumasjan (✉) • I.M. Welpe
Technische Universität München, Lehrstuhl für Strategie und Organisation, Arcisstr. 21, 80333 Munich, Germany
e-mail: andranik.tumasjan@tum.de; welpe@tum.de

© Springer International Publishing AG 2017   129
K. Jacob et al. (eds.), *Liquid Legal*, Management for Professionals,
DOI 10.1007/978-3-319-45868-7_9

To create value for their internal clients, corporate lawyers need not only a thorough understanding of the abstract commercial goals of the organization, but they also need to act entrepreneurially in recognizing, evaluating, and exploiting opportunities for value creation (Tumasjan et al. 2013). Entrepreneurial behavior in organizations can be defined as "the extent to which individual workers proactively engage in the creation, introduction, and application of opportunities at work, marked by taking business-related risks" (De Jong et al. 2013, p. 982). Management research provides a rich basis of evidence on the individual and organizational factors that foster such entrepreneurial and value-creative behaviors. Using such evidence-based knowledge (Pfeffer and Sutton 2006) will provide legal departments with concrete and tested indications for "running legal as a business".

In this chapter, we present selected *findings* from management research and identify the individual precursors (i.e., individual mindsets) as well as organizational antecedents (i.e., structural components) for enhancing entrepreneurial behavior in organizations. Moreover, we provide suggestions for how both individual and organizational antecedents can be *measured* in legal departments (and organizations in general) for assessing the status quo and providing a discussion basis for potential change. We conclude by showing how these insights can be combined with the notion of the *co-creative enterprise* (Ramaswamy and Gouillart 2010) to outline how legal departments can discover and exploit value creation opportunities together with their internal clients.

2   Individual Antecedents: The Role of Promotion vs. Prevention Focus Mindsets

Stereotypes and anecdotal evidence of the legal profession describe lawyers as mainly focusing on preventing negative outcomes for their companies rather than searching for business opportunities: "As a lawyer, a big part of your job is to forecast every conceivable thing that can go wrong for your client, then protect against it. To remove ambiguity and uncertainty. With whatever time you've got left, you focus on putting the legal structure in place to maximize the upside. But that's nearly always second to protecting against the downside." (Fields 2013, para. 7). This focus, of course, stems from lawyers' education and their primary tasks in business, i.e., advising internal clients and mitigating commercial risks.

However, if legal departments want to substantially contribute to business value, they need to think and act entrepreneurially, which involves acting proactively and opportunity-focused in accordance to their clients' business needs. The distinction between a focus on security and (potential) losses vs. riskiness and (potential) gains has been shown to be a central part of individuals' mindsets in research on *regulatory focus theory* (Higgins 2006).

Regulatory focus theory posits that individuals use two different mindsets to guide their behavior: promotion vs. prevention focus (Higgins 1998). In a promotion focus, individuals concentrate on gains, advancement, growth, and positive outcomes. They act with an open mindset toward novel opportunities, consider

	Promotion focus	Prevention focus
Underlying motives	Advancement, growth, and accomplishment	Security, safety, and responsibility
Goals or standards	Maximal goals: hopes and ideals	Minimal goals: duties and obligations
Salient outcomes	Attaining hits and avoiding misses	Attaining correct rejections and avoiding false alarms
Means	Eagerness means	Vigilance means

Fig. 1 Dimensions of regulatory focus theory (Higgins 1997): promotion vs. prevention focus. Reprinted from the *Journal of Business Venturing, 27, 622–636, A. Tumasjan & R. Braun, "In the eye of the beholder: How regulatory focus and self-efficacy interact in influencing opportunity recognition"*, Copyright 2012, with permission from Elsevier

many different alternatives, and "think big". In contrast, in a prevention focus, individuals concentrate on losses, security, safety, and negative outcomes. They exhibit high vigilance, are prone to behave and think conservatively, and focus on details and accurateness (Halvorson and Higgins 2013). Individuals act in both mindsets—depending on the task and situation—but usually, one of the mindsets is dominant. The difference between promotion and prevention focus are summarized in Fig. 1.

Research examining the influence of regulatory focus on (work) behavior generally demonstrates that a promotion focus is associated with innovation, creativity, opportunity recognition, and change-related organizational citizenship behaviors. In contrast, a prevention focus is associated with safety behaviors, risk-aversion, and maintenance-related organizational citizenship behaviors (e.g., Lanaj et al. 2012; Strobel et al. 2013). Moreover, it has been shown that it is a promotion focus rather than prevention focus that positively influences entrepreneurial behavior, and in particular the recognition of novel business opportunities (Hmieleski and Baron 2008; Tumasjan and Braun 2012).

Although promotion and prevention focus are stable individual characteristics, they still can be influenced situationally to a certain extent. In this vein, leadership behavior and team climates play an important role in shaping employees promotion and prevention focused behavior (e.g., Neubert et al. 2008; Wallace and Chen 2006). A teams' group climate for safety (i.e., an emphasis on safety rules and regulations) has shown to significantly increase employees prevention focus (Wallace and Chen 2006). Moreover, leaders' promotion vs. prevention focus also influences employee behavior independent from employees' stable regulatory focus. In a study by Wu et al. (2008), leaders' promotion focus instilled promotion-focused behavior in their employees fostering employees' creative behavior (Tang et al. 2015). Overall, the extent to which individuals act in a promotion vs. prevention focused mindset depends not only on their stable characteristics but also on situational cues within the organization. In sum, all these findings imply that firms have the possibility to influence their employees' promotion vs. prevention focus mindsets at work through leadership and team climate. In turn, promotion vs. prevention focus will influence how employees approach and accomplish their work.

For legal departments in particular, these findings offer concrete managerial implications. First, leadership in legal teams has to balance promotion and prevention-focused behaviors. Usually, legal teams will focus on the prevention and safety side when giving legal advice to their internal clients. However, leaders need to make their team members aware of the importance of promotion-focused thinking when working with clients. That does not imply that legal department employees have to solely act in a promotion-focused way. Rather it is important that depending on the stage or situation of internal client advice, promotion and prevention-focused thinking need to be balanced. For instance, in contract management, internal clients (e.g., sales) will, due to their role and incentive structure, focus on the opportunities that a certain deal will create for the company. In contrast, the legal employees' role is to focus on the risks and problems that a contract may create. In such situations, legal department leaders may encourage their employees to think proactively about the best ways of value creation with the client rather than focusing exclusively on "what may go wrong". Moreover, a proactive, promotion-focused approach may involve by searching for further opportunities for value creation that the internal client may have overlooked. Thus, rather than only securing against "errors of commission" (i.e., making mistakes), legal employees may create additional value by ensuring "errors of omission" (i.e., losing potential gains from a deal; Crowe and Higgins 1997).

Second, legal managers' leadership behavior will influence the extent to which legal department employees will act promotion-focused, and, in turn, entrepreneurially or opportunity-oriented. Leaders thus need to act as role models for opportunity-focused behavior to encourage employees to think in terms of value creation rather than "merely" avoiding mistakes or risks associated with business deals. By their role modeling, leaders' open-minded, promotion-focused mindset will transfer to their employees and instill a stronger focus on finding opportunities and different alternatives for legal departments' internal clients. There exist a variety of training methods for fostering a promotion focus in individuals which may be readily applied by leaders and employees alike (Halvorson and Higgins 2013). Training interventions may use techniques such as focusing on the gains (rather than only the losses) that can be obtained by a project, concentrating on one's future aspirations or making lists of the positive sides of envisioned goals (e.g., providing a new service) to enhance promotion focus (see Halvorson and Higgins 2013; Strobel et al. 2016).

Third, acting in a promotion-focused way also means being open to change and embracing innovations. Stereotypically, both managers and employees of legal departments are usually not known as being technological early adopters or proponents of change. However, especially in times of rapid technological developments (e.g., digitization), a promotion-focused attitude in legal departments is important to keep abreast of and implement technological innovations for legal issues (e.g., automatization of contract management or more generally innovations under the label of "Legal Tech"). Importantly, a promotion focus positively influences such behaviors—termed proactive strategic scanning—i.e. "proactively surveying the organization's environment to identify ways to ensure a fit between the organization and its environment, such as identifying ways the organization might respond to emerging markets or actively searching the environment for future organizational threats and opportunities" (Parker and Collins 2010, p. 637). Thus, adopting a promotion-focused mindset may encourage employees to proactively search and make suggestions for implementation of legal innovations that will contribute to increased productivity and, ultimately, to business success.

Finally, in leading legal teams it is advisable to cultivate both high promotion and prevention orientation depending on the issue or phase at hand. Maintaining both orientations concurrently may be considered a form of *ambidexterity*. Ambidexterity—a concept that was initially used to describe the ability to equally use both the left and the right hand—has been introduced to explain the creation and management of innovations (Raisch and Birkinshaw 2008). Proponents of the ambidexterity concept argue that for organizations to foster innovations both *exploitation* (i.e., focus on refining existing solutions) and *exploration* (i.e., search for novel solutions) are important for successful innovation. Similarly, managers and employees of legal departments should strive for mastering promotion and prevention focused acting to create business value. To achieve ambidexterity, organizations or teams can use two basic approaches: structural ambidexterity or contextual ambidexterity (Raisch and Birkinshaw 2008). Transferred to our example of legal teams, structural ambidexterity may involve creating separate groups of individuals or teams that follow a promotion vs. prevention-oriented work style. Thus, when cooperating and coordinating, the promotion-focused groups may counterbalance the prevention-oriented individuals in decision-making. On the other hand, contextual ambidexterity refers to switching between a promotion vs. prevention focus within one team or individual. Thus, this approach requires managers and employees to achieve both high promotion and prevention focus simultaneously and switch between both depending on the situation. Recently, research has shown that *ambidextrous leadership*, i.e., leading in a way that highly encourages both a) behaviors that are related to experimentation, innovation, and risk-taking (i.e., promotion-focused behaviors) as well as b) behaviors related to sticking to plans, routine behaviors, and attention to mistakes (i.e., prevention-focused behaviors) fosters team innovation (Zacher and Rosing 2015). This finding implies that it is both possible and advisable for leaders to achieve high levels of both orientations and switch between them to foster innovative behaviors.

The extent to which individuals/teams have a promotion and prevention focus at work can readily be measured by existing assessment instruments. For this purpose, Wallace et al. (2009) have developed the *regulatory focus at work scale*, a survey instrument that assesses promotion and prevention focus at work with 12 Likert-style questions. Using this instrument, teams can assess the degree to which the two mindsets are pronounced in their members' work behaviors and thus have a starting basis for a discussion about potential change opportunities.

3   Organizational Antecedents: Insights from Corporate Entrepreneurship and Organizational Culture

While individual and team mindsets are important as the microfoundations of entrepreneurial behavior, the structural antecedents given by organizations may facilitate or hinder the translation of mindsets into actual work behavior. Regarding the facilitating or enabling antecedents of entrepreneurial behavior in organizations, the corporate entrepreneurship literature offers important insights for organizational structures.

In a comprehensive study of middle managers' perceptions of an enabling environment for entrepreneurial behavior in organizations, five overarching organizational factors were identified: management support, work discretion, rewards, time availability, and organizational boundaries (Hornsby et al. 2002). *Management support* describes senior managers' fostering behaviors of entrepreneurial behavior involving, for instance, the receptiveness of new ideas, quick adoption of improved working methods, support of cross-functional collaboration, and support for "experimental" projects (with the knowledge that some will inevitably fail). *Work discretion* refers to being granted high levels of autonomy in one's work, which is exemplified by allowing the usage of one's own work methods, discretion in judgment, and freedom from "double checking" all decisions. *Rewards* describe the reinforcement of high performance and innovation by one's leaders, such as, for instance, results-based rewards, increased job responsibilities following high job performance, and the recognition for high performance by one's managers. *Time availability* refers to having time not only for pressing issues and routine work, but also for thinking about wider organizational problems, for long-term problem solving or developing new ideas. Finally, the dimension of *organizational boundaries* captures the presence of clear expectations of work outcomes and performance, such as standards for evaluation of innovativeness, agreements on expected outputs, and performance feedback (Hornsby et al. 2002). The extent to which these antecedents in terms of organizational structure are present in a legal department and the firm as a whole will influence the extent to which legal departments will embrace entrepreneurial behavior.

To measure the five factors mentioned above in teams and organizations directly, Kuratko et al. (2014) provide a readily available diagnostic tool, namely the *Corporate Entrepreneurship Assessment Instrument (CEAI)*. Using this instrument, teams or business units may calculate their scores and compare them with other teams/units or the entire organization to identify gaps that need to be closed in terms of the structural facilitators. Another possible mode of administration of this instrument would be to answer the questions twice: first, regarding the current state (which is the way the CEAI is usually administered), and second, regarding the preferred state for fostering individuals' entrepreneurial or innovative behaviors.

By doing so, teams can identify gaps between current and preferred states, which in turn can be used as a basis of discussion within the team and with managers to prepare potential structural change.

A related measurement instrument that can be used to assess dimensions of structural antecedents for team innovation is the *Organizational Culture Assessment Instrument (OCAI)* developed by Cameron and Quinn (2006). Despite the reference to *organizations*, this instrument can also be applied to teams, units, departments or other parts of an organization. The OCAI covers six central dimensions, namely the dominant organizational characteristics, organizational leadership, employee management, organization glue, strategic emphases, and criteria of success. The obtained scores (to be rated in a current state and preferred state format) will give teams an indication of their dominant culture which can then be gauged regarding its fit with desired entrepreneurial or innovative behaviors. Specifically, four archetypes of cultural orientations can be assessed: clan, adhocracy, hierarchy, and market (for a detailed account see Cameron and Quinn 2006). A recent meta-analysis supports the notion that these cultural orientations are differentially associated with relevant organizational outcomes, such as innovation, product quality, growth, and employee job satisfaction (Hartnell et al. 2011).

In sum, as described above, management research provides ample evidence-based indications for fostering entrepreneurial behavior in teams and organizations. To put all the presented insights in a coherent and deployable framework, we will use the notion of the *co-creative enterprise* to describe how the principles in terms of individual mindsets and structural conditions can be put to work.

4 Putting It All Together: A Co-creative Approach to Management

How can the insights developed above be combined and applied in a coherent management framework? In our view, the *co-creation approach* to management (Ramaswamy and Gouillart 2010) offers a general paradigm in which the factors identified above can be summarized and implemented for managing processes in legal departments (and in organizations in general). The co-creation approach aims at bringing together all stakeholders involved in a certain process and improving their interactional patterns. Rather than merely searching for process improvements in all single steps involved in product or service delivery and optimizing their efficiency (e.g., Six Sigma), co-creation focuses on what the stakeholders of a process (e.g., employees, customers, suppliers, distributors) experience and how this experience can be altered for better results for everyone involved.

The authors propose four simple steps that firms or departments may take in a co-creational approach (Ramaswamy and Gouillart 2010): first, all relevant stakeholders that are involved or influenced by a process (e.g., contract management) have to be identified. Second, the current interactions of the stakeholders need to be mapped out and visualized (e.g., how are the stakeholders currently interacting within the process). Third, all involved stakeholders share their current experiences with the process in workshops and generate ideas how to improve those interactions (e.g., how are legal and sales interacting in contract creation and how can disparate repository systems across regions be integrated). Fourth, firms then can implement ideas for improvement using platforms where the discussion regarding further improvements of interactions can continue (e.g., integration of contract creation, negotiation, and repository on one platform and continuing dialog on the platform forum about further improvements).

This latter point is crucial: the co-creation paradigm is very much about an ongoing dialog between stakeholders about interaction improvement, i.e., a dialog that needs to be sustainably continued (rather than be seen as a one-shot project) to be effective in the long run. The co-creation paradigm builds on the firm conviction that people are inherently motivated to proactively create and find opportunities to change their environment for the better—key characteristics of entrepreneurial behavior (Tumasjan et al. 2011). It is, in fact, a matter of giving people autonomy, providing platforms for dialog, and the means for implementation. With the continuing technological developments in the digital age (Welpe et al. 2010; Sprenger et al. 2014), all three ingredients are easier than ever to implement. In particular, with the proliferation of digital tools such as company social networks (e.g., Zyncro), collaboration platforms (e.g., Slack) or voting apps (e.g., Pollcode) the facilitative nature of the co-creation paradigm can readily be brought to life in a structured way. However, such tools alone will not serve as a panacea and will likely remain unused unless they fit with an organizational logic that truly cherishes a culture of co-creation. The time is ripe to create such an environment—it may lay the groundwork for legal departments to empower both individuals' promotion-focused thinking as well as unleash the potential for entrepreneurial acting.

Liquid Legal Context
by Dr. Dierk Schindler, Dr. Roger Strathausen, Kai Jacob

When introducing a KPI-driven environment, there is an inherent risk to default to what may be called "traditional" metrics, typically centered around financials, e.g. cost, variable spend, outside counsel cost etc. Such a reductionist approach enforces a narrow and self-reflective view, instead of a holistic perspective. As Tumasjan and Welpe state: *"To create value for their internal clients, corporate lawyers need not only a thorough understanding of the abstract commercial goals of the organization, but they also need to act entrepreneurially in recognizing, evaluating, and exploiting opportunities for value creation."*

The authors calibrate the discussion well, right from the beginning: This is not only about the dimension of finding entrepreneurially minded people; of course, one needs to understand the individual precursors (i.e., individual mindsets) that need to be found and developed. This is as much about

(continued)

understanding and creating the organizational antecedents (i.e., structural components) for enhancing entrepreneurial behavior in organizations.

As to the individual side of things, Tumasjan and Welpe make reference to the promotion vs. prevention focused mindset and what makes up one or the other. A great guide for developing and hiring talent which bridges right into the article of Escher, who talks about changing the stereotype when hiring lawyers. They also underline the critical importance of creating the right mindset in the managerial ranks of the department—leading by example is key!

As to the organizational antecedents, the authors draw on research that has identified five key elements for creating an enabling environment for entrepreneurial behavior in organizations: management support, work discretion, rewards, time availability, and organizational boundaries. What does an organization look like that enables entrepreneurial behavior? Tumasjan and Welpe call out the co-creation approach that aims at bringing together all stakeholders involved in a certain process and improving their interactional patterns. Adding innovation and value will replace the mere and siloed improvement of the status quo.

If that is future mindset of individuals in the legal industry, will there even be the opportunity of developing them into other parts of the corporation? *"Yes"* says Chomicka!

References

Cameron, K. S., & Quinn, R. E. (2006). *Diagnosing and changing organizational culture.* San Francisco: Jossey-Bass.

Crowe, E., & Higgins, E. T. (1997). Regulatory focus and strategic inclinations: promotion and prevention in decision-making. *Organizational Behavior and Human Decision Processes, 69,* 117–132.

De Jong, J. P., Parker, S. K., Wennekers, S., & Wu, C. H. (2013). Entrepreneurial behavior in organizations: Does job design matter? *Entrepreneurship Theory and Practice, 39,* 981–995.

Fields, J. (2013). *Why most lawyers make terrible entrepreneurs.* Available at http://www.jonathanfields.com/why-most-lawyers-make-terrible-entrepreneurs/

Halvorson, H. G., & Higgins, E. T. (2013). Do you play to win--or to not lose? *Harvard Business Review, 91,* 117–120.

Hartnell, C. A., Ou, A. Y., & Kinicki, A. (2011). Organizational culture and organizational effectiveness: A meta-analytic investigation of the competing values framework's theoretical suppositions. *Journal of Applied Psychology, 96,* 677–694.

Higgins, E. T. (1997). Beyond pleasure and pain. *American Psychologist, 52,* 1280–1300.

Higgins, E. T. (1998). Promotion and prevention: Regulatory focus as a motivational principle. *Advances in Experimental Social Psychology, 30,* 1–46.

Higgins, E. T. (2006). Value from hedonic experience and engagement. *Psychological Review, 113,* 439–460.

Hmieleski, K. M., & Baron, R. A. (2008). Regulatory focus and new venture performance: A study of entrepreneurial opportunity exploitation under conditions of risk versus uncertainty. *Strategic Entrepreneurship Journal, 2,* 285–299.

Hornsby, J. S., Kuratko, D. F., & Zahra, S. A. (2002). Middle managers' perception of the internal environment for corporate entrepreneurship: Assessing a measurement scale. *Journal of Business Venturing, 17*, 253–273.

Kuratko, D. F., Hornsby, J. S., & Covin, J. G. (2014). Diagnosing a firm's internal environment for corporate entrepreneurship. *Business Horizons, 57*, 37–47.

Lanaj, K., Chang, C. H., & Johnson, R. E. (2012). Regulatory focus and work-related outcomes: A review and meta-analysis. *Psychological Bulletin, 138*, 998–1034.

Nabarro (2011). *General counsel: Vague about value?* London: Author.

Neubert, M. J., Kacmar, K. M., Carlson, D. S., Chonko, L. B., & Roberts, J. A. (2008). Regulatory focus as a mediator of the influence of initiating structure and servant leadership on employee behavior. *Journal of Applied Psychology, 93*(6), 1220–1233.

Parker, S. K., & Collins, C. G. (2010). Taking stock: Integrating and differentiating multiple proactive behaviors. *Journal of Management, 36*, 633–662.

Pfeffer, J., & Sutton, R. I. (2006). Evidence-based management. *Harvard Business Review, 84*, 63–74.

Raisch, S., & Birkinshaw, J. (2008). Organizational ambidexterity: Antecedents, outcomes, and moderators. *Journal of Management, 34*, 375–409.

Ramaswamy, V., & Gouillart, F. (2010). Building the co-creative enterprise. *Harvard Business Review, 88*, 100–109.

Sprenger, T. O., Sandner, P. G., Tumasjan, A., & Welpe, I. M. (2014). News or noise? Using Twitter to identify and understand company-specific news flow. *Journal of Business Finance & Accounting, 41*, 791–830.

Strobel, M., Tumasjan, A., Spörrle, M., & Welpe, I. M. (2013). The future starts today, not tomorrow: How future focus promotes organizational citizenship behaviors. *Human Relations, 66*, 829–856.

Strobel, M., Tumasjan, A., Spörrle, M., & Welpe, I. M. (2016). *Proactive strategic behavior throughout the organization: How future focus fosters proactive strategic scanning* (Working paper).

Tang, M., Werner, C., Tumasjan, A., Cao, G., Shen, J., Shi, J., & Spörrle, M. (2015). Creative expression and its evaluation on work related verbal tasks: Comparison of Chinese and German samples. *Journal of Creative Behavior.* doi:10.1002/jocb.134.

Tumasjan, A., & Braun, R. (2012). In the eye of the beholder: How regulatory focus and self-efficacy interact in influencing opportunity recognition. *Journal of Business Venturing, 27*, 622–636.

Tumasjan, A., Strobel, M., & Welpe, I. M. (2011). Employer brand building for start-ups: Which job attributes do employees value most? *Zeitschrift für Betriebswirtschaft, 81*, 111–136.

Tumasjan, A., Welpe, I., & Spörrle, M. (2013). Easy now, desirable later: The moderating role of temporal distance in opportunity evaluation and exploitation. *Entrepreneurship Theory and Practice, 37*, 859–888.

Wallace, C., & Chen, G. (2006). A multilevel integration of personality, climate, self-regulation, and performance. *Personnel Psychology, 59*, 529–557.

Wallace, J. C., Johnson, P. D., & Frazier, M. L. (2009). An examination of the factorial, construct, and predictive validity and utility of the regulatory focus at work scale. *Journal of Organizational Behavior, 30*, 805–831.

Welpe, I. M., Tumasjan, A., & Strobel, M. (2010). Construal Level Theory-Eine Theorie für die Grenzenlose Unternehmung? (Construal level theory – A theory for the boundaryless organization?). *Zeitschrift für betriebswirtschaftliche Forschung (zfbf) Sonderheft, 62*, 84–105.

Wu, C., McMullen, J. S., Neubert, M. J., & Yi, X. (2008). The influence of leader regulatory focus on employee creativity. *Journal of Business Venturing, 23*, 587–602.

Zacher, H., & Rosing, K. (2015). Ambidextrous leadership and team innovation. *Leadership & Organization Development Journal, 36*, 54–68.

Dr. Andranik Tumasjan is a postdoctoral scholar at the Technical University of Munich, TUM School of management. His research focuses on innovative organizational and entrepreneurial behavior, strategic human resource management, the future of work design, and the implications of digitization for management. His work has been published in leading academic management journals and covered in the media, such as the *Harvard Business Review, Süddeutsche Zeitung* or *Huffington Post.* He graduated from the Ludwig Maximilians University of Munich and received a doctoral degree in management from the Technical University of Munich. As a fellow of the China Scholarship Program, he studied at Nanjing University (China), and was a visiting scholar at Columbia University (New York) and the University of California, Los Angeles.

Prof. Dr. Isabell M. Welpe holds the Chair of Strategy and Organization at the Technical University of Munich and is the Head of the Bavarian Institute for Higher Education Research and Planning. Her research interests are in New Public Management, leadership, future concepts of work and organisations, impact of digital technologies and social media and strategic innovation. She studied management at the Ludwig-Maximilians-Universität in Munich, Germany and at the Massachusetts Institute of Technology, Boston, USA. She completed an additional MSc at the London School of Economics before finishing her PhD at the University of Regensburg. She has been a visiting professor at the Keck Graduate Institute, Claremont, USA and a postdoctoral fellow at the Carlson School of Management at the University of Minnesota. Before taking over the Chair of Strategy and Organization at the Technische Universität München, she worked at the Max Planck Institute for Economics.

A Rose by Any Other Name Would Smell as Sweet: The New Legal Pro-Occupations in the Construction Sector

Barbara Chomicka

Abstract

The occupational golden age of the legal profession is said to have come to an end. The eBay dispute resolution site resolves 60 m complaints a year. Changes in the law are making it easier for accounting practices, estate agents, building societies, banks and others to offer legal services on the side. Companies are cutting back their in-house legal departments or deciding they no longer want to maintain one.

We are therefore on the brink of a period of fundamental and irreversible change in the way that legal expertise is available both within organizations and in society. In the long-term future we will neither need nor want lawyers to think and work in the way they did in the twentieth century and earlier.

In response to these challenges, lawyers are trying to rethink the traditional ways of working, by making legal work more transparent and client-friendly, providing demonstrable value for money and delivering to firm performance indicators. Law firms have started charging clients the same for more work, or less for the same work, shedding staff or keeping the same number and paying (most of them) less.

But this will not be sufficient to halt the current decline. Lawyers must look beyond the traditional channels of providing professional services and appropriate opportunities in other fields, even if they are not immediate neighbors, by re-defining their professional requirements to include legal education and training.

"A rose by any other name would smell as sweet" is a frequently referenced line from William Shakespeare's play *Romeo and Juliet* (1597), in which Juliet argues that it does not matter that her lover Romeo is from the rival house of Montague, that is, that his name is "Montague."

B. Chomicka (✉)
Arcadis, London, UK
e-mail: bchomicka@gmail.com

© Springer International Publishing AG 2017
K. Jacob et al. (eds.), *Liquid Legal*, Management for Professionals,
DOI 10.1007/978-3-319-45868-7_10

One of the potential opportunities is offered by commercial contracting in construction, a sector almost entirely dominated by non-legal staff, standard forms of contracts and established processes and contractual boundaries. What if a contract administrator, contract manager or even a portfolio, program, or project manager, rather than being a construction professional with an appreciation of legal issues, happens to be a lawyer trained in basic construction matters? A rose by any other name would smell as sweet.

There are, however, fundamental issues preventing many lawyers from grasping the opportunity and venturing into traditionally non-legal roles in construction, namely the low public opinion of lawyers, professional peer pressure, personal expectations and—the last taboo in the twenty-first century—pay.

1   Introduction

John Marquess, Chairman, chief executive and general counsel of Legalgard, in his paper on dishonest legal bills (1994) recalls a scene from a film he watched with his 8-year-old daughter which drove the audience "absolutely wild": this was the first official dinosaur murder in *Jurassic Park* (1993), which involved a lawyer being plucked right off the toilet and eaten by a runaway Tyrannosaurus rex. During the discussion that followed the film, his daughter noted: "I thought he would have passed him by just as a matter of professional courtesy." While we are all familiar with this line, as it appears in many common jokes amongst lawyers involving a range of sharks and vultures, the selection of a stereotypical lawyer as the first victim of a fairly banal behemoth of the prehistoric world was probably not coincidental.

According to Susskind and Susskind (2015), the legal profession as we know it today is an artefact built to meet a particular set of needs in a print-based industrial society. As we progress into a technology-based Internet society, the legal profession, or any profession in its current form, will no longer be able to satisfy the needs of society: professions are unaffordable, often antiquated, the expertise of the best is enjoyed only by a few, and their work is not transparent. For these and many other reasons, today's lawyers should be, and will be, displaced by feasible alternatives.

In the film, the unfortunate individual devoured by the Tyrannosaurus rex was Donald Gennaro, a lawyer sent by Cowan, Swain & Ross to inspect Jurassic Park, who was also the general counsel for InGen. In the scene, once the Tyrannosaurus rex knocks the hut down around him, Gennaro, having approximately 10 seconds of life remaining, readies himself to be eaten: he is calm, and makes sure his hair is slicked back. He seems to be particularly unsurprised about the event, which adds to the general horror of the scene. The television channel MTV rated the act as ninth in their list of "9 Most Horrific Deaths in the *Jurassic Park* Movies" (2013).

Gennaro, a stereotypical lawyer, is likely to have spent his life amassing intellectual credentials; he is probably a graduate of an elite university, with a

CV full of Latin honors. He made the law review at a top law school and has clerked for federal judges. By choosing this educational and career path, he was promised job security, steady career progression, and was guaranteed a fairly comfortable life in return for spending a lot of time being rather bored. Then suddenly his hut is destroyed—not only by a Tyrannosaurus rex, but also by today's key drivers of change in the legal services market: with the eBay dispute resolution site resolving 60 millions complaints a year, changes in the law are making it easier for accounting practices, estate agents, building societies, banks and others to offer legal services on the side.

Faced with extinction in the stomach of a roaring dinosaur, Gennaro had the same amount of time left that the American runner Florence Griffith-Joyner needed in 1988 to complete a 100-metre dash. Gennaro, however, remained still. Moreover, having being caught in the act he did not seem to even contemplate an attempt at a lucky escape, focusing instead on preparing to die.

Unlike Gennaro, the lawyers listening to the presentation by Des Hudson, the Law Society's chief executive, were shocked at the realization that their days were numbered when he told his audience that "survival is not compulsory" (Hilton 2013). Drawing an analogy between the optometry and legal services markets, he brought to the attendees' attention the consequences of the Opticians Act 1985, which repealed the legal monopoly for opticians on sight tests and the dispensing of spectacles. In 1985 there were 3500 independent optical outlets enjoying a 65 % market share by revenue. In 2010, there were 3750 independents, with the market share reduced to 27.5 %, while the market itself grew by 80 % (Baksi 2012). The growth in the optometry market was not driven by the nation's eyesight suddenly getting worse, but because of the innovation in provision of services: the advertising of the benefits of proactive eye care, the introduction of new products such as disposable contact lenses, the promotion of glasses as a fashion accessory and, according to WebMD, their potential to reduce wrinkles ("Don't squint—get reading glasses!" (Bouchez 2008)).

Although it is highly unlikely that any innovation in legal services carries the potential for improving one's looks, it definitely creates the potential for an increased awareness of legal issues, encouraging individuals and businesses to take a more proactive stance with regard to their legal health. The innovation in law may take many forms, from the restructuring and rationalization of old ways of working to a transformation in the way that legal expertise is made available within an organization or industry, or in society as a whole. While both propositions attract deserved scrutiny among legal entrepreneurs and visionaries, there is one aspect of the latter which appears to remain overlooked: in their evolution, lawyers are able to not only draw analogies from the work of others and carry the lessons learned into their own area, but also to appropriate opportunities in other fields, even if they are not immediate neighbors, by re-defining their professional requirements to include legal education and training. As suggested by Susskind and Susskind (2015), if we think more widely and strategically about professionalism in general it is not at all clear where the boundaries of the professions lie, nor in accordance with what criteria they can be delimited. The steady evolution of all the professions—the emergence of new ones and the exit of obsolete ones, the overlapping and constant rubbing of shoulders—creates an opportunity for lawyers to encroach on other, non-legal professional territories, especially in sectors identified as having a low representation of professionals with a legal background.

Construction is one of the few uncharted waters. While in other sectors there might be complaints that lawyers are too intrusive, in construction lawyers are very rare and remote, called in as "rottweilers" to sort out problems, usually when it is too late to achieve a good resolution (with the overarching question: "Whose budget does it come from?"). Construction contract administration and management teams are usually "unspoilt" by law degrees and often separated from their corporate in-house legal departments by hundreds of miles, in a literal sense (providing there is an in-house legal function at all). No surprise then, that according to Arcadis (2015), the number of formal disputes in construction is increasing on an annual basis: the most common cause of construction disputes globally, for the third consecutive year, is (1) failure to administer the contract properly. This is followed by (2) poorly drafted or incomplete and unsubstantiated claims, (3) errors and/or omissions in the contract document, (4) failure to understand and/or comply with its contractual obligations by the employer, contractor and subcontractor and (5) failure to make interim awards on extensions of time and compensation. There is certainly a scarcity of professional staff in the industry in general, and an over-reliance on contract professionals with limited legal awareness in favor of a construction site-based background. A greater involvement of contract professionals with legal background offers, at a minimum, a promise of ample resolution of at least two causes which made it to the top five in 2015, namely poorly drafted claims and failure to understand contractual obligations. Considering the average value ($51 m) and length (13.2 months) of a construction dispute, the potential benefits to the industry of legally trained professional staff taking over contract administration and management roles are immense.

The introduction of a legally trained contracting team could be a very strong market proposition for the corporate built asset consultancy, with the potential to improve customer choice and service, ensure compliance, improve the company's bottom line and deliver better outcomes. It offers opportunities for the fundamental re-definition of legal roles in the new, leaner corporate structures in the construction industry, has the potential to generate new ideas and methods and extend the boundaries of contract administration and management in construction.

Although this opportunity exists, only a handful of lawyers express an interest in traditionally non-legal roles in construction. Contracting in general, and the construction sector in particular, is not perceived as an attractive career choice for someone with a legal education and training, and the reasons for this situation are complex. A careful consideration of various aspects of legal work indicates that certain myths and external pressures, such as social stereotyping and peer pressure, and personal ones, such as inflated social and pay expectations, represent a forceful challenge to new ideas and opportunities for lawyers. As pointed out by the English economist John Maynard Keynes (1935), "the difficulty lies not so much in developing new ideas as in escaping from the old ones." It seems that a recognition and consideration of these issues may offer inspiration to those considering creating or taking up traditionally non-legal jobs in construction.

2   "The First Thing We Do, Let's Kill All the Lawyers", Shakespeare (1591), *Henry VI Part 2*

Any respectable insight into the legal profession in the United Kingdom seems to take as a starting point these words, uttered in *Henry VI Part 2* by Dick the butcher, a somewhat minor Shakespearean character. Contrary to popular belief, this proposal was not designed to restore sanity to commercial life. Rather, it was intended to eliminate those who might stand in the way of the revolution that was contemplated, thus underlining the important role that lawyers can play in society. Despite its alleged intent, the line is widely used today to illustrate the low public opinion of lawyers.

The public perception of lawyers as self-interested "fat cats" has proved difficult to shift. In the UK, in the recent survey of the most trusted professions, it emerged that more people would trust hairdressers (69 %) to tell the truth than lawyers (51 %) (IPSOS MORI 2016). Similar studies in the U.S.A. have indicated that people rate the honesty and ethical standards of a building contractor higher than those of a lawyer (25 % and 21 % respectively, (Gallup 2015)). However, in the light of the results of earlier editions of the Gallup survey (which has been running since 1976) this can be viewed as a big improvement from the 13 % score reported in 1999 and 2009. One of the root causes of this situation is clients' negative experience when using lawyers directly. According to research by Which? The Consumers' Association, based in the United Kingdom (2005), one in six consumers of legal services considered the service they had received to be "poor". The main causes for complaint were unexpectedly high bills and the failure of many lawyers to listen to customers' opinions, while other common grievances included rudeness, arrogance and poor communication of the progress of case (Bedlow 2006). This negative image, and the resulting public attitude towards lawyers, has proved to be important in the current battle for increased legal aid funds, competition for work with "paralegals" or potential employment outside traditional legal positions.

Maitland Kalton, senior partner in Kaltons, in an interview with Derek Bedlow (2006) for the *Law Society Gazette*, noted low levels of morale in parts of the profession as the main impediment to the efforts of legal firms, departments and campaign groups to improve lawyers' service to their clients. The evidence suggests that 40 % of lawyers are unhappy with their career choice, and, according to Kalton, "that's not only very sad, it is very costly for law firms". In the last decade, the very nature of legal work has evolved from craft to commerce; work that was formerly intellectual has slowly become purely commercial, and an aptitude for schmoozing has become more important than brainpower to professional advancement in legal work, resulting in severe disappointment with the job. Ideas about innovation, change, the appropriation of other professional domains, excellence in client service or the application of Key Performance Indicators (KPIs) in legal services are useless if one cannot maintain a satisfied and motivated workforce. And the scale of the problem makes it impossible to overlook. A study by Johns Hopkins University found that among more than 100 occupations studied, lawyers were three times more likely to suffer from depression than any other profession (David 2011). According to C. Stuart Mauney, from the Lawyers Helping Lawyers Commission (undated), the rate of substance abuse among lawyers is twice that of the general population. The reasons behind this statistic are usually identified as work-related stress and the requirement for lawyers to work long hours to establish themselves. It should also be mentioned that there is a general tendency for law students to suffer from depression. Reports suggest that nearly 40 % of law students are dealing with some form of depression.

If not addressed, depression can develop into thoughts of suicide. Statistics indicate that lawyers are 1.33 times more likely to commit suicide than the average person, which puts them between fourth and eighth on the various lists of the 10 professions with the highest suicide rates, usually just behind professionals with easy access to prescription drugs, such as dentists, pharmacists and physicians, in terms of the highest per capita suicide rate. According to Tom Roberts, mental health blogger (2015), "It is a middle-aged, white trial lawyer who is most likely to kill himself". The significant increase in the rates of depression and suicide among legal professionals in recent years has led to the implementation of mandatory psychological evaluations for lawyers in certain US states. Obviously not all lawyers suffer from depression and suicidal ideation; it just happens to be more common in this particular occupation. Any job is stressful, but there are underlying aspects of the legal profession that explain why lawyers cannot deal with the stresses and demands of their job as successfully as others. It is possible that the personal expectations of people who enter the profession, particularly in relation to job security and the expectation that a law degree automatically entitles one to a six-figure salary, play an important part.

The disillusionment about the legal profession starts with the number of traditional legal job opportunities per legal graduate. The growth of the legal workforce seems to be following Moore's law, based on an observation by Gordon Moore, co-founder of Intel and Fairchild Semiconductor, that the number of transistors in a dense integrated circuit doubles approximately every 2 years (Moore 1965): there are simply many more lawyers than there are traditional legal work opportunities. According to Matt Leichter (2013), attorney and proprietor of the blog *Law School Tuition Bubble*, in the U.S.A. it is estimated that there are more than two law graduates for every traditional job opening. For example in 2013, in the US state of Michigan there were 6.48 law graduates for each job vacancy, in Delaware 4.20 for each vacancy and even in New York there were 2.92 graduates for each vacancy. There is a common joke in the legal profession that the closest that the majority of law graduates will come to being employed at the bar is by working as baristas, clearly assuming that legal jobs are more desirable than coffee-making ones. Interestingly enough, when Costa Coffee advertised for three full-time and five part-time baristas to staff a new shop in the Mapperley area of Nottingham, UK, the company received applications from 1701 applicants in two months, some of whom had 10–15 years' experience in retail (Benedictus 2013). While this example is a fascinating anomaly, especially in a city the size of Nottingham, it illustrates the level of competition in the job market. Applying for a job which might be perceived as an easy alternative to a traditional legal career is no longer a default option for a lawyer. It is possible, of course, that if the job advertisement was run in the immediate aftermath of the Liebeck v. McDonald's Restaurants, the "hot coffee lawsuit", a law graduate could argue their way into the position by highlighting their unique awareness of the legal risk associated with serving coffee.

In addition to the general goals for a career there is, of course, the issue of compensation.

Law is generally perceived to be a highly privileged profession, and the financial rewards of legal work have lodged themselves in the public imagination. However, in reality those in the profession who can really afford a luxurious lifestyle constitute a relatively small percentage of the legal population. In an interview with Burkeman (2010), a barrister sheds some light on the "real" salary for legal work, with its self-employed status, chambers rent and variable income depending on caseload: "Last year I made around £45,000, but that includes VAT, and 20 % of it goes to chambers rent, then income tax on top". The following year (2011), four years after graduation, he reported earning £60,000 (including VAT and before payment of chambers rent). Lawyers generally earn less than people think they do, and less than what they imagine their salary is going to be when they graduate. This is exemplified in the salary expectation mentioned by a legal professional in a career query e-mailed to Adams (2013), author of *A Manual of Style for Contract Drafting* and a popular blog, in which an unnamed assistant attorney expressed the view that he would expect to be paid more than £55,000 4 years into a legal career. This sum is well above what majority of contract administrators in construction are paid, but also much more than the market realistically pays the majority of lawyers early in their careers in the traditional legal professions.

Fortunately for many, the connection between happiness and money is to a large degree relative. As a general rule, people are happiest to earn more than other people rather than more per se, even if they are earning less than they otherwise might. Happiness is comparison-based, and it matters greatly with whom one choose to compare oneself. For many non-corporate lawyers it is fine to earn less than, say, their corporate peers; for example, the barrister cited earlier stated: "I am interested in money to have a nice life, but I'm not interested in being wealthy. Which is lucky, because most criminal barristers don't get paid as much as people think we do [. . .] The top commercial lawyers have high-powered clients and charge top fees – they're the ones who earn hundreds of thousands a year".

If one compares legal positions listed on americasjobsexchange.com against the median rewards offered by these positions across the board collated by payscale.com, only a handful of these roles offer a starting salary higher than that offered, for example, to a certified industrial maintenance mechanic (median £36,000 per annum). From a commonsense perspective there is nothing wrong with this situation: there are fewer people with mechanical skills than with law degrees, but from the perspective of a person who has just made an upfront investment of £100,000 for their legal education this might be a rude awakening.

Becoming a lawyer requires significant education, and therefore significant financial investment. An average legal professional is said to graduate with a £100,000 of debt. It is interesting in this context to note the average debt burden carried by other respected professionals. Architects, for example, are also said to accumulate £100,000 of student debt before they are legally allowed to use the title "architect", as do doctors and dentists before they are allowed to practice. Even in professions that do not require a university education, there is a significant upfront investment necessary: for example, pilots have to spend up to £100,000 in order to train (Burkeman 2010)'. An architect, four years after graduation, can expect to be paid, on average, £35,000, a similar salary to that of a legal professional. For the majority of professionals there is no direct link between the investment and the subsequent rewards. However, the difference between these professions goes beyond their social and economic significance. Being an architect or a doctor, for many practitioners, is seen as a labor of love and not simply labor for a wage. It involves considerably more than holding down a job, an ethos very different from that embodied by many people who choose to go to law school. While legal work is a true personal passion for some, there is a significant legacy from earlier generations, for whom the law functioned as a kind of psychological safety net for the ambitious and upwardly mobile—whatever your life plan was originally, you could rest assured that law school would be there if your plans fell through: one was, after all, an admissions test and six semesters away from upper-middle-class respectability.

By comparison, a construction contract administrator with a starting median salary of £25,000 can expect this to increase to £45,000 with experience. After 10 years of practice, as a senior contracts manager they will enjoy between £50,000 and £70,000 a year, with some corporate contracts administrators in construction enjoying higher salaries and performance-related bonuses. The role usually comes with a car allowance and other benefits.

In many industries there is a natural tendency to recruit qualified lawyers for contracting roles. This has never been the case in the construction sector. Construction is rarely a field considered for employment by prime legal professionals, and even the largest, most prestigious global corporations operating in the built asset domain have less than a handful of lawyers working outside their (slim) in-house legal teams. Wearing safety boots (even occasionally) instead of Manolo Blahniks, or a high-visibility vest over one's business suit, from time to time might not be everyone's vision of professional success. And this is despite the safety footwear being paid for by the employer under The Personal Protective Equipment Regulations 2002 and the Personal Protective Equipment at Work Regulations 1992 (as amended).

The potential of the construction industry to attract prime legal talent is further diminished by the fact that within the legal profession, in-house lawyers are perceived as "lesser beings": contract lawyers have a low status among the "proper lawyers", and for many general counsels, commercial contracting is way down their list of priorities and resources (Cummins 2010). Moving "in-house" is perceived as a one-way street, with the perception that one will be "out of practice" for a few years, ultimately hindering the possibility of a future career path in a traditional legal role. According to Harrison Barnes, chief executive of the BCG Attorney Search, the decision "to go in-house" is deemed to be one of the most significant career decisions a lawyer can make. Recognising the benefits of this choice, such as "more interesting work, shorter hours, potentially lucrative stock options, and the opportunity to be on the business side in a corporate environment" (Barnes undated), he quotes one of his recruiters providing advice to a friend ("three years out of a top Ivy League law school and working for arguably one of the top two or three law firms in the United States"): "Are you sure about the in-house thing? (...) kind of look at the option with the same sort of circumspection that you might view a vasectomy: It may be reversible, but you'd better be darned sure about it anyway." Barnes further suggests that once you go in-house "your legal skills are likely to deteriorate", "it is very difficult to move to another in-house job" and that "you may have to work as hard in-house as you did in a law firm".

Law firms are relatively hierarchical institutions, with the work funneled up the chain of command, while in-house legal departments or contracting departments tend to adopt a flatter model. In-house lawyers "often talk to the person doing the work" (Manch and Shannon 2006) or—even worse—do the work themselves, as is the case among, for example, lawyers working in contract manager positions in the oil and gas or IT industries. The universal preference for in-house lawyers to be generalists stands in sharp contrast to law firms' preference for specialists. And while in any other profession a generalist is deemed to specialize in "everything" (a general practitioner or family doctor being the prime example), in the legal world, "As a generalist, you will be an expert in nothing" (Barnes undated). The reason such threats resonate with the legal community is a persisting stereotype of what it means to "practice law" rather than selecting a job best suited to one's credentials, skills, abilities and lifestyle.

3   Conclusions

Coming back to our question: what if, in the construction industry, a contract administrator, contract manager or even a portfolio, program or project manager, rather than being a construction professional with an appreciation of legal issues happens to be a law practitioner trained in basic construction? Construction industry products and processes haven't really changed that much in the last thousand years, with Newton's law of universal gravitation being the main principle followed religiously throughout the sector, thus making it fairly easy to grasp. In the majority of underdeveloped countries a person can build their house themselves, and they usually do, which is one of the main reasons behind a shortage of professionals in this sector. The occupational requirements for contract professionals in construction do not include any formal legal training, other than an appreciation of the legal issues. As market conditions have become more complex, this approach is being reconsidered by large built asset corporate businesses. So far, the challenge of attracting professionals with legal training has prevented any meaningful change from taking place, and, as discussed above, the reasons for this situation are complex.

Unlike the legal services sector, the construction market is witnessing a significant rebound. Construction spending, especially in the public sector, continues to increase. It is widely known that, for example, the US transport infrastructure system, much of which was built in the 1950s, is in dire need of a significant overhaul, and alternative transportation systems such as light rail and busways have moved to the forefront as the North American highway system reaches full capacity (Arcadis 2015). Contrary to the common belief among lawyers, construction contracting is anything but boring. Globally, there is a radical rethink of strategy and delivery across the major contracts, following the significant reduction in oil price, high-profile corruption scandals in South America and China, the consequences of tenders priced in the immediate aftermath of the 2008/2009 financial crisis, a rising global cost base and strain upon the supply chain, a scarcity of labor and an increase in cross-border and multi-jurisdiction activity, as well as increasing exposure to more "force majeure" and "neutral event" circumstances. With construction projects increasingly being aggregated into big complicated programs, attracting additional risk as well as political and public attention, high-visibility disputes are not an option for their owners. Owners of mega-programs have turned to alternative project delivery, increased project controls and early intervention to mitigate disputes to help manage that risk. The contracting community has to follow suit, and a greater involvement of satisfied and professionally fulfilled legally trained professionals offers an opportunity for the industry to deliver excellent customer service.

Liquid Legal Context
by Dr. Dierk Schindler, Dr. Roger Strathausen, Kai Jacob

Chomicka looks at the pressure on the legal industry from a totally different angle. A lot is being said about lawyers needing to pick up business skills in many forms in order to carry them back into their own environment as it transforms (or to transform it). Chomicka points out one aspect which is often overlooked: in their evolution, lawyers are able to not only draw analogies from the work of others and carry the lessons learned into their own area, but they can—and should—also carry their new, extended skills to appropriate opportunities in other fields, re-defining the professional requirements in those fields to include legal education and training.

Enhancing the curriculum and practice of other professions with legal skills and thereby opening those fields as a new career opportunities for lawyers? A "hostile takeover" of a function triggered by pressure? Or a win-win-opportunity for both sides? Definitely the latter, says Chomicka

(continued)

and illustrates her theses very thoughtfully and pointedly using the construction industry as an example.

We have heard about the need for lawyers to acquire new skills like project management and other business skills to have a future in their jobs, as we recall the articles of Meents and Markfort. We are now hearing that lawyers become contenders for jobs outside their traditional function. But Chomicka adds further to the case by saying that this is not only about new types of jobs, but also often better paid jobs, as this might be the jump for lawyers from a supporting role into a business creation role, which typically has access to better remuneration packages.

This line of thought reminds us of another way how lawyers can directly influence the top-line of the company—by turning Legal from a cost-center into a profit-center. How this can be achieved is vividly described by Roux-Chenu and de Rocca-Serra in her inspiring article on their journey at Cap Gemini, on how Legal can be and become a true business enabler.

References

Adams, K. (2013). From lawyer to contract-management professional: A one-way trip? *Adams Drafting*, May 9. Available at: http://www.adamsdrafting.com/from-lawyer-to-contract-management-professional-a-one-way-trip/. Accessed 31 March 2016.

Arcadis. (2015). *Global construction disputes report*. Available at: https://www.arcadis.com/en/united-kingdom/our-perspectives/construction-disputes-rise-in-value-over-60-percent-to51million/. Accessed 31 March 2016.

Baksi, C. (2012). Should doom merchants have gone to Specsavers? *The Law Society Gazette*, 6 January. Available at: http://www.lawgazette.co.uk/analysis/should-doom-merchants-have-gone-to-specsavers/63667.fullarticle. Accessed 31 March 2016.

Barnes, H. (undated). The 'Dark Side' of Going In-house. *BCG Search*. Available at: http://www.bcgsearch.com/article/60637/The-dark-Side-Of-Going-In-House/. Accessed 31 March 2016.

Bedlow, D. (2006). From zero to hero. *The Law Society Gazette*, 17 November. Available at: http://www.lawgazette.co.uk/analysis/from-zero-to-hero/2064.fullarticle. Accessed 31 March 2016.

Benedictus, L. (2013). Why did 1,701 people apply for just eight barista jobs? *Guardian*, 20 February. Available at: http://www.theguardian.com/lifeandstyle/2013/feb/20/1701-people-apply-for-eight-barista-jobs. Accessed 31 March 2016.

Blake, N. (2013). 9 Most Horrific Deaths in the *Jurassic Park* movies. *MTV*. Available at: http://www.mtv.com/news/2815374/jurassic-park-death-scenes/. Accessed 31 March 2016.

Bouchez, C. (2008). 23 Ways to Reduce Wrinkles. *WebMD*. Available at: http://www.webmd.com/beauty/wrinkles/23-ways-to-reduce-wrinkles?page=2. Accessed 31 March 2016.

Burkeman, O. (2010). Because you're worth it. *Guardian*, 20 November. Available at: http://www.theguardian.com/money/2010/nov/20/what-people-earn. Accessed 31 March 2016.

Cummins, T. (2010). The role of lawyers in contract management – Part II. *Commitment Matters*. Available at: http://commitmentmatters.com/2010/01/08/the-role-of-lawyers-in-contract-management-part-ii/. Accessed 31 March 2016.

David, T. (2011). Can lawyers learn to be happy? *Practical Lawyer, 57*(4), 29.

Gallup. (2015). *Honesty/Ethics in Professions.* Available at: http://www.gallup.com/poll/1654/honesty-ethics-professions.aspx. Accessed 31 March 2016.

Hilton, A. (2013). Lawyers are facing a tough task making a case for the survival of their profession. *Independent*, 11 May. Available at: http://www.independent.co.uk/news/business/comment/anthony-hilton-lawyers-are-facing-a-tough-task-making-a-case-for-the-survival-of-their-profession-8611980.html. Accessed 31 March 2016.

IPSOS MORI. (2016). Politicians are still trusted less than estate agents, journalists and bankers. *Ipsos MORI Veracity Index 2015: Trust in Professions.* Available at: https://www.ipsos-mori.com/researchpublications/researcharchive/3685/Politicians-are-still-trusted-less-than-estate-agents-journalists-and-bankers.aspx. Accessed 31 March 2016.

Jurassic Park. (1993). *Dir. Steven Spielberg.* USA: Universal Pictures.

Keynes, J. M. (1935). *The general theory of employment, interest and money.* London: Macmillan.

Leichter, M. (2013). Most States Saw Lawyer Surplus Grow from 2009 to 2011. *The American Law Daily*, May 14. Available at: http://www.americanlawyer.com/id=1202600046114. Accessed 31 March 2016.

Manch, S. G., & Shannon, M. P. (2006). *Maximizing law firm profitability: Hiring, training and developing.* New York: Law Journal Press.

Marquess, J. J. (1994). Legal audits and dishonest legal bills. *Hofstra Law Review, 22,* 3, Article 3. Available at: http://scholarlycommons.law.hofstra.edu/hlr/vol22/iss3/3. Accessed 31 March 2016.

Mauney, C. S. (undated). *The lawyers' epidemic: Depression, suicide and substance abuse.* Greenville, SC: Gallivan, White and Boyd. Available at: http://www.scbar.org/Portals/0/Outline%20for%20Lawyers'%20Epidemic.pdf. Accessed 31 March 2016.

Moore, G. E. (1965, April 19). Cramming more components onto integrated circuits. *Electronics*, 114–117. Available at: http://www.cs.utexas.edu/~fussell/courses/cs352h/papers/moore.pdf. Accessed 31 March 2016.

Roberts, T. (2015). Why are lawyers killing themselves? *Tom Speaks Out*, [blog], 31 July 2015. Available at: http://www.tomspeaksout.com/3/post/2015/07/why-are-lawyers-killing-themselves.html. Accessed 31 March 2016.

Shakespeare, W. (1591). *Henry VI, Part 2.*

Susskind, R., & Susskind, D. (2015). *The future of professions: How technology will transform the work of human experts.* Oxford: Oxford University Press.

Barbara Chomicka is a trusted advisor and international authority on project management and contract administration. She is a Board Director of the International Association for Contract and Commercial Management (IACCM) and Chair of the IACCM Construction and Engineering Community providing global leadership and promoting development of the global construction and engineering sector.

She exemplifies an approach to life as a project manager that everything that we face is a project—a collaborative enterprise requiring the right methods to resolve it. In her thought-provoking presentations, she promotes a 360-degree duty of care inside and outside of work.

Liquid Legal: Organization 4.0: Using Legal Competency for Building Fluid & Innovation-Driven Structures

Gerrit Mauch

Abstract

Innovation-driven organizations are characterized by their adaptability to the environment. A combination of flexible processes and stable social interactions with the environment enable the development of adaptability. The interaction of the product "labor" must be imagined beyond organizational boundaries and be adapted for the existing frameworks of the organization.

This calls for employees who act in a self-reflective way and who are willing to consider the daily context critically. Such employees monitor the product "labor", identifying degrees of freedom for their personal development, design options in their work performance and their personal responsibility of their conduct. Conversely, this means that personal reflexive qualities of employees are required to allow for the development of strong innovative organizations.

How can organizations enable the development of this type of person within their own ranks, and what can organizations do to set up a stable framework for work relationships despite of permanent critical observations?

1 Taylorism: Once a Brilliant Idea

To this day, organizations in developed countries are mostly characterized by production organization theories, aiming at the optimization of the value chain rather than its modification. Talk of innovation in organizations frequently turns out to be no more than an improvement of the value chain. The spirit of Taylorism is inherent in the most common management theories.

G. Mauch (✉)
RETENCON AG, Freystr. 4, 80802 München, Germany
e-mail: gerrit.mauch@retencon.de

© Springer International Publishing AG 2017
K. Jacob et al. (eds.), *Liquid Legal*, Management for Professionals,
DOI 10.1007/978-3-319-45868-7_11

All economic inefficiencies can be solved brilliantly by separating thinking (reserved for the management) and action, as well as by separating functionalities in production and services. The simplification of complicated structures seems to be the logical consequence of our perception of cause effect. Occurring side effects of the common management theories such as conflicts within departments, different rationalities within organizations, or relationships between superiors and employees are perceived as deficiencies of the acting person rather than a deficiency of the principle of Taylorism. The globalized, dynamic, networked progress breaks the value chain. For example, a search engine developer can suddenly become a car manufacturer, turn car manufacturers into suppliers, or even transform a car manufacturer into a software developer. Many organizations continue to look at last century's methods to figure out how to handle innovation in a positive way. Rituals and dogma of Taylorism and Fordism[1] in corporate governance satisfy managers' longing to resolve every problem by means of reduction. In an environment of changed conditions for decision making, where coalitions of interest become more complex and motivation changes all the time, such a way of thinking is the real culprit for blocking innovation.

1.1   The Future World Is VUCA[2]

Today top managers and their organizations act in environments in which information ceases to have any prognostic significance. The consequences are volatility, uncertainty, complexity and ambiguity: VUCA. In the end, it is all about two parameters: How much information about a particular situation is available, and to what extent can I estimate the consequences of my actions? In principle, this means giving volatile frameworks sufficient fluctuation buffers and giving uncertain situations a solid amount of information. Complex developments are counteracted by a combination of information and resources. Back in the beginning of the

---

[1] See http://www.humanecology.ch: **Taylorism and Fordism:** Frederick W. Taylor (1856–1915) was an American engineer who sketched a system of the scientific management which should entail a maximum in achievement by means of a working rationalization. It founded on empiric data which Taylor won in the course of time studies and motion studies in workers who worked according to his appraisal already fairly efficiently. Besides, every activity became in her smallest components disassembles and as a result examines each of these components how it could be explained best of all, i. e. with the slightest time involved. The principles culminate in the technical implementing of Ford image of line production.

[2] See Wikipedia: **VUCA** is an acronym used to describe or reflect on the volatility, uncertainty, complexity and ambiguity of general conditions and situations. The notion of VUCA was introduced by the U.S. Army War College to describe the more volatile, uncertain, complex and ambiguous multilateral world which resulted from the end of the Cold War. The common usage of the term VUCA began in the 1990s and derives from military vocabulary. It has been subsequently used in emerging ideas in strategic leadership that apply to wide range of organizations, including everything from for-profit corporations to education.

nineteenth century, even Clausewitz urged the military leader to explain complex situations in a simple way, but not to think in an easy way.

People who think about the future, such as philosophical essayist Nassim Taleb and his interpretation of epistemology, no longer apply the logic of value chain. Today, the evolutionary power of organizations supersedes process creation. Nassim Taleb is trying to figure out how the robust tayloristic system can lead to development of versatile, adaptable and thus resilient organizations. Taylor's attempt to control the dynamic of systems by creating a self-similar structure depicting the economic reality, is opposed by Taleb's model of evolutionary development. Taylor's idea copies seemingly essential points of economic reality, thus creating a self-similar copy of what we consider necessary. In contrast, Taleb attempts to establish an idea for the reorganization of rules, norms and principles which establish a framework, but do not claim to dominate all contingencies. The shape of a treetop is not necessarily as important as its environment which allows the tree to grow and bear fruit.

Once, a Bavarian forest farmer said to me: *"Only change what you are able to change."* [3]

The difference between Taylorism and the thinking of Nassim Taleb can be explained by means of a stone—its structure reminds us of rocks or even mountains. The benefit of such simplification is apparent. Complicated structures become transparent and manageable. There is a danger to succumb to misconceptions, if the management of such simplification is taken for granted. Due to self-similarity, attributes of mountains such as danger of avalanches, are eliminated. Such a fractal invites misconception and ignorance of seemingly irrelevant information. The stone displays a deceptive similarity to reality, however without the identity of the mountain. The increasing dynamic of markets unmasks Taylor's fractal.

Organizations exposed to the complexities and dynamics of megatrends, like humans who are exposed to forces of nature, can permanently resist development pressure, once they are able to develop self-similar systems from within. In Taleb's view, there is an evolutionary correlation, making biology and economics face similar challenges: both disciplines try to explain survival and innovation in an unpredictable world. The evolution resolves this by constant self-reflection about the available resources and the possibilities of the environment. Next to that, the system develops alternatives for the most different scenarios. For enterprises this means owning an idea, rather than the solution for the recombination of products and processes. A new culture of feedback and dialogue is the precondition for that.

Nassim Taleb appeals to organizations, asking them to rethink their visions and strategies. He calls on the companies to also think about the unthinkable and to develop skills and tools which allow to think in a frame of diversity. The aim is to be prepared for the unforeseeable. He calls this *antifragility.*[4] It is not about all-encompassing solution mechanics, but rather about the idea of facing the

---

[3] See Sepp Spann, http://www.cluster-forstholzbayern.de/
[4] Refer Taleb (2012), pp. 231–259.

environment in a reflexive manner. The forest farmer, quoted before, plants different kinds of fruit trees around his forest, knowing that parasites prefer special kinds of wood. Longer distances between individual trees increase the probability of birds catching the insects. In his view, fewer parasites mean a greater number of healthy trees, making the entire forest more resistant to changing adverse weather conditions. The amount of birds in the orchard are indicators for how well his system functions. In addition, he casually mentions the fruit's suitability to make Schnapps and jam as an attractive sideline of business for the family. In a sequentially operating system, the symptoms of pest infestation would have been combated with chemical pesticides. Initially, this would have worked, but would also have caused a negative effect on the entire ecosystem. Poisoned insects means fewer birds, fewer birds means less seeds in the forest, less seeds in the forest means less growth etc.

If the actions of a forest farmer secure survival in difficult situations, how can an organization benefit from this thought process? In relation to our economic behavior this would mean a transformation of tayloristic and fordistic social models into Taleb's world[5] to allow for the development of innovation-driven organizations, organizations that are at ease with technical issues of flawless performance. The majority of organizations are well organized for creating optimal conditions for production of goods and the provision of services. The lever for change lies within employees' behavior and can be shaped by the design of modern employment. Due to a lack of experience with a VUCA work environment, one can only speculate about the changed expectations with regard to employment and its future; it certainly won't be as linear as labor research has predicted in the 1990s of last century.[6]

1.2   Only Change, What You Are Able to Change

As consultants we observe the effect of a changing economic landscape on the creation of employment. If we look at employment, we put change in the context of *"open innovation"*. Rather than in a laboratory situation like those found in a traditional R&D department, which is more or less a closed laboratory situation, in open innovation, the process of "embodied knowledge" allows an exchange between the environment and the institution. This exchange allows the environment, such as a consumer but also software programs, to look behind the scenes of a company. The boundaries blur between inner and outer world. Does this mean that, to date, inside an organization these rules—rules of communication and interaction, interpretation and action—have been addressed in the context of open innovation dialogues? What are the circumstances in which organizations are able to change their own rules? Will they be able to determine the consumer regulations of an

---

[5]Refer Taleb (2010), pp. 85–99.
[6]Refer Robertson (2014).

organization in the future? Who will make this change and bring them in line with the company's interests? In our work, we discovered that this can only be the task of Legal, both at the present time and in the future. In order to ensure that legality is upheld Legal must transform from being the interpreter to becoming the creator of conditions required for new thinking. In labor law, Legal will no longer be the formal converter, but it will take on the role of the designer of formal working conditions—and that requires new thinking. Legal has to redefine its mission.

1.2.1 Theseus' Ship

The philosophical parable of Theseus[7] highlights a different aspect of change. The legend starts with Theseus' departure to kill the Minotaur. In the course of the odyssey, every plank of his ship is being replaced. It is subject to ongoing change. The ancient philosophers discussed whether the repaired ship was still identical with the original one and what impact this answer would have on Theseus' story. The original state at the beginning of the voyage ceased to exist, but the function and basic system still existed without any restrictions. I don't want to continue the argument, but it clarifies the factors for change and identity. This ideal, that stability presents the unchanged functionality and yet still permits change, presents three important aspects of transformation:

1. A temporal dimension—the transformation lasted the entire trip
2. A functional dimension—the ship remained a ship
3. A social dimension—the discourse on the meaning of travel and its effects

We will focus on number 3., in particular on the question: How does behavior change in relation to its context? How can plank by plank be exchanged, how can a system of self-empowerment develop without questioning the learned norm? It means that the modification of rules becomes the norm rather than the exception.[8] Philosophers discussed the factors time and functionality and the social question underlying change. Already back in the 1960s, Talcott Parsons und Niklas Luhmann tried getting to grips systemically with the transformation of the "structure mountain" into a stone, as described in the previous paragraph.

They were satisfied with the sociological role of the describing observer. Their intentions weren't to resolve anything, but rather than to help to understand the status of actions. They provided sorting instructions as in a puzzle: First, start with the pieces around the edges or with the sky. It became apparent that this these kind of hints can help clarify even complex pictures. However, this approach requires mainly time and social awareness. In his book *"Organisation for Complexity"*,[9] Niels Pflägling describes the ideas of sociology and merges them with the aspects of change. He refers to this as a social, functional and temporal gap (see footnote 3).

---

[7]See J.J. Abrams, S. & Dost - Das Schiff des Theseus, 2013.
[8]Refer Luhmann (1984).
[9]Refer Pflägling (2015), pp 66–67 u. 217–220.

The social gap appears when management decisions prioritize functional and temporal dimensions, negating the social process. Decisions and procedures are being accelerated, but excluding social interaction can lead to pressure resulting in anxiety. Learning processes are being blocked which can kill creativity and inventive spirit. Changes made under pressure can result in no more than successful reflexes, but they will never match the quality of sustainable inventions. The VW scandal following manipulation of car emissions is an example of what can happen when social gaps are not prevented. This means the risk of innovation does not lie in the risks of a functional environment, but in the social acts of actors. In the future, the focus of legal needs to align more to the consideration of social interaction and less to the formal processes that describe this interaction. However: How can we recognize the difference?

The Social Act

The *"social act"* [10] in organizations is defined by interaction with one another via communication, thereby creating relationships and identity. Personal flexibility and relationship structures are frequently regarded as rivals. This may also be the case for rigid and clear concepts—a circle remains a circle. However, this does not apply to relationships between companies and people or societies. Relationships can lose their power if they are being formalized rather than being based on trust.

A legal contract (i.e. an employment contract) may be a suitable instrument to close gaps in trust. However, it can turn into a boomerang if it becomes incomprehensible for the contractual partners, or if it creates the impression that the contract is more in favor of one of the contractual partners. Trust is created by a process of exchange of information and power. Thereby, relationship means sharing of information within a community. In Organizations that are deemed to be innovative we observe a different kind of exchange and collective awareness. In the past few years, our social relationships have transformed from a hierarchy of doers and executives to the desire for relationships at eye level. It is not surprising that an agile movement group in Germany named itself *"eye level"* [11] for a film project.

1.3 Labor Subjectification or How Privacy Enters Organizations

In the future, the transformation of employment must take place at eye level. This can be facilitated by flexible work design on the one hand, and variable working hours on the other hand. Both points are regulated by state regulations and employment agreements, today, and they are designed in the spirit of Taylor. Separation of doers and executives in the production process can be compared to the bargaining parties in the area of employment, who are trying to regulate the respective shares in the workforce by means of institutionalized negotiation rituals. In this case,

---

[10]Refer Luhmann (1984).

[11]See http://augenhoehe-wege.de.

collective action is understood to be a mandate for the representation of interests. Collective awareness of a seemingly new generation of employees is oriented towards a common feel-good atmosphere resembling the Communards—however, without of the commitment to change existing systems fundamentally. Collective behavior seems to aim at establishing a micro system within the system, rather than trying to change the system itself.[12]

So called "New Work" organizations prioritize teamwork, implementing the 4 'Cs[13]—critical thinking, communication, collaboration and creativity. The question of participation will certainly play a major role in the development of companies. The significance of existing mechanisms representing work-related macroeconomic issues will remain uncertain for the future. The individual employees want to determine their employment quality in discourse with others, rather than being represented by the solidarity idea of trade unions. In this case, autonomous work doesn't seem to have anything in common with classic neoliberal thinking, while both might look the same from the outside.[14]

This transformation can be explained by pluralization and individualization of structures in household and family. When it comes to the development of the ego, mankind has just started to emancipate him or herself during the last centuries, starting with renaissance and enlightenment. Additional factors are the decline of Ford's social model and the rapidly progressing digitization of our environment. The latter has led to the (practically unnoticed) removal of boundaries between private life and work. The tendency towards more flexible work environments and the variable usage of time relating to work performance lead to subjectification of employment.

Looking at *"crowd–intelligence"* as a product designer, we realize that crowd intelligence intuitively performs this role in relation to employment, too. Consumers naturally exercise their rights to participate in product design; equally, employees want to participate in the world of employment personally and creatively, rather than being represented by unions. The catchword *"democratic enterprise"* haunts the workforce of today's organizations that are deemed to be particularly innovative. It is often overlooked that in those innovative organizations the traditional formalized functions of regulated participation which are part of our democratic system are non-existent. Andrea Nahles, German Minister for Employment, once cuttingly commented: *"works council over table tennis"*; but the need for table tennis seems to win. The possibility of satisfying personal needs through employment increases expectations in personified employment offers. The 180-degree-turn of the labor market, induced by demographics and prosperity of the economy (e.g. Germany), fueled to raise expectations. This unveils a paradox. The wealth of offers increases the employee's worry of making the wrong career choice. Neuroscience explains this by means of evolution. Ancestors who ran away

---

[12] According Brühl and Pollozek (2015).

[13] According Farooq and Carroll (2007); NEA (2010).

[14] Refer Pflägling (2015).

when they heard rustling in the bush survived—and thus passed on their genes—, not those whose curiosity made them run into the bush.[15]

Simultaneously, there is a desire for individuality and the need to have one's decision made by someone else. There is also a desire for stability for the own life i.e. salary on the one hand and a maximum of self-development on the other hand. The first criterion, applicants look at in organizations, is their robustness, rather than their innovative capability in global economy. This behavior of employees possibly determines the strength of the innovation overall. It also means that the risk of innovation does not lie in the perceived risk from the functional environment, but in the consequences from social acts, as defined above. In the future, legal needs to focus on aligning to the considerations of social interaction and less on the formal processes that describe this interaction.

Matthias Horx has created the term *"flexurity"*,[16] explaining the alternation between stability and flexibility. Mastering both elements is a challenge for modern HR departments. Balancing subjectification and individualization of personnel management with securing collective accomplishments for the entire staff. At this point there is a need for a "creator" who understands that the element of security can only form basic conditions. Only the power of an institutional function can enable such a transformation process in organizations. Future oriented organizations need a switchboard that understands the different needs of people and can couple them with the specific necessities of one's own enterprise to design the labor framework required.

It can be compared to the cultivating influence of the forest farmer, who generates income from a plot of mountain forest. If cultivation did not take place, we would face a jungle which is insignificant for the economy. Nowadays, top management is in the role of the forest farmer. Employment lawyers are in higher demand than ever to trigger these processes and guide the whole management team. Though, seemingly paradox, outsiders frequently experience legislation as a jungle with pitfalls, or they have the impression that lawyers prefer sitting between two chairs, or brooding over legislative texts. However, as soon as the fog of blurred perception has lifted, the potential of creative power of labor and social legislation for the organization become apparent, and thus the potential creative power of the designing lawyer.

Let us use the picture of a tetris-game to explain the challenge for a designing function. At the current level, falling shapes had to be fitted into a particular pattern. Successful execution means good result. Success depends on speedy recognition of individual patterns and of matching the parts with the correct positions. Translated into our process thinking this means that on one level the same pieces are recurring and we optimize the time to move these. Yet, our reality is changing, we seem to have mastered a new level. Now, pieces which are unknown to us, are descending more dynamically. Just as the tetris player trains his spacial thinking and improves

---

[15]Refer Spörer and Prieß (2013), pp. 89–94.
[16]Refer Horx (2005), pp. 52–82.

his handling in order to master the next levels, Legal will have to understand rules, norms and principles as stable social interactions, rather than corporate risk minimization.

The player must place seven different blocks in a rectangle, so Legal can use seven principles for change. The possibility to rotate the blocks leads to an almost infinite range of alternative solutions. Therefore Legal can use this concept of seven principles for change. The leeway predetermined by Legal reflects the possible twists in the game. So Legal *must* have an idea for the recombination of norms and principles into new rules. The Seven Principles for providing innovations driven structures (in support of Hanjo Gergs[17]) are:

1. Know thyself—willingness for self-reflection of management
2. Communication and networking—dialogue leads to change
3. Allow diversity and paradoxes—learn to love contradictions
4. Doubts and forget—get rid of old ideas, to separate the known and proven
5. Explore and experiment—develop awareness and curiosity
6. Establish error and feedback culture—learn from mistakes and successes
7. Perseverance and thinking in systems—thinking in social action

[18]We distinguish the application of the seven principles on (i) the role and (ii) the task of labor law. In the short run, the main tasks and processes of HR will remain unchanged, despite of progressing digitalization and advancing technology; they will be optimized and secured in the traditional way. However, beyond that modern personnel management must embrace the transformation of organization in terms of change ability, demography, employer brand, leadership and corporate culture. These are the four chances and challenges with their HR must handle.

Transformation of organizations will need to happen by means of adopting new teaching and learning methods, which should follow Maria Montessori's principles of self-empowerment: *"Help me to do it by myself."* Therefore, time and result must be separated in the learning process; for the teaching process it means, asking questions rather than teaching solutions. This also entails dissolving the surreptitious tunnel vision towards the younger generations.

The German comedy *"we are the new generation"*[19] is about a commune of a group of elderly people that deal with the generation conflict, an issue which also professional organizations will have to face in the future. It is equally important to consider how the majority of staff can work towards a retirement age of 70 years whilst maintaining the company's performance.

---

[17]Refer Gergs (2016).
[18]Refer Hedderich (2011).
[19]See http://www.imdb.com/title/tt3777462/

We must distinguish between the brand product of a company and the product job of an organization which has to be sold in a jobseeker's market. This approach is more radical than depictions of current employer branding strategies.

The final transformation task concerns the continuing development of corporate culture; since the latter can only be considered retrospectively, leadership models and management development according to Taleb have to be understood as an evolution and thus must be constantly re-developed.

Today, we can only speculate about the changed expectations of future employment, since there is no linear development of employment that can be encountered. Feeling involved in tasks and responsibilities is the first indicator for staff identification with their organizations and their willingness to tackle change. The Matthias Horx Future Institute summarizes poignantly: The reevaluation of community will have an impact on organizations. At all levels, proven command structures are wobbling in the face of a workforce growing with community orientation, a crowd offering diverse innovations, and leadership trainees who climb the career ladder with entirely different principles.[20]

The peer-to-peer interaction is crucial for leaders who at most had to deal with management cybernetics. The community votes and negotiates the role and task, just the way old-school unions were dreaming about once—but it is an entirely different method. The acquisition of role and task presumably stems from an immense self-confidence, a kind of technical superiority of ensuing generations. Revolt of the cobblestones, the sharp distinction between capital and drudgery, the idea of dialogue creeps into our nation's organizations in its new disguise, the web. This kind of exchange still lacks many attributes of a reflexive discourse, but it shows effect. Corporate management needs to be convinced not to use legislation or contracts to shift risks onto someone else, but to understand legislation and contracts as the tools for stability, thus allowing for growth. Nowadays, standardized work specifications and availability of workforce, restrictions in decision making and a lack of room to maneuver don't seem to promote innovation any more.

The work requirements are leaning towards indirect control and self-organization. This has massive feedback effects on corporate culture. Organizations opting for more community have to be willing to learn. New forms of collaboration require new openness and transparency, the functional structure is replaced by "We". Company internal silos don't seem to be necessary anymore.

The systemic approach of observing, understanding and changing has been developed into deciding, development of ideas and trying out. This approach has ceased to be in the hands of a privileged person; now is the time to claim for the dialogue of a "We-collective".[21]

---

[20]See Horx (2015).

[21]According Brühl and Pollozek (2015).

1.3.1 Next Practice by a French Hotel Company

Creating a dialogue space to allow for change has already been discovered by two smart Frenchmen who founded a European hotel chain at the end of the 1960s of last century.

Their service idea was built on the idea of *"new work"*.[22] I take this example deliberately to illustrate that the new features do not depend on a technical innovation, but rather on the idea behind it. I agree with the thesis which has been developed at the DGFP Lab 2014: Sharing responsibility and having trust. Tomorrow's successful employee thinks "We". He or she actively demands other opinions, uses them and faces others respectfully, expecting the same fundamental understanding from others. How did the founders of the hotel chain solve this thesis? Rather than copying existing hotel concepts, they wanted to bring the industrial revolution into the hotel business.

They realized during the development phase that they could not be part of the existing hospitality business in 1969 which justified itself by means of its own norms and rules. Forty years ago, a bathroom as a part of the hotel room, good traffic links or a swimming pool, was still a privilege seen only in 5 star hotels. At the time, in hospitality, it was unthinkable to offer these services for a large number of travelers. The two founders of a hotel chain covered the existing concepts and quickly realized that the standardization of processes and the flexibility of service provided the key to a profitable hotel brand. They *exchanged the planks of the ship*, without compromising its functionality in the process. Their credo: *"Faire la course en tête"—lead the field from the front*[23] could only be realized if they were more innovative and faster than their competitors.

In their view, they were able to be faster and more innovative if they were questioning themselves and, above all, if they gave employees a chance to discuss and question their system. Soon, they would learn that employees may have good ideas, but they were lacking the courage to discuss these. This allowed for the creation of company values right at the start of a new organization.

These values were considered the entry ticket into a protected dialogue space. Anyone could retire into this space who was able to explain their actions and behavior conclusively with a value. In that case, there wasn't going to be a sanction. One of the founders is said to have uttered: *"Values make sense only if they are useless"*,[24] alluding to the sword of political games in organizations. This danger exists if from values undefined rules originate. Singles or parts of the organization can abuse values thus for own interests. Five of the values that had been introduced didn't carry explanations of what the value canon meant, but consciously explained what wasn't intended. Long word loops were omitted, in order to avoid taking away employees' orientation.

---

[22]See DGFB Lab 2014 Thesenpapier, Mitreden, Mitdenken, Mitgestalten im Unternehmen von morgen!

[23]Refer to Virginie Luc (1999).

[24]Refer to Accor reaching for the impossible 1967–2007, 2007.

This construction was tested during a discussion of company goals, which showed conflicts just like the magic square of business studies. The transparency and openness in which value conflicts are addressed in the hospitality business is unique, up to today.

Since then, the company has not formulated many rules regarding service delivery to the guest. These five values underpin the spirit and behavior towards guests. Not every employee or manager may understand this, but the ability for innovation has been imprinted in the company's DNA. A pattern which can be described retrospectively as culture. The Latin stem for *"colere"* means "to build, to order or to care for/nurture". This term became the center of discourse of culture in society and economy during the last 200 years. It now describes a certain moral behavior in comparison to an uncontrolled and random approach. The farmer tending his fields was considered uncultured since he didn't take the time to reflect his moral ideals and to cultivate them. This is at the center of the task which is presented to the legal function in the organization. Both, thinking about how the world might perceive the company's actions, and determining what is economically feasible touches moral boundaries.

1.4 Correlation of Task, Relation and Mind Model

As already described role and task create workplace identity and so does job functionality. Together with the company's big picture of business it will become the deeper meaning of employment. The supporting principle is each individual's contribution to act: are my actions related to the company's success, are they useful in relation to customer value and do they make sense in the overall picture of the organization. Management leaders never get tired of talking about the "big picture"—but they do not talk about the frame of work identity. In consulting, we explain the term "identity" as an act of social construction: oneself or another person is grasped in a web of meaning. The quest for identity has a universal and a cultural-specific dimension. It is always about producing a correlation between subjective "inside" and social "outside", i.e. the production of an individual social orientation.

In current management theories, results from roles and tasks, in combination with the company's vision, provide a practical and exemplary work environment. Is this really the case? Employee satisfaction is understood in terms of the usual economic theories and the respective measuring methods (e.g. morale of the team), as the exchange of a caring framework in turn for the performance of the individual. In the discussion about the design of the working environment of the future, the above is subsumed under the term *"work life balance"*. But in the context of the New Work movement, private life and working life become unified. It is called "work life romance", as for example the Audi AG presents itself on the company's homepage with the statement: Some call it work, we call it passion!

In our work, we describe the potential built by the mental model of identity, by means of a matrix. We limit the space of identity, resulting in four directions from which employment may stem, similar to those of a compass. Employee and organization are on opposing sides of one axis, and *"attractors and repellors"*[25] on opposing sides of the other axis. This compass doesn't dissolve the demand for change, but it shows where employees and company are located in its dynamics. Innovative organizations emerge by the observing, understanding and locating of social actions within the framework of mental models. This means that the inter-action between the macro level (organization), the meso level (potency of attractor & repellor) and the micro-level are (the individual) analyzed and understood. The mental model is developed from evaluating task and role based on motives and norms.[26] Nature has so far been a good example for change. We understand very little about a tree's growth and we have equally little control over the development of companies. However, companies can deal with the ecosystem by recognizing it as both, growth and stagnation processes. An organization should concentrate on those conditions they can change. We introduced in our consultation the term "reflexivity". For us, this means revising rules, principles and practices.

Taking a closer look at the organizational level and at individual motives, we can see three modes of action on each side regarding the factor work. On the organi-zation side there are: vision, structure and culture. These mechanisms form a macro-level. On the individual's side, the macro level meets the micro, i.e. the employee's modes of "should", "can", and "want". Thus, the meso level is the intermediate identity. In the research of complexity, the force that allows for a stable pattern in a dynamic system is called *"the Attractor"*. Attractors are community-building patterns, such as rituals or principles. An attractor can bring stability to a world out of order. In an experiment with flashing bulbs this can be shown. The light bulbs are not connected in this experiment but after a certain time a solid flashing pattern forms in all lamps. It acts as if the bulbs have an awareness. This physical process is geared towards certain bulbs (*"the Attractor"*). The attractors cannot be determined in advance, it is impossible to predict what patterns are triggered. However, statements can be made, regarding which actions destabilize the pattern. In a dynamic or social system, a number of employees moves towards a number of states or relationships. Each social interaction in a group tends towards this in the course of the enterprise development pattern. The force that dissolves the pattern, is known as *"The Repellor"*, as it has a repelling effect.

In 4.0 organizations both poles seem to contract and de-contract like a beating heart, due to blurred boundaries between work and life. On the side of the individual there is more usage of subjective potentials and resources. The transformation of work capital into work effort gradually ceases to be the obligation of an organizations' control systems, it rather becomes the actor's obligation. The actor doesn't strive for renewal of existing legislation; instead, he needs a work life tailored to his personal circumstances in life. The dynamics of this system allow for the stability of these relationships. The resulting status will then remain near this

---

[25]Refer Knapp (2013), pp. 134–144.
[26]Refer Hartman (1967).

attractor. An attractor then appears to be interpretable culture. Colloquially, the term "pattern" of the organization is used. Relationships are a state towards which systems move.[27]

1.4.1 Subjectification of Work and Meaning for the Collective

On the meta-level, two developments indicate a rough direction. The creation of certain types of employment, such as permanent freelancers, or the distinction of structure, such as age, qualification etc. Often, this is presented as something new, but upon closer examination it becomes clear that Tayloristic employment organizations constitute our economy's backbone; there is still sufficient flexibility and potential for optimization to carry the transformation of our society. The increasing disintegration of the value chain leads to virtual workforce focusing on one product or service relationship; however, they cease to be on-site due to their special and functional disintegration.[28]

Contrary to predictions of work sociologists, it is not a social void like Pflägings definition of systems, rather it seems like Theseus ship: some planks must be replaced to ensure the functionality of work. When the old "planks" have been filled, this leads to a renewal of the identity of work.

Consider the example of the Sparda Bank in Munich. The business model of banking got under pressure, given low interest rate periods and loan comparison internet portals. The future of the bank is uncertain, however, the organization has still a model for the near future. In recent years, the bank has begun to offer new jobs which not only fulfilled the role and responsibilities of a bank employee, but it also recruited people who have special skills in addition to their experience as an employee of the bank. The combination of the special skills of employees and the existing infrastructure of the company are being used by the organization for its own transformation process. Today the bank develops consulting teams that handle different questions put forward by small and medium-sized enterprises. The task of HR was to lead the change in the employee selection procedure, the change in the payment scheme and towards a renewed personnel development. Legal had to develop contracts for new positions and performance schemes that are synchronized with the existing contracts. The intervention had to capture the individual expectations of the organization by means of rules and regulations. Changes in private life and societal consequences of digitization lead to transformation of the work environment.[29]

The example illustrates how employment can change. Oriented to potential and interaction, work can change the subjective quality of professional actions. It develops a new idea of the working identity. Sparda remains the provider of a frame for a co-op commercial model. The resolution of existing working time structures, the significance of life-long learning and technological progress will

---

[27]Refer Knapp (2013), pp. 134–144.

[28]According ISF Munich Nick Kratzer (2003).

[29]Refer Kötter et al. (2015).

accelerate the change of the working identity even further. The Legal function becomes the intermediary of the transformation.

Movements such as the grassroots community seem to take control of the executive's mandate, in order to soften legal requirements of employment law or even to avoid them entirely. It remains to be seen whether subjectification and flexibilization contribute to the development of work quality. How can there be a new and fair distribution of existing risks for the organization under the aspect of subjectification of labor? The transformation of work will lead to modified work environments and new job profiles, or it might even lead to their dissolution. At first glance, companies that introduce a flexible and individual approach in designing work environments seem to be more innovative and thus able to withstand a dynamic environment better. Legal has to keep an eye on both tendencies and be prepared to stop risk regulation by writing down every eventuality; instead, Legal should assume the mandate and foster the ability to actively create room for flexibility and to manage the risk associated with it.

Legal will thereby facilitate the continuous development and marketing of the product labor; Legal will co-create the organization's attractiveness and will thus contribute to its survival, similar to the forces of evolution.

1.5   How Companies Organize Their Own Transformation

I would like to outline this by looking at the practice of social activity and transformation in companies, rather than as a theory in social science.

Imagine yourself as hunter who suddenly sets his sight on the silhouette of a duck. If you aim at the duck, you won't hit it. The bang of your gun would scare the duck away before the bullet could reach it. A hunter is familiar with this problem. He has to fire at a fictive trajectory of the duck. Does this mean that innovation is hitting a fiction? What distinguishes innovative companies? A high degree of intuitive adaptability and a hunter's experience. How can individual skills turn into corporate goals? How can companies motivate employees to chase after a fiction which above all depends on factors that cannot be influenced?

Our work environments will be redesigned and this means transformation. HR will have to stop their reactive role of offering employment and will instead have to design a product which is both stable and can leave room for development, using social and labor legislation. HR does not yet use the "New Works" platform much, due to a fatal miscalculation of demographics or due to old prejudices regarding the competency of HR. Based on our consulting experience in employee loyalty projects, we would say today, that the creation of an interrelationship via individual development and security is the strategic key to corporate innovation. An innovative enterprise culture must ensure development of the individual—and must unite collectives of individuals at the same time into a comprehensive "We". Professional life and personal life must melt. The integration of a future professional life requires a new mindset, a new mental model allow the innovative organizational models to work and to foster free self-development within a stable "We-context".

As specified above, HR has seven levers at its disposal to create such an interrelationship. To set the seven levers well, effective managers (HR, Legal etc.) must have understood the correlations of social acts and gaps on the macro, meso and micro level. An example of misunderstanding, in history, is the production line process of Ford: the assembly-line production with a new separation of tasks and activities. The time saved lead to the afore-mentioned social gaps. The attempt to fill these gaps with money was effective in the short run, but it led to a wage spiral in the long run, rather than to the identification with the Ford brand. This means the employee's identification with the company can be regulated via work tasks. If tasks are interchangeable or standardized, as in production or service, it doesn't matter where or in which organization it is performed. Ford's understanding has evolved to now appreciating the connection between loyalty and work task. Today, in production, there is teamwork—a backwards roll to Fordism. The application of multiple skills and the resulting increase in responsibility in production is supposed to lead to stronger identification with the task. Employees will not only want to execute sensible activities, but they will also want to determine these in the future. The catchwords *"Sociocratie"* or *"Holocratie"* develop into trends in the organizational theory of tomorrow. The director of an IT service organization once explained the following to me: *"I actually don't care how other people work. It was just important to me that I didn't want to work like this."*

HR and its sovereignty in the world of employment transforms into a being the designer aided by instruments of legislation. This means for HR to leave behind a sequential view of its organization and to reorient itself. If the approach of disruptive innovation is taken seriously, the newly formed labor market offers vast opportunities for changing one's job profile. How can HR lead this transformation? The challenge of a fluid network economy lies in defining new working time models and places, because in times of the "knowledge society", creativity cannot be tied anymore to the models of optimization related to production standards. As places to work become more and more adaptable, the creation of the firm working sphere also has a new relevance. This is not only a question of designers, but it is just as relevant for the juridical frame. The future staff of a "next" professional life and innovation culture wants to work and be led differently. Enterprises must appeal to new motives, to a changed thinking about achievement. Classical organizational structures and career paths disappear from new and adaptable working models. To be armed for the huge complexity that comes with such a development, enterprises must raise their own complexity. The new communication patterns and employer-to-employee relationships require a modus operandi of variety and diversity. The mindset of the future workforce is not hardcoded to a given identity from a role or a job or to fixed expectations, but it relates to the legitimacies of a network economy. At the same time, this has to be compatible with the self-relation of the employees.

Employment law and its proponents—mainly in HR—seem to oppose the degrees of freedom, of a dynamic development by means of an array of principles almost as solid as concrete. This is where the discussion about too much bureaucracy frequently begins; it is sometimes used to dissolve a fight for rights of employees. I believe this is the wrong approach. It is not a question of having too many laws, but of whether we are prepared to view our guidelines and regulations as a system of repression or as a buffet of design opportunities. Well, I speak with the naivety of a non-lawyer and I am surrounded by a cloud of ignorance when it comes to all kinds of risks. I am also wishing for someone at my side who evaluates the risk of my environment and who excludes every risk innate to innovations, a risk relating to employees' behavior. Leaders who hide behind the line of legal counsels lack courage. In the future, leaders will have to stand in front of that line and decide for themselves whether employment contracts have 20 pages or maybe just 2.

HR and employment lawyers will have to decide how to coach leaders to enable them to distinguish between necessities of regulations and scope for innovation. Leadership must not withdraw from compliance rules and their application. Freeing leaders from their straight jacket of perfection and their superman role may enable this. Moreover, it must be possible to control different sides of power constellations such as influence, reputation and compliance. Leaders were drilled to have their staff on board. Temporarily, this became dictum in every management meeting. There was a perception that the right and legally correct information sufficed to change the acting people.

Organizations are structured by rules—rules of communication and interaction, of interpretation and action.[30] In the future, HR and employment law staff will have to ask themselves how organizations can change their rules. Is there such a thing as a rule for modification and evolution?[31] Up to the 1990s, sociology and business science observed the transformation of employment in organizations from the point of view of organizational rationalization strategies in the capitalist society. On the side of economics, the term "Change Management" (see Levin's phase model) entered organizations. It seems that only a minority of consultants or leaders was given the key to change and only they were able to initiate change. The term empowerment meant giving the individual tasks but without giving them responsibility, as well. Former generations tried to fight for their rights to participate in work outside entrance gates of companies.

A team of young entrepreneurs like Larry Page, Sergey Brin and Mark Zuckerberg introduced a new understanding of power and responsibility, first related to their own role and then also with a view to the teams in their start-up companies. Their approach hasn't changed as they became the multimillionaire CEO, and as the company exploded in terms of size. Such patterns contradict the thesis that company development depends on the size of staff or on sequential planning of processes. The attitude of a framework-giving institution determines whether companies are innovative or not. Whether it has democratic legitimation or follows a capitalist founder motive is not relevant for the transformation of employment. It does become critical though, that the moral perception of rules is

---

[30]Refer Moldaschel (2006).
[31]Refer Moldaschel (2006).

	Production organization	Transformation organization
Function	Routine tasks: balance or eliminate disturbances	Analysis of disturbances to allow for transformation of regulations
Criteria	Effectiveness and efficiency of the operational target tracking	Creation of transformation willingness and ability
Typical instances	R&D, Production, Personnel, Controlling, Marketing	Organization development, in-house consulting, project management, coaching, think tanks

Fig. 1 Difference between production and change organisation. Adapted from M. Moldaschel

trumped by the chance of renewal. The moral use of power in organizations will be the determining factor.

The crucial question for the development of employment will be: how can a newly understood power of collective decision making replace the existing idea of production process improvement, thereby leading to a change in employment culture? Ulf Brandes, one of the "New Work" drivers, writes in his book "Management Y": new innovation approaches such as "Design Thinking" comprise methods and tools as well as employment-cultural recommendations.[32] Success and innovation don't depend on regulations; the design of rules which guide the interaction between the world in front of and the world behind the façade of companies. In his opinion it is a question of the distribution of and participation in decision making power.

The change of perspective on the employers' side can be supported by distinguishing organizational regulations as to whether they are (i) primarily part of operational tasks or (ii) their permanent evaluation and adaptation. Manfred Moldaschl picks up on that in his approach of institutional reflexivity; however, his distinction between a production organization and a transformation organization is portrayed in an ideal-typical way (Fig. 1).[33]

Can Legal and its principles of order help recreate a seemingly lost stability and tranquility? The natural distance between a term such as innovation and a collection of principles such as legal texts might explain why not many people see a connection. We do see a connection of innovation and Legal for the future, because for us Legal will be a navigation aid. In fact, innovation and Legal must meet on a new surface, which acts as catalyzer. On the level of employment, which creates stable relations through task and role in a company. On the level of organization, in order to build new frames of learning and change. It takes more than job description and a salary. In fact, the job itself must be considered a product, which has to prove itself in a tough market.

---

[32]Refer Ulf Brandes (2015), pp. 41–59.
[33]Refer Faust et al. (2005), pp. 355–382.

2   Conclusion, Liquid Legal Can Only Develop If Theodor Storm's Statement Is Taken Seriously: *"Authority as well as trust can't be rocked more than by a feeling of being treated unjustly."*[34]

There is an increasing need for self-empowerment and continuing self-transformation, not just in terms of employee behavior, but also for organizations. This is a common theme in the theory of modernization and organization. Legal is in the unique position to provide institutional observation criteria which allow for determining the extent and the quality of change. Equally, Legal can accelerate or block the dynamics of change by how well and creative it adapts, develops and applies functional best practices enabling adherence to rules and norms. In fluid organizations, this task becomes an innovation task, if the content of norms, rules or principles is not just evaluated by their flat content, but above all by a reflexive process in the context of the organization, the product "job" and the employees' subjective expectations of teamwork.

In the future, jobs will cease to be the focus of organizations in favor of the individual in his or her occupation; any organization getting to grips with that will become anti-fragile and will develop a new working and learning culture. A culture based on the exchange of knowledge and with the inherent power that comes from relationships on eye level. A culture in which the principles are made clear, in which transparency prevents hidden agendas and in which a participation of all, regardless of their abilities within a function. No potentials or contribution will be separated from the development of a company.

Liquid Legal Context
By Dr. Dierk Schindler, Kai Jacob and Dr. Roger Strathausen

Mauch reminds of a fundamental role for legal in the transformation of the future working environment, which will be defined by VUCA: volatility, uncertainty, complexity and ambiguity. Success of organizations will depend on their adaptability. There needs to be a constant recombination of product and processes. Thus, the traditional security for individuals of a static correlation of their work to *the* product will fade.

Instead, open innovation and the modification of the rules that govern a working relationship will be the norm—not the exception. What does this mean for the employment lawyer? Mauch calls upon the role of legal in the future of employment as one that changes from an interpreter of regulations around current conditions to becoming the creator of them. Horx' theory around "flexury", the alternation between stability and flexibility comes to mind.

(continued)

---

[34]Theodor Storm an Dorothea Jensen, April 1866.

Mauch's broad thinking around the future workplace and its DNA creates correlations to Tumasjan and Welpe describing the settings of a co-creative enterprise—indeed a joint task of HR and legal, or as Mauch puts it: *"HR in the world of employment transforms into a designer aided by instruments of legislation."* And Legal must step up as the co-creator.

References

Abrams, J. J., & Dost, D. (2013). *Ship of Theseus*. Amsterdam: Mullhollands Books.
Brühl, K., & Pollozek, S. (2015). *Die neue Wir Kultur*. Frankfurt: Zukunftsinstitut.
DGFB Lab 2014 Thesenpapier. Mitreden, Mitdenken, Mitgestalten im Unternehmen von morgen!
Farooq, U., & Carroll, J. M. (2007). Supporting creativity with awareness in distributed collaboration.
Faust, M., Funder, M., & Moldaschl, M. (2005). *Die "Organisation" der Arbeit* (pp. 355–382). München.
Gergs, H.-J. (2016). *Die Kunst der kontinuierichen Selbsterneuerung*, 1. Auflage (pp. 52–144). Weinheim: Beltz Verlag.
Hartman, R. S. (1967). *The structure of value: Foundations of scientific axiology*.
Hedderich, I. (2011). *Einführung in die Montessori Pädagogik*. Reinhardt Ernst.
Horx, M. (2005). *Wie wir leben werden* (pp. 52–82). Frankfurt: Campus.
Horx, M. (2015). *5 Thesen zur Zukunft von Arbeit*. Frankfurt: Zukunftsinstitut 9/2015
ISF Munich Nick Kratzer. (2003). *Flexibilisierung und Subjektivierung von Arbeit*. München.
Knapp, N. (2013). *Kompass neues Denken*. Hamburg: rororo.
Kötter, R., Kursawe, M., Schöning, P., & Klingenberg, M. (2015). *Design your life*. Campus.
Luc, V. (1999). *Never take no for an answer*. Paris: Édittions Albin Michel.
Luhmann, N. (1984). *Soziale Systeme. Grundriß einer allgemeinen Theorie*. Frankfurt am Main: Suhrkamp.
Moldaschel, M. (2006). *Institutionelle Reflexivität*. Chemnitz.
NEA. (2010). Preparing 21st Century Students for a Global Society
Pflägling, N. (2015). *Komplexithoden* (3rd ed., pp. 67–68 & 217–221). München, Redline.
Robertson, B. J. (2014). Hologracy—The new management system for a rapidly changing world, 2014—Part one
Spörer, S., & Prieß, A. (2013). *Führen mit dem Omega Prinzip* (pp. 89–94). Haufe.
Taleb, N. N. (2010). *The black Swan* (6th ed.). München: DTV Verlag.
Taleb, N. N. (2012). *Antifragile—Things that gain from disorder* (3rd ed., pp. 231–259). München.
Ulf Brandes. (2015). *Management Y* (pp. 41–59). Campus.

List of Websites

www.augenhoehe-wege.de
www.imdb.com/title/tt3777462/
www.cluster-forstholzbayern.de
www.zukunftsinstitut.de/artikel/die-neue-wir-kultur/

Gerrit Mauch   The sociologist is Chief Academic Officer and consultant to the RETENCON AG in Munich. The company advises organizations on matters of employee engagement and loyalty. One of his special areas of interests is the transformation of enterprises with the help of a new learning and teaching culture. As an experienced human resources manager, he also accompanied senior ranks in organizations on matters of HR development. Mauch is a multiple award winner as a coach and training specialist. His awards include the "Initiativpreis Fort- und Weiterbildung" of the DIHK (2004), the "Chief Learning Officer-Award" of the trade magazine "Wirtschaft & Weiterbildung" and the "International German Training Award in Gold and Silver".

Change Management for Lawyers: What Legal Management Can Learn from Business Management

Arne Byberg

Abstract

The market for legal services is undergoing radical change which also impacts in-house legal departments. A number of chapters in this book address change that is already ongoing or imminent for legal departments, but how do you best go about managing this change? Lawyers are notoriously skeptical when it comes to change, and this is true for both in-house lawyers and their private practice peers. Practically no law school teaches change management, so most lawyers in management roles have only the management training offered by their respective corporations as basis for managing change in their legal departments—and many struggle with change. The most career-defining questions for many lawyer managers are simply: "Will the change I'm planning succeed? Can I overcome the inherent resistance to change among my lawyers? What can I do to improve the likelihood of successful change?" Fortunately, change management theory and experience exist which can be leveraged, and this chapter will help you estimate the likelihood of success for your change project—before you get in too deep.

1   Introduction to the Topic

"Change management for lawyers"—it may sound like a contradiction in terms. Lawyers are notoriously skeptical about change and, while there are honorable exceptions, my experience is that the general public is more right than wrong when thinking of the legal community as change-resistant. My favorite quote to this point is a Danish Supreme Court Judge allegedly having stated that he was resisting all

A. Byberg (✉)
EVRY, Inkognitogata 9, 0258 Oslo, Norway
e-mail: enra@arnebyberg.com

© Springer International Publishing AG 2017
K. Jacob et al. (eds.), *Liquid Legal*, Management for Professionals,
DOI 10.1007/978-3-319-45868-7_12

change—including change for the better! I cannot vouch for the veracity of the anecdote, but even if it is not true, it could be. My experience is that most people engaging with lawyer communities have a couple of examples in the same direction, but rarely as dogmatic.

Exactly why lawyers are perceived as change skeptics I would not really know, and it probably is more of a social anthropology study for someone to consider. But the commercial reality for the manager of lawyers and legal teams—who usually is a lawyer, as well—is change pressures coming from all directions, at an increasing pace. More often than not, the change pressures on legal teams simply reflect increasing market pressures on their clients. As the clients experience innovation and efficiency pressures, they expect their legal advisors to work faster, better and more efficiently as well. And rightfully so, in my opinion. The entire legal industry, in-house as well as private practice, are dealing with a new paradigm where legal services are perceived as exactly that—services. The notion of legal advice being some kind of "dark art", too complex for commercial scrutiny, is fading fast. The market demands operationally efficient legal services and we start seeing legal services becoming increasingly operationalized like Finance, HR and IT services. We see legal services getting segmented into the classic, bespoke "high-end" or "complex" legal services dominated by higher cost law firms, and new areas of "low-end" or "commoditizable" legal services where the key is critical mass and new players are challenging the classic law firms with innovative delivery and cost models. In my opinion, it is more than overdue to start thinking about legal services in more classic Gartner Group terms of services simply being a factor of "people, processes and technology". In fact, the classic legal industry has focused nearly exclusively on the people element and not much on process and technology at all. When I see legal teams struggling with change management I often find the main perceived challenge being cost or resource scarcity, while the real challenge is need for better utilization (or even introduction!) of process and technology in teams that traditionally focused almost exclusively on people. In business terms, the legal community has been "throwing people at the problem" for too long. Getting the mix right will be a critical success factor for the lawyer managers going forward, and while every team works on finding out which mix is optimal for them and their clients, I am convinced this is an area with continued need for change management strategies and execution for years to come.

2 Change Management Basics

Change Management is a huge topic by itself, and I am not going to spend much time on the basics, because I know many lawyer managers have access to standard Change Management training from their employers or elsewhere. My focus will be on how to anticipate the likelihood of successful change rather than the nuts and bolts of how to implement/execute the change. However, the very basics are needed to appreciate the rest of the article, so here we go: Change Management in a Nutshell!

Fig. 1 Illustration of a typical business application of the Kübler-Ross model. A search for "kübler-ross change curve" on Google.com will return hundreds of applied variations of this curve

Commonly accepted theory suggest that when you are affected by change, you are likely to experience a series of typical emotional reactions, first simplified in a model by Swiss psychiatrist Elisabeth Kübler-Ross in 1969.[1] Brilliantly simple, the Kübler-Ross model works on the most banal changes (e.g. you lost your permanent parking space at work) as well as the most existential (e.g. you have been diagnosed with a potentially lethal disease). It goes roughly like this:

Denial—The first reaction is denial. In this stage individuals believe the news is somehow mistaken, and cling to a false, preferable reality.

Anger—When the individual recognizes that denial cannot continue, they become frustrated. Certain psychological responses of a person undergoing this phase would be: "Why me? It's not fair!"; "How can this happen to me?"; "Who is to blame?"; "Why would this happen?".

Bargaining—The third stage involves the hope that the individual can avoid or negotiate mitigations to the rejected change. Usually, the negotiation for an extended status quo is made in exchange for reformation.

Depression—"I'm so sad, why bother with anything?"; "It's over soon, so what's the point?" During the fourth stage, the individual becomes saddened by the inevitability.

Acceptance—"It's going to be okay."; "I can't fight it, I may as well prepare for it."; "Nothing is impossible." In this last stage, individuals embrace the unavoidable future (Fig. 1).

In my experience, most people swiftly acknowledge the relevance of the model, and it is pretty easy for anyone to think of an example of recent change that triggered a response pattern along the lines of this model. Obviously, any manager implementing change will have to take this pattern into consideration, because organizations consist of real people who will have real feelings about the change affecting them. The manager who can shepherd a team through the emotional rollercoaster is a very valuable asset to his or her organization. Most of Change

---

[1]Elisabeth Kübler-Ross: On Death and Dying: What the Dying Have to Teach Doctors, Nurses, Clergy and Their Own Families (1969).

Management theory out there seems to focus on these stages and how to deal with the challenges of each.

Existing Change Management theory is very useful, in fact extremely useful if you have not come across it before, but I still think there is a significant shortcoming when applied to commercial settings like business or law. The Kübler-Ross model and similar adaptations are based on the premise of an inevitable outcome. I.e. painful as it may be to move from denial through acceptance, the change will eventually prevail. Which makes sense when you think about Kübler-Ross studying the field of acceptance of death (which, alas, is inevitable), but certainly is not always the case in business or law, where there frequently is so much resistance that the change fails. In other words, the use of a Kübler-Ross type model in planning change may trick you into thinking that you will be successful in the end—which is simply not true. Which leads me to the main topic of this article.

3   Can You Assess Whether the Change Will Succeed: Before You Get Started?

If we had a crystal ball, looking into the future, we would of course not have started projects that eventually turn out not to succeed. Alas, such devices are not part of the lawyer manager's common toolkit, so consider this: is the risk of failure the reason you have not started on the change project you secretly think is needed? Will your management provide "air cover" to fend off escalations caused by change resistance or fear? Would you be a little more courageous if you had a good way of assessing the likelihood of success before you started the project? Well, you are not alone, but there is help. Several years ago I stumbled across a methodology that has been useful for several change projects. Unlike many change management methodologies—which mostly focus on how to execute, or implement the change—this methodology solely focuses on assessing the likelihood of success before you get started. Meet Gleicher's formula for change:

$$D*V*F > R$$

Now, before you totally freak out and reach for the algebra book, don't worry. It is not nearly as complex as it reads, and you do not need much math knowledge to put it to practical use. Let's face it: lawyers are mostly not great mathematicians and I'm certainly no exception, but I have found it very helpful. Gleicher's formula is in fact fascinatingly simple, so stay with me.

D is the Dissatisfaction with the current situation
V is the Vision of how the change will improve things
F is the First Steps towards the Vision
R is Resistance to change.

Hence, the D*V*F>R formula roughly means that the combination of your Vision of how things will improve, the team's dissatisfaction with the current situation and the First Steps you can offer up—in aggregate—needs to be greater than the team's inherent resistance to change. If it is not, your project will likely succumb to the change resistance and fail.

The formula for change's origin is usually credited David Gleicher, while he was working at consulting firm Arthur D. Little in the early 1960s, and later refined by Kathie Dannemiller in the 1980s.[2]

4 Applying Gleicher's Formula in Practice

I have found Gleicher's formula for change very useful, but it is admittedly difficult to appreciate as a theoretical model alone. Applying it to a practical example really helps, and that is what I will do in the following.

Assume for a moment that you are the manager of an in-house team of 20 lawyers (could be 2 or 200, the principles are the same). The lawyers mostly support commercial transactions, but do some compliance work as well. You have inherited the team from a manager who left on short notice and the morale of the team is not great, but stable. Now, your legal function management and business clients have asked for information about the volume of deals the team support, deal velocity data and the team's value-add to the business. But there is practically no information to be found. Each team member supports deals upon request, typically as sales reps approach them deal by deal. Each lawyer stores the contracts on their own PC and uses MS Outlook to send and receive documents. Effectively, there is no workflow tool and no central repository. Your predecessor set up a Sharepoint and asked each lawyer to upload their main redline versions plus executed contracts so that at least Finance could have access to the executed documents as a basis for revenue recognition, but adoption was poor and the lawyers explained how they are too busy to deal with the administrative burden of uploading documents to a Sharepoint when the PC hard drives are managed by central backup anyway. Does the example sound familiar? A variation of this example case is the sad reality of deal support in too many companies, and even if you are not caught in this particular predicament, you are likely aware of some company and in-house departments operating similarly to the example.

Fortunately, your employer has a creative resource that is willing to help (could be a Chief-of-Staff, Operations Lead, or a visionary GC or senior manager). When you explain the situation, your creative resource suggests implementing an IT solution that covers contracting workflow (aka knowing who supports which deals) and contracts repository (aka finding those executed documents without ever having to go through the embarrassing ritual of asking the other party for a copy ever again).

---

[2]https://en.wikipedia.org/wiki/Formula_for_change

You have found a commercial IT solution that provides both workflow management and repository, and you have secured budget for the project—let's call it project "Deal Performance". But when you announce this to the team they show a surprising lack of enthusiasm for project Deal Performance. In fact, you get the feeling that they don't see any need at all for changing the way they work in supporting deals. Your creative resource suggests you do a Gleicher test on likelihood of successful change before you start implementation of Deal Performance as the company's new workflow and repository solution.

4.1 Vision

I always recommend starting with the vision. The vision should be reasonably aligned with the organization's overall strategy and priorities, or at the very least not be in conflict with them. It sounds banal, but too often managers skip over this step and get a surprise during the change implementation. All professional organizations have strategies and priorities, but they may not be equally well communicated or understood in all parts of the organization. Or they can be outdated or too general for practical application. Sometimes the search for strategy and priorities can even reveal that different stakeholders in the organization are in fact not aligned around a common set of strategy and priorities at all, and while it may not be your job to fix that, it will be very important to know before you set out on a change journey—for several reasons. First, change projects with real impact often need a degree of management "air cover", which you are more likely to receive if you have aligned the change vision with the organization's strategy and priorities and found supportive stakeholders at the management level. Second, any lack of alignment on strategy and priorities in the organization is likely to impact the assessment of resistance if you have to deal with resistance to change not only from the affected team but also resistance from the stakeholders not aligned with the strategy and priorities you based the vision on.

The change agent—i.e. the person driving the change—must be responsible for the Vision, and in our example it is you. A potential pitfall for the vision owner is to believe that the need for change and the associated benefits are obvious and do not need precise articulation. The benefits of change may eventually be self-evident to you, but remember that others may not have spent as much time analyzing the challenge as you have; and frankly, one person or team's benefit may turn out to be another person or team's disadvantage. So before you start any significant change project you should test the vision on some trusted colleagues.

Now, for project Deal Performance, you swiftly confirm the company's strategy and priorities. The CEO has recently released a strategy to grow sales in a particular market, and the Legal function you belong to has been tasked with making your company easier to contract with and reduce average negotiation time with 20 % by the end of the year for deals in the target market. Having a contract workflow tool and central contracts repository will be helpful in terms of implementing the strategy and the Legal Department management will prioritize the project. You take down the following key elements for the Vision:

- Deal Performance will show who is supporting which deal and make it easier for the managers to allocate workload among team members.
- Proper allocation of workload will improve utilization of the team member's available time.
- Deal Performance will help in identifying deals where negotiations are taking a long time, and support pro-active manager intervention to drive difficult deals to closure.
- The repository function will help Finance find the executed documents.

We'll revisit these below, when pulling it all together and testing the formula.

4.2 Dissatisfaction

Let's then move on to dissatisfaction. What we are looking for here is any dissatisfaction with the current state. Dissatisfaction is normally nothing to strive for, but in terms of Gleicher's formula, having some dissatisfaction with the current state is in fact a good thing. It is good, because it can help overcome resistance to change—but clearly dissatisfaction is only helpful to the extent it will be addressed by the change.

For project Deal Performance you take down the following key dissatisfaction:

- Legal management is dissatisfied with not knowing who supports which deals.
- Legal management and sales management are not happy about deal velocity in the priority market.
- Finance are unhappy with the fragmented storage of executed contracts.

We will revisit these observations below, when pulling it all together and testing the formula.

4.3 First Steps

This is an interesting part of the formula, which, I have to admit, I have been struggling with sometimes. The underlying point is that human behaviors gravitate so strongly back to existing patterns and habits, that even if the vision is very compelling and dissatisfaction significant—people are mostly just going to continue doing what they have been doing. The vision becomes a "pie in the sky" without first steps, and the cynics will soon undermine the vision by adding to the resistance. Comments like "Great idea, but I want to see it before I believe it" will start undermining the project. First steps are the first, tangible or practical proof that the change is actually coming, which becomes helpful validation for those working on the change project and provides hope for the most dissatisfied. But—let's face it—first steps also kick starts the denial phase of the Kübler-Ross model for those affected by the change: "Really? Are we starting the change already? Shouldn't someone think more about whether this change is a good idea, first...?"

For project Deal Performance you have not thought of any specific first steps. Thus, we will address this topic again below.

It is worth commenting here that timing of communication is in my experience really quite key for First steps. If there is only a short time from when you announce the change project until it has been implemented the need for first steps is dramatically reduced (imagine: "we have all lost our parking spaces and your entrance cards to the garage will not work in the morning"—hardly need for first steps here...). And conversely, if there is a very long time from the time of announcing the change project until it has been implemented, the more important first steps will be.

4.4   Resistance

First steps lead us nicely into the core element of Gleicher's formula: Resistance to change. Realizing that change nearly always has an element of resistance is vital to change planning and change management. All too many change projects have failed because they do not take the resistance to change seriously. The change agent is always at risk of being seduced by his or her vision and overlook resistance elements. In fact, I know very complex organizations where I would argue that any change will meet some resistance—even change for the better (remember the Danish judge...?). An example of this is where some brave new middle manager initiates change that most agree is clearly for the better—thereby upsetting anyone who should have initiated the obvious change earlier (typically his predecessors or peer managers). It's a long way of saying: always assume there will be some resistance to change and do your best to identify the resistance before you start on your change journey.

Resistance mapping can be done in many ways—from elaborate Stakeholder Mapping exercises with location mapping and intensity mapping—to informal watercooler discussions and corporate chatter. I wouldn't even try to recommend a best practice for picking up on resistance, except if there has been a recognizable failed attempt to change in the past. If there has been a failed change project in the area you are planning a change, you may be lucky and find a post mortem analysis for the project. However, few organizations are good at documenting their failures, so you may have to do a kind of after-the-fact analysis by tracking down the people involved in the project, i.e. the ones who tried to implement the failed change—and interview them. Try to find out which Resistance eventually stopped the change, whether the resistance was known before the project started and which steps were taken to deal with the resistance. This post mortem analysis is important for the obvious reason: avoid making the same mistake twice. But also for a subtler reason. In my experience, every time you fail to bring about change it seems to me that it gets more difficult next time around. It is almost like organizations learn, and every failed change project tends to harden the resistance to change. Hence, you may be better off assigning more weight to the resistance elements if there were past failures than if we are talking about a novel and new change.

So how about our project Deal Performance then? You already know that there has been a failed change project (your predecessor's attempt to have main redlines and executed documents uploaded to a Sharepoint—that the team is not using). So first red light: you have to assume some hardened resistance. For simplicity, let's assume there are no post mortem analysis or past project members, so you have to gather the resistance info informally. Recently, you have brought the past project and the poor Sharepoint adoption up as a topic when talking to team members and other stakeholders. You take down the following key observations:

- Most deal supporting lawyers do not see the value in using the Sharepoint, because they are on top of the deals they are working on and can always find the executed documents from their local hard drives whenever anyone asks for them.
- All deal supporting lawyers claim they work as hard and fast as they can and blame slow negotiations on customer or internal business clients for slow closing deals.
- Some deal supporting lawyers share that they are uncomfortable with having management reading their redlined documents.
- Most deal supporting lawyers explain that they are usually deeply engaged in the next deal by the time the first deal closes, so uploading executed documents to the Sharepoint is considered an unnecessary administrative burden.
- Most deal supporting lawyers express some "big brother" concerns that management will use workflow data points to monitor their performance in a simplified way that does not recognize the uniqueness/complexity of each negotiation.

4.5 Putting It All on the Scale

Now, this is where it gets interesting. The key observations you have collected about project Deal Performance in the areas of Vision, Dissatisfaction, First Steps and Resistance must be put on the virtual scale. Will the R(esistance) outweigh the combined value of V*D*F?

Having discussed Gleicher's formula with a wide population of managers over the years, this is where we always end up in a bit of debate. Overly simplified, I divide them into the "Engineering School" and the "Lawyering School" of legal team managers. Those trending towards the "Engineering School" just cannot help themselves adding numerical values to the items on the scale. Sometimes, they would even weigh the items, which surely complicate the process of comparing vision, dissatisfaction and first steps with resistance items. I am not a big fan of adding numerical values to the identified items, and I will openly admit that I belong to the second school, recognizing that the items identified under V, D, F and

Fig. 2 An illustration of initial assessment, with missing first steps

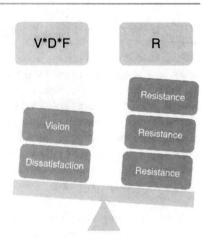

R are not all apples and cannot be directly compared 1:1, nor "weighed", in a natural science manner. Rather, I will argue that comparing "apples and oranges" arguments—that are all relevant but carry different weight—lies at the core of classic legal training, and is something legally trained managers are actually quite good at. In legal method terms we sometimes refer to this step in legal reasoning as a "concrete evaluation of the specific facts of the case" or "holistic assessment of all the relevant facts" or something similar. My point is that this is core to legal method in most jurisdictions and whereas lawyers are not well trained on change management the step of putting all relevant items on the scale is right in the sweet spot for most lawyer managers.

Nevertheless, balancing the combined value of V*D*F against R has some challenges, and there are some pitfalls. The first pitfall is not realizing that the formula reads V*D*F on purpose, and it is definitely not V + D + F. The difference being that if either of the factors equals zero you are in trouble. That is, no matter how much Dissatisfaction you have or which well-planned First steps you can offer, you will fail if there is no Vision. And same logic, if there is zero dissatisfaction or no first steps. Gleicher's formula basically warns you that if either of the V, D of F factors are zero you will to fail (Fig. 2).

Let's try it with the Deal Performance example:

V*D*F	R
Vision	Resistance
• Deal Performance will show who is supporting which deal and make it easier for the managers to allocate workload among team members.	• Most deal supporting lawyers do not see the value in using the sharepoint, because they are on top of the deals they are working on and can always find the executed documents from their local hard drives whenever anyone asks for them.
• Proper allocation of workload will improve utilization of the team member's available time.	• All deal supporting lawyers claims they work as hard and fast as they can and blame slow
• Deal Performance will identify deals where negotiations are taking a long time, and	negotiations on customer or internal business

(continued)

support pro-active manager intervention to drive difficult deals to closure.
• The repository function will help Finance find the executed documents.

Dissatisfaction
• Legal management is dissatisfied with not knowing who supports which deals.
• Legal management and sales management are not happy about deal velocity in the priority market.
• Finance are unhappy with the fragmented storage of executed contracts.

First steps
• None.

clients for slow closing deals.
• Some deal supporting lawyers share that they are uncomfortable with having management reading their redlined documents.
• Most deal supporting lawyers explain that they are usually deeply engaged in the next deal by the time the first deal closes, so uploading executed documents to the sharepoint is considered an unnecessary administrative burden.
• Most deal supporting lawyers express some "big brother" concerns that management will use workflow data points to monitor their performance in an overly simplified way that does not recognize the uniqueness/complexity of each negotiation.

So what to make of this? The first observation is that having no first steps is a problem. Better deal with that immediately. As you think through the implementation project, two potential first steps come to mind:

1. you can enforce the uploading of executed contracts to the Sharepoint while waiting for the Deal Performance solution to be implemented, or
2. you can set up a generic emailbox (e.g. contracts@yourcompany.com) and tell the deal supporting lawyers to simply copy/forward this generic emailbox when they deal with executed documents at the final stage of the deal support.

Your concern with #1 is that it will not be popular with the deal support team and you first think the second option is less controversial (but also less useful as it will be more work migrating executed contracts from the generic emailbox to the new system than from the Sharepoint). However, discussing your findings with your creative resource, you realize that option #1 has an interesting double effect, because it both, serves as first steps, and may increase the dissatisfaction with the current situation—which can be a good thing in terms of Gleicher's formula. You are still uncertain whether increasing dissatisfaction is needed, and you are a bit concerned it can be perceived as too "Machiavellian", so you would really prefer option #2 for first steps. On the other hand, the sum of the resistance items is really quite substantial, and you doubt that the combined value of your VDF factors outweigh the resistance factors.

You re-consult the creative resource, who quickly points out that not only do the resistance items seem to outweigh the VDF items, but additionally there seems to be an imbalance when it comes to whom the issues concern. Your creative resource illustrate it like this:

Category	Issue	Team member concern?	Mgmt concern?
Vision	Deal Performance will show who is supporting which deal and make it easier for the managers to allocate workload among team members.		X
Vision	Deal Performance will show who is supporting which deal and make it easier for the managers to allocate workload among team members.		X
Vision	Deal Performance will identify deals where negotiations are taking long time, and support pro-active manager intervention to drive difficult deals to closure.		X
Vision	The repository function will help Finance find the executed documents.		X
Dissatisfaction	Legal management is dissatisfied with not knowing who supports which deals.		X
Dissatisfaction	Legal management and sales management are not happy about deal velocity in the priority market.		X
Dissatisfaction	Finance are unhappy with the fragmented storage of executed contracts.		X
First steps	Generic emailbox.		X
Resistance	Most deal supporting lawyers do not see the value in using the sharepoint, because they are on top of the deals they are working on and can always find the executed documents from their local hard drives whenever anyone asks for them.	X	
Resistance	All deal supporting lawyers claims they work as hard and fast as they can and blame slow negotiations on customer or internal business clients for slow closing deals.	X	
Resistance	Some deal supporting lawyers share that they are uncomfortable with having management reading their redlined documents.	X	
Resistance	Most deal supporting lawyers explain that they are usually deeply engaged in the next deal by the time the first deal close, so uploading executed documents to the sharepoint is considered an unnecessary administrative burden.	X	
Resistance	Most deal supporting lawyers express some "big brother" concerns that management will use workflow data points to monitor their performance in an overly simplified way that does not recognize the uniqueness/complexity of each negotiation.	X	

Some changes are just like this, that all of the resistance comes from the team or individuals most affected by the change, while the vision, dissatisfaction and first steps focus on the need of the management, owners or other pan-organizational stakeholders. And the risk with this constellation is that the entire change projects ends up in a "us" vs "them" battle where the change agent ends up in the middle—relying solely on the managements will and ability to force or "marshal" the change on the affected team. Your creative resource suggest that you try adding weight to the VDF side and that you consider if there are VDF items concerning the team members that you may have overlooked (i.e. not only think about VDF from the management perspective).

4.6 Re-Assessment

Re-thinking the vision and looking over notes from interviews with the team, you realize there is a pattern of concerns with in-equal workload balance in general and holiday coverage in particular. Having no contracting workflow tool, some team members feel they regularly are assigned more deals than others. Plus, when it is time for holiday coverage, each team member will have to forward all relevant drafts to the colleague covering the deal while the first team member is on holiday—and similarly the colleague will have to return all updated drafts when the holiday is over. In both instances, there is room for error. Follow-up calls to locate missing drafts or legacy documents during holiday are more the rule than the exception. If all current drafts and executed documents were available in a centralized system, holiday coverage will be a smoother process. Not to mention sudden absence due to sickness or other abruptions, in which all team members will benefit from relying less on the individual team members' hard drives.

You decide to include fair workflow assignment and improved deal coverage during holiday and sickness as vision items benefiting the team members.

Regarding dissatisfaction and first steps, your creative resource conversations have led you to the conclusion that it is better to enforce the Sharepoint upload until the new contracts workflow and repository solution is in place. It is better to take the pain now and have a central collection of executed documents that can be transferred to the new repository in an automated fashion (batch upload or similar), than to let things slide and try to convince the team to dig out old documents from their hard drives when the new system is available. Furthermore, you are pretty sure that the team members will welcome the move from a rudimentary Sharepoint solution to the sleeker, new system, adding weight to the VDF side of the equation in Gleicher's formula.

Your creative resource did not ask you to revisit the resistance items, but when looking over you think there is actually room to reduce some of the concerns by reducing the uncertainty about the use of the data in productivity assessment of the team. You work swiftly with Legal Management to create a framework for which data points the Deal Performance system will report, and how the data will be used in performance assessment. Several team members are positive about the increased clarity, and some are looking forward to objective data points showing how hard they work and their value add. Overall, you are convinced that the sum of resistance items has reduced, and that the increase in vision, dissatisfaction and first steps

Fig. 3 An illustration of final assessment, including first steps and resistance mitigation

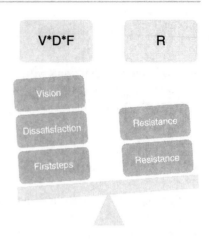

items will be sufficient to tip the scale. You're ready to begin project Deal Performance (Fig. 3).

5   Conclusion

"Culture eats Strategy for Breakfast" is a frequently used management quote usually attributed to the iconic Peter Drucker. And rarely is it more true than when an organization is faced with profound change. At the same time, it has never been more dangerous for businesses to remain static, being subject to change rather than driving change.

Whether it is culture, politics or just human nature that keeps adding challenges in your specific situation, I hope that you will find Gleicher's formula to be of some help as a framework and methodology—or simply structure for thought. Good luck!

> **Liquid Legal Context**
> by Dr. Dierk Schindler, Dr. Roger Strathausen, Kai Jacob
> Whatever angle we take to the transformation of the legal industry, it is a fact that it brings about change in fundamental ways and at large scale to individuals that work in the industry. "Known territory", one is tempted to say, as we are all somewhat literate in the traditional methods of change management.
> Byberg, accepts that—but makes a convincing case why we need to look beyond proven models like e.g. the Kübler-Ross-curve. He identifies a short-coming in models like that, if they are applied in commercial settings, like business or in legal. Commercial reality has the potential power to make change fail.

(continued)

This is why the author proposes to use a different approach to change and to assess first, if there is even a chance to make it happen. He advocates to use Gleicher's formula, which basically helps to answer the question whether the team's dissatisfaction with the current situation and the first steps for improvement you can offer—in aggregate—are greater than the team's inherent resistance to change. If not—don't waste your resources and the team's goodwill until you have a better plan.

Byberg concludes with a tangible example that allows for taking his approach to practice. Yet, let's also test his approach by applying it to the impressive journey that Roux-Chenu and de Rocca-Serra took their team on, turning legal into a profit center.

Arne Byberg is General Counsel at EVRY, a leading IT company in the Nordics with headquarter in Oslo, Norway. Prior to joining EVRY, Arne was Associate General Counsel at Hewlett-Packard (HP), Palo Alto, California. At HP, Arne worked extensively with Innovation and Strategic Solutions, as well as Legal Management, in several global roles. Arne is a member of the Board of Directors of the International Association for Contract and Commercial Management (IACCM). His academic background is from Bergen University (Norway), Bond University (Australia) and Stanford University (USA). Arne is a member of the Bar Association in Oslo, Norway.

The Legal Department: From Business Enabler to Business Creator

Isabelle Roux-Chenu and Elisa de Rocca-Serra

Abstract

"Legal still needs to earn the right to exist." Those were a senior Capgemini executive's introductory words in his speech at the 2013 Group Legal Forum. Beyond the provocative tone, this challenge has been an ongoing driver of the Capgemini's Legal function.

It is increasingly necessary that legal departments demonstrate their value to the company, lest they be seen as a mere cost center and be treated as such. Legal has often times been dubbed the "sales prevention team" by allegedly being too risk-adverse, appearing as a hindrance to the sales executives' desire of a quick closing or occasionally viewed as a scapegoat for lost bids. It is critical to change this perception so internal clients realize that Legal is not only protecting the company's interests but also is a "sales and profit enhancing team."

The modern legal department must reinvent itself and change the rules of the game through innovation, being proactive with its internal and external clients, and demonstrating that it can be a business creator and not merely an enabler.

Bringing business discipline to the legal department has been the ambition of the Capgemini Group's General Counsel and her teams for the last 19 years, and in November 2015 it led to Capgemini's legal department receiving four Trophy awards ("*Trophées du Droit*") at the in-house legal team contest organized by the French magazine "*Directeur Juridique & Financier*". This annual event rewards professional and innovative legal departments in France, gathering the most important members of the French legal community. These awards, related to transactions, innovation, contract management, and best international legal team, reflect the Capgemini legal department's accomplishments and the hard work and contributions made by all legal team members over the years in France and abroad.

I. Roux-Chenu • E. de Rocca-Serra (✉)
Capgemini, Paris, France
e-mail: isabelle.roux-chenu@capgemini.com; elisa.de-rocca-serra@capgemini.com

© Springer International Publishing AG 2017
K. Jacob et al. (eds.), *Liquid Legal*, Management for Professionals,
DOI 10.1007/978-3-319-45868-7_13

1   Develop Internal Conditions for Innovation

Capgemini's legal department seeks to offer the best possible work environment and career opportunities to its team members through a dedicated career-management program not only focused on expertise, but also strongly encouraging creativity and innovation. Innovation originates in people, and a department can only be innovative if its members are individually driven to be creative and rewarded for it. Working for an IT and consulting company such as Capgemini is a strong driver for innovation. However, any legal department, regardless of the industry, should favor an environment conducive to innovation. This is not necessarily a budget issue as constrained budgets can in certain circumstances foster creative ideas.

1.1   The Right Team

International Capgemini's legal department was created in 1998 on the 30th anniversary of the Group, which employed 30,000 persons at the time. Despite being headquartered in France, the Capgemini legal department was never thought of being limited to French lawyers. It was "born with an international DNA" from day 1, recruiting lawyers from different jurisdictions who formed the nucleus of what would later become the Capgemini global legal department with 280 team members, in December 2015.

Diversity Diversity is a foundation for innovation. Beyond its international DNA, a deliberate effort is made within the legal department to bring balance to the team. At the end of 2015, the headquarters' legal department was composed of members from seven nationalities, 50 % non-French. The ambition was to equally cover all national common law and civil law as well as numerous languages. Familiarity with cultural diversity enables fluid and productive interaction with lawyers and business colleagues all around the world.

Gender It is worth noting that in many countries the legal function is largely composed of women lawyers but only some of them reach a General Counsel position. This was never the case within Capgemini. The legal department is divided into five regions plus the headquarters, and there is a perfect gender parity at this managerial level. Although perfect parity was not a specific goal, allowing talented women to take responsibilities in the legal department was always the Group General Counsel's ambition. She is also the founder and lead of "Women@Capgemini," the Group Gender Balance Program. The underlying principle in promotion of lawyers was always to give equal opportunities to all team members, regardless of their gender or ethnicity. In addition, internal promotion is encouraged, and every time an appointment is opened, priority is given to existing talent over external hires. Most General Counsels were appointed internally, hence allowing the promotion of talented women who had grown within the community.

A few years ago, the General Counsel of a small geography moved to another position. It was decided to wait for 2 years to replace him in order to allow a talented but less experienced female lawyer to prepare for the role. During this time, a senior lawyer from another jurisdiction was appointed as interim General Counsel. This was a "win-win" situation, since it gave the interim lawyer a unique opportunity to act as a General Counsel, a role unavailable at the time in his own geography, while the future General Counsel could be trained and promoted.

Backgrounds Legal cannot any longer include exclusively lawyers but must be open to and enriched by new complementary profiles. The Capgemini legal department, which includes a contract management team, is composed of a diversity of profiles, lawyers and non-lawyers with diverse backgrounds (delivery, finance, risk management). This allows the department to provide better analyses while having an in-depth understanding of other functions and their expectations. The legal department itself benefits from the opportunity for its entire team to develop talent. Non-lawyers are being trained on legal matters and lawyers can expand their expertise. It also enhances the possibility for lawyers to evolve outside of legal functions if so motivated.

Mobility In order to foster exchanges between local legal departments and headquarters, a rotation program was created in 2003. Members from local legal departments are seconded for a few weeks or months to the Paris headquarters. This program gives them the opportunity to better understand Capgemini Group's priorities and policies. It also enables local best practices—brought by the rotation lawyer—to be rolled out through the entire legal community. Allowing local lawyers to gain a corporate perspective is an extremely valuable exposure, while it helps headquarters lawyers to keep a link with the day-to-day local operational constraints and ensure that current processes are well suited. At the end of 2015, almost all local legal departments of Capgemini had sent lawyers in rotation to the headquarters. Beneficiaries' profile and level of experience are diverse, as not only senior lawyers, are eligible for the program. "Game changers" are highly valued across Capgemini, and the rotation lawyers' contribution is diverse and valuable. Examples of contributions range from the drafting of a "Legal Department Welcome Kit" suggested by a junior lawyer sharing her experience on the information she would have liked to receive upon joining, to contributions to the legal department strategy, subject matter expertise or methodologies. The rotation program initiated at Group level aims also to be applied between the local legal departments to enhance relationships.

Financial Arbitrage Facing an increasing number of requests for legal support in a Group experiencing a strong internal and external expansion, albeit in a restrictive budgetary environment, Capgemini created the Rightshore® economic model. This model allows the legal department to provide in-depth, high-quality legal advice at limited costs. The Rightshore® economic model is a financial arbitrage defining the optimal location of resources in terms of labor costs, in each main type of legal activity adapted to our needs (contracts review, negotiation, trackers, templates, and policies drafting, etc.). Today the four Rightshore® locations: Brazil, India, Poland and Guatemala, are a unique opportunity for the headquarters legal department and most local ones to work closely with colleagues from these four countries.

Open Mind Open-mindedness is important in the search for talent, devoid of hierarchical considerations. A well-run organization must allow talent to shine, and leveraging talent globally is particularly meaningful to enhance small teams' performance. It is widely recognized that bringing together different people with various academic backgrounds and level of experience fosters innovation and helps the team to think outside of the box. It is essential as well to recognize successful initiatives taken by an individual and to give due credit for ideas and contributions of each member of the department. This mindset encourages the younger generation to speak up and propose initiatives that more experienced colleagues would not necessarily have thought of; it is the combination of all members that allows the team to push innovative projects.

1.2   Within the Right Organization, with Clear Goals and Priorities

One Team Capgemini's legal department members work together globally as "One Team" solely reporting to five regional General Counsels and ultimately to the Group General Counsel, without any hierarchical link to operational management. In 2009, this organization replaced the dual reporting lines to Group General Counsel and to the local management. It was done to preserve the independence of the legal function while maintaining the proximity of the local legal team to their local internal clients. It has allowed the entire legal team to be driven by common guidelines and a unique impulse. The "One Team" concept recognizes a person's sense of belonging to one team and one's greater commitment if his or her realm moves from local to global. The objective is to give each team member the opportunity to be visible at a global level as no local budget boundaries prevent involvement in global projects. Within Capgemini, General Counsels are requested to invest 70 % of their time on local and 30 % on global matters.

Legal Priorities Each year, the Group General Counsel sets the "Legal Priorities" which are distributed to all members of the legal department. It reflects the main directions given by the Group Chairman and CEO and his team, and sets the main strategic goals and realizations expected from all legal team members. It allows the General Counsels to define the KPIs of their team members. In the 2012 Legal Priorities for example, each team member was directed to discuss suggestions for innovation or improvement of the legal department with their General Counsel, who was requested to elevate them to the Group General Counsel.

Leader Profiles Since 2011, all lawyers are assessed along common "Leader Profile" criteria defined at the Group level: "Business Pioneer", focusing on proactively facilitating business initiatives in new markets and geographies, "Profit Shaper", focusing on risk awareness, and operational excellence turning business into margin, and "People Leader" focusing on leadership characteristics.

When these Leader Profiles were introduced, they did not necessarily appear well suited to the legal function, so the General Counsels worked on making these Leader Profiles a driver for the legal community. Today these Leader Profiles shape the entire legal team's attitude and focus.

Global Legal Awards The legal department must be driven by motivated members, and all in the team are encouraged to make themselves, their teammates, and their contributions visible. "Legal Awards," following the Leader Profile categories, were created to reward individuals or teams worldwide for their achievements. The "People Leader" Legal Award for example rewards federating and inspiring members of the legal department who deliver excellence on a global scale.

Candidates for Legal Awards are usually nominated by the General Counsels but may also be referred by colleagues or even other departments. Legal Awards are a chance for small countries or for young lawyers to make themselves visible as they reward initiatives, subject matter expertise, or processes in all domains. In 2014, a local team won a Legal Award in the Business Pioneer category for their program called "Data Protection for Delivery," which helped delivery teams identify and deal with data protection issues. This program has had an exceptional impact on team spirit with effective and proactive collaboration between several areas of the company not previously in contact in that specific country. The program increased delivery, risk, and commercial teams' awareness with regard to personal data and helped them to respond effectively to client requirements. It was based on an industrialized process, and now all projects in that country use the same template and follow the same procedures to identify the requirements for the management of personal data, and it will be deployed globally. The creation of the global Legal Awards has accelerated the emergence of a company spirit and generates a healthy emulation within the entire legal community.

1.3   With Powerful Tools and Methodologies

Much efficiency today is derived from appropriate tools, good knowledge management, and processes, all of which are even more relevant in a virtual team environment. Numerous legal initiatives and working groups were created within

Capgemini's legal department to enable the sharing of good practices and to seek opportunities for an ongoing, cost-effective improvement of the legal function. Moreover, volunteers in charge of a legal initiative are offered a great opportunity to develop their leadership skills at the Group level.

Tools The Capgemini legal department uses a number of tools such as an "Electronic Management System", a "SharePoint" or a "Contract Management" solution. The decision to invest in a much-needed global Electronic Management System was made years ago to manage and file according to the same taxonomy, the vast amount of documents and information created or received every day within the legal department worldwide. The decision was to customize one of the readily available document management tools for Capgemini's specific needs. Today, the Electronic Management System is used by the entire legal community, with the persistent goal to improve response time, security, and user experience within the legal department.

As communication and information sharing are critical within a global team, Legal also needed a tool to help local and headquarters' legal departments to better interact with each other. One of the reasons that led to the creation of the Legal function's SharePoint was the desire to allow each department (local and headquarters) to present its team and share its best practices freely. Such showcasing encourages the teams to see what other departments are doing, and to share knowledge. This tool is also the perfect place to promote initiatives such as the "Legal Practice Groups" and "Legal Initiatives" developed within the legal department. SharePoint also gives centralized access to all the data a team member needs, such as policies and guidelines, templates or team member lists and roles.

Legal Technology Group Technology is not necessarily a natural area for lawyers, but a global department is bound to include team members with a passion for technology. Within the Capgemini legal department, it was proposed that a few team members gather in a dedicated work group (the "Legal Tech Group"). The five-member team, led by a local General Counsel, was mandated to regularly monitor all tools used by the department, and to make recommendations on how to keep them best suited to its needs. As Legal Tech Group members have a good understanding of technology as well as of the legal department's needs, they can best evaluate tools capable of improving its efficiency. The legal department owns and has access to significant knowledge and data that could be valuable for other functions and should be made available to them through tool interconnection. As a consequence, the Legal Tech Group is also expected to focus on the legal department's tools interactivity with those of other functions and departments.

Legal Practice Groups Strong expertise is necessary in a global legal department, and knowledge sharing and teamwork must be pushed continually. When budgets are constrained and resources scarce, one must leverage existing expertise and deploy it worldwide. Mapping of resources, capabilities and aspirations is key to locating and leveraging talent. Within the Capgemini legal department, cross-border networks of experts, the "Legal Practice Groups", were created in 2011 to offer all members worldwide the opportunity to work together and develop their specific skills and expertise. The first Legal Practice Groups focused on subject matter expertise (Labor law, Intellectual Property, and Data Privacy), specific services lines (Financial Services, Cloud, and Outsourcing) or internal processes (Capgemini Group Contracting Principles). As success rests on the interest and desire to learn, participation to Legal Practice Groups is based on the willingness to join a group of lawyers and non-lawyers specialized in certain domains. Legal Practice Groups are expected to gather people who have an in-depth knowledge of the applicability of their expertise in the business, and to be a laboratory for new ideas. Legal Practice Groups are also used to develop legal training to be made available within the Group.

Legal Practice Groups' nimbleness helps bridge the resource shortage, as experts may not be available in every geography. Participating in a Legal Practice Group is an excellent opportunity for senior experts to lead the team as Chair or Co-Chair, and for lawyers in small jurisdictions to benefit from a network of specialists outside their own area of expertise and geography. For example, when Capgemini started doing business in a particular geography, it had a limited legal knowledge of the constraints to operate there and no business case for the creation of a dedicated legal department. The creation of a dedicated Legal Practice Group was the occasion to bring together the current and past experience of a number of lawyers who had worked on deals involving such geography, and to develop expertise in a very short time. Not all Legal Practice Groups will last, and some of them can evolve into a specialty, such as the Data Protection Legal Practice Group, which evolved into a network of Data Protection Officers. Innovation stems also from the opening of Legal Practice Groups to experts outside of the legal department when the subject requires Legal to rely on, for example, a specific technical expertise.

These initiatives allow all team members who wish to develop a capability to find the time and place to do so. Thinking outside of the box must be encouraged, and the Capgemini legal department allows its team members to develop ideas that positively contribute to the department, even if these ideas are not necessarily directly linked to their day-to-day assignment.

Webinars In addition to regular global messages, on-boarding sessions, e-learning and local training required for lawyers to maintain their local qualification to the bar, webinars are organized each semester, directed towards the entire legal community. These webinars may focus on legal developments, new processes (legal, financial, human resources, etc.), or initiatives by local teams, and are a unique chance for all 280 members of the team to be together and hear the same message. The format is lively and allows for interactions between the speakers and the participants. Due to time zone differences, two webinars are organized on the same day to facilitate attendance by a maximum of participants; attendance usually is above 80 %.

Legal Forum Every year, the Legal Forum physically gathers for 3 days, all local General Counsels, as well as several of their team members. Legal Forums are a great opportunity to strengthen relationships between the different local Legal teams. Numerous presentations and workshops allow them to share knowledge as well as local innovations or initiatives and increase their legal skills. Moreover, the Legal Forum is an unrivaled occasion to bring team members closer while fostering the spirit of "One Team" within Legal. It is an occasion to ask to Group leaders to present their strategy and expectations for the legal department or to present an innovation or a new service offering.

The right team within the right organization, with clear goals and objectives and powerful methodologies and tools are the first conditions on which Capgemini legal department bases its innovation strategy.

2 Be Proactive and Bring Value to Internal and External Clients

The role of Legal has changed. Times are long gone when the legal department was mostly waiting for internal requests. From being reactive, it has become pro-active and anticipates the needs of its internal and external clients as well as market evolutions. In the fast-evolving IT industry, one needs to anticipate at a very early stage future requirements for legal support.

The legal department interacts with almost all functions, such as sales, delivery, strategy, risk, communication, or human resources on a large variety of topics, and contributes to cohesiveness cross the organization. This central role must be used to create bridges with the other Group functions, and Capgemini's legal department strives to maintain good communication and relationships with them, while continually seeking how it can bring value.

2.1 Develop Internal and External Communication

Part of leadership at all levels is effective communication. Several channels were put in place to ensure that the legal department is close to the business and that communication is plentiful and fluid.

Global and Local Intranet Pages Legal has a global intranet page while each local department has also its own page on local intranets. The purpose of these pages, regularly updated, is to be the first image of the legal department, presenting its organization as well as its mission statement: *"Whichever country you might be in and whatever your role in Capgemini is, the legal community strives to work with you as true business partner as well as trusted adviser. Our mission is to contribute to the Group's development by facilitating profitable business through professional,* *responsive and pragmatic legal advice and contract management support to all the Group's activities."*

"Fiona Booklet" Leveraging a local initiative from a junior lawyer, a booklet named *"Fiona meets the Legal Department"* has been created with the aim to present the legal department to the sales and delivery communities in an innovative form. The innovation comes from the format, the creation of a cartoon figure, Fiona, the story telling, and from the humorous tone. The booklet tells the story of Fiona, a junior sales or delivery representative recently hired by Capgemini who is regularly confronted with legal issues. It addresses basic questions such as: When is a contract concluded? What are the legal issues in a contract? This local initiative was rapidly turned into a global initiative and the booklet is now available world-wide. This was so successful that another booklet covering data privacy topics was created, *"Fiona meets Data Protection."*

Legal Ease "Legal Ease" are simple one-page articles posted regularly on the Capgemini intranet, with the motto, *"Legal cannot get easier than this!"* Again, it was started as a local initiative and was quickly turned global. Local legal departments are encouraged to create their own Legal Ease covering local matters, and a global Legal Ease is prepared for subjects with a global relevance. Through Legal Ease, global and local legal teams keep the business teams informed about various legal issues, tips, tricks and developments relevant in everyday business. Topics range from signing Non-Disclosure Agreements, to a new law on payment terms, and from open source software to parent company guarantees. These articles are very useful and can be used as pre-drafted answers to business teams. Many legal team members also add a link to the Legal Ease page on their internal signature, increasing the awareness of the initiative.

Global Survey The headquarters legal department launched internal surveys to rate the services it renders and the importance of Legal to the success of Capgemini's business. The surveys are sent to the communities interacting with Legal, rating accessibility, respect of deadlines, legal expertise, understanding of business issues, advice communication and quality of work. Broader questions about the role expected from Legal as well as its contribution to the success of the business are also very valuable as they help determine the position of the legal department within the company. Suggested improvements regarding skills and expertise allow for the anticipation of business needs. These surveys led to specific action plans, which helped develop today's legal department. In the 2008 global survey, almost half of the respondents indicated that a contract management function should be systematically implemented for complex and/or big deals, which contributed to the creation of the contract management function within Legal.

External Communication The legal department of a multinational company has a role to play in the market at many levels, by sharing ideas, writing papers, contributing to the training of attorneys to be qualified, and networking in the market place. Capgemini's Group General Counsel participates in numerous events. She initiated the reunion of General Counsels of other large multinationals headquartered in France to discuss marketplace issues. This gathering evolved into the Commission of CAC40, a reunion of the General Counsels of the 40 largest companies on the Paris stock exchange, which she co-leads with another multinational company's General Counsel. The initial impetus was her ambition to join forces with other General Counsels of multinationals to lobby on the question of the recognition of the status of in-house counsel in the marketplace, and the lack of "attorney-client privilege" resulting from the Akzo Nobel case law at a time where France's President had commissioned a study on the reform of the legal profession including in-house counsels. More generally, she wanted to reinforce the legal function in corporations and also ensure that Group General Counsels would meet as regularly as CEOs and CFOs do, to allow them to discuss best practices or regulatory changes. Capgemini Group's General Counsel is also a member of the European board of the International Association of Conflict Prevention and Resolution. Capgemini legal department members are strongly encouraged to participate in numerous events, and be speakers at marketplace events on specific themes such as data privacy, intellectual property or contract management matters or at sessions organized by other multinationals. It is important to benchmark and exchange views in the marketplace and to contribute thought leadership on specific topics relevant to one's industry.

2.2   Develop Strong Relationships with Internal Clients

Capgemini's legal department makes it a priority to create strong and meaningful relationships with its internal clients. Each member of the department is individually encouraged to create personal connections and to build trust with his or her internal clients.

"Legal to" Programs The "Legal to" programs are targeted communication channels launched in 2011 by the Capgemini legal department to improve the relations with other functions such as sales and delivery. These programs are dedicated to a function, with a specific focus on its particular needs and expectations. Each "Legal to" program is led by a regional or local General Counsel and a senior stakeholder from the function targeted, and all programs pursue the objective to create strong bonds between both communities. Each program is specific, but all of them focus on relationship improvement, on providing valuable deliverables for both communities, and on anticipating future needs. The legal team's primary interest is to understand how it can improve the level of services provided to each function beyond sharing information, and to increase internal customers' satisfaction.

Legal to Sales The "Legal to Sales" program was initially focused on enhancing Capgemini's chances to win deals as "One Team" through improved collaboration between Legal and Sales. One important prerequisite was to help each function understand the other's interests and motivators. This program was the beginning of a greater collaboration between both communities on several common topics such as training (Sales/Legal negotiation workshops) and communication (internal videos showing significant achievements of both communities working together). In 2015, Legal and Sales worked together on a negotiation strategy initiative as well as on governance proposals. The first deliverable was a guide named "Negotiation for Success", produced by senior members of Legal and Sales communities working closely together to elaborate a unique pathway to success. By creating links and promoting its availability, Legal took a deliberate step toward Sales to be seen as more than a subject matter expert. In turn, regular interaction with the sales community helps Legal understand Sales' expectations from the legal community and Sales' priorities.

Legal to Delivery The "Legal to Delivery" program, also launched in 2011, focused mainly on how Legal can help delivery move forward after a contract is signed. Business relationships are governed by contracts, yet often times after a contract is signed, it is not readily accessible to the people who need it, preventing the capture of the full value of agreements. In March 2015, a joint pilot was launched for the preparation of contracts summaries ("Contract Briefings") for all new contracts signed in selected countries above a certain value threshold.

The success of the "Legal to" programs led to the creation of other programs such as the "Legal to Procurement" program mainly focusing on processes and templates or the "Legal to HR" program which is dedicated to the relationship with the human resources department. The Legal to HR program led in particular to the harmonization of terms and conditions contained in all employment contracts across service lines in the largest geographies. Contents of the "Legal to" programs are also evolving continually, and the next step is to make the programs more bilateral, asking the other functions to increase their contribution to the awareness of the legal community.

Relationship Attorneys Capgemini Group is organized in a number of service lines, so-called Strategic Business Units (SBUs). The Capgemini legal department, like many others, is however, organized by geographies, so a specific role had to be created to facilitate the relationship and interaction of the legal department with the different SBUs, hence the "Relationship Attorney". The objective is to strengthen the connection between SBUs and Legal (at the headquarters level and in the regions), to enhance intimacy, and ensure the sharing of important information between the SBUs and the legal department. The Relationship Attorney in each SBU is free to pursue these objectives at his or her own discretion but at a minimum he or she must create proximity with the business in the SBU and facilitate the legal team's integration through bilateral information sharing.

To the extent that the Relationship Attorney has visibility on upcoming deals, part of the role is to promptly inform the General Counsels of the regions involved in such deals. The role might involve some problem solving, e.g., on a global deal where the Relationship Attorney must help to identify which legal team should be assigned. The Relationship Attorney must also refer to the relevant Legal team new matters not yet addressed requiring legal assistance. Being visible is critical, and the Relationship Attorney must represent the legal team at the SBU Kick Offs and at important meetings, either as a participant, a contributor, or presenter. The Relationship Attorney is also required to provide legal information to the SBU CEO and management team when appropriate—for example, about new legal developments or global legal initiatives—and provide strategic and tactical legal advice on issues that may arise during SBU management meetings.

It is important to stress that this networking and coordinating role is in addition to the lawyer's daily work in the SBU. As a member of the regional legal department, he or she must therefore be one of the key lawyers on the SBU's deals and other legal matters. The role is usually suitable for a Deputy General Counsel or Associate General Counsel. The Relationship Attorney is appointed by the Group General Counsel, and the role is expected to evolve over time and with experience. In creating the Relationship Attorneys, the intent was to give a position to a senior member of the legal department at an international level while not creating a sectorial General Counsel position which would have created a confusing double matrix and undermined the position of General Counsels who need to remain the leaders in their respective geographies. Relationship Attorneys rotate periodically, every 2 or 3 years, to diversify assignments and perspectives.

2.3   External Client Satisfaction

Ensuring the legal department's optimal performance for its internal clients is not the only undertaking. Legal in Capgemini is also concerned with external client satisfaction, and part of the department's objectives is to maintain collaborative relations with external clients and accelerating contract closure, critical in contract negotiations.

For new offerings and business models, such as cloud computing contracts, several business stakeholders have acknowledged that internal lawyers may help enhance external clients' understanding of the offering and clarify certain concerns. Legal is valued in the pre-sales phase as part of the expert team facing the client, and it must be involved at an early stage in order to craft the most appropriate contractual set-up.

Part of the post-signature contract management initiative also stems from the desire to manage external clients' expectations, by ensuring that contracts are delivered in conformity with the agreements signed and in close collaboration with the client.

2.4 Conclusion

Constant focus on proactivity and internal and external client satisfaction is crucial for the legal department to be considered as a business enabler.

3 Evolve from Business Enabler to Business Creator

Every legal department should be striving to be more than a business enabler, but to be a business creator in order to make a real difference. Capgemini's Legal interacts with the whole ecosystem, i.e., not only with all internal functions, but also with clients, vendors, and alliances partners. This unique central position allows Legal to have a 360° view, to foresee the needs of the market, and to develop solutions for its internal and external clients in Rightshore® contract management services.

3.1 Contract Compliance and Optimization

The legal department must be aligned with the Group's strategy. When the Capgemini Group communicated its "Industrialization/Intimacy/Innovation" program a few years ago, the Group General Counsel announced that the legal department would contribute to the growth strategy, and this led to the creation of a dedicated service line named "Contract Compliance & Optimization" or, CCO. Together with one of the General Counsels and one of its senior lawyers, Capgemini Group General Counsel initiated, in partnership with Capgemini's "Business Process Outsourcing" (BPO) strategic business unit, a new service and suite of products combining: (1) legal expertise in dealing with contracts; (2) BPO processes, delivery methods and locations; and (3) a forward-thinking approach to handling contract-related tasks, focused not just on labor arbitrage but on real, tangible business outcomes as part of its value proposition.

The idea was to assist all stakeholders with a consistent reading and understanding of contractual terms, to follow and track contracts, and to ensure they are properly amended when the scope of the services evolves. It led to the creation of a contract retention program in which contracts brought to CCO are kept and encoded according to a specific taxonomy that allows searching and data mining.

Although contracts are the basis of every relationship between clients, vendors, or alliance partners, and in spite of their key role in the business chain, they are often one of the least protected assets in a company. Companies routinely allocate significant resources, costing time and money, to negotiate, assess and approve contracts. Unfortunately, despite this massive upfront investment, once the contract is signed, it is too often kept in a closet, not properly leveraged, and not retrieved unless a litigation starts. It was therefore decided to create the CCO service line in order to offer a turnkey solution allowing effective execution and management of contracts, securing maximum financial returns and operational effectiveness.

Visibility Contracts are increasingly complex and in many cases extremely voluminous. Typical IT contracts may contain between 300 and 1000 individual obligations or requirements. Contracts contain clauses, terms, conditions, commitments and milestones that must be tracked and managed over the contract's life to maximize business benefits and minimize associated costs and risks. Without a systematic approach to extracting, monitoring, auctioning and reporting on these obligations, the company faces delivery and reputational risks, as well as the risk of cost overruns. CCO provides key stakeholders with a crystal-clear view of contracts, and a tool for the effective management of large, complex contracts from signature to change orders and renewals. It is not just a reporting system, but a way to categorize and prioritize the contracts' important features and tie them to the drivers of the desired business outcome. It also allows the preparation of reports and recommendations to continually optimize the contract's monitoring and performance.

Control CCO monitors contracts in real time with commitment reminders sent in advance to mitigate the risk of non-compliance. These reminders put parties to the contract on par, minimizes the waste of management time, and enhances the relationship with clients as it support compliance with contractual terms. CCO tracks buy- and sell-side obligations and milestones while leveraging discounts, bonuses and performance credits and earn-backs. This tracking provides for tangible, quantifiable results, e.g., a reduction in contract cycle time, review resources, and cost. CCO also addresses scope evolutions by putting in place a process to systematically initiate and draft contractual amendments (so called "Change Order Management"), including collecting approvals to signing and archiving contracts. It also proactively handles price adjustments, preserving margins, and freeing up resources for other business areas. In addition, the CCO team can respond to ad-hoc queries and prepare contract summaries.

Value Significant profitability can be gained by simply exerting control of existing contracts. Enterprise-wide accessibility allows every employee to minimize contract deficiencies and enhance decision-making capabilities. New opportunities are not missed, and if the possibility of dispute arises, Capgemini can readily have a clear view of its contractual obligations. Greater compliance with contractual terms generates substantial revenue over time, and contracts delivered exactly as negotiated deliver better value. CCO also facilitates the production of powerful data analytics and reports, because once contracts are entered into the contract management tools, it provides useful management tools such as comparisons, effective research and benchmarks. In addition, CCO improves client satisfaction by enhancing compliance with contractual terms and adapting the contract to client's evolving needs or requests.

CCO is led by a multinational team of experts, delivering profitable performance through proactive operational and contractual monitoring. The CCO team is today headed by the senior lawyer who contributed to launch the initiative. All members of the legal department are encouraged to work closely with the CCO team and to assess the type of work to be externalized to CCO. The services are available in six languages: English, French, German, Spanish, Portuguese, and Dutch. For Capgemini's Legal it was a key initiative leading to the visible creation of value for the Group internally and it also proved that the legal department should be seen as a business creator and not only a cost center.

This service line was so successful internally, that responding to several external clients' demands, Capgemini now offers a dedicated CCO service to help them manage vendors, partners or any issue within the full contract lifecycle.

3.2   Contract Management

Even if Capgemini's legal department focuses on centralizing initiatives to avoid duplications, it recognizes that complementary initiatives can yield outstanding results. Beside the CCO initiative, the Group General Counsel initiated a contract management program "on-site" complementing the CCO program. It mainly started by assisting delivery teams post contract signature and thereafter evolved as a useful program to assist in shaping contracts, analyzing risks, writing schedules, participating in contract negotiations, and accelerating closing. Contract managers are contract specialists, lawyers, and non-lawyers, who have a vast understanding of contract negotiations and performance, and are trained on legal and financial issues, with an understanding of risks.

The program started in a jurisdiction where an internal study was conducted at the end of 2011 to understand the reasons why difficult projects resulted in cash "evaporation". The study discovered that Capgemini was investing heavily in the contract pre-signing phase and, after signature, contracts were gathering dust. It also identified that the delivery team focused its efforts on the performance of services, often without having a systematic and consistent approach in regards the terms and conditions of the contract itself.

As a result, the local legal department proposed an action plan and, in early 2012, the fondation was established of what is today Capgemini's strong area of on-site contract management aimed at maximizing the financial return of contracts. Initiated by the local General Counsel, the deployment started with a single person experienced in complex projects and PMOs directly involved in projects, and financed by the legal department. The idea was to start small, demonstrate real tangible value for internal clients and grow as demand developed. It should be emphasized that this economic model demands that a contract manager be assigned to, and be part of the project team.

The strategy also looked for "quick wins" which helped gain credibility among internal stakeholders who then started financing the use of contract management services. These "quick wins" helped raise projects' profitability through strong management and contract negotiation. As often with process changes, resistance was encountered initially from the delivery teams. However, it was quickly over-come thanks to strong communication, the creation of alliances, and, most importantly, thanks to quick positive results. Those results included the release of billings and the collection of amounts withheld by the clients, the signature of acceptance certificates by clients, the effective negotiation of change requests and penalties, as well as contract readjustments.

The model proved successful and yielded rapid results. In the first year (2012), the financial benefits amounted to several million euros, fueling the team's growth from 2013 onwards. In addition, the contract management team, having earned the local CFO's trust, started to centralize the process to review, approve, and file the documents presented for bookings in the pilot country. Today contract management is on the business critical path, since no revenue can be booked nor any contract started in that country without the Contract Management's "green light".

This approach leverages CCO capabilities by assigning an onshore contract manager, working on all projects considered complex or particularly risky, side-by-side with the delivery teams, to improve financial performance. CCO teams are systematically in charge of documents and metadata management for all contracts.

The development of contract management was achieved jointly with delivery by focusing on four pillars: finance, scope, evidence, and risk management. It resulted in internal clients' high satisfaction and demand for more support by Contract Management. In 2014, the local contract management team won the "Profit Shaper" Capgemini Legal Award as well as an external award. This model, combining on-site contract management with CCO capabilities, is currently being deployed in most of the Capgemini Group.

3.3 Cybersecurity Offering

Last but not least, Legal should also be ready to help the company to develop new offerings.

One local legal department recently demonstrated its ability to act as a true business enabler to help a local Business Unit build a cybersecurity offering (360° Cybersecurity Strategy). This offering leverages the business unit's technical capabilities, the legal clout of a well-known external law firm and an insurance broker. The role of the internal legal department was decisive in structuring this security offering which offers clients an appropriate and complete cybersecurity incident prevention program. At the project's inception, the business unit stakeholders shared with the local General Counsel the difficulties to market the existing cybersecurity services. Legal helped reposition the offering and combined it with the skills of complementary market players to leverage each partner's potential customer base. The program rests on three legs. The first leg is the technical conditions designed to limit the risks of unauthorized access, data losses or failures of critical IT infrastructure; the second one is the legal and contractual framework applicable to the critical IT infrastructure; and the third is insurance coverage for cybersecurity incidents.

This type of initiative is again possible because the legal department plays a central role in the company and is thus well aware of client, vendor, and alliance ecosystem, as well as litigation and regulations. This example proves that it is possible for Legal to generate significant opportunities and demonstrate legal departments' value to the business teams.

4 Not a Conclusion, But a Step on an On-Going Journey

Times have changed and the role of General Counsels in Europe has grown, similar to their American counterparts'. The Legal function, faced with the increasing importance of laws and regulations in a globalized world driven by fast-moving technology and innovation, has evolved from a reactive to a pro-active role. It ought to be closely associated with the company's business development and management from the inception, and no longer limited to formalize contracts and agreements. That implies a considerable evolution of the talent in legal departments, with non-lawyers bringing an in-depth expertise in all areas of the company's business. It also opens many opportunities to General Counsels and their teams to embrace additional and complementary roles such as Data Privacy Officer, Risk Manager, Ethics & Compliance Officer, and even Head of Internal Audit, to move from business enabler to business creator roles beyond support functions. Several such occurrences happened in Capgemini, and in particular the former Group General Counsel, co-author of this chapter, became Group Head of Commercial & Contract Management. That global business role was recently created to help win, retain and grow profitable business through commercial negotiation and optimized contract management. Agility and flexibility in contracts becomes a must to adapt to fast evolving client demands, market trends and technology. Reporting directly to the Group Chairman and CEO, it was the natural evolution of the "Contract Compliance & Optimization" service line and the emerging global contract management function. It is not a unique case as two other General Counsels of CAC40 companies have recently accepted managerial roles with P&L responsibility, a trend in line with North America.

One secret of game-changing players, be they individuals, movements or corporations, is to turn upside down what is taken for granted. Viewing corporate Legal as a business driver rather than a grim cost center is one such revolution.

Liquid Legal Context
by Dr. Dierk Schindler, Dr. Roger Strathausen, Kai Jacob
   Roux-Chenu and de Rocca-Serra tell an authentic and inspiring story about how Capgemini turned their legal department into a profit center. The step stones are straight forward, and it all starts with creating the prerequisites for innovation. The authors thereby deliver the practice proof point to what Tumasjan and Welpe have developed based on research: the co-creative enterprise as the foundation for entrepreneurial behavior.

(continued)

It is fascinating to find those individual concepts that often come towards us in isolation—or even diminished to buzzwords—in a direct business context. Diversity (in its many forms), internationality, mobility and breadth of background (non-lawyers!) create the innovative mix to get into a position to succeed. A strong and well developed organization, clear goals and priorities and a clearly defined leader profile are the step stones to success and directly link into what Pauleau, Roquilly and Collard have established as a KPI-framework to develop a performance driven organization. Last but not least, legal technology as the enabler to scale, but also to connect legal to the other parts of the organization.

Another aspect that sticks out from the article is the emphasis on client feedback—internally and even externally. If the company culture is right and the leadership is strong, overcoming the fear of open and honest constructive feedback should be doable—specifically if in return you get direct input as to what works and what does not yet work. Is this not what we typically (have to) do to other departments as we guard the integrity of the business? Why not making feedback a mutual thing?

Von Alemann takes us all the way to a part of the legal industry that often gets overlooked—despite representing a very large part of the business: SME's, i.e. companies that either have a very small or even no legal inhouse function. What does change and opportunity in our industry look like for them?

Isabelle Roux-Chenu a Capgemini Corporate VP and former Group General Counsel, is Head of Group Commercial & Contract Management and Senior Advisor to the Group Chairman & CEO.

She founded and leads Women@Capgemini, the Group Gender Balance program.

A member of the New York and Paris Bars, she co-founded the Commission of the CAC 40 General Counsels, and is a member of the CPR European Executive Board and a board member of *Droit & Croissance*.

In the renowned annual French Legal Trophies, she received three Gold Trophies successively for Group International Legal Team, Transactions and Innovation, and a Silver Trophy for Contract Management.

Elisa de Rocca-Serra is an Assistant General Counsel at Capgemini. She joined Capgemini Headquarters in 2008 and is today responsible for framework agreements with global clients. Specialized in international business law, she has more than 13 years' experience in the Information Technology industry. She started her career working for a software editor before joining the service industry. She is passionate about contributing to the promotion of the Legal function and on how to show the value and contribution that in-house lawyers can bring to their company growth.

Legal Tech Will Radically Change the Way SMEs Handle Legal: How SMEs Can Run Legal as Effectively and Professionally as Large Corporations

Sven von Alemann

Abstract

Legal departments of all sizes are facing challenges around technology and liberalization, triggered by what is described as the "more-for-less" or "better, faster, cheaper" challenge. Surprisingly, the focus in literature and practice is almost exclusively on large legal departments. However, there are fundamental differences between legal departments in large corporations and the legal function in small and mid-sized enterprises (SMEs). SMEs generally more often use the help of external counsel. Small legal departments usually have a lesser degree of specialization and are much closer aligned with other departments, like Sales and Finance. In some cases, SMEs also have a higher tolerance of risk-taking. Often, there is a lack of clear processes and policies, resulting in more communication and ad-hoc coordination. These challenges affect SMEs without a legal department even more. Such SMEs have the additional challenge of information asymmetry when hiring an external lawyer, they usually have no dedicated legal budget and are lacking structured documentation of legal data. So how can SMEs effectively run Legal as a Business? This is only possible with the effective use of technology, something which is still often rejected by lawyers (also in small legal departments). Technology in the legal services market, or Legal Tech, will enable SMEs to run Legal as a Business, just as large corporations. Legal Tech thus offers opportunities for new and innovative legal services providers to successfully enter into the legal services market.

S. von Alemann (✉)
rfrnz, Giselastraße 10, 80802 Munich, Germany
e-mail: sven@rfrnz.com

1   Introduction

Many industries got turned upside down in the last years by technology and innovation. Currently, the financial sector and the insurance market are subject to disruptive technology innovation. Only one industry seemed to be immune against radical innovation: the legal services industry. Business models of law firms remained generally stable with a focus on individualized and specialized legal advice to clients based on hourly rates. Even after the financial crisis in 2008, law firms generally continued to operate under this same business model, although they faced increased pressure on their rates. On the other side of the market, legal departments have continued to be an insulated branch in companies and success-fully claimed to be different and special from other departments. Therefore, legal departments often refrain from using the standard processes and reporting tools or the same metrics that apply to other corporate departments. Legal departments defend their position as a gatekeeper for legal advice. In the last years, however, researchers, practitioners and experts have started to think, develop and implement innovative ideas for the legal market that will radically change how law firms, legal departments and vendors of legal tools operate.

For the legal function in companies, this may seem part of the usual up and down of the last decades. For most of the twentieth century, legal departments mainly served as switchboard to distribute all prestigious work to one or very few outside counsel who were considered to be the only ones capable of handling complex and important tasks, while day-to-day and routine work was kept in-house. Then, since the 1980s, the legal functions and their General Counsel (GC) gained more power (Ribstein 2012). At that time, clients wanted to regain their control over costs but also over the legal know-how relevant to their business. Also, more competition emerged between big law firms which gave Chief Legal Officers (CLOs) power in the buyer's market. Recently, however, the legal departments themselves face increasing pressure again—not from the outside, but from senior management which demands that the legal function should cut down costs, both for headcount and in their budgets for external counsel. Additionally they are requested to use management best practices, data analytics and alternative services providers, and generally balance risk with cost. In other words, senior management effectively requests their legal functions to be run as a business. This does not only affect large legal departments, which are often in the focus of attention, but also small companies and their legal functions.

In this article, we will analyze the challenges of small companies to run their legal function, and we will examine how they can react with the help of technology. The following Sect. 2 will discuss the current challenges in the legal market and whether these challenges are cyclical or structural. Section 3 will describe the differences between large and small legal departments and what these differences mean for small legal departments or small companies without legal departments. Section 4 finally outlines how small companies can tackle these challenges and describes the elements a perfect solution for small companies would need to have.

2 Challenges in the Legal Market

Let's first take a look at the challenges the legal market is generally facing and why these are important for legal corporate functions. Many authors conclude that legal departments have to deal with a situation that is often called "more-for-less" or "better, faster, cheaper". There are, according to legal futurist *Richard Susskind*, three parts to this situation: First of all, because of economic conditions, General Counsel are under pressure from their management to reduce the number of lawyers in their teams. Secondly, they are also required by their chief executives to cut the spending for external counsel. Finally, the regulatory requirements for doing business continue to increase, resulting in the need for more advice for the companies. These conflicting elements put legal departments into the difficult situation of handling more work with less headcount and less support from external sources. Other authors make the same observation. Galbenski and Barringer (2013) identified the "better, faster, cheaper" challenge, which describes the same situation, as one of seven trends in the legal services market. And Callier and Reeb (2015) also observed that in the legal services market, legal departments face increasing budget constraints resulting in more insourcing and less outsourcing. However, there are also critical voices. Hartung and Gärtner (2015) doubt that the "less" part of this observation—the budget and headcount cuts—can actually be observed in the market while agreeing that the workload for legal departments increases.

The more-for-less (or "better, faster, cheaper") challenge will affect the way GCs are purchasing legal services. They will increasingly look for alternative ways of sourcing or billing and will be open to handle outside counsel relationships in new ways, if they are able to receive legal services in a similar quality but at lower costs. Accordingly, an increasing amount of time and effort will be spent on sourcing management and unbundling of legal tasks. This is a result of the more-for-less challenge and it will bring legal project management into the focus as one of the main tasks for legal services providers. *Susskind* described unbundling as the evolution of legal services through five different stages: from bespoke to standardized, systematized, packaged and commoditized services (Susskind 2013). He explained that, when moving from bespoke to commoditized, the cost of legal service comes down, the price becomes more certain, the time taken to complete work reduces and the quality goes up—which may be in favor of the client but not for law firms operating under the traditional sole-source/billable hour/cost-plus business model. Since the different stages of legal services may exist simultaneously for any matter, dispute or deal, it is possible to decompose them into a set of constituent tasks. According to *Susskind*, the different tasks may then be sourced from alternative and multiple sources which may not only include off-shoring or outsourcing, but also computerizing or sourcing with no qualified lawyers involved at all.

Another challenge that legal departments will have to deal with in the future is the increased pressure to use information technology. Information technology will create new possibilities of how legal work is done, from online marketplaces to machine learning, embedded legal knowledge and big data. Technology will be developed and used for different aspects of the legal market, from Do-it-yourself-law websites, document assembly, online dispute resolution, legal data analysis to computational law; it will be present in many areas, just like in other markets already today. Legal departments will have to introduce many of these technologies, either of their own accord or because of outside pressure.

But there is also good news for legal departments. With increasing competition among legal services providers, the legal market has turned into a buyer's market (Callier and Reeb 2015) and legal departments therefore have a strong position in that market. Ribstein (2012) described the development of increased power of in-house lawyers as they become the purchasing agents in an expanded market for legal information. However, he also expected that in-house lawyers will ultimately find their own power eroding because of products and services that replace customized legal advice with standardized technology. In his opinion, the place where this is most likely to begin is large corporations, for several reasons: they have large data sets which they can use, their buying power represent a large share of the demand side of the market, they do not have misaligned incentives like law firms (spending more time on a matter means more hours to bill) and finally they are less impeded by disadvantageous regulation (Ribstein 2012). I strongly agree with his view but would go even further: in my opinion, such innovation will start with small and mid-sized enterprises (SMEs). According to Clayton Christensen (1997), disruptive innovation usually starts at the low end of the market, and that will also be the case in the legal market.

The second question with regard to these challenges is: will they go away? Since the legal function experienced ups and downs before, one may wonder if this is only a phase which will disappear sooner or later. I am convinced that these challenges are not cyclical but structural. Once management has gained the insight that legal departments need to act more like other corporate functions, it is highly unlikely that this mindset will change back to the previous. And once they see that legal functions can operate with less headcount and budget, they will show little willingness to increase legal spending again. Another reason is technology. Technology not only enables management to better analyze all aspects of the company, including the costs and budgets of the legal departments. Management will also require legal departments to deploy and utilize technology more effectively. Legal departments will change the way they work and will not look back.

3 Big vs. Small Legal Departments or No Legal at All?

Challenges, risks and opportunities for the legal function are usually described for large legal departments. However, there are fundamental differences between legal departments in large corporations and legal departments in small and mid-sized enterprises. These differences will be outlined in the following. For the purpose of this article, small legal departments are considered to be legal departments with 1–5 inhouse legal counsel.

The first major difference between large and small companies is the budget available to small legal departments. Usually, budgets for small legal departments are significantly lower than for large legal departments, when looking at them in absolute terms. This does not only limit the number of inhouse lawyers that can be hired. It also affects spending on external counsel, both in the overall volume of work that can be given to external counsel and the choice of external counsel. Small legal departments are more likely to hire smaller or mid-sized firms with lower hourly rates than big law firms. Start-ups with sufficient funding in hyper-growth mode or situations when bet-the-company decisions have to be taken may be an exception. This makes it more demanding for GCs of smaller legal departments to find the right external counsel and agree on rates with them. While it is safe to say that clients, when hiring a big law firm, more often than not receive adequate quality in the legal advice for their money, this relatively safe bet becomes less likely the smaller the firm and the cheaper the rates are. Of course there are many mid-sized and small law firms in the market which provide the same or even better quality as big law firms. However, it does require more knowledge of the market and experience to find these firms. This results in a higher need for effectively managing external counsel to control the costs, a task which collides with the headcount and time limitations that small legal departments face.

A second difference between large and small companies is the degree of specialization of lawyers in small legal departments. Generally, the bigger a legal department, the higher this specialization tends to be. A bigger legal department is able to employ and also required to have a number of specialists for different fields of law, e.g. for employment law, corporate law, commercial law. In smaller legal departments, because of their limited size, inhouse lawyers tend to be generalists. This has the advantage that each member of the legal team can take on every matter that comes in, and work can be distributed efficiently between the inhouse lawyers. The disadvantage is, however, that special topics will have to be given to external experts, unless it is decided not to review a specific question in depth.

This relates to the next difference: the degree of risk-taking. Generally, smaller legal departments tend to have a higher tolerance of taking risks. This usually reflects the management style and personality of smaller companies which is often more entrepreneurial. It may also be the result of a high workload paired with a limited budget and headcount. While such higher risk tolerance is probably true for many smaller entrepreneurial and startup companies, it may not always be the case for established small family businesses (research shows that family firms are taking risk to a lesser extent than non-family firms, Zahra (2005)).

For small legal departments, communication is not only important in order to know what attitude management has towards risk-taking. The need to constantly communicate with other departments of the company may be even more important for members of small legal departments than for members of bigger legal departments. That is because small legal departments—as opposed to large legal departments—usually do not have a formalized process for alignment with other departments. Through communication, members of small legal departments can therefore detect legal issues early and prevent non-compliance instead of only reacting to legal problems after they are discovered. By communicating with other corporate functions as business partners, legal departments of all sizes can actively shape the direction of the business, for example by providing options, by communicating legal problems early and by making sure all stakeholders are involved.

Finally, there is a difference in the use of tools and processes. Due to budget restrictions, smaller legal departments are often not able to develop own IT systems like large legal departments can. Usually they are also not able to purchase powerful but expensive Enterprise Legal Management (ELM) software suites that may support them in their operations. Management may also not be willing to purchase solutions that require substantial implementation efforts. On the other hand, especially small legal departments need effective tools to manage their affairs and compensate for their limited budgets and headcount.

When discussing the functioning and operations of legal departments, irrespective of size, we usually only cover a part of all businesses because the majority of businesses do not have an inhouse legal function at all. While there are no detailed numbers on the percentage of companies with legal functions, it can be assumed that SMEs usually do not have an inhouse legal function if they have less than 250 employees, because of the relative high cost of inhouse counsel.

How many businesses belong to that category? The answer is, the absolute majority of all businesses: SMEs in the EU employ a total of about 88.8 million employees, this represents 99.8 % of all active enterprises in the EU. The following data shows how the 21.57 million SMEs in Europe can be structured (Figs. 1, 2 and 3).

In the United States in 2011, 99.7 % of the 5,68 million employer firms had less than 500 workers (which is the threshold for the SME definition in the US) and 89.8 % of these firms had less than 20 workers (US Census Bureau, http://www.census.gov/econ/susb/). When adding the nonemployer firms—22.7 million in

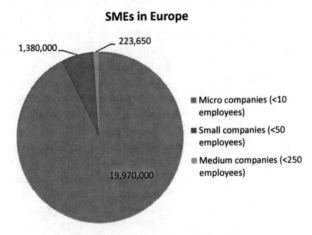

Fig. 1 SMEs in Europe. Annual report on European SMEs 2013/2014, July 2014, European Commission, http://www.ifm-bonn.org/fileadmin/data/redaktion/statistik/unternehmensbestand/dokumente/KMU-D_2009-2013_EU-Def.pdf, Accessed July 2016

GDP contribution of SMEs in the EU in 2013

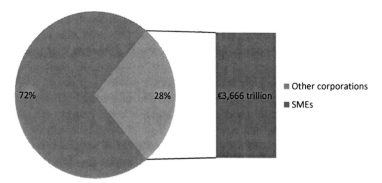

Fig. 2 GDP contribution of SMEs in the EU in 2013. Annual report on European SMEs 2013/ 2014, July 2014, European Commission, http://www.ifm-bonn.org/fileadmin/data/redaktion/ statistik/unternehmensbestand/dokumente/KMU-D_2009-2013_EU-Def.pdf, Accessed July 2016

SMEs in Germany in 2015

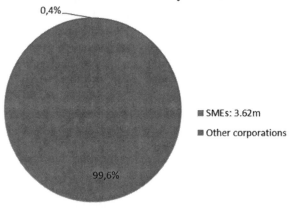

Fig. 3 SMEs in Germany in 2015. Statistisches Bundesamt: Sonderauswertung des Unternehmensregisters 2009 bis 2013 im Auftrag des IfM Bonn, Wiesbaden, 2015; Berechnungen des IfM Bonn, http://www.ifm-bonn.org/statistiken/mittelstand-im-ueberblick/#accordion=0& tab=1, Accessed July 2016

2012—, the share of U.S. businesses with less than 500 workers increases to 99.9 %, and the share of firms with less than 20 workers increases to 98 %. It can be assumed that at least the latter group of firms does not have an inhouse legal function due to its size.

Businesses without any inhouse legal function have additional challenges when dealing with legal issues. Especially the use of service providers, in the form of external counsel or legal software, is substantially different for them as opposed to SMEs with a legal department. In inhouse legal functions, the point of contact for external counsel or providers of legal technology are the inhouse counsel: they are lawyers themselves and can communicate on a level playing field. If non-lawyers communicate with external counsel or use legal technology, however, there is usually an information asymmetry which has to be taken into account. Examples of such information asymmetry include fact finding, the advice itself, the language which is used, the software interface or the invoicing and how it is communicated. Also, there is usually no dedicated budget for legal issues and no continuous dealing with legal topics. Instead, legal topics are handled when they arise and once they become pressing. This often affects the administration and management of legal documents. It is not uncommon that the legal documentation in small companies is not well organized and may even be non-compliant. Because of the only ad-hoc involvement of external counsel, legal issues are often not identified early but may become critical due to late targeting. This leads to more costs for legal advice than initially estimated.

4   How Can Small Companies "Run Legal as a Business"? Legal Tech!

How can small companies and their legal departments deal with the challenges described above and run their legal function as a business? For answering this question, we will first describe what "Running Legal as a Business" means for small companies (A). Secondly, we will outline the specific problems they need to solve and how they can tackle them with the use of technology (B). Finally, we will give a high-level overview of the solutions that are already available (C), and a description what a perfect solution for small companies can look like (D).

A. What exactly does it mean to run Legal as a Business? It means that the legal department is measured up to the same level of scrutiny as other corporate functions, is using similar processes and tools like other corporate functions, and applies comparable metrics as other corporate functions. This will only work if there are no structural differences between the legal function and other corporate functions, so that the same scrutiny, tools and metrics can apply. There are some undeniable differences between the legal function and other corporate functions: the legal function is not a profit center, it deals with many different types of issues relating to legal, risks and compliance on behalf of the entire company, and its members usually require a highly specialized education which makes it almost impossible to regularly exchange employees with other departments. However, other corporate functions like Finance or Information Technology have similar characteristics, yet they are usually much more integrated into the company system of measurable business standards. Since characteristics like specialized knowledge, dealing with (ad hoc) company risks and the lack of profit-generation are not exclusive for Legal but also apply to other corporate functions, these characteristics cannot serve as convincing arguments for a structural difference of the legal function. The differences between the legal department and other corporate functions, therefore, do not justify treating Legal as a function sui generis which operates with its own processes and does not apply the metrics other departments adhere to.

B. So, if legal departments can generally be treated similar to other corporate functions, which specific problems do especially small companies need to solve when running their legal department as a business or when they do not have a legal department at all?

(1) The first thing small companies will have to do is applying meaningful metrics to the operation of their legal department or legal affairs. Measuring the performance of the legal department, the quality of work of outside counsel, the price of outside counsel, the total workload, the sources of legal issues in the company, the time it takes for matters to be processed, the common deviations from standard contract templates, or the correlation between complexity of contract negotiation and total contract value (just to give a few examples) is crucial for management's ability to scrutinize the functioning of the legal department or of the legal processes, and to make decisions on targets, budgets or headcount.

(2) Metrics and KPIs can only be obtained when there is data that can be analyzed. Therefore, small companies will need to store and organize their relevant legal data in a way that it can be effectively accessed, standardized and analyzed. This can be done with services that are comparable to data room providers like High Q—cloud-based and secure storage that is intuitive and easy-to-use.

(3) Furthermore, in order to gain more control over the legal budget, an effective vendor management system for managing legal services providers should be used. Small companies use external counsel proportionally more often due to their limited inhouse legal capacity, which increases the need to effectively choose, engage, control, monitor and manage their outside counsel. This challenge has several aspects.

On the one hand, vendor management is usually done very effectively by procurement departments, but small companies may not have a dedicated procurement department with the appropriate processes in place. On the other hand, legal departments are reluctant to introduce processes which were not specifically designed for Legal. Procurement departments choose vendors based on clear metrics like price and performance. Clients, however, usually choose specific attorneys (and not law firms) based on trust. Such a trusted relationship might not be considered to fit into a system which chooses service providers based on a catalogue of metrics. However, much of the work of small companies is commoditized work for which the trust factor is less relevant than the measurable performance indicators. An effective system to help with choosing, monitoring and managing external counsel would, therefore, help aligning legal departments with standard business practices. This effect can already be seen in larger legal departments which use detailed panels of preferred providers from which they choose their legal services providers, ranging from small boutique firms to big law firms.

Also, small companies *without* legal departments often have even more difficulties to find a suitable lawyer and—once they have used one legal service provider—tend to stay with it. Here again information asymmetry is the key issue: for a non-lawyer, it can be very difficult to judge the quality of a lawyer and the appropriate time to spend on a specific matter. Monitoring and managing external counsel is also difficult for them for the same reason. A system for managing external counsel would, therefore, be needed to overcome this information asymmetry in order to effectively help small companies without legal departments. Such a system would need to suggest a lawyer to the company based on relevant information like area of expertise, price and experience. It would also need to provide trust for the company that this lawyer delivers high-quality work. The system would act as a trusted agent for the company to find a suitable lawyer.

(4) When planning the budget for the legal department or for legal affairs, it has to be taken into account that legal costs often arise out of unplanned events like litigation, compliance issues or other legal problems that were not foreseen. That is why a simple correlation between target budget and actual spend is often not helpful. Budgets, therefore, are planned more effectively if the support function of the legal department is adequately taken into account. That means, calculation of the legal budget should not simply consider the spending of the previous years, but the costs for legal affairs need to be calculated on the basis of the companies' type of business and the legal risk of every corporate function. This is relevant for small companies, because they regularly have longer periods with little or no legal spend. Nevertheless, also companies with a small or no legal department should ensure that enough accruals are set up for legal costs.

All of these challenges need effective systems in place—which is why technology will play a crucial role for small companies when dealing with legal affairs. Metrics, data storage and analysis, managing external counsel and controlling the legal spend can be done with IT systems that are tailored for the legal needs of small companies. Technology for the legal market is usually branded as Legal Tech. Legal Tech will be the driver for change in the legal services market.

C. What kind of solutions are already on the market for small legal departments? There are solutions available for different aspects of these problems. One category can be summarized as "lawyer-matching" services, i.e. connecting clients, who seek for legal advice, to lawyers. The effective use of such services enables SMEs to find suitable outside counsel and manage them better. Other solutions on the market support legal departments in specific tasks, like legal billing, contract analysis, legal document creation, contract negotiation or claim management. There are also software solutions for Legal Case Management (LCM) or Contract Management Solutions (CMS), or software suites for ELM. Many of the software solutions have in common that they are suitable more for larger legal departments than for small companies. They also often focus on services for legal departments, so small companies without a legal function will have difficulties using them.

D. This leads to the question which attributes a perfect solution for small companies would need to have. Small companies need a one-stop-shop for all their legal needs, a *digital legal department*. This service would be targeted at companies without a legal department, but could of course also be used when there is a small legal department in place. A crucial point is that it needs to be designed to be usable for non-lawyers, so that the information asymmetry barrier is removed. The whole user interface needs to take into account that non-lawyers, who do not know the legal jargon nor want to dive deep into legal theory, are using it. This can be achieved by allowing the users to create a request with their own words, even by speech. Also, a graphical interface will be used without detailed questions in "legalese". Natural language processing (NLP) and speech recognition will enable the system to understand the customer's request and contact the customer for additional details. The system needs to focus on providing seamless help for their customers.

(1) The *digital legal department* will handle all legal topics for the customer. This will be done through a combination of technology and human expertise. The technology will enable the system to automate requests whenever possible. At the same time, human expertise will make sure that customers receive a high-quality advice. A customer request will first be processed by the system, categorized and standardized. The more standard the customer request is, e.g. topics like incorporation of a company or drafting of General Terms and Conditions (GTC) for a web shop, the more effective an automatization will be. The level of automatization that can be achieved will increase as Artificial Intelligence (AI) technologies like machine learning and deep neural networks advance. After the request is processed by the system and if it cannot be solved by an automated process, an attorney will contact the customer and provide him with the solution for his request. For this, a partner attorney network needs to be established. It will need to be ensured that this partner network consists only of high-quality and experienced attorneys. Customers will need to have the same level of trust in these external counsel as if they were recommended by personal contacts. This could, for example, be guaranteed by an extensive vetting system for the partner counsel network and by an effective rating system for the services of partner counsel. Such rating system however needs to be more sophisticated than a simple 5-star system by customers. The ideal solution will be a curated rating system where the service provider helps in reviewing the performance of the outside counsel.

(2) An important barrier for small companies to seek advice from outside counsel when facing legal issues are the intransparent and unforeseeable costs of lawyers. Therefore, an alternative pricing model must be applied instead of the traditional hourly rates model. The solution could be a monthly subscription fee for legal advice, or service packages with fixed fees for certain topics (e.g. creation of standard GTC, incorporation of a company with standard incorporation documents). Customers will be

invoiced by the *digital legal department*, but the revenue will be shared between the platform and the involved partner attorney.

(3) A third aspect to such a solution will be the effective management of the legal data of the company. Legal data includes all data that is relevant for legal or regulatory purposes. The benefit of an effective legal data management is that external counsel are in turn enabled to provide a better and more effective service, because they can access the relevant and standardized legal data and communicate with the client through the service. If the company, for example, needs GTC for its web shop, the external counsel can access the data of the company to see what other terms and conditions already exist, where the registered seat of the company is, if and which open source licenses apply, if contracts with vendors are in place, etc. Identification of the relevant legal data will be done with the help of AI technologies such as machine learning and deep learning. Of course, data protection legislation will have to be taken into account, and data may, for example, only be stored and handled on servers in the customer's country. With a structured data base of all legal data, small companies can also be provided with metrics on all aspects of their legal affairs, or they can be benchmarked against the competition or market. Using and analyzing the legal data will also help inhouse lawyers or decision-makers in a company to judge whether legal support is required.

(4) The service may also offer legal project management tools to effectively manage projects that may involve different legal service providers. Legal service may be provided by lawyers with different specialization who contribute to a specific project. Especially when mandating smaller law firms or sole practitioners, it is likely that not all legal fields are covered by one firm or one person. In order to make sure that all participating professionals work together without friction (even if they come from different firms and have not previously worked together), such legal projects need to be managed effectively. This can be organized with IT tools; such tools already exist for general project management in the market. Not only lawyers with different specialty fields may be involved in a project when tasks are unbundled; different legal service providers including non-lawyers, professionals from other jurisdictions or even software could also be involved. This diverse supply chain needs to be managed by an ideal solution for small companies.

(5) Finally, there may also be interfaces to other IT systems of the company, e.g. the Enterprise Resource Planning (ERP) like SAP or Customer Relationship Management (CRM) like salesforce.com. This way, not only legal risks may be detected early, but also smart contracts may be implemented that perform certain tasks automatically, like contract renewals and terminations or supply ordering.

(6) But even if the *digital legal department* as a one-stop solution for SMEs' legal needs is not (yet) on the market, SMEs need tools to help them tackle specific legal tasks and processes. An automatization of as many processes

as possible enables SMEs and their GCs to concentrate on tasks that require human expertise. Dedicated tools for automatization should be used for tasks like analyzing contracts or deciding if legal action should be taken in a specific case. These tasks can be automated with the help of AI technologies to perform work that used to be done by paralegals or junior inhouse counsel. IT tools can perform such tasks faster and even with more reliability than human experts. When using such tools, SMEs and their legal functions can balance the disadvantage they used to have against large corporations and large legal departments: The difference in size between large and small legal departments becomes less relevant when more and more tasks and processes are automated with affordable IT tools.

5   Conclusion

The future of Legal is in technology. Legal can only run as a business if effective IT tools and processes are used. This does not only apply to large corporation, but it is even more important for small companies without legal departments. For these companies—which form the majority of businesses in all major economies, Legal Tech will be the key to run their legal affairs as any other business processes even without having an inhouse legal function. Legal Tech will enable small companies to effectively tackle the challenges they are confronted with today and in the near future. Providers of Legal Tech solutions will benefit from this disruptive innovation. One example for the attributes of a successful Legal Tech solution for SMEs is a *digital legal department*. There will be many more Legal Tech products that will effectively solve the needs of lawyers, clients and companies.

Legal Tech will change the way Legal is done in the future, for inhouse legal departments, small companies, lawyers and other legal service providers.

Liquid Legal Context
by Dr. Dierk Schindler, Dr. Roger Strathausen, Kai Jacob

With his article, von Alemann covers a huge gap that often occurs in the public debate about the transformation in the legal industry. Typically big law firms and large companies with sizeable legal departments lead the discussion and are subject to research—while there are thousands and thousands of small and midsize enterprises (SME) that form the backbone of the economy and that only have a very small legal inhouse function—or do not employ lawyers at all.

For SMEs, legal management contains a much larger degree of vendor management, i.e. dealing with optimizing the value that can be obtained from using external legal service providers, traditionally outside counsel. Contrary

(continued)

to many, von Alemann expects the rapidly materializing opportunity to replace bespoke and customized legal advice by standardized technology to play out in the area of the SMEs as well. The legal budget is lower in the first place and thus the economic pressure to embrace new opportunities is higher. At the same time, the barrier of non-lawyers talking to (external) lawyers in order to resolve a legal issue in a business oriented manner is even higher— what an opportunity if that could be resolved by means of technology!

So what would be the optimal technology-based solution for SMEs with a small—or even no—legal department? According to von Alemann, it is what he calls a "digital legal department". The whole user interface needs to take into account that non-lawyers, who do not know the legal jargon nor want to dive deep into legal theory, are using it. Natural language processing (NLP) and speech recognition will enable the system to understand the customer's request and contact the customer for additional details.

This is actually quite intriguing even for a "large company" legal manager: what if your team could literally "talk to" technology that would then translate the request, connect it to the sources in which or by which the solution can be found, and comes back once the solution has been generated? What helps SMEs to cope with legal demand in the first place is an enormous lever for efficiency and cost effectiveness for more sizeable legal departments.

Adding the enormous combined buying power of the SMEs in the legal industry to the opportunity technology provides to them, easily translate into a big economic threat to the business models of law firms. This is why Meents and Allen, representing one of the big law firms, view transformation as a call to action to define value in a new way that goes far beyond the "cost lense".

References

Callier, M., & Reeb, A. (2015). The industrial age of law: Operationalizing legal practice through process improvement. *Oregon Law Review, 93*, 853–925.

Christensen, C. M. (1997). *The innovator's dilemma.* Boston: Harvard Business School Press.

Galbenski, D. J., & Barringer, D. (2013). *Legal visionaries: How to make their innovations work for you.* https://www.amazon.com/Legal-Visionaries-make-their-innovations/dp/1484075366.

Hartung, M., & Gärtner, A. (2015). Das "More for less"-Paradox. *Deutscher AnwaltSpiegel, 25*, 15–18.

Ribstein, L. E. (2012). Delawyering the corporation. *Wisconsin Law Review, 2012*, 305–331.

Susskind, R. (2013). *Tomorrow's lawyers: An introduction to your future.* Oxford: Oxford University Press.

Zahra, S. A. (2005). Entrepreneurial risk taking in family firms. *Family Business Review, 18*(1), 23–40.

Dr. Sven von Alemann is an attorney-turned-entrepreneur and founder of early stage Legal Tech startup rfrnz, which provides contract analysis based on Artificial Intelligence techniques like machine learning and deep neural networks. He is an experienced attorney in IT/IP law. Before founding rfrnz, Sven held positions as Associate at the law firm McDermott Will & Emery, Legal Counsel at Fujitsu and Senior Legal Counsel at SAP Hybris. Sven obtained an LL. M. from the University of Christchurch (2003), his Ph.D. from the University of Hanover (2008) and an Executive MBA from the Technical University in Munich (2015).

The Value of Everything: How to Measure and Deliver Legal Value?

Jan Geert Meents and Stephen Allen

Abstract

Oscar Wilde famously described a cynic as someone who knows *". . .the price of everything and the value of nothing"*. Legal departments have allowed themselves to become the focus of such cynicism, seen as a (high) cost, rarely able to articulate the value of what they do.

Measuring cost is important, legal functions need to be more efficient and their failure to do so has only increased the level of scrutiny they face.

Almost all commentary on legal departments, to date, has focused on the cost of legal and its failure to leverage technology and alternative ways of working.

However, if everything is viewed only through the "cost lens" then effectiveness is often overlooked—and 'value' not understood.

What, therefore, is "legal value" and how do we measure and deliver it? In answering these questions, we will also consider *Why do companies "buy law"* and *What should their return on investment be?*

1 Costs Are, Currently, Everything

As our industry stands today, there remains an unblinking focus on the cost of legal services. There are many reasons for this:

J.G. Meents (✉)
DLA Piper UK LLP, Maximilianstraße 2, 80539 Munich, Germany
e-mail: jan.meents@dlapiper.com

S. Allen
LexFuturus, London, UK
e-mail: Stephen@lexfuturus.com

© Springer International Publishing AG 2017
K. Jacob et al. (eds.), *Liquid Legal*, Management for Professionals,
DOI 10.1007/978-3-319-45868-7_15

1.1   Perception (Versus Reality)

The "cost" of lawyers has been, in equal part, a source of humor and frustration for many business people. However, if we take a step back and look at legal cost compared to other areas of business expenditure, we will see that it does not represent a major area of cost, for most organizations. A survey by PwC in 2013 revealed that, on average, cost of legal (both the cost of the in-house legal team and the fees paid to external legal advisors) was just less than 1 % of revenue. This figure rises to almost 2 % for highly regulated businesses but drops to around 0.3 % of revenue for simpler business models, such as retailers.

By comparison, as a percentage of revenue (Table 1).

So why is the cost of legal seemingly such an issue?

1.2   Historical Prejudice

Although not the case today, historically in-house legal teams have been seen as "the department that likes to say no". Many avoid going to legal for this reason. We all know this view was unfair then and is wildly out of line with the reality of what most in-house lawyers offer today. However, the perception does remain amongst many in business, unjustly.

Those who do go to legal, and then engage external lawyers, have found the lack of precision when agreeing on the potential fee a reason for unease. Further frustration is created through the wide spectrum of fees charged for work of a similar type.

If someone's livelihood is based on the number of hours they spend and the pages they fill—then are they not going to have more meetings and write more letters? Again, this is a case of *perception versus reality*. Lawyers work incredibly hard for their clients and in most cases, will self-regulate the amount of time spent that is added to the final bill—generally applying further discounts before issuing it.

1.3   Modernizing the Production Process But. . .

The issue of cost is continually cited by many market commentators as a need for lawyers to modernize (most strikingly by Professor Susskind in a number of books, including *"The End of Lawyers?"*). Industry *"gurus"* claim that applying new

Table 1 LexFuturus Research—Support Department Costs—v—Revenue, 2015

Area	% of revenue
Information technology	3.4
Marketing	2.8
Finance function	2.7
Legal	*0.9*

business concepts—such as *"lean six sigma"*, technology, project management or even artificial intelligence—would drive down the cost of production.

However, here again the "dictate of the hourly rate" holds the industry back. New ways of working will require investment, some of which will be significant. If, however, "hours worked" remains the sole metric of choice—such investment is difficult to justify.

In order to encourage the investment needed to ultimately reduce the cost of production, legal services must be bought and sold differently. But how?

1.4 The Great Procurement Experiment

In recent years we have seen a growing number of procurement departments getting involved in buying legal services. For want of a universal metric, procurement professionals have resorted to comparing hourly rates and discounting as a means to drive down cost. Most law firms have trimmed or, in some cases, even eradicated margins to meet the criteria necessary to continuing working for some clients. The suppliers have, by and large, met the challenge thus far but little margin remains for this to continue.

1.5 Now Adding the Global Financial Crisis to the Mix

Post the Global Financial Crisis (GFC), we have seen further pressure on "legal cost". Whilst, comparatively, legal remains a small area of business expenditure for most organizations, it has come under much greater scrutiny post the GFC.

There are two main drivers for this: regulatory burden, and pressure on business to reduce cost (Fig. 1).

Post the GFC, all businesses have focused even more keenly on cost, and the target for potential further areas of cost reduction has fallen on *legal*. Having already looked at applying process, technology or outsourcing efficiencies to other support functions—such as finance, marketing, IT and HR—legal had been largely left alone, not only because it was a comparatively small area of business expenditure, but also due to the fact that legal cost (unlike HR, Finance and IT) is only partly spent internally, while an equal percentage spent on external lawyers.

Fig. 1 LexFuturus 2015

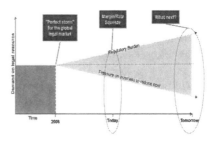

Savings gained by putting finance or HR teams into shared service centers were not available when looking at the legal team, and therefore those teams were left largely untouched.

The second reason why legal has risen up the agenda is that the burden of regulation has burgeoned since the GFC. Companies just have more law and regulation to deal with than before and this trend is set to continue. Examples would be the great volume of financial market regulation on banks, anti-bribery and anti-corruption laws or additional and renewed data protection regulation. The impact of the increase in regulation is further compounded by the requirements it places on organizations in complying with it.

Further, it is no longer sufficient to have policies in place to set out how the business is to comply with the regulations. Adopting the model established by Sarbanes-Oxley, organizations now need to be able to demonstrative "active compliance"—tracking policy, documentation, adherence and deviation. The expense and effort of compliance is far greater than it was previously, adding cost and even further scrutiny.

However, as every in house lawyer knows, the penalties for non-compliance are far greater than before the GFC. The fines are no longer symbolic and are ever more punitive. The maximum fine in the UK for a data protection breach used to be £5000—it can be up to 4 % of annual global revenue under the new General Data Protection Regulation (GDPR). The penalties for directors now include the threat of custodial sentences. Being non-compliant is not an option. The burden of risk escalates at the very same time when the need to reduce legal cost increases.

So what is next? What should in-house lawyers be focusing on?

2   Value of Everything

All this focus on cost is, ultimately, limiting for in-house legal teams. If in-house lawyers are to "run legal as a business" they need to change the perception of what they do as being a cost and instead look at it as an investment, which is driving value for the business. In order to achieve that, they have to be able to articulate, target and measure legal value. To assess the investment in legal, we have to better understand the value of legal. How can it be measured? Where should investment be made?

To understand this better, we first have to ask why do businesses buy legal.
Businesses buy legal for two reasons:

1. to help ensure that money doesn't go out of the business—*value leakage*; or
2. to help secure money comes into the business—*value realization*

Ultimately all efforts of legal should be directed to help ensure that the business prevents *value leakage* and secures *value realization*.

So, we have identified a value metric that legal can be measured by, but where does this value come from?

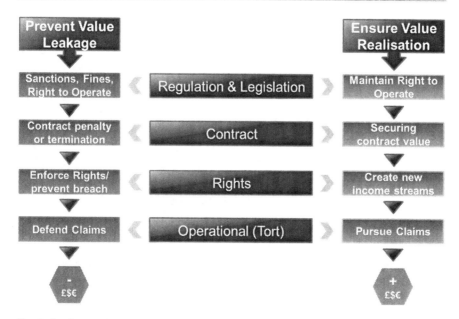

Fig. 2 LexFuturus 2014

Legal's role is to protect the business from risk. We often talk about *legal risk,* but when running legal as a business and looking at our role as creating legal value, we shouldn't be focused on "legal risk". Instead, the focus should be on what the risks of the business are and how they are crystallized in law.

As set out below, business risk is crystallized in law in four ways (Fig. 2):

1. Business Risk can be crystallized in **Regulation and Legislation**. Value can be lost through the business' failure to observe its obligations—as a consequence of which it could find itself fined, its operations limited, or its right to operate lost.
2. **Contracts** crystallize obligations which, if not met, could lead to penalties or termination, but they also enshrine rights that need to be secured in order to realize value.
3. **Rights** need to be enforced and breaches prevented.
4. Things happen, **operationally,** within all businesses and claims need to be both, defended and pursued.

Therein lies the challenge for the in-house legal team. Whilst there are business risks crystallized in law, and the responsibility for remedying failure sits with legal—these risks materialize within the operational parts of the business.

Things that trigger a risk event rarely go wrong in legal. Typically, a breach of contract occurs based on acts or omissions in the business, while the contract itself might be perfectly legally sound. Equally, the business may breach a policy or

Fig. 3 LexFuturus 2012

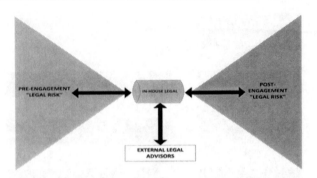

regulation even though legal has highlighted that risk in a policy manual or during training.

These risks are realized before legal is involved—("Pre-Engagement Legal Risk"); or after legal has been involved ("Post-Engagement Legal Risk") (Fig. 3).

In relative terms, the impact of value leakage or value realization on the profit and loss of an organization is higher than the cost of legal.

2.1 Running Legal as a Business

Therefore, if we are to run legal as a business, we need to start looking at the value impact legal can have. Companies need to be able to prioritize where they invest ("legal spend") and then look at the return on investment that it provides for the business.

This may mean that companies no longer look at how we reduce expenditure on legal cost from $100 to say $90 but, instead, they will look at what return on investment spending $100 delivers to the business and what the impact of increasing or decreasing expenditure may have on legal value realized. Would spending $90 still deliver the same return or would spending $110 deliver exponentially more?

What if legal were to measure and report the amount of legal value realized instead of how much was spent on costs?

If legal were able to measure, report and make decisions on where to "invest" *legal spend*, based on legal value realized, then they would be operating as a business.

2.1.1 Measuring Legal Value

So, all that is left now is how to measure legal value?

There are two ways to do this. One is to adopt a lawyerly approach by trying to identify the direct impact of the legal involvement in any outcome. To do this, you need to be able to calculate the value outcome to the business, had legal not been engaged (the *"but for legal"* question) and then be able to demonstrate that either

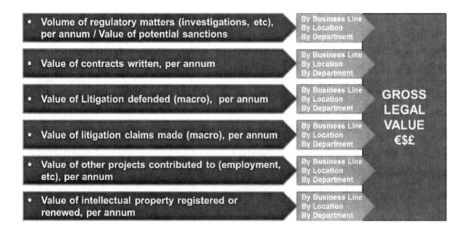

Fig. 4 LexFuturus 2015

Value Leakage would have occurred or Value Realization would not have been ensured, if had the legal team not been involved.

To do this, it is necessary to map the sources of legal demand, benchmark the outcomes and then repurpose the legal function to drive the outcomes that directly delivered value—i.e. ensure that "value in" happens and that "value out" doesn't happen.

This is a method that requires a large investment in time and systems to track. It is also a level of measurement that the rest of the business does not go into.

We can learn here from how marketing, procurement, finance or any other area of the business articulate their contribution. By adopting such an approach, legal can demonstrate the contribution it had made towards business outcomes.

To identify this value, it is necessary to collate data relevant to your business, an example of which is set out below (Fig. 4).

As this table sets out, gross legal value can be assessed through: recording and articulating the value of regulatory matters worked on (in terms of fines or sanctions); or the value of contracts written by legal; the value of litigation defended or pursued.

Recording this information by business line, and/or location, and/or department will aid the quality of data collected.

3   Conclusion

If we were to run legal as a business, we wouldn't just concentrate on cost. Managing cost is an important part of business but it must be managed in conjunction with realizing returns for the business. We need to focus on delivering legal value.

Therefore instead of calling this cost, call it spend. Look at how that spend is invested in terms of the true value it delivers to the business: does it assist the business to secure that money comes in, or does it protect the business against needlessly allowing money to flow out?

Decide where to invest to drive maximum value and use this as your business case to ensure that you have the funds necessary to invest to drive further value in the future.

Don't be a cynic. Know the value of everything.

Liquid Legal Context
By Dr. Dierk Schindler, Dr. Roger Strathausen, Kai Jacob

Meents and Allen challenge the very common and inhibiting fact that legal departments are mainly managed with an overemphasis on the cost-dimension. They conclude that if everything is viewed only through the "cost lens" then effectiveness is often overlooked—and "value" not under-stood. If cost is the perception and the center of the metrics we offer, we should not be surprised that we fuel the prejudice that lawyers need supervision when spending the company's money.

Even beyond that, as long as hourly rates, lawyers per billion of revenue etc. are the focus of C-level debates, any innovation offered will be viewed mainly in terms of how it can reduce cost—rather than in the context of the value it can provide to the department and the business at large. Meents and Allen point out the paradox in which corporate legal functions find themselves: ever increasing cost pressure while regulation explodes and compliance with new laws becomes ever more complex—and non-compliance ever more costly.

In order to break the vicious circle, the authors offer a change of perspective, based on the question: why do companies buy law? It is all about securing value, either by preventing value leakage from or by securing value creation for the company. The call to action is to cease stopping at legal cost—but rather call it legal spend and answer question if it was a reasonable investment into securing value for the company and if it was worth it. This directly links into the push towards value-based KPI's and performance management that Pauleau, Roquilly and Collard have established, as well as Timmer's concept on managing the legal function.

Dr. Jan Geert Meents is a partner in the Munich office of DLA Piper. As a technology lawyer, Jan has over 15 years of experience advising IT companies and national and international businesses in IT-related matters. His practice covers a combination of corporate, intellectual property and other legal issues specific to the technology sector. Jan has published numerous articles on tech law related matters and has co-edited the standard compendium for IT lawyers in Germany and a book on legal aspects of cloud computing. Jan is a frequent speaker at tech conferences and holds a lectureship on IT contract law at the University of Oldenburg.

Stephen Allen "A highly experienced operational and transformational business leader who has been at the very vanguard of delivering legal market change and is internationally recognized as a leading expert and innovator.

He worked as a lawyer both in private practice and in-house during early career, before crossing the board table to become Managing Director of two divisions of Orange-France Télécom in the UK and Continental Europe.

Stephen led PwC's legal market advisory practice, internationally, advising and delivering value-led change programs for law firms and corporate legal functions.

Most recently devised and created the Service Delivery & Quality Function at DLA Piper."

The Value Add of Legal Departments in Disputes: Making a Business Case Rather Than Providing Pure Legal Advise

Ulrich Hagel

Abstract

Legal Departments are usually involved when it comes to Business-to-Business (B2B) disputes. They provide legal opinions on the subject matter at hand, consult on the available dispute resolution mechanisms and are the interfaces to the external law firms. However, disputes are usually not the companies' core business, and thus the commercial aspects of solving disputes are predominant for the company. The following article describes how disputes can be looked at commercially and how they can be run as a Business Case. The article also describes the role and responsibility of the Legal Department in such a Business Case, and several Tools that assist the Legal Department in increasing their contribution to efficient and effective dispute resolution.

Todays Legal Departments need to add value to their corporations through supporting the business in delivering both a sustainable bottom line and improvements and protections to transactions (Fig. 1).[1]

This applies especially in dispute situations as any Euro in dispute that has been resolved has a direct impact on the bottom line. Legal Departments can add value to their corporations in dispute situations by focussing on risk reduction and profit maximization rather than running litigations.

---

[1]Desjardins (2016).

U. Hagel (✉)
KonsensKanzlei Berlin, Linienstraße 106, 10115 Berlin, Germany
e-mail: u.hagel@konsenskanzlei.de

K. Jacob et al. (eds.), *Liquid Legal*, Management for Professionals,
DOI 10.1007/978-3-319-45868-7_16

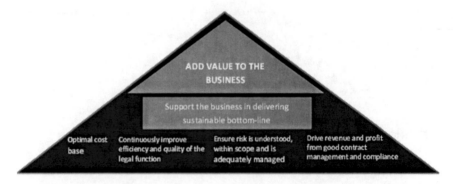

Fig. 1 The value pyramid of the Legal Department (Desjardins 2016)

1   Business Disputes

A dispute is a disagreement, a conflict or controversy.[2] Business disputes are all disputes related to either the corporation or the business transactions (Fig. 2). *Internal business conflicts* are conflicts within a business enterprise and include (1) conflicts between Business Units, Divisions and affiliates of a company, (2) workplace disputes[3] and (3) disputes between shareholders.[4] *External business conflicts* are those of the business enterprise with external parties, be it other business enterprises (B2B-conflicts), authorities (B2A-conflicts) or consumers (B2C-conflicts). Disputes can also be differentiated by the context (e.g. legal disputes are disagreements as to rights[5]) or the type of conflict (e.g. relationship conflicts, data conflicts, value conflicts, interest conflicts, structural conflicts, strategy conflicts).[6] Legal Departments are usually involved in external business disputes but might also get involved in internal business conflicts.

---

[2]Conflict or Controversy: The Black's Law Dictionary: What is a Dispute, retrieved from the internet on April 22nd, 2016 http://thelawdictionary.org/dispute/

[3]E.g. between employees, employee and employer, between or within teams, employer and works council.

[4]Hagel (2012), pp. 127 et seq.

[5]Schreuer (2008), pp. 960 (978): "A dispute will be legal if the claim is based on treaties, legislation and other sources of law and if remedies such as restitution or damages are sought".

[6]The Circle of Conflicts: Moore (2014), pp. 106 et seq.

Business Conflicts					
Internal Conflicts =„Intra-Business-Conflicts"			**External Conflicts** = Conflicts between business subjects („Inter-Business-Conflicts")		
Internal Business-conflicts between Business Units or affiliates of a company	Workplace Conflicts	Shareholder Conflicts	Between independent companies = **B2B-Conflicts**	Between Companies and Consumers = **B2C-Conflicts**	Between Companies and Third Parties (e.g. administration = **B2A-Conflicts**)

Fig. 2 Overview on business conflicts (Hagel 2011, p. 128)

2   The Traditional Role of the Legal Department in Solving Disputes

When the going gets tough, the business is asking the Legal Department for advice, help and support. Management wants to get an evaluation of the risks and/or opportunities of the dispute, based on either the law or the contract. It is the role of the Legal Department to provide such advice. In case external advice is needed, the Legal Department selects the external law firm[7] and provide the interface between the external lawyers and the business. External advice might be required for the following reasons:

1. the in-house Legal Department cannot provide the requested expertise (area of law or jurisdiction), or
2. the in-House Legal Department does not have sufficient resources to provide the legal advice within the required time frame, or
3. a second opinion is required.

In the event, the dispute cannot be solved through negotiation, the Legal Department advises on the next possible steps to be taken in order to resolve the dispute. Usually the in-house counsel will check the dispute resolution clause of the underlying contract and will advise accordingly. In case disputes do not relate to contracts, the in-house counsel will check the applicable law and advise accordingly.

---

[7]Legal departments can choose law firms either directly or from a pre-selected panel of law firms. For the selection of the external counsel, they can also invite several law firms for offers and presentations (beauty contest).

3   Disputes from a Commercial View Point

"Winning lawsuits is not the goal, minimizing risks and maximizing profit is the goal".[8] This citation describes perfectly the commercial view on business disputes. It considers several aspects (e.g. financial returns, relationship, reputation) and dimensions (e.g. individual case, long-term) at the same time.

3.1   Maximized Profit

The profit (P) is the difference between the financial return (R) and the invested dispute costs (C):

$$P = R - C$$

At first glance the formula sounds pretty simple. However, the variables R and C are not independent but linked to each other. The Legal Department needs to identify the dispute resolution process with the highest return on investment. This can either be evaluated on an individual case basis, a business relationship basis or a holistic enterprise basis. The following example may illustrate the different dimensions:

> Company A bought equipment from Company B. The equipment is defective. The parties disagree on the root-cause and thus the responsibility for the defect rectification. As company B is not willing to repair the equipment, company A repairs the equipment on its costs (5 M€). A claims the incurred costs from B.

With respect to the individual case, the profit of A is maximized when the difference between the costs to settle the claim and the compensation received from B is the highest. The settlement costs are not to be confused with the repair costs of 5 M€ which is the face value of the claim. The costs to settle are the costs needed to resolve the dispute. They comprise the own costs to work out the claim file, costs for external support (e.g. external lawyers, technical experts), administration fees for court or dispute resolution providers.[9] Assumed B would offer to settle in out of court negotiations for 2.5 M€ and A had invested 200 K€ in own resources and a technical expert, the "profit"[10] for A would be 2.3 M€. If in comparison A had sued B in arbitration and got 3 M€ awarded, but had to spend 1 M€ in own costs, external lawyers, arbitration fees and technical experts, the profit would only be 2 M€ (Fig. 3).

---

[8]Dauer, Edward A., CPR 1982, S. xviii.

[9]E.g. fees for arbitrators and arbitration institutes, mediators and mediation institutes, adjudicators and adjudication institutes, dispute boards.

[10]In fact it is a reduction of A's loss by 2,3 M€ as A incurred 5 M€ as a loss by rectifying the equipment.

Dispute Resolution	Return	Costs	Profit
Negotiated Settlement	2.5 M€	0.2 M€	2.3 M€
Arbitration	3.0 M€	1.0 M€	2.0 M€

Fig. 3 Comparison of profit in case example

In this example, maximizing profit would mean to settle during negotiations instead of fighting the claim through in arbitration.[11] It is thus of importance that the in-house counsel can easily evaluate the costs to come for all available dispute resolution processes and recommend the best suited process (as described in detail under Sect. 4.3). The cost calculator (Fig. 27) is a good supporting tool in that regard.

The problem in maximizing the profit lies in the uncertainty. A definite comparison can only be made hindsight and only when an award is rendered, i.e. party A declined the settlement offer of B. However, A has to decide on whether to settle out of court or not before the award. A's decision at that moment in time can only be based on assumptions, expectations and experience. The evaluation of the expected result of the arbitration is the task of the Legal Department in collaboration with the other functions.[12] How to run the calculation of the expected value is shown below under Sect. 4.3.2.

However, for dispute settlement considerations, focusing on the individual case is not sufficient. Sustainable profitability is the goal. When claiming B, A is running the risk to overexcite the demand, causing B to terminate the business relationship with A. This might cause consequential costs for A, such as resourcing costs, higher prizes, etc. Maximizing the long-term profitability of A requires to consider such potential consequences as well.

3.2 Minimized Risk

Declaring risk minimization the goal of dispute management implies that the term "risk" does not include positive effects of an uncertainty (=opportunities) as can be found in some risk definitions.[13] With respect to disputes, risk can thus be defined as an uncertainty that an actual return on an investment will be lower than the expected return.

In case of an offensive claim[14] there is uncertainty on the outcome. When the claim is submitted, the other party can either accept, partially accept, reject or even

---

[11]For a detailed cost comparison of Court Litigation, Arbitration and Mediation, see: Hagel (2013), chapter 2.16.

[12]Depending on case and organizational structure, this could be Project Management, Procurement, Finance, and/or Engineering.

[13]PMBOK 5th edition (2013) defines risk as "an uncertain event or condition that, if it occurs, has a positive or negative effect on one or more project objectives"; for the different risk definitions see Hillson and Simon (2012), p. 3f; Maytonera (2013), p. 109.

[14]An offensive claim is a claim against another party. A defensive claim is a claim received from another party.

counterclaim.[15] In case of rejection or a counterclaim, the claimant may waive the claim or take legal action. If the claimant takes legal action, the outcome (award) is uncertain. In the best case, A could win in total with reimbursement of the investment costs; in the worst case A could lose all and is even obliged to reimburse B the investment costs.

3.3   Maximizing Profit While Minimizing Risks

The goal in dispute management is to minimize the risks while maximizing the profit. In the example, the uncertainty can be reduced or even be excluded at several stages; however, the impact on the profit is different. Not claiming B at all would reduce any uncertainty right from the start, but does so at the expense of not getting any profit/reduction of loss. Accepting the settlement offer of B also eliminates uncertainty; but also the chance to get the full amount claimed from B. Fighting it through to a final award eliminates uncertainty by risking to get a lower profit than by settling out of court or even by risking to make further losses.[16]

4   How Legal Departments Turn Disputes into Business Cases

4.1   Dispute Avoidance

Except for rare cases, avoiding conflicts and disputes makes commercial sense. In order to effectively avoid conflicts, the main causes of disputes need to be known. Disputes are often caused by miscommunication. Parties communicate (1) on the wrong subjects, (2) in the wrong way and (3) at the wrong time.

4.1.1   Wrong Subject: Positions Instead of Interests
In order to achieve good and sustainable results, whether in contract negotiations or conflict negotiations, it is essential that the parties express their interests rather than their positions. When entering into mutual contractual obligations, the parties expect a certain return. Those expectations are based on the parties interests. In order to achieve a sustainable business relationship, the interests need to be satisfied. However, during contract negotiations, the parties usually argue on positions rather than openly communicating their interests. This in turn leads to unsatisfied expectations and finally to frustration. Conflicts are the inevitable

---

[15]Further consequences might include (without being exhaustive): stop of production, termination of business relationship, involvement of media.

[16]Further losses can be incurred by losing own investment costs and compensating the investment costs of the opponent(s).

consequence. This can be avoided by an interest-based negotiation.[17] As it often is difficult for the parties to determine their interests, it might be helpful to involve a neutral person to structure the negotiation and help the parties to identify their interests in order to create solutions for mutual gain ("Deal-Mediation").[18]

4.1.2 Wrong Way: Clarity Is Key

Communication
Communication implies the risk of misunderstandings. Besides the issue of losing information on the way from the sender to the receiver,[19] the usage of different "frequencies" is a major source for misunderstandings.

According to Friedemann Schulz von Thun's "four-ear-model" (Fig. 4), each statement contains four messages:

1. Factual information
2. a self statement,
3. a relationship indicator,
4. an appeal

Each of the four messages is sent on a different frequency. In order to have a flawless communication, sender and receiver must tune to the same frequency. Unfortunately, each statement contains all four messages at the same time and is thus sent on four different frequencies. Often, sender and receiver are using different frequencies. The sender for example just wanted to send factual information ("The light is green") while the receiver heard an appeal ("you better drive

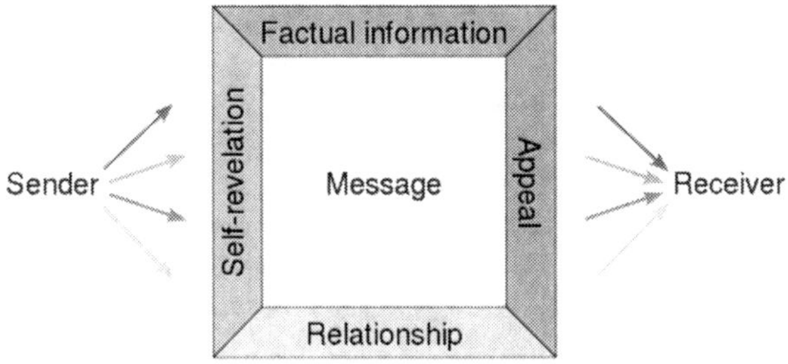

Fig. 4 Communication square by Schulz von Thun

---

[17]"Focus on interests, not positions" is the second principle of the Harvard concept on principled negotiations: *Fisher/Ury/Patton* Getting to Yes (1991).

[18]More details on Deal-Mediation: Peppet (2004), pp. 283 et seq.; Berkel (2015), p. 4; Hagel (2014a), § 1 Rn 18; Hagel (2016), § 151 Rn 1.

[19]Not all of the information that the sender intends to send is actually received on the other side. Losses occur at any transformation point of the transmission process. For oral communication, the first transformation takes place from the brain to the mouth of the sender. The sender only says a portion of what he intended to say. From what he said, only a portion is received by the ear of the receiver of which only a portion is used by the receiver's brain in order to understand.

now"). Awareness of the available frequencies and clarity on the message helps to reduce the risk of misunderstandings and disputes in consequence. It is the task of the Legal Department to advise the Business on the different frequencies of communication and (1) to draft clear contracts and letters and (2) to interpret received messages in accordance with the four frequencies and get clarity from the sender on the intended message.

Contract Drafting

Drafting contracts is an art. Especially lawyers usually see the goal in drafting contracts to hold in court ("the water-proof contract") and protect the client by focusing on passive clauses.[20] The addressee of the lawyers is the judge to rule the case if anything goes wrong.[21] From a business perspective however, the purpose of contracts is to guide the contracting parties in achieving the underlying business objectives and minimizing the risk of failure. Business people would expect the contract to be addressed to them to ensure that nothing goes wrong. Due to this mismatch of expectations with respect to the purpose of a contract, it is not surprising that contract interpretation is still one of the major sources of contract litigation[22] and that the failure to understand the contractual obligations remains under the top five root-causes for disputes.[23] In order to prevent misunderstandings, contracts need to be user-friendly and clear. It is the role of the Legal Department to ensure that contracts are drafted in a manner that enables the parties to perform their contractual scope and minimize the risk of non-performance. The better the parties understand the contract, the more they act accordingly and the less they enter into conflicts. A better contract understanding can be achieved by (1) plain language, (2) user-friendly layout and (3) visualization.[24]

4.1.3 Wrong Time: Always Too Late

Communication in dispute situations usually takes place when the problems cannot be hidden any longer. This behaviour is due to the conflict adverseness and the corresponding desire for harmony, the inability to admit failures and the hope that issues might disappear over time. In consequence, issues and potential risks are not addressed early on, and the parties are not able to commonly mitigate the risks. When the issue gets obvious, the parties start blaming each other and the spiral of

---

[20]Contract clauses can be differentiated by active clauses (which describe the roles and responsibilities with respect to contract performance) and passive clauses (which describe the consequences of non-performance): see IACCM, Contract and Commercial Management—The operational Guide, p. 123, 366, 522; Haapio and Siedel (2013), pp. 84 et seq.

[21]Mamula and Hagel (2015), p. 472; Haapio (2013), p. 2; Stark and Choplin (2012).

[22]Passera (2012), p. 376.

[23]According to the Arcadis Global Construction Disputes Report 2015 "Failure to understand and/or comply with its contractual obligations by the employer/contractor/subcontractor" is worldwide ranking no. 4 as cause of disputes and interestingly in Common Law countries it ranks even worse (US no. 3, UK no. 2).

[24]In more detail: Mamula and Hagel (2015), p. 473.

escalation is triggered. To avoid such situations, it is, besides other functions, the task of the Legal Department to create a business relationship between the contracting parties based on trust and transparency rather than mistrust and confidentiality. The contribution of the Legal Department in building a trustful relationship starts by drafting contracts in a collaborative way.[25] In dispute situations, the Legal Department can brake the spiral of "naming, blaming and claiming"[26] by encouraging the business to admit responsibility where necessary.

4.2   Contract Management

In most cases, the people involved in negotiating the contract are no longer involved in the contract execution, and the responsibility is transferred from the Sales Department (respective Purchasing Department) to the Project Management Department. From a Contract Management point of view, it is essential that the knowledge gained during the negotiation process is being transferred to the team executing the contract. The Legal Department plays a core role in the transition phase,[27] helping to fully understand the obligations entered into under the contract by summarizing the major rights and obligations of the parties, the stories behind the clauses and the expressed intent of the parties. Usually this is done at the Project Kick-off-Meeting. At the beginning of the execution phase, the Project Team allocates the roles and responsibilities of functions and individuals with respect to all contractual obligations.[28] During the further execution of the contract, it might be helpful to organize regular Contract Awareness Workshops to explain to the team which contractual clauses are important for the upcoming milestone/phase, what the pitfalls are and also to remind the team what the parties originally intended when signing the contract.

4.3   Dispute Resolution

Even with perfect Contract Management, conflicts cannot be avoided. "Resolve claims when they're big enough to see and small enough to solve,"[29] is the guiding principle on Dispute Resolution. It starts with an early identification, continues with

---

[25]More details on relational contract theories: *Diathesopoulos,* Relational contract theory and management contracts: A paradigm for the application of the Theory of the Norms, MPRA paper no. 24028, online at https://mpra.ub.uni-muenchen.de/24028/, retrieved on March 28, 2016.

[26]Felstiner et al., p. 631.

[27]More details on the Transition: Cummins et al. (2011), pp. 519 et seq.

[28]This can e.g. be done in a Contractual Obligation Matrix, which lists all contractual clauses, assigns responsibilities, milestones and due dates. See also: Reid (2004), p. 40.

[29]PWC (2014), p. 4.

a risk evaluation, the selection and application of the appropriate dispute resolution mechanism, and ends up with a settlement or decision by a third party.

4.3.1   Early Identification of Disputes

Contractual disputes usually arise when the parties to a contract have conflicting views on the responsibilities for non-performances, contract breaches or contract changes. The described sources for conflicts have in common that the "as is" deviates from the "to be", at least in one parties' view. In order to identify contractual deviations, a permanent monitoring of the contractual performance is essential. The root cause of deviations and the responsible party must be identified. If the analysis shows that the deviation is caused by the other contracting party, the communication process should be started in accordance with the contractual requirements.[30] In case the contracting party does not assume responsibility, the dispute needs to be resolved in accordance with the following steps.

4.3.2   Risk Evaluation (Getting Close to the Crystal Ball)

When the (potential) dispute has been identified, the risk (or opportunity) needs to be evaluated in order to "translate" the Dispute into commercial terms, usually financial figures for Management to decide on how to proceed.

When approaching disputes, many outside counsels, as well as still some in-house counsel, focus on legal issues, litigation strategy and winning. Most in-house counsel and management, however, approach Disputes from the viewpoint of costs, probability of success, and the potential value of the Dispute either in terms of potential benefit or potential loss. They also consider whether, when and at what costs settlement is feasible and makes commercial sense.

In the following, building up the Risk Analysis is described step by step.

Case Example

A consortium consisting of company "A" and company "B" has entered into a contract for the delivery of 25 oil platforms to Customer "C". A is responsible to manufacture and deliver 15 platforms and B is responsible to manufacture and deliver 10 platforms. The scope split between A and B is that both are responsible for designing different parts of the platform (e.g. A being responsible for the accommodation container, the drilling equipment, etc.). However when the platforms are designed, both companies manufacture complete platforms. The contract with C foresees a joint and several liability of the consortium members A and B towards C.

Under the partnership agreement between A and B, the parties have agreed that each party is responsible and liable for its scope. The party who has delivered the respective platform will rectify defects; the costs of rectification, however, shall be borne by the party being responsible for the defect (= having caused the defect). Liability for damages between the consortium partners is limited to 1 M€ per

---

[30]E.g. Form Requirements, Notification Periods, Communication Channels.

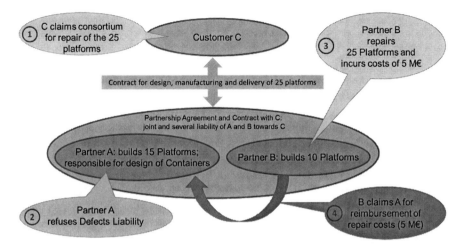

Fig. 5 Illustration of case example (author's own material)

event. Three arbitrators shall finally settle all disputes arising out of, or in connection with, the partnership agreement under the Rules of Arbitration of the International Chamber of Commerce.

The customer notified the consortium of a defect of the accommodation containers. According to the customer, the wooden floor of the container is rotten due to water which got into the container. A, being responsible for the design of the container, refuses to repair its 15 platforms. B repairs all 25 platforms and incurs repair costs of 5 M€. As B holds A responsible for the design of the containers and thus the defect, B claims A for reimbursement of the 5 M€ (Fig. 5).

In the claim negotiations, A argues that the floor was damaged because C floods the containers when cleaning them. Even if there is a defect, it would just be a manufacturing defect, not a design defect, and thus, even in the worst case, A assumes that it only has to pay for 15 out of the 25 repaired platforms. A further argues that any liability between the consortium partners is limited to 1 M€. Finally, A argues that any warranty claims of C were time-barred and that B repaired without being obliged to do so. B replies that in fact A's design caused the defect, that the limitation of liability does not apply for recourse claims under the joint and several liability, and that C's defect liability claim was not time-barred as negotiations took place. At the end of long claim negotiations A made a last and final offer to settle the case for 1.2 M€.

Management of B is asking the Legal Department whether to accept the settlement offer or what an arbitration would result in. Management of A want to know from it's Legal Department if a risk provision needs to be booked, and if yes, for which amount.

In order to answer their respective management, both Legal Departments need to perform a litigation risk analysis.

Step 1: Building Up the Tree

In a first step, the dispute needs to be transformed into the decision tree. In order to do so, the issues relevant to the outcome need to be determined. Such issues are the decision-"nodes". All nodes need to be brought into a logical order. This order is not necessarily the sequence of a legal subsumption, but ensures that all relevant aspects are considered before the end of a branch. Each node is marked either with a "+" for the potential answer "yes" or a "−" for the potential answer "no".[31]

Usually, the decision follows a certain logic from left to right. Starting with the central fact based issue (e.g. Defect, Delay, Infringement), followed by some legal pre-conditions, and ending with the quantum. In order to simplify the decision tree, it is recommended to use all issues leading to a direct result (usually a dismissal of a claim) as early as possible. In our example, the claim will fully be dismissed if either there is no defect or the claim is time-barred, thus the nodes "defect" and "time-barred" are used at the beginning. Only in case there is a defect, the question whether it is a design defect is relevant, and only in case there is a liability, the question of a limitation of liability needs to be answered. In consequence, the decision tree for the case at hand looks as shown in Fig. 6.

Scenario 1 reflects the claim scenario where there is a defect but the claim is time-barred. In this case, a judge would dismiss the case, and the outcome for the claimant ("scenario value") would be 0 €.

In scenario 2, there is a defect, the claim is not time-barred, the defect is a design defect and the limitation of liability kicks in. In such a case the scenario value (=potential award) is 1 M€.

Scenario 3 shows the best case for the claimant, where there is a defect, which is a design defect, no time-barrage and no limitation of liability, leading to a scenario value of 5 M€.

In scenarios 4 and 5, there is a defect which is not a design defect, and the claim is not time-barred. In scenario 4, the limitation kicks in, whereas in scenario 5, it does not. This leads to a scenario value for scenario 4 of 1 M€ and for scenario 5 of 4 M€.

Fig. 6 Decision tree without probabilities (author's own material)

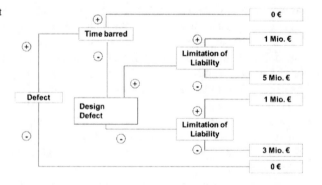

---

[31]Risse (2009), p. 461 (463).

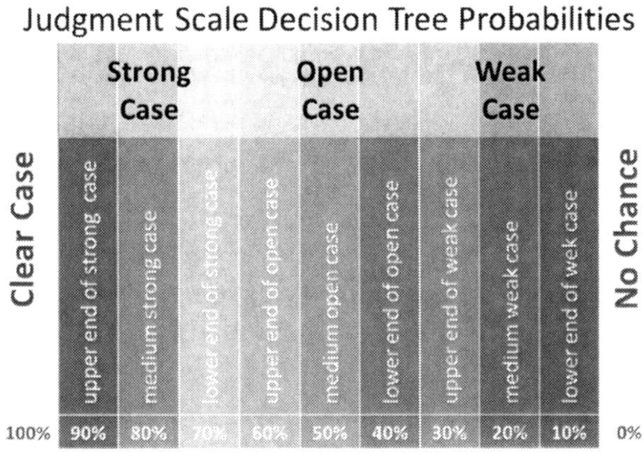

Fig. 7 Judgment scale for decision tree probabilities (author's own material)

Scenario 6 is the worst case for the claimant, as there is not even a defect. The scenario value is 0 €.

This first, quite simple step of building the Decision Tree, allows the Legal Department to provide its management with an easy-to-digest comprehensive overview which provides a basis for a focussed discussion. It shows the potential results as well as the respective pre-conditions.

Step 2: Adding Probabilities

In a second step, percentages are attached to the branches of the scenarios, representing the probability that a court or arbitration tribunal will follow the respective argument.

Attaching probabilities is the most difficult part, especially for lawyers. In order to get a sufficient approximation of the probabilities, the in-house counsel may ask themselves or the external lawyer two simple questions. The first one is: "Do we have a strong case, an open case, or a weak case with respect to the respective issue (node)?" The second question is; "Is our strong/open/weak case at the upper or lower limit, or about in the middle?" Based on the answer to the two questions, percentages from 10 % (lower end of a weak case) to 90 % (upper end of a strong case) can be allocated. A clear case will be valued at 100 % and a "no case" will be valued at 0 % (Fig. 7):

Party B evaluates the case as follows:

The probability that a defect can be proven is 80 %, and with a probability of another 80 % it can be proven that the defect is a design defect. The argument that the claim is time-barred has a likelihood to succeed of 30 %. The argument that the limitation of liability is not applicable on the rectification costs has a slightly better chance to be heard and is thus evaluated at 60 %. Inserting the respective probabilities into the decision tree would lead to the decision tree shown in Fig. 8.

The probabilities for each node needs to add up to 100 %[32] (Node 1 "Defect" yes ("+") 80 % + no ("−") 20 % = 100 %).

---

[32]Calihan et al. (2004), p. 7 (footnote 7).

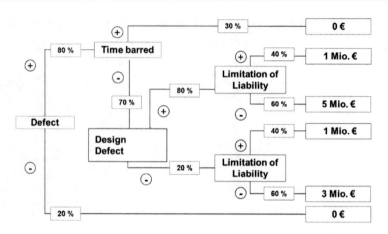

Fig. 8 Decision tree with probabilities (author's own material)

Step 3: Running the Calculation

The next step is pure mathematics. Two ways of calculating the expected value are available, the Compound Probability Method[33] and the Roll-Back Method.[34]

The **Compound Probability Method** calculates the probability of each claim scenario by multiplying the individual probabilities comprising that claim scenario. In the example, for claim scenario 1 (Defect yes but claim time-barred), the compound probability equals 24 % because the first outcome (Defect) was assessed with 80 % and the second outcome (time-barred) with 30 % (80 % × 30 % = 24 %). In other words, there is a 24 % chance of claim scenario 1 occurring.

Similarly, the compound probability of claim scenario 2 is:

$$80\% \times 70\% \times 80\% \times 40\% = 17.92\%.$$

All compound probabilities of the possible claim scenarios (in our example 6 scenarios) need to add up to 100 %.[35] This counter-check shows that all potential cases have been considered.

With the compound probabilities of the claim scenarios, the expected values of the scenarios can be calculated by multiplying the compound probability with the scenario value. In the example (see Fig. 8), the likelihood that a court awards 5 M€ (scenario 3) is 26.88 %, thus the expected value of such scenario is 1.344 M€ (26.88 % × 5 M€). In order to get the expected value of the claim in total, the expected values of all claim scenarios need to be added up. In the example, the expected value of the claim is 1.769 M€ (see Fig. 9). The expected value will not be awarded by any court as only 0 €, 1 M€, 3 M€ or 5 M€ can be awarded, but it is

---

[33]Calihan et al. (2004), p. 7.

[34]Calihan et al. (2004), p. 9.

[35]Hagel (2011), p. 69; Bühring-Uhle et al. (2009), p. 100.

Claim Scenario	Individual Probability				Compound Probability	Scenario Value	Scenario Expected Value
1	80%	30%			24,00%	0 €	0 €
2	80%	70%	80%	40%	17,92%	1.000.000 €	179.200 €
3	80%	70%	80%	60%	26,88%	5.000.000 €	1.344.000 €
4	80%	70%	20%	40%	4,48%	1.000.000 €	44.800 €
5	80%	70%	20%	60%	6,72%	3.000.000 €	201.600 €
6	20%				20,00%	0 €	0 €
					100%	Expected Value of Claim	1.769.600 €

Fig. 9 Overview on claim scenarios and calculation of the expected value (author's own material)

an average value of a simulation of 100 awards on the specific case. It considers the uncertainties and the different probabilities.

Besides the Compound Probability Method, the calculation can also be run by the **Roll-Back Method**[36] (see Fig. 10), by which an expected value is calculated on each node, beginning at the right side of the tree and rolling-back towards the left, resulting in the expected value of the claim. The most far right node is calculated first. In the example, the two nodes dealing with the question on whether the limitation of liability is applicable are at the same level. Taking the upper pair first: When the limitation of liability applies, 1 M€ would be the result. The probability is 40 %. In case the limitation does not apply, the result is 5 M€ with a probability of 60 %. Both branches added $(0.4 \times 1 \text{ M€} + 0.6 \times 5 \text{ m€})$ result in 3.4 M€ as shown at the respective decision node in Fig. 10. The same is true for the question on the limitation of liability in case there is a defect other than a design defect. In this case, limitation results in 1 M€ with a probability of 40 %, and no limitation of liability results in 3 M€ (only 15 platforms of A need to be reimbursed by $A => 15/25 \times 5 \text{ M€} = 3 \text{ M€}$) with a probability of 40 %. The branches added up results in $0.4 \times 1 \text{ M€} + 0.6 \times 3 \text{ M€} = 2.2 \text{ M€}$. The same way of calculation is now used for the next node to the left. $0.8 \times 3.4 \text{ M€} + 0.2 \times 2.2 \text{ M€} = 3.16 \text{ M€}$. At the end, the total expected value of 1.769.600 € is shown at the very left. As can be seen, the Roll-Back Method and the Compound Probability Method lead to the same result.

Step 4: Considering the Investment Costs

The Legal Department has to provide Management with a clear advise whether to pursue a claim in any formal dispute resolution process, or whether to enter into a negotiated settlement. For such advise, the expected outcome of the claim itself is not sufficient. To get the full financial picture, the invested claim costs, and a potential reimbursement of such costs by the opponent, need to be considered as well as the cash-flow of all such costs. In order to get an award, B needs to sue A which will cause costs on both sides. A and B will be represented/supported by external lawyers, the court/arbitration fees need to be paid and the parties will incur own costs (transactional costs as well as opportunity costs). In the example, ICC

---

[36]Victor (2014), pp. 736 and 738; Shenoy (1993), p. 323.

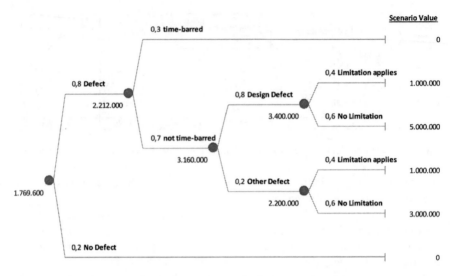

Fig. 10 Decision tree using the Roll-Back Method (author's own material)

arbitration had been chosen. With an amount in dispute of 5 M€ and 3 arbitrators, the administration fee is 45,015 €,[37] the fees for arbitrators are in a range of 98–425 K€,[38] which would lead to a worst case scenario of 470 K€ (45 K€ +425 K€). In addition, lawyer fees of 41 K€[39] and internal costs of 264 K€ need to be considered. The internal costs are calculated based on the assumption that the claim team, consisting of members of different functions, will spend 200 h/month for 11 (not consecutive) months[40] at an hourly rate of 120 €.[41] According to Art. 37 (4) ICC Rules, "the final award shall fix the costs of the arbitration and decide which of the parties shall bear them or in what proportion they shall be borne by the parties". Art. 37 (5) ICC Rules states: "In making decisions as to costs, the arbitral tribunal may take into account such circumstances as it considers relevant, including the extent to which each party has conducted the arbitration in an expeditious and cost-effective manner". In the worst case this means that all costs (administration, arbitrators and external lawyers[42]) are to be borne by the losing party (Fig. 11).

---

[37] Actually the ICC cost calculator works with US $. For simplification, an exchange rate of 1:1 is assumed.

[38] See cost-calculator of the ICC: http://www.iccwbo.org/Products-and-Services/Arbitration-and-ADR/Arbitration/Cost-and-payment/Cost-calculator/

[39] The fee for external lawyers is based on the German Lawyers Compensation Act (RVG). In international arbitrations, the external lawyers are usually remunerated on an hourly basis, and increasingly on fixed fee arrangements.

[40] Two rounds of written statements with 3 months each, further 3 months for preparing evidence (witnesses and experts) and 2 months for hearings and post hearing briefs.

[41] See for further details: Hagel (2013), chapter 2.16, pp. 235 et seq.

[42] Further relevant costs are not considered in the example (e.g. experts, reimbursable costs of the parties, such as in-house counsel costs).

Type of Costs	Amount based on a claim amount of 5.000.000 €	Advances	Reimbursable	Worst-Case
Administration Costs	ICC: 45.015 US$ Arbitrator Min. 98.301 US$ Arbitrator Max. 425.700 US$	A and B share 370 KUS$	yes	470.715 €
Lawyers	41.260 €	A and B	yes	82.520 €
Transactional Costs	264.000 €	A and B	no	264.000 €
Total				817,235 €

Fig. 11 Overview on investment costs and cash-flow for arbitration (author's own material)

Further investment costs may need to be considered, depending on the specific circumstances. They may include opportunity costs, interests, further transactional costs and costs of taking evidence. As these investment costs vary significantly, they are not included in the calculated example.

Considering the investment costs for the arbitration minus the reimbursable costs in each claim scenario will lead to different expected arbitration values. In case the plaintiff wins the full claim amount of 5 M€ as well as the cost award, the internal costs of 264 K€ are still not reimbursable and need to be deducted from the scenario value reflecting the net result of the award. In the calculation (Fig. 12), the cost allocation follows the ratio of win/loose. The decision tree considering the investment costs is shown in Fig. 12.

By taking the investment costs into consideration, the expected value decreases by 0.63 M€, resulting in 1.13 M€ (see Fig. 13).

Besides the expected value of the claim, the probability distribution is also of importance for taking an informed decision. Such probability distribution shows the magnitude and likelihood of each risk/opportunity.[43] The graph perfectly demonstrates that, even though in average a positive outcome of 1.13 M€ is to be expected, the likelihood of incurring a loss of 0.81 M€ is pretty high with 44 %. The likelihood of getting more than the expected value is only 33.6 %, whereas the likelihood to get less is 66.4 %. However, in the event the award is above the expected value, it will either be 1.25 M€ or even 3.59 M€ more than expected. In case the award is below the expected value, it will either deviate by 0.89 M€ with a still positive outcome (0.24 M€) or by 1.94 M€ and a negative result (0.81 M€) (Fig. 14).

With any settlement above 1.32 M€,[44] B is on average better off settling the dispute, rather than fighting it through in arbitration. Any € above the expected value

---

[43]Victor (1990), chapter 17, p. 13, available under http://www.litigationrisk.com/Litigation%20Risk%20Analysis(tm)%20and%20ADR.pdf, retrieved on March 28, 2016.

[44]In case A incurs further costs prior to the settlement, those costs need to be taken into account.

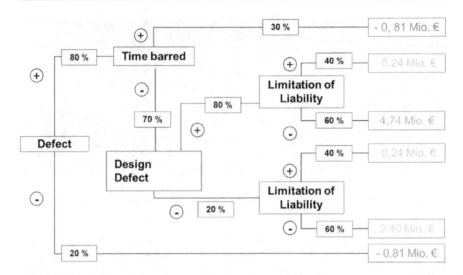

Fig. 12 Decision tree with probabilities including investment costs (author's own material)

Claim Scenario	Individual Probability				Compound Probability	Scenario Value	Scenario Expected Value
1	80%	30%			24,00%	-810.000 €	-194.400 €
2	80%	70%	80%	40%	17,92%	240.000 €	43.008 €
3	80%	70%	80%	60%	26,88%	4.740.000 €	1.274.112 €
4	80%	70%	20%	40%	4,48%	240.000 €	10.752 €
5	80%	70%	20%	60%	6,72%	2.400.000 €	161.280 €
6	20%				20,00%	-810.000 €	-162.000 €
					100%	Expected Value of Claim	1.132.752 €

Fig. 13 Overview on claim scenarios and calculation of the expected value including investment costs (author's own material)

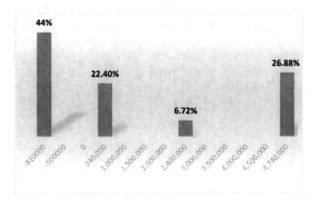

Fig. 14 Risk distribution (author's own material)

is increasing the bottom-line profit. However, with respect to risk minimization, the risk distribution cannot be ignored. There is a higher likelihood to get less than the expected value and a high risk of even incurring a (further) loss of 0.81 M€.

As a negotiated settlement requires the agreement of the other party (A), B needs to change perspective in order to identify whether there is a "Zone of a Potential Agreement" (ZOPA). In principle, A needs to perform the same calculation in order to determine the risk and a respective risk provision. However, the outcomes would be different as the cost burden is different. In case A wins, A would still face a loss of the investment costs of 0.264 M € and, in the worst case, A would have to payout the claim-amount, reimburse the costs of B (except for B's transaction costs) and bear the own transaction costs, resulting in a loss of 5.81 M€. Applying the decision tree and the respective calculation, the risk value for A is approximately 2.2 M€ (Figs. 15 and 16).

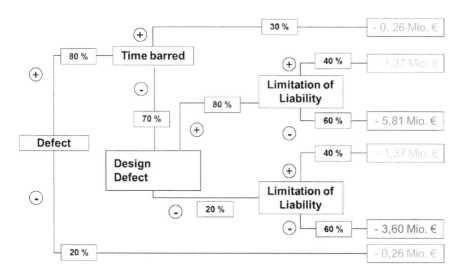

Fig. 15 Decision tree with probabilities and investment costs from A's perspective (author's own material)

Claim Scenario	Individual Probability				Compound Probability	Scenario Value	Scenario Expected Value
1	80%	30%			24,00%	-260.000 €	-62.400 €
2	80%	70%	80%	40%	17,92%	-1.370.000 €	-245.504 €
3	80%	70%	80%	60%	26,88%	-5.810.000 €	-1.561.728 €
4	80%	70%	20%	40%	4,48%	-1.370.000 €	-61.376 €
5	80%	70%	20%	60%	6,72%	-3.600.000 €	-241.920 €
6	20%				20,00%	-260.000 €	-52.000 €
					100%	Expected Value of Claim	-2.224.928 €

Fig. 16 Overview on claim scenarios and calculation of the expected value from A's perspective (author's own material)

Claim Scenario	Individual Probability				Compound Probability	Scenario Value	Scenario Expected Value
1	70%	40%			28,00%	-260.000 €	-72.800 €
2	70%	60%	70%	50%	14,70%	-1.370.000 €	-201.390 €
3	70%	60%	70%	50%	14,70%	-5.810.000 €	-854.070 €
4	70%	60%	30%	50%	6,30%	-1.370.000 €	-86.310 €
5	70%	60%	30%	50%	6,30%	-3.600.000 €	-226.800 €
6	30%				30,00%	-260.000 €	-78.000 €
					100%	Expected Value of Claim	-1.519.370 €

Fig. 17 Overview on claim scenarios and calculation of the expected value from A's perspective with different probabilities (author's own material)

Based on these evaluations, the ZOPA would be from 1.13 M€ (expected claim value for B) to 2.2 M€ (expected claim value for A), as any settlement amount in-between would be a "win" for both parties. Most likely, A's evaluation would look different as each party usually is more confident, or even over-optimistic, with respect to its own arguments. The decision nodes remain the same, and applying probabilities of 10 % more favorable for A at each node would result in an expected risk for A of 1.52 M€ (Fig. 16). This would still result in a "win-win" scenario as the ZOPA would be from 1.13 to 1.52 M€ (Fig. 17).

Running a risk analysis with a decision tree has the following benefits, not only for the Legal Department:

1. It provides a framework to identify the key legal and factual issues and uncertainties of a claim;
2. It provides a framework to identify the probabilities of the identified issues;
3. It forces Legal Counsel to assess the probabilities;
4. It provides a model to identify the possible outcomes of claims;
5. It improves the quality of the claim evaluation by making the process transparent and standardised;
6. it visualizes the lines of argumentation;
7. it helps to stay focused during negotiations;
8. it helps to identify the issues having the highest impact on the claim result[45]
9. It enables the Expected Value of the claim to be calculated;
10. it helps to calculate risk provisions and to provide transparency for the auditors; and
11. It provides a model to determine the value of the claim or Best Alternative to a Negotiated Agreement (BATNA) and the ZOPA

---

[45]By using the sensitivity analysis based on the decision tree; further details on the sensitivity analysis: Hagel (2011), p. 72.

4.3.3 Frontloading: Selection of the Appropriate Dispute Resolution Mechanism

When the parties cannot settle disputes, an independent third party needs to be involved, unless the demanding party does not want to pursue the demand any further, which is often seen as the "Worst Alternative to a Negotiated Agreement" (WATNA).[46]

Overview on Dispute Resolution Processes

There are various possibilities available to get a third party involved in the resolution of a dispute (Fig. 18):

In **Delegated Processes**, the parties refer the outcome of the dispute to a third party. The result of such process is a (preliminary) binding decision of the third party:

Court Litigation is a process for handling disputes in the state court system. Litigation can be initiated by a party without the consent of the opponent(s), and it is the fallback procedure when the parties do not agree on any other dispute resolution process.

Arbitration is a proceeding in which an impartial arbitrator (or a panel of several arbitrators) resolves a dispute by a final and binding decision (award).

Expert Determination is a procedure in which a dispute between the parties is submitted to one or more experts who make a determination on the matter referred to them by the parties. The determination is binding, unless the parties have agreed otherwise.

Adjudication is a process by which the parties to a dispute submit their differences to the decision of an impartial person (adjudicator) or group appointed by mutual consent or statutory provision. The adjudicator's decision is binding unless or

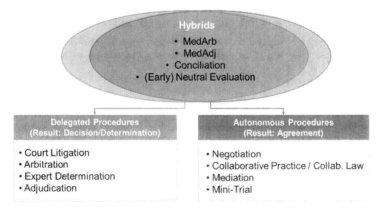

Fig. 18 Overview on dispute resolution processes (Hagel 2016, § 149 Rn 1)

---

[46]More on WATNA and BATNA (Best Alternative to a Negotiated Agreement): Blake et al. (2014), pp. 186 et seq.

until the dispute is finally determined by court proceedings, arbitration or by agreement of the parties via negotiation or mediation. If a party chooses to pursue subsequent proceedings, the dispute will be heard afresh—not as "appeal" of the adjudicator's findings.

In a **Consensual Process**, the parties remain in control of the outcome of the dispute, as the result is a settlement agreement of the parties.

Negotiation is a voluntary and usually informal process in which parties discuss the issues with the aim to reach a mutually acceptable agreement to resolve the issues raised.

Mediation is a structured, interest-based process, whereby two or more parties to a dispute attempt by themselves, on a voluntary basis, to reach an agreement on the settlement of their dispute with the assistance of a mediator who is not empowered to decide the case.[47]

Collaborative Practice/Law is an out-of-court settlement process where parties and their external consultants[48] try to reach an agreement satisfying the needs of all parties involved. If the parties cannot settle the case and engage in contested litigation, their consultants (in Collaborative Law their external lawyers) cannot represent them in court.

Mini-Trial is a private process where each party makes a brief presentation of the case as if they were at a trial. Representatives (usually high-level business executives) from each side with the authority to settle the dispute observe the presentations.[49] At the end of the presentations, the representatives attempt to settle the dispute in negotiation. A neutral person, usually a mediator who assists the executives in the negotiation, can lead the mini-trial.

Hybrid processes are a combination of delegated and consensual processes. The combination is either sequential,[50] or the delegation is limited to render a recommendation. This recommendation then needs the consensus of the parties to get binding.

---

[47]Article 3 EC-Directive 2008/52/EC on certain aspects of mediation in civil and commercial matters defines mediation as follows: "Mediation" means a structured process, however named or referred to, whereby two or more parties to a dispute attempt by themselves, on a voluntary basis, to reach an agreement on the settlement of their dispute with the assistance of a mediator. This process may be (1) initiated by the parties or (2) suggested or ordered by a court or (3) prescribed by the law of a Member State. It includes mediation conducted by a judge who is not responsible for any judicial proceedings concerning the dispute in question. It excludes attempts made by the court or the judge seized to settle a dispute in the course of judicial proceedings concerning the dispute in question.

More detail on the definition of mediation: Hagel (2014a).

[48]In case of Collaborative Law, external lawyers support the parties.

[49]Weise, Representing the Corporation, 2000-2 Supplement, 8-Ex-74.

[50]For various different sequential combinations of mediation and other ADR processes, see: *Reeves* Mediation plus: Don't leave money on the table, Advocate 2015.

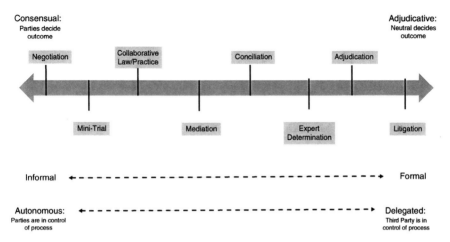

Fig. 19 The spectrum of dispute resolution processes (author's own material)

MedArb is a combination of Mediation and Arbitration. The process involves the same person who first acts as a mediator, and, if the parties cannot reach a settlement, then acts as an arbitrator, rendering a final and binding award.

MedAdj is a combination of Mediation and Adjudication. The process involves the same person who first acts as a mediator, and, if the parties cannot reach a settlement then acts as an adjudicator, rendering a preliminary binding award.[51]

Conciliation is a negotiation process led by a third party (conciliator). In case no settlement can be reached, the conciliator makes a non-binding settlement proposal.

(Early) Neutral Evaluation provides the parties with a preliminary assessment of facts, evidence or legal merits to serve as a basis for further negotiation.

Dispute resolution processes cannot only be differentiated by the result of the process (decision or consensus) (Fig. 19), but also by numerous other criteria, such as[52]:

- time,
- cost,
- confidentiality of the proceeding,
- neutrality of the forum,
- enforceability of the result (decision or agreement),
- usability/feasibility for non-justiciable disputes,

---

[51]See in detail: Lembcke (2009), p. 122.

[52]Non exhaustive listing; the working group "B2B Disputes" of the Round Table Mediation & Conflict Management of the German Economy ("RTMKM") has identified 47 relevant differentiation criteria for the selection of the appropriate dispute resolution process; see also: CPR European Mediation and ADR Guide (2015), p. 6.

- possibility to appeal,
- flexibility of the proceedings,
- formality of the process,
- involvement of the parties in the process.

Systematic Selection of the Appropriate Dispute Resolution Process

Since processes differ, none of them is suited for all disputes. However, for each dispute (and the interests of the disputants with respect to the resolution process), there is a most suitable process available.[53]

Proposing the right process to resolve the dispute at hand is the task of the Legal Department. This requires detailed knowledge of all available processes[54] as well as a structured approach to select the appropriate process. Traditionally, when negotiations on solving contractual disputes fail, the dispute resolution process foreseen under the respective contract is applied. Contractual dispute resolution clauses should, however, be regarded as a recommendation as well as a fallback solution when the parties *cannot* agree on a more suitable dispute resolution process to be applied in the specific case, if there is such a process. Clauses are usually drafted for all potential contractual disputes, and they might not perfectly fit to the specific dispute. The task of the Legal Department is thus to check the best suitable dispute resolution process first and then to check whether it is in line with the one foreseen under the contract, or whether a specific agreement on a deviating dispute resolution process is needed. In order to identify the most appropriate dispute resolution process for the individual dispute and the interests of the party with respect to its resolution, Legal Departments as well as providers/institutions have developed several tools.

Checklist

A simple tool to identify the most appropriate dispute resolution process is a checklist. The checklist covers the criteria that differentiate the dispute resolution processes. It might address the interests of one's own company, or even the (potential) interests of all involved parties. The ADR Case Evaluation Worksheet of Motorola can demonstrate both, the listing of the differentiation criteria, as well as the possibility to enter both (all) parties interests.[55] One question asks whether a speedy resolution is important to Motorola,[56] another whether the advantages of delay run heavily in favor of one side.[57] The International Institute for Conflict Prevention & Resolution ("CPR") has also issued such a checklist.[58] In this

---

[53]Sander and Goldberg (1994), pp. 49–68.

[54]Freyer and Sayler (2000), Chapter 9, p. 171.

[55]Reilly and MacKenzie (1999), p. 147.

[56]Section 1 e: Reilly and MacKenzie, p. 151; which speaks for ADR instead of litigation.

[57]Section 2 f. Reilly and MacKenzie, p. 152; which might speak against ADR.

[58]CPR ADR SUITABILITY GUIDE (Featuring Mediation Analysis Screen) (2006) https://www.cpradr.org/Portals/0/Resources/ADR%20Tools/Tools/ADR%20Suitability%20Screen.pdf, retrieved on March 28, 2016.

7.   Do the parties only seek a neutral evaluation on the extent of damages or
      other specific issue?

      ___   a)   Very likely.
      ___   b)   A possibility.
      ___   c)   Very unlikely.

            COMMENTARY

            A more evaluative form of consensual ADR – such as early neutral
            evaluation or fact-finding – may be a more appropriate option than
            mediation in some instances. (See Section 2: Matrix of Other
            Nonbinding Processes).

Fig. 20 Excerpt from the CPR ADR suitability guide

checklist, commentaries are added to explain the purpose of the question and to lead
the user to the most appropriate process, depending on the answer (Fig. 20).

Flow-Chart

Another possibility to identify the right dispute resolution process is by flow-chart
with decision nodes that guide to a specific process dependent on the decisions
taken at the differentiation nodes (Figs. 21 and 22). The disadvantage of such flow-
chart is the single-criterion structure. The flow-chart sorts out certain processes
based on one criterion, even though one of the processes singled out might overall
be the most appropriate. In addition, parties often do not know what they really need
as they are basing the answer to the question raised in the decision nodes of the flow
chart on their position rather than their interest. The outcome of a process is one
differentiation criterion (settlement agreement, decision or determination). When
asked, whether a decision is needed/wanted, parties tend to agree as prior settlement
negotiations have failed. However, asking the parties why a decision is important
for them, the parties express their interest to settle the dispute, which can also be
achieved by consensual processes.

Overview Matrix

An overview on the different processes with respect to the differentiation criteria in
an overview matrix has the advantage that all processes can easily be benchmarked
based on the selected criteria.[59] Based on this overview, the party can make an
informed decision (Fig. 23).[60]

Software Based Tools

More sophisticated than the previously described tools are software tools such as
the "Dispute Resolution Recommendation Matrix (DRRM)" of Bombardier Transportation[61] which automatically provide recommendations for dispute resolution

---

[59]See also the Overview of the CPR in: CPR European Mediation and ADR Guide (2015), p. 8.

[60]*Weise* Representing the Company, 2000-2 Supplement, 8-Ex-46, Exhibit 3.

[61]Detailed description of the tool: Hagel and Steinbrecher (2014), p. 53.

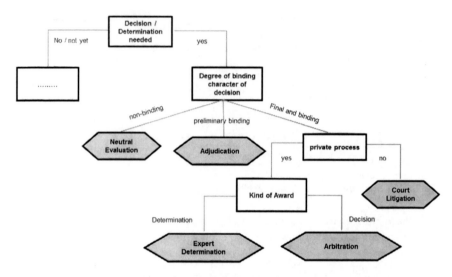

Fig. 21 Flow-chart for identification of dispute resolution process (author's own material)

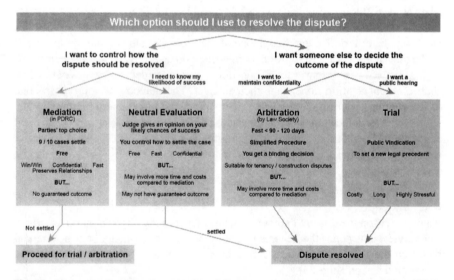

Fig. 22 Alternative flow-chart on selection of dispute resolution process (Quek and Choo 2012). Quek and Choo, Lawgazette 2012-09: Mediation Advocacy for Civil Disputes in the Subordinate Courts: Perspectives from the Bench, retrieved from internet on March 28, 2016, http://www. lawgazette.com.sg/2012-09/files/images/20120918145347895.jpg

Dispute Resolution Process	Result of Proceeding	Involved third party	Confidentiality of Process	Binding Character	Prior agreement on process needed	Suitable for non-justiciable disputes
Negotiation	Settlement Agreement	-	yes	-	- (possible)	yes
Mini-Trial	Settlement Agreement	No third party needed but possible	yes	-	needed	yes
Mediation	Settlement Agreement	Mediator	yes	-	needed	yes
Conciliation	Proposal	Conciliator	yes	non-binding	needed	yes
Adjudication	decision	Adjudicator	yes	Preliminary binding	needed	no
Expert Determination	Determi-nation	Expert	yes	Binding	needed	no
Arbitration	decision	Arbitrator	yes	Binding	needed	no
Court Litigation	decision	Judge (Jury)	no	Binding	Not needed	no

Fig. 23 Overview matrix on dispute resolution processes (based on Hagel 2011, p. 129)

processes to be applied on the specific case. The recommendation matrix facilitates rationale decision making in multiple ways.

1. The tool filters out the procedural options not fitting to the individual dispute.
2. The tool enables the user to compare the procedural options in light of the claim at issue.
3. The tool makes a rational recommendation on the selection of one or more processes.
4. The tool advises on actions to be taken or issues to be considered, based on the answers given in the specific case.

The tool is divided in three parts:

Part 1: Filter Function
Part 2: Evaluation and recommendation of the most appropriate resolution process(es)
Part 3: Further recommendations based on the answers given in combination with the recommended process

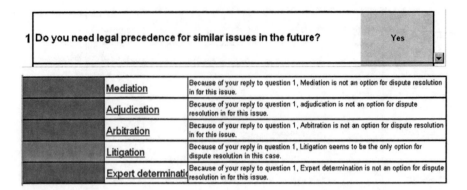

Fig. 24 Example for a recommendation rendered in part 1 of the DRRM (Hagel and Steinbrecher 2014, p. 62)

Part 1 filters out such cases where alternative dispute resolution processes are not appropriate, either due to the applicable law or due to the specific requirements of the respective claim. Dependent on the answers, one or more dispute resolution procedures will be filtered out by marking such procedure "red" and giving the explanation for the exclusion. The filtering is based on several questions, touching various issues. If, for example, the answer to the question whether legal precedence is needed is "yes", the tool refers to court litigation as the only suitable dispute resolution process (Fig. 24).

In Part 2, the dispute resolution processes are compared with respect to answers given in a questionnaire. The questions address facts (e.g. cross-border dispute; number of parties involved) as well as interests (e.g. confidentiality). After having answered all questions by clicking on the boxes, the tool will provide an overview on the scoring of the different dispute resolution processes and based thereon it will automatically make two recommendations (Fig. 25).

The application of the recommendation made by the tool is not mandatory but a counter-check.

In Part 3, the tool automatically addresses the needs expressed in answering the questionnaire in part 2. Example: If question number 9 ("Is confidentiality important in your dispute") is answered with yes, and mediation has been recommended by the tool, a further recommendation is made, stating: "In order to achieve confidentiality as desired according to question 9, a Confidentiality Agreement needs to be signed!". Such further recommendation is needed as under most jurisdictions, mediation is not automatically or by law confidential.[62]

---

[62]Example Germany: Even though mediation is defined to be a confidential process (Art 1 I MediationsG), only the mediator is obliged to keep confidentiality (Art 4 MediationsG), neither the parties nor any other third party (e.g. lawyers, experts). See also: Hagel (2014a) § 1 Rdn 6 et seq.

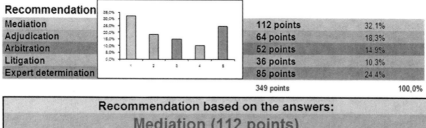

Recommendation			
Mediation		112 points	32.1%
Adjudication		64 points	18.3%
Arbitration		52 points	14.9%
Litigation		36 points	10.3%
Expert determination		85 points	24.4%
		349 points	100.0%

Recommendation based on the answers:
Mediation (112 points)
The second-best solution is Expert determination (85 points)

Fig. 25 Example for recommendation rendered in part 2 of the DRRM (Hagel and Steinbrecher 2014, pp. 63 and 64)

Dispute Resolution Spider

The Dispute Resolution Spider provides a further visualization of the different processes available to the dispute at hand.[63]

All relevant aspects can be shown in a spider chart. This allows comparing different potential scenarios. In the example (Fig. 26), the following categories are shown:

1. Financial aspects

    All financial aspects are listed separately in the respective currency using the same scale. For the Claim Value, Counterclaim Value and Expected Value, the amounts will be the same for all different dispute resolution mechanisms, unless parts of the claim/counterclaim will only be claimed under certain procedures (e.g. consequential damages will be claimed as maximum plausible position in negotiation and mediation but, due to limited success expectations under the applicable law, not in court or arbitration).
    a. face value of the claim in dispute: shows the face value of the claim as submitted to the counterpart or filed at court
    b. face value of the counterclaim: shows the face value of the counterclaim as submitted to the counterpart or filed at court
    c. expected value: shows the result of the Decision Tree. It can either be shown for the claim and counterclaim separately or consolidated
    d. internal costs to resolve the Dispute: shows the sum of the internal costs to resolve the dispute, including transactional costs and opportunity costs
    e. external costs to resolve the Dispute: shows the sum of the external costs to resolve the dispute, including external advisors and consultants and administration fees (Fig. 27)
2. Escalation Level of the Dispute: shows the level of escalation according to Glasl's escalation model: Hardening (1), Polarization and debate (2), Deeds, not words (3), Concern for image and coalition (4), Loss of face (5), threats (6),

---

[63]See also: Hagel (2014b), p. 108 (112).

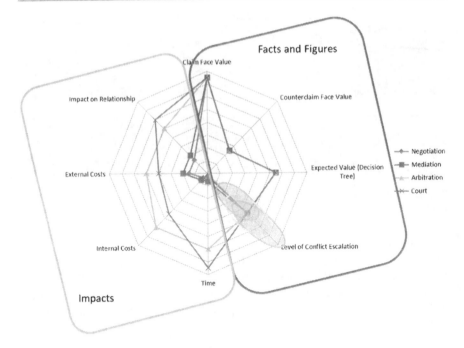

Fig. 26 The Dispute Resolution Spider (author's own material)

Limited destruction (7), Fragmentation (8), Together into the abyss (9). The Circles show the span where a certain dispute resolution mechanism can be applied in order to identify the mechanisms available for the individual dispute.

3. Expected time to resolve the Dispute: On this axle, the average time to resolve similar disputes in the respective processes is shown. B2B Mediations usually take up to 3 months for preparation, including the selection of the mediator and 2 days of mediation. Arbitrations last at least 2 years, not seldom up to 5 years. Average times for the different instances of Court Litigation can be found in official statistics.

From a business perspective, the (potential) length of a process is important for several reasons:

- it shows when a cash-in or cash-out with respect to the amount in dispute is to be expected
- it can be used as a basis to calculate interests on the claim amount
- it will form part of the cost calculation for the internal and external costs. In such a case however, a further analysis is needed to show the net time of involvement, as the parties usually are not involved fulltime during the whole proceeding. The chart (Fig. 28) gives an indication on how to perform such an analysis. In the example (Fig. 28), Mediation, Arbitration and Court Litigation are compared with respect to the net time of involvement of a party to the dispute. Mediation usually requires a 3 months preparation, including the selection of the mediator, the preparation of the mediation statement and the

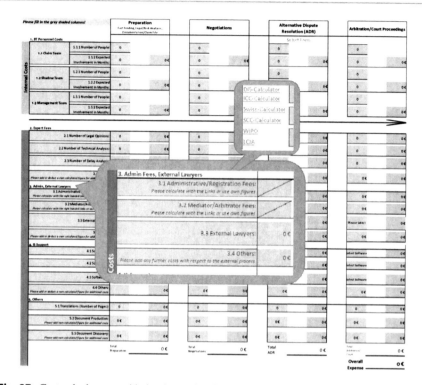

Fig. 27 Cost calculator considering internal and external costs at different stages of the dispute resolution (author's own material)

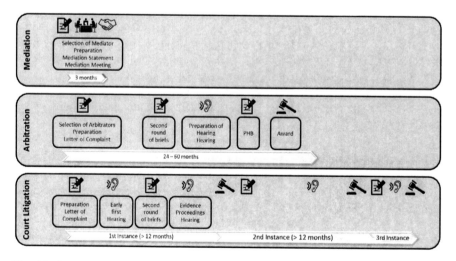

Fig. 28 Overview on duration of Mediation, Arbitration and Court Litigation (adapted from Hagel 2014b, p. 236)

mediation session(s). Arbitration requires at least 3 months of preparation for the claimant, including selection of the own party appointed arbitrator and drafting the letter of complaint. During the constitution of the tribunal, the parties' involvement is less intensive. At the second round of briefs, the parties are heavily involved with the full claim team. During the evidence proceedings (e.g. witness statements and expert opinions), only the relevant functions of the parties are involved. Party representatives attend the arbitration hearing(s) and the preparation of the post hearing brief ("PHB") The analysis of the award requires at least the involvement of the party's Legal Department. In Court proceedings, the parties' involvement is less intensive compared to arbitrations, as the judge(s) are not appointed by the parties, the expert is appointed by the court and the witnesses have to give oral testimonies in a witness hearing led by the judge(s).

4. The expected Impact on the Business Relationship

When choosing the appropriate dispute resolution process, the (potential or expected) impact on the business relationship needs to be considered.

Further aspects can be added to the spider, such as, but not limited to, "Impact on Cash-Flow", "Availability of Resources (e.g. key people, tools)".

The spider diagram provides a "helicopter view", showing the differences of the several dispute resolution processes with respect to the differentiation criteria. At the same time, the spider shows relevant measurable facts (e.g. amount in dispute). In doing so, it provides within one chart all relevant information to make an informed decision on which process to apply.

Consultation of a Neutral Conflict Manager

In a dispute situation, the disputants need to agree on the dispute resolution process to be applied on the individual dispute, unless the contractually agreed resolution process remains the preferred choice of all parties to the conflict. In order to achieve such an agreement, it might be helpful to get a neutral advice of a Conflict Manager. The German Arbitration Institute ("DIS") has developed a conflict clarification procedure,[64] where a conflict manager nominated by the DIS together with the parties clarifies the issue of how and with the help of which neutral third party a dispute should be resolved.

4.3.4 Running the Dispute Resolution Process

When the process is chosen, it needs to be executed by the parties. A good preparation with respect to the case but also the process is mandatory. The Legal Department selects the external legal advisors,[65] supports the business in finding the

---

[64]DIS Conflict Management Rules (DIS-KMO).

[65]For requirements to external (legal) advisors from a user's perspective, see: *Round Table Mediation & Conflict Management of the German Economy*, SchiedsVZ 2012, pp. 254 et seq.

third parties needed for the process,[66] and further consultants.[67] Preparation of briefs and statements but also of witnesses and experts falls under the responsibility of the Legal Department. The Legal Department also accompanies the internal client during the Dispute Resolution process.

4.3.5 Settling the Dispute

It is in the best interest of all parties to attempt to settle their differences through negotiation rather than resorting to more expensive and longer lasting forms of dispute resolution such as arbitration or litigation. As a negotiation draws to a close, pressure builds to finalize or conclude the settlement. However, what appeared to be a fair deal in the heat of negotiation, may later, with the wisdom of hindsight, prove to be insufficient. It is the task of the Legal Department to coach the negotiation team in comparing the settlement proposal with the BATNA.[68] As long as the settlement proposal is commercially more beneficial to the party, the negotiated settlement should be preferred. The commercial view should, however, not be limited to the settlement amount but should include the right timing for a settlement as well as a value-optimization.[69] When the dispute comes to a settlement, the Legal Department takes over the drafting of the settlement agreement, considering the recommendations on Contract Drafting under the section "Contract Drafting".

5 Conclusion

With respect to Dispute Management, the role of the Legal Department has dramatically changed. While providing pure legal advise was sufficient in the past, the Legal Department has become the key driver in adding value to the business in the context of disputes. This is true for dispute avoidance as well as dispute resolution.

Beyond the traditional tasks of the Legal Department, it nowadays needs to

- ensure that the parties focus on interests rather than positions when negotiating a contract;
- ensure that contracts are drafted in a way that everybody involved in the execution of the contract clearly understands the rights and obligations;
- evaluate risks and opportunities of disputes by a thorough risk analysis;
- know the spectrum of dispute resolution processes;
- select the appropriate dispute resolution process;
- drive the resolution process;
- work out the BATNA and WATNA and
- advise with regards to a commercial beneficial settlement.

---

[66]E.g. Mediator, Arbitrator, Adjudicator.

[67]Claim specialists, Forensic Experts.

[68]Best Alternative to a Negotiated Agreement.

[69]Items might have different values for the parties and are thus a chance to escape the pure distributive bargaining towards an integrative consensual solution.

In order to do so, in-house counsel need to see the bigger picture. This requires education beyond legal studies. No wonder, in-house counsel are more often not only qualified lawyers but hold an MBA degree at the same time. Business Acumen is essential to put disputes in a commercial rather than emotional or legal perspective. Reducing costs by e.g. selecting the most appropriate dispute resolution process and maximizing the return by e.g. increasing the BATNA are assets, the in-house counsel can contribute. Focusing on the specific interests of the parties rather than just looking for legal justice generates sustainable profitability.

The new role of the in-house counsel with respect to disputes can be described as being the:

- **Active Listener**, identifying the interests of the parties rather than their positions when negotiating a contract;
- **Designer**, drafting contracts with a clear structure, plein language, fresh layout and visualizations;
- **Translator**, helping the business to understand legal terms and legal concepts in the different law systems;
- **Coach**, supporting the negotiation teams to avoid misunderstandings in communication and falling into the traps of psychological biases;
- **Manager**, orchestrating the claim team to achieve the best result possible;
- **Consultant**, providing clear and concise legal advise

or simply the Legal Expert with a business focus.

Legal Departments approaching Disputes in the manner described above will add value to the business and support a sustainable bottom line of the corporation by minimizing risks and maximizing profits.

Liquid Legal Context
By Dr. Dierk Schindler, Dr. Roger Strathausen, Kai Jacob

Legal inhouse departments are typically focused on supporting top-line growth by adding value to transactions. Hagel rightfully emphasizes that any Euro spent or saved on disputes has an even larger impact, as it directly impacts the bottom line. A dispute clearly is a prime example of the importance for a lawyer to be a proficient risk manager whose job it is to evaluate the risk of a dispute and to translate it into a realistic resolution strategy that minimizes risk and maximizes profit.

In several articles we learn about the need to look at contracts differently, to move away from a pseudo adversarial tool to a sound basis constructed to support a mutual business outcome. Haapio and Barton make a very strong and substantive case for that. Typically, this goes along with the criticism that most contracts are drafted "for the judge", for litigation. Hagel calls out another myth which is talked about much less: the fact that due to passive

(continued)

clauses and the lack of focus on the business purpose and clarity around it, contracts that are seemingly drafted for litigation actually *cause* litigation. Contract interpretation is still one of the major sources of contract litigation and the failure to understand the contractual obligations remains to be under the top five root-causes for disputes.

Hagel's approach is instructive, as he also calls out the various means of avoiding conflict and litigation in the first place. When he refers to the principle of talking about interests rather than positions, when he points out the risks of gaps in communication and also the timing around bringing up a conflict, we again see an image of lawyers acting as holistic business advisors with a big picture in mind, rather than experts that know the law.

Reading the article and letting the very logical and mathematical approach sink in, one inadvertently bridges back to Bues and Matthaei who show the significant capabilities of legal tech, already today. Why not taking the human factor and the emotion out of the dispute and rely on artificial intelligence and contract data to determine the "ZOPA"—the "Zone Of Potential Agreement"?

References

Berkel, G. (2015). Deal mediation. *Zeitschrift für Konfliktmanagement (ZKM)*, 4–7.

Blake, S., Browne, J., & Sime, S. (2014). *A practical approach to alternative dispute resolution* (3rd ed.). Oxford, UK: Oxford University Press.

Bühring-Uhle, C., Eidenmüller, H., & Nelle, A. (2009). *Verhandlungsmanagement*. München, Germany: Beck.

Calihan, R., Dent, J. & Victor, M. (2004). The role of risk analysis in dispute and litigation management. In *27th Annual Forum on Franchising*. http://www.litigationrisk.com/Paper%20on%20Risk%20Analysis%20for%20ABA%20Forum%20on%20Franchising.pdf. Accessed 25 Sept 2016.

Cummins, T., David, M., & Kawamoto, K. (2011). *Contract and commercial management—The operational guide*. Zaltbommel, NL: Van Haren.

Desjardins, D. (2016). *A perspective of value: Forging new connections between Legal Departments and Law Firms* (pp. 77–82). ACC Docket.

Felstiner, W., Abel, R. & Sarat, A. The emergence of disputes: Naming, blaming, claiming. *The Law & Society Review, 15*(3/4), 631-654. http://media.leidenuniv.nl/legacy/Felstiner_Abel_Sarat%20(1981)_Naming.pdf. Accessed 25 Sept 2016.

Freyer, D. & Sayler, R. (2000). Commercial disputes. In N. Atlas, S. Huber & W. Trachte-Huber (Eds.), *Alternative dispute resolution—The litigator's handbook*. American Bar Association.

Haapio, H. (2013). *Next generation contracts: A paradigm shift*. Helsinki, Finland: Lexpert Ltd.

Haapio, H., & Siedel, G. (2013). *A short guide to contract risk*. Farnham, England: Gower.

Hagel, U. (2011). Der Unternehmensjurist als Risikomanager. *German Arbitration Journal (SchiedsVZ)*, 65–75.

Hagel, U. (2012). *Es geht auch anders*. Jahrbuch Deutscher AnwaltSpiegel 2011/2012. Stuttgart, Germany: German Law Publishers.

Hagel, U. (2013). Kosten und Nutzen der Mediation bei Konflikten zwischen Unternehmen. In T. Trenczek, D. Berning, & C. Lenz (Eds.), *Mediation und Konfliktmanagement*. Baden-Baden, Germany: Nomos.

Hagel, U. (2014a). Commentary on § 1 MediationsG. In J. Klowait, & U. Gläßer (Eds.), *Mediationsgesetz – Handkommentar*. Baden-Baden, Germany: Nomos.

Hagel, U. (2014b). Effizienzgewinnung durch rationale Auswahl des Streitbeilegungsverfahrens. *Zeitschrift für Konfliktmanagement (ZKM)*, 108–113.

Hagel, U. (2016). Mediation bei gesellschaftsrechtlichen Streitigkeiten. In M. Born, N. Ghassemi-Tabar, & B. Gehle (Eds.), *Münchener Handbuch des Gesellschaftsrechts, Band 7, Corporate Litigation* (5th ed.). Beck: München, Germany.

Hagel, U., & Steinbrecher, A. (2014). Systematik der Verfahrenswahl—die toolgestützte Wahl des geeigneten Konfliktbeilegungsverfahrens. In U. Gläßer, L. Kirchhoff, & F. Wendenburg (Eds.), *Konfliktmanagement in der Wirtschaft*. Baden-Baden, Germany: Nomos.

Hillson, D. A., & Simon, P. W. (2012). *Practical project risk management: The ATOM Methodology* (2nd ed.). Vienna: Management Concepts.

Lembcke, M. (2009). MedAdj — Mediation in Baustreitigkeiten durch Adjudikation? *Zeitschrift für Konfliktmanagement (ZKM)*, 122–125.

Mamula, T. & Hagel, U. (2015). The design of commercial conditions—Layout, visualization, language. In E. Schweighofer, F. Kummer & W. Hötzendorfer (Eds.), *Co-operation*. Wien, Austria:OCG.

Maytonera, E. (2013). Perspectives on managing risk and uncertainty. In D. Lowe (Ed.), *Commercial management: Theory and practice*. Wiley-Blackwell: Chichester, UK.

Moore, C. (2014). *The mediation process: Practical strategies for resolving conflict* (4th ed.). San Francisco: Jossey-Bass.

Passera, S. (2012). Enhancing contract usability and user experience through visualization – An experimental evaluation. In E. Banissi, et al. (Eds.), *16th International Conference on Information Visualisation, IV2012*, 11–13 July 2012, Montpellier, France (pp. 376–382). Los Alamitos, CA: IEEE Computer Society.

Peppet, S. (2004). Contract formation in imperfect markets: Should we use mediators in deals? *Ohio State Journal on Dispute Resolution, 19*(2), 283-367. https://kb.osu.edu/dspace/bitstream/handle/1811/77174/OSJDR_V19N2_0283.pdf?sequence=1. Accessed 25 Sept 2016.

PWC. (2014). Resolving capital project disputes: Adopting a business case approach. https://www.pwc.com/gx/en/capital-projects-infrastructure/publications/assets/pdfs/pwc-resolving-capital-project-disputes.pdf. Accessed 25 Sept 2016.

Reid, T. (2004). How to construct a contract compliance matrix. In *Contract management* (pp. 40–44). http://fundassist.flinders.edu.au/uploads/docs/Sample_Compliance_Matrix.pdf. Accessed 25 Sept 2016.

Reilly, T., & MacKenzie, D. (1999). *ADR in the corporate environment: A practical guide for designing alternative dispute resolution systems*. North York, Canada: CCH Canadian.

Risse, J. (2009). Procedural risk analysis: An ADR-tool in arbitration proceedings. In G. Zeiler, I. Welser, et al. (Eds.), *Austrian Arbitration Yearbook 2009* (pp. 461–470). Vienna: Manz'sche Verlags- und Universitätsbuchhandlung.

Sander, F., & Goldberg, S. (1994). Fitting the forum to the fuss: A user-friendly guide to selecting an ADR-procedure. *Negotiation Journal, 10*(1), 49–68.

Schreuer, C. (2008). What is a legal dispute. In I. Buffard, J. Crawford, A. Pellet, & S. Wittich (Eds.), *International law between universalism and fragmentation. Festschrift in Honour of Gerhard Hafner* (pp. 959–980). Leiden, NL: Martinus Nijhoff Publishers.

Shenoy, P. (1993). Information sets in decision theory. In M. Clarke, R. Kruse, & S. Moral (Eds.), *Symbolic and quantitative approaches to reasoning and uncertainty* (pp. 318–325). Berlin, Germany: Springer-Verlag.

Stark, D., & Choplin, J. (2012). Dysfunctional contracts and the laws and practices that enable them: An empirical analysis. http://www.works.bepress.com/debra_stark/6/. Accessed 28 Mar 2016.

Victor, M. (1990). Litigation risk analysis and ADR. In J. Wilkinson (Ed.), *Donovan Leisure Newton & Irvine ADR Practice Book*. http://www.litigationrisk.com/Litigation%20Risk%20Analysis(tm)%20and%20ADR.pdf. Accessed 25 Sept 2016.

Victor, M. (2014). Decision tree analysis: A means of reducing litigation uncertainty and facilitating good settlements. *Georgia State University Law Review, 31*(4), Article 3. http://readingroom.law.gsu.edu/gsulr/vol31/iss4/3. Accessed 25 Sept 2016.

Dr. Ulrich Hagel In-house Counsel at Bombardier Transportation, Mediator and Attorney at Law at KonsensKanzlei Berlin. Dr. Hagel studied Law and Business Administration at the University of Bayreuth. After having worked as an Attorney at Law in Stuttgart, he joined Bombardier Transportation in 1998. As Head of Claim Governance, Litigations & Procurement Support, he is working conceptually on conflict management processes and tools, but is also operationally leading complex disputes in negotiations, ADR-processes, arbitrations and litigations.

Dr. Hagel is Academic Director at the Dresden International University (DIU) for the MBA Program "International Commercial & Contract Management" and lecturer at EBS Executive Education in Oestrich-Winkel. He has published several articles on Conflict Management, Contract Management and Compliance and is co-editor of the German Arbitration Journal ("SchiedsVZ"), founding member of the Round Table Mediation and Conflict Management of the German Industry ("RTMKM") and a member of several advisory boards (German Arbitration Institute "DIS", Bucerius Center on the Legal Profession "CLP" at Bucerius Law School Hamburg, the online magazines "Deutscher AnwaltSpiegel" and "Dispute Resolution").

The Future of In-House Legal Departments and Their Impact on the Legal Market: Four Theses for General Counsels, and One for Law Firms

Markus Hartung and Arne Gärtner

Abstract
The legal market is in a state of flux. The "more-for-less" challenge, digitization, Artificial Intelligence (AI) and Big Data, technology, growing compliance needs, the rise of new business models and the growing emphasis on efficiency are only some of the trends that shake up the traditional structures of legal departments and their relationship with law firms and alternative providers of legal services. These significant changes have an undeniable impact on the legal market in its entirety.

From our perspective, the future of legal services will be driven through companies (as clients), maybe even through in-house legal departments. They decide if law firms are holding up to their promise of delivering value for money and will thereby survive the hypercompetitive market, they decide which technologies are useful in the long run, and they decide which services should be provided internally and which should be outsourced to law firms or alternative providers of legal services. Legal departments' sphere of influence has never been greater, both within the company and with regard to the relationship between companies and law firms.

This chapter introduces four theses on the structure and processes of companies, and one thesis relevant for law firms on how they can position themselves in the market.

M. Hartung
Bucerius Center on the Legal Profession, Hamburg, Germany
e-mail: markushartung@me.com

A. Gärtner (✉)
Linklaters LLP, Frankfurt, Germany
e-mail: arne.gaertner@linklaters.com

© Springer International Publishing AG 2017
K. Jacob et al. (eds.), *Liquid Legal*, Management for Professionals,
DOI 10.1007/978-3-319-45868-7_17

1   Introduction: A Bit of History

In general, legal departments' importance has grown significantly over the past 10 years. In-house counsels nowadays provide legal advice not only with regard to strategic decisions, big transactions and major litigation, but also on a day-to-day basis as a business partner for internal clients. Most General Counsels (GCs) are either part of the managing board or report directly to the CEO. The procurement of legal services has been in the hands of in-house lawyers for some time now. Thereby, the image of the legal department has clearly changed, as well: from being perceived as an antiquated department, a semi-academic ivory tower in the company, to being perceived as a modern, well-managed service provider to internal clients. Hence today, the added value of legal departments is commonly accepted, and many in-house lawyers are fully integrated into the day-to-day business of the company.

One reason for this change is the ever increasing importance of legal risk. When in 2013 Accenture asked executives from 446 organizations across seven industries and two public services subsectors which risks they foresaw rising most over the next 2 years, 62 % of the respondents named legal risks first, followed by business risks (52 %), regulatory requirements (49 %), market risks (47 %), credit risks, operational risks and strategic risks (all together 46 %, see Accenture 2013 Global Risk Management Study: Risk Management for an Era of Greater Uncertainty). The increasing significance of legal risk means that legal departments are becoming more and more important in multinational companies. Although legal and compliance risks are not exclusively owned by the legal department, executives understand the importance of involving the legal department when it comes to managing risk and making legally compliant decisions.

These seem like golden times for GCs and their legal departments. However, the growing prominence and changing role of legal departments does not necessarily lead to a growing budget. What is known as the "more-for-less" challenge describes the expectation of most companies to manage the growing need for legal advice with a shrinking, or at least stagnant, budget. This leads to a greater emphasis on efficiency in legal departments.

2   The "More-for-Less" Challenge: Does It Exist?

The "more-for-less" challenge has been around for several years now and seems to be widely accepted by both external and in-house lawyers. However, there is not much data available to verify this assumption. That is why in 2015 the Bucerius Center on the Legal Profession (Bucerius CLP) carried out a survey to test the "more-for-less" hypothesis (more details in Hartung/Gaertner, The "more-for-less" paradox, in: Business Law Magazine No. 1, 3 March 2016, p. 21 et seq.). We asked 700 in-house lawyers from companies based in Germany to complete a short questionnaire, of these 700 nearly 10 % participated in the study. What we discovered is that only one part of the hypothesis is true; 80 % of in-house lawyers stated that the legal department's workload grew (+3 to +10 %) or grew significantly (more than +10 %) during the last 3 years. This demonstrates that legal departments today have to provide more legal services. When we asked about the available resources (both internal and external), one third of participants answered that the budgets for external counsel, as well as the number of in-house lawyers, remained almost the same. When it comes to internal resources however, we observed growth; in our study, 40 % of the participants answered that the number of lawyers in their team grew or grew significantly during the last 3 years. In a different study, carried out by the German Magazine Juve Rechtsmarkt in 2014/2015, 442 executives from the areas legal, IP, compliance and tax were asked the same question, of these, 60 % answered correspondingly (see Juve Rechtsmarkt 02/2015). When it comes to external resources, nearly 40 % of in-house lawyers in our study stated that budgets are on the decrease. In a nutshell, we cannot find enough evidence to support the "more-for-less hypothesis", at least not in Germany. That is why we assert that the term "more-for-less" is not completely correct, and should be changed to "more-for-the-same". The expression "more-for-the-same" also captures the greater need for efficiency. We will further use the expression "more-for-less" when we describe the past, going forward we will use the "more-for-the-same" expression.

3   Why This Chapter?

In this chapter, we are going to examine trends that affect the future of the legal market. Firstly, we shall focus on legal departments. We have developed four hypotheses that summarize what we think reflect the most relevant trends for legal departments. At the end, we will introduce a fifth hypothesis on general developments in the legal market, and especially on the role of law firms in the future.

3.1   The Consequences of Ongoing Economic Pressure

The "more-for-less", or "more-for-the-same" challenge remains the basic principle with regard to the management of legal departments. Although our study on the "more-for-less" challenge indicated that "only" 60 % of the in-house counsel are directly confronted with this challenge, most GCs try to manage their department in a more efficient and effective way and thereby avoid waste and duplication. Nearly 80 % of in-house counsel who participated in our study try to handle the "more-for-less" challenge by improving efficiency within the department and, at the same time, cutting budgets for external counsel.

    This has not always been the case. When GCs were confronted for the first time with the expectations of their CEOs or CFOs that they should reduce their budgets, they focused on "low-hanging fruits" and negotiated price reductions with law firms. Since, as a result of the financial crisis of 2007–2008, the M&A market collapsed and law firms, therefore, lost a significant part of their transaction-related business, GCs were in a good position to demand such price reductions. For the first time, companies were in the driving seat of their relationship with law firms. Altogether it seemed that GCs were successfully saving costs.

However, price reductions are only part of the first stage of change; a stage which Richard Susskind calls the "denial", or "hoping for no real change" stage (see his book Tomorrow's Lawyers, 2013). GCs realized that these short-term orientated measures were not sufficient to improve efficiency in the legal department and cut costs; rumour has it that in some cases, law firms apparently found ways to add more hours to their bills and therefore the cost of external counsel remained the same.

Another reaction to deal with the "more-for-less" challenge was to establish long-term relationships with law firms and alternative legal services providers. By establishing panels, or even alliances, with only a few law firms who would handle most of their work, GCs motivated their suppliers to look at their relationship on a long term basis and therefore invest more in the relationship. If law firms were promised a significant share of external counsel budgets, GCs assumed that there would be an alignment of incentives between legal departments and law firms.

4   The Next Stage

The next "stage of development", Susskind calls it "re-sourcing", was characterized by the re-evaluation of the way legal services are delivered. Companies began the quest for greater overall efficiency and an optimal balance between "make and buy" (not "make or buy") of legal services. A significant part of this quest was the multi-sourcing of legal services and working differently. The underlying precondition for greater efficiency is to first of all break down, or "decompose" the production process of legal services and, as a second step, identify the best sourcing option. Hence, through the decomposition and modularization of the legal production process, GCs laid the foundations for plural and/or multi-sourcing. This approach to produce legal services is also known as the "production-line approach" (see Sako/Chondrakis/Vaaler 2013, "How do Firms Make-and-Buy? The Case of Legal Services Sourcing by Fortune 500 Companies").

Through the unbundling and modularization of services, our understanding of the production process, or assembly line, of legal services grew significantly. GCs today no longer accept the delivery of legal services in a black box, but only as a more or less bundled set of activities, like due diligence, contract drafting or negotiation. Thus they regularly use different sourcing options and no longer outsource bundled requests to only one law firm.

Disaggregation on the one hand requires technology that supports half human, half automated production processes and on the other hand leads to new technology, because when it is more and more possible to provide parts of the supply chain of legal services without the human factor, new IT-driven business models arise. Of course one has to recognize that standardized solutions are not perfect and not a 100 % solution, but quite often, an 80 % solution is sufficient. GCs using the Pareto principle, or 80–20 rule, is surely something new.

These considerations lead to the first hypothesis:

Economic pressure and therefore the need for optimization will remain high ("more-for-the-same"). This leads to an increasingly disaggregated value chain of legal services, where everything that can be done with the help of IT will be done with IT – even if it is no longer a 100 % solution. In combination with a modern IT infrastructure, legal knowledge itself will increasingly become a commodity.

4.1 Collaboration and Knowledge Sharing Remain a Driver for Efficiency

The need for efficiency in turn leads to a greater emphasis on collaboration and knowledge sharing in legal departments. The basic idea behind knowledge sharing and collaboration is to avoid duplication and superfluous work, especially with regard to external counsel, and thereby to considerably improve the use of resources.

According to the resource-based view in strategic management (see Barney 1991), intangible resources, such as legal knowledge, have the potential to become a primary sources of competitive advantage, as long as they fulfil the VRIN criteria (valuable, rare, inimitable, non-substitutable). Legal departments who understand the value of those resources and facilitate knowledge sharing and collaboration will not only avoid duplication, but, more importantly, provide benefits to the entire company.

The concept of the resource-based view will in the long-run foster a different perspective on the balance of legal services provided internally and externally. Whereas the decision on how to strike the "make and buy" balance currently depends, amongst other factors, on different production costs, in the future, the question will be whether or not the service is strategically important such that it could provide a competitive advantage for the company. Companies will focus on strategically necessary and important services and will mostly outsource non-strategic services. Knowledge management and sharing are key to the successful implementation of resource-based management of the legal department.

Both knowledge sharing and collaboration are further driven by technology. Modern IT-platforms simplify knowledge sharing across borders and across different parts of a company. They also provide tools for collaboration, so called "collaboration platforms". A major part of knowledge management in legal departments usually lies in the area of contract management. All types of contract can be part of a legal knowledge management tool. When assisted by IT, companies, especially large companies, can develop their own "automated document assembly" tools. Of course this requires investment, and many companies are still not used to investing in Legal IT. In the future, however, automated document assembly will replace handmade contract drafting. If GCs are not prepared to invest in bespoke solutions for automated document assembly, they can cooperate with providers of so-called "self-service platforms", like LegalZoom, Rocket Lawyer or LawPivot.

Knowledge sharing and collaboration work not only within a company but also across different companies. There are providers of networking platforms, like Legal OnRamp or AdvanceLaw, that assist in-house counsel from different companies to share knowledge.

These considerations lead to the second hypothesis:

Modern IT platforms will further support collaboration and knowledge sharing among in-house counsel and also between companies. Contract drafting and management will be standardized and automated. Furthermore, legal department management will focus on strategically important resources.

4.2   The Trend of Centralization Will Reverse

For a long time, companies have centralized large parts of the legal function. Before that, companies used to have independent legal departments in each country and in each subsidiary. Today, all these departments are connected and run by GCs of the parent company. GCs are leading the company-wide legal department by functional and sometimes also by disciplinary guidance.

The trend of centralization started when companies realized the savings potential of demand aggregation. Their combined buying power, and therefore position in negotiations with law firms, was a lot higher when their demand for legal services was combined. Another reason for centralization was to support collaboration and knowledge sharing. Furthermore, companies wanted to centralize legal risk management to more effectively prevent non-compliant behaviour.

From an economic perspective, centralization leads to positive economies of scale and scope. Despite the positive effects of centralization, centralization also leads to higher coordination costs because all the activities of the legal function need to be coordinated and controlled. Decentralization, on the other hand, leads to costs of autonomy because decentralized units work completely independently from individual procurement processes and IT infrastructures. GCs therefore always need to manage the trade-off between the positive and negative effects of centralization and decentralization.

Albeit that many GCs, for the reasons mentioned above, have tended towards centralization, we assume that this trend will reverse in the future. A major problem for a centralized legal department is that in-house counsel are too far away from the day-to-day business of their internal clients. Lack of knowledge of the internal clients' business itself leads to increased coordination costs. In addition, companies have realized, or will realize, that centralized departments with no direct link to day-to-day operations are cost-intensive, and therefore it is in many cases more reasonable to mandate external counsel than to keep the work in-house.

We assume that companies will therefore differentiate between centralization and decentralization, and define which services should be provided within the centralized legal department and which services should be provided directly by lawyers working in decentralized units. There are some roles that need to be part of the centralized legal department, for example lawyers who directly advise the management board, like corporate and M&A lawyers. Furthermore, most parts of the legal department's operations, like IT, HR, knowledge management and procurement, should remain in the centralized legal department. With regard to the day-to-day operations of the company, lawyers will be embedded directly in the business. Besides, there is a third breed of lawyers; lawyers specializing in legal project management. Project management lawyers are part of the centralized legal department but work on different projects all over the company.

This will lead to more in-house lawyers working within the day-to-day operations of the company. With the help of centralized functions like knowledge management, IT and procurement, companies are able to combine the advantages of a decentralized legal unit, that gives advice on a day-to-day basis with a deep understanding of the business of their internal clients, and centralized lawyers specializing in single fields of expertise. All this will be facilitated through modern IT-platforms, efficient processes and a centralized approach to legal services sourcing.

These considerations lead to the third hypothesis:

> The concept of a large centralized legal department with sometimes hundreds of lawyers is out-of-date. In the future most in-house counsel (nota bene: not always lawyers!) will work with their clients on a day-to-day basis. In-house counsel acting like external counsel will no longer be the standard. Only a few lawyers, in addition to business functions, will remain in the centralized legal department where they act as trusted advisors to the board.

4.3   KPIs Help to Measure the Performance

Another trend which we have previously discussed is the growing interest of CFOs and CEOs in the overall performance of the legal department. There are mainly two reasons for the growing interest: (1) companies nowadays understand that the legal function needs to be completely integrated in the processes and operations of the company to ensure that its compliance needs are managed professionally. A separate legal department that operates like an external law firm is no longer acceptable. (2) The costs of the legal department should not be neglected when companies try to become more efficient. The legal department is under the same economic pressure as every other department.

This interest leads to a growing use of KPIs in legal departments. KPIs help the CFO or CEO to examine the efficiency, effectiveness and overall performance of the legal department. KPIs measuring the effectiveness of legal departments and KPIs measuring the efficiency are two very different means. The main difference is that KPIs measuring the effectiveness try to measure the output of the legal function, e.g. in terms of less litigation or lesser exposure to legal risks. KPIs measuring the efficiency focus on whether the legal department makes the most out of limited resources.

The performance of the legal department is not only measured by internal KPIs, but also by benchmarking data from other legal departments. Typical KPIs which are used to manage the legal department are: percentages of legal spending from revenue; outside legal expenses; percentages of cases successfully solved; or number of in-house lawyers per 1000 employees. Sadly, one of the most important contributions a well-run legal department makes is difficult to measure—the legal risks avoided in terms of dollars (see Morrison 2008).

For GCs, both types of KPIs, those measuring effectiveness and those measuring efficiency, are a valid way to measure their departments' contribution to the long-term success of their companies. GCs who try to revolt against KPIs will increasingly come under question from the management board.

This leads to the fourth hypothesis:

> Legal functions operating without metrics to measure their performance are no longer acceptable. Even risk management needs to be included in the key performance indicators in order to measure success and make the performance of the legal department visible to the CEOs or CFOs of large corporations.

4.4 The Future of Law Firms: Structure or People

Much has been said and written about the future of law firms: we seem to know everything about the future of the profession; we know a lot about the challenges brought forward through LegalTech and AI; we know which segments of the legal market are at risk; we have read about taxonomies of law firms, commentaries on recent figures and financial results year on year. If you want to, you could spend days going through literature. This book, and in particular this chapter, however, approaches the future of law firms from a different perspective.

This perspective comes purely from the client's side, as we have described it above. No particularities of law firms or legal markets have been taken into account, we have simply taken the client or consumer's point of view. That makes things different. Taking a story which was used in Richard Susskind's "Tomorrow's lawyers" as a starting point: the following considerations don't focus on the product, i.e. the wonderful drilling machines of Black & Decker, but rather on the hole in the wall, which is the client's interest.

When we talk about the legal function of a corporation, we mean everything that forms part of risk and legal management (incl. enabling business opportunities) with regard to the proper and successful surviving and thriving of the company.

The legal function, as described above (and in an ideal world), is a rational, transparent and measurable set of rules and procedures. The workforce consists of lawyers, paralegals, project managers, technical assistants and many other capable people who are able to fulfil certain tasks. Whether or not the legal function is managed by a lawyer is not the main point. The proper running of a legal function requires first and foremost structuring skills, then certain (legal, project, financial, economic and all sorts of other) management skills, and the ability to decide on the most appropriate resource for a certain piece of work (or a set of tasks), independent of your own capacity or role. We do not rule out that lawyers could head-up legal functions, but what they learn and how they think does not make them the first choice for these functions.

What about GCs? Nowadays, most GCs are lawyers. Is this a necessary prerequisite for a GC? Rather not. The GC has to advise the board on the best, or most appropriate, way forward with regard to risk and compliance management. Many legal and/or regulatory questions have to be taken into account. However, a GC who only focuses on legal issues would miss the point. Hence, being a lawyer can be one of the preconditions of being a good GC but it is not a *conditio sine qua non*.

Bearing in mind what we've said above about the structure of modern in-house legal departments (and assuming that companies are prepared to reorganize their legal function accordingly!), our hypothesis is this: in B2B and in "normal times", only law firms that are prepared and ready to form a truly integrated part of the client's value chain have a chance to survive. For the rest, it will be rather difficult.

These considerations lead to our final hypothesis:

> What is true for in-house counsel is true for external counsel as well. Generalists giving abstract legal advice will become rare, and most external counsel will be working in the value chain of their clients advising on day-to-day questions. Together with their in-house clients, they will be responsible for the effective risk management of their clients. Only a few generalists will survive in the marketplace and act as trusted advisors. On the other hand, specialists and lawyers focusing on project management will still find their niche in the legal market.

4.5 Between Normal Times and Times of Crisis

All our considerations are based on what we call "normal times". By that we mean everything other than a crisis, or on a positive note, everything which supports the ongoing business of a company, like: producing and selling goods and/or services and keeping the operation up and running. We talk about a value chain, or the sequence of events which, at the end, turns effort into turnover for the company. The legal function, and external legal services, play an important role in this value chain as their task is to keep the (legal and sometimes non-legal) risk levels down.

Assuming that companies organize their legal and risk function along the lines described in this and in other chapters of this book, we can conclude that law firms have to align themselves with their clients. Their structure, their people, their processes, even their locations and office fit-out has to be organized with a view to clients' needs far more than it is today. Should law firms be big or small, global or local? The answer to this question very much depends on what is needed. Interestingly enough, this exercise has not yet been undertaken, bar some exceptions. Future considerations do not revolve so much around the questions of local presence vs. global span, all-lawyers or diverse workgroups, but rather around what is needed to properly run a legal function, from a company's perspective.

5   Crisis and People

When a crisis comes, things change. By crisis, we mean major events with the potential to seriously threaten the company, maybe even its existence, and what is sometimes called "bet the company" or "bet the firm" issue. The "Siemens-Crisis" (some 10 years ago) or the "Volkswagen-Crisis" are good examples of what we mean. These types of crises happen when internal processes designed to avoid certain "situations" fail. In this case, it seems that everything we've said above (or what is said about the perfect or modern structure of a legal function) no longer applies.

Why is this? It seems to us that a crisis defies any process or plan. It was Helmuth von Moltke who said "*no plan of operations extends with any certainty beyond the first contact with the main hostile force*", or, in a shorter version (and often attributed to Napoleon): "*No battle plan ever survives contact with the enemy*".

Hence, when it comes to a crisis, i.e. to something which surpasses all processes regarding the value chain, our discussions on modern legal function structure etc. are not really helpful because they do not work in reality. Companies may train their people how to behave in a dawn raid, and it may even help nervous employees to act calmly, but it will not avoid the crisis.

In times of crises, we should not talk about B2B. What we have said about B2B is not applicable to the nervous CEO with regard to his function, or for helping the board to get it right when faced with an unfriendly takeover or an internal investigation. Advising board members in these situations is closer to B2C business, and here is room for all sorts of lawyers who are truly great and empathic advisers. Why B2C? Because the nervous CEO, or board members, are closer to a (sophisticated or informed) private customer who evaluates and appreciates lawyers' services. When things get tough, CEOs will not be calling the procurement department to help find the most cost-efficient lawyer.

In practice, this means that in certain situations the success of the legal function (and its external advisers) depends on the abilities of the people (lawyers, paralegals, other jurists etc.) to cope with and be able to read and understand situations, and to take or recommend appropriate decisions. What do these people look like, what is their profile? Recently, Jordan Furlong issued a paper "How to be a legal marvel", describing the most important attributes and characteristics for successful professionals. He mentioned collaboration skills, customer service, emotional intelligence, financial literacy, process improvement, relationship building, technological affinity and time management—in short: leadership qualities. This is similar to research from the Bucerius Center on the Legal Profession done a couple of years ago on the most important areas in which successful lawyers, in-house or in private practice, have to excel: business acumen, ownership and legal management, accountability, rigour, risk and cost management.

Having said all this, what are the consequences? These are the key messages and takeaways for law firm managers or in-house legal department managers: companies will have to structure and organize their legal functions to respond to the hypotheses discussed above; and external providers of legal services will have to fit neatly into the value chain.

Note, however, that processes and structure won't save the company's life in a crisis. It is instead the human workforce that makes the difference.

Liquid Legal Context

By Dr. Dierk Schindler, Dr. Roger Strathausen, Kai Jacob

Hartung and Gärtner provide a compact overview on the main forces that drive change in the legal market: Economic pressure, IT providing opportunities for automation as much as for collaboration and knowledge sharing, the decentralization of legal departments and the gravitation—or rather push—towards metrics-based performance management.

It is fascinating how the kaleidoscope of voices from forward thinking authors starts to paint a consistent picture around those four theses:

- On the economic pressure, we have had clear voices explain that and why it exists—starting with Fawcett in his foreword. At the same time, Ross and Bassli have shown us means of getting a higher return on investment on every Euro that we spend on purchasing legal services.
- As to the game-changing opportunities in modern legal tech, Bues and Matthaei have given us a concise overview on the opportunities that develop at ever increasing speed.
- On the trend to decentralize and up-level the legal human resources, we have heard Markfort introducing the polycentric approach in law firms, while Tumasjan and Welpe have shown us the way to develop an entrepreneurial DNA in a legal department.
- Pauleau, Roquilly and Collard have built a clear and tangible case for why and how to introduce a KPI-based performance management, while Meents has taken a stab at how law firms need to help clients to see the value in the services of a law firm, rather than remaining solely focused on the price-tag.

As we talk about the rapid and fundamental change in the ratio of external legal services that inhouse departments use and what we expect in terms of value for the money, the question arises: what is the best way to procure them? Mascello talks about how customers professionally procure legal services today.

Refererences

Barney, J. (1991) Firm resources and sustained competitive advantage. *Journal of Management, 17* (1).

Morrison, R. (2008). *Missing and elusive metrics.* GC New York. http://gcnewyork.com/columns08/061908morrison.html.

Markus Hartung is director of the Bucerius Center on the Legal Profession (CLP), a think tank on topics regarding the further development of legal markets. His special expertise lies in market development and trends, management and strategic leadership as well as corporate governance of law firms, combined with the regulatory requirements of various legal markets. Since 2006 he is member of the Committee on Professional Regulation of the German Bar Association, chairing this committee since January 2011. He is a regular conference-speaker on leadership, management topics and professional ethics and has written numerous articles and book chapters on these topics.

Arne Gärtner is a Project Manager at Linklaters within the global Business Improvement team. After a 9 month secondment to the London office, he is now responsible for Legal Project Management in Germany. He also supports the delivery of the firm's continuous improvement and efficiency strategy in the German offices. Until summer 2015, he was a Research Assistant at the Bucerius Center on the Legal Profession at Bucerius Law School in Hamburg and has served as a fellow there ever since.

Arne studied Business Administration (Diplom-Kaufmann) at the University of Potsdam and Mediation (M.A.) at the European University Viadrina, Frankfurt (Oder). He also wrote a doctoral thesis on "Strategic Management of Legal Departments in multinational Corporations—Value add Options of Professional Service Departments".

Procurement of Legal Services: How Customers Professionally Procure Legal Services Today

Bruno Mascello

Abstract

When companies need legal services, they typically turn to outside counsel and law firms ("buy"; BigLaw). Increasingly, larger companies start or enlarge the work force of their legal departments to perform the required legal services ("make"; insourcing). As a new option, the legal branches of the big auditing firms (Big Four) and alternative legal service providers (NewLaw, e.g., LPO) are also being considered. Depending on the customer's (The term "customer" is uniformly applied to both clients of outside counsel and internal customers of legal departments to express the view that providing legal advice is considered a service with customer orientation in either case.) experience and whether or not a company has its own legal department, the purchase of these services, which in particular includes the selection process on the one hand, and the appointment and management of attorneys on the other hand, may occur differently. However, the questions to be raised and the topics to be addressed in this context remain the same. Although the relationship between customer and outside counsel will continue to be diverse, it is mutually beneficial to understand both sides and to recognize the different facets of such a relationship. Further, in any event such legal services and advice cannot stand alone but must fit into an overall solution for the customer's problem and the challenge he is facing. This article seeks to provide a first overview and to systematically investigate the questions to be posed during the professional procurement of legal services from third party providers, be it outside counsel and law firms or other alternative suppliers. (This article is based on the following publication: Mascello, Bruno (2015) Beschaffung von Rechtsdienstleistungen und Management externer Anwälte, Schulthess Zürich (also to be published in English soon). There, you can find further comments and explanations, sources and references as well as an

B. Mascello (✉)
Executive School of the University of St. Gallen, Holzstrasse 15, CH-9010 St. Gallen, Switzerland
e-mail: bruno.mascello@unisg.ch

© Springer International Publishing AG 2017
K. Jacob et al. (eds.), *Liquid Legal*, Management for Professionals,
DOI 10.1007/978-3-319-45868-7_18

extensive bibliography. For the sake of readability and brevity, this article uses the masculine form of pronouns only, but the feminine form should always be understood to be included as well.)

1 Introduction

The mere addressing and answering of legal issues from a subject-matter expertise perspective only, is no longer enough for a lawyer to succeed in a law firm. The same applies when looking at legal departments, i.e. the head of a legal department and his team, when servicing their internal clients. The legal challenges are not only increasing in number, but are also becoming more international, complex and sophisticated. Thus, to run a law firm and a legal department properly requires not only legal expertise, but the consideration of the economic and operational point of view as well.

A company has to approach systematically the questions of how it intends to provide the necessary legal services and how it will make them available. It can either produce the legal services itself ("make") or acquire them from third parties ("buy"). If a company has decided to hire a third party, i.e. to outsource the work, the questions will arise as to whom such order is being assigned and according to what terms the work is to be completed. Now, as before, external law firms and outside counsel continue to play a significant role in the provision of legal services. As a consequence, the expenditure incurred for this type of service is becoming of greater importance to companies and to the entire economy. Hence, the professional procurement of legal services is inevitable for a customer.

2 A Changing Legal Market

2.1 General Remarks

The financial crisis of 2008 served as a game-changer in the legal market. Many of the law firms hoped—and some still do today—that the negative effects that were unleashed would represent an interim economic lull only, that the effect of this recession would soon abate and the "golden age" return. This financial crisis, however, has also caused structural, irreversible changes in the legal market. It has especially raised sensitivity and awareness with respect to the relationship between law firms and their customers. This in turn affects how companies organize themselves for the purpose of obtaining the necessary legal services. The processes set in motion by the market changes are thus not only temporary in nature; rather, they will remain and may even become more profound. These processes represent a "new normal" that has to be understood and to be adjusted to.

2.2   Complex Trend Pyramid

Changes have always affected the legal services market. The situation today, however, is in many ways different: the changes are more diverse, occurring on many fronts and simultaneously, showing greater dynamism and intensity, and are characterized by a structural rather than a cyclical nature. In order to understand these complex changes, it is imperative to outline the various trends in a more simplified way by making use of the trend pyramid as set out in Fig. 1.

Looking at the legal market in a strict sense, this is characterized by the following three major changes: liberalization, globalization and increasing application of technology. The legal market shows only a slow but continuous trend towards liberalization: for example, consulting bans and the lawyers' monopoly are being further relaxed, and barriers to entering the market are being eliminated. The economy is growing and expanding, the markets are becoming more global, and customers' business operations are becoming increasingly more international, particularly as they are entering more and more new markets (especially also SME). In connection with this, regulation and complexity of legal issues are also expanding. Technology is playing an increasingly important role for the efficient provision of legal services, and the technological possibilities are already much more advanced. This helps with the rising cost pressure, the fragmentation of the value chain in the production of legal services (disaggregation), and the improvement of knowledge management.

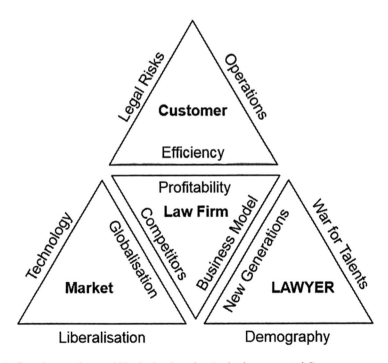

Fig. 1 Complex trend pyramid in the legal market (author's own material)

Since legal staff comprise—at least for now—the most important resource for the creation of legal services, the changes in the labour market for lawyers are of great importance. These are mainly characterized by the following three criteria: demography, a shortage of talent (war for talents) and a new generation of employees. With the demographic shift in the age pyramid—compared to the baby boomer generation—fewer and fewer workers will be available to future labour markets. With this quantitative change, circumstances will be accentuated in the future. Not only will outstanding talents continue to be rare and sought after, but less qualified staff will become less available, too. The migration of foreign workers will not really contribute to relieving the situation. Considering that soon, the majority of the employees will come from the so-called Generation Y, it would be advisable to deal with their needs and motivation at an early stage. For members of that generation, for example, the so-called "work-life balance" has a higher priority; they want more flexible and interactive work and ask for different working time models, alternative career models as well as training and education.

The law firms today are challenged on three important fronts: changing and increasing competition in the legal market, declining profitability and the question of finding the right business model. The number of lawyers is increasing steadily, which—from a mere quantitative perspective—is already leading to increased competition among lawyers. Further, the competitive environment has become more varied and more complex, e.g. by the appearance of alternative legal service providers, which are not considered traditional law firms. In addition, to achieve or exceed profitability targets, law firms will be forced to organize themselves more professionally across the board by applying best practices when running an enterprise. Further, the current business model of large business law firms, which are organized like a pyramid and take advantage of the so-called leverage rate, is being called into question. Previous work and working time models seem to have lost their appeal for recent generations, and the broadly applied "up-or-out" career model is not as promising and accepted any more as it may have been in the past.

2.3   Trends with Customers

One of the biggest changes will take place at the customer level. This is relevant since ultimately they are the source that triggers the demand for legal services in the legal market. Customers are facing the following challenges, the resolution of which they may pass on, in one form or another, to outside counsel and to other service providers: the continuous increase in legal risks, a compulsory increase in efficiency and the need for the optimization of operations.

The growing juridification of business life and the rise in regulatory efforts calls, on the one hand, for legal advisers with a sense for the whole (generalists), and, on the other hand, for the processing of vast amounts of information, which requires an increased use of specialists. New topics are emerging and are becoming more important (e.g. compliance, corporate governance, regulatory issues and, in my opinion, also risk management). The globalization of business is accompanied by other hazards (e.g. penalties) which require better control of the legal framework. Hence, customers have an interest in externalizing these legal risks, which especially affects all legal service providers directly. This may lead to growing legal budgets in companies.

Despite the corresponding growing budget for legal expenses, however, both cost-savings pressure and the need to increase efficiency are also on the rise for general counsel, hence their growing demand for effective cost management. This means that legal departments have to deliver more than before ("more for less"), and even more efficiently than before, that is: "better, faster and cheaper". Finally, legal departments have to demonstrate how they contribute to the execution of the corporate strategy and how they generate added value (including applying suitable KPI). All these new demands will be passed on to their legal service providers.

Despite the increasing demands in substantive terms, the management of a legal department today requires much more than simply being able to answer internal customers' legal questions. The criteria for an optimal management of the legal function have become more varied, in particular from an operational point of view. As a result of requesting efficiency improvements in the legal department, the operational issues with respect to the provision of legal services are increasingly coming into focus. The required back office operations are being structured in a more professional way, they are being reorganized and made more efficient. The organization is carried out along the value chain and the relevant processes of the company. Moreover, the purchase of services is becoming more professional (e.g. involvement of the procurement department, tender processes and requests for proposals, focusing on preferred suppliers, considering suppliers with lower rates), and alternatives to law firms are being considered (e.g. LPOs). The previously applied hourly fee model for outside counsel will increasingly be called into question, and alternative compensation models may increasingly be taken into account.

Today, moreover, other trends are noticeable. For instance, the work previously outsourced to law firms is increasingly being taken back again and dealt with by internal resources (insourcing). The composition of the law firms mandated by the companies is being rearranged or their number is being reduced (convergence or panel). Further, smaller and less expensive law firms are increasingly being considered. Dealing with law firms is becoming more professional and institutionalized, compensations are being negotiated in a new and harder way (alternative fee arrangements) and new legal service providers, i.e. providers that are not traditional law firms, are also being considered (legal process outsourcing).

2.4 Positioning of the Legal Department

The roles of the general counsel and in-house counsel are also subject to constant change. On the one hand, the growing legalization and regulation in each industry means that the legal department is playing an increasingly important role in the company. On the other hand, legal is losing the status of a singular function and must, similarly to other business units and functions, constantly prove to be an efficient and cost-effective service provider.

Today, the legal department has a more prominent position in the company. In particular, the general counsel is now perceived as a risk manager. He is also expected to provide general problem-solving beyond legal subject-matter tasks and to act as a co-designer of the company's strategic development. Consequently, legal strategies are being integrated into corporate strategies. The presence of outside counsel in the business is being reduced and, to the extent possible, the provision of legal services is being lowered to the level of a commodity.

The importance of a legal department and thus the value of legal advice provided within a company can be determined by the position of its general counsel in the leadership hierarchy. There are different views on whether and how a general counsel should be represented, or be present, at the (extended) executive level or in board meetings. There seems to be a trend in different countries that the general counsel should participate as an advisor in board meetings and have a "seat at the table" of the executive management of the company. This ensures a systematic and timely involvement of the general counsel and ties him into the business responsibility.

3   Legal Sourcing

3.1   Procurement of Legal Services as an Operational Task

The mandate of a legal department ideally includes the responsibility for the complete delivery of services with respect to legal issues in the company. Various options are available to a company to cover its demands for legal services. From a company's point of view, it is basically irrelevant whether these services are rendered through internal (make) or external resources (buy). It is only relevant that the company obtains a legally correct and adequate solution for the required purposes, which is sufficiently customized, customer-oriented and cost-efficient.

Accordingly, an essential component of operating a legal department is the purchase of legal services and the management of outside counsel. The general counsel has become the actual buyer and an informed customer of the outside counsel. In this way, the otherwise existing information asymmetry between non-lawyers and outside counsel can be reduced or avoided. The involvement of external consultants is often connected to the fact that the related costs are associated with the legal department and therefore these expenses are allocated internally to this function. Because these costs typically account for a share of the annual legal department's cost, the related impact on the budget ought not to be underestimated. These costs appear regularly on the CFO's radar, and the general counsel is required to provide the necessary information and explanations. Thus, a policy that regulates, in particular, the provision of legal services by the legal department and the integration of these services into the value chain of the company, can significantly increase the efficiency and effectiveness as well as the standing of a legal department.

3.2   Options to Procure Legal Services

Whether and how someone should do a job does not only depend on whether or not he can actually do it. Rather, the question is whether or not it is efficient to perform the task. Since there are various ways of doing a job, there is the desire to do it as optimally as possible—depending on the specific needs on an individual basis. Consequently, the various service providers must be carefully selected and coordinated in order to ensure smooth cooperation. The need for coordination is also reflected in the many terms used to describe the various methods of legal sourcing. In order to reduce the confusion around these terms, it may make sense to organize and define the key terms as suggested in Fig. 2. It can mainly be distinguished by the service provider (make or buy) and the place of provision (out-, near- or offshoring). In my view, "rightsourcing" seems to be the proper generic umbrella term, since it addresses in the best and most neutral way possible both "make" and "buy" variants, including the sub-varieties and also the decision-making process for the most efficient and effective way and place of service provision, i.e. in terms of personnel, financials and time.

3.3   Legal Department vs. Other Legal Services Providers

An organized legal department will first carefully analyze the overall legal services a company may need, and then identify the tasks and core competencies that should stay in-house and not be outsourced. Then it must assess whether a particular activity is of high strategic importance for a company and could have a significant financial impact on the balance sheet. Consequently, this activity may comprise a relevant threat to the company's reputation, represent an important competitive advantage, or could, in general, have a major impact on the company with respect to other risk aspects.

Further, an increasing number of innovative customers do not only consider traditional law firms but also any other legal service providers that have become

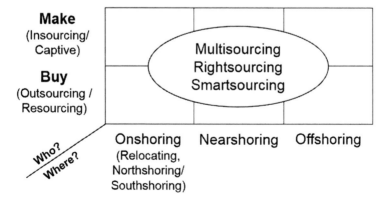

Fig. 2 Terminology in legal sourcing (author's own material)

available in the market by now. The decision may depend on the question as to which core activities need to be performed by qualified lawyers only. When considering the entire value chain to produce legal services, it is not necessary for all steps to be performed by qualified lawyers alone. The competitors of the big external law firms ("Big Law") that offer the same or similar services as law firms, but at more favorable terms, include the legal branches of the big audit and accounting firms (the so-called "Big Four") on the one hand, and all other providers in the financial sector on the other hand. These providers also cover all those providers that offer their customers certain selected legal services only (e.g., banking institutions, legal protection insurance and fiduciary companies).

In addition to these alternative legal service providers, a next level of development is evolving. Third parties only perform certain parts of the entire value chain for the creation of legal services by offering new concepts and business models. These suppliers complement the legal market with new competition—initially mainly in the low-price segment, i.e. the consumer/retail legal services market—and are designated as "New Law".

Numerous and different drivers and reasons exist for deciding in favor of "make" or "buy" on the one hand, as well as for mandating a law firm or an alternative legal service provider on the other hand. The decision will depend on the respective company, legal department and individual situation. In any event, an attentive external legal service provider should make sure that he understands the customer's analysis and motivation when offering his services, since the customer defines the playground for business. It may be relevant for all outside service providers to note that there seems to exist a tendency in different countries to increasingly insource tasks which are associated with the expansion of the in-house legal department. The interest in doing more with internal resources particularly also concerns tasks in connection with transactions (e.g. M&A). This is also cost-driven, considering that an hour of an outside counsel may cost up to three times as much as an hour of an in-house counsel (Fig. 3).

Fig. 3 Provider of legal services (author's own material)

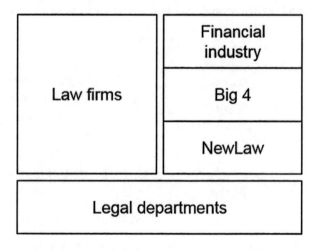

3.4   Relevance of Project Management

The disaggregation of the value chain and the consideration of various service providers require one key skill: project management. Neither legal departments nor law firms usually address the important question determining success, namely, who will assume the procurement of the various individual components of work and who will coordinate them with each other to form a logical and functioning whole at the end. Securing functioning interfaces and the perfect co-ordination and integration of the single pieces into an overall solution, which is certainly facilitated significantly through the utilization of IT, will ultimately decide whether and to what extent the efficiency and quality gains envisaged by the unbundling of services will be achieved. The designation "one-stop shop" will therefore no longer only apply to a full range supplier from a technical perspective, i.e. covering all legal subject-matters; rather, this will now also include related services of a non-legal nature, with which someone—for example, a law firm—assumes responsibility for delivering and supporting work and projects from a single source. This includes in particular the responsibility for the selection, coordination and the reassembly of all partial services into a whole, single result, no matter who provided or produced the individual services. However, such a service requires knowledge and experience in project management, which may create new job profiles like those of a legal project manager (Fig. 4).

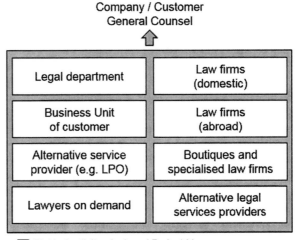

Fig. 4 Field of activities of a legal project manager (author's own material)

4   Professional Procurement Process

4.1   Drivers

Nowadays, a customer procures external legal services in a much more professional way. In doing so, several objectives are being pursued: the customer ensures, among other things, a detailed analysis of the legal market, an improvement of the purchasing terms and a reduction of process-related costs, and as a further result, a reduction of total expenditures (i.e. total cost of ownership). Improved information gathering and reduction of the number of suppliers provides increased transparency of the framework agreements and cost structure, which in turn allows the customer to achieve more efficient supplier evaluation and control. Moreover, legal departments are required to explain why they still outsource work and why external resources cannot be procured more cheaply. CFOs then often refer to the business consulting industry, which already suffered from and adapted to the new procurement principles earlier.

4.2   Procurement Process in Ten Steps

The purchase of legal services features a few special facets. It is therefore necessary to separately address the underlying steps a customer typically faces in this particular procurement process. Outside counsel claim that the procurement of legal services cannot be compared with the purchase of simple commodities like screws. They then often refer to the key elements of the relationship such as trust, independence and the attorney-client-privilege. However, there is no sensible reason why the procurement of legal services should escape—even tough—price discussions, as long as this does not materially affect the performance. A customer may reasonably assume to be informed by its suppliers when and how such a consequence is linked to the expected and agreed performance.

It does not matter how large a customer is, whether it has its own legal department, how many people are employed and how big the available budget is for the procurement of external legal services. During procurement and when dealing with outside law firms, every customer will regularly be confronted with the same or similar questions and problems, which will become relevant to a greater or lesser extent, depending on the individual situation. Therefore, customers follow an organized procurement process, which can be divided into ten steps encompassing the entire cycle, starting from initiating the process and ending with the evaluation as set out in Fig. 5.

It is important for legal service providers, in particular outside counsel, to know and to understand this process and to realize that most of it is handled behind customers' closed doors without their involvement. Therefore, it becomes even more important for potential suppliers that customers are able to identify them as prospective participants in the procurement process at all. Once a supplier has received a request for proposal, he must understand which time window is available

Fig. 5 Professional
procurement process in ten
steps (author's own material)

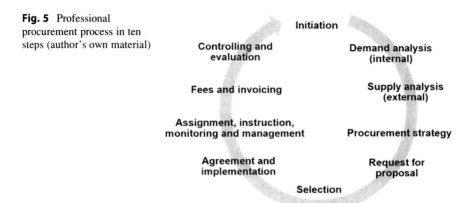

and what is required for a successful pitch. A customer, being part of defining the very procurement strategy, may also decide to install a so-called "legal panel" with preferred law firm providers. The same may be established for alternative providers.

4.3 Role of the Procurement Department

In order to execute a project for the procurement of legal services, identifying dedicated resources, setting up a company-wide project team and finding and making available the right people with the required knowledge, experience and skills should be considered. Tasks, competencies and responsibilities must be defined for and allocated to each role. Trust and loyalty are of great importance here. The team has to draw up a detailed project plan with timelines, milestones and deliverables. Measurement criteria, as well as the process, have to be defined.

Further, the extent of involvement of any existing procurement department should be determined. In companies, the bundling of supplier management by the purchasing or procurement department has long been accepted as standard and is considered best practice. By now, however, there is already talk of the electronically supported procurement of legal services (e-sourcing). Legal departments have often been spared from the usual cost-cutting exercises; on the contrary, often they could even expand their resources. In the eyes of CEOs and CFOs, their general counsel—and in this respect not particularly actively supported by their outside counsel—have demonstrated far too little seriousness in dealing with their own cost-saving measures. As a consequence, general counsel are now seconded by the procurement department. This is not a discussion about procurement now becoming the decision-maker when it comes to mandating outside counsel. Rather, in my view, general counsel should welcome cooperation with these new partners, recognize their expertise and specifically use them to improve their overall efficiency. This ranges from tasks associated with the processing of a mandate (e.g., payment, accounting and controlling activities) to logistical support (e.g., in the planning of the process or the preparation of tender documents) and covers the analysis and evaluation of different data and numbers (e.g. for KPI).

For outside counsel and their newly established so-called business development departments, understanding the customer's internal procurement process is paramount. This fosters a better understanding of the potential points of contact (touch points) on the one hand, and the timing and the extent of any involvement with the customer on the other hand. If suppliers are organizing themselves, customers should in fact rapidly get a team ready as well, i.e. one that includes specialists like procurement people, to negotiate with their suppliers on an equal footing.

4.4   Gender Diversity

Similarly to the question as to whether the procurement department should play a role in buying legal services, a gender-related factor needs also to be taken into consideration. Large and international companies have already been facing the obligation to pay attention to diversity requirements, for example, in connection with the requirements related to Corporate Social Responsibility programs. This plays a particularly important role when recruiting employees in order to avoid any unjustified discrimination. In this respect, however, gender represents merely one of the many elements of diversity.

There are three good reasons why it should be in the best interest of a law firm to take the "gender factor" seriously into account. First, there are direct economic reasons for the importance of the requirement for a gender-mixed composition of the workforce. It could be shown that mixed teams are more innovative, successful and profitable. Second, a gender-mixed composition of a law firm (gender diversity) plays an important role for customers when it comes to assigning mandates. The large law firms' up-or-out model and the fact that today only a few women have achieved partner status in law firms inevitably leads to the conclusion that many female outside counsel leave the law firms before reaching the partnership level. By going in-house and switching to the other side of the table, they now become informed buyers. Third, gender-related differences in behavior exist when outside counsel are selected; i.e. when procuring legal services, female general counsel do not rank the same criteria as important as their male counterparts do. For male general counsel reputation, personal relationships and trust are important; female general counsel, however, put more emphasis on the requirement that outside counsel understand their business and their needs, respond quickly and communicate effectively and efficiently.

5   Management of Law Firms

5.1   Framework Agreements

Once a complex tender process has been conducted and the desired law firm is selected, I recommend that the result obtained is contractually sealed in order to facilitate implementation and to avoid any misunderstandings. Framework agreements are particularly useful in those cases when it is expected that there will be regular assignments between the parties in the future and that the points to be negotiated will be repeated. Such agreements also make sense when multiple parties are involved—such as in international law firms with different locations or in a network of law firms. With the one-time negotiation of all key points set down in a framework agreement, the subsequent process of placing orders should be facilitated and become more efficient. This will also replace the retention and engagement letters prepared by the law firms. If a framework agreement is to fulfil its purpose, it should be designed in a detailed way and must, from a content point of view, be more than just a letter of intent. It should, inter alia, provide information on the range of services and the content of the work (including accessibility), conflicts of interest, the nature and extent of staffing and team structures, communications and reporting as well as contact persons, fees and compensable work and expenses (in particular the extent of it) and invoicing (including outside counsel retention and billing guidelines).

5.2   Control of Law Firms

A company has already achieved a great deal with the proper selection and adequate instruction of outside counsel. However, this reflects only one side of the coin. In order to achieve the goals—especially the financial ones—related to the procurement of outside counsel services, a continuous management of the lawyers and the related mandates is required. Otherwise, there is a risk that hard-fought and successfully negotiated positions, as well as the attained rights and benefits that accompany them, may ultimately not be enforced and realized. This management task requires time and resources, and that must be considered in the annual budget and underlying structures of a legal department. The increasing monitoring of the relationship with outside counsel is based on the assumption that they may perform more efficiently and effectively when obligated to keep their customers informed. This customer behavior is based on the fact that cost controls have become more important for them as well, which is why regular reporting and updates by suppliers on the status of actual costs versus the agreed budget is necessary. Furthermore, outside counsel has to provide summaries on the assigned mandates to identify possible alternative resolutions during a mandate and to perform a critical assessment at the end of a mandate (post-mortem evaluation) in order to map out any room for improvement for future cases.

5.3 Alternative Fee Arrangements

If an outside counsel is entrusted with a mandate, it is quite common that it will be settled and paid for on the basis of hourly fees. At most, the hourly rate may be further graded depending on the subject area, country or seniority of the lawyer, and apparently also on gender. When charged by the hour, the customer is paying solely for the lawyer's activities, which is basically paying for the lawyer having worked. However, an efficient and qualitatively accurate performance of the lawyer is neither agreed upon nor guaranteed. The customer thus has an interest in building an appropriate incentive structure to steer a lawyer's performance in these areas. From a customer's point of view, a fee should not be calculated according to the time spent on a mandate (input) but rather on the basis of the benefit or (added) value the lawyer has generated for the customer (output).

Various developments show, however, that alternative remuneration methods are steadily on the rise, which will lead to changes in the future. Customers are demanding more cost transparency and they expect explanations regarding the fee compensation system. This is probably not least of all due to CEOs and CFOs demanding that such models should be applied. These models often do not only deliver cost savings, but also promise better performance by outside counsel. Further, alternative billing methods are based on the presumption that someone who claims to be a specialist or an expert (here: for legal advice) should know how much time is required for the completion of pre-defined tasks.

Fixed fees are the easiest way to use an alternative fee arrangement (AFA). For the avoidance of doubt, discounts or rebates as well as blended rates are not considered to be an AFA. With such mechanisms, a general price reduction is granted on existing standard hourly rates only. With so-called "volume discounts", a discount will be granted—in terms of a loyalty rebate—upon reaching an agreed sales target. Therefore these mechanisms do not constitute a real alternative compensation model since they do not change the incentive model. The same applies to cost and budget estimates, since they are often not binding and simply constitute an indication of the expected total fees. For the sake of argument, however, these mechanisms are not worthless and should be viewed as an appreciable attempt to provide at least some comfort to the customer.

5.4 Invoicing and Evaluation

After a legal service provider is invited to present itself and its services, then also successfully wins a pitch and does an excellent job throughout the mandate, there is one final moment of truth left: the invoice. This last element should not ruin the valuable reputation a provider has built up with a customer over a long period before. Unfortunately, reality is somehow different, and it is not unusual that customers are surprised with this very last item of deliverables. This is a pity since it goes against the cheapest form of customer acquisition and retention: customer satisfaction that leads to re-mandating a service provider on the one hand, and providing recommendations and references to further potential customers on the other hand. Customers maintaining a panel of service providers usually conduct evaluation reviews every year to assess whether the selection is still adequate. If required, e.g., when the service is not as promised or agreed upon, the required corrective measures are taken.

6 Final Remarks

The business relationship between customers and outside counsel has not changed much over many decades. Recent years, however, have seen the emergence of a "new normal". This is primarily driven by the customers, who are supported in their intent to bring about modifications to the current situation by new legal service providers, which are also interested in creating a substantial change in the legal industry. It remains to be seen what consequences these changes will ultimately generate.

The good news for legal service providers is that customer demand for legal services will continue to exist since there are no substitutes for it. What has changed or will change, however, is the following: the role of general counsel has changed; customers and legal departments are improving efficiency and optimizing both staff deployment and the volume of work; less outsourcing to third parties is expected and is being replaced by more insourcing; the procurement of legal services is changing and being professionalized; and finally, price amendments, increased demands and changes in technology are likely to occur.

The role of in-house counsel will have to change and adjust accordingly. This does not only create duties and pressure, but also offers a vast variety of new opportunities and exciting tasks that must be exploited and executed.

Liquid Legal Context
By Dr. Dierk Schindler, Dr. Roger Strathausen, Kai Jacob
Mascello provides a great overview on the changed and further changing dynamics around the cost of providing legal services for legal departments—whether incurred by "building" the services inhouse, or by "buying" them on the market. He points out the structural changes in the legal market and consolidates those dynamics into a very insightful graphic that connects the impact on all main elements: lawyers, law-firms, customers and the broader legal market.

The author determines liberalization, globalization and the increasing application of technology as the fundamental forces that disrupt the market, very much in line with what we have just heard from Hartung and Gärtner. The liberalization brings about not only new players (e.g. LPO's), but also opens up the market for new leaders in services: think of Ross' suggestion of

(continued)

legal advice or a law firm at some point potentially becoming one branch of the services of an LPO. While globalization increases the pressure on local legal service providers, the polycentric approach that might be part of the answer to the challenge (see Markfort) makes it even more complex. Is this development building a case for the big accounting and audit firms that—as Sako points out—have by far the largest global presence?

Mascello also asks the question as to what all of this means for the positioning of the legal department. No more hiding behind a strong CFO, it is time to lead for legal departments, we have heard Fawcett state. Mucic expands that notion to the fundamental impact lawyers and legal inhouse work has on the culture of a company. As many traditional legal services are becoming candidates for automation or even a legal commodity, it is critical to position the legal department beyond a mere "problem solver". It is vital that we are able to credibly explain its integration into the corporate strategy and its value creation for the company.

Mascello provides a clear overview on the various sources for legal services and what a professionalized procurement process looks like. This makes a strong case for professionalizing the operations of legal departments by introducing a legal operations function. Brenton is a true leader in shaping this function and driving towards a standard model of legal operations, also by means of founding the non-profit organization and collaboration platform CLOC.

Bruno Mascello is Vice-Director at the Executive School of the University of St. Gallen. He conducts research, teaches and publishes with a special focus on law and management topics. Before, he worked as an attorney in an international law firm and for many years in-house in various senior management positions in an international financial services company. He is a qualified lawyer, admitted to the Swiss Bar, and runs a private practice. He studied law (including Dr. iur.) at the University of St. Gallen, completed an Executive MBA and received his LL.M. from New York University School of Law.

CLOC: Joining Forces to Drive Transformation in Legal: Bringing Together the Legal Ecosystem

Connie Brenton

Abstract
Many corporate legal departments still run in much the same way they always have, failing to keep up with the changing needs of the modern marketplace. In today's fast-moving and competitive markets, where companies need to enter into new types of agreements and relationships with customers and partners, this is no longer good enough. Corporations need innovative strategy and cutting-edge execution from their legal departments.

Everyone leading a legal department, today, must define their goals. Do they want to focus simply on being an effective and capable legal department? Or do they want to think like a business, and focus on growth, innovation, and opportunity? The further they go from the traditional, limited model of corporate legal teams, the greater the potential impact on the organization—but the greater the risk.

The non-profit group CLOC (Corporate Legal Operations Consortium) is a direct response to that challenge. It is a collaborative, community-driven organization of legal professionals focused on defining the future of corporate legal departments. The association is focused on modernizing, streamlining and amplifying the Legal Operations role within the legal ecosystem.

C. Brenton (✉)
Corporate Legal Operations Consortium, Las Vegas, NV, USA
e-mail: connie.brenton@netapp.com

© Springer International Publishing AG 2017
K. Jacob et al. (eds.), *Liquid Legal*, Management for Professionals,
DOI 10.1007/978-3-319-45868-7_19

1   Rethinking the Corporate Legal Department

1.1   Three Types of Legal Departments

There are few parts of the modern corporation that can be more conservative, defensive, and conventional than the legal department. That type of approach is now out-of-date and no longer sustainable. Consider an analogy with the IT department. No company could succeed if the CIO focused only on fixing what was broken, without setting a vision for the company's technology future. Yet, that is exactly how many legal teams operate, however—in a completely reactive mode. No business would succeed that way.

Legal teams today define their mission in three possible ways:

- **As a function.** Still the dominant model for many companies, this is the narrowest possible interpretation of the corporate legal role. These teams view themselves as owning only issues and processes tied directly to legal work. They don't focus much, if at all, on the broader context of their organization, responding only to legal work reactively, as it pours into their departments.
- **As a service.** For more progressive legal teams, the emphasis is on internal service. In this model, the business leaders within the company are the clients. Success is judged by how effective the team is at satisfying internal client needs efficiently and repeatedly. Teams following this model tend to think of themselves as problem-solvers and partners within the business.
- **As a true business unit**. These teams don't simply solve the problems that their internal clients bring them—they anticipate and plan. They don't just try to run more efficiently—they innovate and experiment. They listen to their "customers"—the internal client teams—but don't limit their contributions simply to addressing their issues. Their numbers are fewer, but growing.

1.2   Bringing a Business Mindset to Legal

The emergence of new categories of technology and service providers, combined with heightened pressure for transparency, have brought the industry to what can only be described as a tipping point. This increased role of legal departments— accompanied by heightened demand for more efficient delivery of legal services, availability of technology, and new entrants to the legal ecosystem—has rendered it impossible to maintain the status quo.

It's time to start running legal departments like a business. The General Counsels of today's legal departments must find ways to add value, deliver premium legal and business consulting services to their internal customers, and provide a competitive advantage to their companies.

To address this need, they are increasingly adding a new function to their management teams—the Corporate Legal Operations Executive, a COO for legal. This new role, for the first time, gave a business focus to the legal department.

Because it was a new role in inhouse legal departments, training was acquired either on-the-job or through sharing best practices with others new to the role.

Today's Corporate Legal Operations Executives face significant challenges as they seek to transform and modernize their departments. The shift from thinking about Legal as functional or service unit to considering it as a true business unit is immense. It requires a huge leap forward in culture, approach, and skills. The core challenges for these leaders fall into a few core areas:

Change the Culture and Skill Set To shift towards a business unit model requires a big shift in the culture and composition of the legal team. It means stepping back from the mindset of "legal experts" to include other priorities, skills, and focus areas. Take any group of smart corporate lawyers and certain qualities are likely to be well-represented: intelligence, motivation, attention to detail. Others might be harder to find: innovation, risk-taking, entrepreneurship. To make the change work, leaders not only need to shift the priorities they set for their organization, they may need to bring in new contributors to the team who don't come from traditional legal backgrounds.

Set Clear Goals There is no growth or evolution possible without goal-setting and measurement. This starts by setting the right goals. What are the things that matter the most to the team? Is it speed of execution? Service to internal clients? Innovation in processes and practices? Goal-setting can be a shallow and limited exercise at some companies. Done right, it is a powerful opportunity to focus objectives and get aligned as an organization.

Define and Track the Right Metrics Once the right goals are in place, then begins the hard work of measuring and tracking your results over time. This is the only way to drive progress and change, but it is also a very uncomfortable practice for many legal departments. In many cases, the data may not exist—it can simply be something that is not currently tracked. It takes time and effort to create a true dashboard that actually speaks to performance against goals, but it is worth it.

Connect to Internal Customers How successful would a business be if it simply waited for customers to walk in? Yet, that is how many legal departments operate. Possibly the biggest key to running a legal department like an effective business is engagement. This means, first of all, engaging with internal customers. Do you meet regularly with your stakeholders around the business to understand their context and to identify ways you can help? Do you adapt your processes to fit them, rather than expect them to change how they work? The goal is to be engaged and connected with stakeholders and to foster a lasting relationship with them.

Engage with Partners It also means engaging with potential partners. Don't look at other companies' legal teams as competitive threats but as potential allies. It makes sense to create relationships and connections across the industry because some threats and opportunities require collective action.

Manage the Value Chain To be effective, every business must optimize its value chain. This means deciding what is created internally, what is outsourced, and everything is combined to deliver value to the customer in a cost-effective way. Is the team working with the right suppliers? Are they supporting the same strategy and goals? Are business terms structured in the right way?

2 Realizing the Vision: The Corporate Legal Operations Consortium

In 2010, a group of legal professionals from Fortune 500 companies across the country got together with the goal of codifying and bringing these principles to life in the modern legal department. Since its inception, the Corporate Legal Operations Consortium—or CLOC—has been charting this relatively new territory in collaborative fashion. It has been seeking new ways to enable efficiency, simplicity, and impact within legal departments. The organization's mission is to drive innovation and sharing of best practices across legal teams.

Today, CLOC has become an incorporated entity and is the first legal association to open its doors to the entire legal ecosystem—General Counsels, law firms, technology providers, managed service providers, legal associations, venture capitalists, law schools, students, and others interested in its mission. Initially formed by members from companies in California and the Pacific Northwest, CLOC has expanded to include members from around the world.

2.1 Focusing on the Basics

The CLOC team began by focusing on simple, core challenges that are common to all legal departments. One of the first was around billing. How could law firm billing be managed in a more consistent and effective way?

Traditionally, faced different billing terms from client to client, resulting in time and resources wasted. In keeping with CLOC's mission to drive efficiency and simplicity, it sought to standardize the industry around routine and administrative tasks, leaving time for attorneys to focus on bespoke legal work. This particular goal has been furthered by the creation of a comprehensive set of billing guidelines.

The result: a process that once required significant time and resources for both, inhouse and outside counsel, has now been made simpler. This is precisely the type of efficiency gain that CLOC strives to facilitate.

CLOC's billing guidelines are driven by its goal to simplify and create efficiencies across legal departments. Legal departments do not compete on efficiencies. There is no need to recreate documents across departments of different companies. A concise set of guidelines makes things easier for everyone.

2.2   Defining the Role and Focus of Legal Operations

The CLOC team has worked to define the elements of Legal Operations (Fig. 1):

- **Strategic Planning:** Create a long-term strategy, aligning yearly goals and corresponding metrics.
- **Financial Management:** Manage the departmental budget. Track accruals and forecasting. Work with Finance to identify spending trends, potential cost savings and efficiency opportunities.
- **Vendor Management:** Create a vendor management program to ensure quality outside counsel support at the right rates and under optimal fee arrangements. Hold regular business reviews. Negotiate fee agreements. Drive governance of billing guidelines.

Fig. 1 This graphic is available online here: http://cloc.org/what-is-legal-operations/

- **Data Analytics:** Collect and analyze *relevant* data from department tools and industry sources, define objectives to provide metrics and dashboards that drive efficiencies and optimize spend, etc.
- **Technology Support:** Create a long-term technology roadmap including tools such as e-billing/matter management, contract management, content management, IP management, business process management, e-signature, board management, compliance management, legal hold, subsidiary management, etc.
- **Alternative Support Models:** Drive departmental efficiency by leveraging managed services, LPOs, and other service providers.
- **Knowledge Management:** Enable efficiencies by creating seamless access to legal and department institutional knowledge through the organization and centralization of key templates, policies, processes, memos, and other learnings.
- **Professional Development and Team Building:** Deliver improved GC Staff and overall team performance by globalizing the team and creating a culture of growth, development, collaboration and accountability.
- **Communications:** Work collaboratively across the legal ecosystem to create consistent global processes, from onboarding to complex project management support. Publish regular departmental communication, plan and execute all-hands.
- **Global Data Governance/Records Management:** Create a records management program including a record retention schedule, policies and processes.
- **Litigation Support:** Support e-discovery, legal hold, document review.
- **Cross-Functional Alignment:** Create and drive relationships with other key company functions, such as HR, IT, Finance and Workplace Resources. Represent the Legal organization at CLOC.

2.3   Evangelizing the Legal Operations Role Across the Industry

Another significant function of CLOC has been to help drive awareness and understanding of Legal Operations across the industry. A decade ago, most corporate attorneys would not have been able to articulate what the Legal Operations role was or why it was important. Thanks in large part to the work of CLOC, it now holds a prominent spot on the legal industry map.

Significantly, CLOC's championing of Legal Operations professionals has propelled those professionals upward. They are now trusted advisors to their General Counsels, holding places among legal executive staff. Further still, the value of the role is being recognized beyond the in-house space, as Legal Operations directors are being added to law firms as well.

CLOC members have been active in speaking to broad audiences about their roles, experiences, and aspirations for the future of the industry. The range of talent among current Operations executives is diverse; about one-third have JDs, one-third have MBAs, and another third has both. Their backgrounds range from traditional legal roles to finance to technology. However, as the role increases in prominence and law schools begin adding an operations curriculum on the heels of

CLOC's education-driven Institute, the legal profession will begin to embrace this career path from the outset.

CLOC has similarly been driving awareness of the sort of changes that spurred them to create the organization in the first place. CLOC members have collaborated on presentations at high-profile events around the world—ACC, CxO/CLOC, IACCM, P3, and others—to explain the changes the industry has been seeing and why awareness of those changes is so important. This is another indicator that the operations role is becoming a force.

In these forums, Legal Operations experts have explained exactly what is driving such inhouse change: the evolution of the General Counsel role, combined with the increased prevalence of legal technology and legal service providers, has driven the inhouse department as we know it to a tipping point. What was once a model of slow growth and change in corporate legal departments has quickly transformed into a sink-or-swim environment, where legal departments either start to drive competitive advantage or lose out to the emerging non-traditional providers. CLOC members are teaching others how to swim.

Liquid Legal Context
By Dr. Dierk Schindler, Dr. Roger Strathausen, Kai Jacob
Show me what you offer and how you do it, and I tell you who you are.
Brenton provides a tangible litmus test for legal departments to determine how far they have progressed into the future state: still a traditional function? Already a service? Or even a true business unit?

All authors agree that the General Counsels of today must find ways to create value, deliver premium legal and also business consulting services to their internal customers, so that their departments provide a competitive advantage to their companies. Against that background, Brenton details out the—still emerging—new function of Corporate Legal Operations, a COO for legal.

We are watching legal transformation in motion, when we read the story of how they established CLOC, starting in 2010 with a group of like-minded professionals that had a similar role and/or vision for a legal operations function, to now be the first legal association to open its doors to the entire legal ecosystem—General Counsels, law firms, technology providers, managed service providers, legal associations, venture capitalists, law schools, students, and others interested in its mission.

The need for an operations role in Legal is obvious, if we just look at the quite brutal forces and the pace of change, but also if we admit the complexity that comes with it. Today's call to action on legal is not evolutionary, it is disruptive in every possible way: process innovation and outsourcing become the new normal; legal tech is a must, not an option; performance management

(continued)

to ensure true creation of business value is mandatory. While front-facing players in a department need to change to master the challenges that come with that in day-to-day practice, there is also a vital need for a function that establishes and constantly improves the operational platform on which an inhouse department can step up to the task.

Besides the functional role of a COO for legal, Jacob adds to the profile when he identifies that *"we need people that are technical affine, process minded and open to new technology"*. Is the *"Legal Information Manager"* the new norm?

Connie Brenton is a pioneer in Legal Operations and widely regarded as one of the world's foremost experts on legal industry innovation. For more than 5 years she has served as Chief of Staff and Director of Legal Operations at NetApp Inc. (NASDAQ: NTAP), a Fortune 500 data management and storage provider. She is the co-founder of the Corporate Legal Operations Consortium (CLOC), an innovative and global Legal Operations Association. Connie holds a JD, MBA, and BA in Economics.

Legal Information Management (LIM) Strategy: How to Transform a Legal Department

Kai Jacob

Abstract

Using both, his personal experience as a Lawyer, Contract Manager and Intrapreneur, and empirical data gathered in interviews, panels and private conversations, the author, together with his team, developed a framework concerning Legal Information Management (LIM). The article will describe LIM as a continuum, moving us from the pre-digital phase to a state of full information-enablement. In doing so, the article aims to de-mystify the digital revolution. The reader will be faced with practical examples of digitalization and should feel motivated to reflect his own situation. LIM does not require in depth knowledge of information technology (IT), but curiosity and openness to change—qualities best exemplified by Faust, the main character in Goethe's play, and his quest for wisdom:

So that I may perceive whatever holds
The world together in its inmost folds (Johann Wolfgang Goethe's play "FAUST")

1   Introduction

Reading legal tech blogs or attending legal tech conferences and meetings, one might get the impression that it is actually too late for us corporate lawyers to adapt. Supposedly, we are too slow and too arrogant to change, and we are already

K. Jacob (✉)
SAP SE, Walldorf, Germany
e-mail: kai.jacob@sap.com

© Springer International Publishing AG 2017
K. Jacob et al. (eds.), *Liquid Legal*, Management for Professionals,
DOI 10.1007/978-3-319-45868-7_20

surrounded by legal robots[1] and hackers[2] who are faster and smarter than us and will do our jobs in the future. And maybe there's some truth to that—maybe the time for the pampered average lawyer doing average lawyer stuff is coming to an end. But for some of us, for us legal entrepreneurs and innovators who keep an open mind, who listen and learn, I believe the journey has only just started! We are excited because we understand that we have the historical chance to participate in something extraordinary: *the transformation of a whole industry.* The enormous speed with which the legal tech market matures and delivers technical solutions that threaten the status quo must be an inspiration and a call to action for us! Legal start-up companies have new ideas, they experiment, build solutions fast, and when they fail (as happens to most start-ups across all industries)—the next and even smarter generation of entrepreneurs comes along and continues the work, based on lessons learned—and so the innovation cycle continues. . .

One could become dizzy following the development of this rather young Legal Tech industry that started in the 80s with legal expert systems, followed by legal ontologies, but that since then emerged into areas which sound unfamiliar, not to say awkward for most lawyers still: machine learning, artificial intelligence, neural learning, NLP etc.

My advice is to forget all the buzzwords and concentrate on the *here and now.* If we understand the basic principles on what our future will be built on, we will learn, grow and adapt as we go. We lawyers do not have to become programmers, but developing a basic skillset on how applications are built is crucial to shape and benefit from the transformation of legal departments.

In my article I will argue that Legal Information Management (LIM) is the key differentiator in a progressing competitive environment, and that legal departments/ law firms who are "information enabled" will have a strategic advantage over those who hesitantly wait. I will describe what I call a "LIM strategy": the aim to easily get access in real-time to all relevant information that is required to perform the legal department's work in the most effective and efficient way. Using SAP as example, I will elaborate what it is, what we have achieved, where we want to go next, and how we can get there.

I predict that antiquated department structures will dissolve, and that legal will transform into an amalgam of skills overcoming the weaknesses created by today's functional silos. This transformation requires a fundamental shift in mind-sets and can only be achieved if motivated people, who understand their business process and are open to new information technology, collaborate and openly exchange ideas. Tomorrow's lawyer will be part of a "liquid legal" team—able to adapt quickly and easily to changing business needs.

---

[1]Topic of the Bucerius Law School conference "Mensch vs. Machines" or the Robot Lawyer on www.donotpay.co.uk

[2]Are Hackers the Future Lawyers? http://www.newsbtc.com/2016/06/26/hackers-future-lawyers-maybe/

2 What Is Going on?

In 2005, Thomas L. Friedman[3] famously described the "flattening effect" globalization has on people around the world. In such a flat world, we expect digitalization to dissolve antiquated organizational structures and flatten also knowledge asymmetries in a way that will allow many operational tasks to be carried out by lower skilled people, and increasingly even by machines. We see a widening gap between "knowledge workers", skilled with scarce expertise, and "regular workers", who once started on a lower transactional level, but progressively take over superior jobs and now being best described as "application workers". The gap between the two groups of workers is bridged by IT—Information Technology. With the help of IT, we are able to transform information and data into components of knowledge that an application worker can be trained to apply or that can even be used to run autonomous processes. The fundamental change is, a shift from a traditional knowledge transfer, to a new form of collaboration, where knowledge worker, application worker and machines, are requested to find the optimal way of working together—and ideally continuously improve the optimal mix of collaboration, under the heading "machine learning".

3 Truth Be Told

I want to tell it like it is, by starting with a fictitious interview (inspired by real events and conversations) in which I ask imagined colleagues (from in-house legal department and law firm) about their experience and give them an opportunity to speak freely about their specific needs and challenges. I will then elaborate on the points they brought up and give details and explanations in the discursive part of the article.

3.1 A Fictitious Interview (... and Real Pain)

Moderator: There is so much talk about the "end of lawyers" in legal tech publications, so I want to kick off with this question: What it is like to work as a legal professional in today's legal world?

In-house legal: We work endless hours, and it seems we are always behind, constantly trying to catch up with the work, trying to get on top of our emails, projects, tasks... The regular working hours stated in my labor contract are far from reality. There is rarely anyone in my company who works less than 60 hours a week!

Law firm legal: Worse – I feel like I could not do my job the way it should be done even if I worked 80 hours a week! It is frustrating to always find yourself behind

---

[3]Friedman (2005).

schedule. Getting pushed from all sides to deliver, being confronted with unreasonable timelines, oftentimes being involved only in the very last minute – it's just crazy. Instead of fighting the fire, I would rather like to prevent the fire or even better, eliminate the causes of fire. I would rather, to stay in this picture, invest my time in installing an early fire warning system, so I can use my freed up time to do the interesting things, the things that would truly add value for my clients.

Moderator: Why all this time pressure and communication overload? How do you get engaged and how do you work? In other words, what is your current infrastructure like – can you describe how you work with IT?

Inhouse Legal: To be honest, our infrastructure is a mess. We have portals, share drives, a team server, a solution here and a tool there, and a whole lot of Apps nobody uses. They all look different, they follow different structures, they are neither intuitive nor easy to learn – all too complex. So I have decided to organize myself differently: I have all my tasks organized in Outlook, documents I work on are stored in folders on my private share drive (so I can work from home and on travel), important things I need to remember are captured in OneNote – everything well organized so I can find easily everything I need to do my job. I don't work with IT – only to replace my hardware every third year.

Law firm legal: Same here. I would work differently if the systems were built by someone who has a clue about how I work. All these overly complex solutions we are forced to use bring no real benefit to me – I admit they make sense from a company perspective, so things are centrally organized and structured and so on – but hey: at what cost? They bother me to work in a tool that requires 10 clicks to open the document, the performance is lousy, so I have to wait endlessly – only to find out that they sent the wrong version… I don't want to come across as a technophobe – I'm interested and open for IT solutions. But as long as the tools are not "Google like" simple, my idiosyncratic no-technology way of working is superior and faster! Send me your stuff via e-mail or fax (yes, we still use faxes a lot!), and I turn it around as fast as I can.

Moderator: Could you give us a concrete example, e.g. how do you manage your contracts today?

Law firm legal: How many times have I heard and read about "The year of Contract Management." Okay – so where are the legal software solutions that make our life easier? We are waiting now for decades and it is still a pain to find relevant information. I remember the software provider who promised us to manage all our contracts in one place. Too good to be true, we thought, and we were right: after the consultants declared successful delivery of the implementation project, they left… there is still no real owner assigned, no power-user trained, and no help desk available! I would be amazed if more than 20 % of our contracts are in the system.

In-house legal: That reminds me of our own project. We implemented a beautiful, well designed and thought-through Contract Management Solution for our Procurement Department – only to find out during deployment that no one in the Procurement Department is actually willing to work outside of emails, shared drives and file cabinets. As there was no push from the top management, the tool silently died – like so many other initiatives. We weren't lazy – over the years we introduced many tools that support our daily business. But looking at the big picture that is exactly our problem today: we have more than 30 Apps and none of them is consistently used.

3.2   The Basis: Contracts

When I started my career at Lufthansa System, as the Lawyer responsible for legal matters in the procurement department, I asked my boss: "Where do we store our contracts?" and the answer was: "in SAP". Digging deeper, I said: "Well, in the SAP system, we have some data, such as the start- and end date of the contract and the contract volume, but where is the contract itself and all other necessary information that allows us to manage the contract?". The answer came unexpected: "Ahh, you mean the "paper"! You'll find it in the file cabinet down the hallway, and the important contract data is in this Excel which we have on our team share!"

That has been my first fundamental observation regarding our profession: legal information (here: contracts) is loosely managed in systems that are not designed for this job: SAP and Microsoft!

In SAP's ERP (e.g. MM or SD) only very few header data is stored, sometimes together with a scanned version of the document, attached to a "leading SAP business object" such as the Sales Order or Purchase Order. Microsoft's Excel is supposed to allow for complex calculations, and is misused by people around the world as a workaround for any kind of contract related project -, obligation- and risk management.

3.3   Building a Contract Management Solution

Around that time, I came across the quote from a corporate CEO in the US who had just acquired a company:

> If you are not in control of your contracts, you are not in control of your business.

It is as simple as this: contracts are—besides people—the main asset of each and every enterprise! You hire and fire people, you buy goods, you sell products, you partner with others—in short: whatever a company does is in the end based on contracts. Contracts are the lifeblood of any business, and to bring contracts back into the center of our daily work became my profession.

When I joined SAP in 2008, I asked the same question again. The answer I got from SAP employees was even more striking: "The 'contract' **is** the 'sales order'". The "legal (paper) document" doesn't even exist in people's vocabulary. No kidding - just pick up any dictionary at SAP. Once you challenge them, they might openly admit that in their processes the contract paper comes "out of the blue"—provided by some legal colleagues or contract manager. So if people are talking about "contracts," you better ask: What do you mean, the "technical" order or the "legal" document?

Missing the contract as an object in your ERP system is a problem for various reasons:

- The contract is widely ignored as a reference document—important information is kept elsewhere (e.g. in Excel)), creating a significant grey zone in which all sorts of shortfalls and liabilities might start to pile up
- The contract is not actively managed (no automated reminders, alerts, no reporting etc.) bearing the risk of a drain of potential revenues
- The contract is not easily accessible in case of questions, making contract research a cumbersome and time consuming undertaking

So how did SAP and its customers manage contracts back in 2008? Well, simply ask the question to peers in your own company and you will receive answers which at first do not sound too bad. But as soon as the curtain lifts, the worrying truth appears: contracts were managed in disparate systems following heterogeneous processes. Which means according to the CEO quoted above: most companies are not in control!

Of course, companies' most critical contracts will always be managed by dedicated teams with high manual effort. But if you dare to ask about the full contract landscape, you might get puzzled looks. So my team and I, backed up by my boss, the General Counsel Field, decided to embark on our mission to close this contract gap for SAP—and for its customers.

True to the motto: *If nothing exists, build something,* we started to design our new Contract Management Solution (CMS) and teamed up with SAP's partner organization, called GEPG, who had similar problems in managing their hundreds of partner agreements. Shortly after we introduced our ideas to the Quote-to-Cash team, an initiative aiming to streamline SAP's end-to-end sales processes, we agreed to join forces and contributed a solution that closed the gap between the Sales Side (Opportunity/Quote/Deal Approval) and the Finance Side (Order booking, Invoicing, Cash collection). Within just one year, a team consisting of Legal and IT people created CMS from scratch—based on SAP standard technology.

From a very basic Graphical User Interface (GUI), the application matured in a few years to a web-based version and is currently in its 7th release, serving more than 15,000 users, covering more than 500,000 contracts and in peak times producing several thousands of contracts a day.

In order to gain back "control of our business", we did three fundamental things:

- We designed a solution that covers ALL contracts, excluding only HR, applying the 80/20 rule. Up to 80 % of all displayed fields in CMS were common for all contracts—only 20 % were customized for special areas of engagement (procurement, OEM business, partner business).
- We conducted a "full contract landscape analysis". We asked all CFO's to fill-out a simple online questionnaire related to the contracts in their area of

responsibility. Within a couple of weeks we were able to report back the full picture and knew now our targets.

- We established and rolled-out a Global SAP Contracting Policy that gave us the mandate to ensure that all contracts follow the same processes, are stored only in CMS or a GCMS[4] approved alternative system. Moreover, the Policy set out the task to bring all legacy contracts into our system. And last but not least, it gave us the authority to manage all legal templates in CMS as well.

We kept our promise and identified all contract types by end of 2015. While we are still on-boarding some laggards to our system, the vast majority of contracts have been managed well for a couple of years now.

Since the inception of CMS, we faced resistance to change and were confronted with long lists of reasons for why CMS would not work for the one or other contract type. We listened and tried to improve as much as possible: we beautified the UI (user interface), significantly increased the performance, reduced unnecessary fields, reorganized the attachment tab for better usability and so on. But an unsatisfying adoption of CMS remained our top challenge.

Facing the threat of low adoption, we implemented three main innovations:

1. Without logging on to the SAP network, any SAP employee can leverage the Contract Request Form (CRF) using smartphones, tablets, laptops or PCs. With minimal data entry, thanks to drop-down lists and auto fill tailored to the type of request, the user provides the required information and attaches any necessary forms. Customized workflow rules move the request to a contract specialist that either creates a "case" in CMS, which triggers the creation of a contract, or simply responds to the requester and then closes the request. CRF's are deployed globally and are allowing SAP to save money, while better structuring the work of the Contract Management teams worldwide.
2. With the Document Approval Workflow (DAW) we added a flexible, mobile enabled, ad-hoc workflow to CMS, allowing for legal or other specialized parties approvals in case of a deviation from the legal template. The superior user experiences positively changed the perception of CMS and raised the adoption.
3. Finally, the introduction of DocuSign, as preferred eSignature partner, not only reduced our internal processes by 25 min in average and 30€ hard saving, but also allowed us to significantly reduce the overall cycle time of the transaction.

With the above three measures, we were able to reduce the processing time from 180 min per transaction down to 10 min in average—with instances of "no touch", where contracts are created fully autonomously. We learned a lot in these last 5 years, but most importantly, it gave us a plan for the future.

---

[4]Global Contract Management Services team reporting into the General Counsel Field.

3.4 The Future Contracting Management Solution

Our CMS was just a first step! In being true to our company's motto, we are striving to *improve people's life*, and allow all our customers to *run better*! So we set out on the mission to add CMS to the SAP standard, so all SAP customers would benefit from our work and close the same gap in their process landscape that we were able to fill with CMS.

We imagine LCMS, our proposed new Legal Content Management Solution, to be more than just a next generation of CMS. LCMS is meant to provide a central layer for all legal content, highly flexible in its use and powered by a document assembly engine. Thus LCMS provides full transparency on the digital content, speeds up processes and gives the agility to adapt easily to the ever changing business needs.

3.5 Legal Information

Returning to the CEO, it seems nowadays his quote should be adjusted:

> If you are not in control of your legal information, you are not in control of your business!

Information constantly increases in value, simply because access to information allows companies to act and react way faster in an environment in which speed is of the essence.

Any organization is challenged to scrutinize itself and perform a health check once in a while, as the inevitable stereotype request to "do more with less" will come. The CFOs rightfully ask: "Can't this job be done more efficiently and effectively? Can we automate parts of the process or introduce extended self-service capacity? Can we outsource to a third party?" This pressure is new for legal departments and causes waves of unbelieving astonishment. The lawyer's typical answer "it depends" was never more true: it depends on the legal department's willingness and openness to embark on the transformational journey.

3.5.1 Control Your Data!

The first thing every legal department should focus on is to gain full control of its legal infrastructure: no data, no insights. So the basis for a successful transformation lies in the ability to make use of your legal teams' data, what we call your legal information. This is all but easy, especially as we are challenged with the phenomenon of information overload. The world's information is doubling every 3 years, while the processing power of our computers (aka *Moore's Law*) only doubles every roughly 2 years. This is aggravated by the fact that 80 % of the information the world produces every day is unstructured, while most computer programs are only able to process structured information. One could argue that the rise of super computers such as IBM's Watson, or in-memory platform, such as SAP's HANA might soon be able to process unstructured information the same way structured data is processed today.

Waiting can be a strategy—but for legal professionals, waiting is a strategy that will lead right into unemployment. In my mind, we lawyers should grasp the opportunity to train these machines! We can make our jobs easier, find new work and make ourselves once again indispensable by helping to create more autonomous and automated workflows—and not arguing against them.

3.5.2 Information-Enablement

Irrespective of what legal practice you work in, in-house, law firm or alternative legal provider, a unified legal information strategy is the key to success! We describe Legal Information Management (LIM) as the way to gain full control of all relevant legal information—by leveraging your company's ERP system, your central enterprise documents system and any legal system you might have—if you have none, make or buy!

That might sound a bit vague for some or overly ambitious for others, but in essence it is no less than the answer to the digital revolution that is upon us. Legal Information Management organizes what we do, prescribes how we do it and allows us to measure how well we do it—providing full transparency of our performance as legal department.

While special knowledge about the law is still considered the key component of our LIM strategy, LIM is more: LIM encompasses everything the legal function needs to know or can re-use.

The biggest challenge for a user is to distinguish between "valuable information" and what we call "noise". Everything a legal profession needs to know or can re-use is in fact already there—it is just hidden under a mess of useless, unstructured, ambiguous data! So the work starts with a kind of "spring cleaning" in which we tidy up our entire legal information system in order to become truly information-enabled.[5]

In 2014 we launched an initiative called Legal Excellence (LEX) which aims to "information-enable" legal. Legal excellence can be achieved if

> all information follows the same data structure,
> is semantically categorized,
> stored in a central database and
> automatically discoverable, re-usable and adaptable.

Or in short: every piece of information that is required to perform a certain task must be readily available and accessible in real-time, instantly. Once "information-enabled" in such a way, loosely based on Salim Ismail, your organization is ready for non-linear growth, thus capable of adapting to all future challenges.

At SAP we information-enabled a team of lawyers, who used to manage their tasks for years in Excel lists, exchanged only via eMails and who stored important

---

[5]Ismail (2014).

information on a team share drive. Applying our LEX strategy we replaced Excel by a central database, instead of eMail we set up workflows and a link in the tool which allows them to easily access their stored documents. The Case Management App was rather simple—but the results were amazing.

On the surface we just fixed a broken process, but soon, people who worked in the new environment cherished the new easy insights they got by just using a common platform. They engaged more actively in the tool, gained deeper knowledge about the process and came up with ideas how to improve the whole system. Later, they started to explore the new information source, which resulted in innovative ideas for App's that went far beyond the initial request...

This examples shows, once people get deeply involved, we sometimes experience the so called TAV paradigm:

TRANSPARENCY = *people understand and see the full picture on what a solution does*
AGENCY = *they take ownership and learn how to proficiently use the solution*
VIRTUOSITY = *some are eager to bring the solution to the next level or start experimenting new solutions*

Take any business process: Once the workarounds are replaced and e.g. the Excel converted to an information-enabled environment, owned by people that are technical affine, process minded and open to new technology, then todays' boundaries are no longer valid. Since its inception, LEX has incubated up ca. 30 Apps that help our organization to run better, faster and cheaper.

Another example we often use to illustrate the progressive information-enablement of legal is how we work with documents.

3.5.3 From Folders to Artificial Intelligence

Becoming information-enabled means to get as much as possible out of the information that surrounds you. Take any document created in MS Word—a contract, for instance. The Word file is obviously in a digital format—it's not paper anymore. But the information provided is limited to what you can read on screen: words, formatting (if correctly applied) and some layout.

When MS Word was introduced, it revolutionized the world—with formatting, people were, for the first time, able to see what they finally will get (WYSIWYG, what you see is what you get) once the document was printed. But is such a document information-enabled when it comes to automation? Do we actually control how the content of the document—the clauses—are used? We don't! And when it comes to contract automation, MS Word actually is a source of errors.

Information-enablement is about making the right pieces of information useable by a computer—the ones we need to solve a problem. Although MS Word is a powerful tool, it is pretty much a "black box", if your aim is to control the content that is in the file.

You cannot easily report on those files or measure its degree of deviation from a perceived standard. We can count the words or compare versions—but do not gain real insights.

So, in order to organize the growing amount of MS Word files, people started to assign sophisticated names to the files. Most started with adding a date code

20160712_filename

to have all files in ascending order, others came up with acronyms to better structure the content

20160712_CUSTOMER_SALES_EULA_V19_FINAL

Very disciplined teams even managed to apply the same standard file naming convention all over the world—but a missing letter or number or false acronym could crash your system.

Inevitable, as soon as the number of files managed by their filenames exceeds a certain threshold, folder structures were added.

Some started with years or quarters ("2015" or "Q2_2016"), some used the customer names (in alphabetical order) to structure content. Sub-folders were supposed to support the main folder structure (the examples are limitless: "Archive"; "Final", "Draft" etc.).

That was the situation we found when we started our legal transformation—content management was a private domain, managed only by some lose naming conventions. . .

We experimented, and found a simple solution for managing files by adding a unique ID stamp on "box" I.e. each and every document.

This ID could not accidentally be removed from the file, as it was embedded in the file itself and not in the file name. As we were able to identify the document, we established automated workflows instead of attaching files to eMails. This improvement brought significant transparency into a process that was considered almost unpredictable. From its launch to only a few weeks later, we experienced high adoption—higher than any other tool we launched before.

Until that point, we had still followed the normal continuous improvement cycles of traditional software development. We measured, assessed root causes, changed for the better, deployed, conducted trainings etc.—but it was getting more and more difficult to improve processes which were already at a decent level of maturity.

The situation we found ourselves in was similar to that described by Clayton Christensen in "Innovators Dilemma".[6] Our thinking was centered on the question of how to improve the status quo? Until the question was raised, "why don't we just open the box?".

Only after we understood our real challenge (i.e. >4400 word files were actively used, were of low structure and were failing on the attempt to automate or

---

[6]Christensen (1997).

manipulate Word in a scalable way), we came up with the idea to change the paradigm and get rid of Word. De-Word-ification is the term we introduced to describe our bold vision of a legal department that is banning the use of Word.

We bring full transparency to the content, by decomposing the legal templates into their core components, the clause or text blocks.

This "little move" has a significant impact: It allows our Lawyers to disassemble the content of more than 4000 World templates into their core components: clauses or content blocks. These hundred-thousands of content blocks, organized by attributes, can be re-used to create unlimited new outputs "on the fly"—instantly. SAP now possesses the agility to react more quickly to the ever changing needs of Sales. And knowing every detail of all our contracts will change the sales game and reveal exponential opportunities.

Our next aim is to create the document model. Today's content is organized in a way that it is understood by humans. In the near future, content will be structured in a way that can easily be read and understood by machines—independent from national languages. So the attribute "language" only instructs the machine to output a specific document in a specific language—we just need to formalize the information. Once we transform text into a formula, mistakes will become obvious because the system will stop working. We will create a simple rule engine that allows end-users to set up the rules, to run tests, refine or learn, and then we can finally extract information and monitor every aspect on how legal content has been used!

For the sake of completeness a word on artificial intelligence or AI. Marvin Minsky provided us with a definition for AI : "The building of computer programs which perform tasks which are, for the moment, performed in a more satisfactory way by humans because they require high level mental processes such as: perception learning, memory organization and critical reasoning."[7] I believe we reached the inflection point and therefore it is about time to change.

So what started as an excursion on how to manage documents can serve as an example for what Richard Susskind described as the disassembling of legal tasks. Colleagues who used to handcraft contracts, by using their own templates, harnessing their private clause library and storing the documents in their own folder system, for the first time now gain access to a central template repository—where all legal colleagues share templates. In a second step, the template itself is split up in clauses, allowing lower skilled people to make use of their pre-approved clauses. As a result,

- the amount of legal work is significantly reduced
- time to contract is shortened
- content can be re-used
- usage of clauses can be tracked
- contracts are available in self-service
- new roles are created: e.g. clause owner

---

[7]Marvin Lee Minsky, quote taken from the PhD Thesis of Samuel Hiard, 2012.

Based on data that is produced in the course of the legal transaction, the team can now asses and make fact based decisions about which contract aspects are critical and require legal approval and which aspects can be outsourced or taken over by a machine. Teams using LIM are not afraid of losing their jobs, to the contrary: Such teams are invaluable because they have proven their ability to transform and thus are ready for the future.

4   Conclusion

Teams who dedicate their whole attention only on fixing the urgent topics will most certainly achieve one thing: a joint burn-out. Whereas clever teams of our age will free up time to work on the important topics. Information is everywhere and our focus should be to transform passive data into active information and such information into insights to better steer our profession in a digital (if not golden) future.

The indispensable foundation for such a transformation is leadership, both on a personal as well as on an executive level. Identifying the right people or teams and providing them with title, mandate and budget is the crucial first step—the rest will follow.

Liquid Legal Context
By Dr. Dierk Schindler, Dr. Roger Strathausen, Kai Jacob

Jacob argues that defining your legal departments unified legal information strategy is not only necessary, but the perfect starting point for the digital transformation. Such a strategy provides deep insights in what your team is doing, and why it matters. Decomposing legal work (as described by Richard Susskind) and identifying the person (or automated process) best equipped to deliver each activity is what in-house legal departments should focus on. And you can only do this with reliable facts & numbers!

"Information-enable legal"—what does that mean? Why are some teams seemingly 10 times faster, better and cheaper than others?

Jacob warns not solely to add tools to an already overly complex and heterogeneous system landscape. Where there is no market leader, MAKE, where there is one, BUY. Two other aspects should also be closely monitored as part of your Legal Information strategy: first, the integration of all tools in order to support a central dashboard as proposed by Timmer. But secondly, and no less important, let's continue to think about how companies will effectively interact in future. Will there be something like a "Central Legal Platform", setting the standard in services, collaboration, the use of templates and other legal technology?

Let's have another look into Legal Tech industry, based on the overview provided by Zetterberg/Wojcik.

References

Christensen, C. M. (1997). *The innovator's dilemma: When new technologies cause great firms to fail*. Boston: Harvard Business School Press.
Friedman, T. L. (2005). *The world is flat: A brief history of the twenty-first century*. New York: Farrar, Straus and Giroux.
Ismail, S., Malone, M. S., & van Geest, Y. (2014). *Exponential organizations: Why new organizations are ten times better, faster, and cheaper than yours (and what to do about it)*. New York: Diversion Books.

Kai Jacob Head of Global Contract & Legal Information Management, IACCM VP of EMEA

Kai a lawyer by education, joined SAP in 2008 and heads the Global Contract Management Services team since 2011. In 2015, he assumed additional responsibility for Legal Information Management, aiming to support the digital transformation of the legal function. Kai joined IACCM (International Association of Contract and Commercial Management) in 2004, became a member of its Board of Directors in 2012, and since January 2014 has been serving as Officer & Vice Chair EMEA. Kai is a regular speaker at conferences and engaged in various round-tables, boards and initiatives in support of his vision of LIQUID LEGAL.

Technology Is Changing the Way Legal Works: A Look at How Technology Is Driving Better Business Practices in Legal

Ulf Zetterberg and Christina Wojcik

Abstract

A new breed of lawyer is trailblazing new paths in in-house legal leadership. They are not simply paving the paths that have always existed, they are leveraging technology that delivers artificial intelligence to get access to information faster, create productivity efficiencies, and improve business practices and outcomes through reporting and metrics.

1 Introduction

Whether lawyers like it or not, new and emerging technologies are changing the way legal departments operate. To be an integral part of the business, in-house legal counsel need to strategically align their legal thinking with business outcomes, which are quantified by data and tracked by metrics, and both are captured and managed through the use of technology. Leveraging technology to process and report on data helps outline the activities of the department team members. Technology can be used to demonstrate specific service level targets, ensure proper billing and invoicing procedures, allow for faster analytics across large amounts of data, and can generally add clarity and efficiency across the business.

That being said, legal is still an industry with laggards in technology adoption. The technology being adopted is primarily productivity-centric (mobile, office automation) and security-centric. One study[1] shows that priorities for technology investment for the legal industry consistently fall into these categories:

---

[1]Legal Efficiency 2015, Raconteur.com, p. 11.

U. Zetterberg • C. Wojcik (✉)
Seal Software, San Francisco, CA, USA
e-mail: christina.wojcik@seal-software.com

© Springer International Publishing AG 2017
K. Jacob et al. (eds.), *Liquid Legal*, Management for Professionals,
DOI 10.1007/978-3-319-45868-7_21

- Network security and firewall protection
- Hardware upgrades (mobile phones, laptops or tablets)
- Remote work technologies (video conferencing and cloud collaboration)
- BYOD policies/portable device security

The takeaway from these trends in technology investment is that the legal profession remains generally focused on "KTLO" activities, otherwise known as "keeping the lights on." These are infrastructure investments in office automation and communications, so lawyers can perform the functions they are currently doing more efficiently.

That same data also shows secondary investment in applications specific for legal operations. More aggressive and contemporary legal firms and legal operations are implementing these technologies, including:

- Case and matter management
- ERP or business management with billing functionality and financial analytics
- eDiscovery and litigation management
- Timesheet and expense management
- CRM and customer management
- Marketing and email outreach management
- Human Resources Management (HRM)

These technologies do help lawyers work more efficiently and remove some of the paper from operations, lowering costs, shortening time for various functions, and reducing errors. If lawyers are not considering these technologies, and some are still not, they are wasting time and are less efficient than their competitors and is essentially *paving the cow paths* to improve performance.

But there is an entirely new type of software, very different than office automation or efficiency tools, and it changes the way lawyers work. It leverages a new set of technologies referred to as Artificial Intelligence (AI), and combines Machine Learning (ML) and Natural Language Processing (NLP) to help lawyers change what they do in their engagement with clients, not just make what they do more efficient. In the legal world where time is literally money (at a hefty hourly rate), being able to solve challenges with the aid of AI is critical.

So what do all those techy terms mean for us lawyers? They essentially mean that you can now teach the software the way you would teach a junior associate a new discipline. You provide it with examples (can be positive and negative) to allow it to learn how to find the relevant information. No more key word search (although you can still do that), no proximity searches (although that's in there too)—we are talking about learning about the types and styles of language used through semantic analysis and Deep Neural Networks. Neural Networks and semantic analysis instructs the software to recognize when different words and sentence structures mean the same thing.

This new technology:

- Allows lawyers to remove manual, tedious and error prone document capture, review and data extraction/management functions;

- shortens processing time and lowers labor review costs for clients, as it allows the highly trained lawyers to spend more time providing high value services to clients vs. coordinating and managing manual document reviews or data analysis; and
- forces lawyers and their clients to rethink the traditional methods and scope of information capture.

2   Lawyers 2.0

The new breed of lawyers, who were raised on next generation user interfaces (UI) that allow for self-taught adoption and easily maneuverability, are rising through the ranks of their profession. They are well poised to adopt new technology and request product improvements based on their understanding of other platforms, both within the legal tech space, but also from other technology.

Unfortunately, adoption of new technology by many lawyers with years under their belt is often more challenging. So where to begin? The first step is to closely scrutinize usability. Not every member of the team needs to fully understand all of the features, functions, and behind the scenes programming that goes into delivering important answers. Identify members of your team that have different levels of legal and technical acumen and assign specific user roles. The General Counsel of a large legal department likely does not need to know much more than that the information they seek is readily accessible and that their business intelligence tools can be leveraged to produce cool reports that can be used during executive meetings. However, having that General Counsel actively supporting the use of technology will set the tone at the top. The daily users of the tools will need a much higher involvement in training and interaction with the platform. Overall, determine if you can get to the answers you need within a few clicks. If you cannot, go back and see if there are other configuration options or, perhaps, there may be better software platform for you.

The key to make any lawyer a "Lawyer 2.0" is to eliminate the fear of embracing new technology. Moreover, to embrace new technology, not EVERY member of a group needs to be a super end-user. The key is to ensure that a strategic mix of the team are able to understand and utilize the technology for the benefit of the entire department, thereby ensuring maximum efficiency and ultimate and successful return on investment.

3   How Does Technology Enable Legal to Run More Like a Business?

The answer is in the reporting and ability to quantify data. Having access and visibility into legal operations is a key initiative among legal practices that understand the value of running legal like a business. Efficiency, cost savings and leveraging limited resources is the name of the game, and bottlenecks and inefficiencies can be clearly identified by reviewing and understanding that information.

The ability to run reports and analytics on the business grants access and visibility into information, including process information, financial information, and contract information. It fuels the insight and analysis to make better business decisions and improve overall business performance. Reporting also ensures that a legal department can be *proactive* in its approach to risk management.

Process studies and financial reporting can help decision making, but harnessing and quantifying the legal provisions within contracts tends to be more challenging. We find that few organizations know with any degree of confidence how many contracts they have, where they are located and what provisions they contain. Even those who can answer some of the more basic contractual questions (e.g. how many active contracts do you have with company X and when do they terminate) cannot find similar answers when new questions are posed (e.g. how many active contracts do you have with company X that address data breaches). Leveraging new types of AI technologies to find contracts and extracting key pieces of information, in an automated fashion, is an absolute game changer for the legal profession.

Now that the system has found the information and extracted the data, the next step is to figure out what the information means. This often means loading it into a business intelligence (BI) tool or contract lifecycle management (CLM) software. With a BI tool, organizations can visualize data, report and run additional analytics. They can also enter the more interesting space of predictive analytics. Analytics tells us what's happened today and yesterday, and then leverages the patterns in this information to predict future behavior or outcomes. BI tools also allow us to present the big data outputs of contract analysis in ways that business users, not highly skilled analysts or data scientists, can intuitively access, understand and use.

An example of some very useful predictive analytics with contracts is when an organization can compare their standard language against all of the provisions actually negotiated and executed upon. When doing this, users can begin to see that some percentage of the time, a specific provision is changed to a consistent alternative clause or if bespoke "new" language was created. Now, if they take that information and use it to assume the same trend will continue in the future, they can then take action by considering offering the alternative clause as the primary provision, thus reducing the negotiation time. This reduction in negotiation time can lead to a more efficient contracting process and earlier revenue recognition as well as a stronger relationship with the other party (because you may be viewed as more reasonable in your approach to negotiation). Corrective action can also be taken against the person insisting on creating bespoke language to ensure they properly follow the contracting playbook.

Having this contract data, users can also set a baseline for acceptable language and behavior in contracting, and measure against that baseline as improvements are implemented. This is typical business practice but rarely adopted as a legal practice. By looking at all of your contracts and seeing where deviations from the standard occurred, and by how many rounds of negotiations it took to reach the final executed copy, you can improve upon the metrics to gain more value and accurately assess the cumulative impact of changes made.

By uploading contractual information or creating and negotiating a contract within the analytics software, the legal department can now create reports to determine areas of inefficiencies and their impact, and improve upon those areas. Examples include number of review iterations, deviations from standards, average turn-around time, etc. With this level of insight, legal departments and the organizations they serve can quickly start gaining a competitive advantage by turning contracts around more quickly and achieving additional cost savings.

AI tools also help with revenue recognition and tracking. By tracking the information in the agreements, an organization can receive the full value of its expertly-negotiated terms, such as discounts or rebates, and avoid the penalties of lost information, which may include erroneous payments or missed expiration dates. This revenue recognition provides legal department's hard numbers to build a business case for initiatives such as performance bonuses and increasing headcount.

More importantly, if a legal department truly wants to serve the business, it must transform itself and understand which activities bring value and at what cost. It must have the data to answer the question: "Does my current course of action bring the biggest value to my organization?" Rather than speculating that something creates risk, it can now provide clear data to support or refute such proposition.

4 What Is Machine Learning (ML) and Natural Language Processing (NLP)?

To make contract discovery and analysis work accurately and efficiently, there are several technologies that need to be used together. This includes NLP, which uses complex rules sets and statistical analysis for the identification of terms and provisions in the discovery and initial data extraction, and ML, which uses combinations of algorithms to support the creation of custom extraction policies and trains the system on the specific language, products, provisions, and clauses for a particular organization.

The system learns through examples, processing multiple contracts over time and receiving feedback on how it identifies various components of a contract. As a consequence, the system becomes more effective and increasingly precise in finding what it is seeking. These systems don't just "find," using keyword search or text matching, but they "think," using combinations of words and phrases to deduce concepts and gist, and then they are taught if they are right or wrong, and that information goes into the learning aspect. This is where the idea of *intelligent machines* emerges.

There are also new techniques in the field of AI called "deep learning" that uses Neural Networks in much the same way as the human brain. One form of Neural Network is called Convolutional Neural Networks (CNN). By using CNN it's possible to reduce the computing power required (i.e. reducing the size of the "brain") and increase the speed at which the system can learn, as a key element of any system is its ability to learn quickly and accurately. This is critical when large organizations sorting through 10,000s to 100,000s of documents to find important pieces of information.

As discussed, it takes the right combinations of NLP, ML, the right set of algorithms with technology that makes them all work together. Important to all of this is the data visualization platform which will present information intuitively in order for a system to work properly. Fortunately for legal professionals, these systems not only exist, but are solving big problems for many organizations today.

It is interesting to see how Intelligent Contracting plays out in practice. Take for example "Change of Control" provisions. Change of Control is a critical field in all mergers and acquisitions transactions, but the provisions can easily hide in assignment or termination provisions, be their own distinct provisions, or hide in plain sight with non-standard language. Take the following examples of Change of Control provisions:

Assignment. *Company shall not assign, delegate or otherwise transfer the agreement or any of its rights or obligations under the agreement without prior written consent. A Change of Control shall be considered an assignment for the purposes of this provision. Any non-conformance with this section shall constitute a breach and immediate termination.*

Change of Control. *In the event of a reorganization, merger or consolidation that results in the transfer of 50 % or more of the voting authority or a sale of all or substantially all of the assets of the Company to another person or entity, this contract shall terminate.*

Termination for Reduction in Ownership. *In the event that Company's Aggregate Ownership Interest is less than five percent (5 %), Client shall have the right to terminate this Agreement immediately by giving ninety (90) days' written notice of termination to Company.*

To add another wrinkle, let's consider Change Control language. Change of Control provisions are much different than Change Control language which often describes the process of how to change the type, nature, delivery, etc. of work define/described in a Statement of Work (SOW) or similar type contract. This process can be pages and pages long, so the below is significantly consolidated for illustrative purposes:

Change Control. *Should there be any changes suggested under this statement of work (SOW), those changes shall be considered out of scope and an amendment to this SOW or a new SOW shall be required.*

Now the question becomes, how does NLP and ML help with these variations? Imagine you are the General Counsel of a highly acquisitive company, and after multiple acquisitions, you recognize that many of your contracts have Change of Control provisions and you need to determine which contracts are potentially terminated due to the new company structure. You have prioritized your supplier agreements as the starting point to begin to determine where Change of Control comes into play. The challenge is, you have over 10,000 suppliers with each supplier having over 20 contracts associated with the relationship, so essentially 200,000 contracts to sort through. The options are to hire a team of lawyers to begin the sorting process (and finding the budget to do so), teaching the software to find the contracts you require, or do nothing and hope for the best.

Since "doing nothing" is not an option as legal counsel during an acquisition, only the first two options are viable. Here is how the math will break down for hiring a team of lawyers to look through your contracts:

Outside Counsel Fees

Number of contracts	200,000
Number of lawyers	1
Cost per hour	~$200
Time to complete	+7000 days (assuming 4 docs reviewed per hour)
Cost	+$17,000,000
Cost per contract	$85 per contract

Legal Process Outsourcing Resources

Number of contracts	200,000
Number of lawyers	1
Cost per hour	~$30
Time to complete	+7000 days (assuming 4 docs reviewed per hour)
Cost	+$2,000,000
Cost per contract	$10 per contract

Now, consider teaching software to do the manual process of sorting through the contracts so the lawyers only need to review the contracts that contain the language, and the language includes the various standard and nonstandard language, yet excludes the Change Control language because the software recognizes that the intent of the Change of Control language is different, even if some of the proximity of the words is similar.

What you're left with is under 10,000 contracts that can be sorted by those that may terminate in order to begin the renegotiation process or tagged as "inactive". This type of sorting can typically be managed in-house and only requires the cost of the software.

In-house legal departments whom can articulate this of result is much more likely to be allocated budget for new technology investments because the return on investment is clear.

5   Do the Robots Come in Peace?

Based on the above example, you can see that the good news is that solutions based on artificial intelligence, sometimes called "robots," prove to be invaluable business partners when it comes to legal counsel support. They allow the legal department to sort through an extraordinary amount of data without disrupting day-to-day operations or deliverables. When a business event occurs and the general counsel wants to know the impact, in-house counsel would historically have to "stop the presses," and turn 100 % of their attention to finding and sifting through thousands of contracts and identify those impacted. This process disrupts contract negotiation and day-to-day legal operations. It also prevents the organization from achieving its strategic objective. However, with the robot, you simply tell/teach it what you're looking for, and it responds with the information you need in order to analyze the issue using your legal judgment and ultimately deliver a reasoned, efficient, and effective result.

6   Business Case for Legal Investing in Technology: From Cost Center to Revenue Enabler

Contracts are an organization's number one economic asset, yet they are often some of the most neglected assets within the organization. According to the Aberdeen Group[2] and the IACCM,[3] most organizations suffer significantly from revenue leakage and incorrect/improper invoicing, which, depending on the size of the organization results in millions of Euros/USD/GBPs of lost revenue opportunities. To combat this loss, organizations must have access, visibility and a disciplined approach to contract management and oversight.

Legal has the opportunity to become heroes if they are able to help (re)gain even 1 % of this leakage from their sales contracts.

When we break sales contracts down into their very basics, they dictate every facet of the business relationship with a customer:

1. Define the products and services sold or licensed
2. Specify a period of time
3. Sets the price and the payment terms
4. Describes the service and support levels to be provided
5. Outlines discounts
6. Contains an inventory of legal terms and conditions

But among these types of agreements there are many missed revenue opportunities. This is according to the Aberdeen Group, which conducted a study of

---

[2] Aberdeen Group, Best-in-Class Performance in Contract Management, July 2015.
[3] IACCM, Top Ten Ways of Avoiding Contract Value Leakage, Nov 2013.

250 organizations and discovered that 3 % of invoices are entered incorrectly: with inaccurate prices, incorrect quantities or missing products.

Another 4–9 % of revenue is lost due to other types of revenue leakage due to poor contracting according to Aberdeen and the IACCM. Aberdeen defines revenue leakage as *"revenue lost from regulatory penalties, missed deadlines, collection failures, maverick pricing, lost sales and transaction errors."*

The challenge with maintaining oversight to contracts does not come in when all contacts are the exact same documents with the exact same commitments. The challenge occurs when contracts are negotiated creating non-standard clauses. Common non-standard clauses include:

- Custom pricing;
- unique payment terms; and
- one-off performance obligations.

To overcome this challenge, organizations must be able to capture and report on the sales contracts across the enterprise. These issues get trickier when organizations analyze who within their organization negotiates these agreements—is it the legal department or the line of business? When is the legal department engaged (if ever) in these seemingly straightforward and standard agreements?

Another challenge is tracking discounting. According to Aberdeen, when discounts are offered to customers who meet certain volume commitments, payment timeframes or other milestones create a huge opportunity for revenue leakage.

- Discounts may be offered if customers can meet certain volume commitments, payment timeframes or other guidelines; and
- often times discounts are provided/granted even though customers do not hit targeted milestones and this lack of visibility can result in significant revenue reduction (up to 10 % per deal according to Aberdeen).

Three other terms cause opportunity for lengthening or recreating sales cycles and revenue leakage.

- Renewal: If there is not a clear understanding of term or termination, a "sure thing" renewal can disappear;
- Most Favored Nations: "I promise that you will always have the best pricing we offer." Nearly impossible for most organizations to manage; and
- Payment: These provisions and revenue recognition can go hand in hand.

7   But Isn't Sending Legal Work to Low Cost/Offshore Locations Still an Innovative Approach?

No. Not unless your offshore provider is offering an underlying technology to drive value to the work being performed. Most Legal Process/Service organizations are making nice margins on performing all commercial transactions manually, and leveraging Excel spreadsheets to capture the results. This methodology is completely outdated for modern information needs, and provisions captured within Excel are static the minute they are entered in the spreadsheet. Classifying contractual provisions in this way does not provide the flexibility needed to coexist with evolving contractual relationships. When new information is needed, such documents need to be reopened, and a new cell needs to be created and reviewed for quality control. There is no way to "future proof" a manual review, to know what you *may* need to know in the future. Things just change too frequently—think of regulatory changes, world events and even policy changes within the organization itself.

What new technology allows for is the querying of the system to find needed information without having to reopen and reread documents. Simply teach the system through processing examples and providing feedback on what you're looking for, and it will search your entire portfolio of documents and identify which contain that information and which do not.

8 What Can Artificial Intelligence Do for Me if There Is a Regulatory Change?

There are many internal and external situations that drive a hard requirement to understand what is in contracts, including lawsuits, data breaches, a financial status downgrade, M&A activity, or a regulatory change, just to name a few. Regulatory events are becoming more prevalent, including accounting changes such as IFRS 15 for revenue recognition and IFRS 16 for the treatment of leases, and also new ones designed to ensure large financial institutes have plans for possible economic downturns, including EBA "write down rules," and, SR 14-1 and "Living Wills" reporting for US-based banking institutions. When a contract discovery and analytics system has found and extracted a set of more common terms from contracts, it can then function as a search engine for contracts. Users can create extraction policies to cover new areas for compliance, and they can do it in a way that is more cost effective and far faster than manual reviewing.

Going back to IFRS 16 as an example, a user can search for lease agreements, then, after they are all found and processed, run search policies for leases with maintenance or services included. The system can find just those items within leases, and allow an organization to make the decision to separate the lease for the asset or assets from the potential services included with that asset. The new system can account for them in a way that meets compliance, and also benefits the financial reporting of the organization. Just imagine the costs of the traditional review in this case, finding all lease agreements, having someone read each one looking for a services element, extracting the details of the asset vs. services leasing, and then passing that to the Legal and Finance teams to restructure the lease for IFRS 16 compliance reporting.

9　Isn't There One Piece of Technology That Can Solve All of Legal's Needs?

The simple answer is no. When you dissect the different components of what the legal department provides to the business, the deliverables are disparate and varied, and so technology applied to these processes has to be as well. Also, technology is moving at an astronomical pace, so that many of the early software offerings for various aspects of legal processes are considered obsolete by today's standards.

For example, what happened to predictive coding? Predictive coding, the term used to describe the early technology for keyword search, filtering and sampling to automate portions of an e-discovery document review was one of the top topics at the legal technology conventions in years past, but now it barely even registers. It quickly went from being the bright and shiny toy on the shelf to relatively obsolete. Predictive coding was utilized by solution providers trying to be innovative by more quickly culling information from the seemingly endless amounts of ESI in eDiscovery, or it was rejected as not being a "perfect" solution by those that chose the pure power of people to review the relevant information.

Predictive coding also faced an uphill battle because it was being sold and marketed to service providers as a way to create efficiency, but the majority of them did not feel the need to try to save their client's money if their clients where happy with "business as usual."

The other problem is that predictive coding was no longer bright and shiny, but became out-of-date technology. The artificial intelligence technology that can power "decision making" in the legal sector now has moved way past early implementations and are at new levels of functionality described above. Also, the decision about using or buying this technology is being removed from the service providers and is being driven by corporate in-house counsel who are demanding increased efficiency.

10　I Can't Use Technology Unless It Gives Me Perfect Results

Outside counsel has this unwarranted notion that information has to be "perfect" in-order for it to drive value to their clients. They believe their clients will accept nothing less, but this notion could not be further from the truth. On the other hand, in-house counsels are quickly becoming sophisticated business people with a clear understanding of risk and risk tolerance. They are increasingly asked to find creative solutions to problems so as not to stop business transactions from progressing. It is not enough to say that a transaction may be risky; counsel must give insight into how to quantify that risk, and whether that risk has been tolerated by the organization in the past.

When it comes to applying artificial intelligence to corporate transactions, most in-house counsel are satisfied with two basic principles: can I find the document I need when I need it, and can I pull the relevant information quickly?

Some of the objectives of eDiscovery, like finding certain documents and pulling out relevant information, simply won't work for corporate transactions. Clustering and removing of seemingly identical documents can lead to catastrophic events if the like documents are simply different by the word "not." Imagine this: you bucket two like contracts and identify them as standard because the clustering technology says they are extremely similar. Upon further inspection, you find the two clauses to read, "Party A shall be liable for any damages arising from negligent performance." The near duplicate reads, "Party A shall not be liable for any damages arising from negligent performance." If those were both put to the side as standard, someone may have just lost his or her job.

11 I've Purchased Legal Technology in the Past and It Failed

There are several reasons why technology is not adopted after purchasing. Let's walk through the standard story of a doomed technology implementation.

An in-house legal person, Jane, needed to purchase a contract lifecycle management tool in order to streamline the contracting process, develop automated workflows, track contracting behavior and better monitor the contractual risks of her organization. Being a good corporate citizen, Jane called her IT and procurement department, explained to them her need and an RFP was immediately generated. The RFP contained some generic needs from Jane, but was mostly left in the hands of procurement to run and then source the solution. After months of negotiation and forced cost reductions from the provider, a solution was selected. The documentation for the solution included a "refined" wish list of user needs, melding the needs of legal, IT and procurement into a more common ground solution. The solution was then put in the hands of the IT department to install. Six months (more likely: one year later), Jane has her shiny new software that is "ready to go." Unfortunately, the software was no longer tailored to meet Jane's specific needs, she doesn't understand how to use it, it doesn't contain any data from her legacy contracts and, most of all, it takes her three times as long to create and negotiate a contract as it did before. Jane decides never to use the software again and goes back to her old methods. Six months later, in her performance review, she was asked why she sponsored a substantial software implementation that was never adopted or used.

The question becomes: did the software fail? No, it worked perfectly as designed. Did the process for giving the people the greatest opportunity for success throughout the entire process fail? Likely, yes.

To successfully source and purchase technology, in-house legal needs to be very involved during the entire process, by successfully covering these five steps in the procurement of contract management software.

Step 1: Answer the following questions:

- Why do you think you need the software?
- What do you expect it do in order to support your role?
- What change management processes are going to be put in place to ensure adoption?

These questions ensure that all parties are clear on the objectives of the purchase. They are expected to get past one of the most significant hurdles of any software implementation: getting users to change what they are doing and adopt the new system.

Step 2: Understand what's in existing current contracts. The biggest challenges organization's face is not knowing where their contracts are located, not fully understanding what has been negotiated. This leads to:

- Poor CLM software design. If you don't know if your payment terms are 30, 60, 90 days or payment due upon completion, your system is not going to be able to capture this information; and
- an inability to leverage previously negotiated terms, to know what fallback or alternative language has been acceptable in the past.

Step 3: Work very closely with Procurement and IT. Unfortunately, Legal, IT and Procurement have different goals and metrics, which can lead to a breakdown of communications and poor outcomes. Procurement is often goaled on how well they were able to source the closest solution at the lowest price, as measured by achieved discount levels.

Often times the best solution is overlooked because of an inferior product offered at a lower price, and therefore Legal is already starting at a disadvantage. IT often understands and focuses on the bells and whistles of a technology, forgetting that a lot of legal professionals lack the experience or need for all the functionality. What is left is a super cool looking tool that is completely ill suited for Legal's actual need. An ideal solution is adaptable to the needs of ALL of its users and includes adequate work flow and security based controls to permit diverse users unique access.

Step 4. Consider if you are ready to leapfrog old technology. Many legal departments are coming to the understanding that even though they are moving in the direction of behaving more like a business, there are still some practices which their department simply won't ever be able to adopt. This may be because of management, resources, funding, cultural attitudes. What if there were a world that allows legal professionals to continue their current rogue behavior and methodology, but rely on technology to fill the gaps?

That world exists, and it is becoming bigger and stronger every day. For example, with contract search and discovery tools, users can negotiate contracts using bespoke language, change templates, use different wording than their colleagues, and the technology will still be able to provide access and visibility into the meaning of those contracts and provisions. With this type of technology and search capabilities, coupled with BI the need for complex, antiquated CLM tools become questionable.

Most in house counsel simply want to do a Google-like search and find answers to their questions, and with new technology, this is possible.

Step 5: Identify who, and in which role they are expected to use the tool, and then map the roles to the requirements of the business. There are usually several levels of user role in most organizations, including:

- The Administrative User who possesses carte blanche access to anything and everything the technology has to offer; it should be given to a very, very limited number of people;
- The Super Users, who are able to control a lot of the functionality and may know some advance features of the product; and
- Business Users, who are able to perform their day to day tasks within guard rails, meaning they are only able to do just enough to be productive, yet to stay out of trouble.

Step 6: Focus on the change management with the users. Ask yourself and your team how user friendly the software is which you installed. If it's not user friendly, or complicated to maneuver through the UI, then expect an uphill battle when it comes to getting people to use the tool.

If the UI is challenging, you need to determine how you are going to encourage your team to adopt and use the software. There is debate as to whether the carrot or stick (or both) approach is the better method, but this is one of the areas in which legal typically fails to behave like the rest of the business.

Most divisions within a large organization are responsible for meeting specific metrics or key performance indicators as part of the employee assessment. Legal rarely has this type of oversight and understanding into how their team is performing. Leveraging the software allows for the manager of the legal department to better understand their activities without having to rely on an antiquated billing practice brought over from the law firm days to assess their work. By using the *carrot* method, employees are rewarded for demonstrating the use of and competence in leveraging the technology. By using the *stick* method, employees receive a punishment or penalty for lack of adoption.

If there is no methodology in place for change management for using the software, the software is likely to fail. The failure may be due to poor UI design and clunky workflows. The software failure is typically blamed on the vendor, therefore the legal department, or in this case "Jane," will go to her IT and Procurement colleagues and declare: "the software you bought doesn't work - go find a new one that does." And the cycle continues.

There is a ray of hope with this process. A lot of the new technology coming to market doesn't require extensive change management as the UI's are much easier to use and developed with the user in mind.

12   Conclusion

In-house legal professionals are at a crossroads. Do they adopt emerging technology and come forth as leaders and innovators as they more closely align themselves with true business needs, or do they practice business as usual and assume their competition is doing the same?

Organizations are realizing they can apply technology to improve the basic processes they perform today, essentially paving the cow paths, but there are new technologies now available that change the processes themselves, creating innovations, not just deploying automation, in the way they work.

The truth is that robots and artificial intelligence are here to support the practice of law, and the former innovators are finding it hard to adopt to modern practices. Good legal training, judgement and counsel will always be critical for every organization, but robots and artificial intelligence can be used to automate laborious and costly tasks such as contract reviews and data analysis. It is the *innovators*, the individuals that are willing to adopt new technology and put in the effort to make it successful, that will take the legal profession to the next level and ultimately survive.

Liquid Legal Context
By Dr. Dierk Schindler, Dr. Roger Strathausen, Kai Jacob

Wojcik and Zetterberg start with calling out an important tension point that exists in the transformation of Legal: Lawyers tend to be laggards in embracing technology. What are the implications? The first thing that comes to mind is that this will slow down the gains in efficiency and cost effectiveness that can be produced from legal tech. Yet, the authors also point us to a second, equally important consequence: technology is the precondition to obtain the metrics on the operational work of lawyers which are required to embark into a KPI-driven and performance-managed future.

So in today's transforming industry, we actually face a double-hurdle—the use of technology itself and the cultural aspect of embracing a metrics-oriented and performance-defined world as positive, rather than a threat. Pauleau, Roquilly and Collard, as well as Timmer provide specific ideas on how to build define KPI's, develop metrics and dashboards that immediately create value also for the operational lawyers themselves, thereby lowering the barrier of accepting them as part of the job. In terms of embracing a digitized world with legal tech being the basis of it all, rather than the isolated fix for a specific task, Wojcik and Zetterberg keep it simple and straight: rigorous focus on usability is key!

But the authors take us one important step further: Introducing tech that is usable and generating the data via reports from it is one thing. However, carefully considering and putting a lot of brainpower into determining what it actually tells us, is crucial. Beyond that, finding ways to not only explain the past, but being able to leverage technology to derive trends and to predict future developments would be creating true and unique value as a legal business partner. As we follow Wojcik and Zetterberg on the journey through the opportunities provided by legal tech, their bold statement is that mere outsourcing and offshoring of legal work to low-cost locations is not innovative anymore—if it has ever been. Don't fight the cost battle, when value is at stake.

(continued)

It is the innovator, the individual that is willing to adopt new technology and put in the effort to make it successful, that will take the legal profession to the next level and ultimately survive, the authors conclude, and connect our minds back to the need of an entrepreneurial mindset that Tumasjan and Welpe have explained and that Chomicka and Roux-Chenu/de Rocca-Serra have made vivid when describing their journeys. It is now time to learn from Timmer what a dashboard for the legal function can look like and how to get there.

Ulf Zetterberg co-founded Seal Software in 2010 and drives the company's overall strategy and execution. He brings over 25 years of enterprise software and services experience in both corporate and entrepreneurial environments. As a serial entrepreneur, Ulf is passionate about innovation and growth, and is driven by and committed to a strong customer-first culture. Prior to Seal, Ulf held senior executive positions at companies like OpenText, Legato, EMC, Kazeon and Proact. Ulf studied Economics at Stockholm University.

Christina Wojcik leads the Legal Service Channels division, globally, at Seal Software. As VP of Legal Services, she engages with legal industry partners to create best-in-class solutions to meet the complex contractual needs of Fortune 1000 organizations. As Practice Executive, Contract Management at IBM, Christina was responsible for Contract Management Strategy & Best Practices at IBM. She worked closely with Fortune 500 companies to replace high-risk, manually-intensive contract management processes with proven, scalable technology that delivers complete risk oversight and obligation management to legal organizations, while streamlining the end-to-end process, thereby increasing revenue and reducing costs.

Look to the Moon: Managing and Monitoring the Legal Function

Ivar Timmer

Abstract

A legal department's objective is to support an organization in reaching its objectives, by seizing legal opportunity whenever possible and identifying and mitigating legal risks intelligently. To do this effectively, a proactive and structured approach is essential. Although times are changing, many legal departments still have a long way to go. Developing and maintaining a *legal dashboard*, in some shape or form, should be one of the first steps in taking a more structured approach to managing the legal function. Where the term legal dashboard is currently used mainly for tools to control legal spend, a complete dashboard should also encompass sources of legal risk and legal opportunity. Only if a legal department has a clear and shared view of the current and, as much as possible, future status of the legal function can there be sensible discussion on setting legal priorities and directing limited resources to where they are most needed. A legal dashboard will facilitate discussion not only within a legal department, but also with other organizational departments. The central idea of this article is that collaboration and structured discussion are essential for legal quality to emerge.

1   Introduction

A business is an organization involved in the provision of goods or services to customers. Obviously, a legal department is by definition always *part* of a business and not a business in itself. However, if we regard a legal department *as* a business,

I. Timmer (✉)
Amsterdam University of Applied Sciences, Windroosplein 122, 1018ZW Amsterdam, Netherlands
e-mail: i.timmer@hva.nl

© Springer International Publishing AG 2017   341
K. Jacob et al. (eds.), *Liquid Legal*, Management for Professionals,
DOI 10.1007/978-3-319-45868-7_22

its service would be providing legal expertise and advice to one customer only: the organization of which it is part.

To most, "running legal as a business" will mean something like: applying principles and good practices of business management to legal departments. In short, we can call management of the work of legal professionals[1] and of closely related processes *legal management.* Many legal professionals have mixed emotions when it comes to legal management. All will understand that it is necessary, but when it comes to their own work being managed there is often a tension. At the core of legal craftsmanship is the ability to appreciate differences between individual cases, while the word "management" is loaded with associations of Fordism and Taylorism, standardization and efficiency. These associations somehow intuitively conflict with the notion of legal craftsmanship. This may explain the, often tacit, resistance that legal professionals feel when it comes to legal management. Legal managers should be aware of this tension. They should respect professional judgment whenever possible. "Micromanaging" professionals is a bad idea. Legal professionals, on the other hand, have to understand that a legal department should operate as a team and make maximum use of available means. In a complex organization, this will always require coordination and prioritization. Therefore, it is an illusion that there can be a legal department without legal management. The only choice is between poor or better legal management. Because the way in which the delivery of legal services is organized could greatly improve quality, efficacy, speed and cost efficiency, legal professionals should simply *want* good legal management.

The tension between management and professional craftsmanship is far from unique to the legal world. It can be observed in many other sectors, especially where professions have a similar knowledge intensive character, such as in the educational and medical professions. Law firm managers, court managers and general counsel therefore have a lot in common with medical directors and educational managers. Consequently, legal management could learn from health care management and educational management, and vice versa.

2   Credence Services

Legal services in general, including legal services provided by in-house legal departments, could be characterized as *credence services*: services whose utility impact and quality are, at least partially, difficult or impossible for customers to

---

[1]The term legal professional is used here as a generic term for professionals with legal expertise, working either in classic legal professions (judges, lawyers, prosecutors) or "modern legal professions" (in-house counsel, legal specialists working for non-profit organizations or government, et cetera). Terminology on legal professions is often confusing when used across jurisdictions. For example, in the US, almost all in-house counsel are also members of the bar and therefore "lawyers", while in other jurisdictions this is not the case. Throughout the text, I will specify which type of legal professionals I mean, when this does not follow clearly from the context.

ascertain. An essential element of a credence service is the *information asymmetry* between service provider and consumers. Everyone who owns a car without knowing about cars has experience with a credence service when taking it to the garage and being charged for maintenance and repairs that only car professionals understand. In many situations, it will be obvious to other organizational constituents that legal expertise is required, but it will be difficult for them to judge the extent to which this is necessary. The quality of the service rendered will be especially difficult to judge. The actions of professionals from the legal department will always have some immediate results, but legal services are frequently intended to prevent future problems. It will then take time before it becomes apparent whether or not problems indeed arise. If they do not, it cannot logically be said that *therefore* the legal service was good. If they do arise, setting and circumstances may have changed fundamentally, making it hard to establish a causal connection. Additionally, the service may have been rendered by people who have long left the organization.

Thus, a legal department is, to a certain extent, more than other departments such as Human Resources or Finance, a black box to the rest of the organization. From this perspective of credence services, it is easy to understand why legal departments, as various empirical studies show (KPMG 2014; RSG/BLP 2012), find it difficult to demonstrate their added value to the organization. Part of the solution to this problem lies in reducing the information asymmetry by continuously explaining the strategy a legal department applies to managing the legal function. For this, a shared view of the legal function within the legal department is essential, combined with clear and consistent communication to management and other departments.

3 Structure

This article discusses how a legal dashboard can help improve the efficiency and effectiveness of a legal department and demonstrate the added value of legal. I advocate that configuring some form of a legal dashboard is one of the first things a legal department should do to optimize management of the legal function. First, I will discuss legal thinking and traditional legal education and the influence they have on the legal profession and legal practice. I will then go on to elaborate on the concept of legal departments, the legal function and managing the legal function, concluding with the benefits and pitfalls of a legal dashboard. Throughout the article, the focus is on commercial organizations, although many concepts will apply equally to public and non-profit organizations.

4   Legal Thinking, Legal Education and Research

Legal thinking implies having specialized knowledge of the law and legal concepts, and being able to approach legal problems using a variety of analytical methods. Throughout the ages, the law and legal culture have hugely benefited the development of individuals, organizations and democratic societies. Although one can, even in the most advanced legal cultures, be critical of many aspects of the law, an advanced and balanced legal system raises the overall standards of justice and fairness in society. Studies also show that the efficacy and independence of a country's legal system contribute significantly to a country's economic prosperity (cf. Veld and Voigt 2003). With regard to businesses, the common law and civil law traditions are converging under the influence of globalization. Although important differences remain, the laws and regulations that apply to businesses in Western countries therefore share many similarities.

A legal system needs legal professionals. Legal education has a long history, starting before Roman times. Law was among the first studies taught at modern universities. Legal education thus has a long tradition. In the Western world, despite differences in legal systems, it has remarkably similar features and is strongly connected to the admission to classical legal professions. There have been several studies on the strengths and weaknesses of legal education and law schools. An influential study is the 2007 report by the Carnegie Foundation for the Advancement of Teaching on Legal education in North America (Sullivan et al. 2012). Some of its most important conclusions will hold true for legal education in almost all Western countries. Because education strongly influences professional culture, we analyze some of these in the light of the topic of this book: legal professionals working at an in-house legal department.

5   Legal Thinking

Becoming a proficient legal thinker takes time and effort. At the core of legal thinking is the ability to determine whether or not an individual case is in accordance with a general rule. To master this analytical skill, law students learn many different sets of rules and study countless individual cases. As the Carnegie report observes, law school provides rapid socialization into the standards of legal thinking:

> Law schools are impressive educational institutions. In a relatively short period of time, they are able to impart a distinctive habit of thinking that forms the basis for their students' development as legal professionals. (Sullivan et al. 2012, p. 5)

Law schools reach this result, the report continues, primarily through the medium of a single form of teaching: the case-dialogue method.[2] One could say that, for a large part, legal students are trained to be "case solvers". In my research, I

---

[2]Legal education in civil law systems will differ in some respects, but the case-dialogue method is equally important in these countries.

have come across managers without a legal background working in legal environments. One joked about his colleagues in the management team who did have a legal background:

> When somebody throws them a case, they will drop everything and instantly start debating about its nuances and consequences. Comes in handy if you want to distract them, but not if you have urgent organizational matters at hand.

The risk of training case solvers is also that they may develop a tendency to react only when a case is presented to them. Seen in this light, it is not surprising that the criticism of in-house counsel is often that they are too *reactive*, acting only when presented with a problem. The preventive and proactive law movements that have originated in the US and Scandinavia are attempts to structurally counter this tendency and encourage legal professionals to direct their efforts to preventing problems, rather than acting when they have arisen. Preventive law originated in the US in the 1960s, with professor Louis M. Brown as its founding father. The name "preventive law" draws a parallel with the distinction between curative and preventive medicine and the saying: "an ounce of prevention is worth a pound of cure". Several Scandinavian scholars and practitioners elaborated on this line of thought from the 1990s onward and founded the Nordic School for Proactive Law.[3] The word proactive, as opposed to preventive, emphasizes that legal professionals should actively identify situations where the law and legal means can be applied usefully at an early stage. Being proactive is vital to effective legal management. Legal prevention can often indeed prevent legal trouble. Of course, not all problems can be avoided, but this line of thought is valuable and deserves greater attention among legal professionals and in legal education.

As legal education is based to a large extent on the case-dialogue method, it is interesting to note that cases are usually examples of "bad case" or "worst case scenarios". Psychology teaches us that frequent exposure to a specific type of examples will change the way a person thinks. When confronted with a certain situation, people will overrate the likelihood of scenarios that are similar to examples to which they have frequently been exposed, compared to other possible scenarios: the so-called "availability bias". A large part of this happens subconsciously. In reality, legal professionals will know that the chances of a worst case scenario being realized are slim, but their education may have shaped their mind such that they overrate these chances. Traditional legal education might therefore be partially responsible for increasing the risk averseness of legal professionals. Other experiences and training will also have an effect, so it remains to be seen whether legal professionals, especially operating in corporate settings, are truly more risk-averse than other professionals, as is often claimed by business people.[4]

---

[3]See http://www.proactivelaw.org/

[4]For example, a recent analysis by global executive search firm Russell Reynolds, focusing on successful executives, finds no notable differences between Chief Executive Officers, Chief Financial Officers and Chief Legal Officers, see: http://www.russellreynolds.com/sites/default/files/calm-risk-taker_attributes_for_success_in_todays_new_legal_environment.pdf

The stereotype of the "legal department as the business prevention department" is more likely to have originated from involving the legal department too late in business initiatives, rather than from the risk averseness of legal professionals. For this late involvement, both the business and the legal departments might be to blame.

6   Non-Legal Aspects

The Carnegie report makes another important observation about legal education. In the case-dialogue method, important elements that fall outside the strictly legal domain often do not receive proper attention:

> Students discover that to "think like a lawyer" means redefining messy situations of actual or potential conflict as opportunities for advancing a client's cause through legal argument before a judge or through negotiation. By contrast, the task of connecting these conclusions with the rich complexity of actual situations that involve full-dimensional people, let alone the job of thinking through the social consequences or ethical aspects of the conclusions, remains outside the case-dialogue method. Issues such as the social needs or matters of justice involved in cases do get attention in some case-dialogue classrooms, but these issues are almost always treated as addenda. (Sullivan et al. 2012, p. 6)

For the purpose of this book, we can substitute "social needs or matters of justice" for "the role that law and lawyers play within organizations" or "legal management". Although there are some relevant differences between different countries and legal traditions,[5] as well as some interesting exceptions and initiatives,[6] legal management normally plays no or just a negligible role in the curriculum of law schools. Even most of the students who specifically want to pursue a career as in-house counsel will therefore leave law school without in-depth knowledge of legal management. It is noteworthy that legal education has changed relatively little over the past decades, while legal practice has seen some important changes. For the purposes of this book, the most important change is the power shift from law firms to in-house counsel that some call the most important change in the legal profession in the last decades.[7]

Attention for legal management is scarce not only in legal education, but also in legal research. The majority of legal scholars conducts research on substantive legal

---

[5]An important difference is that in Anglo-Saxon systems, law is often a graduate study, while in continental systems t is also an undergraduate study.

[6]Since the 1970s, the University of Denver offers the Master of Science in Legal Administration. Other universities are, partly in response to the Carnegie report and following debate, starting to offer courses in legal management. For example, Columbia University offers the course "Navigating the Challenges Faced by In-House Counsel". The author of this article has led the project to set up the post-experience master's program Legal Management at the Amsterdam University of Applied Sciences, running since 2012.

[7]See Simmons and Dinnage (2011), p. 79.

matters. Although the number of studies and publications on legal management and related subjects is growing, it is still relatively low. The upsurge in interest in empirical legal studies[8] is a promising development in this respect. Outside the academic arena, consultancy firms and law firms are doing some empirical work on legal management. However, this type of research is less objective than academic research, and the resources are usually limited. A substantial increase in independent academic research is therefore desirable, especially now that technology can be expected to change legal practice in important ways. Independent research would provide practitioners with valuable and reliable insights and would also strengthen research into substantive legal matters. As any in-house counsel knows, there can be great differences between the intended goals of legislation and regulation and the way these work out in practice. Research into "corporate legal management" will contribute to identifying important discrepancies between theory and practice. To conduct research in the field of legal management, the abundance of General Counsel networks around the globe is a good starting point. One could say that these networks, often very active, underline the desire that professionals have for knowledge on "evidence-based legal management".

The above is not intended as "law school bashing". Traditional legal education and substantive legal research are valuable and essential to the legal profession. Change is hard in any organization, and law schools filled with strong-headed academics who cultivate valuable traditions are probably among the toughest environments. As the Carnegie report puts it:

Law school curriculum reform is a tedious and often frustrating task and seems to work best when modest changes are made at the margin by adding one or two additional courses.

Still, no matter how difficult, it would be wise to make some more fundamental changes in law school curricula. Training students to be critical legal thinkers will always be the basis of any law school curriculum, but this curriculum should be supplemented, more than in the current situation, with elements that are not "strictly legal", such as ethics, societal impact of the law and legal management. It goes without saying that law schools can only provide a basis for work in legal practice. Every knowledge-intensive profession requires ample "learning on the job", but law schools should strive to provide students with a strong and all-round foundation, as the influence of education on professional culture is profound. It is possible, and in some respects: plausible, that the side effects of "typical legal education" account for part of the standard criticism of legal professionals: too reactive, case-oriented, sometimes too risk-averse and with too little attention for managerial aspects. In-house counsel now have to acquire the knowledge and skills needed for a proactive, integrative and business-wise approach to legal management after they leave law school.

---

[8]See, for example, the website of the Society for Empirical Legal Studies, Cornell University, founded in 2006, at http://www.lawschool.cornell.edu/SELS/index.cfm

7   The Rise of the Legal Department

Over the past decades, there has been a shift in power from law firms to in-house counsel and legal departments. In many western countries, in-house counsel had strong positions at the beginning of the twentieth century. Over the course of the twentieth century, the modern law firm emerged, growing in size and strength and able to attract the brightest young minds. Simultaneously, the position of in-house counsel weakened, and companies increasingly turned to outside law firms for important legal issues. Starting around the 1980s, globalization, a long list of corporate scandals, increased regulation and growing attention for legal risk management strengthened the role of in-house counsel again. Legal departments have since grown in size and are professionalizing their management. This development, together with the economic crisis and the resulting need to cut costs on legal spend, has weakened the position of law firms that in the decades before had seen continuous growth in both size and profits.

To put things into perspective, it is important to realize that the vast majority of businesses does not have a legal department. Small businesses only hire legal counsel when confronted with specific legal issues. Medium-sized businesses usually rely on outside counsel to provide them with legal expertise. It is only when an organization has reached considerable size and complexity that it becomes an economically sound decision to set up an in-house legal department. Organizations involved in activities that bear particularly complex legal aspects will reach this point sooner, others later. Even in modern economies, it is not uncommon for businesses to have several hundred employees and no in-house counsel.[9] From this, it follows logically that organizations that have a sizeable legal department will be large and complex and/or operate in a complex legal environment.

There are many factors that influence the size of a legal department, such as whether or not the company is publicly traded, its corporate culture and how well the legal department is managed. The amount of regulation and the nature of the sector are crucial factors. Organizations in the financial sector or oil and gas companies will have considerably larger legal departments than a retail company that sells relatively straight forward fast moving consumer goods. The world's largest legal departments comprise several hundred to over a thousand in-house counsel. These are exceptions, as most legal departments are relatively small. For some of its working groups, the Association for Corporate Counsel rates a legal department as big if it has over 40 in-house counsel. Generally, in Western countries, the number of large law firms exceeds the number of large in-house

---

[9]However, in many countries the corporate secretary will often, yet not necessarily, have a legal background.

legal departments, and the total number of in-house counsel will be relatively small, compared to that of legal professionals working for law firms.[10]

8 Profit or Cost Center?

The reason why organizations usually do not have large (legal) departments is simple: they cost money. A legal department performs a support function within the business and does not generate direct revenue. From around 2005, there has been some debate on transforming legal departments into profit centers, referring to the recovery programs initiated by, inter alia, the legal departments of DuPont, Tyco and Michelin.[11] In these programs, legal departments pursued actions against insurers, infringers of their intellectual property rights, suppliers acting in violation of competition law and partners that failed to honor their contractual obligations. These programs sometimes brought in more than the entire legal budget. Exercised with prudence, recovery programs can be a sensible and recommendable initiative. However, exercised too rigidly, recovery programs can harm business relations, for example if dubious claims are also being pursued. Furthermore, some successful programs may have resulted primarily from "deferred legal maintenance". Finally, not every organization will lend itself to a successful recovery program. Normally, a legal department may save money, but not make money.

9 Future Growth

The size of legal departments can be expected to grow in the coming years, partially because of the autonomous growth of legal work within large organizations, and partially because they may insource more work that they previously outsourced. However, there will be a natural limit to this growth. A larger department offers in-house counsel the possibility to specialize in different subjects, but there will always be work that does not come around often enough to justify specialization. Although legal departments may not grow much larger, to the detriment of law firms, this does not mean that the relationship between them will not continue to change. Legal departments are increasing their demands on law firms, and procurement of legal services by outside counsel is likely to professionalize further in the near future. Recent years have seen legal departments sometimes making drastic choices in panel management. The market in which law firms operate can be expected to become even more competitive, but it is not likely that we will see

---

[10]In a project by the research program Legal Management of the Amsterdam University of Applied Sciences, Dutch legal practice was charted (www.atlasrechtspraktijk.nl). In the Netherlands, there are approximately 4–5.000 legal professionals working for in-house legal departments, compared to about 18–19,000 legal professionals working for law firms.

[11]See http://www.reedsmith.com/Recoveries-Can-Turn-Legal-Departments-Into-Profit-Centers-09-04-2013/

"the end of the law firm" in the near future. Outsourcing work to law firms will continue to have inherent benefits, providing a more objective view that will often be demanded by organizational stakeholders when it comes to important decisions. Also, most companies will have a natural tendency to prefer a percentage of variable costs (outside counsel) over fixed costs (in-house counsel), making it easier to cut back in costs when necessary.

From the above follows the challenge that legal departments face. With limited resources, they have to support large and complex organizations in optimizing the legal function. As a complicating factor, law schools have not prepared in-house counsel optimally for this task, and research into this subject is relatively scarce. The organizations they serve will regard the legal department as a cost center—and not as a profit center—that provides services that are difficult to evaluate on efficacy and quality by outsiders and are sometimes seen as hindering business. A manager of a legal department will ask the question: "How do we continuously convince the organization of our added value, while it is hard for other departments to completely understand what we do and what the quality of our services is, but easy to see what we cost?" To successfully take on this challenge, a shared view of the legal function and a legal department's strategy will be essential. Consistently communicating this view will reduce the information asymmetry that inevitably, by the nature of the services rendered, exists between the legal department and other organizational constituents.

10 An Organization's Legal Function

A legal department's task is to support a business in reaching its objectives, by maximizing the legal upside of an organization's activities and minimizing the legal downside, or: "optimizing the organization's legal function". An organization's legal function involves *all* legal aspects, connected to *all* its activities and is performed by many organizational constituents. Ultimately, general management will be responsible for managing the legal function, but a legal department obviously plays an essential role, together with a compliance department and possibly a department for contract management or corporate social responsibility. From here on, we will refer to all departments that have specialized legal expertise as the (extended) legal department.

Some of the most important aspects of the legal function are:

10.1 Contracts

As a rule, every large organization juggles a dazzling amount of contracts, and their variety and the number of employees involved in negotiating and executing those contracts are equally dazzling. Sales, procurement, human resources and research and development and all other business units and departments will all have their own contracting needs. Contracts are the strings in the complex legal web of employees, suppliers, contractors, consultants, temporary workers, service providers, outsourcers, brokers, intermediaries and agents of which modern organizations are made. Hence, controlling the life cycles of all contracts in an organization is extremely complex and will involve many different processes. The responsibility for contract-related processes will always be distributed across several departments, requiring effective coordination between the legal department, contract management and other departments involved. A reactive legal department may feel responsible only for the legal quality of a contract on which it has been asked to advise. As contracts are one of the primary sources of both legal risk and legal opportunity, a proactive legal department should play an active and initiating role in continuously improving the organizations contracting and contract management processes.

10.2 Compliance

As mentioned above, the amount of legislation and regulation that an organization has to comply with depends on its size, legal structure and the nature of an organization's activities. Generally, most large organizations experience the amount of regulation with which they have to comply as ever increasing. Non-compliance with legal norms accounts for some of the largest corporate scandals in recent years, with the Volkswagen emissions scandal as the most recent addition to this long list. It is therefore not surprising that legal professionals consider legislative and regulatory issues one of the most concerning factors. Again, responsibility for this part of the legal function will be distributed across several departments. Both operations, compliance and legal play vital roles. As with contracts and contract management, compliance demands a lot of organizational discipline and has complex managerial aspects. Compliance is, of course, not limited to external legal norms. Internal rules and corporate social responsibility policies that an organization strives to uphold are equally important.

10.3 Protecting Assets

The law provides various instruments that an organization can deploy to protect its assets. Choosing a specific organizational legal structure may transfer risk and protect the parent organization from the possible losses and liability of a subsidiary. Another example is the protection of an organization's ideas and inventions through the use of intellectual property rights.

10.4 Preventing Liability

The legal function also encompasses the general prevention of liability for possible torts by the organization. Torts may vary from inadvertently violating a competitor's intellectual property rights or causing environmental pollution to not responding adequately to a claim by an employee that has been sexually harassed by a manager. As Bagley and Savage[12] advise, an organization's management should implement an ongoing educational program and monitoring aimed at reducing the risks of tort liability. The contents of such program should depend on the organization's specific activities and the possible risks that these activities present. A legal department should play a proactive and advisory role with regard to such programs.

10.5 Promoting Organizational Integrity

Last but not least, promoting organizational integrity is an important aspect of the legal function. It may be unwise or unethical to pursue certain initiatives, even if not prohibited by clear rules. All departments should continuously strive to act in an ethical manner, but the connection between law, legal norms and ethics clearly shows that a legal department has a special task in ensuring that the organization maintains ethical standards.

11   Legal Opportunity and Legal Risk

Any events that occur on aspects of the legal function listed above will have positive or negative effects on organizational objectives. Positive effects may be labeled legal opportunity, while negative effects may be labeled legal risk. In practice, a large part of managing the legal function will consist of managing legal risks: preventing negative effects. Events may also lead to disputes between the organization and third parties or employees. Handling disputes and conflicts could be regarded as managing legal risk. A dispute is not in itself a legal risk, as the risk is found in the underlying root cause of the dispute, but could be regarded as a risk that will possibly materialize. Of course, a legal risk that becomes reality will materialize in consequences that are not of a legal nature, such as financial or reputational damage. Theoretically, it is hard to give an exact definition of legal risk. Instead of spending time and effort defining its exact scope in an abstract way, a more sensible approach would be to regard it as one of many meaningful perspectives on risk that should be operationalized in practice (see Mahler 2007).

Although a great deal of a legal department's daily activities consist of managing legal risks, there are also many situations where there is no or little legal risk, and in-house counsel will primarily assist in using the law and legal means to achieve positive effects: seizing legal opportunity. An example would be if research showed that the organization is eligible for a government subsidy for a business venture it would have undertaken anyhow. Figure 1 shows the basic elements of managing the legal function.

---

[12]Bagley and Savage (2009).

Management of the legal function

Fig. 1 Elements of managing the legal function

12 Recipes for Success?

Organizational performance and management are complex subjects to research. The same goes for managing the legal function. In the everyday life of organizations, a million factors continuously interact. Isolating factors and measuring their impact on (parts of) the performance of organizations is extremely difficult. Many management books and gurus promise simple recipes for success, sometimes marketed with claims that research has proven their effectiveness. In reality, there is little hard evidence on "what really works" with regard to organizational performance. A lot of management research that does claim to have found simple recipes for success can be questioned methodologically. Few describe the flaws of a substantial amount of management and business research better than Phil Rosenzweig in *"The Halo Effect, or how managers let themselves be deceived"*.[13]

Rosenzweig's central point is that a lot of business research is "pseudoscience" because it uses material of a subjective nature as a basis, such as articles from newspapers, popular business journals and interviews with managers and professionals. In essence, these sources are all subjective and susceptible to the halo effect. The halo effect is a cognitive bias in which an observer's overall impression of an entity influences the observer's feelings and thoughts about that entity's character or properties. With regard to businesses, this will mean that an observer judges all or many aspects of an organization as good, or even excellent, because the organization's overall results are good. In reality, organizations will

---

[13]Rosenzweig (2007).

often have good overall results *in spite of* flawed strategies or policies on aspects. If the input for a study is contaminated by the halo effect, it does not matter how impressive and sophisticated the analytical methods are used to analyze.

Rosenzweig gives many examples where successful companies are described as having an excellent strategy or HR policy 1 year, while the unchanged strategy or policy is fiercely criticized the next year, only because overall results have changed. The impact of the halo effect is profound and happens subconsciously. Even some of the most famous books and articles on management suffer from the defect that Rosenzweig illuminates.

Apart from using a "garbage in-garbage out" methodology, management books and business research can also cloak a limited understanding by using vague and ambiguous terms. Rosenzweig quotes physicist Richard Feynman, stating that many fields have a tendency for pomposity, dressing up issues that are not fully understood with complicated-sounding terms. With regard to a particular philosopher, Feynman remarked:

> It isn't the philosophy that gets me, it's the pomposity. If they'd just laugh at themselves! If they'd just say, "I think it's like this, but Von Leipzig thought it was like that, and he had a good shot at it, too.

Business and management science too seldom demonstrate the relativization that Feynman recommends here, and no field, legal management being no exception, is immune to pomposity. It is good practice to always keep this lesson in mind, especially when reading publications and research that also serve marketing purposes.

13   Systematic and Data-Driven

So, what *does* really work in (legal) management? As Rosenzweig remarks: "nothing works all the time". Effective management is dependent on the context of organizations and managers should adjust their practices and decisions to fit this context. Simple recipes for success do not exist. It is perfectly fine to simply try a new policy and see if it has effect. However, systematic management will require setting specific goals before implementing a new policy, and systematically measuring and evaluating its effectiveness. Experts will agree that generally there are basic "common sense conditions" that have to be fulfilled before there can be effective and systematic management of any organizational function. One of the most important conditions will be that an organizational function cannot be properly managed when there is no clear view and understanding of its components. Management is, for a large part, the art of directing limited resources to where they are most effective and beneficial. If there is an incomplete view and only partial information, this cannot be done in any sensible manner. These preconditions could be summarized as the need for good management to be systematic and, at least to a certain extent, data-driven. With regard to legal management, a legal department cannot sensibly prioritize legal risks and opportunities if it does not have a clear view of the organization's activities and the connected legal aspects. As mentioned before, in-house counsel are sometimes accused of having a too reactive stance, responding only when problems have already arisen. The approach that the preventive and proactive law movements advocate to counter this tendency will always require legal departments to have an overview of the organization's legal function.

In-house counsel will not happily admit that they lack a clear view. However, it is not uncommon to find that a legal department does not have a clear idea of what activities are undertaken by a certain department or subsidiary, even if it is plausible that it may perform activities that present considerable legal risk. Not having a clear idea is one thing and can be pardoned if the department has limited capacity. However, not *wanting* or *striving* to know what is going on within the organization is unacceptable. This may be a somewhat understandable survival tactic for an understaffed department ("we did not know and they did not come to us for advice, so we cannot be held responsible"), but it is not optimal management of the legal function. Effective legal management is directing the legal analytical power and good judgment that the in-house counsel of a legal department have to offer to where it is needed most. Hence, being able to perform a basic assessment of the most important legal risks and opportunities is a precondition for effective legal management. To achieve this, a legal department should constantly be communicating with other departments and business units, analyzing possible gaps between current and desired situations.

14   Visualizing the Legal Function

To facilitate communication within the legal department and explain the role of the legal department to other business units, it is useful to create a visualization of the legal function. As Haapio and Barton convincingly explain in this book, visualizations can be a powerful communication tool. There are many ways to visualize an organization's legal function. It will be a good idea to attune the visualization to (risk) management methodologies already in place within the organization. Another option would be to simply use the organizational chart as a starting point. The picture below uses a generic model for visualizing the legal function, based on Michael Porter's classical model of the value chain. Every element of the value chain is linked to a set of questions about basic legal aspects. If a legal department were to start from scratch, these questions could be the basis for a first "legal inventory". Depending on the answers and the context of the organization, relevant legal risks and opportunities should then be assessed and priorities set (Fig. 2).

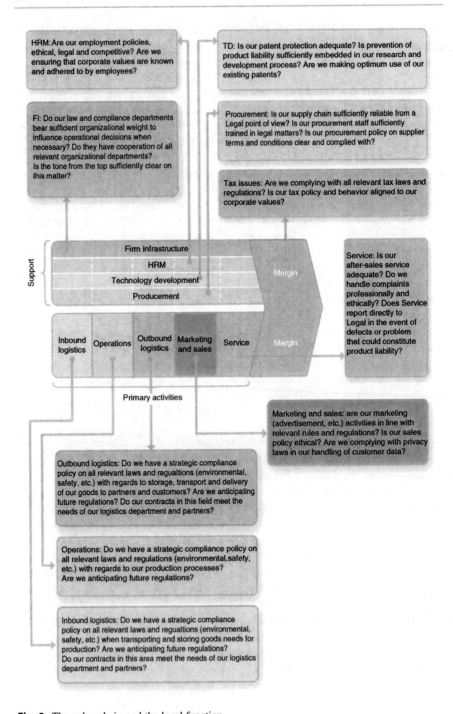

Fig. 2 The value chain and the legal function

15   Legal Dashboard

The visualization of the legal function can be a starting point for configuring a legal dashboard. The term legal dashboard is used in a broad sense here: a support tool for legal management that grants insight into key aspects of the legal function through performance metrics for which data is periodically collected, thus providing a dynamic view on the legal function. Most legal departments will have some performance metrics in place, at least on internal headcount and on legal spend. However, various surveys (cf. Blickstein 2015) indicate that most legal departments still have a long way to go in professionalizing their legal management in other areas. Configuring a legal dashboard that does not only focus on costs, but also on performance metrics that improve legal quality and thus enhance the legal function, is a first step towards professionalizing legal management. A dashboard can become more balanced and refined as management of the legal function professionalizes further. A basic legal dashboard should at least incorporate core legal issues: issues that are critical to mission and strategy of the organization. If Volkswagen were to set up a legal dashboard now, they would surely have to incorporate targets on complying with emission standards. For a research organization, non-disclosure agreements on a particular new product could be a core issue, for which a 100 % target may be desirable. For a financial institution, training all staff on new regulations may be essential. Once all core issues have been covered, the dashboard may be expanded to other areas.

Information and data for the dashboard may be collected from a variety of systems, such as HR systems, procurement and contract databases. With the continuing digitalization of organizations, the possibilities of collecting important data without much effort will continue to grow in the coming years. Big data and preventive e-discovery techniques open up possibilities to use unstructured data as input. Although objective data and performance indicators are essential elements of a legal dashboard, it is important to remain vigilant about whether they are truly representative of the actual state of the legal function and do not have unintended side-effects. Performance indicators always bear a risk of acting as so-called "perverse incentives": producing results that are contrary to the intentions behind the indicator. Under French colonial rule, a bounty was introduced for rat tails in Vietnam, which did not lead to the extermination of rats, but to people breeding rats. In the context of a legal department, a performance indicator rewarding fast handling of claims could lead to a reduction in legal quality, or unwanted settlements.

A critical approach is also important because performance indicators, even if not acting as perverse incentives, can have a ritualizing effect and create the illusion of being in control. The most important advantage of a legal dashboard is not insight into the state of the legal function that it offers, however valuable. The biggest plus is the constant communication within the legal department and between the legal department and other departments necessary to keep the dashboard up to date. This communication enables the legal department to be truly proactive, anticipate changes in strategy and external developments, and constantly attune its services to the needs of the organization. Quality management within organizations sometimes has a tendency to develop into "tick-box exercises". The founding father of quality management, William Edwards Deming, would have been horrified, as he always stressed the importance of cooperation and collaboration as the most important precondition for true quality to emerge.

16   Conclusion

To conclude, a professional legal department should configure some form of legal dashboard as a tool to optimize legal management. A dashboard is a symptom, rather than the cause of good legal management. It is important to remember that a dashboard is never more than a tool. Zen Buddhists say that it is the fool who mistakes the finger pointing at the moon for the moon itself. Similarly, a legal dashboard only points towards the state of the legal function and is not the state of the legal function itself. However, if used systematically and over longer periods of time, a dashboard will provide insight into the development of the legal function that will enable a legal department to effectively communicate its added value and improvements in the state of the legal function. A dashboard will promote consistent communication with other departments and thus reduce the information asymmetry that is inherent to providing legal services. Professional legal management makes most of limited resources, by prioritizing proactively and systematically, rather than simply responding to the organization's requests. Ultimately, this will lead to greater customer satisfaction, with the ultimate customer being the organization itself.

Liquid Legal Context
By Dr. Dierk Schindler, Dr. Roger Strathausen, Kai Jacob

Introducing his article, Timmer puts his finger on a hot spot in the world of legal management: the conflict between legal craftsmanship, i.e. the ability to appreciate differences between individual cases, and "management", which is loaded with associations of Fordism and Taylorism, standardization and efficiency. The two seem to be pointing to a very different mindset and approach, which according to Timmer may explain the, often tacit, resistance that legal professionals feel when it comes to legal management.

However, hiding behind the legal craftsmanship will inevitably lead to upholding the "black box" that exists around legal services for the rest of the organization. Is this tendency based on pure unwillingness or even fear on the part of the legal organization? Timmer leads us to a different answer: it is the lack of building out the competencies. Lawyers are not trained to be legal managers, it is simply neither part of the university curriculum nor at the center of legal research.

(continued)

Well, if Legal is mainly a cost center, a cost of doing business that large and complex organizations (have to) accept, while the vast majority of SME's tend to go without (or with a minimally staffed) legal department, why then the effort to go beyond cost management? Timmer, like many other authors, rightfully points to the fact that taking a holistic view to a modern legal function reveals that legal is not just about managing risk (and the cost for doing that), but also about exploiting opportunity.

So, is then not the simple answer to pull out the management books and adopt some standard practices that have long been researched and described? Timmer takes side with Phil Rosenzweig who fundamentally questions a lot of business research as "pseudoscience", as it uses material of a subjective nature as a basis and is therefore exposed to the "halo-effect". This means that an observer tends to assess most aspects of an organization as good, just because the organization's overall results are good, while in reality, organizations will often have good overall results in spite of flawed strategies or policies on certain aspects of it.

Timmer recommends a well-founded model that combines monitoring "common sense conditions" (i.e. what needs to be in place for any organization) with what is needed to communicate the basics on legal risk and opportunity. In terms of structuring the dashboard, the author recommends to visualize the function by showing where and how it correlates with other departments. Configuring a legal dashboard that does not only focus on cost, but also on performance metrics geared to improve legal quality and thus to enhance the legal function, is a first step. The dashboard can become more balanced and refined as management of the legal function professionalizes further.

References

Bagley, C. E., & Savage, D. W. (2009). *Managers and the legal environment, strategies for the 21st century*. Boston MA [bei Bagley].

Blickstein. (2015). Blickstein Group, in cooperation with Huron legal. *Findings from the 8th Annual Law Department Operations Survey*, December 2015, http://blicksteingroup.com/wp-content/uploads/2015/11/LDO-Survey-Supplement-Dec-2015.pdf

KPMG. (2014). Over the horizon: How corporate counsel are crossing frontiers to address new challenges.

Mahler, T. (2007). *Defining legal risk*. Paper presented at the conference "Commercial Contracting for Strategic Advantage – Potentials and Prospects", Turku University of Applied Sciences 2007, pp. 10–31. Available at: http://papers.ssrn.com/sol3/papers.cfm?abstract_id=1014364

Rosenzweig, P. (2007). *The halo effect: How managers let themselves be deceived* (1st ed.). New York: Free Press.

RSG/BLP. (2012). RSG Consulting/Berwin Leighton Paisner, Managing legal risk effectively – an evolving approach, A collection of insights from General Counsel.

Simmons, O. S., & Dinnage, J. D. (2011). Innkeepers: A unifying theory of the in-house counsel role. *Seton Hall Law Review, 41*, 79.

Sullivan, W. M., Anne, C., Wegner, J. W., Bond, L., & Shulman, L. S. (2012). Carnegie Foundation for the Advancement of Teaching. In W. M. Sullivan, et al. (Eds.) *Educating lawyers, preparation for the profession of law*. San Francisco.

Veld, P., & Voigt, S. (2003). *Economic growth and judicial independence: Cross country evidence using a new set of indicators* (Working Paper No. 906). Munich: Center for Economic Studies.

Ivar Timmer is an associate professor at the Amsterdam Research Center for Societal Innovation (ARISI), part of the Amsterdam University of Applied Sciences (AUAS). He has been the project leader for the development of the master (LLM) and research program in Legal Management that the ARISI hosts (since 2012). He has previously worked as an in-house counsel and has experience as lecturer in contract law and administrative law. His research focuses on legal risk management and legal process management. He is the co-author of two books (in Dutch) on legal management and legal project management, as well as two books on the law of contracts and torts. He is currently conducting a PhD research on legal risk management.

Building a Legal Department in a Metrics-Driven World: A Guide to Finding the Best Candidates for the Legal Departments of the Future

W. Jon Escher

Abstract

In-house legal departments will continue to experience pressure to meet or exceed performance standards across the full spectrum of the legal services they provide. This can only be accomplished if legal managers and their HR colleagues can identify and recruit high quality lawyers who will succeed in a metrics-driven environment. Traditional reliance on academic credentials and "brand name" law firm training is insufficient. Companies will need to develop tools to identify candidates with business literacy, efficient work habits, business-friendly communication skills, well developed risk assessment analytics, and practical judgment. Identifying such candidates requires a combination of new screening techniques and a substantially better use of the traditional interview process. Hiring mistakes are costly, time consuming, and damaging to a legal department's reputation within the company. Fortunately, several resources are at hand, from psycho-metric testing to effective interview engagements, that greatly enhance the prospects of successful recruiting.

Legal departments around the world are busy creating, implementing and refining performance evaluation models to better assess how their legal departments are satisfying client demand and advancing the business objectives of their companies. At the root of this effort is the basic concept of *measurement*. Companies are utilizing quantifiable performance ratings to evaluate the effectiveness of the legal function. From meeting budgets, managing work-flow, and providing responsive services to improving cross-functional communication and harnessing efficiencies from outside counsel, legal departments all over the world are turning to metrics, metrics, and more metrics.

W.J. Escher (✉)
Solutus Legal Search, Redwood City, CA, USA
e-mail: jon@solutuslegal.com

© Springer International Publishing AG 2017
K. Jacob et al. (eds.), *Liquid Legal*, Management for Professionals,
DOI 10.1007/978-3-319-45868-7_23

This development raises the question as to whether general counsels and hiring managers should change the way they evaluate candidates for open positions in their legal departments. Is the traditional method of relying on a standard resume, the in-person interview, and pro-forma post-interview reference checks an adequate way to evaluate whether or not a candidate possesses those attributes that will succeed in a metrics-driven environment? Put another way, is the traditional candidate vetting process in alignment with the methods now being used to measure the overall effectiveness of the legal department? After all, no legal department can succeed in a metrics-driven world if the lawyers who comprise it are themselves improperly vetted on the very criteria the department itself will be measured against.

1 The Traditional Vetting Process

For decades most in-house legal departments have relied on a three-pronged vetting system: (1) evaluation of the candidate's credentials and experience as revealed on the resume to assess advanced reasoning aptitude and substantive skill set compatibility; (2) the in-person interview to assess cultural fit; and (3) the pro-forma post-interview reference check to make sure there is nothing glaringly wrong with the candidate that the first two parts of the system failed to reveal.

Within these three prongs, most hiring managers placed significant emphasis on only a couple of key components. As for the resume, the single most important factor has always been academic credentials. Sometimes to an exclusionary degree, but always to a significant degree, employers relied on the prestige of the candidate's law school and his performance within the law school to assess general levels of intelligence and advanced legal reasoning. The more prestigious the better, and the higher the class rank the better. Such credentials served as certification of the candidates' ability to navigate complex legal issues and also to excel at legal writing and drafting. In short, the credentials established the candidates' high quality lawyering skills.

The credentials could be augmented by a work experience (including the reputation and prestige of previous employers) that confirmed the above assessment, or the work experience could dilute the value of the credential in certain rare cases. More often the traditional system looked at work experience in a purely utilitarian light. Is the experience relevant to the type of work that the candidate would perform at the company? If it is and the credentials are strong, then the evaluation of the resume often would come to a quick end.

Once the candidate cleared the credential and work experience hurdles, the in-person interview was primarily used for two purposes. First, to gently probe the quality of the candidate's lawyering skills to confirm the positive assessment. Second, and more importantly, to determine if the candidate's personality would fit with the company's culture. Under the traditional method, this was a necessarily vague and subjective assessment which all too often boiled down to whether or not the general counsel or hiring manager felt "comfortable" with the candidate. Whenever such an assessment is made without reference to some defined criteria, many people do the natural thing: they find themselves more "comfortable" with a candidate who is most like themselves. Hiring in one's own image is among the most common results of the traditional vetting process.

Finally, the traditional method would use the post-interview reference check in a fairly perfunctory way to basically (and briefly) allow the reference to confirm the Hiring Manager's positive view of the candidate. Many companies traditionally do not even initiate the reference checking process until they have made an offer, making the offer conditional on the positive reference. Given that it is the candidates themselves who provide the references, a negative reference is extremely unlikely. In fact, in the over 25 years of my experience in the legal search business and the thousands of placements made during that period, I can only recall one instance where an offer was rescinded as a result of a negative reference. In short, as traditionally used, the post-interview reference check is a pro-forma waste of time.

Given the limitations of the traditional method, it is hardly surprising that some companies are moving to a different system utilizing different tools to assess potential candidates. Also not surprisingly, many of these tools are beginning to incorporate the very metrics that now help to define a legal department's success. In short, companies are now beginning to *measure* the suitability of potential candidates.

2 What to Measure

The Association of Corporate Counsel ("ACC") provides on their website a sample Legal Department Client Satisfaction Survey. While every company would want to customize their own survey, the ACC survey does an excellent job of setting forth those categories of legal department performance that are of critical importance to the client. The survey then asks the client to rate the legal department on a numeric scale in each category. Our own experience as legal search consultants confirms that the categories identified by ACC are the ones emphasized over and over again by our corporate clients. What are the categories that legal departments will be judged on?

1. *Aptitude and Drafting Skills.* This is the bread and butter of lawyering. Clients look to their lawyers to have the ability to provide, in essence, the correct legal answer to a wide variety of problems that arise in the business. Lawyers must be capable of advanced legal reasoning, they must know the law, and, because so many in-house positions are transactional in nature, clients look to lawyers to effectively memorialize business agreements. By "effectively" the clients mean that the lawyers will draft agreements that accurately reflect the business understanding while, at the same time, shielding the company from undue risk,

ambiguity, and misunderstanding. The ability of lawyers to deliver the core competencies of lawyering is a primary criterion that clients will assess, and one the lawyers themselves often believe that clients are not necessarily qualified to measure.

2. *Risk Assessment and Business Literacy.* One recurring concern that clients often express is that their in-house lawyers are not "business savvy" enough and do not place their legal analysis within a larger business context, which would help the client to appropriately assess various risk factors. The ACC Client Survey poses this question in multiple ways, including asking the client to rate the lawyers on the following proposition: "Demonstrating commitment to helping me find a way to achieve my business objectives instead of just saying -no-." Of course, it is not possible for lawyers to score well in this category unless they have a deep understanding of the business itself. In turn, it is not possible for lawyers to possess such an understanding unless they are familiar with basic business and accounting concepts. Clients will measure a lawyer's aptitude in this area.

3. *Communication Skills.* Every in-house client survey I have ever reviewed contains multiple questions concerning a lawyer's ability to effectively communicate within the company. This means being able to explain complex legal concepts in terms that non-lawyers can understand. It also means being honest, straight-forward and candid with clients. Lawyers will be judged on their ability to effectively communicate in three basic settings: the group meeting, one-on-one meetings, and brief written summaries. High competency in aptitude and risk assessment/legal writing skills will be wasted if the lawyer is unable to communicate to the client in ways the client can understand.

4. *Responsiveness/Time Management.* Time and again, clients will emphasize the importance of a lawyer's responsiveness, which is another way of saying that they value lawyers who can effectively manage their time and prioritize their work in a way so that the client receives the advice and counsel they need in a timely manner. The threshold requirement is one of accessibility. Lawyers cannot be responsive to clients if they are not accessible. But it also means that lawyers must effectively manage clients' expectations. Over-promising and under-delivering in terms of responsiveness will result in a low rating.

5. *Cost Containment and Managing Outside Counsel.* Legal services are expensive, and lawyers are increasingly held accountable for containing the cost of these services. Of all the categories which are subject to numeric rating, this is perhaps the easiest to measure. There is a budget, and the lawyers will be held accountable for meeting it. The single biggest variable in doing so is the cost of outside counsel. In order to succeed in the in-house setting, lawyers must be able to take advantage of the expertise outside counsel provides while staying within budget. How they do this is not typically visible to the in-house client. But whether or not they do it is painfully obvious. Bottom lines simply don't lie.

6. *Collaboration and Teamwork.* This category is perhaps the most subjective of all, and it is the one that typically produces asymmetrical results on client surveys. But it remains one of the most critical. Some constituencies within a company might think a lawyer is collaborative and an effective teammate.

Others quite simply may find it hard to get along with a particular lawyer (and vice versa!). Nevertheless, this criterion looms large in the minds of the clients and is a prominent feature of any assessment.

So then, the question arises, how does one measure potential candidates' ability to achieve a high score on client surveys once they become an integrated member of an in-house legal team?

3 How to Measure

A cursory review of the above criteria demonstrates the traditional three-pronged method of vetting potential candidates is seriously insufficient. Can a resume, an in-person interview, and a perfunctory reference check provide sufficient insight into a candidate's ability in all of these categories, or even some of them? Let's review the measuring tools we have at hand (in the order in which they should be used) to improve the vetting process.

3.1 The Resume

Every evaluation of a potential candidate begins with a review of the resume (we will assume for purposes of this chapter that the resume describes a skill set that is relevant to the open position). And, while limited in its utility, the resume remains the single most (although not exclusive) tool for measuring one aspect of aptitude: advanced legal reasoning. The experience of most general counsels and hiring managers is that academic credentials and law school performance are reasonably reliable indicators of high achievement in the area of advanced legal reasoning. A good law school and strong performance within law school generally correlate to the ability to navigate complex legal concepts and wed them to complex fact patterns to arrive at sound legal results. After all, in order to achieve these credentials, candidates have already gone through a battery of advanced reasoning tests to be admitted to law school and to perform well once they are there.

However, the resume is a poor measuring device to assess almost every other attribute that will be important to achieving success in a legal department. Many general counsels are tempted to also assume that, if the candidate's early career has been spent at a top-flight law firm, s/he will necessarily have acquired the training to become an adept drafter of contracts and other legal documents. Unfortunately, the correlation between high prestige law firm training and high aptitude for drafting skills is substantially more tenuous than the correlation between advance legal reasoning and academic credentials. As a result, many of our clients now look to a customized writing exercise (discussed below) as better tool for measuring drafting performance.

Many clients are also tempted to look at the work history on a resume and draw conclusions about a candidate's employment stability. Lots of moves tend to be a red flag for many clients, suggesting that the candidate might be a job-hopping malcontent. However, in today's world, there are so many perfectly legitimate reasons for cycling through several positions that drawing such a conclusion from the resume would not be fair to the candidate.

And, of course, with respect to every other attribute that will be measured (risk assessment/business literacy, communication, collaboration, time management, etc.), the resume is practically useless as a vetting tool. Fortunately, there are other tools available to measure these other important qualities.

3.2   The Written Exercise/Drafting Skills

It is important at the outset to distinguish the written exercise from a writing sample. Many clients (although certainly not the majority) do ask candidates to provide a writing sample, typically after the initial interview. This request gives the candidate wide latitude to choose a writing sample that may or may not have been written under a tight deadline, may or may not have been written with the help of others, and may or may not have been edited by a third party. In short, the writing sample may not either be representative of the type of drafting the candidate will be asked to undertake in the company, or even be substantially the candidate's own work product. There is a much better way.

We are seeing a clear trend among our clients to ask candidates to take a written exercise (many still shy away from the word "test"). The exercise can take several forms. Some clients ask the candidates to mark up a draft agreement that the client may have purposefully sprinkled with errors, both substantive and typographical. Other clients present the candidate with a term sheet and ask the candidate to draft an agreement reflective of the terms. Each client can determine what is the best type of exercise to present, but it is important that the exercise be designed to reveal drafting skills of the candidates that are *relevant* to the work they will be asked to perform. Typically, the candidate is given a time deadline in which complete the exercise (often the candidate will be asked to block out a two hour window where the exercise will be emailed to them and they will have to email it back within the two hours).

Our clients who use these written exercises have found them to be hugely valuable vetting tools that are most appropriately administered before the in-person interviews (although potentially after a phone screen). These are so valuable that we also recommend that the clients administer another much briefer written exercise to measure the candidate's ability to write internal communications to non-lawyers explaining a legal concept. This is usually a brief two or three paragraph email the candidate might be asked to write to the head of sales explaining new revenue recognition rules, for example.

3.3   Psycho-Metric Testing: Advanced Reasoning and Personality

These types of tests have been around for a long time and have made very few in-roads into the vetting process of lawyers. Part of the reason may be that the credentials on the resume are usually viewed as sufficient for establishing advanced reasoning capabilities. Another reason is that lawyers are skeptical of personality tests generally and feel they are too generic and easily gamed.

These objections have some force to them but we believe these tests can be helpful in certain circumstances, particularly in those companies where the tests have been found to be useful in vetting candidates for other functions. The personality tests can help identify potential strengths or weaknesses in the area of collaboration and teamwork. The advanced reasoning tests can also help to clarify the nature and scope of a candidate's reasoning abilities, particularly if a candidate possesses less than stellar academic credentials but otherwise appears to have solid and relevant experience. Rather than simply rejecting such a candidate, an advanced reasoning test might prove useful in establishing that candidate's capabilities. Each client will have to determine for itself whether the use of such tests is appropriate, but they should be considered as part of the mix.

3.4 The Interview

Now comes the truly hard part. There is simply no way around the acknowledgement that the interview is the single most important, and single most squandered, tool for vetting candidates. Properly conducted, the interview can shed light on nearly every category of importance. Unfortunately, more often than not, the interview devolves into a rambling exchange of potentially relevant (or not) anecdotes. The interviewer either achieves that level of "comfort" with the candidate or not. More often than not, the main criteria that are so important to the metrics-driven environment in which we operate are barely explored.

Interviewers need to have a plan for each interview. Our own experience teaches us that the interview is particularly valuable as a measuring tool for the following criteria: risk assessment/business literacy; communication skills; responsiveness/time management; cost containment/management of outside counsel; and collaboration and teamwork. Of course, the interview can also probe the issues of advanced reasoning and the candidate's understanding and mastery of relevant legal principles.

Time and space constraints prohibit setting forth a comprehensive list of all the questions that could be asked in an interview to elicit valuable information, but when formulating an approach to the interview, the interviewer might consider alternating between more general questions and more specific ones. In my own experience, I have found that when testing for risk assessment and business literacy, open-ended questions tend to elicit very useful answers. For example, I might ask the candidates to generally describe the business models of the various companies where they have worked. In their answers I look for an understanding of how the products are developed, how they come to market, how they are priced, how they are sold and distributed. In short I'm seeking from the candidate evidence that the candidate understands the business context within which the legal advice is rendered. Similarly, I might ask an open ended question to a candidate who worked on a M&A deal: "Why did your client buy that company?" A surprising number of candidates can struggle with that answer.

Conversely, I have found more specific questions are useful when measuring the criteria of responsiveness/time management and cost containment/management of outside counsel. For example, I might give the candidate a list of three or four projects that could be on their plate and ask them to specifically prioritize their approach and give me an idea of how long they might take to complete each task. I will also ask them to give me hard numbers on the cost of outside counsel for various assignments and what they think is reasonable for outside counsel to charge. Of course, they must demonstrate an understanding of the market for fixed fee arrangements and discounts.

When it comes to communication, there is nothing like the art of listening. A candidate won't be good at communicating if they aren't good at listening (and an interviewer won't be good at measuring a candidate's communication skills if they aren't good at listening either). The threshold issue is this: is the candidate listening to the question and responding to the question that is asked rather than answering some unasked question that the candidate would prefer to answer? If they are on track, then I have found it useful to ask a very direct question: "Pretend I am on the sales team, please describe to me the potential risk to the company if we agree to this indemnity provision (insert an appropriate indemnity clause)." Do they respond clearly, concisely, respectfully and in a manner that a non-lawyer can understand?

It is important to remember that communication within a company takes place in three principal settings: the group meeting; one-on-ones; and written communications. We have already tested for written communication and the interview handles the one-on-one. How about the meeting setting? How can we measure whether a candidate will function effectively in the group meeting with all of its unpredictable conversational flows, protocols, and frustrations! The group interview is the answer. As part of the interview process, many of our clients have found that in addition to one-on-ones, it is valuable to subject the candidate to a group interview to see how they handle over-talk and whether they can be inclusive and respectful when fielding comments or questions they might find irrelevant. Do they interrupt? How do they handle interruption? Can they effectively insert themselves during cross-talk? Will they let people have their say or try to shortcut the conversation? Success in meetings is a key component that informs how the client will evaluate a member of the legal department. The interview process should attempt to partially replicate that setting to see how the candidate manages it.

Collaboration and teamwork are the most difficult criteria to measure. As noted above, psycho-metric personality tests can be potentially useful. The interview can also give you a sense of a candidate's collaborative skills, but it is very unlikely that a candidate will overtly demonstrate bad teamwork tendencies. Since this is such an important criterion, rather than just trust to hope, it is important to turn to third party testimony. This is the one area where the under-used reference check can be very valuable.

3.5 The Reference Check

As noted above, it is important to conduct the reference check at a point in the process where it can be of use, rather than as an afterthought once the offer has been extended. Ideally, in addition to the references that the candidate provides, it is very useful to "back channel" the candidate with others who may have worked with the candidate but who are not on the official reference list. Of course, this can be tricky, and clients must be mindful of keeping a candidacy confidential. But if recourse to an unofficial reference is available and appropriate, it is wise to contact that reference.

Once the list of references is complete, what is the best way of utilizing this resource? Again, it is important to have a plan and prepared questions rather than the open-ended "how was Jane Doe to work with, was she a good colleague?" We have found that the best approach is to ask the reference to cite specific examples of a candidate's performance in each of the relevant categories. For example, "can you give me an example of an instance where Jane Doe ran into some uncooperative colleagues on a particular matter and describe how she navigated to a successful outcome?" "How does she perform in a meeting context, and can you give me an example that illustrates her style of communication within the meeting context?"

3.6 Damning with Faint Praise

The way references answer these questions can be very illuminating. Very rarely will they say anything overtly negative. However, if they can't readily retrieve any examples that illustrate the topic at hand or if they don't seem very interested in even trying, that can be an indicator of a lukewarm feeling about the candidate. Of course, they just may be too busy to invest the time in giving you a substantive answer in which case it is best to move on to another reference. More often, a reference who is not that enthusiastic about a candidate, will heavily qualify their praise of a candidate. A heavily qualified reference is usually a warning sign.

4 Conclusion

We all know that bad hiring decisions are costly, both in economic terms and in the reputational currency of the legal department. Getting it right is probably the single most important responsibility of a general counsel. Good hiring decisions require two things: (1) a thoughtful process that aligns the criteria for selection with the criteria to which the legal department as a whole is subjected; and (2) a core acknowledgement that tools other than the judgment and instincts of the general counsel and/or the hiring manager are required. Establishing such a process takes a bit of doing and a modest investment of time and effort and training. In larger companies, the human resources departments can help in creating customized screening and assessment tools. Many larger companies are also adding legal operations managers who bring consistency and efficiency to the recruiting process.

More and more companies are discovering that once such a recruiting infrastructure is in place, the legal department and the company as a whole will benefit immeasurably.

Liquid Legal Context
By Dr. Dierk Schindler, Dr. Roger Strathausen, Kai Jacob

As we have taken deep dives into creating different, entrepreneurial-minded environments for lawyers (Tumasjan and Welpe), as we have learned about the unstoppable force of change and opportunity that comes with legal tech (e.g. Markfort, Wojcik and Zetterberg, Bues and Matthaei) and as we have learned about the different and new types of roles (Brenton) and skills that are needed, there is a glaring question in front of us: How do we hire against a profile that needs to encompass all of the skills needed to work in this new environment?

Escher taps into the wealth of his experience in advising clients globally in hiring legal talent. He calls an end to the traditional three-pronged approach to hiring: credentials, culture fit, pro-forma reference check. He is brutally honest when he sums up that, too often, we basically look at the lawyering skills plus a gut feel on the culture fit, based on a personal conversation, when we take a hiring decision.

Escher offers a very tangible and practical guide as to "what to measure" in the hiring process. He also adds recommendations on how to do it. Reading his conclusions and recommendations, they are in line with what we can derive from the other articles in terms of skills and mindset required. When technology shaves off the repetitive and standardized part of the jobs in the legal industry, next to technology, talent becomes an even more important asset than ever before. Then, a planful, objective and well developed approach is an obvious key to success.

W. Jon Escher is the Co-Founder of Solutus Legal Search, a premier legal search firm based in California and operating internationally to assist companies and law firms in recruiting top legal talent.

Jon is a graduate of Stanford University and the University of California Hastings College of Law. Jon practiced law in a top Boston law firm and served for 7 years as Assistant General Counsel to Tyco International.

A recognized expert in the legal search field, Jon is a frequent speaker on panels and at law schools throughout the United States.

Business-Friendly Contracting: How Simplification and Visualization Can Help Bring It to Practice

Helena Haapio and Thomas D. Barton

Abstract

One thesis of this book is that the legal function within businesses will shift from a paradigm of security to one of opportunity. This chapter embraces that likelihood in the context of business contracting, where voices calling for a major shift are starting to surface. It explores how contracts can be used to reach better outcomes and relationships, not just safer ones. It introduces the concept of business-friendly contracting, highlighting the need for contracts to be seen as business tools rather than exclusively as legal tools, and working as business enablers rather than obstacles. By changing the design of contracts and the ways in which those contracts are communicated—through simplification and visualization, for example—legal and business operations can be better integrated. Contracts can then be more useful to business, and contract provisions can actually become more secure by becoming easier to negotiate and implement.

1 Introduction

In the hands of the lawyers who traditionally draft contracting documents, the primary goal for contracts is that they be "legal-friendly:" legal formalities should be observed by invoking specialized vocabulary, and legal risks should be allocated

The Authors are grateful to Leila Hamhoum for her editorial assistance.

H. Haapio (✉)
Department of Economics and Business Law, University of Vaasa, Vaasa, Finland

Lexpert Ltd, Helsinki, Finland
e-mail: helena.haapio@lexpert.com

T.D. Barton
California Western School of Law, San Diego, CA, USA
e-mail: tdb@cwsl.edu

© Springer International Publishing AG 2017   371
K. Jacob et al. (eds.), *Liquid Legal*, Management for Professionals,
DOI 10.1007/978-3-319-45868-7_24

clearly between opposing parties. Each lawyer typically seeks to limit liability for his or her client, and to shift business as well as legal risks to the other side.

This chapter describes and urges a different vision: to make contracting "business-friendly." Business-friendly contracting must ensure that the agreement can be legally enforced; but it should do so using language that is comprehensible to everyone involved in forming and implementing the exchange. Furthermore, business-friendly contracting stresses the value-enhancing possibilities of contracting relationships that are collaborative rather than adversarial. Transitioning from legal-friendly to business-friendly contracting can be achieved by practicing long-standing methods of Preventive and Proactive Law ("PPL"), as well as fast-emerging principles of Contract Design. By changing the design as well as the mentality of contracting, legal and business operations can be more strongly linked; hidden value may be revealed; and contracts can become *more* secure even as those new opportunities are explored.

Section 2 below introduces the evolution of traditional contracting into business-friendly contracting by describing the work of the International Association for Contract and Commercial Management (IACCM). IACCM (2015a) summarizes "10 Pitfalls" which characterize traditional contracting (*See also* Hughes 2015). Section 3 then describes how these pitfalls can be transformed into business-friendly contracting through PPL and the emerging tools of Contract Design: simplification, visualization, and collaboration. Section 4 offers examples of using these techniques in corporate practice and in related research. Working together, business and legal can co-create business-friendly documents of many sorts: certainly contracts, but also proposals, disclosures, bylaws, policies, and "How We Work" guides. The PPL/Business-Friendly ideas and methods further the joint ends of opportunity and security through stronger clarity, participation, understanding of underlying strategic significance, and collaboration.

2   Traditional Contracting Versus Business-Friendly Contracting

The chart below depicts the "10 Pitfalls" that IACCM identifies as snaring practitioners into traditional contracting practices. Collectively, the pitfalls reflect what IACCM annual surveys of its members prove: that negotiators all over the world spend much of their time preparing for failure rather than securing success and opportunity.[1] (*See* IACCM 2014a, 2015b; Bergman 2015) Year after year, limitation of liability and indemnification clauses have retained their top positions in the most negotiated contract terms. Yet instead of providing the desired security and certainty, this focus may actually lead to lost opportunity, value erosion, and

---

[1]The most recent Top Negotiated Terms 2015 survey was undertaken by IACCM during May–August 2015, with replies representing more than 10,000 negotiators based in over 100 countries. The respondents reflect primarily large organizations, mostly doing business internationally (IACCM 2015b, pp. 6, 9).

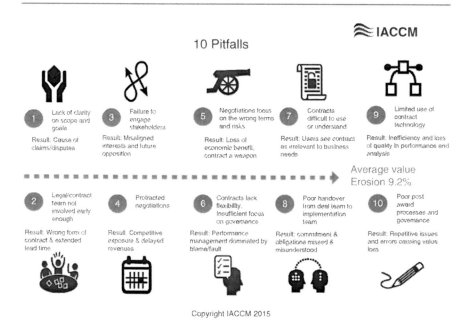

Fig. 1 10 Pitfalls (Cummins 2015). Copyright IACCM 2015. Used with permission

conflict. Time and money are being spent on lengthy negotiations over legal issues, when the focus should be on business issues and how the parties can succeed together—goals that this chapter hopes to further. Figure 1 shows IACCM's description of the 10 Pitfalls.

Noting that the pitfalls lead to average value erosion of over 9 %,[2] IACCM seeks the transformation of each pitfall into a positive "Attribute" of successful contracting. Figure 2 is IACCM's depiction of the completed transformation of Pitfalls to Attributes.

This chapter fully shares the goal of transforming contract Pitfalls to contract Attributes. But how can that be accomplished? We explore in Sect. 2.2 below how PPL methods and mentality can help to achieve this evolution from traditional to what we term business-friendly contracting. First, however, we will identify common themes among the Pitfalls, describing the dysfunctional cycle that can come to characterize traditional contracting.

2.1 The Need for Simplified Language and Fewer Self-Protective Clauses

We first enter the traditional contracting cycle through a combination of Pitfall #7, that "contracts [are] difficult to use or understand," resulting in "users see[ing]

---

[2]This statistic, and others in IACCM (2015a), is drawn from IACCM research with its global, cross-industry membership, representing more than 12,000 organizations. *See* IACCM (2015a), p. 4.

Fig. 2 Pitfalls to Attributes (Cummins 2015). Copyright IACCM 2015. Used with permission

contracts as irrelevant to business needs;" and Pitfall #5, that "negotiations focus on the wrong terms and risks," resulting in "loss of economic benefit" and turning contracts into "a weapon." Pitfall #7 (difficult to use) and Pitfall #5 (too aggressive and adversarial) stem from the same root causes: an exaggerated concern among lawyers for the security of the transaction, and a failure to imagine that transactional security can actually be more strongly enhanced by using *different* methods than burdening the document with overly-elaborated legal language focusing on failure, disputes, and remedies.

Lawyers and business managers alike should realize the destructive impacts of jargon-laden, self-protective contract language. Such language can: (1) impair implementation of the contract; and (2) lead eventually to missed value and opportunities in the economic exchange itself (Cummins 2015). The way in which concern for *security* is addressed, in other words, ends up undermining *opportunity*. This opposition between security and opportunity, however, is not inherent or necessary. It can be transcended through simplification, visualization, and better-integrated communication between business and legal—as well as among all parts of a business and its contractual partners.

2.1.1   Impaired Functionality; Challenges in Contract Implementation

The *business* functionality of contracts can be impaired when their drafters use language that pays too much attention to *legal* functionality. Difficult language and self-protective content go hand in hand in this privileging of legal needs over business needs. When lawyers draft contracts, they often focus too strongly on imagined courtroom settings, rather than the far more immediate business settings. Their attention is too often directed on whether their language would prevail in court if its meaning were disputed by other lawyers. So lawyers tend to write contract terms for other legal professionals, not for the delivery teams and project managers who need documents they can easily work with and act upon. As a consequence, the contract implementers may create their own "translations" of those contracts, widening the gap between what the contract says (what Stewart Macaulay calls the "paper deal") and what the original business planners and negotiators *mean* for the exchange (the "real deal") (Macaulay 2003).

That disjuncture of language between the paper deal and the real deal can lead to confusion and possible contract breaches. Worse, it may *legalize the resolution* of problems that otherwise might have been dealt with through business flexibility and compromise. Because the paper deal elaborates legal language and concepts, Pitfall #6 is commonplace: contracts' "lack of flexibility" with an "insufficient focus on governance." As a result, "performance management [becomes] dominated by blame/fault" that characterizes legal outcomes. Once a problem arises, if *business practice* does not accord with the *legal interpretation* of the contract document, then the contract has the potential of being turned into a courtroom weapon by one party or the other. To guard against such courtroom losses, however, both sides "weaponize" the contract even further through Pitfall #5: they insert the self-protective substantive provisions of disclaimers, indemnities, and liquidated damages.

2.1.2 Missed Value and Opportunities

The exaggerated focus on legal needs at the expense of business needs is reflected in Pitfall #4: "protracted negotiations" leading to the dangers of "competitive exposure and delayed revenues." Those lengthy negotiations and missed opportunities again often stem from the difficult language that is routinely used in contracts. The language can needlessly isolate lawyers and business negotiators from one another, because business negotiators cannot readily participate fully in creating the legal agreements that should be memorializing the discussions among contracting parties.[3] Pitfall #1 is the ironic result: a "lack of clarity on scope and goals," causing claims and disputes. The contract is both *over*written (with self-protective clauses) and *under*written (lacking sufficient attention to the core terms of the actual economic exchange). At least in part, the complexity of contract language drives a wedge between legal and business functions, which is reflected in Pitfalls #2 and #3: the legal/contract team is not involved early enough, and vital stakeholders are not sufficiently engaged.

---

[3] According to Deepak Malhotra, in the process, many key decisions have been left to the lawyers, even in areas where business managers and subject matter experts could (and should) have made an important contribution; the latter, according to Malhotra, are in a much stronger position to negotiate *better* outcomes and relationships, not just *safer* ones. *See* Malhotra (2012), pp. 363–364. Emphasis added.

Engaging stakeholders and broadening the use of contracts is difficult, however, so long as contracts are burdened by language that is largely decipherable only by legal and contracts experts. Poor communication and integration at the front end then may be repeated both at implementation and when business conditions require a change in the contract terms. Adding to the challenges is the limited use of contract technology, Pitfall #9, resulting in "inefficiency and loss of quality in performance and analysis". The consequences include Pitfall #8, "poor handover from deal team to implementation team," resulting in "commitment and obligations missed and misunderstood;" and Pitfall #10, "poor post-award processes and governance," leading to "repetitive issues and errors causing value loss."

2.2 Transitioning to Business-Friendly Contracting

The end-result of the traditional contracting cycle—repetitive errors and losses and considerable value erosion—serves well to introduce the ideas of PPL. PPL is comprised of two main components, namely "Preventive Law" and "Proactive Law." Preventive Law focuses on dysfunctional cycles that generate recurring losses. It seeks to identify and understand the conflicting elements of a system, as we have done above, that, unless somehow resolved, will continue to generate problems.[4] Proactive Law adds a focus to achieving positive goals and value.[5] Together, PPL can alter mentalities and harness tools toward smoother operations and successful outcomes.

2.2.1 Preventive Law

Traditionally, the focus in the legal field has been on the past, mainly on failures and how to react to them through legal proceedings, remedies to force compliance, sanctions, punishment, fines, and so on. Preventive Law promotes a different approach: one where the focus is on the future and on using the law and legal skills to prevent disputes and eliminate causes of problems (Barton 2007). In doing so, Preventive Law has similarities with preventive medicine, a branch of medical science dealing with methods of preventing the occurrence of disease—here, the "disease" of legal trouble, disputes, and litigation. Preventive Law thus emphasizes the lawyer's role as a planner, advisor, or problem solver. In the words of Dauer (1988): "Litigation law is mostly law. Preventive law is mostly facts. And the critical time for preventive lawyering is when those facts are first being born. As a lawyer speaking to business people, I would have one request of them: Please let us be involved in the making of those facts."

Table 1 illustrates the shift of mindset and focus that the proponents of Preventive Law have proposed since the 1950s.

---

[4]For a general overview and elaboration of preventive and problem solving methods, *see* Barton (2009).

[5]For the background of Preventive Law and Proactive Law, *see* Haapio (2008, 2013a, 2013b) and Berger-Walliser and Østergaard (2012).

Table 1 Preventive law: shifting focus from the past to the future (Haapio 2013b, p. 39)

Focus away from	Focus toward
• the past	• the future
• minimizing cost	• eliminating causes
• winning in court	• preventing litigation
• lawyers as fighters	• lawyers as advisors, planners and problem-solvers

2.2.2 Proactive Law and Proactive Contracting

With the development of what is now known as the Proactive Law approach, a new dimension was added to Preventive Law. In addition to minimizing problems and risk, the proactive approach focuses on enabling success and enhancing opportunities. Using the medical analogy, in the proactive approach the focus is not just on preventing problems or "legal ill-health". The goal is to promote "legal well-being": embedding legal knowledge and skills in corporate culture, strategy and everyday actions to actively promote success, ensure desired outcomes, balance risk with reward, and prevent problems. (Haapio 2013b, p. 39).

The approaches specifically called Proactive Contracting and Proactive Law emerged in the Nordic countries, initiated by a small team of Finnish researchers and practitioners (one of this chapter's authors being among them) in the late 1990s and early 2000s.[6] In the context of contracting, the pioneers of the approach merged quality and risk management principles with Preventive Law, thereby adding the *promotive* dimension to the preventive dimension. This laid the conceptual foundation for a new way of thinking: "proactivity=prevention plus"[7]. The goal of Proactive Contracting, according to Soile Pohjonen (2002, p. v), is that the contracting parties achieve the goal of their collaboration in accordance with their will. This requires, Pohjonen continues, above all, a careful investigation of their goal and will, and the skill to create a clear and legally robust framework for their implementation.

---

[6]The first publication mentioning the proactive approach was "Quality Improvement through Proactive Contracting" by Haapio (1998). Since then, a growing body of literature, conferences, and books has contributed to the further development of the approach. The early experiments led to the formation of the Nordic School of Proactive Law, http://www.proactivelaw.org and of the Proactive ThinkTank, www.proactivethinktank.com. The mission of the ThinkTank is to provide a forum for business leaders, lawyers, academics and other professionals to discuss, develop and promote the proactive management of relationships, contracts and risks and the prevention of legal uncertainties and disputes. (*See* ProActive ThinkTank mission statement 2007). The Nordic School's and ProActive ThinkTank's conferences have led to the publication of several books, including Wahlgren (2006); Nystén-Haarala (2008); Haapio (2008) and Berger-Walliser and Østergaard (2012). Collaboration between participants in the Nordic School, the ProActive ThinkTank, and legal scholars in the United States has enriched the proactive approach and expanded its reach. These undertakings have explored the use of the law for competitive advantage and the interaction between law and strategy; *see, e.g.* Siedel and Haapio (2010, 2011) and DiMatteo et al. (2012). For the history of the Proactive Law movement, *see also* Berger-Walliser (2012), with references.

[7]Also used in the form "proactive=preventive plus promotive".

Table 2 Proactive law: shifting focus from prevention to promotion (Haapio 2013b, p. 41)

Focus not just on	Focus also on
• rules, legal tools: helping the parties to comply with the rules	• goals, managerial tools: enabling the parties to reach their objectives
• minimizing risks, problems, disputes, losses	• maximizing opportunities, desired outcomes, benefits
• preventing causes of failure and negative effects	• promoting drivers of success and positive effects
• lawyers as advisors, practicing preventive law; the law office as a preventive law laboratory (*See* Brown 1956)	• lawyers as designers and coaches, working with clients as part of cross-professional teams (*See* Haapio 2006, p. 30)

Table 2 illustrates the shift of mindset and focus that the proponents of Proactive Law have proposed.

Proactive Law literature has addressed extensively the reasons and objectives of its call for a paradigm shift; less addressed is how to make it happen (Berger-Walliser 2012, p. 31).[8] This chapter represents a step toward effecting the paradigm shift: turning Proactive Law into practice.

The promotive dimension of the proactive approach has a positive and constructive emphasis. It involves using contracts to *enable the parties to reach their business objectives*. In order to do so, contracts must be usable and well suited for their purposes. For business, the contract itself is not the goal: its successful implementation is the goal (*See* Haapio 2013b; Ertel 2004, p. 62).[9]

2.2.3 Moving Away from Traditional Contracting

The diagnosis of the Pitfalls of traditional contracting identifies an ongoing dynamic of personnel who fail to communicate early enough, and with enough shared vocabulary, to align contracting documents well enough with the real aims of the parties. The elements of the traditional contracting system speak different languages, and focus on different goals. Such diversity of function is not necessarily bad: division of labor is efficiency-enhancing *so long as the various parts of the system can communicate well with one another*. But that does not happen fully in traditional contracting. The language used in contracts artificially *raises* information costs. The vocabulary is so specialized, and the text is so packed with

---

[8]What is needed, according to Berger-Walliser (2012), are case studies, identification of best practices, and more distinctive methods and tools to turn Proactive Law into practice. According to Thomas D. Barton (2008, pp. 41–42), when contracts lawyers envision a potential problem, they tend to revert to the dominant legal paradigm in their analysis: "the lawyerly imagination looks backward rather than forward, in order to prevail in the courtroom [...] they rearrange the present contract language so as to be able to *win* that legal contest. [...] What is needed instead is a mentality toward *preempting* the problem from arising—reducing the client's risk *even while being proactive toward achieving the client's goals*." See also DiMatteo et al. (2012), p. 106.

[9]*Similarly*, EESC (2009), p. 32 (§ 6.11): "The life cycle of a piece of legislation does not begin with the drafting of a proposal or end when it has been formally adopted. A piece of legislation is not the goal; its successful implementation is."

legal concepts rather than business language, that the contract cannot effectively speak to many people on the business side who are in charge of planning, pricing, negotiating, or implementing the agreement or passing its terms on to sub-contractors. According to IACCM research, more than 9 out of 10 managers admit that they find contracts difficult to read or understand (IACCM 2015a, p. 6). Furthermore, the felt need to produce traditional legal language in contracts diverts drafters' attention away from the needed integration among those who construct the business transaction, and those who must carry it out.

The proactive suggestions for remedying this dysfunction are several. In this chapter, we focus on three of them: simplification of contract language and design; visualization; and collaborative contracting. Each of these methods reduces the barriers to effective communications within an organization, and between contracting parties. They make concepts and ideas more accessible, and they prompt stronger cooperation and flexibility.

Section 3 will summarize each of these three methods; together, they are important parts of a broader PPL-inspired move toward business-friendly contracting. Section 4 will offer examples where business-friendly approaches have been implemented.

3 Business-Friendly Tools: Simplification, Visualization, and Collaboration

If your company's current contracts are complex, you are not alone. Many top managers recognize a growing problem that contracting processes and documents are complex—too complex for companies' own personnel as well as customers and suppliers to handle. This is especially true for small and medium sized enterprises (SMEs).[10] On the sell-side, the consequence can be fewer winning bids, lost sales, and value erosion during implementation. On the buy-side, if the bidding process or documents seem too complicated or time consuming, there will be no SME bidders. Further, if the bidders do not understand the contracts they enter into, misunderstanding easily leads to a breakdown in relationships, and poor or late delivery. According to surveys conducted by the IACCM, major areas of weaknesses include:

- disagreements over contract scope;
- performance failures due to over-commitment or disagreement over what was committed; and
- inappropriate contract structures (*See* IACCM 2014a, 2015b; Bergman 2015).

---

[10]Recent research in both private and public procurement confirms that for many SMEs, contracts are overly legalistic and difficult to work with. *See, e.g.*, Patajoki (2013) and Haapio (2013a).

As surveyed below, the tools of simplification, visualization, and collaboration can begin to address these weaknesses by clarifying terms, and by improving communication among contract negotiators, drafters, and implementers.

3.1   Simplification

Most of us have probably been told that our contracts are not simple; they are too long, too complex, and hard to work with. If we want to prevent misunderstanding, disagreements, and other pitfalls, what can we do to simplify our contracts?[11]

To begin with, we can start to see ourselves and contracts differently: ourselves as *designers* and contracts as *business tools*. Contracts contain vital business information, not just legal provisions. They are also about roles, responsibilities, and requirements that need to be translated into action and procedures and timelines that need to be followed. When we see the role of contracts as *communication tools*, it becomes obvious that contracts need to be *designed*, not just drafted.

In our previous work, we have looked into what business lawyers can learn from *design thinking* (Haapio 2013a; Berger-Walliser et al. 2017) in general and *information designers* (Haapio and Passera 2013)[12] in particular. In the following, we will look into some tools and methods that we can borrow from the designers' toolbox.

In any (re)design project, the designer takes the user's situation as the point of departure. Irrespective of what one seeks to simplify, the effort needs to start with the users. A simple contract is one that is considered simple by its intended users. Different users have different backgrounds, skills, competencies, needs, and expectations. Contracts offer themselves as a particularly interesting field of simplification, because of their two quite different audiences: business users and legal users. Traditionally, the focus of contract crafters has been on the needs and expectations of the legal users, such as courts and arbitrators who may be asked to interpret the contract in case of a dispute. In this chapter, our focus is not primarily on such users; it is on those users who are not lawyers or contracts professionals. For them, any contract, even one that may seem simple and familiar to an expert, may be too complex and intimidating. And let's admit it: most contracts today are not simple even for the experts.

A systematic approach to contract simplification can be based on three key building blocks developed by Siegel and Etzkorn (2013) in their book *Simple*: (1) empathy with the users' needs and expectations; (2) clarity through the use of both plain language and design; and (3) distillation of the communication, boiling it down to its essence. These three key requirements are illustrated in Fig. 3.

---

[11] Simple, for the purposes of this chapter, means *not complex* or *complicated*. By simplification we mean making contracts *less complex* or *complicated*—they may still not become simple.

[12] *See generally* the movement toward using design methods and tools in legal context, *e.g.*, Margaret Hagan, http://www.margarethagan.com (Accessed September 26, 2016) and Szabo (2010).

Fig. 3 The three building blocks of simplicity (The idea of the image is adapted from Siegel and Etzkorn 2013, p. 49)

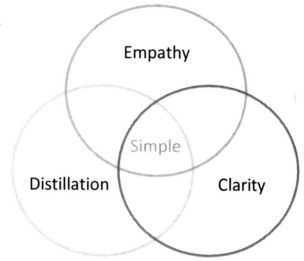

To simplify business users' experience of contracts, two approaches predominate: either hiding complexity by providing a better "user interface;" or changing contracts themselves to make them less complex. Information design scholarship divides the available methods into two categories: *optimization*, which includes plain language and clear typography that improve but may not fundamentally change a given document; and *transformation*, which includes a range of more radical strategies such as distillation, abstraction, layering and visualization (Waller 2011c).

Layering is a particularly useful method for contracts, as it allows adaptation to multiple user needs. As the term suggests, layering creates alternative strata of information that vary in depth or style: in the context of contracts, one layer might include the text of the contract as is; another the headings or keywords of each clause; and a layer between these two might show in laymen's terms what the clause means. Layering responds not only to differing needs of different users, but also to the needs of one user at different times, when either careful study may be needed, or just a quick reminder of some general points. It also can express information in different formats—for example icons or images versus words (For practical examples, see e.g., Waller 2015, pp. 13–16).

Creative Commons (http://creativecommons.org) is perhaps the best-known example: their copyright licenses incorporate a three-layer design seeking to ensure that both the creators of works and their users can understand their rights.[13] Clicking on the icons reveals a plain-language version of the license terms: the icons inform

---

[13]For an image of the three layers of Creative Commons licenses ("Legal Code," "Human Readable," and "Machine Readable"), *see* Creative Commons (2015).

users about the possibilities and limitations of, for instance, sharing or remixing the licensed content.[14] If additional information is required, the full text is also available just one click away. There is the so-called Legal Code (the "lawyer readable" version, the full license), the Commons Deed (the "human readable" version), and the "machine readable" version of the license, with the Commons Deed acting "as a user-friendly interface to the Legal Code beneath" (*See* Creative Commons 2015).

3.2 Visualization

"Visualization" builds on the goals and methods of simplification, by employing visual images to supplement textual language. Graphs, charts, timelines, diagrams, flowcharts, decision-trees—all of these and more can depict information in easily digested formats (Barton et al. 2013; *See also* Passera et al. 2013; Passera and Haapio 2013a, b; Haapio and Passera 2013). "Such techniques could be used directly *in* a contract, as part of the drafting process. Or visualization can be *about* a contract, a separate document that assists all those who are involved in the planning, review, or approval of a contract or in monitoring or implementing its terms." (Barton et al. 2013, p. 48)

The aims of visualization have been summarized as follows:

1. Clarifying what written language does not manage to fully explain;
2. Making the logic and structure of the documents more visible;
3. Giving both overview and insight into complex terms and processes;
4. Supporting evidence, analysis, explanation, and reasoning in complex settings;
5. Providing an alternative access structure to the contents, especially to the non-experts working with the document;
6. Helping the parties articulate tacit assumptions and clarify and align expectations; and
7. Engaging stakeholders who have been alienated by the conventional look and feel of contracts. (Passera et al. 2013)

Like the tools available in simplification, one need not be professionally trained in design to make helpful use of visualization methods. Even simple charts or diagrams can further the goals of more easily understood documents, and prompt better communication. For more complex relationships, working with a professional information designer can be especially helpful.

Depicted below is one example of such a successful collaboration (Barton et al. 2015). Figure 4 illustrates the gradual transfer of ownership—together with particular business and legal risks, rights, and duties—over a 15 year contractual relationship between a supplier and purchaser of equipment (This figure first

---

[14]For an icon summarizing the dimensions and choices of licenses, *see* http://wisesearch.weebly.com/uploads/1/1/3/6/11361394/1762233_orig.gif (Accessed September 26, 2016).

Transfer of ownership, risks, costs and responsibilities

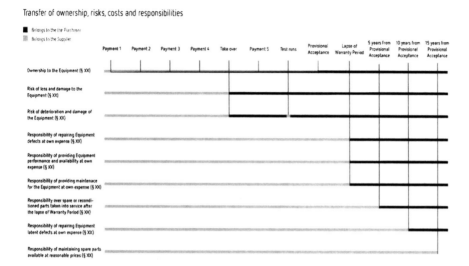

Fig. 4 Multiple timelines showing transfer of ownership and the allocation of risk, cost, and responsibilities between parties (© 2012. Aalto University. Image by Stefania Passera. Used with permission.)

appeared in Passera et al. 2013, p. 43). The multiple timeline shows the schedule of behaviors and events, starting with periodic payments from the buyer and extending beyond the lapse of the warranty, plotted against their shifting responsibilities. The information is displayed in a format that is easy to follow, encouraging ongoing use of the contract to monitor implementation over the years.

3.3 Collaboration

"Collaboration" in contracting is the simple idea that parties to a contract are better off thinking of themselves and working as partners, rather than as adversaries (Mosten 2009. *See also* Barton 2012, 2016). Collaboration is directly linked with the methods and goals of PPL: "better relationships, better communication, and contextual understandings that will prevent problems and facilitate success" (Barton 2012).

Collaboration explicitly recognizes that contracting embraces personal relationships, as well as legal and economic ties. As depicted below in Fig. 5, contracting should be thought of as three overlapping spheres that work together.

As suggested above in this chapter, various barriers can drive apart the "legal" and "business" spheres. Perhaps in part because of that lack of integration, neither lawyers nor business managers typically acknowledge fully the human relationships that importantly accompany the negotiation and implementation of a deal (Barton 2012). Collaborative contracting consciously reflects on those ties, and

Fig. 5 The three
relationships of contracting
(This *diagram* also appears in
Barton et al. 2015, p. 17.)

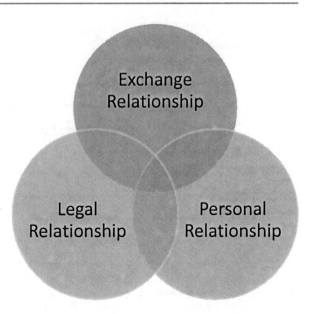

attempts to reunite the legal, economic, and personal relational spheres toward mutual benefit.

Should collaborative intentions and expected practices be part of the actual contract documents? The advantages of doing so were emphasized by Jacqui Crawford of Rolls-Royce: the parties disclose from the outset their respective interests, their baseline expectations, and a process for addressing and managing the changes that will inevitably occur over the life of a long term contract (Cummins and Crawford 2010). Revealing underlying interests advances both the economic exchange perspective and the relational perspective. It also promotes finding win-win solutions where problems emerge.

> In drafting the document, the parties can express both the general intentions they have worked out during the planning/negotiation stage, and also include as much detail as possible about the process that they have devised for periodic communication. Statements of their relational expectations should go beyond labels, but also be open-ended to set up basic norm expectations. (Barton 2012)

These norm expectations could include any or all of the following: to share more information about underlying interests; to work toward sharing risks in a balanced way, so as to satisfy *both* sides of those party interests; to hold periodic meetings following contract formation, so as to monitor performance quality; and to be open to one another's needs for flexibility in meeting commitments (Barton 2012). Jennejohn (2008) has researched specific examples of collaboration, extracted from contracts between parties like Cisco & KMPG, Coca-Cola & Synomyx, and Intel & Phoenix Technologies. These companies adopted communication enhancing measures like interacting teams, exchange of on-site personnel, and creation of a joint research steering committee. To measure the success of these efforts, they included general benchmarking clauses with specific metrics. Finally, they established helpful feedback loops to improve long-term performance. Would such collaborative terms be warranted in *every* contract? Not necessarily: importantly, collaborative terms can be used selectively. Some of the provisions above are more demanding of time, money, and organizational coordination than others (Barton 2012).

As we have written before, successful collaboration is more than just good intentions. It involves a mentality and skills that may be relatively unfamiliar or even uncomfortable. For lawyers, it means that they address more than the language in contracting documents:

> Healthy economic and personal relationships need not rely solely on legal rights. Where lawyers work toward making the economic and personal relationships stronger, therefore, the burden of dealing with risks does not fall exclusively on airtight legal language in the contract. Lawyers should therefore embrace the value of non-legal communication. That in turn requires that the lawyers learn much more about the economic exchanges that are the subject of the contracts. They should treat their clients more like partners who are capable of contributing significantly to the success of the lawyer's efforts. (Barton et al. 2015, p. 19)

As to managers, "collaboration requires first that they not abdicate too much responsibility for formal contract processes to their lawyers" (Barton et al. 2015, p. 19). Furthermore:

> Managers should also understand the worlds of their employees and any subcontractors. Managers should flatten hierarchies that, for example, prevent production or sales personnel from making suggestions about the terms of prospective contracts or the implementation of existing contracts. Finally, managers should invest time in talking with contractual counterparts about contract goals, risks, and implementation. In many cases managers should not be reluctant to share information about the economic or strategic interests that prompt willingness to enter into a contract. The underlying interests of a company do not give away negotiation strategies—it does not mean that a manager invites exploitation. Instead, managers should explain the broader interests of their company as a prelude to negotiating the contract. (Barton et al. 2015, pp. 19–20)

These ideas can be startling, and resisted, because they seem to contradict so much conventional wisdom about proper negotiating style and the power that is assumed to flow from possessing secret information. True, one should not normally disclose the "reservation point" below which one would terminate negotiations. But sharing one's interests and basic goals with a contracting counterpart is virtually a precondition to discovering "win-win" possibilities. All value in exchange flows from learning that another person values something more highly than we are able and willing to supply. Unless people communicate what they want, those needs and possible value-enhancing exchanges may never become visible. Further, unless the deeper interests are disclosed, parties may never consider unconventional ways— contract terms apart from price—by which both parties may emerge even more satisfied with the transaction. The mutual exchange of information is thus a precursor to immediate value-creation, but also to longer-term relationships. How does one convince a skeptical contracting counterpart of the wisdom of this approach? The unilateral disclosure of one's own underlying interests, coupled with an offer to listen to the interests of a contracting counterpart, is an important step toward realizing hidden value and better relationships.

In Sect. 4 below, we offer some examples in which the tools of business-friendly contracting have been effectively used.

4 Business-Friendly Contracting: Examples and Implementation

User-centered design, simplification, and visualization have already made their way to some practitioners' ways of working. In the field of consumer contracts, experiments have proven how loan documents and credit card agreements can benefit from a new, more user-friendly approach (US Consumer Financial Protection Bureau CFPB 2011; Siegel and Etzkorn 2013). Further projects have aimed to simplify, for example, an online game's terms of service, a rail network's disclaimer, and a law firm's standard terms of engagement (Clarity2010 Blog; UK Office of Fair Trading OFT 2011). Several projects have looked into the simplification of online Terms & Conditions, end-user licenses, and privacy policies through the use of icons (For a summary, *see* Lannerö 2013).

The proponents of plain language (Felsenfeld and Siegel 1981; Kimble 2006, 2012), simplification (Waller 2011a, b; Etzkorn 2011), minimalism (Hetrick 2008) and lean contracting (Weatherley 2005; Siedel and Haapio 2010, 2011) have suggested major changes in document design and drafting, but until recently, not much seems to have happened in the specific field of contracting. Instead, the trend seems to have been toward *more* complex contracts. For example, in the 1980s a typical credit card contract was perhaps a page and a half or two pages long—but now it may easily cover 20–30 pages.

4.1 Case Studies of Business-Friendly Contracting and Simplified Contracts

Even in the commercial contracting arena, however, some pioneering organizations and innovative professionals have experimented with simpler contracting processes and documents.

4.1.1 Scottish and Newcastle: The Pathclearer Approach

The Pathclearer approach developed by the in-house legal team at Scottish & Newcastle plc (S&N) offers a first example. The legal team at S&N found that in many cases, detailed contract terms were unnecessary, and that too much detail could actually be an obstacle to doing business. S&N developed an innovative approach which helped reduce paperwork and better identify legal risk (Colquhoun

2007; Weatherley 2005. *See also* Siedel and Haapio 2011, pp. 119–121). They moved from conventional contracts—tens of pages and exhibits full of dense text—to brief texts, such as the Pathclearer Supply Agreement: a brief letter agreement that drastically reduced the length and complexity of the contract.

4.1.2   Agilent Technologies: The 50/50/500 Plan

Another example of contract simplification is offered by Dave Barton (2008)[15], Director of Contracts at Agilent Technologies. For Agilent Technologies' Customer Contracts organization, the goal of *simplicity in agreements* was not enough. In what they called a "50/50/500 Plan", they set numerical goals: reduce the length of most common agreements by at least 50 %; reduce negotiation cycle time by 50 %; and provide more empowerment on contract terms for deals of $500,000 or less. In one example, a services division had previously consolidated six different exhibits describing six different services into one long document of 17 pages. The comprehensive document was efficient in some ways for Agilent: they did not need to worry about which set of terms and conditions to use when preparing quotes and processing customer orders. *However,* less complexity for Agilent meant more complexity for customers: rarely did a customer require more than one of the services described in the contract. Agilent was routinely sending its customers a 17-page document of which, at most, three pages might apply to their particular needs. The document did not fully take into account its multiple users, and as a result some users had to waste time determining which part of the document was pertinent to their particular transaction.

As part of their 50 % simplification goal in the *50/50/500 Plan*, Agilent broke the document apart and re-drafted it into six separate documents, none longer than three pages. The resulting contract was much less complex for the customer. At the same time, Agilent's contracts organization increased its capacity to focus on higher value-added business relationships and issues. According to Dave Barton (2008): "The plan restored a sense of purpose in alignment with corporate goals, and this has reinvigorated a great sense of pride."

4.1.3   IBM Cloud Services

IBM recently simplified their contract for cloud services offerings, reducing a contract that once was between 30 and 90 pages long, to a contract that is a mere two pages. This project was named a finalist for the 2014 IACCM Innovation Award for Operational Improvement. Based on the positive market feedback regarding the simplified Cloud Services Agreement (CSA), IBM has extended the simplified contracting approach and now has a short, simple, modular master contract based upon the CSA which applies to all of IBM's offerings, including Cloud, Machines, Appliances, Software and Services (IACCM 2014c). According to Neil Abrams, Assistant General Counsel at IBM, they learned that using a shorter contract takes much less time for the customers and their lawyers. Where there

---

[15]No relation to this Chapter's co-author of the same surname.

needs to be some negotiation, that can be done faster too (Reisinger 2014). When he began the task, Abrams was the head lawyer for software. Now he is an assistant GC assigned to look for ways to transform the client experience, including simplifying more contracts—all part of the legal team's focus on helping their business satisfy clients and innovate (Reisinger 2014). Webcast recordings illustrating the process and its outcomes are available at the IACCM website (IACCM 2014b, 2015c).

4.1.4   The New Engineering Contract (NEC)

A noteworthy example of using visuals to guide the use and interpretation of complex commercial contracts comes from the UK: the NEC family of contracts. This set of documents consists of several contracts designed for procuring a diverse range of services and goods, plus associated guidance notes and flow charts that assist in the understanding of those contracts. Originally launched in 1993 under the name of the "New Engineering Contract", NEC has been praised for its collabora-tive and integrated working approach to procurement. The implementation of NEC3 contracts reportedly has resulted in major benefits for projects both nation-ally and internationally in terms of time, cost savings and improved quality (*See* NEC 2014b, c, d). In their comparison between NEC and FIDIC conditions, the publishers of NEC praise their standard form of contract by noting: "It is probably fair to say that FIDIC focuses on liabilities and risk in the manner of traditional contracts, whereas NEC requires and enables a more proactive and collaborative approach" (NEC 2014a, p. 2). The NEC publishers also highlight that "a feature of NEC is the drafting in plain English and providing for clarity and flexibility. NEC attempts to eliminate the use of legal terms and instead provides for simple language, and gives words their natural meaning" (NEC 2014a, p. 2).

4.1.5   Rolls Royce, plc.

At the IACCM Academic Forum of 2013, Shad Haddad (Lead Commercial Officer of Rolls-Royce plc.) presented a paper that reflected on contract visualization in infrastructure development, from both pre- and post-contract award perspectives (Haddad 2013). He first asked about an organization's purpose in entering into a contract: is it to enforce in court or arbitration various obligations on the other party and gain compensation for their failure in undertaking them; or is it rather to provide a statement or formal commitment to the undertakings of the organization's own obligations? Without giving an answer, he then pondered whether the overly complicated "legalese" way of drawing up contracts provides for adequate clarity and accurate interpretation of the obligations of the parties, especially in an already complex project. He concluded that visualizations can help integrate law (espe-cially Proactive Law) and contract management, and transform legal documents into enabling instruments. His paper included examples of how visualization techniques can provide the parties with clarity on what they require and what they should deliver, thereby helping to promote contractual compliance and shape the procurement process.

4.2   Research on Contract Simplification and Visualization

In different parts of the world, pioneering scholars have started to experiment with user-centered contract design and contract visualization. Michael Curtotti and Eric McCreath of the Australian National University have developed prototype tools for visualizing contract definitions in different ways (Curtotti and McCreath 2012). Stefania Passera, at Aalto University, has developed and prototyped visual contracts in collaboration with private and public organizations.[16] Together with Michael Curtotti and one of this chapter's authors, she has experimented with a prototype of automated contract visualization (Passera et al. 2014). At Stanford University, Margaret Hagan and George Triantis are working with students to tackle consumer-contract design challenges, studying, among other things, principles of contract design, communication design, and behavioral economics to understand the dynamics of how lay people interact with legal text and choices.[17]

Researchers who have viewed contracting as an ongoing, common sense-making process between the parties have found that visualization can play an important role in helping the contract parties avoid misunderstandings and inadvertent non-compliance (Passera et al. 2014). Contract visualization has been presented as a way to implement a proactive approach to contracting and law, helping the parties not only to prevent disputes and litigation, but also to enhance the likelihood of successful business outcomes and a mutually beneficial relationship (Passera et al. 2014). The usability and user-experience of the new contract prototypes are in the process of being evaluated. Early case studies are preliminary but encouraging: they clearly indicate positive results and a strong user preference for a simplified and visualized contract as opposed to a traditional, text-only version (Passera 2012, 2014, 2015; Passera and Haapio 2013a, b).

The new approach obviously involves risks. As regards visualization, questions such as potential conflicts between text and images need to be resolved. Some of these questions can be resolved contractually, and others require further investigation. More prototypes, user tests and research are required to analyze, for example, which methods work best for which users or contexts. In any case, the early results indicate that the benefits outweigh the risks, and that much can be gained by merging contract design with information design and visualization.

---

[16]For examples of the published results of this work, *see* the web pages of M!ND research group, http://www.mindspace.fi/en/contract-visu/ and Why contracts need visualization? http://www.mindspace.fi/en/english-why-contracts-need-visualization/

[17]Legal Design Lab: Consumer Contracts, https://law.stanford.edu/courses/legal-design-lab-consumer-contracts/

5   Conclusion

Security and opportunity are not necessarily mutually exclusive. Even while the authors of this chapter welcome a shift toward a paradigm of opportunity, that new emphasis need not come at the expense of a secure foundation of contractual agreement. Our chapter has demonstrated how employing the principles and methods of PPL—especially simplification, visualization, and collaboration—can *enhance* security and opportunity simultaneously.

Advancing security and opportunity together in contracting is possible because PPL methods can transcend what causes security and opportunity to *appear* as inherently opposed: the traditional divergence in outlook, goals, and language between law and business. Framing contract goals as prevailing in court or limiting legal damages will emphasize standardized, litigation-tested disclaimers and indemnification clauses—exactly those terms that IACCM finds to be high on the agendas of many legally-focused contracts negotiators. A moment's reflection, however, reveals how stifling of opportunities those clauses are likely to be. They suggest on their face a mentality of self-protection through rigidity, and veiled threats to bring the power of the law against a contract partner—hardly an environment that encourages innovation.

In contrast is the business mentality that seeks stronger (and typically longer-enduring) economic and personal relationships with another party. A relational focus will *expect* occasional disruptions in contractual implementation. This focus will also accept the need to be flexible and accommodating, based on a reservoir of trust and long-term mutual benefit.

Although a relational mentality may be uppermost in the minds of those who negotiate the *real* deal, it is not often expressed in the *paper* deal. When economic and relational intentions are formalized into legal contracts, everyday language is translated and communications norms are transformed. The agreements suddenly become inaccessible to non-experts—those who must implement the agreement as well as those who may have negotiated the deal. Furthermore, communication expectations may be disrupted, or rendered self-protective or suspicious—all in the name of ensuring legally "the security of contracts." Little wonder, then, that security and opportunity appear opposed to one another. Where business and legal language and communication styles are so strongly compartmentalized, security and opportunity are never part of a shared agenda.

In every realm of law, PPL methods seek a healthy integration of stronger personal engagement, attention to factual environments, and legal possibilities. PPL aims not only to prevent legal disputes by better long-range planning and design, but also to enable parties to reach individual goals, mutual benefits, and new opportunities. PPL examines the systemic, patterned interactions of people to uncover and explain recurring points of friction or lost value. It then suggests interventions by which the revealed dissonance is resolved—and often transcended toward greater possibilities.

So also in our examination of contracting: diagnosis of traditional patterns reveals lost value through failure of adequate communication, which in turn is caused by an exaggerated and unnecessary separation of business and legal professionals. The "treatment" suggested in this chapter is simplification and visualization of contracting language, plus the creation of collaborative structures and practices. If implemented, these PPL interventions may enhance security of agreements through greater understanding, flexibility and trust. Simultaneously, they can facilitate collaborative refinements and new business opportunities for each contracting partner.

Liquid Legal Context

By Dr. Dierk Schindler, Dr. Roger Strathausen, Kai Jacob

Haapio and Barton translate the sometimes abstract concept of lawyers needing to be more proactive, rather than only preventive, more opportunity rather than risk focused into the core of a lawyer's work: Contracting. They pick up the growing demand on lawyers to view contracts less as a legal tool, but rather as a business tool. They then take us on a journey what contract drafting with the mindset of a business enabler can look like. While stating clearly that contracts today are centered (sometimes purely) around meeting legal standards, the authors leave no doubt that they are not making a case to sacrifice enforceability for the benefit of speed or ease of doing business.

Taking the "10 pitfalls" in contracting, that IACCM has established by research, and pointing to the massive business value erosion that comes with them, Haapio and Barton establish a few common denominators that underlie those pitfalls: the need for simplified language and less self-protective clauses; the need to shift to a balance between preventive law and proactive law and thereby towards business friendly contracting.

Yet, what are the specific levers to pull? First, simplification is being called out and Haapio and Barton start with a call to action that lawyers should view themselves as designers who create rather a business tool than a contract. Second, visualization, as a technique to be used in contracts, aiming at making key information accessible to business stakeholders in an efficient way. Third, collaboration, meaning the simple idea that parties to a contract are better off thinking of themselves and acting as partners, rather than as adversaries.

As Haapio and Barton then point to very practical means of moving towards and implementing such a new way of contracting, it again becomes clear how interrelated the many aspects of the transformation in the legal industry are. Legal tech is the key to rise above the budget and efficiency pressure; at the same time it is the enabler to gain metrics that make a KPI-based performance management possible. In sum, this—when enabled by a professional legal operations function—allows for a truly new profile of a lawyer, who then must bring very different skills to the table than traditionally sought for. Freeing the lawyer from the ghosts of the past will create space to embrace new concepts around business enablement—like simplification, visualization and collaboration in contracting.

References

Barton, D. (2008). *Using measurements to drive organizational value.* Contracting Excellence, November 2008. International Association for Contract and Commercial Management IACCM. http://www2.iaccm.com/resources/?id=8030. Accessed 26 Sept 2016.

Barton, T. D. (2007). Three modes of legal problem solving–and what to do about them in legal education. *California Western Law Review, 43,* 389–416. http://works.bepress.com/thomas_barton/10/. Accessed 26 Sept 2016.

Barton, T. D. (2008). A paradigm shift in legal thinking. Six contrasts of traditional and preventive/proactive legal thought. In H. Haapio (Ed.), *A proactive approach to contracting and law* (pp. 35–42). Turku, Finland: International Association for Contract and Commercial Management & Turku University of Applied Sciences.

Barton, T. D. (2009). *Preventive law and problem-solving: Lawyering for the future.* Lake Mary, FL: Vandeplas Publishing.

Barton, T. D. (2012). Collaborative contracting as preventive/proactive law. In G. Berger-Walliser & K. Østergaard (Eds.), *Proactive law in a business environment* (pp. 107–127). Copenhagen, Denmark: DJØF Publishing.

Barton, T. D. (2016). Re-designing law and lawyering for the information age. *Notre Dame Journal of Law, Ethics & Public Policy, 30,* 101–134.

Barton, T. D., Berger-Walliser, G., & Haapio, H. (2013). Visualization: Seeing contracts for what they are, and what they could become. *Journal of Law, Business & Ethics, 9,* 47–63.

Barton, T. D., Haapio, H., & Borisova, T. (2015). Flexibility and stability in contracts. *Lapland Law Review, Issue 2,* 8–28. http://www.ulapland.fi/InEnglish/Units/Faculty-of-Law/Research/Lapland-Law-Review/Issues/Issue-2,-2015. Accessed 26 Sept 2016.

Berger-Walliser, G. (2012). The past and future of proactive law: An overview of the development of the proactive law movement. In G. Berger-Walliser & K. Østergaard (Eds.), *Proactive law in a business environment* (pp. 13–31). Copenhagen, Denmark: DJØF Publishing.

Berger-Walliser, G., & Østergaard, K. (Eds.). (2012). *Proactive law in a business environment.* Copenhagen, Denmark: DJØF Publishing.

Berger-Walliser, G., Barton, T., & Haapio, H. (2017). From visualization to legal design: A collaborative and creative process. *American Business Law Journal, 54*(2) (forthcoming). Manuscript available at http://ssrn.com/abstract=2841030. Accessed 26 Sept 2016.

Bergman, J. (2015). 2015 top terms in negotiating – review & analysis – AMERICAS 2015. https://www.iaccm.com/resources/?id=8856 (for members only). Accessed 26 Sept 2016.

Brown, L. M. (1956). The law office. A preventive law laboratory. *University of Pennsylvania Law Review, 104*(7), 940–953.

Clarity2010 Blog. http://blog.clarity2010.com. Accessed 26 Sept 2016.

Colquhoun, G. (2007, January). A clearer way to deal. *The Journal,* 45.

Creative Commons. (2015). About the licenses. http://creativecommons.org/licenses. Accessed 26 Sept 2016.

Cummins, T. (2015). Commercial excellence. Presentation at IACCM Finland event, Helsinki 14 September 2015.

Cummins, T., & Crawford, J. (2010, April 8). *Collaborative contracting: Is it achievable? Webinar conducted under the auspices of IACCM.* http://www2.iaccm.com/resources/?id=3446 (for members only). Accessed 26 Sept 2016.

Curtotti, M., & McCreath, E. (2012). *Enhancing the visualization of law.* Paper presented at the 2012 Law via the Internet Twentieth Anniversary Conference, Cornell University, 9 October 2012. http://ssrn.com/abstract=2160614. Accessed 26 Sept 2016.

Dauer, E. A. (1988, September). *Corporate legal health: Preventive law dictates going to root causes to prevent claims from arising.* Preventive Law Reporter, p. 12.

DiMatteo, L., Siedel, G., & Haapio, H. (2012). Strategic contracting: Examining the business-legal interface. In G. Berger-Walliser & K. Østergaard (Eds.), *Proactive law in a business environment* (pp. 59–106). Copenhagen, Denmark: DJØF Publishing.

EESC. (2009). Opinion of the European Economic and Social Committee on 'The pro-active law approach: a further step towards better regulation at EU level'. *Official Journal of the European Union*, 2009/C175/05, 26–33. http://eur-lex.europa.eu/legal-content/EN/TXT/PDF/?uri=CELEX:52008IE1905&from=EN. Accessed 26 Sept 2016.

Ertel, D. (2004). Getting past yes: Negotiating as if implementation mattered. *Harvard Business Review*, 82(11), 60–68.

Etzkorn, I. A. (2011, August). Ten commandments of simplification. *Center for Plain Language*. http://bustthefacts.blogspot.fi/2011/08/ten-commandments-of-simplification.html. Accessed 26 Sept 2016.

Felsenfeld, C., & Siegel, A. (1981). *Writing contracts in plain English*. St. Paul, MN: West Publishing Company.

Haapio, H. (2006). Introduction to proactive law. In P. Wahlgren (Ed.), *A proactive approach. Scandinavian studies in law* (Vol. 49, pp. 21–34). Stockholm, Sweden: Stockholm Institute for Scandinavian Law. http://www.scandinavianlaw.se/pdf/49-2.pdf. Accessed 26 Sept 2016.

Haapio, H. (2013a). Good contracts: Bringing design thinking into contract design. In J. Chittenden (Ed.), *Proceedings of the 2013 IACCM Academic Forum* (pp. 95–136). Ridgefield, CT: International Association for Contract and Commercial Management. http://www.iaccm.com/resources/?id=4958 (for members only). Accessed 26 Sept 2016.

Haapio, H. (2013b). *Next generation contracts: A paradigm shift*. Helsinki, Finland: Lexpert Ltd.

Haapio, H. (1998). *Quality improvement through proactive contracting: Contracts are too important to be left to lawyers!* Proceedings of Annual Quality Congress (AQC), American Society for Quality (ASQ), Philadelphia, PA, 52, May 1998, pp. 243–248.

Haapio, H. (Ed.). (2008). *A proactive approach to contracting and law*. Turku, Finland: International Association for Contract and Commercial Management & Turku University of Applied Sciences.

Haapio, H., & Passera, S. (2013, May 15). *Visual law: What lawyers need to learn from information designers*. VoxPopuLII Blog. Legal Information Institute, Cornell University Law School. http://blog.law.cornell.edu/voxpop/2013/05/15/visual-law-what-lawyers-need-to-learn-from-information-designers/. Accessed 26 Sept 2016

Haddad, S. (2013). Integration of law and contract management – Applying Contract visualization. In J. Chittenden (Ed.), *Proceedings of the 2013 IACCM Academic Forum* (pp. 52–73). Ridgefield, CT: International Association for Contract and Commercial Management. http://www.iaccm.com/resources/?id=4958 (for members only). Accessed 26 Sept 2016.

Hetrick, P. K. (2008). Drafting common interest community documents: Minimalism in an era of micromanagement. *Campbell Law Review*, 30(3), 409–435. http://scholarship.law.campbell.edu/cgi/viewcontent.cgi?article=1472&context=clr. Accessed 30 March 2016.

Hughes, S. (2015, March 6). Commercial excellence: Ten pitfalls to avoid in contracting. *IACCM Ask The Expert*. International Association for Contract and Commercial Management IACCM. https://www.iaccm.com/resources/?id=8451 (for members only). Accessed 30 March 2016.

IACCM. (2014a). 2013/2014 top terms. *International Association for Contract and Commercial Management IACCM*, 23 May 2014. https://www.iaccm.com/resources/?id=7619. Accessed 30 March 2016.

IACCM. (2014b). The IACCM innovation awards: Celebrating excellence & innovation in contracting. *International Association for Contract and Commercial Management IACCM*, 19 September 2014. https://www.iaccm.com/resources/?id=7840. Accessed 30 March 2016.

IACCM. (2014c). IBM - Finalist - Operational improvement award. *News* 6 December 2014, International Association for Contract and Commercial Management IACCM. https://www2.iaccm.com/resources/?id=8288. Accessed 30 March 2016.

IACCM. (2015a). *Commercial excellence: Ten pitfalls to avoid in contracting*. [Booklet] Ridgefield, CT: International Association for Contract and Commercial Management.

IACCM. (2015b). Top negotiated terms 2015: No news is bad news. *International Association for Contract and Commercial Management IACCM*. http://www2.iaccm.com/resources/?id=8930 (for members only). Accessed 30 March 2016.

IACCM. (2015c). *Webinar - Innovative contract management: How to infuse simplification into your contracts.* 1 December 2015, International Association for Contract and Commercial Management IACCM. https://www2.iaccm.com/resources/?id=8997 (for members only). Accessed 30 March 2016.

Jennejohn, M. (2008). Collaboration, innovation, and contract design. *Stanford Journal of Law, Business & Finance, 14*(1), 83–150.

Kimble, J. (2012). *Writing for dollars, writing to please. The case for plain language in business, government, and law.* Durham, NC: Carolina Academic Press.

Kimble, J. (2006). *Lifting the fog of legalese.* Durham, NC: Carolina Academic Press.

Lannerö, P. (2013, April 30). *Fighting the biggest lie on the Internet: Common terms beta proposal.* Stockholm, Sweden: Metamatrix. http://www.commonterms.net/commonterms_beta_proposal.pdf. Accessed 30 March 2016.

Macaulay, S. (2003). The real and the paper deal: Empirical pictures of relationships, complexity, and the urge for transparent simple rules. *The Modern Law Review, 66*(1), 44–79. doi:10.1111/1468-2230.6601003. http://www.law.wisc.edu/facstaff/macaulay/papers/real_paper.pdf. Accessed 26 Sept 2016.

Malhotra, D. (2012). Great deal, terrible contract: The case for negotiator involvement in the contracting phase. In B. M. Goldman & D. L. Shapiro (Eds.), *The psychology of negotiations in the 21st century workplace. New challenges and new solutions* (pp. 363–398). New York, NY: Routledge.

Mosten, F. S. (2009). *Collaborative divorce handbook: Helping families without going to court.* San Francisco, CA: Jossey-Bass.

NEC. (2014a). *A comparison of NEC and FIDIC.* https://www.neccontract.com/getmedia/2bd4ffb9-8e1e-4684-af86-1d913152f10d/A-comparison-of-NEC-and-FIDIC-by-Rob-Gerrard.pdf.aspx. Accessed 26 Sept 2016.

NEC. (2014b). *About NEC.* https://www.neccontract.com/About-NEC. Accessed 26 Sept 2016.

NEC. (2014c). *Products.* https://www.neccontract.com/Products. Accessed 26 Sept 2016.

NEC. (2014d). *Why NEC3?* https://www.neccontract.com/About-NEC/Why-NEC. Accessed 30 March 2016.

Nystén-Haarala, S. (Ed.). (2008). *Corporate contracting capabilities. Conference proceeding and other writings.* University of Joensuu Publications in Law, No 21. Joensuu, Finland: University of Joensuu.

Passera, S. (2012). Enhancing contract usability and user experience through visualization – An experimental evaluation. In E. Banissi, et al. (Eds.), *16th International Conference on Information Visualisation, IV2012,* 11–13 July 2012, Montpellier, France (pp. 376–382). Los Alamitos, CA: IEEE Computer Society.

Passera, S. (2014). *Contract understanding and usability test.* Aalto University School of Science & International Association for Contract & Commercial Management. https://www2.iaccm.com/resources/?id=7877 (for members only). Accessed 26 Sept 2016.

Passera, S. (2015). Make your contracts visual and user-centered. In: *FIMECC UXUS final report 1/2015 – User Experience and Usability in Complex Systems – UXUS* (pp. 181–186). FIMECC Publications Series No. 8. http://hightech.fimecc.com/results/final-report-uxus-user-experience-and-usability-in-complex-systems. Accessed 26 Sept 2016.

Passera, S., & Haapio, H. (2013a). Transforming contracts from legal rules to user-centered communication tools: A human-information interaction challenge. *Communication Design Quarterly, 1*(3), 38–45. http://sigdoc.acm.org/wp-content/uploads/2012/09/CDQ-April-1-3-FINAL.pdf. Accessed 26 Sept 2016.

Passera, S., & Haapio, H. (2013b). The quest for clarity – how visualisation improves the usability and user experience of contracts. In M. L. Huang & W. Huang (Eds.), *Innovative approaches of data visualisation and visual analytics.* (Advances in data mining and database management (ADMDM) series, pp. 191–217). Hershey, PA: IGI Global.

Passera, S., Haapio, H., & Barton, T. D. (2013). Innovating contract practices: Merging contract design with information design. In J. Chittenden (Ed.), *Proceedings of the 2013 IACCM Academic Forum* (pp. 29–51). Ridgefield, CT: International Association for Contract and

Commercial Management. http://www.iaccm.com/resources/?id=4958 (for members only). Accessed 26 Sept 2016.

Passera, S., Haapio, H., & Curtotti, M. (2014). Making the meaning of contracts visible – Automating contract visualization. In E. Schweighofer, F. Kummer, & W. Hötzendorfer (Eds.), *Transparenz. Tagungsband des 17. Internationalen Rechtsinformatik Symposions IRIS 2014/Transparency. Proceedings of the 17th International Legal Informatics Symposium IRIS 2014* (pp. 443–450). Wien, Austria: Österreichische Computer Gesellschaft OCG.

Patajoki, U. (2013, August 27). *Towards a successful contractual relationship. Public service procurement from a small business perspective.* Master's Thesis, Aalto University, School of Science, Degree Programme in Information Networks. http://tuta.aalto.fi/en/midcom-serveattachmentguid-1e47559bc2ceb62755911e4a2f4dd39aba9b4fdb4fd/ulla_patajoki_masters_thesis_final.pdf. Accessed 26 Sept 2016.

Pohjonen, S. (2002). Johdanto [Introduction]. In S. Pohjonen (Ed.), *Ennakoiva sopiminen – liiketoimien suunnittelu, toteuttaminen ja riskien hallinta [Proactive contracting – planning, implementing and managing risk in business transactions]* (pp. v–xiii). Helsinki, Finland: WSOY Lakitieto.

ProActive ThinkTank mission statement. (2007). http://www.juridicum.su.se/proactivelaw/main/thinktank/missionstatement.pdf. Accessed 26 Sept 2016.

Reisinger, S. (2014, December 16). *How IBM shrunk a complex contract down to 2 pages.* https://www2.iaccm.com/resources/?id=8527 (for members only). Accessed 26 Sept 2016.

Siedel, G., & Haapio, H. (2011). *Proactive law for managers: A hidden source of competitive advantage.* Farnham, England: Gower.

Siedel, G. J., & Haapio, H. (2010). Using proactive law for competitive advantage. *American Business Law Journal, 47*(4), 641–686. doi:10.1111/j.1744-1714.2010.01106.x.

Siegel, A., & Etzkorn, I. (2013). *Simple - Conquering the crisis of complexity.* New York, NY: Twelve.

Szabo, N. (2010). Design thinking in legal practice management. *Design Management Review, 21* (3), 44–46. doi:10.1111/j.1948-7169.2010.00078.x.

UK Office of Fair Trading (OFT). (2011, March 2011). *Consumer contracts – What you need to know.* OFT1318. http://webarchive.nationalarchives.gov.uk/20140402142426/http://www.oft.gov.uk/shared_oft/market-studies/consumercontracts/OFT1318_Consumer_Contracts_1.pdf. Accessed 26 Sept 2016.

US Consumer Financial Protection Bureau (CFPB). (2011, December 7). CFPB aims to simplify credit card agreements. Agency announces plans to pilot test prototype agreement; Invites public to weigh in. http://www.consumerfinance.gov/about-us/newsroom/consumer-financial-protection-bureau-aims-to-simplify-credit-card-agreements. Accessed 26 Sept 2016.

Wahlgren, P. (Ed.). (2006). *A proactive approach* (Scandinavian studies in law, Vol. 49). Stockholm, Sweden: Stockholm Institute for Scandinavian Law.

Waller, R. (2011a). *Information design: How the disciplines work together* (Technical paper 14). Simplification Centre. http://www.simplificationcentre.org.uk/downloads/papers/SC14DisciplinesTogether.pdf. Accessed 26 Sept 2016.

Waller, R. (2011b) *What makes a good document? The criteria we use* (Technical paper 2). Simplification Centre. http://www.simplificationcentre.org.uk/downloads/papers/SC2CriteriaGoodDoc_v2.pdf. Accessed 26 Sept 2016.

Waller, R. (2011c). *Simplification: What is gained and what is lost* (Technical paper 1). Simplification Centre. http://www.simplificationcentre.org.uk/downloads/papers/SC1SimplificationGainedLost-v2.pdf. Accessed 26 Sept 2016.

Waller, R. (2015). *Layout for legislation* (Technical paper 15). Simplification Centre. http://www.simplificationcentre.org.uk/downloads/papers/SC15LayoutLegislation-v2.pdf. Accessed 26 Sept 2016.

Weatherley, S. (2005, October–December). Pathclearer: A more commercial approach to drafting commercial contracts. *PLC Law Department Quarterly*, 39–46. http://www.clarity-international.net/documents/Pathclearer%20article%20in%20PLC-3.pdf. Accessed 26 Sept 2016.

Helena Haapio is an Associate Professor of Business Law at the University of Vaasa and International Contract Counsel at Lexpert Ltd. Based in Helsinki, Finland, she consults worldwide. She is a contract innovator and a pioneer of the proactive approach, where contracts and the law are seen as enablers rather than obstacles. She has for many years promoted the use of simplification and visualization in commercial contracts. Her multi-disciplinary research focuses on ways to enhance the functionality and usability of contracts. She is a member of the Advisory Council of the IACCM. She also acts as arbitrator in contract disputes.

Thomas D. Barton is a professor of law at California Western School of Law in San Diego, California. He lectures in the U.S. and abroad on a variety of topics, including Contracts, legal theory, and the prevention of legal problems. His latest research seeks methods for using emerging technology to help the legal system function better in the Information Age, including making contracts and legal rules more accessible through visualization.

Running the Legal Department with Business Discipline: Applying Business Best Practices to the Corporate Legal Function

Liam Brown, Kunoor Chopra, Pratik Patel, Jack Diggle, Peter Eilhauer, Suzanne Ganier, and Ron Dappen

Abstract

Running a successful business is difficult—ask any CEO. First you must face the reality of where you stand today. Then you need to develop a point of view about where you want to be in the future, by when, and design a strategic plan that sets out what you will do to get there—but just as importantly, what you choose *not* to do. You must prioritize the initiatives you will focus on, sequence their order, and build consensus, alignment and buy-in—both internal and external to the department—without which your plans will not succeed. Then you must execute. You must constantly measure, improve and course correct. You must analyze and manage your costs. You must scan the technology horizon in order to respond to threats and take advantage of opportunities. You must recruit, train, retain, and even inspire your people. You must decide what to build and what to buy. And you must do all these things at the speed of business! This article examines how leading legal departments are tackling the "more for less" challenge that they face by adopting applicable business disciplines from other corporate functions.

1 Introduction

Successful legal departments are addressing the growing "more for less" challenge by adopting proven, relevant practices from other business functions. The most effective General Counsel and senior legal department leaders have stepped into

L. Brown (✉) • K. Chopra • P. Patel • J. Diggle • P. Eilhauer • S. Ganier • R. Dappen
Elevate Services, Inc., 10250 Constellation Blvd., Suite 2815, Los Angeles, CA 90067, USA
e-mail: liam.brown@elevateservices.com; kunoor.chopra@elevateservices.com; pratik.
patel@elevateservices.com; jack.diggle@elevateservices.com; peter.eilhauer@elevateservices.
com; suzanne.ganier@elevateservices.com; ron.dappen@elevateservices.com

© Springer International Publishing AG 2017
K. Jacob et al. (eds.), *Liquid Legal*, Management for Professionals,
DOI 10.1007/978-3-319-45868-7_25

their "C-suite of Legal" shoes, running the legal department with business discipline.

As any C-suite executive will attest, running a successful company or function is challenging, but fortunately the world of business has already developed, tested, and documented a range of applicable best practices that can be studied and applied. With few exceptions, executives succeed by adapting and applying proven strategies and tactics that have stood the test of time.

The good news for legal department leaders seeking to run their department successfully is that they too can draw on this rich base of best practices. Not only are best practices inherently effective, they are understood by other business leaders outside of the legal department—in Sales, Finance, Operations, HR and so on—which facilitates communication, understanding, cooperation, and even respect between the General Counsel and other executives in the company's C-suite.

So, what are these business disciplines specifically, and how are they being applied in leading legal departments? They fall into several major categories: strategy, systems and processes, use of technology, people and organization, right-sourcing, spend and supplier management, and metrics.

2 Strategy: Determining Where You Are and Where You Want to Go

"Failure to plan is a plan to fail." This maxim applies to the legal department as much as it does to any business. Successful legal departments don't just plan quarter by quarter or initiative by initiative, they look further ahead, developing multi-year strategy roadmaps linked to company strategy, stakeholder input, and objective assessment data including benchmarking.

Well-developed strategy roadmaps do several things:

- Articulate a realistic picture of the department's current state
- Lay out a purpose and vision that aligns with the strategy of the company overall
- Set specific goals that align with and support the overall goals of the company
- Identify and prioritize initiatives and measures of success for achieving those goals

One of the best strategic roadmaps we've ever seen (see Fig. 1) was created by the NetApp Legal senior leadership team, under the guidance of Matthew Fawcett, GC, who literally held 100 meetings in 100 days to take stock of the legal department's current state when he first stepped into his role.

The most effective strategy plans are designed to enable the business, manage risk and cost, and clearly communicate to all members of the legal department what the priorities are—and are not—and what is expected of them. The strategy plan should connect the overall goals of the company and other departments to the goals of the legal department, cascading to the departmental priorities, then down to team and individual goals, linked to metrics that will be used to measure performance.

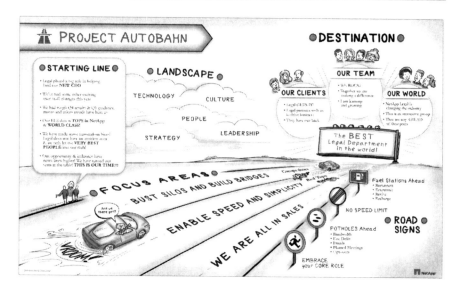

Fig. 1 Illustrated summary of NetApp's strategy roadmap, dubbed "Project Autobahn" (Source: NetApp Legal)

In our experience, determining which initiatives to prioritize and deciding on their sequence is complex because many factors must be considered. There is no "one size fits all" decision framework, but key areas of consideration include:

- Understanding and supporting the strategic activities of the business
- Identifying areas of risk to manage, and to what extent to manage them
- Carefully planning the sequence of initiatives, which may reveal that some activities need to happen in the right order to prepare the way for others in terms of technology, processes, staffing, and even change management
- Analyzing costs and effort involved, identifying relatively "easy wins" that can fund costlier subsequent initiatives.
- Being realistic about what can be achieved over what time-frame, effective change management and pacing, to foster buy-in, build momentum and avoid burning out in-house staff

A strategy is only as good as what you do with it, and successful legal departments are characterized by a distinctive ability to put their plans into action. Not only do the GCs of these companies achieve real operational improvements in their legal department, but they also gain the respect of the rest of the company C-suite, who understand and respect the value of this business discipline.

Developing a strategy requires starting out by understanding the department's current state, then developing a shared point of view about an improved future state, and finally, creating a multi-year roadmap to get there.

A clear understanding of the department's current state requires subjective input from relevant stakeholders, objective measures, and peer benchmarking (Fig. 2). The best legal departments measure key performance indicators (i.e., metrics) that provide objective information about how the department is performing. We will discuss metrics in more detail in Sect. 8.

Gathering subjective input can be difficult, but it is essential to do so in a structured manner in order to develop a true picture of the performance and effectiveness of the department, without bias or relying on anecdote. Subjective or qualitative information should be gathered using online surveys (see Fig. 3, an example from the legal department of BlueScope Steel, a multinational steel company) or through interviews with the in-house legal team, colleagues in Sales, Finance, Procurement, HR and other key groups, customers, and the company's legal service providers (law firms and non-law firms).[1]

Fig. 2 Strategic planning process (Source: Elevate)

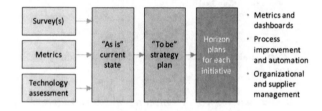

Fig. 3 Example results of online survey question (Source: Elevate)

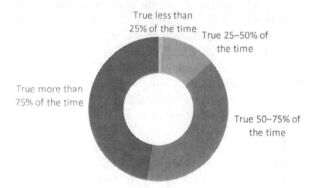

---

[1]Disclaimer: As the founder of a number of legal technology and service providers that are not law firms, I take it as a given that most effective legal departments now use both law firms and non-law firm legal service providers.

	Early Stage	Maturing	Mature	Best Practice
Business Alignment	• No team specialism • Reactive services coverage model based on business demand • No assessment of legal risks	• Business aligned structure • Service provided based on subjective analysis of key legal risks for the business • More proactive legal involvement in all steps of business lifecycle	• Business aligned relationship teams, with shared teams providing consistent delivery by practice area • Formal risk assessment sets parameters of legal service coverage • Some formal embedding of legal management into business boards	• Framework service agreements with business incorporating SLAs • Legal work guided by clear understanding of commercial benefits / legal risk to business • Presence of legal in all key business function boards enabling advice 'at source'
Resource Management	• Limited in-house team, 'pass-through' service to external counsel • Law firms provide both overflow resourcing and capability coverage	• In-house capability grown to match BAU demand, large projects still cause significant disruption • Firms still used heavily regardless of value / complexity • Formal role definitions for in-house teams, but inconsistent	• Internal and external resourcing decisions increasingly based on work value / complexity and understanding of volumes • Some understanding and use of alternative legal service providers (ALSPs) • Simple demand planning • Consistent role definition / work allocation across in-house teams	• All internal and external resourcing choices aligned with assessments of value / complexity of work • ALSPs fully embedded in ecosystem • No use of law firms for capacity; ability to flex resourcing quickly • MI and proactive demand planning supports resourcing decisions
Spend Management	• Uncontrolled external spend • Spend tracking relies entirely on Firm MI • No matter scoping • Engagements on rack-rate fees using Firm Ts&Cs	• Rudimentary efforts to consolidate spend with Firms • One-off spotlights on global spend for budgeting • Scoping, AFAs and bespoke Ts&Cs used for major matters • Ad-hoc invoice review	• Major spend areas designated to tender or consolidate with Firms • Regular spend data updates and analytics at practice area level • Scoping and AFAs extended to lower value matters • In-house Ts&Cs and billing guidelines, consistent approach to invoice review	• Formalized strategy to consolidate or tender at matter-level for all work • Real-time data analytics and scorecards • Automated, widespread usage of scoping and AFAs at all levels of matters • Automated straight-through bill review (third party or in-house), approvals and spend recovery embedded in invoice payments process
Operations, Processes, and Metrics	• No Legal Ops roles and responsibilities, ad-hoc ops issues supported by in-house lawyers and personal assistants • No documented processes	• Appointed Legal Ops roles and responsibilities, focused on back office processes e.g. invoice payments / IT delivery • Isolated efforts to improve processes and streamline spend mapping • KM processes are ad hoc	• Well defined legal processes and guidelines supported by legal project management • Dedication to continuous process improvement • KPIs defined in some areas • KM strategy defined	• Partnership with Firms and ALSPs extends to back office functions • Dedicated strategy and roadmap for improvements in front-to-back office technology and processes • Responsive management by KPIs • Proactive KM approaches adopted consistently
Technology	• Ad-hoc data collation via spreadsheets • Knowledge stored on individual work stations • Fully paper invoices • Hard-copy signatures	• Formalized data and document management on shared drives • Some adoption of e-billing • Contract management and knowhow systems in place, but not updated and used • IP docketing system in place • Formal relationships with e-Discovery providers • E-signature for NDAs / basic agreements	• Enterprise search across all data sources • Centralized contract management and knowhow systems widely used • IP prosecution /patent lifecycle system in place • TAR used occasionally in e-Discovery process • Integrated matter management / e-billing • Formal technology strategy • Fully integrated e-signatures and workflow with contract management system	• Centralized real-time dashboard and analytics capability • Paper based filing eliminated • TAR consistently used for all e-Discovery • Consistent and inter-operable systems architecture • Digital approvals for all legal and non-legal transactions

Fig. 4 Legal department maturity model (Source: Elevate)

In helping legal departments with strategic planning, we often use an operational maturity model (see Fig. 4, an example assessment framework we used with British Telecom's legal department) to: (a) develop a rich picture of the department's current state; (b) provide a framework for discussion of what the future state should be, and then (c) identify what the gaps are. At a summary level, the discussion addresses questions such as:

- How do the current activities of the legal department support the needs and goals of the company overall?
- What needs to be added, changed or discontinued?
- What is the most effective combination of resources, systems and tools to support the company's needs and goals?
- What are feasible next steps that can be taken now to achieve long-term goals?

In support of this assessment process, we typically gather and analyze data on work volumes and cycle times by task and complexity, legal spend and matter type, in order to identify performance trends and perform benchmarking, e.g., an analysis of a client's own portfolio of legal spend data against industry spend data for similar matters supported by similar firms, which can bring objectivity and actionable insights to an area that has historically been opaque and difficult to assess. However, different legal departments must manage different risks and other variables that impact spend, so not all industry-wide benchmarking is relevant. While benchmarking can be conducted as a one-off exercise, it is most impactful when conducted regularly, as shown in Fig. 5, where several months of data are included.

With the benefit of analytics, benchmarking, maturity assessment, and surveys from stakeholders, the legal department will have developed a clear picture of the "As Is" state. It can now start to brainstorm a mental picture of what it wants to look like in the "Future" state. During this facilitated workshop, the legal department will debate what it wants to start doing, what it wants to stop doing, what it wants to do more of or less of, in order to get to that future. The goal is to identify the key initiatives that the legal department wants to prioritize, and to create a one-page strategy plan that can be used to communicate to the whole legal team—see example in Fig. 6 that we helped IMS Health to produce. The framework illustrated here is based on the widely-used Balanced Scorecard approach.

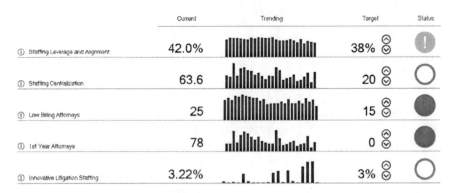

Fig. 5 Example spend benchmarking report (Summary Level), produced using our proprietary spend analytics tool Cael Vision. Similar reports can also be compiled manually, but technology can significantly streamline the administrative burden. (Source: Elevate)

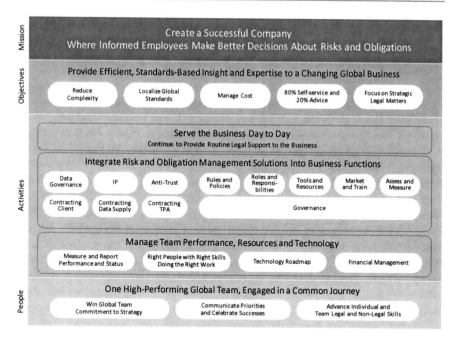

Fig. 6 Legal department strategy plan (Source: IMS Health and Elevate)

3 Systems and Processes: Working Smarter by Design

Efficient systems and processes directly affect the legal team's ability to meet the needs of the business, and they also have a profound effect on job satisfaction and retention. To assess and improve systems and processes, the legal sector has started to use Lean, a systematic method for increasing business value by eliminating waste, and legal project management ("LPM"), a growing trend likely to become table stakes within a few years.

Originally developed by Toyota, Lean is now widely used throughout the business world as a common standard for improving operations of all sorts, including both products and services. When applied to legal work, Lean does several practical things:

- It fosters continuous improvement by leveraging the experience and talent of the individuals closest to the work.
- It focuses the team's attention on the value provided to—and perceived by—clients and stakeholders for whom matters are handled.
- It encourages the development and use of standards and best practices.

Lean is sometimes confused with Six Sigma, a quality improvement approach that was originally developed by Motorola. Both are valuable in different ways, and in fact can be used in conjunction with each other—referred to as "Lean Six Sigma"—but in the legal sector Lean is more relevant because it is focused on improving the value of the output by eliminating process waste, whereas Six Sigma is focused on reducing defects to improve quality.

Lean provides a collection of practical tools and techniques, including defining a problem, mapping the relevant processes, conducting root cause analysis, identifying and implementing solutions, and monitoring corrective actions. These techniques allow the removal of waste and inefficiency in legal work that can take the form of waiting/delays, work that is out of scope, re-work, or "over-lawyering" work.

Using Lean techniques, we have helped NetApp implement systemic improvements in many areas of their legal department. One such was a new approach to client NDAs, which enabled the sales team to engage new clients more quickly, improved compliance, and reduced burden on the lawyers. Process Mapping (a Lean technique, but certainly not exclusive to the Lean approach) revealed a confusing, inefficient "As Is" process that was inherently slow, with too many hand-offs and unclear roles and responsibilities. A Lean question-asking technique called "The Five Whys" identified non-value added steps (waste) in the process. "The Fishbone Analysis" technique identified the resource and technology constraints. Using insights from these Lean techniques, we worked with the lawyers, legal ops team and sales team to simplify and automate a redesigned process whereby NDAs with no client changes—roughly 85 % of the total—can be processed on a self-serve basis using automated e-signature technology. Thus the majority of NDAs that previously took days can now be processed in minutes. The remaining 15 % of NDAs that require some legal review of client comments are routed to an Elevate legal team for review against a playbook. Less than a third of that 15 % segment actually require commercial negotiation and are escalated to the NetApp legal team. After implementing the new process, average time to NDA execution was reduced from five days to less than one hour, and the NetApp lawyer email noise was radically reduced—much to the lawyers' delight—as the new process allows them to focus on fewer than 200 NDAs per annum, compared to 4100 NDAs previously. (See Fig. 7.)

While not all examples of Lean process improvement are as dramatic as this one, substantial incremental improvements are made possible in many areas by tapping the expertise of individuals closest to the work. In addition to the improvements themselves, the Lean approach helps legal team members co-create and co-own the solution, increasing both buy-in and morale.

Improving systems and processes helps legal departments make optimal use of their people. While there are many valid approaches to improving systems and processes, we've seen the Lean approach prove to be effective in legal.

Law departments are increasingly bringing another common business discipline to the toolkit: project management. As with non-legal corporate functions, project management eliminates surprises; improving predictability of timelines, deliverables and budgets. Sophisticated legal departments now expect their law firms and other legal service providers to provide some form of legal project

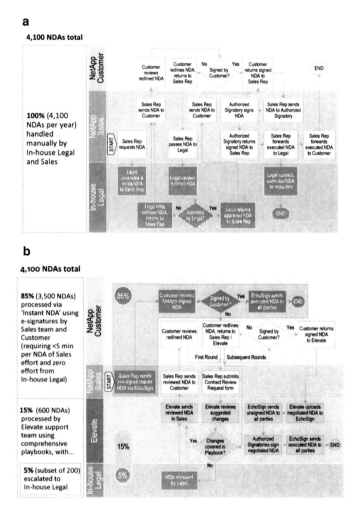

Fig. 7 System and process improvement facilitated by Lean for Legal (Source: NetApp and Elevate). (**a**) Before system and process redesign. (**b**) After system and process redesign

management (LPM), on both hourly and non-hourly fee engagements. More importantly, legal departments expect to benefit from the efficiencies and savings generated from LPM best practices.

They recognize that managing their matters more effectively requires thoughtful consideration of scope and assumptions at the outset, followed by planning and staffing the matter based on those factors, and subsequently revisiting the plan on a regular and frequent basis throughout the lifecycle of each matter. Based on our experience designing and implementing LPM frameworks—see Fig. 8 for an example—as well as providing enabling software for LPM, we expect the LPM trend to become table stakes in the legal market for both law firms and law departments within the next 3–5 years.

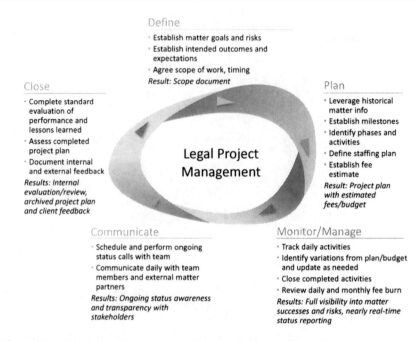

Define
- Establish matter goals and risks
- Establish intended outcomes and expectations
- Agree scope of work, timing

Result: Scope document

Close
- Complete standard evaluation of performance and lessons learned
- Assess completed project plan
- Document internal and external feedback

Results: Internal evaluation/review, archived project plan and client feedback

Legal Project Management

Plan
- Leverage historical matter info
- Establish milestones
- Identify phases and activities
- Define staffing plan
- Establish fee estimate

Result: Project plan with estimated fees/budget

Communicate
- Schedule and perform ongoing status calls with team
- Communicate daily with team members and external matter partners

Results: Ongoing status awareness and transparency with stakeholders

Monitor/Manage
- Track daily activities
- Identify variations from plan/budget and update as needed
- Close completed activities
- Review daily and monthly fee burn

Results: Full visibility into matter successes and risks, nearly real-time status reporting

Fig. 8 Example legal project management framework (Source: Elevate)

The rise of LPM has also enabled more active and real-time collaboration on matters. Historically, lawyers in-house often had to wait until they received a monthly fee invoice to understand in detail how the law firm was spending its time and interpret what progress had been made in the previous month. That scenario was prone to surprises, often resulting in damaged trust and reactive discussions about fees and discounts as the corporate legal department sought to manage its budget. Today, a growing number of technologies enable easy, frequent monitoring of matter progress, hours spent and budgets to actuals, helping in-house teams and outside counsel stay in sync and course correct when needed, before things get out of hand.

Legal departments have begun to use sophisticated but practical approaches to working more effectively, both internally and externally with outside counsel and other providers. By embracing principles found in Lean and LPM, legal leaders are improving systems and processes, leading to better efficiency, outcomes, working relationships and job satisfaction, thus driving better business.

4 Useful Technology: Choosing and Implementing Effective Tools

Ensuring that legal teams have access to the right tools requires understanding the business or lawyer user needs, assessment and planning, selection, investment, implementation and, in some cases, experimentation.

Fig. 9 Key technology elements for legal departments at the time of writing (Source: Elevate)

With the caveat that legal technologies continue to evolve rapidly, the current scope of a legal department's technology framework typically includes the key elements shown in Fig. 9.

To assess the state of a legal department's technology, we start with the technology dimension of the Legal Department Maturity Model to identify the opportunities. While we help GCs use a department-wide assessment to build a comprehensive technology "heat map," we quickly dive into a more detailed technology assessment focused on a specific function or need. For example, if a legal team believes that their contract lifecycle management (CLM) tools need to be updated, they can use this methodology to focus specifically on the selection of a new CLM system:

- Define legal and business outputs or objectives
- Map those objectives to desired technologies, features and workflows
- Explore availability and assess functionality of existing tools, and identify
- Understand actual usage of current tools, barriers to adoption use or other limitations, and identify any training needs to better leverage the current investments
- Perform feature comparison and cost analysis of technology options

Build a business case, project plan and change management plan for new technology purchases, if necessary. Because the world of technology changes quickly, it is important to scan the horizon for new technologies as well as changes to existing tools, including new version releases, mergers and acquisitions of existing products, and, in some cases, "retirement" of existing tools.

Legal departments often rely on outside providers for the implementation of new technologies and training. This gives the legal department access to additional resources and expertise. However, it is important to have people on the team with experience of having implemented that specific technology previously, and who have a crystal clear view of the process that is being automated or supported. This new breed of lawyers could be thought of as "legal engineers." Unfortunately, we see too many legal departments buy technology, e.g. matter management or e-billing systems, which are configured by the technology provider's professional services team without a deep understanding of the company's unique processes—so even if the technology is great, it doesn't ever quite do what the legal department needs it to do, leading to frustration and a misplaced future aversion to technology.

On the other hand, we also see some innovative legal departments experiment with technology, leading the adoption of new versions of existing products, as well as beta testing new tools and even collaborating to design new tools from scratch. This experimentation has ushered in an explosion of legal technologies such as electronic signatures, technology assisted review ("TAR"), auto-extraction of contract metadata, legal spend analysis, and centralized dashboards. Not surprisingly, legal departments that experiment or lead the use of new technology are in the minority; most prefer to let others work out the bugs first. However, the majority can still benefit by following what their experimentally-inclined peers are doing by listening to what they have to say at industry conferences, in articles and awards focused on innovation, and in groups like the Corporate Legal Operations Consortium ("CLOC"), a knowledge-sharing group. (More about CLOC in the following section and elsewhere in this book.)

5 People and Organization: Managing Your Most Valuable Resource

In recent years, sophisticated law departments have been hiring Legal Operations professionals to improve policies and processes, select and implement technologies, manage change, develop and track KPIs (key performance indicators), plan and manage projects and budgets, manage law firm and non-law firm legal service providers, and otherwise drive efficiencies. If the GC is effectively CEO of the legal department, then the Legal Ops head is effectively the legal department's COO, responsible for driving peak performance by coordinating the non-lawyering aspects of how the department functions. In 2015, the Association of Corporate Counsel estimated that about one third of GCs at Fortune 500 companies have Legal Ops staff.

The most senior Legal Ops professionals frequently serve as Chief of Staff to the GC, with responsibility to enhance the performance of the legal department's most valuable resource—its people. The Chief of Staff reinforces and communicates the GC's vision, and the mission, values, and culture of the department. Organizational planning and personnel development strengthens the legal team and the operation in many ways: improving management capabilities, succession planning, fostering teamwork and trust, and increasing job satisfaction and retention. Improved retention reduces the disruption and cost of staff turnover, protecting institutional knowledge and improving the effectiveness of the legal department. Legal Ops leaders serve as champions of culture, ensuring buy-in and adoption of changes and new initiatives among the department's lawyers. Most Legal Ops people are lawyers themselves, but many have formal business training, often JD/MBAs. Legal Ops leaders often attribute their success to their willingness to experiment and risk failure, coupled with confidence in their ability to course correct while initiatives are underway. Successful Legal Ops professionals "get things done" in the legal department from the inside—by partnering with the lawyers.

As part of this relatively new, but quickly growing discipline, many Legal Ops professionals participate actively in groups such as CLOC and the ACC's newly-formed Legal Ops sub-group, which meet regularly to share knowledge, best practices and advice. These groups have developed and published several legal industry guidelines for general use, including billing guidelines and a detailed profile of the Legal Ops and Chief of Staff role, with more guidelines in development, e.g. budget templates, e-signature policy, and GC metrics. More information on CLOC is available on their website at www.cloc.org, and more information on ACC Legal Ops is available at www.acc.com/legalops.

6 Right-Sourcing: Dividing (i.e., Unbundling) and Conquering

GCs are developing frameworks to decide what legal work to eliminate, automate, outsource, or retain in-house. Whether a legal department's people work in-house or as an extension of the department via law firms or other legal service providers, "right-sourcing" makes the best possible use of those resources, ensuring they are engaged in their "highest and best use" by assigning them the work that is most appropriate to their capabilities and cost. Right-sourcing results in improved levels of service to the business, operational efficiency and savings for the legal department, as well as job satisfaction and lawyer retention.

Right-sourcing ties strategic planning, organizational design, and supplier management together. To make right-sourcing decisions, legal departments must assess the factors that impact the appropriate profile and location of the resource. Examples include:

- Whether the work is tied to the competitive advantage of the business
- Risk
- Regulatory considerations, such as cross-border data restrictions
- Specific jurisdiction or practice area knowledge requirements
- Level of knowledge of the business required
- Requirement to interact in-person or during same office hours with the business
- Turnaround time requirements and expectations
- Other dependencies, such as availability of talent or access to proprietary systems required
- Opportunity to automate
- Cost
- Project management and tying the work together

Legal departments now realize that some legal matters are divisible and assign each component of a legal case or transaction to a resource or provider whose capabilities, cost or business model are best suited to that specific task. By "unbundling" legal work, legal departments ensure that lower level work is delegated to more junior resources, freeing up more senior in-house lawyers for work that is more valuable to the business, or more complex work that would ordinarily be sent to outside counsel. This improves the development of junior team members while managing risk appropriately, and it reduces the amount of lower level work being done by senior lawyers, increasing their job satisfaction. In some cases, right-sourcing identifies some work that doesn't need to be done by lawyers and reassigns that work to paralegals or administrators—or doesn't need to be done at all.

Over the last decade legal departments have successfully unbundled litigation matters into value-added, bespoke advisory work, which is sourced from law firms; and repeatable, systematized document review and e-discovery, which is now handled efficiently by a non-law firm provider. With that large spend under control, many legal operations are now applying similar efficiency strategies to due diligence and contracts, including: streamlining processes, implementing technologies for automation, delegating repeatable work to lower cost resources, etc. In addition to significant cost savings and freeing up valuable in-house resources, this also provides several strategic advantages. Robust contract lifecycle management can improve service to the business, increase visibility, reduce risk, and improve compliance. It has enabled a global banking client of ours to support ring-fencing requirements and has enabled a global technology client to shorten speed to revenue by 14 days.

To ensure that work is methodically and efficiently delegated to appropriate resources, we work with our clients to implement formal systems for assigning work requests based on relevant factors of risk/impact and complexity. We have found that it is helpful to designate a "Legal Front Gate" that is the point of contact for stakeholders requesting support. As outlined in Fig. 10, this role uses a pre-defined complexity matrix to assess and assign work to a range of experience levels, as well as collecting metrics on turnaround time, work volumes, SLA compliance and other operational KPIs. In addition to enabling operational reporting, this creates a built-in feedback loop that helps the Legal Front Gate continuously improve criteria and processes for assigning work.

One of our clients, a global metals and mining company, has used this "Legal Front Gate" support model to manage a significant volume of in-house work in both English and French, tapping resources (provided by Elevate) based in the U.S., U.K. and India to support their legal offices in 11 countries worldwide.

Many GCs and Legal Ops leaders leverage non-law firm legal service providers to "extend and enable" their department, supporting a wide variety of day-to-day activities such as contract management, litigation investigatory document review, due diligence, and project management. This enables in-house lawyers to focus on

Legal Front Gate assesses work and tabulates complexity score based on work/task type, transaction complexity, and monetary value of underlying transaction

Work Type	Description	Complexity Level
Drafting, Negotiation	Simple amendment or SOW to existing agreement	1
Drafting, Negotiation	Complex amendment or SOW to existing agreement	3
Drafting, Negotiation	One time procurement – short form	1
Drafting, Negotiation	One time procurement – long form	2
Drafting, Negotiation	Long term procurement agreements – short form	1
Drafting, Negotiation	Long term procurement agreements – long form	2
Drafting, Negotiation	Creation of customized contract for strategic sourcing purpose	3
Drafting, Negotiation	Simple Termination Letter or Agreement	1
Drafting, Negotiation	More complex Termination Letter or Agreement	3
Review of changes to Terms	Review and respond to changes proposed by Supplier to standard terms (topics covered in playbook)	1
Review of changes to Terms	Review and respond to changes proposed by Supplier to standard terms (topics not covered in playbook)	3
Review of changes to Terms	Review of Supplier comments or changes to simple Termination Letter or Agreement	2
Review of changes to Terms	Review of Supplier comments or changes to more complex Termination Letter or Agreement	3
Review, Negotiation Supplier Terms	Review of supplier's simple amendments, SOWs to existing agreements	1
Review, Negotiation Supplier Terms	Review of supplier's complex amendments, SOWs to existing agreements	3

Legal Front Gate assigns work based on complexity score, turnaround time required, and resource availability

Aggregate Complexity Score	Resource Required	Description
1–3	Contracts Specialist / Junior Attorney	3–5 years' experience
3–4	Mid-level Attorney	5–10 years' experience
5–6	Senior Attorney	10+ years' experience

Fig. 10 Legal Front Gate assigning work using complexity matrix (Source: Elevate)

providing the business with exceptional legal services. It also enriches the careers of the in-house team, allowing them to take on more fulfilling challenges while providing hands-on experience delegating and managing work to others—a skill set that will be useful to their future careers.

7 Spend and Supplier Management: Applying Business Savvy to Buying Legal Services

Law firms and other suppliers of legal services constitute the majority of legal department spend, therefore effective legal spend management requires effective supplier management, which has several aspects: systematic use of a panel of law firms and non-law firm legal service providers, an effective engagement letter and billing guidelines, electronic billing tools, a formal program for outside counsel selection and management, and a framework for "legal spend under management."

Buying legal services cost effectively begins with having a range of sound choices in the legal department's panel of providers, then ensuring that work is assigned appropriately depending on the profile of the work. The most effective legal operations use a systematic approach to match matters to appropriate firms and alternative providers based on type of matter, complexity, risk, business impact, and other factors, balancing priorities and outcomes required against cost. Such a system can also facilitate effective alternative fee arrangements.

Implementing an effective engagement letter enables the legal department to reset expectations and terms of engagement across all prior relationships, both formal and informal, with panel firms. When we help clients develop engagement letters and billing guidelines, we recommend a concise charter for working together with outside counsel, including:

- A statement of purpose
- Partnership expectations
- Technology and information security requirements
- Matter and timekeeper procedures
- Billing and invoice submission rules (including resolutions and penalties)
- Budgeting, forecasting and accrual rules
- Staffing guidelines

Also, CLOC has defined a set of standard billing guidelines for use by legal departments across a wide range of industries. These guidelines are publicly available on the CLOC website at cloc.org.

Electronic billing was once seen by legal departments as a nice-to-have technology, but now it is viewed as an essential tool for effective spend management, streamlining the invoice review and approval process, enabling automated rules to help enforce billing guidelines, and making possible sophisticated legal spend analysis and management.

E-billing also increases the efficiency of expert invoice review. Professional invoice review services typically identify 5–10 % savings on legal bills while also reducing the amount of in-house time and resources spent on invoice review. An effective review methodology will check compliance to guidelines, reasonableness of charges, and billing accuracy. In-house lawyers who rarely look forward to checking invoices and negotiating with outside counsel are often relieved to have this responsibility taken up by the legal ops team or a third party service, escalating to them only when necessary. While e-billing and expert invoice review can be used independently of one another, they are substantially more effective when used together.

In addition to cost containment, legal departments can use expert invoice review to gain insights into what lawyers are actually doing, and then use those insights to more efficiently approach certain practices of law. For example, one of our clients used this analysis to identify and selectively assign specific activities to firms that were especially efficient in those areas. Another client used our analysis of invoice line items to calculate benchmarks for flat fee structures, making cost more predictable for certain kinds of matters. In other words, expert invoice review can reveal insights from the massive volume of billing data, which can deliver targeted opportunities to reduce budget uncertainty.

Handling billing data electronically also enables other valuable business practices. For example, we helped the NetApp legal department use their billing data to create an automated system for verifying whether proposed hourly rates for outside counsel lawyers are "fair market value." The system benchmarks proposed rates entered in the e-billing platform against NetApp's historical spend data as well as industry-wide legal spend data.

The legal operations team uses this information to set systematically approved rates in the e-billing system, and they respond to the outside counsel firm with an auto-generated letter informing them of the rates approved by NetApp, advising the firm to respond to NetApp within 14 days if the approved rates pose any concern. This shifts the management burden of initiating any renegotiation from the legal department to outside counsel. The legal department openly invites their outside counsel firms to collaboratively use this benchmarking system with them so firms can proactively determine rates that fall within the objectively determined, approved ranges. With this new approach, the legal department has solved a typical cost management challenge of receiving annual rate increase letters from law firms. Made possible by an e-billing platform, this sophisticated business strategy has lowered costs by an average of 7%, while helping NetApp legal reward outside counsel firms that propose market-appropriate rates (Fig. 11).

Fig. 11 Example of spend analytics benchmarking for a law firm, with timekeeper names redacted for confidentiality (Source: Elevate)

Business everywhere understands that spend management is most effective when coupled with relationship management for a holistic Supplier Relationship Management (SRM) program. This is especially applicable in the legal market, given the nuances, complexity and quality expectations inherent in legal work. In our experience, the best legal department programs for outside counsel management involve an investment of time in a regular rhythm of scheduled business reviews, supported by balanced scorecards (see Fig. 12 for an example used by the NetApp legal department), which measure and report performance across a range of criteria that the legal department values. Such investment delivers high ROI, including: improving the value of legal services delivered, increasing budget transparency and predictability, enabling successful alternative fee arrangements, fostering more objective discussions about law firm performance relative to law department needs, and generally improving working relationships with outside counsel.

Legal departments often wonder how deep to go with SRM. In our experience, it varies depending on the size of the company, the legal department, and the size of panel firm relationships, but we often advise clients to apply an 80/20 rule: the bottom 80 % of spend should be passively managed through analytics, reporting, engagement letters, billing guidelines and bill review, but the top 20 % of spend

Qualitative Analysis		Quantitative Analysis		
Category	**Score**	**Category**	**Performance Details**	**Score**
Subject Matter Expertise	3.5	Staffing Models	• High Partner-leverage (65%) for compliance and products matters • Overall, high partner leverage across all matters (47%)	2
Business Alignment	4			
Responsiveness/ Accessibility	3.5	Staffing Efficiency	• 55 Unique TKs used to provide 1.73 FTEs worth of work (32 TK/FTE); 52% higher than firm portfolio average (21 TKs/FTE) • Legal research activities are being performed by high-level resources at very high rates ($404 WABR);	1
Project Management	4			
Budgeting Accuracy	2.5			
Creativity	3.5			
Proactive Execution	3	Fees/ Costs	• Partner-level rates higher than portfolio averages for compliance and products area ($652/hr. vs. $561/hr.) • Associate-level rates generally in line with Client portfolio averages	2
Aggressiveness to Resolve	1			
Communication	3			
Partnership/ Trustworthiness	3	Compliance	• Paralegal rates well above allowed averages ($246 vs. $100) • Billing precision score is 3.55/5; Ranked 49/77 Firms • Timely, accurate and consistent submission of invoices problematic.	3
Quality and Presentation	3.5			
Results/Outcomes	3			

Fig. 12 Balanced scorecard example used in outside counsel management by NetApp for one of their law firms (Source: NetApp and Elevate)

should be actively managed using regular business reviews, balanced scorecards, alternative fees, etc. In general, focusing on the firms and matters that account for the largest amounts of spend will achieve the largest impact.

These same SRM principles apply to non-law firm legal service providers, including, discovery and document review providers, traditional LPO and other "NewLaw" type providers. As a non-law firm provider of legal services, we actively encourage clients to participate in quarterly and annual business reviews of our performance, using a balanced scorecard.

We have seen law departments realize annual savings of 5–15 % in outside legal spend using SRM programs, which have led to lawyers at both the law firm and the legal department working more effectively and efficiently. It takes time, but by working with outside counsel methodically, an SRM program provides the continuous improvement framework and roadmap to implement other business disciplines, such as better budgeting, project management, alternative fee arrangements, and unbundling or right sourcing legal work.

At a macro level, it is valuable to monitor "legal spend under management," a concept adapted from sourcing organizations, which originally developed the idea of "spend under management" to gauge how much control and effectiveness they have in managing cost. The premise is that the most effective management of spend and service provider performance uses a blend of passive, active and collaborative measures, with increasing levels focus for spend associated with strategic or critical matters. The model we use to advise clients on legal spend under management is shown in Fig. 13.

Within this framework, legal departments should strive to manage almost all spend at the *Visible* level or better. The *Not Managed* category should include only a small percentage of spend, comprised of mostly of one-off spend items or spend controlled by another department. Beyond that threshold, a legal department's passive, active, and collaborative strategies will be influenced by the department's size, scope, and goals. Achieving the ideal state typically takes several years (see Fig. 13c), and we advise legal departments to build this into their strategic plan.

Legal spend management and supplier relationship management go hand in hand, applying business discipline to the business of law. Key elements of this include spend analytics, managed use of a panel of legal service providers (including law firms and others), an effective engagement letter, billing guidelines, electronic billing tools and expert invoice review, and a systematic approach to outside counsel management—all of which can be monitored at a macro level by applying the "legal spend under management" framework. Integrating these disciplines typically delivers 15–35 % savings per annum.

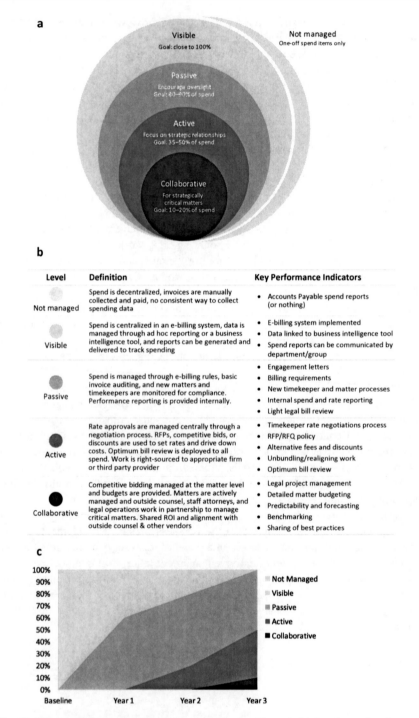

Fig. 13 Legal spend under management model (Source: Elevate). (**a**) Legal spend under management: conceptual framework. (**b**) Legal spend under management: definitions and key performance indicators. (**c**) Legal spend under management: example of multi-year progress

8   Metrics: Measuring What You Manage

So you know where you are today (survey, benchmarking, capability maturity assessment); where you want to go and the route you want to take (mission and strategy); you're driving a well-tuned car for the journey (systems, processes and technology); with the right people in the right seats (organization and people). To ensure you get to where you're heading, on time, you need to keep track of the car's location, direction, speed, and fuel level—and to make course corrections throughout the journey. Likewise, the modern GC uses metrics to monitor how the department is performing. As the business world likes to say, "You can't manage what you don't measure."

In order to be useful, the metrics framework must measure information relevant to the legal department's business goals and objectives. In order to be practical, the scope of measurement must be proportionate to the department's stage of operational maturity. When we help clients develop legal department key performance indicators (KPIs), we recommend focusing energy on collecting and reporting only those measures that inform management decisions or actions. Where possible they should be "forward indicators" giving visibility ahead, rather than "lagging indicators" that only look behind. To understand the whole picture, include measures of both internal and external performance—that is, collect data from within the in-house team, from customers and other stakeholders (see Fig. 14). After distilling law department performance from "anecdata" (anecdotal data) to objective KPIs, we recommend monitoring trends over time and using benchmarks to evaluate where the department stands against peers.

It is important to remember the audience; different metrics may be required by different levels of management. At the strategic level, the GC measures the overall status of the department and progress against major goals and objectives using metrics such as total legal spend as % of revenue or total legal spend per in-house headcount. Meanwhile at the tactical level, more granular metrics help managers to measure day-to-day operations, such as cycle time to execute a contract and volume levels. And at the micro level, which fallback positions are being used most often, in order to continuously improve a contract playbook. Effective reporting generally

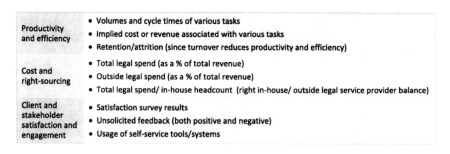

Productivity and efficiency	• Volumes and cycle times of various tasks • Implied cost or revenue associated with various tasks • Retention/attrition (since turnover reduces productivity and efficiency)
Cost and right-sourcing	• Total legal spend (as a % of total revenue) • Outside legal spend (as a % of total revenue) • Total legal spend/ in-house headcount (right in-house/ outside legal service provider balance)
Client and stakeholder satisfaction and engagement	• Satisfaction survey results • Unsolicited feedback (both positive and negative) • Usage of self-service tools/systems

Fig. 14 Example KPI framework with both internal and external dimensions (Source: Elevate)

provides managers with no more than six to ten high level summary metrics and the ability to drill down to more detail levels as needed.

From a business perspective, all relevant metrics measure cost, value, or both in some fashion; where possible, they also enable budgeting and prediction. To use a simple example, metrics on litigation volumes by matter type, complexity and risk profile enable more accurate budgets. On the more sophisticated end of the spectrum, we have helped clients cross-reference litigation portfolio metrics with outside counsel spend data to create a system for selecting panel firms more cost-effectively, depending on matter type, complexity and risk.

Metrics frameworks vary depending on the operational maturity of the legal department. To be of practical use, they must focus on what is currently relevant and feasible to measure that will enable the department to progress to the next stage of development—at which point the metrics framework can be refreshed to address the new current state. To help inform this discussion with legal departments about the ongoing evolution of metrics, we often use the same operational maturity model shown in Fig. 4, earlier in this chapter.

Effective legal operations use data and metrics to manage performance against strategic goals and objectives and to inform decision-making. Smart GCs automate data gathering where possible and take advantage of new technologies that display analysis of the metrics in easy to use dashboards. Automation can reduce the human time and effort required to gather and display relevant data. Many technologies, from e-billing to contract lifecycle management tools, provide some automatic report generation. More advanced operations use centralized dashboard tools and business intelligence technologies to aggregate data from many sources (e.g., e-billing, matter management, contract management, e-signature tools, IP management, etc.), providing a unified interface for real-time reports and ad hoc analysis. See Fig. 15 for examples of Elevate's Cael Vision dashboard and reports for VMware, a technology provider of cloud and virtualization services. These dashboards have helped the VMware legal team to manage their innovative contract lifecycle management approach, including heavy use of electronic signatures (see Fig. 15c).

Regardless of the level of sophistication a legal department has reached, we encourage GCs to adopt the mantra "visibility is valuable," because there is almost always room for material improvement. The most successful GCs know what data they have, what they need, and what they know they want but cannot yet capture (see Fig. 16) in order to drive the objectives they seek—lower cost, higher efficiency, greater predictability and better outcomes. In this context, the key to making data useful is to work towards improving the quality of it, taking incremental steps to move it from the lower right quadrant to the upper left quadrant.

Often the data from the various sources is not easy to tap into in real time, without manipulating in some way, in which case we recommend an analyst develop and document a repeatable methodology to gather and normalize the data so that the dashboards are kept up to date—there is much less value in reports that are used once a year than a live dashboard that is referred to and used proactively to make management predictions and decisions.

In one advanced example of the use of data, Intel's Business Legal group has borrowed and adapted best practices in supply chain management to create units of

a

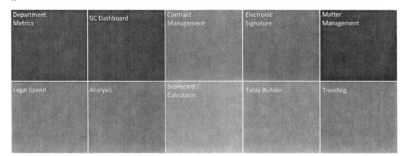

CAEL Vision™

b

c

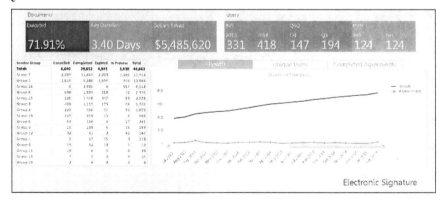

Fig. 15 Example of centralized dashboard, reporting and analysis tool (Source: VMware and Elevate). (**a**) Menu showing reporting and analysis areas. (**b**) Billed hours report. (**c**) Electronic signature usage report

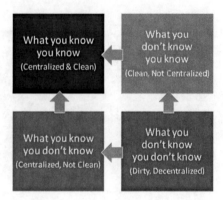

Fig. 16 Different states of data. *Arrows* indicate progress towards greater usefulness (Source: Elevate)

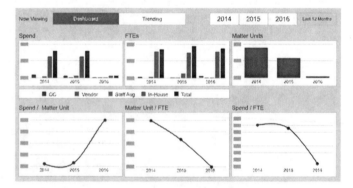

Fig. 17 Intel's legal dashboard uses supply chain best practices to measure value and identify opportunities for efficiency. Values redacted for confidentiality. (Source: Intel's Business Legal group and Elevate)

measure for the throughput of legal work. The idea—still in development—is to create units of measure for volume of work (Matter Units) and lawyer resources (FTEs), based on internal and external Spend, which will enable Intel to monitor trends such as Spend/Matter Unit. Done right, this will help Intel's legal department measure value and identify opportunities for efficiency. (See Fig. 17.)

9   Conclusion

By adapting and applying strategies and tactics that have already stood the test of time in the world of business, the most successful GCs and senior legal department leaders now function as "the C-suite of Legal," running the legal department with business discipline to achieve results. Best practices in strategy, systems and processes, useful technology, people and organization, right-sourcing, spend and supplier management, and metrics improve the effectiveness and efficiency of the legal department and win the respect of colleagues and peers throughout the business.

Liquid Legal Context
By Dr. Dierk Schindler, Dr. Roger Strathausen, Kai Jacob

Brown offers the pure and stringent future vision for a legal department that aims to be run as a business. He basically states that this requires the department to be made up of and to monitor the same elements as the business overall, i.e. strategy, processes and systems, technology, people, budget, a partner ecosystem etc.

If that is the starting point, his point that legal needs to think of its leadership as the "C-suite of legal", is nothing but consistent and it reveals the magnitude of the challenge that legal faces in the transformation. Yet, is the change he describes not too much in one leap, too ambitious a goal to be achieved while keeping the eyes on day-to-day work? This is when Brown offers a Legal Maturity model, which is based on the reality of this being a multi-stage journey and at the same time provides for orientation as to "where we are" on that journey.

Based on his vast amount of experience in building up and leading the new types of LPOs and advising clients on exactly that journey, Brown displays very practical and detailed examples on the various building blocks for running legal as a business, or rather for running legal with business discipline to achieve results that add value to the business.

Liam Brown has spent over 20 years as an advisor and consultant helping general counsel and law firm leaders design and implement successful strategic change programs focused on improving effectiveness and efficiency. He founded Elevate in 2011, a next generation legal service provider with the mission to help corporate legal departments and law firms operate more effectively. He was the Founder, President and CEO of Integreon, Inc., a global legal process outsourcing provider, which he led from startup in 2001 to annual sales of nearly $150 million by 2011, before he sold his stake to the private equity investors to launch Elevate. Prior to Integreon, he was the President, COO and co-founder of Conscium, Inc., a pioneering Web 1.0 legal virtual data room technology company, which he sold in 2001. Liam is a frequent speaker at legal conferences and regularly publishes articles about trends in the legal sector. He is also an active investor in Web 2.0 and Cloud technologies in the legal sector, and an executive coach for founders of startups.

LIQUID LEGAL Manifesto: Changing the State of Aggregation in Legal

Dierk Schindler

Abstract

The fundamental change in the legal industry is often called the end of an era. While this accurately reflects the gravity of the impact, it disguises the huge opportunity this holds for our function. Building on our intrinsic capability of creating trust and stability in business, legal can and should look into the future—as unknown as many things may be—with an optimistic mindset.

Traditional boundaries in our industry and around our function collapse. They are torn down by the *new types* of services offered by legal process outsourcers (LPO's), the *new ways* services are being offered by LPO's and also law firms, and of course the radically *new opportunities* that legal technology brings about.

The new landscape and the new horizons created by the changes open the way for legal to rethink modus operandi. We can and must break free from our self-referential system and find a new balance between our interdependence, i.e. how we relate to the company as a whole, and our independence, i.e. our own self. This will enable us to recalibrate ourselves and strive to create business value straight by our own work and by how we go about it.

As we think about the creation of value and as we embrace the vast opportunity that legal technology holds for us in that respect, our approach to both, primary legal data, and, legal analytics will change. As we introduce smart legal technology to our work that supports our processes on primary legal data, we will automatically be able to generate legal analytics that create unique insights for the company.

In LIQUID LEGAL, collaboration is the new paradigm! Forward looking non-profit organizations will drive us forward; open exchange between inhouse departments will create ideas and confidence when stepping onto unknown territory; academia has a wealth of guidance to offer and legal education an

D. Schindler (✉)
NetApp B.V., Schiphol-Rijk, The Netherlands
e-mail: dierk.schindler@netapp.com

© Springer International Publishing AG 2017
K. Jacob et al. (eds.), *Liquid Legal*, Management for Professionals,
DOI 10.1007/978-3-319-45868-7_26

opportunity to adapt to a rapidly changing profile of lawyers that must be reflected in the curriculum.

The law of gravitation in legal has changed. Maneuvering requires a new vision and new strategies. Leadership is required throughout and leaders need to rethink their traditional approaches and need to welcome the new talent, skills and roles that come into being in legal. We need to run our function with business discipline.

If everything flows, we better change our state of aggregation and become LIQUID LEGAL and, in the spirit of collaboration, continue to share what we learn—to create and add new value.

1   Introduction

Welcome to a time of exponential change, the most amazing time ever to be alive.

This is how Peter H. Diamandis, Co-Founder of the Singularity University, opens his foreword to the inspiring book "Exponential Organizations".[1] Reading this line, the well-conditioned managerial mind immediately gravitates to "change" and then to the many concepts around change management. Yet, there are two elements in this statement that I believe are much more important and, above all, perfectly relevant for where the legal industry is today: *"exponential"* and *"amazing"*.

Why *"exponential"*? In the regular course of events, professions that interact in (or with) corporate environments are being gradually shaped by two forces: first, by their own drive which they develop dependent on the creativity, innovation and ambition of the leaders within the organization and, second, by external forces that voice a new demand or pose a new challenge to which the profession needs to react. There are, however, moments of non-linear disruption. By disruption I mean a pressure to change that pushes beyond the foreseeable next step of improving current state. I mean forces that do so with unsettling power and speed, making leaders realize that the current path will inevitably lead to destruction and that it is therefore unavoidable to pave a new way by taking steps into the unknown. This is where legal is: the speed of transformation is too fast, the change too profound in order to address it with mere improvement of today's state. It is the time when only true innovation will provide adequate answers.

Susskind and Susskind conclude: *"There is a strong sense that the professions, as currently organized, are approaching the end of an era ..."*.[2] They then provide us with the four fundamental characteristics of what they call the end of the professional era:

---

[1]Ismael et al., Exponential Organizations—Why new organizations are ten times better, faster, and cheaper than yours (and what to do about it), New York, 2014, p. 7.

[2]Susskind and Susskind (2015), p. 104.

- "... the move from bespoke service;
- the bypassing of traditional gatekeepers;
- a shift from a reactive approach to professional work; and
- the more-for-less challenge."[3]

It is baffling how well this analysis connects to every single article in this book; but it is not surprising, if we map the four characteristics provided by Susskind and Susskind to what we all can see happening in our industry:

(i) rapidly growing opportunities for standardization and automation;
(ii) commonly and ever more easily accessible legal knowledge;
(iii) a push for a proactive and more constructive ("business") approach of legal; and
(iv) the questioning of the size of legal budgets and the expectation to decrease them.

Why is that then an *"amazing"* time, i.e. something positive? Change—specifically at fast pace—will inevitably create *angst*, rejection and frustration when it comes about. It is human nature and there is no reason to challenge the unsettling effect that change has on organizations and individuals. The current inflection point that the legal industry has reached, however, has a different and much more fundamental make up. We are not just facing ordinary change, e.g. a new structure, a new application, a new process, reacting to budget cuts or whatever else one might typically subsume under "change". We are facing the destruction of traditional boundaries in our profession! This means that the legal industry offers significant opportunity for both, for us leaders in terms of refining our vision and strategy, and also for our teams in terms of what the future work environment and mode of working will look like.

The disruption opens enormous opportunity for the creation of new types of jobs, career options and fully blown business opportunities for service providers, as new tools and skills are being added to the traditional role of a lawyer. Amazing? I believe so! If we just take the example of what decomposing our work and finding better ways to get the "repetitive and boring stuff" done will do to job satisfaction; or if we consider the opportunity for us as leaders to lead our teams to break free from a mostly self-referential legal system[4] and to start working in a business frame of reference. Would it not be amazing, indeed, and much more interesting and fulfilling to be primarily seen and appreciated in the context of the business value we create, rather than the given legal issue we work on, or the amount of cases we deal with, or the cost we incur or the billable hours we invoice?

Legal—in whatever role—will be put much more directly and profoundly into a business frame of mind. Rightfully so, as this is the main point of reference in the

---

[3]Susskind and Susskind (2015), p. 105 (rearranged as a list for ease of reading).
[4]Strathausen, "Masters of Ambiguity: How Legal Can Lead the Business", p. 13.

professional world. When we recently were invited to present the key theses of this book at an international conference, during the lively discussion a senior colleague raised the concern that by the continuous push on legal to become a business function, we needed to watch out for not losing track of the core element of legal—in whatever role, i.e. being the guardian of legality. This is an important plea, indeed. Thus, in order to avoid any misunderstanding, I would like to add two important points of calibration. One as to what we do *not* mean and one as to what we *do* mean by *Liquid Legal*:

First, *Liquid Legal* is *not* meant to be a call for any role in legal to abandon its fundamental function of being an element of the system of law and justice in society at large and business in particular; this is and remains a crucial aspect to the role of a lawyer—specifically in times of change. *"Compliance and protecting our organizations against risk, as true stewards do, have always been and will remain the core tasks of legal, ... The law is the law, and we have to observe it. Period. That core remains stable."*[5]

Second, *Liquid Legal* is, however, a call for any role in legal to embrace even stronger the intrinsic capability which we bring to the table and which is more relevant today, than ever before: to create trust! *"By providing security, fostering trust and enabling people to work together, law is both, an expression and a fundamental driver of human civilization ... Just like the heart pumps blood through physical organisms, legal, by establishing fair and transparent rules among people, departments, lines of businesses, divisions and subsidiaries, can carry trust through business organisms."*[6]

2 The Manifestation of LIQUID LEGAL

2.1 The Expectation on Legal Has Changed: A Good Thing!

2.1.1 An Optimistic Mindset

Despite the inevitable pain, the insecurity caused and the stress infused into our daily lives by the disruptive change we are facing, there are strong reasons to go through it with an optimistic mindset. We just always need to keep in mind that the underlying request is a positive one and that the ultimate aim is a good place to be. The push on legal to *"do things differently"* is in fact just the enabler, the means to win back time from repetitive and self-referential work. The actual goal is to be able to redeploy the time and thus to invest more (in fact most) of our time into activities that add immediate value for others. In short: the underlying request is to *increase legal's relevance!*

So, as we transform our current state, as we change legal's state of aggregation and become *LIQUID LEGAL*, we will preserve our core, but unleash our potential.

---

[5]Mucic, "Foreword: Bridging the Gap—The New Legal", p. v.
[6]Strathausen, "Masters of Ambiguity: How Legal Can Lead the Business", p. 31.

We will stop looking backwards by farming traditions, but instead we will move forward with innovation and a new mindset. We will stop being passengers, but become co-pilots that add direction and additional momentum. *"...'Legal' can be just as effective and innovative as any other part of the company ..."*[7]

Let me provide a—widely known—example to make this more tangible. When I started my current role, heading the legal business support for Europe, Middle East and Africa, my legal team was in a state of constant fire drill. The downsides are obvious, so allow me to summarize it with what I call the three "O"s': *overburdened, over hours, overworked.* The upside, however, is also well known and I call it the *"voodoo-effect"*: No one knows what you really do in detail, if it is all even really needed, but it looks impressive and the belief is that you better do not question the voodoo-master but praise her or him when it is done.

2.1.2 An Example

A core element of our issue at the time was the commonly known problem of the lawyer being called in too late, to then be left to hunt all the information required to get a complete contract done and to finally run after all sign-offs required to be ready for signature—which was then the final logistical challenge. I do not want to take you through the full analysis of the problem and its resolution, but rather illustrate a couple of main points related to changing the expectation on and the perception of legal:

(i) The traditional working mode of the lawyers actually disguised that a full function plus a defined process was missing, i.e. the function of analyzing the full deal (e.g. tender or request for proposal), identifying all specialists required, define their work-packages, determine timelines, make sure all followed the same win-strategy, get all approvals ... let's call it *deal management.* To fix it we defined this role, its basic processes and started to invest headcount in it—rather than continuing to add lawyers to a foggy and disorganized bundle of tasks, most of which they were neither trained nor hired to do.

(ii) The main driver of inefficiency and "heat" on the team was random and typically far too late engagement. We integrated a simple—but mandatory—step into our CRM-tool: sales now needs to answer a few basic questions at opportunity stage, the answers to which indicate whether a lawyer (or deal manager) needs to be involved. We also got access for legal to the CRM-application and established two basic reports: (1) on large opportunities in the pipeline to know what is potentially coming our way—the most basic report sales management is using anyway; and (2) one showing the results and adherence to the registration process.

---

[7]Fawcett, "Foreword: Creating Your Path—Building Towards Liquid Legal", p. ix.

(iii) We established the logging of non-standard requirements in contracts and deals we got involved in—allowing us to automate approval flows and go back to precedents.

So what did we gain? Let us look at some numbers: Over the course of 5 years we *doubled* the run-rate of cases & deals on the team—while *lowering the overall run rate of OPEX by 30 %*! On employee listening surveys we stood out by 10 points in terms of overall satisfaction of the team, satisfaction with management and organized work environment. Well, our peers in other functions were happy, too, as we offered them an organized step-stone and process to deal with the most complex part of our business.

And our internal main client, sales? Next to appreciating all of the above, we saw a remarkable change: Sales started to invite us to their business reviews, i.e. when the business is being analyzed! We were asked to bring our analytics on deal trends, complications and our ideas on how to improve our go to market so that we can win more deals faster. Well, we could simply pull that from our database, but I still could not stop myself from asking the question to our EMEA SVP of Go to Market, Manfred Reitner: "How come you thought about inviting us?" The answer was eye-opening: *"You are the only function that sees all of the most critical deals and contracts holistically and end-to-end; you lead the negotiations with our customers on contracts and you have data on their requirements that no one else has – it would be stupid not to invite you?"* .—Nothing to add.

What was our strategy?

- We had decomposed our traditional way of doing things—accepting the challenge that legal was asked to resolve the issue, regardless of traditional boundaries.
- We had taken another step out of the ivory tower and proposed a change of process in the space of our clients, promising a win-win—earlier engagement and visibility for better service and more controlled traffic on the team.
- We started to use the metrics we gained by way of leveraging simple tools to support our processes—and we offered them also to our clients.

The only open question that keeps getting raised to me every now and then, like a bad memory in the soul of the organization: Why is deal management in legal? I am typically tempted to keep the answer very simple: WHY NOT!?

2.1.3   Time to Act

The expectation on legal has clearly changed and will continue to do so. We must be careful not to get paralyzed and reactive by just staring at the symptoms and accommodating them. Let's leave our traditional sphere and dare to apply new solutions rather than wait for a special invitation.

As Cummins stated in his foreword: *"Knowledge is rapidly becoming an easily accessed commodity. It is the application of knowledge that increasingly has value, which differentiates the 'trusted counsellor' from the 'mere specialist'. Here we have the explanation for that question about the General Counsel; should he or she be the most senior specialist, or perhaps the intermediary who links legal opinion with business context?"* [8]

2.2   Boundaries Collapse: And the Playing Field Is Growing!

The days are gone when the world of legal was protected from intrusion and when the various players in legal had clearly identified and mostly separated roles. Let's take a look beyond the ruins of the castle wall that used to isolate the legal ivory tower for so long—who is out there to challenge the legal kingdom and who are the new contenders for a leadership role in our industry?

2.2.1   LPO's ... and Beyond

The LPO's and their refined business models provide a good starting point, because I believe that they will hold quite a central role in the transformation of legal. Today, LPO's are still mostly seen in the context of outsourcing and alternative resourcing, as being the lever to balance out the mix of fixed and variable expenditure towards the latter. While this undoubtedly will remain core to the added value that a professional outsourcing firm brings to the table, there are three more important elements to their role: (i) their ability to support change-management, (ii) their deep understanding of legal technology and (iii) their changing role towards and in comparison to law firms.

Many articles in this book have made the point that additional skills need to be and are being added rapidly to the various role profiles of lawyers, e.g. project management, process design, leveraging legal technology in general and automation in particular. As Brown rightfully points out: *"Efficient systems and processes directly affect the legal team's ability to meet the needs of the business, and they also have a profound effect on job satisfaction and retention. To assess and improve systems and processes, the legal sector has started to use Lean, a systematic method for increasing business value by eliminating waste, and legal project management ("LPM"), a growing trend likely to become table stakes within a few years."* [9]

Adding the resource constraints and economic pressure to the operational roles in legal, it is evident that it will be next to impossible for legal departments to first develop the skills required, in order to then analyze, decompose, reassess, re-design—in short—to implement all the change required purely with the existing resources. This amounts to the task of changing the tires on a car while driving at full speed. Inevitably, the consequence is that *"[s]ophisticated legal departments now expect their law firms and other legal service providers to provide some form of legal project management (LPM), on both hourly and non-hourly fee engagements. ... we expect the LPM trend to become table stakes in the legal*

---

[8]Cummins, "Foreword: Need a Lawyer? Use a Robot Instead!", p. xiv.

[9]Brown, "Running the Legal Department with Business Discipline", p. 403.

market for both law firms and law departments within the next three to five years."[10]

Let's make no mistake: Beyond finding and leveraging these new abilities with LPO's (and law firms), legal departments will also expect to see a net-positive effect on their cost-structure; they will expect to benefit from the cost-effectiveness in two ways: first, by the improved way of how the work is being done at LPO's and law-firms and, second, by the fact that the work product more often will not be the resolution of a task, but the support to change how a given legal demand is being answered, leading to efficiencies from standardization and automation. Is that fair?—To ask external service providers to seemingly work on making their own traditional work get less? Well, it is the "new world" entering the legal castle and—next to the threat to traditional business models—it opens a totally new range of very tangible business opportunities for legal service providers of whatever kind: *"It is time for law firms to deliver services with the quality of a law firm but with the operational excellence of an outsourcing company."*[11]

2.2.2 Technology

Thereby, we are already half way into the next important shift in boundaries: Technology. We see a rapidly growing scene of legal technology startups—some even talk about an explosion.[12] Roundtables develop around "LegalTech",[13] universities invest in research that crosses from the substance of law to technology[14] and—of course—there is a continuous stream of successful new market entrants in legal technology.

However, the landscape is also quite confusing: While the opportunity that legal technology provides is absolutely evident, it seems to play out as an avalanche of solutions for specific elements of legal work. Matthaei and Bues have provided a very good map on the type of legal technology solutions that are available:

> Broadly, three solution categories can be distinguished within LegalTech: (a) technologies facilitating the access to and processing of legal data and lawyers (b) support solutions, and (c) substantive law solutions. The first category offers solutions which provide a better access to lawyers and legal data ranging from vertical legal marketplaces to legal research and information retrieval. The second category comprises supportive tools which enhance case management and back-office work, ranging from human resources management,

---

[10]Brown, "Running the Legal Department with Business Discipline", p. 405.

[11]Bassli, "Shifting Client Expectations of Law Firms: Morphing Law Firms into Managed Services Providers", p. 59.

[12]http://www.corpcounsel.com/id=1202755396452/Theres-an-Explosion-of-Legal-Startups?slre turn=20160609061123—while there are also voices that rationalize the hype—see the insightful blog at http://associatesmind.com/2016/04/20/not-explosion-legaltech/ that seeks to add clarity to the facts around number of legal startups, the venture capital they get etc.

[13]The one in Munich was co-founded by one of our authors, Dr. Sven von Alemann, meets live in a 6–8 week cadence and is attended in average by 30 people—and that is "just" legal tech based in Munich.

[14]An even nearly complete overview goes far beyond this article; instead let me point to a very insightful blog on work done at Cornell university, by Costantini (2016).

accounting, billing, and financing to business development. The third category includes solutions which support or even replace lawyers in the execution of specific legal tasks.[15]

The legal technology-scene is in the stormy phase of exploring seemingly endless opportunity. It makes us feel a bit like kids in the candy store—and that actually might be true for both, the consumers of legal technology and the providers, as there are so many features needed and as today's rapid development of technology allows for so many new solutions. Is it the new contract management application, the contract extraction, automated contract assembly, a legal knowledge base, workflow automation, AI … Well, probably it is at some point all of the above (and more), but how on earth can this ever changing armada of technology options be monitored, analyzed, understood, down-selected, piloted and then implemented and be maintained by any legal department? Putting the immediate cost challenge to one side, obtaining and keeping an overview plus acquiring the competency to select an implement already goes beyond what an inhouse department can realistically do.

Taking a step back will allow us to realize the fundamental issue—and also the fix. The manifold challenges and the pressure, on the one hand, and the opportunities and the buzz, on the other hand, are a tempting environment to simply jump to a solution immediately. However, what we should do instead, is to spend more time on asking and defining the "why". What are we hoping to get out if a much larger and profound use of legal technology? What we are trying to ultimately achieve? And who are the key stakeholders, i.e. who are we doing it for?

The answer lies beyond the typically invoked cost-benefits, beyond improving response time and SLA and also beyond getting even better feedback from clients. The answer links back to the change in perception of and expectation from legal. Legal is expected (and legal is ready) to change the answer to the question *"why are we here?"* Legal is not just a self-referential system anymore that as such is a platform for others to create value on top of it. Legal is moving to be a value creator by directly linking to the business process! In this context, technology is the lever— a powerful lever, indeed. Technology provides the data, the flexible and easy access to it and the ability to exploit it for immediate insights that drive better decisions. This is easily said—but underlying this statement we find a wide gap from current state to future state. How will we realistically close it and who can realistically do it?

Brenton has pinned it down a first important requirement, as she states that *"[The] increased role of legal departments—accompanied by heightened demand for more efficient delivery of legal services, availability of technology, and new entrants to the legal ecosystem—has rendered it impossible to maintain the status quo. It's time to start running legal departments like a business. … To address this need, they are increasingly adding a new function to their management teams—the*

---

[15]Matthaei and Bues, "LegalTech on the Rise: Technology Changes Legal Work Behaviours, But Does Not Replace Its Profession", p. 91.

Corporate Legal Operations Executive, a COO for legal."[16] With establishing a legal operations function, an inhouse department has defined its interface to the technology market and puts itself into the position to be ready to connect internal demand by the legal sub-functions to both, the market of legal technology and internal IT.[17]

But even having an expert—legal operations—scanning and working the market of legal technology will only provide half of the answer. The question remains how to master the enormous dynamic of the market which makes it hard to take long term investment decisions and which makes it a challenge to manage the complexity of implementation and change management. Here, again, we can close the loop to the future picture of both, LPO's and law firms that Ross and Brown (LPO's) and Meents, Markfort (law firms) and Bassli (inhouse perspective on law firms) have described. Both providers of service to legal departments may well be asked to do this including a Software-as-a-Service-element—and by *expectation* I mean two things, (i) for customers to benefit from the technology upside and (ii) to realize the cost benefit of it! Looking at it from the perspective of legal technology providers—especially in start-up mode—this has tremendous upside, as well. A newly calibrated ecosystem in which law firms and LPO's also work as service providers in terms of technology does open a completely new pathway and becomes a significant multiplier to the market. If you win an LPO with your technology solution, you might have won tens or hundreds of customers.

2.3   Think Data When You Say Technology and Aim at Value, Based on Information

Value needs information—information needs data—data needs technology.

Putting the use of "technology" in context helps us to avoid the slippery slope of jumping too quickly into the weeds of a technical solution, when we should actually be focused on the data we need to obtain to produce the information we require to create the value we are aiming for.

2.3.1   Two Halves to the Whole: Primary Legal Data and Legal Analytics

Before we focus on the value that legal can create by rethinking how we deal with our data, I would like separate to perspectives on data and information in legal: (A) the information that can be produced directly with legal data and the combination thereof (hereafter referred to as *"primary legal data"*) and (B) the information that can be generated by analyzing legal data or the combination thereof (hereafter referred to as *"legal analytics"*). An example for (A) would be a contract

---

[16]Brenton, "CLOC: Joining Forces to Drive Transformation in Legal: Bringing Together the Legal Ecosystem", p. 304.

[17]Of course, the legal operations role is much broader than taking care of legal technology—please see the article of Brenton for a detailed outline of it.

management application—data (e.g. templates and clauses) is being used to create information, i.e. a contract. An example for (B) would be the analysis run in the contract management application to learn things like: how many contracts have been concluded, in which regions, what have been the most negotiated terms etc.?

Why is that important? Well, in a nutshell, value creation from data in a legal department rests on both of those pillars. Indeed, those two pillars are closely interconnected and true value cannot stand stably on just one. Whoever has tried to obtain data for legal analytics from a team while the primary legal data has been inconsistent—or generated outside any application (e.g. manual contracting based on data on c-drives) has experienced the devastating effect this has on the quality of the analysis and thus the usability of the outcome of the legal analytics, or the devastating effect on morale this has had caused by the manual exercise and the time commitment that comes with it. This close interrelation is the reason why the two types of data often get pulled together into one conversation about "legal data" or "legal IT". However, is crucial to keep in mind that they require distinctly different care and attention when being built, maintained and further developed.

Establishing an application for *primary legal data* typically directly integrates into the operational, day-to-day processes of the full team. Going back to the contract management system, it is evident that this will—and should—be one of the most used systems in the team. Mapping the business requirements to the working process of the team will be of paramount importance not only in terms of change management, but also to obtain the efficiency gains and other upsides that are typically part of the project goal when introducing an application for managing primary legal data. What else sticks out as success factor are: agility and fluidity. What I mean by agility is referring to the fact that in today's work environment, *"[o]ur businesses and the underlying information technology must be able to adapt quickly to changing circumstances."*[18] Fluidity, in turn, refers to a need that actually is a hot topic across the IT-industry, not just in legal IT: the ability to process and connect data across the boundaries of individual applications. *"Data, to have value, must be in motion, it must be current, agile and available, integrated as close to the point of decision as possible. You must identify the pinch points and blockages that keep data from moving."*[19] To illustrate this point just think about the question, whether your contract management system is interoperable—and connected—to your company CRM-system? Is it reading (automatically?) from a central source the data on the contractual partner? Do you know the status of a given customer because the contract management application "knows" that from interoperating with the CRM? ... This could be a long list, but the point is clear: in Legal we are quite used to living in a world of broken records—but we can't afford that moving forward, because data is crucial and efficiency is, as well!

Introducing *legal analytics* into the picture, again there is an important distinction to be made. Mostly, legal analytics are used in the context of "managing the

---

[18]Jacob, "Legal Information Management (LIM) Strategy: How to Transform a Legal Department", p. 312.

[19]Dun&Bradstreet, p. 4.

department". This is an important point to professionalize legal management by a regime of goals that are driven by defined KPI's that in turn are based on metrics.[20] Yet, it is as important for a modern legal function to identify legal analytics that create as such value to the business and other functions. This, in fact, is the essential step that overcomes the self-referential system of legal and that frees legal from the position to only measure its own performance and be—by good old tradition— bogged down to justify its spend, its organization, . . . its existence. Let me refer back to my example when we started to do legal analytics on the trends we saw in the largest deals and contract negotiations and how that translated into action to optimize our commercial positions as a company. Interestingly, it was only legal that really could pull it all together—our data and then our ability to interpret it, based on our end-to-end view on the deals was crucial. At the same time we used a combination of data from our applications and from the CRM-tool of the company, i.e. we did not only break through boundaries in terms of what kind of added value legal can deliver, but also in terms of how we collaborate with other business functions—in that case sales operations.

2.3.2   Contributing to the Business Review with Legal Analytics

Thus, in our case a business review on legal and actively supported by legal has the following elements:

1. Engagement ratio & efficiency
2. Speed & effectiveness
3. Traffic (workload)

This is not to state that this selection is necessarily complete or a match for any given situation, but it has proven to work for us and our strategic dialogue with the business and our peer functions.

Engagement Ratio & Efficiency

How are we doing in terms of traction, i.e. how well is our engagement working, which will tell us about efficiency. We require our sales force to "register" large opportunities at an early sales stage. Registration means to answer less than 10 very basic questions online, right in the CRM-application. The report below is one we actually pull from our corporate CRM-system and it displays the process-adherence rate. Thereby we can see two things—an early trend on upcoming workload and how well the process works (Fig. 1).

While this tells us about how well one of our most important interfaces works, we use a similar set of data from our own deal management system that tells us another thing, namely the absolute number of actual new engagements that turn into a "case" on our part, i.e. longer term work for us. We then put this in context over

---

[20]See the broader context provided to that aspect by Brenton, "CLOC: Joining Forces to Drive Transformation in Legal: Bringing Together the Legal Ecosystem", p. 305.

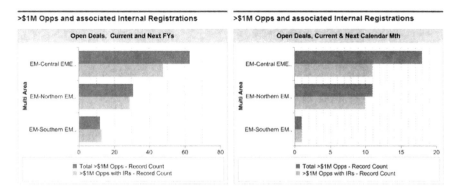

Fig. 1 Engagement and quality of process (own material)

Fig. 2 Engagement on new deals over time (own material)

time and also compared to the previous years to see trends. Thereby we can indicate to the business when we see peaks and why. We also serve as an early indicator; given the latency of complex business turning into a successful sale, we can add to the prediction on the pipeline. Last but not least, again this tells us about actual load (Fig. 2).

Speed & Effectiveness

Complexity on deals or negotiations is interesting to dissect, because it easily translates into complication, i.e. several effects that can slow down to "get the contract or deal done". The most common complications are: (i) identifying and coordinating all stakeholders; (ii) getting functional input and decisions in the time and quality required; and (iii) getting overall approval by higher management ranks on the overall risk and opportunity profile.

As to (i), this is where we have introduced a whole new function to our department—the deal manager—whose job it is, among many other tasks, to drive the right and effective deal team set up.

As to (ii), we have started to pull the reports (Fig. 3) on which stakeholder (by department) owns (meaning is responsible content-wise for) the most deviations, "deviation" meaning a customer request that demands us to move away from a standard position. Why is that interesting? Well, first, if you lead on

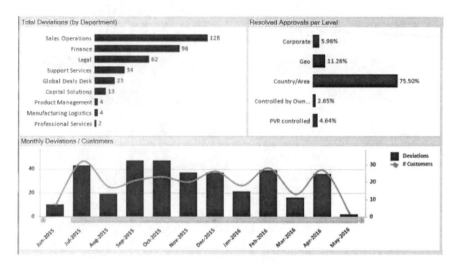

Fig. 3 Deviations from company standard positions (own material)

that deviations-chart as a function, you will want to analyze why that is. So, why is in the example provided below, sales operations generating the most "deviations"? Are they too conservative on certain positions? Are they off market standard? Or are they just diligent? First, it is worth noting that a high number is not a bad thing: If most of those deviations can be dealt with at a low level in the organization, e.g. because there are pre-approved solutions or because decision making power is delegated,—no problem.

At this point (iii) comes into play. In fact, if you take a look at the upper right chart, what I just described seems to be the case: about 75 % of the deviations can be resolved within country, while only 11 % need to be decided at an EMEA-level (we call it "Geo") and only about 6 % need to reach the highest decision level in the company, corporate.

You can imagine that this chart looked very different, when we first introduced it several years ago, but the transparency and detail that we could provide led to several improvement-initiatives, based on the new insights on what makes deals and contract negotiations slow down. Last but not least, the common reflex of explaining and proving that in legal we are not the "nay-sayers" or "complicators" is being extinguished. This message is actually there—we are only in third spot of owning deviations—but it is nothing but a side-effect of analyzing the overall speed of decision-making in the business.

Traffic (Workload)

Of course, keeping track of workload is a key element of information for and about the department. This is when the common struggle is twofold: (i) *how* to obtain relevant data in the first place, without starting to ask the team to become data-clerks, i.e. having to manually enter data into a spreadsheet; and (ii) how to obtain *relevant* data. If, for example, you take an obvious starting point and track the number of cases or deals on the team, there is a huge variable that almost completely undermines the usability of the data: how much effort or time is needed for a case? Is it an NDA or a simple question that can be answered with an email, or is it a month-long negotiation of a multinational multi-million contract?

As to getting to relevant data, the rule of thumb should be simple: legal analytics should be based on data that is being collected automatically, on data that you can pull from the "backdoor" of applications that have been built to support an operational process. In my example above this means, that 90 % of the data is pulled from our application that supports the deal and contracting process or from the CRM-application. The basic rule we had to observe, as we structured our application based on the business requirements we had defined, was to think: "database". Simple rules had to be rigorously applied—well known for IT-experts in building business application—like being careful with too many "free text-fields", as they are hard to analyze and to report on or leveraging drop-downs and tags as much as possible.

What we got were several helpful views that allowed us to understand load and effort better than ever before. By the amount of big deals and negotiations below, we have an initial indicator. As we capture the current deal phase (a drop down-based click) and deal stage, meaning if a deal is active and thus we are at work, or inactive, meaning we wait for external input (again a simple one-click tag), we can get a fairly good understanding about the current load on the team. 233 deals could be an issue, if 200 were active and most of them in the phase "negotiation", when typically the load is the highest on the team. But having 133 active and only 40 in a negotiation state provides a very different picture (Fig. 4).

Against that background, adding the overall case load, i.e. the simple number of "how many requests for legal support have we received" is a very useful additional factor in the equation, as it adds the dimension of small ticket-traffic to the picture (Fig. 5).

Open Deals per #

Stage	Number of Deals
Active	133
Inactive	100
All Items	233

Phase	Number of deals
Contract Negotiation	15
Deal Negotiation	25
Pre-Negotiation	7
Pre-RFP	33
Proposal	151
Protect	2

Chart Title

- Contract Negotiation
- Deal Negotiation
- Pre-Negotiation
- Pre-RFP
- Proposal
- Protect

Fig. 4 Current run-rate of deals on the team (own material)

Fig. 5 Number of support requests on the lawyers per quarter (own material)

The above chart clearly indicates an overall upward trend plus a significant uptick in two parts of the EMEA-region. Overall it is a good thing that we are being sought and found, but are we busy with the right things? Or mostly with repetitive requests that could be standardized or automated?—Yet, let us take a moment here: actually, the information on new requests is less relevant for a business review with our clients, but rather important for us running our function. This is data to analyze and discuss in our functional reviews. Since we have quite a few relevant legal analytics for the business to offer, we have better things to discuss with our clients, than the question if we run our function properly. Based on the value we deliver operationally every day and based on the value we deliver strategically in business conversations, we can request the trust to leave the piece of analyzing ourselves to us. We can dare to say: *"Let's not waste time on self-referential topics – let's talk business."*

2.4   Collaboration Is the New Paradigm!

Embracing the approach of LIQUID LEGAL leads us from an inhouse perspective to changing the dynamics between our internal clients and legal, moving to a new, much more collaborative approach. Collaboration, however, works as the central paradigm in a much broader context in the transformation of the legal industry. I am with Strathausen as he sets out that *"[j]ust like the heart pumps blood through physical organisms, legal, by establishing fair and transparent rules among people, departments, lines of businesses, divisions and subsidiaries, can carry trust through business organisms. Liquid legal is the belief that trust is the essence of business – and that together, we are better off than alone."*[21]

2.4.1   Driven by the Future and by Non-Profit
A prime and very profound example for that new paradigm are future oriented and innovation driven non-profit organizations like CLOC or IACCM. CLOC, as described earlier in this book by Brenton, is based on collaboration at the heart of

---

[21]Strathausen, "Masters of Ambiguity: How Legal Can Lead the Business", p. 31.

the matter—in legal operations: *"[CLOC] is a collaborative, community-driven organization of legal professionals focused on defining the future of corporate legal departments. The Association is focused on modernizing, streamlining and amplifying the Legal Operations role within the legal ecosystem."* [22] ... *"The organization's mission is to drive innovation and sharing of best practices across legal teams."* [23]

IACCM, a widely known global organization in the field of commercial and contract management, has also been founded based on innovation and collaboration. It was the first organization to identify the new opportunity for a function that was emerging from the combination of commerce, i.e. business skills, and contracts, i.e. legal skills. Commercial and contract management has long been (and quite frequently still is today) challenged with the question: Does this belong to legal? ... or somewhere else? The answer of IACCM was to simply rise above the hindrances of traditional silos and rather react to a need in industry practice and to approach with an open mind and the standing invitation to all players—lawyers or not—to come together and collaboratively shape the future. As Cummins has put it in his foreword: *"There will be many changes in the near future. Examples may include on-line courts, industry standard agreements and digital contracts. But fundamental to social progress is the readiness and ability of the legal profession itself to lead the change agenda. Ultimately, human and social progress will not be held back by the reluctance of lawyers to adapt."* [24]

Of course there are many more organizations or informal collaborative circles in our industry—an approach that is on the rise to the benefit of all of us.

2.4.2 Resolving the Riddle Together As Inhouse Departments

Six years ago, when I was embarking with my team on the journey to do commercial legal support differently, by integrating a former business function (deal managers) and by starting to be more focused on technology which supports process and provides metrics, I was aware that this would send my team off to a journey into the unknown. A fine challenge that needed trust and a strong team. During our 2-day workshop to build the strategy and the initiatives to pursue our vision, we did a team building exercise: Splash art! A very dynamic way of creating art, while constantly changing the perspective. Opposed to traditional painting, the canvass is not up on an easel, but put on the floor so that you can access it from all directions. Instead of a fine paintbrush, you use paint in all sorts of containers, from which you then throw, drip, wipe ... the various colors at the canvass at your own pace, rhythm and based on your imagination. We put as many canvasses right next to each other on the floor as we had locations represented on the team—but the paint was flying all over the whole thing. When we were done, we realized that it was one

---

[22] Brenton, "CLOC: Joining Forces to Drive Transformation in Legal: Bringing Together the Legal Ecosystem", p. 303.

[23] Brenton, "CLOC: Joining Forces to Drive Transformation in Legal: Bringing Together the Legal Ecosystem", p. 306.

[24] Cummins, "Foreword: Need a Lawyer? Use a Robot Instead!", p. xiii.

gigantic and stimulating, colorful piece of art—but we also realized that each of the individual canvasses were as well. It worked as a whole and as parts.

This outcome actually was the perfect symbol for our journey, during which we would sometimes feel being distributed on various islands of solution that we would struggle to see fit together until much later when we would be closer to the end-state. Based on that experience, we have engrained the principle of listening and sharing into our professional DNA. Within a company, it happens too easily to confuse your own picture with the whole picture; or simply to forget that one and the same picture looks very differently if you just walk around it. We have found new ways of collaborating with other departments in our company, making cross-team learning and sharing a habit.

Yet again, the same is true with peers outside our own company. Collaboration between inhouse departments or peers is pure gold. To put it simply, it was exactly the spirit of sharing and collaborating when navigate the massive transformation we are facing, that brought Kai Jacob, Roger Strathausen and myself together. We met at an IACCM-conference and realized that we were seeing the same picture, but from different angles. Kai heading a global contract management and operations function, Roger advising clients in change and innovation projects, and I managing an EMEA-wide Legal and a global contract management team. We readily took the extra time to share in regular sessions what we have learned and what we struggled with. Each time, we left our meetings with the strong sense of having gained insights and reassurance that continuing to push towards the unknown was the right thing to do. Collaborate to innovate!

2.4.3 You Gotta Talk: Inhouse, Law Firms and LPO's

Looking at our common picture and looking at it from a law firm perspective, the paradigm of collaboration works well too. It not only points towards the client, but also towards LPO's and legal technology. Bassli has made a strong case about how the interaction between law firm and inhouse needs to deepen: *"In addition to high quality legal services and advice, we need to get insight into the work of the law firms in a way we have never had before. The law firms are full of valuable information and data about the legal services that we procure from them, which could inform in-house teams about the business of the company they work for more broadly. Yet, that information is not being harvested and business is continuing as usual: deal by deal, legal memo by legal memo."* [25] It is obvious that this requires a mutual understanding that a law firm will only obtain by finding ways to learn more profoundly what their clients are seeking.

The same holds true for the relationship between law firms and LPO's. *"Over the next 3–5 years, the challenge and opportunity for LPO providers and their law firm clients is to develop new service delivery models that will drive even greater innovation. It is thus incumbent upon all the key constituent stakeholders in the*

---

[25]Bassli, "Shifting Client Expectations of Law Firms: Morphing Law Firms into Managed Services Providers", p. 60.

legal services industry to find better ways of working together."[26] Law firms continuing to be leading the new ways of delivering substantive legal work for clients; LPO's leading the transformation, process redesign and automation for the same clients; and jointly law firms and LPO's co-piloting the overall transformation with their joint clients in an integrated way. A pretty good match and an obvious call to action—a call to collaborate more profoundly. *"In coming years, there is no doubt we will see even closer collaboration between law firms and LPO providers, with the lines of ownership in the legal services delivery model becoming increasingly blurred as stakeholders invest in and enter into joint ventures with one another."*[27]

2.4.4 Legal Tech

Legal technology will be a huge, if not the most important lever to transform the role of legal and the way lawyers work. *"Technology lies at the core of most of the changes that we are encountering in the professions."*[28] As pointed out earlier in this chapter, we are still living the stormy phase of legal technology. Thus, under the header of collaboration, the main but strong additional request to make is for legal technology providers to continue the collaborative approach with inhouse departments, LPO's and amongst each other. Whether customers of legal technology can cash in on the promise of legal technology will to a large extend depend on the flexibility and interoperability of the various solutions.

2.4.5 Academia

The collaboration of the commercial legal market with legal academia bears huge opportunity for a true win-win. Looking at it from a commercial perspective, the academic world offers a wealth of research, insights and concepts that the legal industry can tap into when navigating through transformation. Change Management, leadership theory, finance and business administration skills etc. come to mind.

The prerequisite for the extended role and influence that Strathausen attributes as a future potential to lawyers, is that the individuals rethink their personal curriculum, their pathway to acquire the skills necessary to fill such an extended role. *"Legal can lead the business because lawyers are masters of ambiguity – trained to see different sides of a matter, to understand varying interests of different parties, and to lay the foundation for win-win situations. When it comes to mergers and acquisitions, to corporate strategy, to product lines and service portfolios, in fact: with regard to all business decisions that require assessing scenarios and weighing alternatives, lawyers should stop limiting themselves to legal aspects only."*[29]

---

[26]Ross, "Legal Process Outsourcing: Redefining the Legal Services Delivery Model", p. 84.

[27]Ross, "Legal Process Outsourcing: Redefining the Legal Services Delivery Model", p. 84.

[28]Susskind and Susskind (2015), p. 109.

[29]Strathausen, "Masters of Ambiguity: How Legal Can Lead the Business", p. 31.

The same applies to the management side of things. Driving a consistent strategy, based on a vision and measured by metrics-based KPI's requires a skill set that universities—while typically not the legal faculty—can provide. Pauleau, Roquilly and Collard rightfully remind us to seek the expertise that is already existing: *"Implementing KPIs is not a one-off exercise. It requires the execution of a transformation program to make the successful transition to running LDs like real Business Units. In this respect, LDs need to follow the guidelines applicable to all business transformation programs."*[30]

Against the background of the decomposition of professional work, i.e. the breaking up of traditional work clusters to enable multisourcing across several professions,[31] Tumasjan and Welpe point at the opportunity that lies in not just putting smaller blocks of tasks back together; they recommend that we rather consider the co-creation approach: *"The co-creation approach aims at bringing together all stakeholders involved in a certain process and improving their interactional patterns. Rather than merely searching for process improvements in all single steps involved in product or service delivery and optimizing their efficiency (e.g., Six Sigma), co-creation focuses on what the stakeholders of a process (e.g., employees, customers, suppliers, distributors) experience and how this experience can be altered for better results for everyone involved."*[32]

Just by acknowledging how many valuable ideas from various authors coming from various academic fields support this book, the huge opportunity becomes evident that academia holds for people working on mastering the transformation in legal.

At the same time there is a challenge ahead in this for our own academic home: the legal faculties. Given the massive spread of how the legal education is structured globally and to which extent certain universities and law schools have already adjusted to the changing landscape in the legal market, any generalizing comment bears a huge risk of imbalance. I think, however, it is fair to say that for the most part, legal faculties are still pending to adjust their curriculum to the changes in the legal industry and to the changing role of a lawyer. We do see the emphasis in the role shifting from *"knowing the law"* to *"knowing the business"* and *"knowing how to orchestrate legal work"*. Legal outsourcing, legal supply chain, legal technology and of course legal management concepts etc.—we should be mindful that for the most part none of this is yet taught at law school. Matthaei and Bues are clear on the competitive advantage—or disadvantage—this can be: *"In order to ensure that lawyers are well equipped for the challenges imposed by LegalTech, legal education needs to amend its curriculum. Many universities and law schools are ill-equipped to train their students on LegalTech and on the applications that are already available. Law schools have to revise their curriculums as part of a larger interdisciplinary approach. They should, for*

---

[30]Pauleau et al., "Key Performance Indicators (KPIs): Run Legal with Business Metrics: Will the Legal of the Future Measure Everything It Does?", p. 124.

[31]See for more detail Susskind and Susskind (2015), p. 122.

[32]Welpe and Tumasjan, "The Legal Entrepreneur: When Do Corporate Lawyers Act Entrepreneurially?", p. 135.

example, introduce LegalTech lectures, courses, clinics, internships, conferences and workshops which provide the theoretical and practical knowledge for the future jobs [. . .]." [33]

However, as Rhodes states in her book "Lawyers as Leaders": *"Although leadership development is now a forty-five billion dollar industry, and an Amazon search reveals close to 88,000 leadership books in print, the topic is largely missing in legal education."* [34] Thus, as much as anyone working in today's legal industry is called upon to leverage broadly the power of research and academia, as much are law schools challenged to rethink their curriculum to include new subjects adapted to prepare young talent better for their future role.

By way of an example we just need to look at Haapio and Barton making the case for transitioning to business friendly contracting by the concept of preventive and proactive law (PPL): *"Preventive Law focuses on dysfunctional cycles that generate recurring losses. It seeks to identify and understand the conflicting elements of a system, [. . .], that, unless somehow resolved, will continue to generate problems. Proactive Law adds a focus to achieving positive goals and value. Together, PPL can alter mentalities and harness tools toward smoother operations and successful outcomes."* [35] A concept developed by the independent power of academia itself, waiting to be leveraged much more broadly in legal curricula as legal transforms.

2.5   It Is Time for a New Vision!

It almost seems odd to write it down, as it is part of any management class: *We, as leaders (situational or managerial) of our function, need to lead our teams into the transformation with a clear vision!*

2.5.1   The Law of Gravitation Has Been Called into Question

Yet, it is not a coincidence that this needs to be called out. Far too long, legal—specifically inhouse legal—has co-existed in the shadow of others, as a self-sufficient system that was "special" and thus quite untouchable and that could thereby surround the business like the moon surrounds earth, kept on track by the mild forces of gravitation, a known companion but also a bit far away. The course is set by planet earth, sometimes a bit defocused by other planets . . . so why bother?

The answer is quite straight forward: The traditional law of gravitation for legal has been called into question! It is quite confusing to imagine what the legal landscape will look like just in 5 years—let alone in ten—or as Cummins puts it, *". . . whether a physical lawyer is needed at all – or whether Robert the lawyer*

---

[33]Matthaei and Bues, "LegalTech on the Rise: Technology Changes Legal Work Behaviours, But Does Not Replace Its Profession", p. 107.

[34]Rhodes (2013), p. 1.

[35]Haapio and Barton, "Business-Friendly Contracting: How Simplification and Visualization Can Help Bring It to Practice", p. 376.

becomes Robot the lawyer."[36] Sometimes it seems that we are surrounded by unstructured forces of change, a lot of questions or daring theses triggered by it, most of them well-founded, but all somewhat based on the unknown of where the wind of change will drive us. Well, *"[i]f one does not know to which port one is sailing, no wind is favorable."*[37]

So there we are, at a moment where we need to take all the scattered pieces of information we can obtain and define a vision of what the future will hold for us, respectively our teams. Do we know for sure? No—but this is why a vision is not a prediction of the future, but a picture of who we, as a function, aspire to be in that future as unclear and unpredictable as the conditions might still be.

2.5.2 The Cornerstones

So what do we know then, that can serve as the cornerstones to define our new vision:

1) We will remain *a function that ultimately supports business outcomes* (while this might be a business for ourselves, if we think beyond the legal inhouse part of the industry).
2) We will leave—or be driven from—the ivory tower by the massive transformation of professions overall; again, legal is not special. Thus, our reason for being must not be derived from our own system, but must instead be based on our will to *create measurable value*.
3) As we are exposed to the forces of efficiency and cost-effectiveness like never before, we will professionalize how we run ourselves—*we will apply business discipline* like any other function.
4) To avoid being haunted by the "do more with less" phantom, we must *embrace the opportunities of legal technology* as much as the opportunities that we can derive from decomposing the work and applying *new labor and co-operation models.*
5) We will not succeed by "throwing technology" at every problem—the investment will be too high, the change pain to big. It is data and information that we need to create outcomes, while technology is the pathway there. Thus *we need a legal information strategy as our compass* for the journey into legal technology.
6) W*e need to be masters of our data and we must make it a habit to actively use it*—for the sake of managing our work and teams better and to enable and underpin our goal to create value for our stakeholders.
7) We are in this together. We have to *invest in and leverage the rapidly growing opportunities for collaboration* in our ecosystem—be it with academia, legal technology, law firms or service providers in our industry.

This might not be complete, but I hope that you look at it as useful crystallization points also derived from this book, useful to get to your vision with your teams.

---

[36]Cummins, "Foreword: Need a Lawyer? Use a Robot Instead!", p. xxii.

[37]Lucius Annaeus Seneca. https://en.wikipedia.org/wiki/Seneca_the_Younger.

A well-defined vision must be the starting point. Pauleau, Roquilly and Collard have rightfully cautioned us to not jump right into goals, KPI and metrics: *"Far too often, legal KPIs are merely based on the data traditionally available within in-house legal teams, without giving adequate consideration to what such KPIs are supposed to demonstrate and to whom. We believe that it is necessary to adopt a "top-down" approach: starting from the vision statement of what the LD should do to be in line with the business strategy, thereby making it possible to identify the objectives to target in order to support this vision."*[38]

2.5.3 Balancing Independence and Interdependence

At a conference recently I had the pleasure to talk to a General Counsel of a large global corporation and we came on to the topic of "the need for a vision" for a legal department. His position was that a vision was not needed, because legal supports the vision and the goals of the company—period. While this is per se true, it is not the answer to the question at hand.

Agreed: the company's primary business is the reason why the legal inhouse department exists, and thus the company goals are a primary reference point. However, we thereby only answer the question "why" we exist, but stopping here would keep us—and our teams—in the dark on "how" we aim to support the company goals and in which spirit. *"The company"* will never determine the DNA of the legal department and its strategy to link the team in the most fruitful way to the company at large and the company goals. This is our job, our duty towards our teams—and our opportunity to step up and strive to determine how we can create the utmost value.[39]

Adding to the picture the transformational forces in the legal industry, defining a vision—a new vision—has never been more urgent. One, if not *the* common denominator of all articles in this book is that the landscape in the legal industry is changing as we speak and will evolve further. The tectonic plates are in motion. This requires a new map that no one will draw up for us—this is upon us. In measuring the changing world of legal, we must make sure that our new map includes all landmarks: inhouse, law firms, LPO's, legal technology, academia, people development etc.

Last but not least, the new vision will also be the anchor point to introduce the combination of and balance between our *independence*, i.e. our own self, and our *interdependence*, i.e. how we relate to the company as a whole.[40] Where are we

---

[38]Pauleau et al., "Key Performance Indicators (KPIs): Run Legal with Business Metrics: Will the Legal of the Future Measure Everything It Does?", p. 113.

[39]In business reality, the lines blur very often between vision, mission, strategy—they get very easily confused; Hambrick and Fredrickson (2005) provide a very good guide on how to detect when this is happening and how to prevent this, taking the element of "strategy" as the center point.

[40]Pauleau et al., p. 9/10 look at this aspect into the performance perspective: *"The legal performance of a company can be understood in two different ways. In a narrow sense, it refers to the performance of its LD, in other words the capacity of that department to achieve its own missions and objectives. This aspect is at the core of the present Chapter. A broader – and perhaps more appropriate – understanding is to see legal performance as the company's ability to deploy legal*

leading as guardians of legality, as fiduciaries of the trust that flows from a legal frame of reference,[41] and where are we supporting as creators of additional value to other frames of reference. Based on a new vision that embraces the new reality and the expanded opportunities for lawyers, legal managers in all ranks have the opportunity—and the duty—to step up as leaders and to show the way.

2.6 Create New Leadership

> All in all, we are witnessing the need for lawyers to broaden their skill set. Not only must they maintain their legal expertise, they also have to sharpen their strategic and business thinking as well as understand and integrate the valuable lessons from their emotional and social intelligence. In one word, they have to become great leaders![42]

Markfort has summed it up nicely, but his statement is as true as it is explosive. Quite typically, and thus also in legal, the managerial ranks are staffed with strong players that have emerged from and developed in the pre-existing setup. In simple terms, we have often seen very good lawyers be rewarded by stepping up to become legal managers. As the role of legal has been well defined and stable for so many years and as the system of legal has been quite closed and independent from the influence from other functions, the role of a legal manager was quite straightforward. This left sufficient room to gravitate quickly to the notion of the working manager; *"less manage – more do"* is not an infrequently used line in legal departments.

2.6.1 Do ... What?

I am not debating the concept that management ranks share the responsibility to carry operational burden—and this does not only apply to legal. However, specifically in the more senior ranks of our profession, the order of priority must be reversed: No department will or should in the long run invest in senior (and thus more expensive) managers and leaders, unless those individuals first and foremost make sure that the team is and stays on board with a new vision of legal, that the individuals are equipped with the skills required to bring it to live and that every lawyer is enabled to leverage and orchestrate the much broader range of resources and tools. On top of that, leaders in legal are called upon to build out a new, much broader and truly interactive interface to peer functions and the business at large. For a future legal leader the harmony of vision, goals, KPI's and metrics needs to be natural, as well as both, the understanding of how to create, define and obtain them,

---

resources [...] and combine them with the other types of resources at its disposal in order to achieve its objectives, in particular its strategic objectives. In this sense, legal performance can be considered as an important factor in the overall performance of the company."

[41] As Strathausen puts it: *"Trust is the ultimate legal currency, and the greatest value delivered by law!"*, Strathausen, "Masters of Ambiguity: How Legal Can Lead the Business", p. 31.

[42] Markfort, "Legal Advisor–Service Provider–Business Partner: Shifting the Mindset of Corporate Lawyers", p. 56.

and, the ability to make them consistently part of the communication internally and externally.

"The General Counsels of today's legal departments must find ways to add value, deliver premium legal and business consulting services to their internal customers, and provide a competitive advantage to their companies."[43] The new challenge for a modern general counsel, as Brenton have defined it, describes the DNA that in fact every senior leader in legal must have. This is why Fawcett makes it a point to refer to his leadership team, when he describes the journey towards the future of legal: *"As a renewed leadership team, we changed the culture of the group from what it had been – a loosely organized collection of lawyers – to a true team of business partners and counselors."*[44]

2.6.2   It's Not Enough to Be a Seasoned Lawyer?

While still remarkable, it is not surprising that on the agenda of the legal all hands that our new GC, Matt Fawcett, ran in his second year at NetApp you would not find a single "legal" topic. It was all about leadership capabilities and the broadening of the mindset towards the role of inhouse legal, the launching of a new vision and the consciousness of being a truly global team. Concepts of authenticity and vulnerability, as key traits of a leader, how to build out and preserve a positive and solution oriented mindset, working across cultures and the department vision to strive to *"be the best"* were discussed in workshops and panel sessions with experts.

This example displays two basic themes that can serve as a general description of the change in leadership expectations in legal:

1) *The traditional core competencies of a lawyer are a given*, they are the basis to be able do the job, but they are not the full qualification to get it and to keep it. Well, if that is true for every single member of the department, what is the message to the managers—or better—the leaders? The same, but exponentiated: Legal and managerial skills are the basis, it is the leadership skills that get you the job, specifically the ability to build a solid strategy on the cornerstones laid out earlier in this article, that carry the new vision.
2) Being *"the best"* is utopia—you will never know; but by making it part of the vision you automatically free up from the legacy, the traditional set up in the legal industry, from being defocused by hunting down trails that many others have used in order to meet benchmarks. You provide your department and the individuals that build it, with the freedom to innovate and to try new approaches, and to accept failure in some instances in order to win and advance overall.

As the expectation on legal is rapidly changing, as the traditional boundaries within and around legal collapse, as technology becomes the new teammate and data the currency for legal to interact with the business, as the vision changes

---

[43]Brenton, "CLOC: Joining Forces to Drive Transformation in Legal: Bringing Together the Legal Ecosystem", p. 304.

[44]Fawcett, "Foreword: Creating Your Path—Building Towards Liquid Legal", p. xi.

fundamentally—how can the DNA and the skillset of a legal leader remain the same? LIQUID LEGAL requires lawyers that are leaders—in whatever function they hold in the organization.

2.7   Redefine Roles, Skills & Career Paths

2.7.1   A Lawyer Is a Lawyer Is a Lawyer . . . Isn't It?

You might share the experience when looking at the majority of job advertisements—be it for inhouse or for a law firm: it very often seems like taking a glimpse back in time. It is all about the traditional hard skills of a lawyer, brushed up to work with more demanding talent that seeks to work more team-oriented and more flexibly.

But, as my grandmother has taught me when I was a kid, when you point to others, four fingers point back at you. As I had worked towards a new vision with my team, had underpinned it with a strategy and goals and was busy working through the initiatives to make it real, one of my senior managers sent me an email with a new version of our job description. "Probably updated in terms of the most current style guide", I thought. But instead, it was completely new, right from the start—which is now titled "Introduction" and reads as follows:

> NetApp Legal is comprised of [. . .] professionals located in 25 offices in 14 countries. Our motto is **"Guide The Business, Guard The Company"** and this is founded on three pillars:
> 1. **Partnership**
> 2. **Service**
> 3. **Integrity**
>
> We strive to act as a **Strategic Business Advisor, End-To-End Business Enabler** and **Risk Management Centre of Excellence** every day.
>   NetApp Legal has built a reputation as a change agent; a department that embraces innovative business models, trusted business partnerships, pioneering service delivery, technology and business process best practices to achieve great things. . . .

As stated above—it is obvious that we have certain expectations in terms of hard skills regarding a lawyer who is joining us and we list those, too, eventually. However and literally: *first and foremost*, we must make it clear that we are looking for a business oriented mindset, a specific personality type and someone who shares our modern interpretation of the role. How could we miss that when calling into the market? How could I have missed that after having gone so far down that route with my team?

A potentially costly flaw that my colleague has pointed out and helped us fix, as Escher reminds us that *"[g]ood hiring decisions require two things: 1) a thoughtful process that aligns the criteria for selection with the criteria to which the legal department as a whole is subjected; and 2) a core acknowledgement that tools other than the judgment and instincts of the general counsel and/or the hiring manager are required."* [45] So it is not surprising that, since we use the updated job description, many candidates have provided unsolicited positive feedback on it, stating that it was not only appealing to them, but that they felt good about knowing very clearly what the hiring department is all about, *before* going into the interview. Against that background, Escher's recommendations on how to conduct more meaningful interviews become even more powerful.

2.7.2   Develop Skills ... But What Skills?

Hiring talent is one thing, but *developing* talent has never been more important than in today's fast paced and rapidly changing work environment for lawyers. As we went through the transition with our team, based on a new vision and now also newly drafted job-profiles, it was evident that we needed to get the best possible handle on the potential of the existing team that was partly quite tenured. To be able to do that we had to close another significant gap: we had to translate our vision, the strategy and the roles into a *skills matrix*. We asked ourselves three questions as design principles:

1. What are the capabilities that are required to do the job (hard skills and soft skills)?
2. How important are they in absolute and in relative terms?
3. What learning and development offerings do we have to work on them?

The end result was a matrix that held about 50 skills, weighted with a factor of importance (1,2,3) and associated to the available means of support, e.g. online or in person trainings offered internally or externally etc. Adding a bit of Excel-magic and the matrix was turned into a self-assessment tool that would generate a spider-web diagram showing the peaks and dents of the respective individual's profile.

This was the first of three pillars on which we have built our development program, the other two being, *on the job experience* (an obligation of the respective manager and the broader leadership team to make it happen) and *mentoring* (a program based on the initiative of the individual and then facilitated by HR).

Beyond the effort that went into building out the substance of our development program, the skills-matrix etc., what have been the key success factors? First, the fact that from the outset this was not a program "by management". We have asked a small delegation of our full team to run this project—by the team for the team. This protected us from the "ivory tower"-risk of management missing the nuances of the operational reality, as much as it tremendously facilitated the acceptance of the end-result by the broader team. Second, we have made the implementation part of the goal sheet of every manager and employee. Every team-member had to do the

---

[45]Escher, "Building a Legal Department in a Metrics Driven World: A Guide to Finding the Best Candidates for the Legal Departments of the Future", p. 369.

self-assessment—while sharing of the results with the respective manager was completely voluntary. Every team member had to have a development plan, linked to the skills-matrix. We got 100 % fulfilment on that goal—it simply made sense, they said.

2.7.3 What Makes a Career

The final question to be answered for creating a basis for a long lasting and mutually beneficial employment relationship is: what does the career path look like? Traditionally, the equation is somewhat like this:

$$Career = (job\ title + job\ level) * size\ of\ the\ team$$

The element of "people management or not" and the size of the team are still a big factor—subjectively and objectively—in what makes a career in legal. Before you disagree, take a moment and test your company on a simple question: Are there useful leadership trainings which are *not* tied to the role of a people manager? I bet that for most companies the answer is *"no"* and you will see my point.

Let's compare that to the future role of senior members in legal departments, or better inhouse leaders. The authors contributing to this book form a harmonic chorus of challenge on any concept that ties seniority to people management or leadership to a management role or power to the size of the team. The future leader in legal will be what, I think, is best described as an *orchestration lawyer*, i.e. an individual with a legal background that is capable to orchestrate a suite of resources in order to create value for the company. Resources, in this context, are defined as budget allocated to get the job done, with an ever smaller part of it being allocated to internal headcount, compared to a larger part being allocated to outside services (LPO or outside counsel) and legal technology. Thus, in LIQUID LEGAL a career will depend on and be built upon the combination of legal skills, business skills and orchestration skills. A fine challenge as *"... successful collaboration is more than just good intentions. It involves a mentality and skills that may be relatively unfamiliar or even uncomfortable."*[46]

The challenge for talent acquisition and talent development in any role in legal practice is evident, and it is certainly not trivial. At the same time, this translates into a rapidly increasing risk of the gap widening between today's common legal education and modern legal practice. It is the joint responsibility of practitioners in the legal industry and academia to collaborate and jointly determine and staff a newly balanced curriculum.

---

[46]Haapio and Barton, "Business-Friendly Contracting: How Simplification and Visualization Can Help Bring It to Practice", p. 385.

3 Run Legal as a Business

3.1 It's an Opportunity

The fundamental change in the legal industry creates tremendous opportunity for lawyers. It creates new business opportunities in the legal services industry (be it at LPO's, in law firms or in legal technology companies). It opens up new roles for lawyers in business functions—Chomicka has made a convincing case for that in her article.[47] Last but not least, it enables—or even calls for—a radically new role description for lawyers in inhouse departments. All of this is based on the evolution of legal, leaving the ivory tower and enjoying the benefits of much closer interaction with all other business functions, changing the perception of legal from "special" to "unique". A broad and collaborative mindset internally and externally, towards service providers, as much as peers and also the academic world, will be the lever to capitalize on those opportunities.

3.2 Run Legal with Business Discipline

Running legal as a business means first and foremost to apply business discipline to legal. Sounds trivial, so what does it mean? The definition I prefer is that business discipline means *to help the business grow in the long term, rather than taking advantage of short term.*[48]

The first element points to *business focus* aiming at *growth.* Engraining business focus into the DNA of legal means to make sure that everyone is clear about why legal exists in a company. The answer is: legal exists in order to create measurable value that supports the company in achieving its goals—after legal ideally has participated actively in shaping them. As stated earlier, this is not about "going fully native", but rather about leveraging our ability to balance the dual role we hold, i.e. to combine the role of guardians of the company with our business enabler role. The business functions are our clients, but the shareholders are our "boss".

The second element is to prioritize the *long term perspective* over the short term gain. This builds on a skill that is typically attributed to lawyers—and rightfully so. We are known to be trained in analyzing, overseeing and admittedly also in being able to create complex systems. Clearly, the point to watch is that we control the risk to translate complexity into complication, as this is rarely truly required to achieve the desired outcome. How can we simplify and streamline business situations to enable speed and simplicity? Long term thinking is the call to action that we consider the broader effects of decisions. While, for example, sales

---

[47]Chomicka, "A Rose by Any Other Name Would Smell as Sweet: The New Legal Pro-Occupations in the Construction Sector", p. 141.

[48]This definition is also provided at http://www.answers.com/Q/What_is_business_discipline?#slide=1.

functions are typically being measured on short term goals, while many stakeholders will be focused on a certain aspect of a contract or deal, our job is it to not only help all of them achieve their goals, but also to explain the interest of the other party to them, to explain the broader context, lay out the options, provide a clear recommendation based on translating the interests ideally into a win-win for both sides.

Bottom line, business discipline provides the perfect bridge for connecting the new interpretation of the role of Legal. It marries the aim of value creation with the role of being a guardian for the company.

3.3   … and the Same Rules Apply

Running legal as a business function emphasizes the importance of managerial effectiveness. Consistent and strong performance has preconditions, but those are well known and just need to be translated into legal. *"Lawyering has become a business and therefore has to follow the rules of business."*[49]

It starts with a *vision* that embraces the new reality in the legal market, the change it requires as well as the opportunity it holds. It needs a clearly cut *mission* statement to frame the new mindset and the redefined roles of lawyers. The *goals* must aim to create value, i.e. they must be related to the company goals and, at the same time, be tied to making progress towards the vision, while clearly defined *key performance indicators* (KPI's), have to enable the leadership, the team and also the business partners at all levels to understand the performance against the goals. Finally, *performance management* has to be based on SMART goals, i.e. measuring is a key factor to success.[50]

Here we look at the additional upside of the rise of legal technology. Embracing legal technology will not only open up the efficiency gains of automation, but it will also create a wealth of data that is generated automatically, as the application gets used. Thus, it is of critical importance to deploy technology that is implemented so that it facilitates the respective process, rather than sitting outside of it and creating "extra effort". Such data will then create a win-win-win: (i) It will add objectivity and credibility to performance management internally to legal; (ii) it will enable anyone in legal to talk to the added value that legal provides to the company; and (iii) it will put legal into a position to generate business information right out of legal, information that no one else has.

---

[49]Markfort, "Legal Advisor–Service Provider–Business Partner: Shifting the Mindset of Corporate Lawyers", p. 49.

[50]Meyer and Gupta, (1994), p. 309/310 provide very good insight, based on research the paradox of measuring performance without exactly knowing what performance is.

3.4   Leaders, Roles and Talent

The new era of legal requires new type of leaders. Put simply: the times are over, when the most senior and hardest working lawyer would eventually become a manager and move up the ranks by law of organizational gravitation. The law of organizational gravitation has changed. Leaders must internalize the new expectation on legal, embrace the opportunity that comes with it and lead the team with a strong vision derived from it. Performance management must be part of the table stakes and the introduction of and then the continuous and close collaboration with legal operations will be crucial to master the challenge to scale, perform and motivate the team. The picture of every leader in legal being part of the "C-suite of legal",[51] creates exactly the right connotation of what calibers are required to lead in the new era.

Hartung and Gärtner are very clear about that to: *"Whether or not the legal function is managed by a lawyer is not the main point. The proper running of a legal function requires first and foremost structuring skills, then certain (legal, project, financial, economic and all sorts of other) management skills, and the ability to decide on the most appropriate resource for a certain piece of work (or a set of tasks), independent of your own capacity or role. We do not rule out that lawyers could head-up legal functions, but what they learn and how they think does not make them the first choice for these functions."*[52]

Legal leaders must be able to redefine roles and to distill the specific skills required to attract, develop and retain talent. Next to managing performance, it is key for legal managers to understand the potential of a person to actually grow and succeed in this very different and ever changing environment. Fortunately, the modern and much more diverse environment in legal holds a much broader range of roles and opportunities. When formerly there was legal work that could lead to an expert career or a people manager career, today technology, automation, outsourcing and the much closer interaction with the other business functions open up a whole suite of new career paths. Just look at the completely new and highly influential role of legal operations.

LIQUID LEGAL: Change Your State of Aggregation

Panta rhei - everything flows.[53]

The expectation on legal has started to change and has redefined the playing field for our function. Adding value to the business, leading the preservation of business culture by the trust we can derive from the concept of law and justice, and creating the opportunity of win-win in contracts are just a few concepts that illustrate the

---

[51]Brown, "Running the Legal Department with Business Discipline", p. 398.

[52]Hartung and Gärtner, "The Future of In-House Legal Departments and Their Impact on the Legal Market: Four Theses for General Counsels, and One 4 for Law Firms", p. 283.

[53]Attributed to Heraclitus—see https://en.wikipedia.org/wiki/Heraclitus.

change. None of this translates well into any stable state, into any traditional concept of "change from A to B and you are done". Adaptability might be the best term to use, reflecting the constant reshaping that the future of legal will require. The "why we exist" and the "how we do our job" will be subject to constant change. Adding technology and the massive change in the legal supply chain, the description of "what we do" will also need to be re-written consistently.

If that that is what we see, if we look at it as our opportunity to lead, if everything flows: we better change our state of aggregation and become LIQUID LEGAL and—in the spirit of collaboration—continue to share what we learn.

References

Costantini, F. (2016). VOXPOPULII. https://blog.law.cornell.edu/voxpop/category/semantic-web-and-law/. Accessed on 15 July 2016.

Dun & Bradstreet. Whitepaper on setting your data in motion. http://www.dnb.com/content/dam/english/dnb-data-insight/setting-your-data-in-motion-whitepaper-final.pdf. Accessed on 15 July 2016.

Hambrick, D. C., & Fredrickson, J. W. (2005). Are you sure you have a strategy? *Academy of Management Executive, 19*(4), 51.

Ismail, S., Malone, M. S., & van Geest, Y. (2014). *Exponential organizations*. New York: Diversion Books.

Meyer, M. W., & Gupta, V. (1994). The performance paradox. *Research in Organizational Behaviour, 16*, 306–369.

Rhode, D. L. (2013). *Lawyers as Leaders*. New York: Oxford University Press.

Susskind, D., & Susskind, R. (2015). *The future of the professions*. New York: Oxford University Press.

Dr. Schindler is the Head of Legal & Deal Management for Europe Middle East & Africa and the Head of Worldwide Contract Management & Services at NetApp, a leading data management company. He has transformed the legal department by combining Legal and Deal Management including the development of a Deal and Case Management application that supports the working processes and provides legal analytics. His teams have been awarded the "IACCM Global Innovation Award" in 2014 and 2015. Between 2009 and 2016, Dr. Schindler also served as a Member of the Board of NetApp Deutschland GmbH, an organization that has acquired top ranks in the Great Place to Work-ranking in 2014 and 1015.

Dr. Schindler regularly presents at both, business and peer group meetings as well as at various universities throughout Europe on the innovation of legal and the vision of LIQUID LEGAL.

CPSIA information can be obtained
at www.ICGtesting.com
Printed in the USA
LVOW10*1923301117
558163LV00004B/18/P